TOYOTA CRESSIDA/CORONA/C...
1970-82 REPAIR MANU...

President	Dean F. Morgantini, S.A.E.
Vice President–Finance	Barry L. Beck
Vice President–Sales	Glenn D. Potere
Managing Editor	Kevin M. G. Maher
Production Manager	Ben Greisler, S.A.E.
Project Managers	Michael Abraham, Will Kessler, A.S.E., Richard Schwartz
Schematics Editor	Lawrence Braun, A.S.E., S.A.E.
Editor	Dawn M. Hoch, S.A.E.

PUBLISHED BY **W. G. NICHOLS, INC.**

Manufactured in USA
© 1997 W. G. Nichols
1020 Andrew Drive
West Chester, PA 19380
ISBN 0-8019-9081-5
Library of Congress Catalog Card No. 97-67988
1234567890 6543210987

Contents

1 GENERAL INFORMATION AND MAINTENANCE

1-2	HOW TO USE THIS BOOK	
1-3	TOOLS AND EQUIPMENT	
1-7	SERVICING YOUR VEHICLE SAFELY	
1-8	FASTENERS, MEASUREMENTS AND CONVERSIONS	
1-14	HISTORY	
1-14	SERIAL NUMBER IDENTIFICATION	
1-21	ROUTINE MAINTENANCE	
1-51	FLUIDS AND LUBRICANTS	
1-63	TRAILER TOWING	
1-64	TOWING THE VEHICLE	
1-65	JACKING	
1-67	JUMP STARTING A DEAD BATTERY	
1-68	HOW TO BUY A USED VEHICLE	

2 ENGINE PERFORMANCE AND TUNE-UP

2-2	SPARK PLUGS AND WIRES
2-9	FIRING ORDERS
2-10	POINT TYPE IGNITION
2-11	TRANSISTORIZED IGNITION
2-13	IGNITION TIMING
2-15	VALVE LASH
2-19	IDLE SPEED AND MIXTURE ADJUSTMENT

3 ENGINE AND ENGINE OVERHAUL

3-2	ENGINE ELECTRICAL SYSTEM
3-20	ENGINE MECHANICAL
3-77	EXHAUST SYSTEM
3-85	COOLING SYSTEM

4 EMISSION CONTROLS

4-2	AIR POLLUTION
4-3	AUTOMOTIVE EMISSIONS
4-5	EMISSION CONTROLS
4-43	VACUUM DIAGRAMS

5 FUEL SYSTEM

5-2	BASIC FUEL SYSTEM DIAGNOSIS
5-2	CARBURETED FUEL SYSTEM
5-13	GASOLINE FUEL INJECTION SYSTEM
5-15	FUEL TANK

6 CHASSIS ELECTRICAL

6-2	UNDERSTANDING AND TROUBLESHOOTING ELECTRICAL SYSTEMS
6-12	HEATER
6-17	ENTERTAINMENT SYSTEM
6-21	WINDSHIELD WIPERS AND WASHERS
6-27	INSTRUMENTS AND SWITCHES
6-34	LIGHTING
6-46	TRAILER WIRING
6-47	CIRCUIT PROTECTION
6-51	WIRING DIAGRAMS

Contents

7-2	MANUAL TRANSMISSION	**7-24**	DRIVELINE
7-4	CLUTCH	**7-28**	REAR AXLE
7-14	AUTOMATIC TRANSMISSION		

CLUTCH AND TRANSMISSION **7**

8-2	WHEELS	**8-16**	REAR SUSPENSION
8-3	FRONT SUSPENSION	**8-24**	STEERING

SUSPENSION AND STEERING **8**

9-2	BRAKE OPERATING SYSTEM	**9-20**	REAR DRUM BRAKES
9-13	FRONT DISC BRAKES	**9-29**	PARKING BRAKE

BRAKES **9**

10-2	EXTERIOR
10-13	INTERIOR

BODY **10**

10-35 GLOSSARY

GLOSSARY

10-39 MASTER INDEX

MASTER INDEX

SAFETY NOTICE

Proper service and repair procedures are vital to the safe, reliable operation of all motor vehicles, as well as the personal safety of those performing repairs. This manual outlines procedures for servicing and repairing vehicles using safe, effective methods. The procedures contain many NOTES, CAUTIONS and WARNINGS which should be followed along with standard procedures to eliminate the possibility of personal injury or improper service which could damage the vehicle or compromise its safety.

It is important to note that the repair procedures and techniques, tools and parts for servicing motor vehicles, as well as the skill and experience of the individual performing the work vary widely. It is not possible to anticipate all of the conceivable ways or conditions under which vehicles may be serviced, or to provide cautions as to all of the possible hazards that may result. Standard and accepted safety precautions and equipment should be used when handling toxic or flammable fluids, and safety goggles or other protection should be used during cutting, grinding, chiseling, prying, or any other process that can cause material removal or projectiles.

Some procedures require the use of tools specially designed for a specific purpose. Before substituting another tool or procedure, you must be completely satisfied that neither your personal safety, nor the performance of the vehicle will be endangered.

Although information in this manual is based on industry sources and is complete as possible at the time of publication, the possibility exists that some vehicle manufacturers made later changes which could not be included here. While striving for total accuracy, W. G. Nichols, Inc. cannot assume responsibility for any errors, changes or omissions that may occur in the compilation of this data.

PART NUMBERS

Part numbers listed in this reference are not recommendations by Chilton for any product by brand name. They are references that can be used with interchange manuals and aftermarket supplier catalogs to locate each brand supplier's discrete part number.

SPECIAL TOOLS

Special tools are recommended by the vehicle manufacturer to perform their specific job. Use has been kept to a minimum, but where absolutely necessary, they are referred to in the text by the part number of the tool manufacturer. These tools can be purchased, under the appropriate part number, from your local dealer or regional distributor, or an equivalent tool can be purchased locally from a tool supplier or parts outlet. Before substituting any tool for the one recommended, read the SAFETY NOTICE at the top of this page.

ACKNOWLEDGMENTS

W. G. Nichols, Inc. expresses appreciation to Toyota Motor Co. for their generous assistance.

1

GENERAL INFORMATION AND MAINTENANCE

HOW TO USE THIS BOOK 1-2
WHERE TO BEGIN 1-2
AVOIDING TROUBLE 1-2
MAINTENANCE OR REPAIR? 1-2
AVOIDING THE MOST COMMON
  MISTAKES 1-2
TOOLS AND EQUIPMENT 1-3
SPECIAL TOOLS 1-6
SERVICING YOUR VEHICLE SAFELY 1-7
DO'S 1-7
DON'TS 1-8
**FASTENERS, MEASUREMENTS AND
  CONVERSIONS** 1-8
BOLTS, NUTS AND OTHER THREADED
  RETAINERS 1-8
TORQUE 1-9
  TORQUE WRENCHES 1-11
  TORQUE ANGLE METERS 1-12
STANDARD AND METRIC
  MEASUREMENTS 1-12
HISTORY 1-14
SERIAL NUMBER IDENTIFICATION 1-14
MODEL IDENTIFICATION 1-14
VEHICLE 1-14
ENGINE 1-14
ROUTINE MAINTENANCE 1-21
AIR CLEANER 1-22
  REMOVAL & INSTALLATION 1-22
FUEL FILTER 1-26
  REMOVAL & INSTALLATION 1-26
FUEL CAP GASKET 1-29
  REMOVAL & INSTALLATION 1-29
PCV VALVE 1-29
  REMOVAL & INSTALLATION 1-29
EVAPORATIVE CANISTER 1-29
  SERVICING 1-29
BATTERY 1-31
  GENERAL MAINTENANCE 1-31
  BATTERY FLUID 1-32
  CABLES 1-33
  CHARGING 1-34
  REPLACEMENT 1-34
BELTS 1-35
  INSPECTION 1-35
HOSES 1-36
  INSPECTION 1-36
  REMOVAL & INSTALLATION 1-37
COOLING SYSTEM 1-38
  LEVEL CHECK 1-38
  INSPECTION 1-38
  DRAIN & REFILL 1-39
AIR CONDITIONING 1-40
  SAFETY PRECAUTIONS 1-40
  GENERAL SERVICING
    PROCEDURES 1-41
  SYSTEM INSPECTION 1-42
  DISCHARGING, EVACUATING &
    CHARGING 1-42
WINDSHIELD WIPERS 1-42
  ELEMENT (REFILL) CARE &
    REPLACEMENT 1-42
TIRES AND WHEELS 1-47
  TIRE ROTATION 1-47
  TIRE DESIGN 1-48
  TIRE STORAGE 1-48
  INFLATION & INSPECTION 1-48
  CARE OF SPECIAL WHEELS 1-50

FLUIDS & LUBRICANTS 1-51
FLUID DISPOSAL 1-51
OIL RECOMMENDATION 1-51
FUEL RECOMMENDATIONS 1-52
ENGINE 1-52
  OIL LEVEL CHECK 1-52
OIL CHANGES 1-52
  OIL & FILTER CHANGE 1-52
MANUAL TRANSMISSION 1-54
  LEVEL CHECK 1-54
  DRAIN & REFILL 1-54
AUTOMATIC TRANSMISSION 1-55
  LEVEL CHECK 1-55
  DRAIN & REFILL 1-55
BRAKE AND CLUTCH MASTER
  CYLINDERS 1-56
  LEVEL CHECK 1-56
DRIVE AXLE 1-57
  LEVEL CHECK 1-57
  DRAIN & REFILL 1-57
STEERING GEAR 1-58
  LEVEL CHECK 1-58
POWER STEERING RESERVOIR 1-59
  LEVEL CHECK 1-59
CHASSIS GREASING 1-59
  EXCEPT CROWN 4M ENGINE 1-59
  CROWN 4M ENGINE 1-59
BODY LUBRICATION 1-59
WHEEL BEARINGS 1-60
  REMOVAL & INSTALLATION 1-60
  PRELOAD ADJUSTMENT 1-62
TRAILER TOWING 1-63
GENERAL RECOMMENDATIONS 1-63
TRAILER WEIGHT 1-63
HITCH (TONGUE) WEIGHT 1-63
COOLING 1-63
  ENGINE 1-63
  TRANSMISSION 1-63
HANDLING A TRAILER 1-64
TOWING THE VEHICLE 1-64
JACKING 1-65
JACKING PRECAUTIONS 1-66
**JUMP STARTING A DEAD
  BATTERY** 1-67
JUMP STARTING PRECAUTIONS 1-67
JUMP STARTING PROCEDURE 1-67
HOW TO BUY A USED VEHICLE 1-68
TIPS 1-68
  USED VEHICLE CHECKLIST 1-68
  ROAD TEST CHECKLIST 1-69
COMPONENT LOCATIONS
  MAINTENANCE COMPONENT
  LOCATIONS—20R ENGINE 1-21
SPECIFICATION CHARTS
  STANDARD TORQUE SPECIFICATIONS AND
    FASTENER MARKINGS 1-10
  ENGINE IDENTIFICATION CHART 1-20
  BATTERY DIMENSIONS (INCHES) 1-35
  TOWING POINTS—1970–77 CHART 1-64
  MAINTENANCE SCHEDULE CHART 1-70
  CAPACITIES CHART 1-72
  ENGLISH TO METRIC CONVERSION
    CHARTS 1-73

HOW TO USE THIS BOOK 1-2
TOOLS AND EQUIPMENT 1-3
SERVICING YOUR VEHICLE SAFELY 1-7
FASTENERS, MEASUREMENTS AND
CONVERSIONS 1-8
HISTORY 1-14
SERIAL NUMBER IDENTIFICATION 1-14
ROUTINE MAINTENANCE 1-21
FLUIDS & LUBRICANTS 1-51
TRAILER TOWING 1-63
TOWING THE VEHICLE 1-64
JACKING 1-65
JUMP STARTING A DEAD BATTERY 1-67
HOW TO BUY A USED VEHICLE 1-68

HOW TO USE THIS BOOK

Chilton's Total Car Care manual is intended to help you learn more about the inner workings of your vehicle while saving you money on its upkeep and operation.

The beginning of the book will likely be referred to the most, since that is where you will find information for maintenance and tune-up. The other sections deal with the more complex systems of your vehicle. Operating systems from engine through brakes are covered to the extent that the average do-it-yourselfer becomes mechanically involved. This book will not explain such things as rebuilding a differential for the simple reason that the expertise required and the investment in special tools make this task uneconomical. It will, however, give you detailed instructions to help you change your own brake pads and shoes, replace spark plugs, and perform many more jobs that can save you money, give you personal satisfaction and help you avoid expensive problems.

A secondary purpose of this book is a reference for owners who want to understand their vehicle and/or their mechanics better. In this case, no tools at all are required.

Where to Begin

Before removing any bolts, read through the entire procedure. This will give you the overall view of what tools and supplies will be required. There is nothing more frustrating than having to walk to the bus stop on Monday morning because you were short one bolt on Sunday afternoon. So read ahead and plan ahead. Each operation should be approached logically and all procedures thoroughly understood before attempting any work.

All sections contain adjustments, maintenance, removal and installation procedures, and in some cases, repair or overhaul procedures. When repair is not considered practical, we tell you how to remove the part and then how to install the new or rebuilt replacement. In this way, you at least save the labor costs. Backyard repair of some components is just not practical.

Avoiding Trouble

Many procedures in this book require you to "label and disconnect . . ." a group of lines, hoses or wires. Don't be lulled into thinking you can remember where everything goes—you won't. If you hook up vacuum or fuel lines incorrectly, the vehicle will run poorly, if at all. If you hook up electrical wiring incorrectly, you may instantly learn a very expensive lesson.

You don't need to know the official or engineering name for each hose or line. A piece of masking tape on the hose and a piece on its fitting will allow you to assign your own label such as the letter A or a short name. As long as you remember your own code, the lines can be reconnected by matching similar letters or names. Do remember that tape will dissolve in gasoline or other fluids; if a component is to be washed or cleaned, use another method of identification. A permanent felt-tipped marker can be very handy for marking metal parts. Remove any tape or paper labels after assembly.

Maintenance or Repair?

It's necessary to mention the difference between maintenance and repair. Maintenance includes routine inspections, adjustments, and replacement of parts which show signs of normal wear. Maintenance compensates for wear or deterioration. Repair implies that something has broken or is not working. A need for repair is often caused by lack of maintenance. Example: draining and refilling the automatic transmission fluid is maintenance recommended by the manufacturer at specific mileage intervals. Failure to do this can ruin the transmission/transaxle, requiring very expensive repairs. While no maintenance program can prevent items from breaking or wearing out, a general rule can be stated: MAINTENANCE IS CHEAPER THAN REPAIR.

Two basic mechanic's rules should be mentioned here. First, whenever the left side of the vehicle or engine is referred to, it is meant to specify the driver's side. Conversely, the right side of the vehicle means the passenger's side. Second, most screws and bolts are removed by turning counterclockwise, and tightened by turning clockwise.

Safety is always the most important rule. Constantly be aware of the dangers involved in working on an automobile and take the proper precautions. See the information in this section regarding SERVICING YOUR VEHICLE SAFELY and the SAFETY NOTICE on the acknowledgment page.

Avoiding the Most Common Mistakes

Pay attention to the instructions provided. There are 3 common mistakes in mechanical work:

1. **Incorrect order of assembly, disassembly or adjustment.** When taking something apart or putting it together, performing steps in the wrong order usually just costs you extra time; however, it CAN break something. Read the entire procedure before beginning disassembly. Perform everything in the order in which the instructions say you should, even if you can't immediately see a reason for it. When you're taking apart something that is very intricate, you might want to draw a picture of how it looks when assembled at one point in order to make sure you get everything back in its proper position. We will supply exploded views whenever possible. When making adjustments, perform them in the proper order; often, one adjustment affects another, and you cannot expect even satisfactory results unless each adjustment is made only when it cannot be changed by any other.

2. **Overtorquing (or undertorquing).** While it is more common for overtorquing to cause damage, undertorquing may allow a fastener to vibrate loose causing serious damage. Especially when dealing with aluminum parts, pay attention to torque specifications and utilize a torque wrench in assembly. If a torque figure is not available, remember that if you are using the right tool to perform the job, you will probably not have to strain yourself to get a fastener tight enough. The pitch of most threads is so slight that the tension you put on the wrench will be multiplied many times in actual force on what you are tightening. A good example of how critical torque is can be seen in the case of spark plug in-

stallation, especially where you are putting the plug into an aluminum cylinder head. Too little torque can fail to crush the gasket, causing leakage of combustion gases and consequent overheating of the plug and engine parts. Too much torque can damage the threads or distort the plug, changing the spark gap.

There are many commercial products available for ensuring that fasteners won't come loose, even if they are not torqued just right (a very common brand is Loctite®). If you're worried about getting something together tight enough to hold, but loose enough to avoid mechanical damage during assembly, one of these products might offer substantial insurance. Before choosing a threadlocking compound, read the label on the package and make sure the product is compatible with the materials, fluids, etc. involved.

3. **Crossthreading.** This occurs when a part such as a bolt is screwed into a nut or casting at the wrong angle and forced. Crossthreading is more likely to occur if access is difficult. It

helps to clean and lubricate fasteners, then to start threading with the part to be installed positioned straight in. Then, start the bolt, spark plug, etc. with your fingers. If you encounter resistance, unscrew the part and start over again at a different angle until it can be inserted and turned several times without much effort. Keep in mind that many parts, especially spark plugs, have tapered threads, so that gentle turning will automatically bring the part you're threading to the proper angle, but only if you don't force it or resist a change in angle. Don't put a wrench on the part until it's been tightened a couple of turns by hand. If you suddenly encounter resistance, and the part has not seated fully, don't force it. Pull it back out to make sure it's clean and threading properly.

Always take your time and be patient; once you have some experience, working on your vehicle may well become an enjoyable hobby.

TOOLS AND EQUIPMENT

Naturally, without the proper tools and equipment it is impossible to properly service your vehicle. It would also be virtually impossible to catalog every tool that you would need to perform all of the operations in this book. Of course, It would be unwise for the amateur to rush out and buy an expensive set of tools on the theory that he/she may need one or more of them at some time.

The best approach is to proceed slowly, gathering a good quality set of those tools that are used most frequently. Don't be misled by the low cost of bargain tools. It is far better to spend a little more for better quality. Forged wrenches, 6 or 12-point sockets and fine tooth ratchets are by far preferable to their less expensive counterparts. As any good mechanic can tell you, there are few worse experiences than trying to work on a vehicle with bad tools. Your monetary savings will be far outweighed by frustration and mangled knuckles.

Begin accumulating those tools that are used most frequently: those associated with routine maintenance and tune-up. In addition to the normal assortment of screwdrivers and pliers, you should have the following tools:

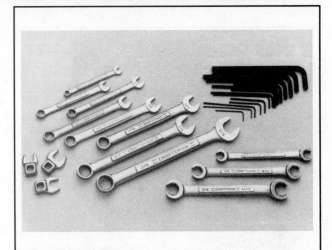

In addition to ratchets, a good set of wrenches and hex keys will be necessary

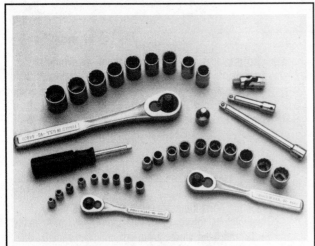

All but the most basic procedures will require an assortment of ratchets and sockets

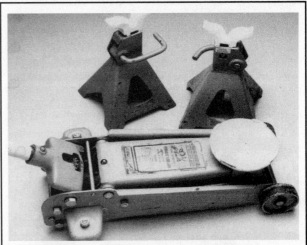

A hydraulic floor jack and a set of jackstands are essential for lifting and supporting the vehicle

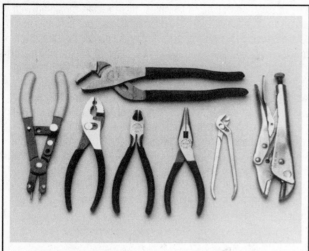

An assortment of pliers, grippers and cutters will be handy for old rusted parts and stripped bolt heads

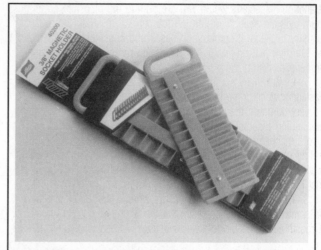

Tools from specialty manufacturers such as Lisle® are designed to make your job easier . . .

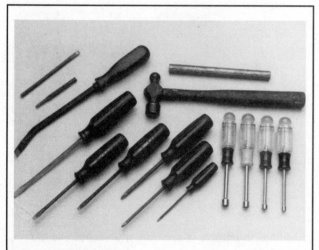

Various drivers, chisels and prybars are great tools to have in your toolbox

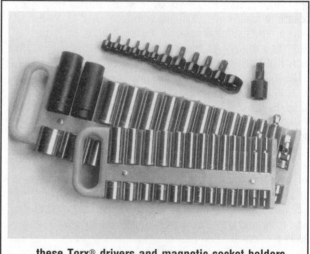

. . . these Torx® drivers and magnetic socket holders are just 2 examples of their handy products

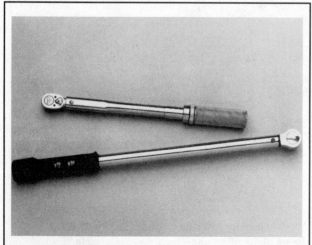

Many repairs will require the use of a torque wrench to assure the components are properly fastened

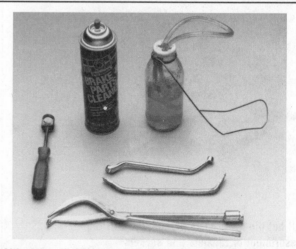

Although not always necessary, using specialized brake tools will save time

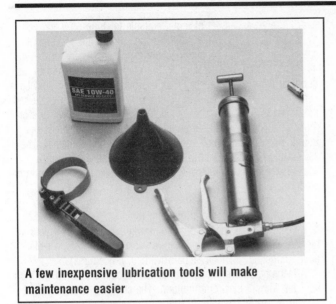

A few inexpensive lubrication tools will make maintenance easier

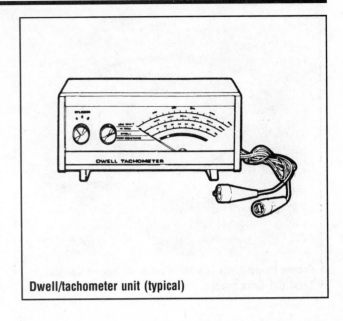

Dwell/tachometer unit (typical)

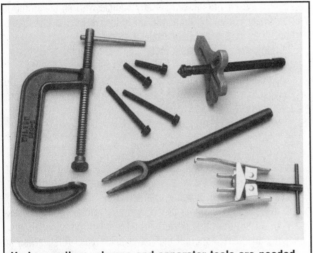

Various pullers, clamps and separator tools are needed for many larger, more complicated repairs

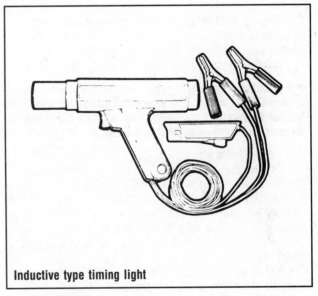

Inductive type timing light

A variety of tools and gauges should be used for spark plug gapping and installation

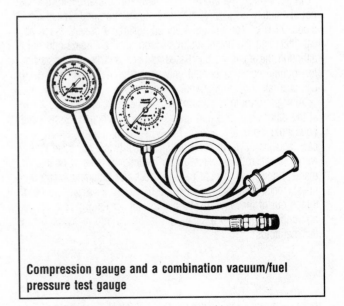

Compression gauge and a combination vacuum/fuel pressure test gauge

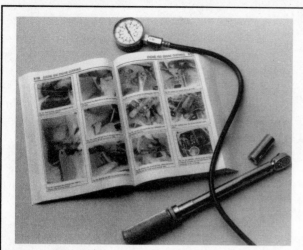

Proper information is vital, so always have a Chilton Total Car Care manual handy

• Wrenches/sockets and combination open end/box end wrenches in sizes from ⅛–¾ in. or 3mm–19mm (depending on whether your vehicle uses standard or metric fasteners) and a ¹³⁄₁₆ in. or ⅝ in. spark plug socket (depending on plug type).

➡️**If possible, buy various length socket drive extensions. Universal-joint and wobble extensions can be extremely useful, but be careful when using them, as they can change the amount of torque applied to the socket.**

• Jackstands for support.
• Oil filter wrench.
• Spout or funnel for pouring fluids.
• Grease gun for chassis lubrication (unless your vehicle is not equipped with any grease fittings—for details, please refer to information on Fluids and Lubricants found later in this section).
• Hydrometer for checking the battery (unless equipped with a sealed, maintenance-free battery).
• A container for draining oil and other fluids.
• Rags for wiping up the inevitable mess.

In addition to the above items there are several others that are not absolutely necessary, but handy to have around. These include Oil Dry® (or an equivalent oil absorbent gravel—such as cat litter) and the usual supply of lubricants, antifreeze and fluids, although these can be purchased as needed. This is a basic list for routine maintenance, but only your personal needs and desire can accurately determine your list of tools.

After performing a few projects on the vehicle, you'll be amazed at the other tools and non-tools on your workbench. Some useful household items are: a large turkey baster or siphon, empty coffee cans and ice trays (to store parts), ball of twine, electrical tape for wiring, small rolls of colored tape for tagging lines or hoses, markers and pens, a note pad, golf tees (for plugging vacuum lines), metal coat hangers or a roll of mechanics's wire (to hold things out of the way), dental pick or similar long, pointed probe, a strong magnet, and a small mirror (to see into recesses and under manifolds).

A more advanced set of tools, suitable for tune-up work, can be drawn up easily. While the tools are slightly more sophisticated, they need not be outrageously expensive. There are several inexpensive tach/dwell meters on the market that are every bit as good for the average mechanic as a professional model. Just be sure that it goes to a least 1200–1500 rpm on the tach scale and that it works on 4, 6 and 8-cylinder engines. (If you own one or more vehicles with a diesel engine, a special tachometer is required since diesels don't use spark plug ignition systems). The key to these purchases is to make them with an eye towards adaptability and wide range. A basic list of tune-up tools could include:

• Tach/dwell meter.
• Spark plug wrench and gapping tool.
• Feeler gauges for valve or point adjustment. (Even if your vehicle does not use points or require valve adjustments, a feeler gauge is helpful for many repair/overhaul procedures).

A tachometer/dwell meter will ensure accurate tune-up work on vehicles without electronic ignition. The choice of a timing light should be made carefully. A light which works on the DC current supplied by the vehicle's battery is the best choice; it should have a xenon tube for brightness. On any vehicle with an electronic ignition system, a timing light with an inductive pickup that clamps around the No. 1 spark plug cable is preferred.

In addition to these basic tools, there are several other tools and gauges you may find useful. These include:

• Compression gauge. The screw-in type is slower to use, but eliminates the possibility of a faulty reading due to escaping pressure.
• Manifold vacuum gauge.
• 12V test light.
• A combination volt/ohmmeter
• Induction Ammeter. This is used for determining whether or not there is current in a wire. These are handy for use if a wire is broken somewhere in a wiring harness.

As a final note, you will probably find a torque wrench necessary for all but the most basic work. The beam type models are perfectly adequate, although the newer click types (breakaway) are easier to use. The click type torque wrenches tend to be more expensive. Also keep in mind that all types of torque wrenches should be periodically checked and/or recalibrated. You will have to decide for yourself which better fits your purpose.

Special Tools

Normally, the use of special factory tools is avoided for repair procedures, since these are not readily available for the do-it-yourself mechanic. When it is possible to perform the job with more commonly available tools, it will be pointed out, but occasionally, a special tool was designed to perform a specific function and should be used. Before substituting another tool, you should be convinced that neither your safety nor the performance of the vehicle will be compromised.

Special tools can usually be purchased from an automotive parts store or from your dealer. In some cases special tools may be available directly from the tool manufacturer.

SERVICING YOUR VEHICLE SAFELY

It is virtually impossible to anticipate all of the hazards involved with automotive maintenance and service, but care and common sense will prevent most accidents.

The rules of safety for mechanics range from "don't smoke around gasoline," to "use the proper tool(s) for the job." The trick to avoiding injuries is to develop safe work habits and to take every possible precaution.

Do's

• Do keep a fire extinguisher and first aid kit handy.

• Do wear safety glasses or goggles when cutting, drilling, grinding or prying, even if you have 20–20 vision. If you wear glasses for the sake of vision, wear safety goggles over your regular glasses.

• Do shield your eyes whenever you work around the battery. Batteries contain sulfuric acid. In case of contact with the eyes or

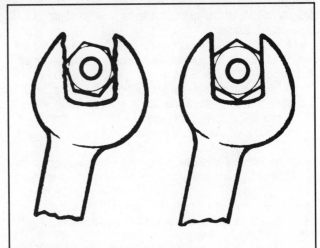

Using the correct size wrench will help prevent the possibility of rounding off a nut

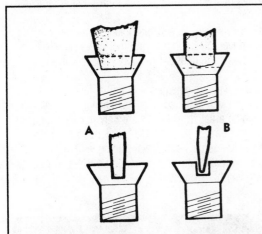

Screwdrivers should be kept in good condition to prevent injury or damage which could result if the blade slips from the screw

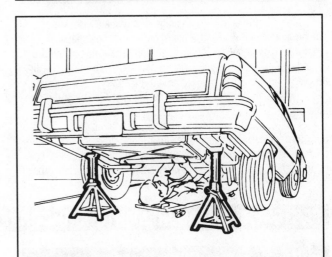

NEVER work under a vehicle unless it is supported using safety stands (jackstands)

Power tools should always be properly grounded

skin, flush the area with water or a mixture of water and baking soda, then seek immediate medical attention.

• Do use safety stands (jackstands) for any undervehicle service. Jacks are for raising vehicles; jackstands are for making sure the vehicle stays raised until you want it to come down. Whenever the vehicle is raised, block the wheels remaining on the ground and set the parking brake.

• Do use adequate ventilation when working with any chemicals or hazardous materials. Like carbon monoxide, the asbestos dust resulting from some brake lining wear can be hazardous in sufficient quantities.

• Do disconnect the negative battery cable when working on the electrical system. The secondary ignition system contains EXTREMELY HIGH VOLTAGE. In some cases it can even exceed 50,000 volts.

• Do follow manufacturer's directions whenever working with potentially hazardous materials. Most chemicals and fluids are poisonous if taken internally.

• Do properly maintain your tools. Loose hammerheads, mushroomed punches and chisels, frayed or poorly grounded electrical cords, excessively worn screwdrivers, spread wrenches (open end), cracked sockets, slipping ratchets, or faulty droplight sockets can cause accidents.

• Likewise, keep your tools clean; a greasy wrench can slip off a bolt head, ruining the bolt and often harming your knuckles in the process.

• Do use the proper size and type of tool for the job at hand. Do select a wrench or socket that fits the nut or bolt. The wrench or socket should sit straight, not cocked.

• Do, when possible, pull on a wrench handle rather than push on it, and adjust your stance to prevent a fall.

• Do be sure that adjustable wrenches are tightly closed on the nut or bolt and pulled so that the force is on the side of the fixed jaw.

• Do strike squarely with a hammer; avoid glancing blows.

• Do set the parking brake and block the drive wheels if the work requires a running engine.

Don'ts

• Don't run the engine in a garage or anywhere else without proper ventilation—EVER! Carbon monoxide is poisonous; it takes a long time to leave the human body and you can build up a deadly supply of it in your system by simply breathing in a little every day. You may not realize you are slowly poisoning yourself. Always use power vents, windows, fans and/or open the garage door.

• Don't work around moving parts while wearing loose clothing. Short sleeves are much safer than long, loose sleeves. Hard-toed shoes with neoprene soles protect your toes and give a better grip on slippery surfaces. Jewelry such as watches, fancy belt buckles, beads or body adornment of any kind is not safe working around a vehicle. Long hair should be tied back under a hat or cap.

• Don't use pockets for toolboxes. A fall or bump can drive a screwdriver deep into your body. Even a rag hanging from your back pocket can wrap around a spinning shaft or fan.

• Don't smoke when working around gasoline, cleaning solvent or other flammable material.

• Don't smoke when working around the battery. When the battery is being charged, it gives off explosive hydrogen gas.

• Don't use gasoline to wash your hands; there are excellent soaps available. Gasoline contains dangerous additives which can enter the body through a cut or through your pores. Gasoline also removes all the natural oils from the skin so that bone dry hands will suck up oil and grease.

• Don't service the air conditioning system unless you are equipped with the necessary tools and training. When liquid or compressed gas refrigerant is released to atmospheric pressure it will absorb heat from whatever it contacts. This will chill or freeze anything it touches. Although refrigerant is normally non-toxic, R-12 becomes a deadly poisonous gas in the presence of an open flame. One good whiff of the vapors from burning refrigerant can be fatal.

• Don't use screwdrivers for anything other than driving screws! A screwdriver used as an prying tool can snap when you least expect it, causing injuries. At the very least, you'll ruin a good screwdriver.

• Don't use a bumper or emergency jack (that little ratchet, scissors, or pantograph jack supplied with the vehicle) for anything other than changing a flat! These jacks are only intended for emergency use out on the road; they are NOT designed as a maintenance tool. If you are serious about maintaining your vehicle yourself, invest in a hydraulic floor jack of at least a 1½ ton capacity, and at least two sturdy jackstands.

FASTENERS, MEASUREMENTS AND CONVERSIONS

Bolts, Nuts and Other Threaded Retainers

Although there are a great variety of fasteners found in the modern car or truck, the most commonly used retainer is the threaded fastener (nuts, bolts, screws, studs, etc). Most threaded retainers may be reused, provided that they are not damaged in use or during the repair. Some retainers (such as stretch bolts or torque prevailing nuts) are designed to deform when tightened or in use and should not be reinstalled.

Whenever possible, we will note any special retainers which should be replaced during a procedure. But you should always inspect the condition of a retainer when it is removed and replace any that show signs of damage. Check all threads for rust or corrosion which can increase the torque necessary to achieve the desired clamp load for which that fastener was originally selected. Additionally, be sure that the driver surface of the fastener has not been compromised by rounding or other damage. In some cases a driver surface may become only partially rounded, allowing the driver to catch in only one direction. In many of these occurrences, a fastener may be installed and tightened, but the driver would not be able to grip and loosen the fastener again. (This could lead to frustration down the line should that component ever need to be disassembled again).

If you must replace a fastener, whether due to design or damage, you must ALWAYS be sure to use the proper replacement. In all cases, a retainer of the same design, material and strength should be used. Markings on the heads of most bolts will help determine the proper strength of the fastener. The same material, thread and pitch must be selected to assure proper installation and safe operation of the vehicle afterwards.

Thread gauges are available to help measure a bolt or stud's thread. Most automotive and hardware stores keep gauges available to help you select the proper size. In a pinch, you can use another nut or bolt for a thread gauge. If the bolt you are replacing is not too badly damaged, you can select a match by finding another bolt which will thread in its place. If you find a nut which threads properly onto the damaged bolt, then use that nut to help select the replacement bolt. If however, the bolt you are replacing is so badly damaged (broken or drilled out) that its threads cannot be used as a gauge, you might start by looking for another bolt (from the same assembly or a similar location on your vehicle) which will thread into the damaged bolt's mounting. If so, the other bolt can be used to select a nut; the nut can then be used to select the replacement bolt.

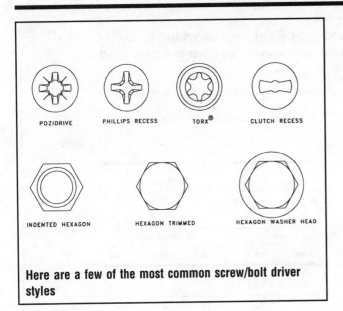

Here are a few of the most common screw/bolt driver styles

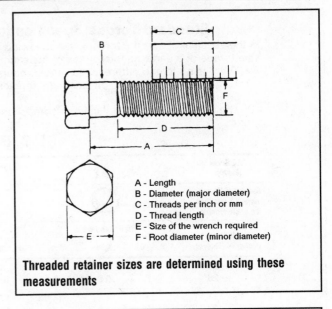

A - Length
B - Diameter (major diameter)
C - Threads per inch or mm
D - Thread length
E - Size of the wrench required
F - Root diameter (minor diameter)

Threaded retainer sizes are determined using these measurements

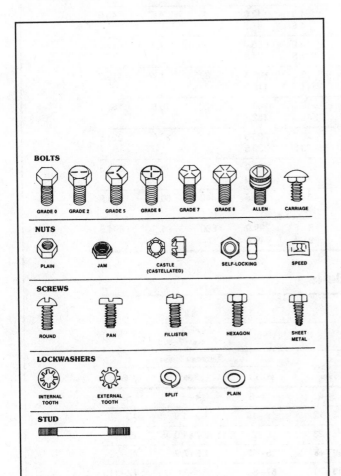

There are many different types of threaded retainers found on vehicles

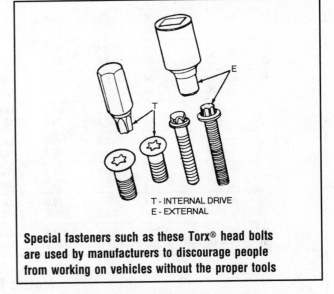

T - INTERNAL DRIVE
E - EXTERNAL

Special fasteners such as these Torx® head bolts are used by manufacturers to discourage people from working on vehicles without the proper tools

In all cases, be absolutely sure you have selected the proper replacement. Don't be shy, you can always ask the store clerk for help.

✳✳ WARNING

Be aware that when you find a bolt with damaged threads, you may also find the nut or drilled hole it was threaded into has also been damaged. If this is the case, you may have to drill and tap the hole, replace the nut or otherwise repair the threads. NEVER try to force a replacement bolt to fit into the damaged threads.

Torque

Torque is defined as the measurement of resistance to turning or rotating. It tends to twist a body about an axis of rotation. A common example of this would be tightening a threaded retainer such as a nut, bolt or screw. Measuring torque is one of the most

Standard Torque Specifications and Fastener Markings

In the absence of specific torques, the following chart can be used as a guide to the maximum safe torque of a particular size/grade of fastener.

- There is no torque difference for fine or coarse threads.
- Torque values are based on clean, dry threads. Reduce the value by 10% if threads are oiled prior to assembly.
- The torque required for aluminum components or fasteners is considerably less.

U.S. Bolts

SAE Grade Number	1 or 2			5			6 or 7		
Number of lines always 2 less than the grade number.									
Bolt Size (Inches)—(Thread)	Ft./Lbs.	Kgm	Nm	Ft./Lbs.	Kgm	Nm	Ft./Lbs.	Kgm	Nm
¼—20	5	0.7	6.8	8	1.1	10.8	10	1.4	13.5
—28	6	0.8	8.1	10	1.4	13.6			
⁵⁄₁₆—18	11	1.5	14.9	17	2.3	23.0	19	2.6	25.8
—24	13	1.8	17.6	19	2.6	25.7			
⅜—16	18	2.5	24.4	31	4.3	42.0	34	4.7	46.0
—24	20	2.75	27.1	35	4.8	47.5			
⁷⁄₁₆—14	28	3.8	37.0	49	6.8	66.4	55	7.6	74.5
—20	30	4.2	40.7	55	7.6	74.5			
½—13	39	5.4	52.8	75	10.4	101.7	85	11.75	115.2
—20	41	5.7	55.6	85	11.7	115.2			
⁹⁄₁₆—12	51	7.0	69.2	110	15.2	149.1	120	16.6	162.7
—18	55	7.6	74.5	120	16.6	162.7			
⅝—11	83	11.5	112.5	150	20.7	203.3	167	23.0	226.5
—18	95	13.1	128.8	170	23.5	230.5			
¾—10	105	14.5	142.3	270	37.3	366.0	280	38.7	379.6
—16	115	15.9	155.9	295	40.8	400.0			
⅞—9	160	22.1	216.9	395	54.6	535.5	440	60.9	596.5
—14	175	24.2	237.2	435	60.1	589.7			
1—8	236	32.5	318.6	590	81.6	799.9	660	91.3	894.8
—14	250	34.6	338.9	660	91.3	849.8			

Metric Bolts

Relative Strength Marking	4.6, 4.8			8.8		
Bolt Markings						
Bolt Size Thread Size x Pitch (mm)	Ft./Lbs.	Kgm	Nm	Ft./Lbs.	Kgm	Nm
6 x 1.0	2–3	.2–.4	3–4	3–6	4–.8	5–8
8 x 1.25	6–8	.8–1	8–12	9–14	1.2–1.9	13–19
10 x 1.25	12–17	1.5–2.3	16–23	20–29	2.7–4.0	27–39
12 x 1.25	21–32	2.9–4.4	29–43	35–53	4.8–7.3	47–72
14 x 1.5	35–52	4.8–7.1	48–70	57–85	7.8–11.7	77–110
16 x 1.5	51–77	7.0–10.6	67–100	90–120	12.4–16.5	130–160
18 x 1.5	74–110	10.2–15.1	100–150	130–170	17.9–23.4	180–230
20 x 1.5	110–140	15.1–19.3	150–190	190–240	26.2–46.9	160–320
22 x 1.5	150–190	22.0–26.2	200–260	250–320	34.5–44.1	340–430
24 x 1.5	190–240	26.2–46.9	260–320	310–410	42.7–56.5	420–550

Standard and metric bolt torque specifications based on bolt strengths—WARNING: use only as a guide

common ways to help assure that a threaded retainer has been properly fastened.

When tightening a threaded fastener, torque is applied in three distinct areas, the head, the bearing surface and the clamp load. About 50 percent of the measured torque is used in overcoming bearing friction. This is the friction between the bearing surface of the bolt head, screw head or nut face and the base material or washer (the surface on which the fastener is rotating). Approximately 40 percent of the applied torque is used in overcoming thread friction. This leaves only about 10 percent of the applied torque to develop a useful clamp load (the force which holds a joint together). This means that friction can account for as much as 90 percent of the applied torque on a fastener.

TORQUE WRENCHES

In most applications, a torque wrench can be used to assure proper installation of a fastener. Torque wrenches come in various designs and most automotive supply stores will carry a variety to suit your needs. A torque wrench should be used any time we supply a specific torque value for a fastener. A torque wrench can also be used if you are following the general guidelines in the accompanying charts. Keep in mind that because there is no worldwide standardization of fasteners, the charts are a general guideline and should be used with caution. Again, the general rule of "if you are using the right tool for the job, you should not have to strain to tighten a fastener" applies here.

Beam Type

The beam type torque wrench is one of the most popular types. It consists of a pointer attached to the head that runs the length of the flexible beam (shaft) to a scale located near the handle. As the wrench is pulled, the beam bends and the pointer indicates the torque using the scale.

Click (Breakaway) Type

Another popular design of torque wrench is the click type. To use the click type wrench you pre-adjust it to a torque setting. Once the torque is reached, the wrench has a reflex signalling fea-

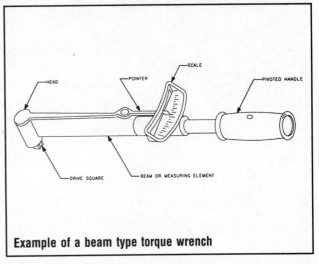

Example of a beam type torque wrench

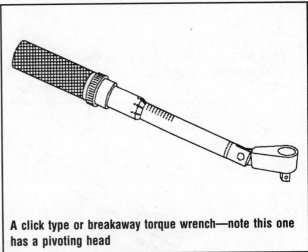

A click type or breakaway torque wrench—note this one has a pivoting head

ture that causes a momentary breakaway of the torque wrench body, sending an impulse to the operator's hand.

Pivot Head Type

Some torque wrenches (usually of the click type) may be equipped with a pivot head which can allow it to be used in areas of limited access. BUT, it must be used properly. To hold a pivot head wrench, grasp the handle lightly, and as you pull on the handle, it should be floated on the pivot point. If the handle comes in contact with the yoke extension during the process of pulling, there is a very good chance the torque readings will be inaccurate because this could alter the wrench loading point. The design of the handle is usually such as to make it inconvenient to deliberately misuse the wrench.

➡ **It should be mentioned that the use of any U-joint, wobble or extension will have an effect on the torque readings, no matter what type of wrench you are using. For the most accurate readings, install the socket directly on the wrench driver. If necessary, straight extensions (which hold a socket directly under the wrench driver) will have the least effect on the torque reading. Avoid any extension that alters the length of the wrench from the handle to the head/driving point (such as a crow's foot). U-joint or Wobble extensions can greatly affect the readings; avoid their use at all times.**

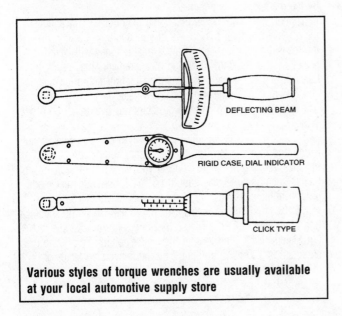

DEFLECTING BEAM

RIGID CASE, DIAL INDICATOR

CLICK TYPE

Various styles of torque wrenches are usually available at your local automotive supply store

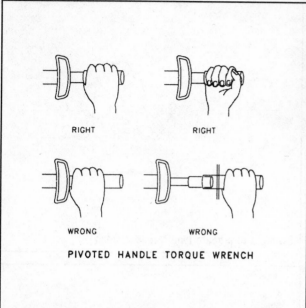

RIGHT RIGHT

WRONG WRONG

PIVOTED HANDLE TORQUE WRENCH

Torque wrenches with pivoting heads must be grasped and used properly to prevent an incorrect reading

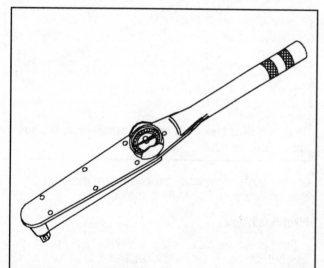

The rigid case (direct reading) torque wrench uses a dial indicator to show torque

Rigid Case (Direct Reading)

A rigid case or direct reading torque wrench is equipped with a dial indicator to show torque values. One advantage of these wrenches is that they can be held at any position on the wrench without affecting accuracy. These wrenches are often preferred because they tend to be compact, easy to read and have a great degree of accuracy.

TORQUE ANGLE METERS

Because the frictional characteristics of each fastener or threaded hole will vary, clamp loads which are based strictly on

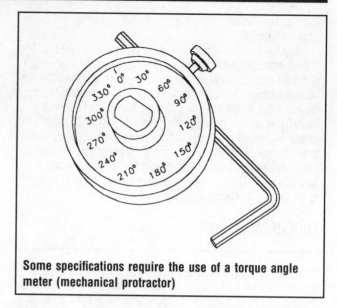

Some specifications require the use of a torque angle meter (mechanical protractor)

torque will vary as well. In most applications, this variance is not significant enough to cause worry. But, in certain applications, a manufacturer's engineers may determine that more precise clamp loads are necessary (such is the case with many aluminum cylinder heads). In these cases, a torque angle method of installation would be specified. When installing fasteners which are torque angle tightened, a predetermined seating torque and standard torque wrench are usually used first to remove any compliance from the joint. The fastener is then tightened the specified additional portion of a turn measured in degrees. A torque angle gauge (mechanical protractor) is used for these applications.

Standard and Metric Measurements

Throughout this manual, specifications are given to help you determine the condition of various components on your vehicle, or to assist you in their installation. Some of the most common measurements include length (in. or cm/mm), torque (ft. lbs., inch lbs. or Nm) and pressure (psi, in. Hg, kPa or mm Hg). In most cases, we strive to provide the proper measurement as determined by the manufacturer's engineers.

Though, in some cases, that value may not be conveniently measured with what is available in your toolbox. Luckily, many of the measuring devices which are available today will have two scales so the Standard or Metric measurements may easily be taken. If any of the various measuring tools which are available to you do not contain the same scale as listed in the specifications, use the accompanying conversion factors to determine the proper value.

The conversion factor chart is used by taking the given specification and multiplying it by the necessary conversion factor. For instance, looking at the first line, if you have a measurement in inches such as "free-play should be 2 in." but your ruler reads only in millimeters, multiply 2 in. by the conversion factor of 25.4 to get the metric equivalent of 50.8mm. Likewise, if the specification was given only in a Metric measurement, for example in Newton Meters (Nm), then look at the center column first. If the measurement is 100 Nm, multiply it by the conversion factor of 0.738 to get 73.8 ft. lbs.

CONVERSION FACTORS

LENGTH–DISTANCE

Inches (in.)	x 25.4	= Millimeters (mm)	x .0394	= Inches
Feet (ft.)	x .305	= Meters (m)	x 3.281	= Feet
Miles	x 1.609	= Kilometers (km)	x .0621	= Miles

VOLUME

Cubic Inches (in3)	x 16.387	= Cubic Centimeters	x .061	= in3
IMP Pints (IMP pt.)	x .568	= Liters (L)	x 1.76	= IMP pt.
IMP Quarts (IMP qt.)	x 1.137	= Liters (L)	x .88	= IMP qt.
IMP Gallons (IMP gal.)	x 4.546	= Liters (L)	x .22	= IMP gal.
IMP Quarts (IMP qt.)	x 1.201	= US Quarts (US qt.)	x .833	= IMP qt.
IMP Gallons (IMP gal.)	x 1.201	= US Gallons (US gal.)	x .833	= IMP gal.
Fl. Ounces	x 29.573	= Milliliters	x .034	= Ounces
US Pints (US pt.)	x .473	= Liters (L)	x 2.113	= Pints
US Quarts (US qt.)	x .946	= Liters (L)	x 1.057	= Quarts
US Gallons (US gal.)	x 3.785	= Liters (L)	x .264	= Gallons

MASS–WEIGHT

Ounces (oz.)	x 28.35	= Grams (g)	x .035	= Ounces
Pounds (lb.)	x .454	= Kilograms (kg)	x 2.205	= Pounds

PRESSURE

Pounds Per Sq. In. (psi)	x 6.895	= Kilopascals (kPa)	x .145	= psi
Inches of Mercury (Hg)	x .4912	= psi	x 2.036	= Hg
Inches of Mercury (Hg)	x 3.377	= Kilopascals (kPa)	x .2961	= Hg
Inches of Water (H_2O)	x .07355	= Inches of Mercury	x 13.783	= H_2O
Inches of Water (H_2O)	x .03613	= psi	x 27.684	= H_2O
Inches of Water (H_2O)	x .248	= Kilopascals (kPa)	x 4.026	= H_2O

TORQUE

Pounds–Force Inches (in–lb)	x .113	= Newton Meters (N·m)	x 8.85	= in–lb
Pounds–Force Feet (ft–lb)	x 1.356	= Newton Meters (N·m)	x .738	= ft–lb

VELOCITY

Miles Per Hour (MPH)	x 1.609	= Kilometers Per Hour (KPH)	x .621	= MPH

POWER

Horsepower (Hp)	x .745	= Kilowatts	x 1.34	= Horsepower

FUEL CONSUMPTION*

Miles Per Gallon IMP (MPG)	x .354	= Kilometers Per Liter (Km/L)
Kilometers Per Liter (Km/L)	x 2.352	= IMP MPG
Miles Per Gallon US (MPG)	x .425	= Kilometers Per Liter (Km/L)
Kilometers Per Liter (Km/L)	x 2.352	= US MPG

*It is common to covert from miles per gallon (mpg) to liters/100 kilometers (1/100 km), where mpg (IMP) x 1/100 km = 282 and mpg (US) x 1/100 km = 235.

TEMPERATURE

Degree Fahrenheit (°F)	= (°C x 1.8) + 32
Degree Celsius (°C)	= (°F – 32) x .56

Standard and metric conversion factors chart

HISTORY

In 1933, the Toyota Automatic Loom Works started an automobile division. Several models, mostly experimental, were produced between 1935 and 1937. Automobile production started on a large scale in 1937 when the Toyota Motor Co. Ltd. was founded. The name for the automobile company was changed from the family name, Toyoda, to Toyota, because a numerologist suggested that this would be a more auspicious name to use for this endeavor. It must have been; by 1947, Toyota had produced 100,000 vehicles. Today Toyota is Japan's largest producer of motor vehicles and ranks among the largest in world production.

It was not until the late 1950s, that Toyota began exporting cars to the United States. Public reception of the Toyopet was rather cool. The car was heavy and under-powered by U.S. standards. Several other models were exported, including the almost indestructible Land Cruiser. It was not until 1965, however, with the introduction of the Corona sedan, that Toyota enjoyed a real success on the U.S. market.

SERIAL NUMBER IDENTIFICATION

Model Identification

◆ **See Figures 1 thru 11 (p. 14–18)**

Toyota's have an identification plate which is located under the hood on the firewall of most models. The models are identified by a code. These codes explain exactly what your vehicle is and has. For example; model number MS55L-KD is a 1968-71 Crown sedan deluxe, with a 2M engine and a 4-speed manual transmission. When you walk into your dealer or local parts store to purchase a part for your vehicle, and are not sure exactly what type of vehicle you drive, the model number and vehicle identification numbers are the key.

MODEL	PRODUCTION PERIOD	ENGINE	TRANSMISSION	
• RT83L·KA/u	7002–7108	8R-C	MTM	4-speed floor shift
• RT83L·KA/c	7002–7101	8R	MTM	4-speed floor shift
• RT83L·KA/c	7102–7108	8R-C	MTM	4-speed floor shift
RT83L·NA/u	7002–7108	8R-C	ATM	3-speed column shift
• RT83L·NA/c	7002–7101	8R	ATM	3-speed column shift
• RT83L·NA/c	7102–7108	8R-C	ATM	3-speed column shift
RT93L·KA/u	7009–7108	8R-C	MTM	4-speed floor shift
• RT93L·KA/c	7009–7101	8R	MTM	4-speed floor shift
• RT93L·KA/c	7102–7108	8R-C	MTM	4-speed floor shift
RT93L·HA/u	7009–7108	8R-C	ATM	3-speed floor shift
• RT93L·HA/c	7009–7101	8R	ATM	3-speed floor shift
• RT93L·HA/c	7102–7108	8R-C	ATM	3-speed floor shift
RT85L·KA	7109–7307	18R-C	MTM	4-speed floor shift
RT85L·NA	7109–7307	18R-C	ATM	3-speed column shift
RT95L·KA	7109–7307	18R-C	MTM	4-speed floor shift
RT95L·HA	7109–7307	18R-C	ATM	3-speed floor shift
RT89L·KA	7208–7307	18R-C	MTM	4-speed floor shift
RT89L·NA	7208–7307	18R-C	ATM	3-speed column shift

* As for the CORONA for Canada, 8R engine was installed up to January 1971, and from February 1971 to August 1971, 8R-C engine was installed.

Fig. 1 Model code identification—1970–73 Corona

Vehicle

◆ **See Figure 12 (p. 19)**

All models have the Vehicle Identification Number (VIN) stamped on a plate which is attached to the left side of the instrument panel. This plate is visible through the windshield.

The VIN is also stamped on a plate in the engine compartment which is usually located on the firewall.

Through 1980 the serial number consists of a series identification number followed by a six-digit production number.

Beginning with 1981 models the serial number consists of seventeen symbols (letters and numbers).

Engine

The engine serial number consists of an engine series identification number, followed by a six-digit production number.

The location of this serial number varies from one engine type to another. Serial numbers may be found in the following locations:

1,900cc (8R-C)

The serial number for this engine is embossed beside the fuel pump on the right side of the engine.

2,000cc (18R-C)

The serial number is stamped on the left side of the engine, behind the dipstick.

2,200 and 2,400cc (20R and 22R)

The serial number is stamped on the left side of the engine, behind the alternator.

2,300, 2,600 and 2,800cc (2M, 4M, 4ME and 5ME)

The serial numbers on these engines are stamped on the right side of the cylinder block, below the oil filter.

MODEL	ENGINE	PRODUCTION PERIOD	CHARACTERISTIC EXPRESSION IN PARTS CATALOG MODEL COLUMN					MODEL NAME
RT104L-KRA	18R-C	7311— 7408	SED	MTM	4F	STD	2D	2000 2-door Sedan
RT104L-HRA	18R-C	7311— 7408	SED	ATM	3FC	STD	2D	2000 2-door Sedan
RT104L-KDA	18R-C	7309— 7408	SED	MTM	4F	DLX	2D	2000 2-door Deluxe Sedan
RT104L-HDA	18R-C	7309— 7408	SED	ATM	3FC	DLX	2D	2000 2-door Deluxe Sedan
RT104L-KDFA	18R-C	7308— 7408	SED	MTM	4F	DLX	4D	2000 4-door Deluxe Sedan
RT104L-HDFA	18R-C	7308— 7408	SED	ATM	3FC	DLX	4D	2000 4-door Deluxe Sedan
RT114L-KDA	18R-C	7308— 7408	HT	MTM	4F	DLX	2D	2000 Hardtop
RT114L-HDA	18R-C	7308— 7408	HT	ATM	3FC	DLX	2D	2000 Hardtop
RT114L-MDA	18R-C	7308— 7403	HT	MTM	5F	DLX	2D	2000 Hardtop SR
RT118L-KDFA	18R-C	7308— 7408	WG	MTM	4F	DLX	4D	2000 Station Wagon
RT118L-HDFA	18R-C	7308— 7408	WG	ATM	3FC	DLX	4D	2000 Station Wagon
RT105L-KRA	20R	7408— 7808	SED	MTM	4F	STD	2D	2200 2-door Sedan
RT105L-HRA	20R	7408— 7808	SED	ATM	3FC	STD	2D	2200 2-door Sedan
RT105L-KDA	20R	7408— 7608	SED	MTM	4F	DLX	2D	2200 2-door Deluxe Sedan
RT105L-HDA	20R	7408— 7608	SED	ATM	3FC	DLX	2D	2200 2-door Deluxe Sedan
RT105L-MDA	20R	7408— 7608	SED	MTM	5F	DLX	2D	2200 2-door Deluxe Sedan E-5
RT105L-KDFA	20R	7408— 7808	SED	MTM	4F	DLX	4D	2200 4-door Deluxe Sedan
RT105L-HDFA	20R	7408— 7605	SED	ATM	3FC	DLX	4D	2200 4-door Deluxe Sedan
RT105L-NDFA	20R	7605— 7808	SED	ATM	3HC	DLX	4D	2200 4-door Deluxe Sedan
RT105L-MDFA	20R	7408— 7808	SED	MTM	5F	DLX	4D	2200 4-door Deluxe Sedan E-5
RT115L-KDA	20R	7408— 7608	HT	MTM	4F	DLX	2D	2200 Hardtop
RT115L-HDA	20R	7408— 7808	HT	ATM	3FC	DLX	2D	2200 Hardtop
RT115L-MDA	20R	7408— 7808	HT	MTM	5F	DLX	2D	2200 Hardtop SR-5
RT119L-KDFA	20R	7408— 7808	WG	MTM	4F	DLX	4D	2200 Station Wagon
RT119L-HDFA	20R	7408— 7605	WG	ATM	3FC	DLX	4D	2200 Station Wagon
RT119L-NDFA	20R	7605— 7808	WG	ATM	3HC	DLX	4D	2200 Station Wagon
RT119L-MDFA	20R	7509— 7808	WG	MTM	5F	DLX	4D	2200 Station Wagon E-5

SED	Sedan	ATM	Automatic transmission
HT	Hardtop	3FC	ATM, 3-speed floor shift
WG	Station Wagon	3HC	ATM, 3-speed column shift
MTM	Manual transmission	STD	Standard type
4F	MTM, 4-speed floor shift	DLX	Deluxe type
5F	MTM, 5-speed floor shift	2D	2-door
		4D	4-door

Fig. 2 Model code identification—1974–78 Corona

TOYOTA CORONA, Sedan

Model	Engine	Production Period	Characteristic Expressions in Catalog Model Column						Model Name
RT134L-TEKDSA	20R	7809—8008	SED	MTM	4F	DLX	USA	LPB	Deluxe Sedan
RT134L-TEMDSA	"	7809—8008	"	"	5F	"	"	"	" "
RT134L-TENDSA	"	7809—8008	"	ATM	3HC	"	"	"	" "
RT134L-TEMESA	"	7809—8008	"	MTM	5F	LE	"	"	Sedan, LE
RT134L-TEHESA	"	7809—8008	"	ATM	3FC	"	"	"	" , "
RT134L-TEHESAX	"	8001—8003	"	"	"	"	"	WPB	" , "
RT134L-TEMDSK	"	7809—8008	"	MTM	5F	DLX	CND	LPB	Deluxe Sedan
RT134L-TENDSK	"	7809—8008	"	ATM	3HC	"	"	"	" "
RT135L-TEMDSA	22R	8008—8112	SED	MTM	5F	DLX	USA	LPB	Deluxe Sedan
RT135L-TEHDSA	"	8008—8112	"	ATM	4FC	"	"	"	" "
RT135L-TEMESA	"	8008—8112	"	MTM	5F	LE	"	"	Sedan, LE
RT135L-TEHESA	"	8008—8112	"	ATM	4FC	"	"	"	" , "

Fig. 3 Model code identification—1979–82 Corona sedan

TOYOTA CORONA, Liftback

Model	Engine	Production Period	Characteristic Expressions in Catalog Model Column						Model Name
RT134L-TLKDSA	20R	7809–8008	LB	MTM	4F	DLX	USA	LPB	Liftback, Deluxe
RT134L-TLMDSA	"	7809–8008	"	"	5F	"	"	"	" , "
RT134L-TLNDSA	"	7809–8008	"	ATM	3HC	"	"	"	" , "
RT134L-TLMESA	"	7809–8008	"	MTM	5F	LE	"	"	" , LE
RT134L-TLHESA	"	7809–8008	"	ATM	3FC	"	"	"	" , "
RT134L-TLMDSK	"	7809–8008	"	MTM	5F	DLX	CND	"	Liftback, Deluxe
RT134L-TLNDSK	"	7809–8008	"	ATM	3HC	"	"	"	" , "
RT135L-TLMESA	22R	8008–8112	LB	MTM	5F	LE	USA	LPB	Liftback, LE
RT135L-TLHESA	"	8008–8112	"	ATM	4FC	'	"	"	" , "
RT135L-TLMESK	"	8008–8112	"	MTM	5F	"	CND	"	" , "
RT135L-TLHESK	"	8008–8112	"	ATM	4FC	"	"	"	" , "

Fig. 4 Model code identification—1979–82 Corona liftback

TOYOTA CORONA, Station Wagon

Model	Engine	Production Period	Characteristic Expressions in Catalog Model Column						Model Name
RT134LG-TWKDSA	20R	7809–7908	WG	MTM	4F	DLX	USA	LPB	Station Wagon, Deluxe
RT134LG-TWMDSA	"	7809–8008	"	"	5F	"	"	"	" , " , "
RT134LG-TWNDSA	"	7809–8008	"	ATM	3HC	'	"	"	" , " , "
RT134LG-TWMESA	"	7809–8008	"	MTM	5F	LE	"	"	" , " , LE
RT134LG-TWHESA	"	7809–8008	"	ATM	3FC	"	"	"	" , " , "
RT134LG-TWMDSK	"	7809–8008	WG	MTM	5F	DLX	CND	"	Station Wagon, Deluxe
RT134LG-TWNDSK	"	7809–8008	"	ATM	3HC	"	"	"	" , " , "
RT135LG-TWMDSA	22R	8008–8112	WG	MTM	5F	DLX	USA	LPB	" , " , "
RT135LG-TWHDSA	"	8008–8112	"	ATM	4FC	"	"	"	" , " , "

SED	Sedan
LB	Liftback
WG	Station Wagon
MTM	Manual transmission
4F	MTM, 4-speed floor shift
5F	MTM, 5-speed floor shift
ATM	Automatic transmission
3HC	ATM, 3-speed column shift
3FC	ATM, 3-speed floor shift
DLX	Deluxe type
LE	LE type
USA	For United States of America
CND	For Canada
LPB	Less Passive Belt
WPB	With Passive Belt

Fig. 5 Model code identification—1979–82 Corona wagon

MODEL	ENGINE	PRODUCTION PERIOD	TRANSMISSION	
RT62L-KA/U	8P-C	6902–7108	MTM	4-speed floor shift
* RT62L-KA/C	8R	6902–7101	MTM	4-speed floor shift
* RT62L-KA/C	8R-C	7102–7108	MTM	4-speed floor shift
RT62L-HA/U	8R-C	6902–7105	ATM	3-speed floor shift
* RT62L-HA/C	8R	6902–7101	ATM	3-speed floor shift
* RT62L-HA/C	8R-C	7102–7108	ATM	3-speed floor shift
RT72L-KA/U	8R-C	6902–7108	MTM	4-speed floor shift
* RT72L-KA/C	8R	6902–7101	MTM	4-speed floor shift
* RT72L-KA/C	8R-C	7102–7108	MTM	4-speed floor shift
RT72L-HA/U	8R-C	6902–7108	ATM	3-speed floor shift
* RT72L-HA/C	8R	6902–7101	ATM	3-speed floor shift
* RT72L-HA/C	8R-C	7102–7108	ATM	3-speed floor shift
RT78L-KA/U	8R-C	6902–7108	MTM	4-speed floor shift
* RT78L-KA/C	8R	7002–7101	MTM	4-speed floor shift
* RT78L-KA/C	8R-C	7102–7108	MTM	4-speed floor shift
RT78L-HA/U	8R-C	6902–7108	ATM	3-speed floor shift
* RT78L-HA/C	8R	7002–7101	ATM	3-speed floor shift
* RT78L-HA/C	8R-C	7102–7108	ATM	3-speed floor shift
RT63L-KA	18R-C	7109–7112	MTM	4-speed floor shift
RT73L-HA	18R-C	7109–7112	ATM	3-speed floor shift
RT73L-KA	18R-C	7109–7112	MTM	4-speed floor shift
RT73L-HA	18R-C	7109–7112	ATM	3-speed floor shift
RT79L-KA	18R-C	7109–7112	MTM	4-speed floor shift
RT79L-HA	18R-C	7109–7112	ATM	3-speed floor shift

As for the TOYOTA CORONA MARK II for Canada, 8R engine was installed up to January 1971, and from February 1971 to August 1971, 8R-C engine was installed.

Fig. 6 Model code identification—1969–72 Corona Mark II

MODEL	ENGINE	PRODUCTION PERIOD	TRANSMISSION		MODEL NAME
MX12L-KDA	2M	7201–7208	MTM	4-speed	Sedan
MX12L-HDA	2M	7201–7208	ATM	3-speed	Sedan
MX22L-KDA	2M	7201–7208	MTM	4-speed	Hardtop
MX22L-HDA	2M	7201–7208	ATM	3-speed	Hardtop
MX28L-KDA	2M	7201–7208	MTM	4-speed	Station Wagon
MX28L-HDA	2M	7201–7208	ATM	3-speed	Station Wagon
MX13L-KDA	4M	7209–7611	MTM	4-speed	Sedan
MX13L-HDA	4M	7209–7611	ATM	3-speed	Sedan
MX23L-KDA	4M	7209–7611	MTM	4-speed	Hardtop
MX23L-HDA	4M	7209–7611	ATM	3-speed	Hardtop
MX29L-KDA	4M	7209–7611	MTM	4-speed	Station Wagon
MX29L-HDA	4M	7209–7611	ATM	3-speed	Station Wagon

SED	Sedan	ATM	Automatic transmission
HT	Hardtop	MTM	Manual transmission
WG	Station Wagon		

Fig. 7 Model code identification—1972–77 Corona Mark II

MODEL	ENGINE	PRODUCTION PERIOD	TRANSMISSION	MODEL NAME
MS55L-KD	2M	6709–7101	MTM 4 speed	Sedan Deluxe
MS55L-ND	2M	6709–7101	ATM 3 speed	Sedan Deluxe
MS53L-K	2M	6709–7101	MTM 4-speed	Station Wagon
MS53L-N	2M	6709–7101	ATM 3 speed	Station Wagon

Fig. 8 Model code identification—1968–71 Crown

MODEL	ENGINE	PRODUCTION PERIOD	TRANSMISSION
MS65L-KDA	4M	7102–7208	MTM 4-speed floor shift
MS65L-NDA	4M	7102–7208	ATM 3 speed column shift
MS75L-KDA	4M	7102–7208	MTM 4-speed floor shift
MS75L-HDA	4M	7102–7208	ATM 3-speed floor shift
MS63L-KA	4M	7102–7208	MTM 4-speed floor shift
MS63L-NA	4M	7102–7208	ATM 3-speed column shift

Fig. 9 Model code identification—1971–72 Crown

Model	Engine	Production Period	Characteristic Expression		Model Name
MX32L-EHNA	4M	7708–7908	SED	L	Sedan
MX32L-EHGA	"	7808–7908	"	LG	"
MX36L-WHNA	"	7708–7908	WG	L	Station Wagon
MX32L-EHNEA	4M-E	7908–8008	SED	L	Sedan
MX32L-EHGEA	"	7908–8008	"	LG	"
MX36L-WHNEA	"	7908–8008	WG	L	Station Wagon

SED	Sedan
WG	Station Wagon
ATM	Automatic transmission
MTM	Manual transmission
L	L type
LG	LG type

Fig. 10 Model code identification—1978–80 Cressida

Model	Engine	Production Period	Characteristic Expression in Catalog Model Column			Model Name
MX62L-XEPMEA	5M-E	8009–8208	SED	ATM	USA	Sedan
MX62L-XEPMEK	"	8009–8208	"	"	CND	"
MX62LG-XWPMEA	"	8009–8208	WG	"	USA	Station Wagon
MX62LG-XWPMEK	"	8108–8208	"	"	CND	" "

SED	Sedan
WG	Station Wagon
MTM	Manual transmission
ATM	Automatic transmission
USA	For United States of America
CND	For Canada

Fig. 11 Model code identification—1981–82 Cressida

VEHICLE IDENTIFICATION

Serial Number Location:
1. On top of dash panel at left "A" Pillar, (See ill.)
2. On fire wall of engine compartment.

Top of Dash on Driver Side

1981-82
17 Digit Serial Number

4th Digit
Engine Series Code

10th Digit
Model Year

J T 2 R T 3 4 G X C X 9 9 9 9 9 9

5th Digit
Car Line

1970-80
10 Digit Serial Number

NOTE: The Last six Digits on the frame number indicate the model year. Refer to Toyota frame number chart for proper year identification.

1st Digit
Engine Series Code

2nd Digit
Car Line

M S 7 5 2 1 2 3 8 9

Fig. 12 The Vehicle Identification Number (VIN) has individual meanings for each character

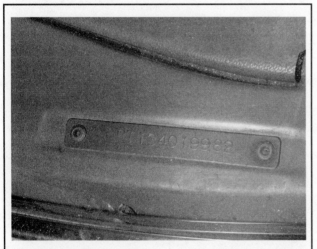

The VIN number is located on a plate attached to the left side of the instrument panel

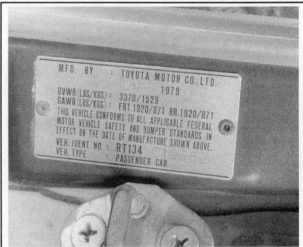

The serial number is on an identification plate on the drivers door jam

The VIN is also stamped on the firewall in the engine compartment

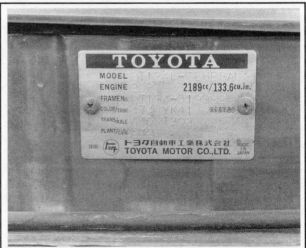

The engine number is located on the model identification plate on the firewall

Engine Idenfication

Model	Year	Displacement (cc/cu in.)	Number of Cylinders	Type	Engine Series Identification
CORONA					
1900	1970–71	1858/113.4	4	OHC	8R-C
2000	1972–74	1908/120.0	4	OHC	18R-C
2200	1975–80	2189/133.0	4	OHC	20R
2400	1981–82	2367/144.4	4	OHC	22R
MARK II					
1900	1970–71	1858/113.4	4	OHC	8R-C
2000	1972	1980/120.0	4	OHC	18R-C
2300	1972 (late)	2258/137.5	6	OHC	2M
2600	1973–76	2563/156.4	6	OHC	4M
CROWN					
2300	1970–71	2258/137.5	6	OHC	2M
2600	1971–72	2563/156.4	6	OHC	4M
CRESSIDA					
2600	1978–79	2563/156.4	6	OHC	4M
2600	1980	2563/156.4	6	OHC	4M-E
2800	1981–82	2759/168.4	6	OHC	5M-E

ROUTINE MAINTENANCE

MAINTENANCE COMPONENT LOCATIONS—20R ENGINE

1. Battery
2. Coolant hose
3. Air cleaner
4. Radiator cap
5. Distributor cap and wires
6. Oil filter cap
7. Thermostat housing
8. PCV valve
9. Fuel filter
10. Washer fluid reservoir
11. Coolant reservoir
12. Accessory drive belt
13. Power steering reservoir
14. Brake master cylinder reservoir
15. Identification plate

Air Cleaner

REMOVAL & INSTALLATION

◆ **See Figures 13, 14, 15, 16 and 16a (p. 22–25)**

The air cleaners used on Toyota vehicles are of the dry element, disposable type. They should never be washed or oiled.

Clean the element every 3,000 miles, or more often under dry, dusty conditions, by using low pressure compressed air. Blow from the inside toward the outside.

✳✳ WARNING

Never use high air pressure to clean the element, as this will probably damage it.

Replace the element every 18,000 miles, (1970–72); every 24,000 miles (1973–74); 25,000 miles (1975–77); 30,000 miles (1978–82); or more often under dry, dusty conditions. Be sure to use the correct one; all Toyota elements are of the same type but they come in a variety of sizes.

To remove the air cleaner element, unfasten the wing nut(s) and clips (if so equipped) on top of the housing and lift off the

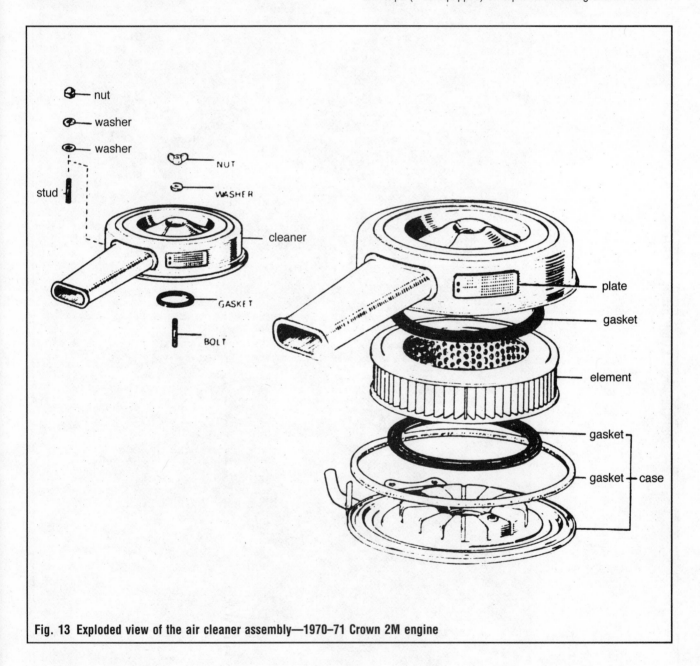

Fig. 13 Exploded view of the air cleaner assembly—1970–71 Crown 2M engine

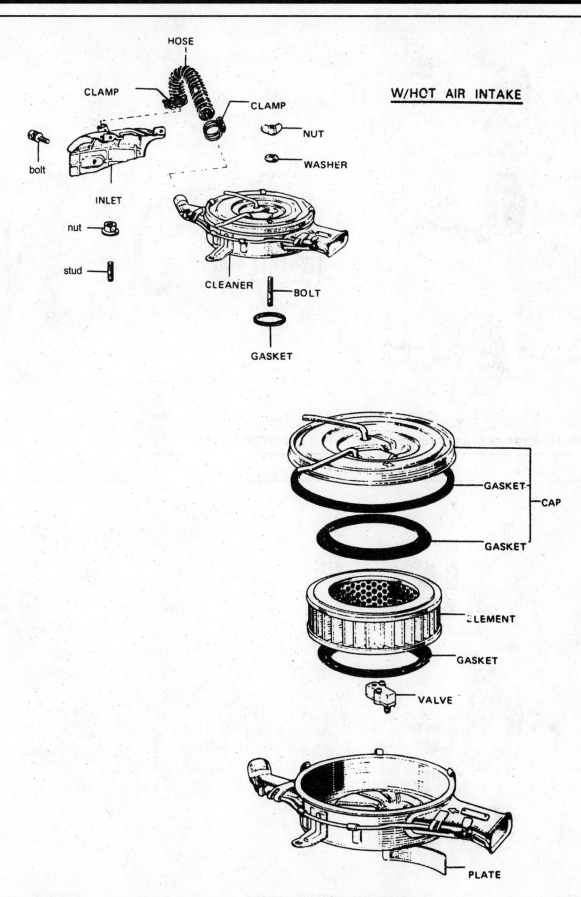

Fig. 14 Exploded view of the air cleaner assembly—1972–74 Crown 2M and 4M engines

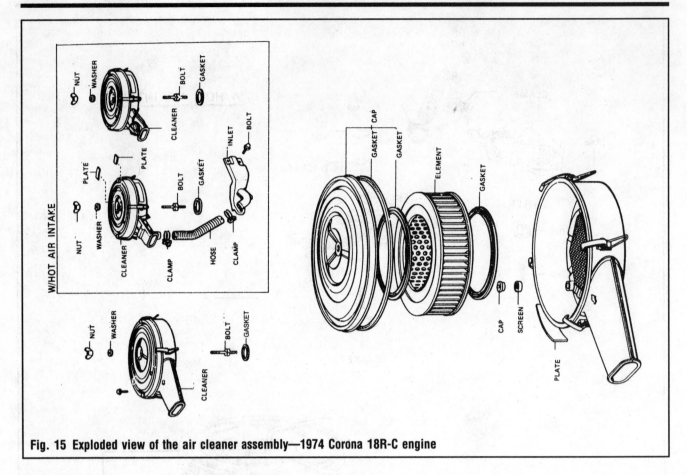

Fig. 15 Exploded view of the air cleaner assembly—1974 Corona 18R-C engine

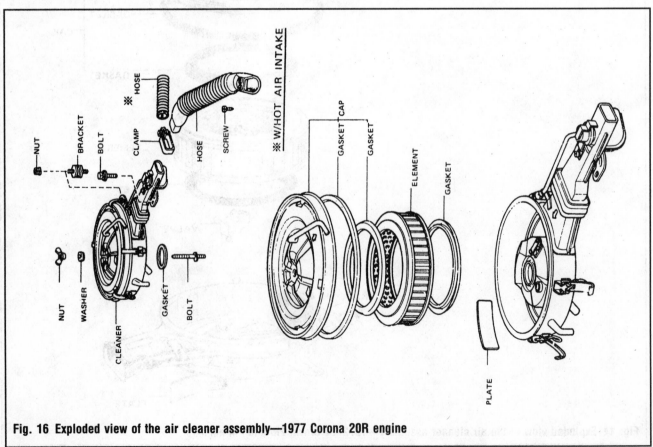

Fig. 16 Exploded view of the air cleaner assembly—1977 Corona 20R engine

Some models have a sticker located on the air cleaner to advise you when to change the air and oil filters

Lift the air cleaner lid off the housing

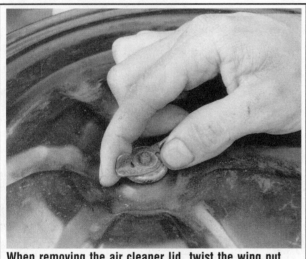

When removing the air cleaner lid, twist the wing nut off . . .

Remove the air cleaner element and replace if necessary

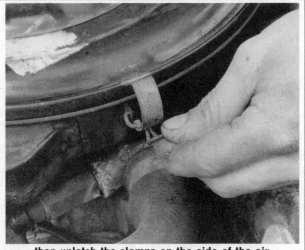

. . . then unlatch the clamps on the side of the air cleaner—20R engine shown, others similar

Fig. 16a When cleaning the air filter element, blow air from the inner side

top section. Set it aside carefully since the emission system hoses are attached to it on some models. Unfasten these hoses first (if so equipped), to remove it entirely from the car. Lift the air cleaner element out for service or replacement.

Installation is the reverse of removal.

Fuel Filter

REMOVAL & INSTALLATION

There are two basic types of fuel filters used on Toyota vehicles. There is the cartridge type (disposable element), and the totally throwaway type.

✳✳ CAUTION

Do not smoke or have an open flame near the vehicle when working on the fuel system.

1970–74 Models

CARTRIDGE TYPE

➧ See Figure 17

The cartridge type filter is located in the fuel line. This service should be performed if the clear of the glass fills up with gasoline or at the maintenance intervals.

1. Loosen and remove the nut on the filter bowl.

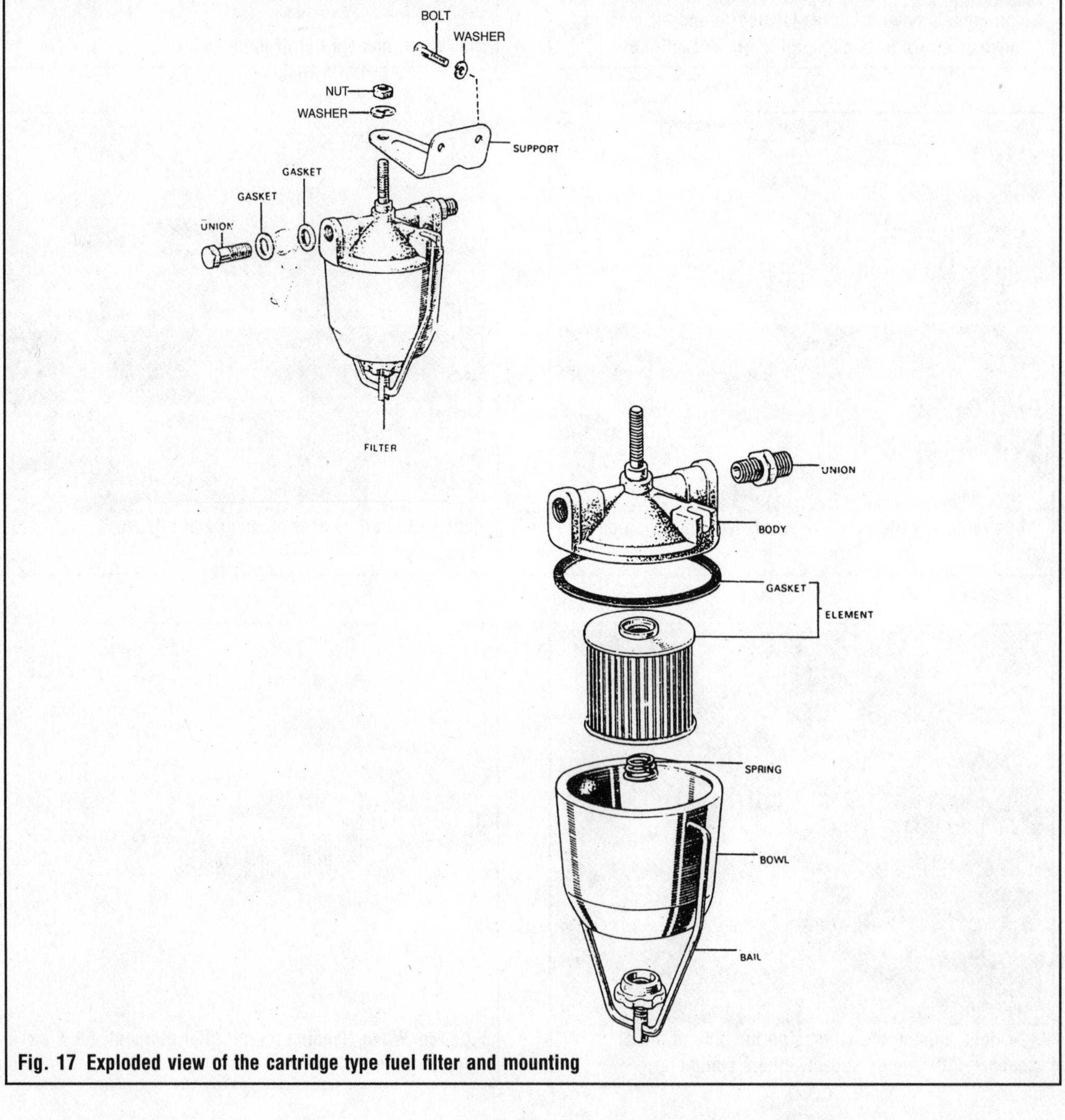

Fig. 17 Exploded view of the cartridge type fuel filter and mounting

2. Withdraw the bowl, element spring, element and gasket.

3. Wash the parts in solvent and examine them for damage.

To install:

4. Install a new filter element and bowl gasket.

5. Install the components in the reverse order of there removal.

6. Seat the bowl by turning it slightly. Tighten the ball nut fully and check for leaks.

THROWAWAY TYPE

◆ **See Figure 18**

1. Place a shop rag around the filter hose and a small container to catch any spilt fuel.

2. Unfasten the fuel intake line. Use a wrench to loosen the attachment nut and another on the opposite side of the filter to keep the filter body from turning in its retaining bracket.

3. Remove the remaining fuel line from the fuel filter in the same manner as you did the first one. Place the container aside.

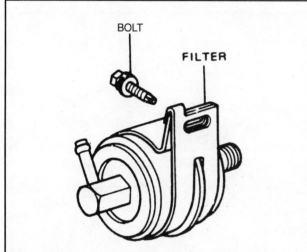

Fig. 18 The first throwaway type fuel filter is metal and bolted on

4. Unbolt the fuel filter and remove it.

To install:

➡**The arrow on the fuel filter should always point toward the carburetor.**

5. Install the filter onto the engine and tighten the mounting bolt.

6. Attach the fuel lines to the filter.

7. Run the engine for a few minutes and check the filter for any leaks.

1975–82 Models

CARBURETED

◆ **See Figure 19**

Starting in 1974, Toyota passenger cars use a see-through type, disposable fuel filter. This filter should be replaced every 2 years or 25,000 miles on the 1975–77 models, 30,000 miles on 1978–82 models, or if the filter seems to be clogged or dirty.

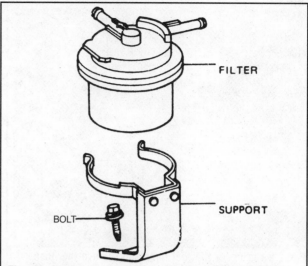

Fig. 19 Another type of disposable fuel filter is plastic, usually retained in a support

The fuel filter on the 1975–82 carburetor models is clamped onto the firewall—20R engine

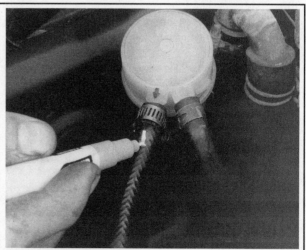

If necessary, place matchmarks on one of the fuel lines to avoid confusion

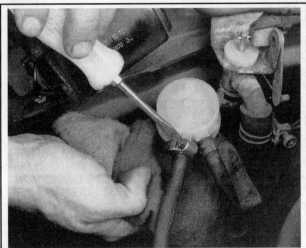

Place a rag under the fuel lines and remove the hose clamps

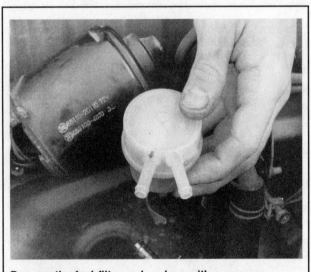

Remove the fuel filter and replace with a new one

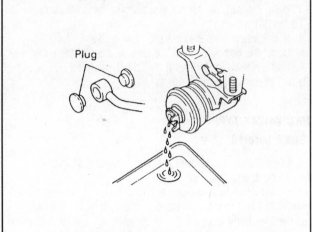

Fig. 20 Place a pan under the delivery pipe to catch the dripping fuel—fuel injected engines shown

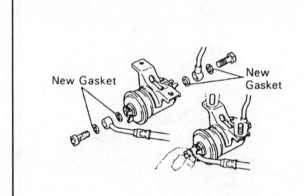

Fig. 21 Always use new gaskets when reconnecting the lines

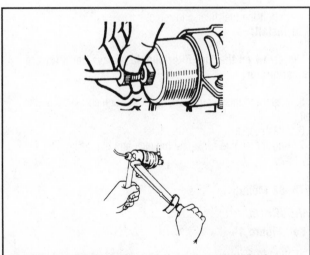

Fig. 22 Hand-tighten the fuel lines first, then final tighten with a torque wrench

1. Place a shop rag around the filter hose and a small container to catch any spilled fuel.

2. Remove the hose clamps from the inlet and outlet hoses.

3. Work the hoses off of the filter necks. Be sure the fuel in the lines is caught in the container. Set the container aside.

4. Snap the filter out of its bracket and replace it with a new one.

➡The arrow on the fuel filter must always point toward the carburetor.

To install:

5. Snap the fuel filter into the retaining bracket.

6. Install the hoses on the filter and tighten the hose clamps.

7. Run the engine for a few minutes and check the filter for any leaks.

FUEL INJECTED

◆ See Figures 20, 21 and 22

1. Unbolt the retaining screws and remove the protective shield for the fuel filter.

2. Place a pan under the delivery pipe (large connection) to catch the dripping fuel and SLOWLY loosen the union bolt to bleed off the fuel pressure.

3. Remove the union bolt and drain the remaining fuel.

4. Disconnect and plug the inlet line.

5. Unbolt and remove the fuel filter.

To install:

➡**When tightening the fuel line bolts to the fuel filter, you must use a torque wrench. The tightening torque is very important, as under or over tightening may cause fuel leakage. Insure that there is not fuel line interference and that there is sufficient clearance between it and any other parts.**

6. Coat the flare unit, union nut and bolt threads with engine oil.

7. Hand-tighten the inlet line to the fuel filter.

8. Install the fuel filter and then tighten the inlet line both to 23–33 ft. lbs. (31–45 Nm).

9. Reconnect the delivery pipe using new gaskets and then tighten the union bolt to 18–25 ft. lbs. (24–34 Nm).

10. Run the engine for a few minutes and check for any fuel leaks.

11. Install the protective shield.

Fuel Cap Gasket

REMOVAL & INSTALLATION

Most Toyotas require the replacement of the fuel filler cap gasket at 60,000 miles (96,558 km). The gasket is important in sealing the filler neck and keeping the vapors from the tank routed through the vapor emission system. Gently pry the gasket off with your fingers or a tool. Install the new gasket and make certain it is not twisted or crimped.

PCV Valve

REMOVAL & INSTALLATION

◆ **See Figures 23 and 24**

The PCV valve regulates crankcase ventilation during various engine operating conditions. At high vacuum (idle speed and partial load range) it will open slightly and at low vacuum (full throttle) it will open fully. This causes vapor to be removed from the crankcase by the engine vacuum and then sucked into the combustion chamber where it is dissipated.

The PCV valve should be replaced every 12 months or 12,000 miles on models made prior to 1972. On the 1972–77 models, inspect the valve every 12 months or 12,000 miles and replace it every 24 months 24,000 miles (whichever occurs first). On the 1978–82 models, replace the PCV valve every 30,000 miles or 24

months. On California models, 1980–82, replace it every 60,000 miles.

1. Check the ventilation hoses for leaks or clogging. Clean or replace as necessary.

2. Locate the PCV valve in the cylinder head cover. Remove it.

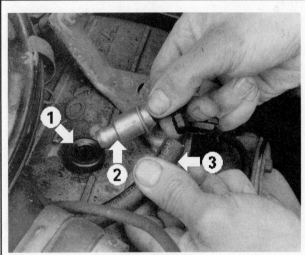

1. Grommet
2. PCV valve
3. Ventilation hose

Pull the PCV valve out of the grommet and remove the ventilation hose from the valve

3. Blow into the crankcase end of the valve. There should be free passage of air through the valve.

4. Blow into the intake manifold end of the valve. There should be little or no passage of air through the valve.

5. If the PCV valve failed either of the preceding two checks, it will require replacement.

6. Inspect the PCV grommet. Replace if necessary.

To install:

7. Insert the PCV valve into the grommet.

8. Place the ventilation hose on the end of the valve.

Evaporative Canister

SERVICING

Check the evaporation control system every 15,000 miles (24,000 km). Check the fuel and vapor lines and the vacuum hoses for proper connections and correct routing, as well as condition. Replace clogged, damaged or deteriorated parts as necessary.

If the charcoal canister is clogged, it may be cleaned using low pressure (no more than 43 psi) compressed air. The entire canister should be replaced every 5 years/50,000 miles (80,450 km) or 60,000 miles (96,540 km) for 1978–82.

1. Label the vacuum lines leading to the canister.

2. Remove the vacuum lines attached to the canister.

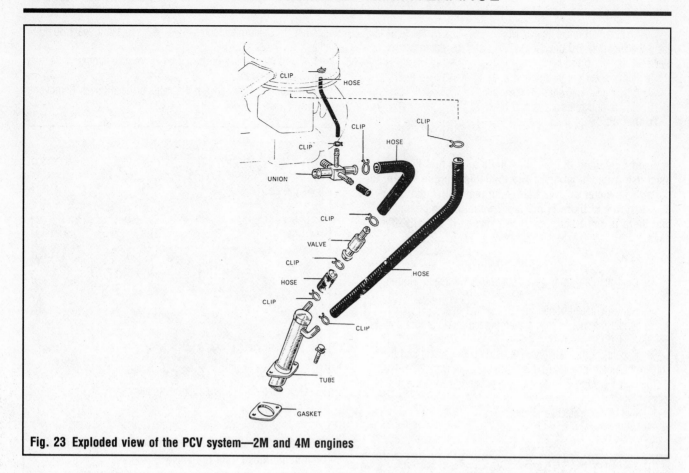

Fig. 23 Exploded view of the PCV system—2M and 4M engines

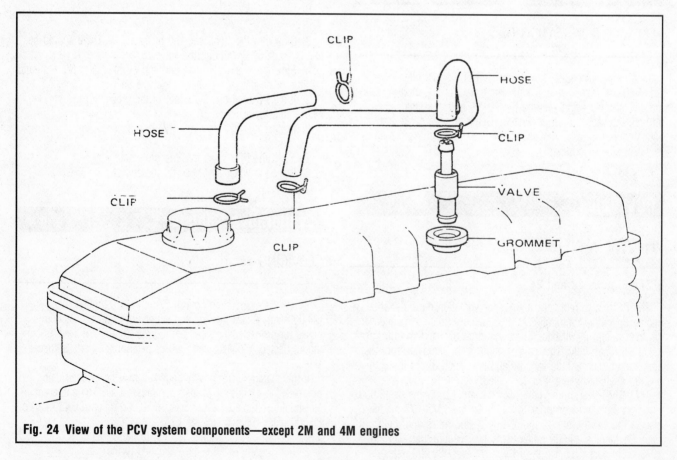

Fig. 24 View of the PCV system components—except 2M and 4M engines

3. Unfasten the retaining bolts from the canister.

4. Lift the canister up and remove the lower hose attached to the unit.

5. Inspect the case for any cracking or damage.

6. Using low pressure compressed air, blow into the tank pipe (flanged end) and check that air flows freely from the other ports.

7. Blow into the purge pipe (next to tank pipe) and check that air does not flow from the other ports. If air does flow, the check valve has failed and the canister must be replaced.

8. Never attempt to flush the canister with fluid or solvent. Low pressure air 43 psi (294 kPa) maximum may be used to evaporate any vapors within the canister. When applying the air, hold a finger over the purge pipe to force all the air out the bottom port.

9. No carbon should come out of the filter at any time. Loose charcoal is a sign of internal failure in the canister.

Battery

GENERAL MAINTENANCE

All batteries, regardless of type, should be carefully secured by a battery hold-down device. If this is not done, the battery terminals or casing may crack from stress applied to the battery during vehicle operation. A battery which is not secured may allow acid to leak out, making it discharge faster; such leaking corrosive acid can also eat away components under the hood. A battery that is not sealed must be checked periodically for electrolyte level. You cannot add water to a sealed maintenance-free battery (though not all maintenance-free batteries are sealed), but a sealed battery must also be checked for proper electrolyte level as indicated by the color of the built-in hydrometer "eye."

Keep the top of the battery clean, as a film of dirt can help completely discharge a battery that is not used for long periods. A solution of baking soda and water may be used for cleaning, but be careful to flush this off with clear water. DO NOT let any of the solution into the filler holes. Baking soda neutralizes battery acid and will de-activate a battery cell.

✳✳ CAUTION

Always use caution when working on or near the battery. Never allow a tool to bridge the gap between the negative and positive battery terminals. Also, be careful not to allow a tool to provide a ground between the positive cable/terminal and any metal component on the vehicle. Either of these conditions will cause a short circuit leading to sparks and possible personal injury.

Batteries in vehicles which are not operated on a regular basis can fall victim to parasitic loads (small current drains which are constantly drawing current from the battery). Normal parasitic loads may drain a battery on a vehicle that is in storage and not used for 6–8 weeks. Vehicles that have additional accessories such as a cellular phone, an alarm system or other devices that increase parasitic load may discharge a battery sooner. If the vehicle is to be stored for 6–8 weeks in a secure area and the alarm system, if present, is not necessary, the negative battery cable should be disconnected at the onset of storage to protect the battery charge.

Remember that constantly discharging and recharging will shorten battery life. Take care not to allow a battery to be needlessly discharged.

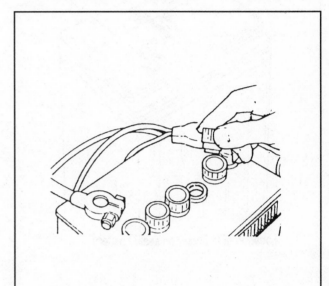

On non-maintenance free batteries, the level can be checked through the case on translucent batteries; the cell caps must be removed on other models

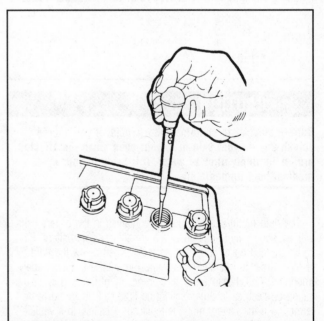

Check the specific gravity of the battery's electrolyte with a hydrometer

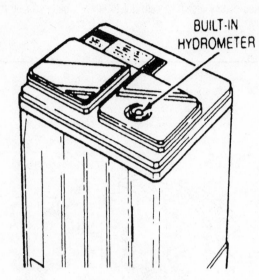

Location of indicator on sealed battery

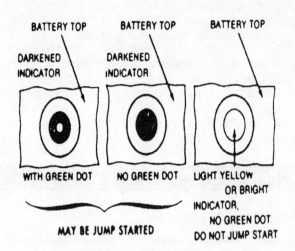

Check the appearance of the charge indicator on top of the battery before attempting a jump start; if it's not green or dark, do not jump start the car

A typical sealed (maintenance-free) battery with a built-in hydrometer—NOTE that the hydrometer eye may vary between battery manufacturers; always refer to the battery's label

BATTERY FLUID

The fluid (sulfuric acid solution) contained in the battery cells will tell you many things about the condition of the battery. Because the cell plates must be kept submerged below the fluid level in order to operate, maintaining the fluid level is extremely important. And, because the specific gravity of the acid is an indication of electrical charge, testing the fluid can be an aid in determining if the battery must be replaced. A battery in a vehicle with a properly operating charging system should require little maintenance, but careful, periodic inspection should reveal problems before they leave you stranded.

Fluid Level

Check the battery electrolyte level at least once a month, or more often in hot weather or during periods of extended vehicle operation. On non-sealed batteries, the level can be checked either through the case on translucent batteries or by removing the cell caps on opaque-cased types. The electrolyte level in each cell should be kept filled to the split ring inside each cell, or the line marked on the outside of the case.

If the level is low, add only distilled water through the opening until the level is correct. Each cell is separate from the others, so each must be checked and filled individually. Distilled water should be used, because the chemicals and minerals found in most drinking water are harmful to the battery and could significantly shorten its life.

If water is added in freezing weather, the vehicle should be driven several miles to allow the water to mix with the electrolyte. Otherwise, the battery could freeze.

Although some maintenance-free batteries have removable cell caps for access to the electrolyte, the electrolyte condition and level on all sealed maintenance-free batteries must be checked using the built-in hydrometer "eye." The exact type of eye varies between battery manufacturers, but most apply a sticker to the battery itself explaining the possible readings. When in doubt, refer to the battery manufacturer's instructions to interpret battery condition using the built-in hydrometer.

➡**Although the readings from built-in hydrometers found in sealed batteries may vary, a green eye usually indicates a properly charged battery with sufficient fluid level. A dark eye is normally an indicator of a battery with sufficient fluid, but one which may be low in charge. And a light or yellow eye is usually an indication that electrolyte supply has dropped below the necessary level for battery (and hydrometer) operation. In this last case, sealed batteries with an insufficient electrolyte level must usually be discarded.**

Specific Gravity

As stated earlier, the specific gravity of a battery's electrolyte level can be used as an indication of battery charge. At least once a year, check the specific gravity of the battery. It should be between 1.20 and 1.26 on the gravity scale. Most auto supply stores carry a variety of inexpensive battery testing hydrometers. These can be used on any non-sealed battery to test the specific gravity in each cell.

The battery testing hydrometer has a squeeze bulb at one end and a nozzle at the other. Battery electrolyte is sucked into the hydrometer until the float is lifted from its seat. The specific gravity is then read by noting the position of the float. If gravity is low in one or more cells, the battery should be slowly charged and checked again to see if the gravity has come up. Generally, if after charging, the specific gravity between any two cells varies more than 50 points (0.50), the battery should be replaced as it can no longer produce sufficient voltage to guarantee proper operation.

On sealed batteries, the built-in hydrometer is the only way of checking specific gravity. Again, check with your battery's manufacturer for proper interpretation of its built-in hydrometer readings.

CABLES

Once a year (or as necessary), the battery terminals and the cable clamps should be cleaned. Loosen the clamps and remove the cables, negative cable first. On batteries with posts on top, the use of a puller specially made for this purpose is recommended. These are inexpensive and available in most auto parts stores. Side terminal battery cables are secured with a small bolt.

Clean the cable clamps and the battery terminal with a wire brush, until all corrosion, grease, etc., is removed and the metal is shiny. It is especially important to clean the inside of the clamp (an old knife is useful here) thoroughly, since a small deposit of foreign material or oxidation there will prevent a sound electrical connection and inhibit either starting or charging. Special tools are available for cleaning these parts, one type for conventional top post batteries and another type for side terminal batteries.

Before installing the cables, loosen the battery hold-down clamp or strap, remove the battery and check the battery tray. Clear it of any debris, and check it for soundness (the battery tray can be cleaned with a baking soda and water solution). Rust should be wire brushed away, and the metal given a couple coats of anti-rust paint. Install the battery and tighten the hold-down

Maintenance is performed with household items and with special tools like this post cleaner

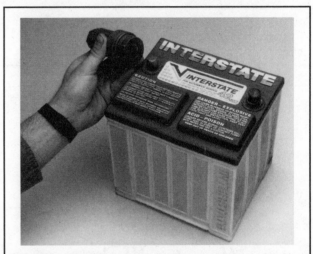

The underside of this special battery tool has a wire brush to clean post terminals

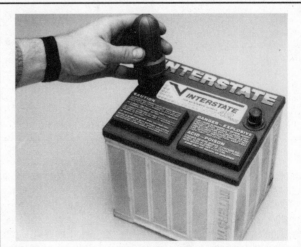

Place the tool over the terminals and twist to clean the post

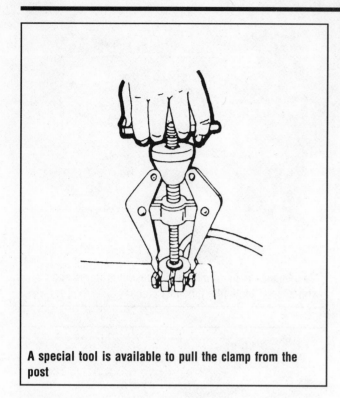

A special tool is available to pull the clamp from the post

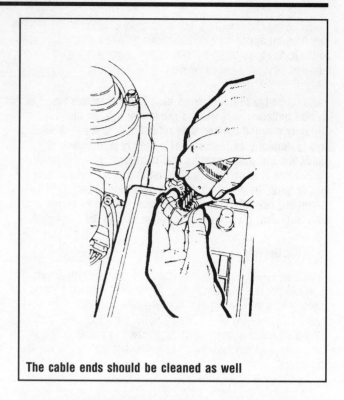

The cable ends should be cleaned as well

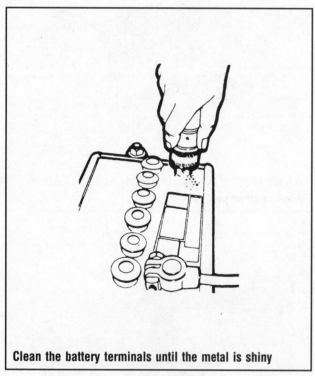

Clean the battery terminals until the metal is shiny

clamp or strap securely. Do not overtighten, as this can crack the battery case.

After the clamps and terminals are clean, reinstall the cables, negative cable last; DO NOT hammer the clamps onto post batteries. Tighten the clamps securely, but do not distort them. Give the clamps and terminals a thin external coating of grease after installation, to retard corrosion.

Check the cables at the same time that the terminals are

cleaned. If the cable insulation is cracked or broken, or if the ends are frayed, the cable should be replaced with a new cable of the same length and gauge.

CHARGING

✳✳ CAUTION

The chemical reaction which takes place in all batteries generates explosive hydrogen gas. A spark can cause the battery to explode and splash acid. To avoid serious personal injury, be sure there is proper ventilation and take appropriate fire safety precautions when connecting, disconnecting, or charging a battery and when using jumper cables.

A battery should be charged at a slow rate to keep the plates inside from getting too hot. However, if some maintenance-free batteries are allowed to discharge until they are almost "dead," they may have to be charged at a high rate to bring them back to "life." Always follow the charger manufacturer's instructions on charging the battery.

REPLACEMENT

When it becomes necessary to replace the battery, select one with a rating equal to or greater than the battery originally installed. Deterioration and just plain aging of the battery cables, starter motor, and associated wires makes the battery's job harder in successive years. The slow increase in electrical resistance over time makes it prudent to install a new battery with a greater capacity than the old.

BATTERY DIMENSIONS (INCHES)

BCI GROUP SIZE	LENGTH	WIDTH	HEIGHT
24	10 1/4	6 13/16	9
24F	10 21/32	6 13/16	9
25	9 1/16	6 7/8	8 7/8
27	12 1/32	6 13/16	8 15/16
27F	12 31/64	6 13/16	8 15/16
35	9 1/16	6 7/8	8 7/8

Belts

INSPECTION

♦ **See Figures 25 and 25a**

Inspect the belts for signs of glazing or cracking. A glazed belt will be perfectly smooth from slippage, while a good belt will have a slight texture of fabric visible. Cracks will usually start at the inner edge of the belt and run outward. All worn or damaged drive belts should be replaced immediately. It is best to replace all drive belts at one time, as a preventive maintenance measure, during this service operation.

At engine tune-up (every 12,000 miles), check the condition of the drive belts and check and adjust belt tension as below:

1. Inspect belts for signs of glazing or cracking. A glazed belt will be perfectly smooth from slippage, while a good belt will have a slight texture of fabric visible. Cracks will usually start at the inner edge of the belt and run outward. Replace the belt at the first sign of cracking or if glazing is severe.

2. Belt tension does not refer to play or droop. By placing your thumb midway between two pulleys, it should be possible to depress each belt about 3/8 to 1/2 inch with 22–24 lbs. of pressure. If the belt can be depressed more than this, or cannot be de-

pressed this much, adjust the tension. Inadequate tension will result in slippage and wear, while excessive tension will damage bearings and cause belts to fray and crack.

To adjust the tension; loosen the pivot and mounting bolts or idler pulley of the component which the belt is driving. Use a soft

Fig. 25a To inspect the belt off the engine, bend it and check for cracks, deterioration, stretching and wear

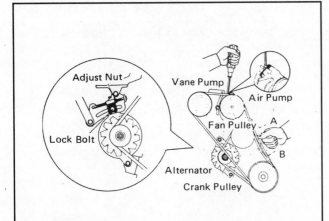

Fig. 25 Inspect the tension at the longest span of the belt. Some components can be tensioned by an adjustment nut, others need to be pried

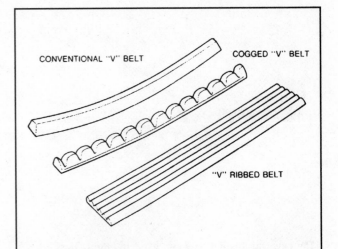

There are typically 3 types of accessory drive belts found on vehicles today

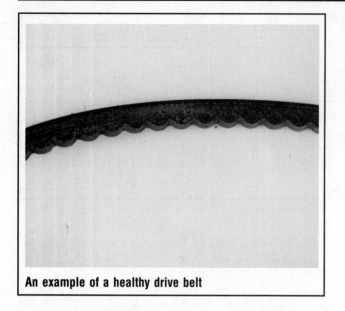

An example of a healthy drive belt

Installing too wide a belt can result in serious belt wear and/or breakage

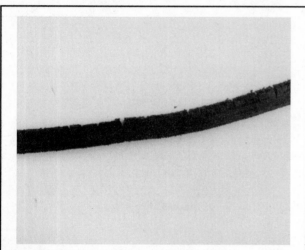

Deep cracks in this belt will cause flex, building up heat that will eventually lead to belt failure

The cover of this belt is worn, exposing the critical reinforcing cords to excessive wear

wooden hammer handle, a broomstick, or the like to pry the component toward or away from the engine until the proper tension is achieved.

✳✳ WARNING

Do not use a screwdriver or other metal device, such as a prybar, as a lever.

Tighten the component mounting bolts securely. If a new belt has been installed, recheck the tension after about 200 miles of driving.

Hoses

INSPECTION

Upper and lower radiator hoses along with the heater hoses should be checked for deterioration, leaks and loose hose clamps at least every 15,000 miles (24,000 km). It is also wise to check the hoses periodically in early spring and at the beginning of the fall or winter when you are performing other maintenance. A quick visual inspection could discover a weakened hose which might have left you stranded if it had remained unrepaired.

Whenever you are checking the hoses, make sure the engine and cooling system are cold. Visually inspect for cracking, rotting or collapsed hoses, and replace as necessary. Run your hand along the length of the hose. If a weak or swollen spot is noted when squeezing the hose wall, the hose should be replaced.

REMOVAL & INSTALLATION

1. Remove the radiator pressure cap.

> ※※ **CAUTION**
>
> Never remove the pressure cap while the engine is running, or personal injury from scalding hot coolant or steam may result. If possible, wait until the engine has cooled to remove the pressure cap. If this is not possible, wrap a thick cloth around the pressure cap and turn it slowly to the stop. Step back while the pressure is released from the cooling system. When you are sure all the pressure has been released, use the cloth to turn and remove the cap.

2. Position a clean container under the radiator and/or engine draincock or plug, then open the drain and allow the cooling system to drain to an appropriate level. For some upper hoses, only

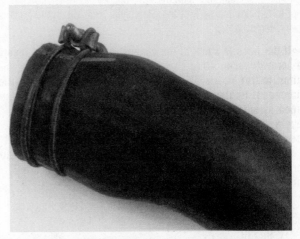

A soft spongy hose (identifiable by the swollen section) will eventually burst and should be replaced

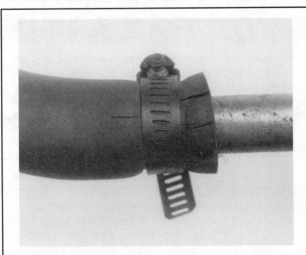

The cracks developing along this hose are a result of age-related hardening

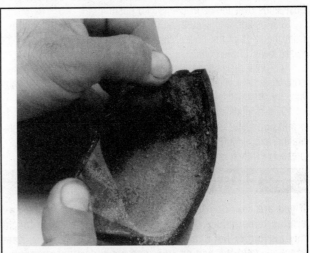

Hoses are likely to deteriorate from the inside if the cooling system is not periodically flushed

a little coolant must be drained. To remove hoses positioned lower on the engine, such as a lower radiator hose, the entire cooling system must be emptied.

> ※※ **CAUTION**
>
> When draining coolant, keep in mind that cats and dogs are attracted by ethylene glycol antifreeze, and are quite likely to drink any that is left in an uncovered container or in puddles on the ground. This will prove fatal in sufficient quantity. Always drain coolant into a sealable container. Coolant may be reused unless it is contaminated or several years old.

3. Loosen the hose clamps at each end of the hose requiring replacement. Clamps are usually either of the spring tension type (which require pliers to squeeze the tabs and loosen) or of the screw tension type (which require screw or hex drivers to loosen). Pull the clamps back on the hose away from the connection.

A hose clamp that is too tight can cause older hoses to separate and tear on either side of the clamp

4. Twist, pull and slide the hose off the fitting, taking care not to damage the neck of the component from which the hose is being removed.

➡️**If the hose is stuck at the connection, do not try to insert a screwdriver or other sharp tool under the hose end in an effort to free it, as the connection and/or hose may become damaged. Heater connections especially may be easily damaged by such a procedure. If the hose is to be replaced, use a single-edged razor blade to make a slice along the portion of the hose which is stuck on the connection, perpendicular to the end of the hose. Do not cut deep so as to prevent damaging the connection. The hose can then be peeled from the connection and discarded.**

5. Clean both hose mounting connections. Inspect the condition of the hose clamps and replace them, if necessary.

To install:

6. Dip the ends of the new hose into clean engine coolant to ease installation.

7. Slide the clamps over the replacement hose, then slide the hose ends over the connections into position.

8. Position and secure the clamps at least ¼ in. (6.35mm) from the ends of the hose. Make sure they are located beyond the raised bead of the connector.

9. Close the radiator or engine drains and properly refill the cooling system with the clean drained engine coolant or a suitable mixture of ethylene glycol coolant and water.

10. If available, install a pressure tester and check for leaks. If a pressure tester is not available, run the engine until normal operating temperature is reached (allowing the system to naturally pressurize), then check for leaks.

✳✳ CAUTION

If you are checking for leaks with the system at normal operating temperature, BE EXTREMELY CAREFUL not to touch any moving or hot engine parts. Once temperature has been reached, shut the engine OFF, and check for leaks around the hose fittings and connections which were removed earlier.

Cooling System

LEVEL CHECK

◆ **See Figure 26**

Dealing with the cooling system can be a dangerous matter unless the proper precautions are observed. It is best to check the coolant level in the radiator when the engine is cold. This is done by removing the radiator cap, on models without an expansion tank, and seeing that the coolant is within two inches of the bottom of the filler neck. On models with an expansion tank, if coolant visible above the MIN mark on the tank, the level is satisfactory. Always be certain that the filler caps on both the radiator and the reservoir are tightly closed.

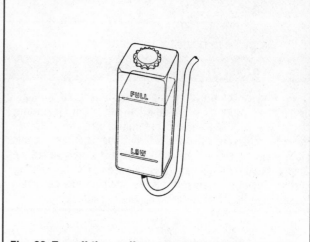

Fig. 26 Top off the cooling system through the reservoir tank

✳✳ CAUTION

When draining engine coolant, keep in mind that cats and dogs are attracted to ethylene glycol antifreeze and could drink any that is left in an uncovered container or in puddles on the ground. This will prove fatal in sufficient quantity. Always drain coolant into a sealable container. Coolant should be reused unless it is contaminated or is several years old.

In the event that the coolant level must be checked when the engine is warm on engines without the expansion tank, place a thick rag over the radiator cap and slowly turn the cap counterclockwise until it reaches the first detent. Allow all the hot steam to escape. This will allow the pressure in the system to drop gradually, preventing an explosion of hot coolant. When the hissing noise stops, remove the cap the rest of the way.

If the coolant level is low, add equal amounts of ethylene glycol based antifreeze and clean water. On models without an expansion tank, add coolant through the radiator filler neck. Fill the expansion tank to the MAX level on cars with that system.

✳✳ WARNING

Never add cold coolant to a hot engine unless the engine is running, to avoid cracking the engine block.

INSPECTION

◆ **See Figures 27 and 28**

If the coolant level is chronically low or rusty, refer to the Troubleshooting chapter for diagnosis of the problem.

The radiator hoses and clamps and the radiator cap should be checked at the same time as the coolant level. Hoses which are brittle, cracked, or swollen should be replaced. Clamps should be

Fig. 27 Pressure test the cooling system with a special tool to check for leaks

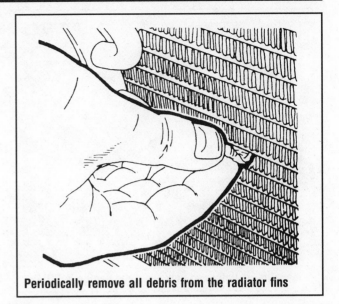

Periodically remove all debris from the radiator fins

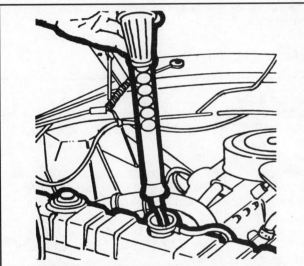

Fig. 28 Coolant protection quality can be checked with an inexpensive float-type tester

checked for tightness (screwdriver tight only. Do not allow the clamp to cut into the hose or crush the fitting). The radiator cap gasket should be checked for any obvious tears, cracks or swelling, or any signs of incorrect seating in the radiator neck.

DRAIN & REFILL

▶ See Figure 28a

Once every 24 months or 24,000 miles, the cooling system should be drained, thoroughly flushed, and refilled. This should be done with the engine cold.

1. Remove the radiator cap.
2. There are usually two drain plugs in the cooling system; one at the bottom of the radiator and one at the rear of the driver's side of the engine. Both should be loosened to allow the coolant to drain.

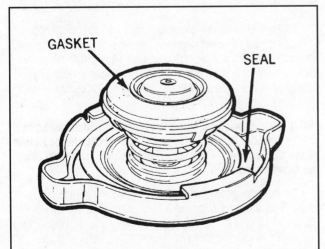

GASKET

SEAL

Be sure the rubber gasket on the radiator cap has a tight seal

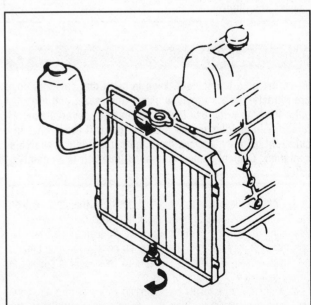

Fig. 28a The cooling system can be drained from the petcock on the bottom of the radiator

Remove the radiator cap only when the engine is COLD

Top off the cooling system with the correct mixture of water and antifreeze

✳✳ CAUTION

When draining the coolant, keep in mind that cats and dogs are attracted by the ethylene glycol antifreeze, and are quite likely to drink any that is left in an uncovered container or in puddles on the ground. This will prove fatal in sufficient quantity. Always drain the coolant into a sealable container. Coolant should be reused unless it is contaminated or several years old.

3. Turn on the heater to its hottest position. This ensures that the heater core is flushed out completely. Flush out the system thoroughly by refilling it with clean water through the radiator opening as it escapes from the two drain cocks. Continue until the water running out is clear. Be sure to clean out the coolant recovery tank as well if your car has one.

4. If the system is badly contaminated with rust or scale, you can use a commercial flushing solution to clear it out. Follow the manufacturer's instructions. Some causes of rust are air in the system, caused by a leaky radiator cap or an insufficiently filled or leaking system; failure to change the coolant regularly; use of excessively hard or soft water; and failure to use a proper mix of antifreeze and water.

5. When the system is clear, allow all the water to drain, then close the drain plugs. Fill the system through the radiator with a 50/50 mix of ethylene glycol type antifreeze and water.

6. Start the engine and top off the radiator with the antifreeze and water mixture. If your car has a coolant recovery tank, fill it half full with the coolant mix.

7. Replace the radiator and coolant tank caps, and check for leaks. When the engine has reached normal operating temperature, shut it off, allow it to cool, then top off the radiator or coolant tank as necessary.

Air Conditioning

➡Be sure to consult the laws in your area before servicing the air conditioning system. In most areas, it is illegal to perform repairs involving refrigerant unless the work is done by a certified technician. Also, it is quite likely that you will not be able to purchase refrigerant without proof of certification.

SAFETY PRECAUTIONS

There are two major hazards associated with air conditioning systems and they both relate to the refrigerant gas. First, the refrigerant gas (R-12) is an extremely cold substance. When exposed to air, it will instantly freeze any surface it comes in contact with, including your eyes. The other hazard relates to fire. Although normally non-toxic, the R-12 gas becomes highly poisonous in the presence of an open flame. One good whiff of the vapor formed by burning R-12 can be fatal. Keep all forms of fire (including cigarettes) well clear of the air conditioning system.

Because of the inherent dangers involved with working on air conditioning systems and R-12 refrigerant, these safety precautions must be strictly followed.

• Avoid contact with a charged refrigeration system, even when working on another part of the air conditioning system or vehicle. If a heavy tool comes into contact with a section of tubing or a heat exchanger, it can easily cause the relatively soft material to rupture.

• When it is necessary to apply force to a fitting which contains refrigerant, as when checking that all system couplings are securely tightened, use a wrench on both parts of the fitting involved, if possible. This will avoid putting torque on refrigerant tubing. (It is also advisable to use tube or line wrenches when tightening these flare nut fittings.)

➡R-12 refrigerant is a chlorofluorocarbon which, when released into the atmosphere, can contribute to the depletion of the ozone layer in the upper atmosphere. Ozone filters out harmful radiation from the sun.

• Do not attempt to discharge the system without the proper tools. Precise control is possible only when using the service gauges and a proper A/C refrigerant recovery station. Wear protective gloves when connecting or disconnecting service gauge hoses.

• Discharge the system only in a well ventilated area, as high concentrations of the gas which might accidentally escape can exclude oxygen and act as an anesthetic. When leak testing or soldering, this is particularly important, as toxic gas is formed when R-12 contacts any flame.

• Never start a system without first verifying that both service valves are properly installed, and that all fittings throughout the system are snugly connected.

• Avoid applying heat to any refrigerant line or storage vessel. Charging may be aided by using water heated to less than 125°F (50°C) to warm the refrigerant container. Never allow a refrigerant storage container to sit out in the sun, or near any other source of heat, such as a radiator or heater.

• Always wear goggles to protect your eyes when working on a system. If refrigerant contacts the eyes, it is advisable in all cases to consult a physician immediately.

• Frostbite from liquid refrigerant should be treated by first gradually warming the area with cool water, and then gently applying petroleum jelly. A physician should be consulted.

• Always keep refrigerant drum fittings capped when not in use. If the container is equipped with a safety cap to protect the valve, make sure the cap is in place when the can is not being used. Avoid sudden shock to the drum, which might occur from dropping it, or from banging a heavy tool against it. Never carry a drum in the passenger compartment of a vehicle.

• Always completely discharge the system into a suitable recovery unit before painting the vehicle (if the paint is to be baked on), or before welding anywhere near refrigerant lines.

• When servicing the system, minimize the time that any refrigerant line or fitting is open to the air in order to prevent moisture or dirt from entering the system. Contaminants such as moisture or dirt can damage internal system components. Always replace O-rings on lines or fittings which are disconnected. Prior to installation coat, but do not soak, replacement O-rings with suitable compressor oil.

GENERAL SERVICING PROCEDURES

➡**It is recommended, and possibly required by law, that a qualified technician perform the following services.**

The most important aspect of air conditioning service is the maintenance of a pure and adequate charge of refrigerant in the system. A refrigeration system cannot function properly if a significant percentage of the charge is lost. Leaks are common because the severe vibration encountered underhood in an automobile can easily cause a sufficient cracking or loosening of the air conditioning fittings; allowing, the extreme operating pressures of the system to force refrigerant out.

The problem can be understood by considering what happens to the system as it is operated with a continuous leak. Because the expansion valve regulates the flow of refrigerant to the evaporator, the level of refrigerant there is fairly constant. The receiver/drier stores any excess refrigerant, and so a loss will first appear there as a reduction in the level of liquid. As this level nears the bottom of the vessel, some refrigerant vapor bubbles will begin to appear in the stream of liquid supplied to the expansion valve. This vapor decreases the capacity of the expansion valve very little as the valve opens to compensate for its presence. As the quantity of liquid in the condenser decreases, the operating pressure will drop there and throughout the high side of the system. As the R-12 continues to be expelled, the pressure available to force the liquid through the expansion valve will continue to decrease, and, eventually, the valve's orifice will prove to be too

much of a restriction for adequate flow even with the needle fully withdrawn.

At this point, low side pressure will start to drop, and a severe reduction in cooling capacity, marked by freeze-up of the evaporator coil, will result. Eventually, the operating pressure of the evaporator will be lower than the pressure of the atmosphere surrounding it, and air will be drawn into the system wherever there are leaks in the low side.

Because all atmospheric air contains at least some moisture, water will enter the system and mix with the R-12 and the oil. Trace amounts of moisture will cause sludging of the oil, and corrosion of the system. Saturation and clogging of the filter/drier, and freezing of the expansion valve orifice will eventually result. As air fills the system to a greater and greater extent, it will interfere more and more with the normal flows of refrigerant and heat.

From this description, it should be obvious that much of the repairman's focus in on detecting leaks, repairing them, and then restoring the purity and quantity of the refrigerant charge. A list of general rules should be followed in addition to all safety precautions:

• Keep all tools as clean and dry as possible.

• Thoroughly purge the service gauges/hoses of air and moisture before connecting them to the system. Keep them capped when not in use.

• Thoroughly clean any refrigerant fitting before disconnecting it, in order to minimize the entrance of dirt into the system.

• Plan any operation that requires opening the system beforehand, in order to minimize the length of time it will be exposed to open air. Cap or seal the open ends to minimize the entrance of foreign material.

• When adding oil, pour it through an extremely clean and dry tube or funnel. Keep the oil capped whenever possible. Do not use oil that has not been kept tightly sealed.

• Use only R-12 refrigerant. Purchase refrigerant intended for use only in automatic air conditioning systems.

• Completely evacuate any system that has been opened for service, or that has leaked sufficiently to draw in moisture and air. This requires evacuating air and moisture with a good vacuum pump for at least one hour. If a system has been open for a considerable length of time it may be advisable to evacuate the system for up to 12 hours (overnight).

• Use a wrench on both halves of a fitting that is to be disconnected, so as to avoid placing torque on any of the refrigerant lines.

• When overhauling a compressor, pour some of the oil into a clean glass and inspect it. If there is evidence of dirt, metal particles, or both, flush all refrigerant components with clean refrigerant before evacuating and recharging the system. In addition, if metal particles are present, the compressor should be replaced.

• Schrader valves may leak only when under full operating pressure. Therefore, if leakage is suspected but cannot be located, operate the system with a full charge of refrigerant and look for leaks from all Schrader valves. Replace any faulty valves.

Additional Preventive Maintenance

USING THE SYSTEM

The easiest and most important preventive maintenance for your A/C system is to be sure that it is used on a regular basis. Running the system for five minutes each month (no matter what the season) will help assure that the seals and all internal components remain lubricated.

ANTIFREEZE

In order to prevent heater core freeze-up during A/C operation, it is necessary to maintain a proper antifreeze protection. Use a hand-held antifreeze tester (hydrometer) to periodically check the condition of the antifreeze in your engine's cooling system.

➡**Antifreeze should not be used longer than the manufacturer specifies.**

RADIATOR CAP

For efficient operation of an air conditioned vehicle's cooling system, the radiator cap should have a holding pressure which meets manufacturer's specifications. A cap which fails to hold these pressures should be replaced.

CONDENSER

Any obstruction of or damage to the condenser configuration will restrict the air flow which is essential to its efficient operation. It is therefore a good rule to keep this unit clean and in proper physical shape.

➡**Bug screens which are mounted in front of the condenser, (unless they are original equipment), are regarded as obstructions.**

CONDENSATION DRAIN TUBE

This single molded drain tube expels the condensation, which accumulates on the bottom of the evaporator housing, into the engine compartment. If this tube is obstructed, the air conditioning performance can be restricted and condensation buildup can spill over onto the vehicle's floor.

SYSTEM INSPECTION

➡**R-12 refrigerant is a chlorofluorocarbon which, when released into the atmosphere, can contribute to the depletion of the ozone layer in the upper atmosphere. Ozone filters out harmful radiation from the sun.**

The easiest and often most important check for the air conditioning system consists of a visual inspection of the system com-

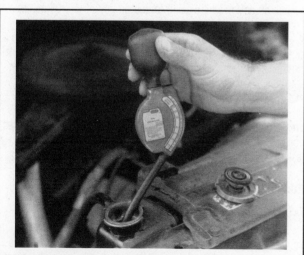

An antifreeze tester can be used to determine the freezing and boiling levels of the coolant

ponents. Visually inspect the air conditioning system for refrigerant leaks, damaged compressor clutch, compressor drive belt tension and condition, plugged evaporator drain tube, blocked condenser fins, disconnected or broken wires, blown fuses, corroded connections and poor insulation.

A refrigerant leak will usually appear as an oily residue at the leakage point in the system. The oily residue soon picks up dust or dirt particles from the surrounding air and appears greasy. Through time, this will build up and appear to be a heavy dirt impregnated grease. Most leaks are caused by damaged or missing O-ring seals at the component connections, damaged charging valve cores or missing service gauge port caps.

For a thorough visual and operational inspection, check the following:

1. Check the surface of the radiator and condenser for dirt, leaves or other material which might block air flow.
2. Check for kinks in hoses and lines. Check the system for leaks.
3. Make sure the drive belt is under the proper tension. When the air conditioning is operating, make sure the drive belt is free of noise or slippage.
4. Make sure the blower motor operates at all appropriate positions, then check for distribution of the air from all outlets with the blower on **HIGH**.

➡**Keep in mind that under conditions of high humidity, air discharged from the A/C vents may not feel as cold as expected, even if the system is working properly. This is because the vaporized moisture in humid air retains heat more effectively than does dry air, making the humid air more difficult to cool.**

Make sure the air passage selection lever is operating correctly. Start the engine and warm it to normal operating temperature, then make sure the hot/cold selection lever is operating correctly.

DISCHARGING, EVACUATING & CHARGING

Discharging, evacuating and charging the air conditioning system must be performed by a properly trained and certified mechanic in a facility equipped with refrigerant recovery/recycling equipment that meets SAE standards for the type of system to be serviced.

If you don't have access to the necessary equipment, we recommend that you take your vehicle to a reputable service station to have the work done. If you still wish to perform repairs on the vehicle, have them discharge the system, then take your vehicle home and perform the necessary work. When you are finished, return the vehicle to the station for evacuation and charging. Just be sure to cap ALL A/C system fittings immediately after opening them and keep them protected until the system is recharged.

Windshield Wipers

ELEMENT (REFILL) CARE & REPLACEMENT

For maximum effectiveness and longest element life, the windshield and wiper blades should be kept clean. Dirt, tree sap, road tar and so on will cause streaking, smearing and blade deterioration if left on the glass. It is advisable to wash the windshield carefully with a commercial glass cleaner at least once a month. Wipe off the rubber blades with the wet rag afterwards. Do not attempt to move wipers across the windshield by hand; damage to the motor and drive mechanism will result.

To inspect and/or replace the wiper blade elements, place the wiper switch in the **LOW** speed position and the ignition switch in the **ACC** position. When the wiper blades are approximately vertical on the windshield, turn the ignition switch to **OFF**.

Examine the wiper blade elements. If they are found to be cracked, broken or torn, they should be replaced immediately. Replacement intervals will vary with usage, although ozone deterioration usually limits element life to about one year. If the wiper pattern is smeared or streaked, or if the blade chatters across the glass, the elements should be replaced. It is easiest and most sensible to replace the elements in pairs.

If your vehicle is equipped with aftermarket blades, there are several different types of refills and your vehicle might have any kind. Aftermarket blades and arms rarely use the exact same type blade or refill as the original equipment. Here are some typical aftermarket blades; not all may be available for your vehicle:

The Anco® type uses a release button that is pushed down to allow the refill to slide out of the yoke jaws. The new refill slides back into the frame and locks in place.

Some Trico® refills are removed by locating where the metal backing strip or the refill is wider. Insert a small screwdriver blade between the frame and metal backing strip. Press down to release the refill from the retaining tab.

Other types of Trico® refills have two metal tabs which are unlocked by squeezing them together. The rubber filler can then be withdrawn from the frame jaws. A new refill is installed by inserting the refill into the front frame jaws and sliding it rearward to engage the remaining frame jaws. There are usually four jaws; be certain when installing that the refill is engaged in all of them. At the end of its travel, the tabs will lock into place on the front jaws of the wiper blade frame.

Another type of refill is made from polycarbonate. The refill has a simple locking device at one end which flexes downward out of the groove into which the jaws of the holder fit, allowing easy release. By sliding the new refill through all the jaws and pushing

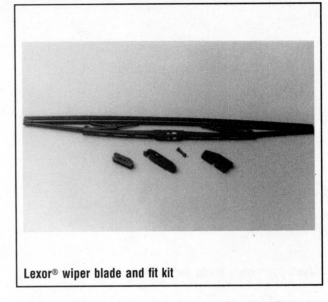

Lexor® wiper blade and fit kit

Pylon® wiper blade and adaptor

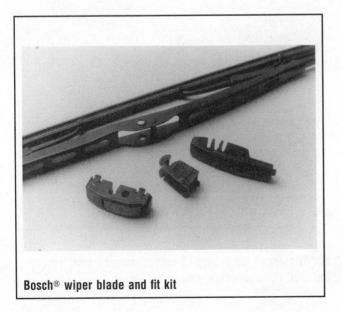

Bosch® wiper blade and fit kit

Trico® wiper blade and fit kit

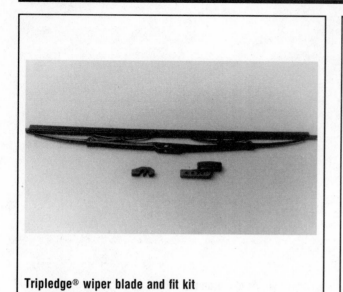

Tripledge® wiper blade and fit kit

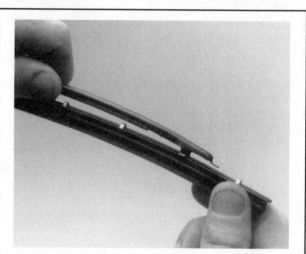

On Trico® wiper blades, the tab at the end of the blade must be turned up . . .

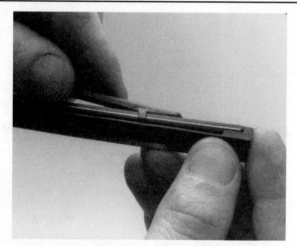

To remove and install a Lexor® wiper blade refill, slip out the old insert and slide in a new one

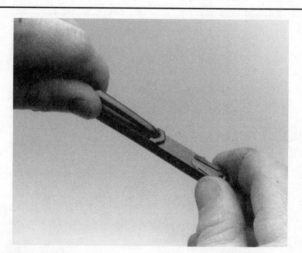

. . . then the insert can be removed. After installing the replacement insert, bend the tab back

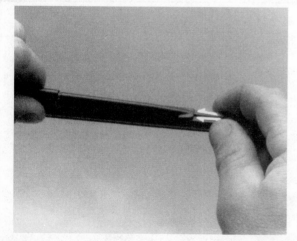

On Pylon® inserts, the clip at the end has to be removed prior to sliding the insert off

The Tripledge® wiper blade insert is removed and installed using a securing clip

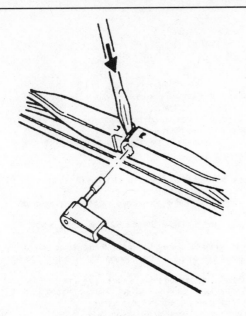

BLADE REPLACEMENT

1. CYCLE ARM AND BLADE ASSEMBLY TO UP POSITION-ON THE WINDSHIELD WHERE REMOVAL OF BLADE ASSEMBLY CAN BE PERFORMED WITHOUT DIFFICULTY. TURN IGNITION KEY OFF AT DESIRED POSITION.

2. TO REMOVE BLADE ASSEMBLY, INSERT SCREWDRIVER IN SLOT, PUSH DOWN ON SPRING LOCK AND PULL BLADE ASSEMBLY FROM PIN (VIEW A)

3. TO INSTALL, PUSH THE BLADE ASSEMBLY ON THE PIN SO THAT THE SPRING LOCK ENGAGES THE PIN (VIEW A). BE SURE THE BLADE ASSEMBLY IS SECURELY ATTACHED TO PIN

VIEW A

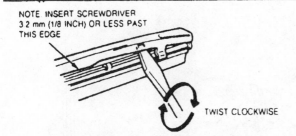

NOTE INSERT SCREWDRIVER 3 2 mm (1/8 INCH) OR LESS PAST THIS EDGE

TWIST CLOCKWISE

ELEMENT REPLACEMENT

1 INSERT SCREWDRIVER BETWEEN THE EDGE OF THE SUPER STRUCTURE AND THE BLADE BACKING DRIP (VIEW B) TWIST SCREWDRIVER SLOWLY UNTIL ELEMENT CLEARS ONE SIDE OF THE SUPER STRUC-TURE CLAW

2 SLIDE THE ELEMENT INTO THE SUPER STRUCTURE CLAWS

VIEW B

4 INSERT ELEMENT INTO ONE SIDE OF THE END CLAWS (VIEW D) AND WITH A ROCKING MOTION PUSH ELEMENT UPWARD UNTIL IT SNAPS IN (VIEW E)

VIEW D

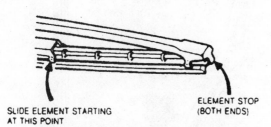

SLIDE ELEMENT STARTING AT THIS POINT

ELEMENT STOP (BOTH ENDS)

3. SLIDE THE ELEMENT INTO THE SUPER STRUCTURE CLAWS, STARTING WITH SECOND SET FROM EITHER END (VIEW C) AND CONTINUE TO SLIDE THE BLADE ELEMENT INTO ALL THE SUPER STRUCTURE CLAWS TO THE ELEMENT STOP (VIEW C)

VIEW C

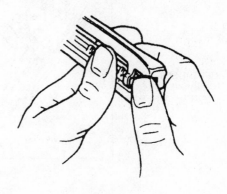

VIEW E

Trico® wiper blade insert (element) replacement

BLADE REPLACEMENT

1. Cycle arm and blade assembly to a position on the windshield where removal of blade assembly can be performed without difficulty. Turn ignition key off at desired position.
2. To remove blade assembly from wiper arm, pull up on spring lock and pull blade assembly from pin (View A). Be sure spring lock is not pulled excessively or it will become distorted.
3. To install, push the blade assembly onto the pin so that the spring lock engages the pin (View A). Be sure the blade assembly is securely attached to pin.

ELEMENT REPLACEMENT

1. In the plastic backing strip which is part of the rubber blade assembly, there is an 11.11mm (7/16 inch) long notch located approximately one inch from either end. Locate either notch.
2. Place the frame of the wiper blade assembly on a firm surface with either notched end of the backing strip visible.
3. Grasp the frame portion of the wiper blade assembly and push down until the blade assembly is tightly bowed.
4. With the blade assembly in the bowed position, grasp the tip of the backing strip firmly, pulling up and twisting C.C.W. at the same time. The backing strip will then snap out of the retaining tab on the end of the frame.
5. Lift the wiper blade assembly from the surface and slide the backing strip down the frame until the notch lines up with the next retaining tab, twist slightly, and the backing strip will snap out. Continue this operation with the remaining tabs until the blade element is completely detached from the frame.
6. To install blade element, reverse the above procedure, making sure all six (6) tabs are locked to the backing strip before installing blade to wiper arm.

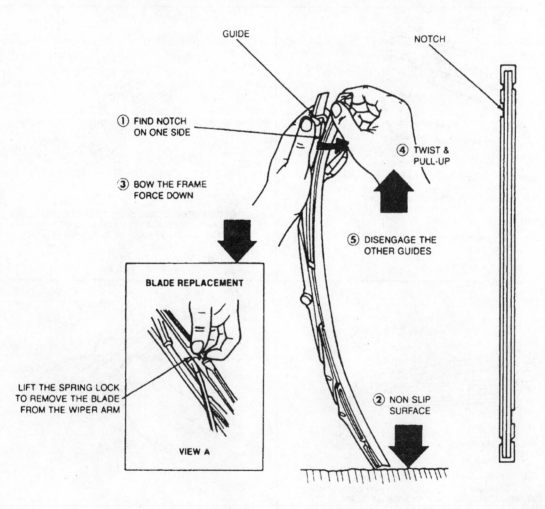

Tridon® wiper blade insert (element) replacement

through the slight resistance when it reaches the end of its travel, the refill will lock into position.

To replace the Tridon® refill, it is necessary to remove the wiper blade. This refill has a plastic backing strip with a notch about 1 in. (25mm) from the end. Hold the blade (frame) on a hard surface so that the frame is tightly bowed. Grip the tip of the backing strip and pull up while twisting counterclockwise. The backing strip will snap out of the retaining tab. Do this for the remaining tabs until the refill is free of the blade. The length of these refills is molded into the end and they should be replaced with identical types.

Regardless of the type of refill used, be sure to follow the part manufacturer's instructions closely. Make sure that all of the frame jaws are engaged as the refill is pushed into place and locked. If the metal blade holder and frame are allowed to touch the glass during wiper operation, the glass will be scratched.

Tires and Wheels

Common sense and good driving habits will afford maximum tire life. Fast starts, sudden stops and hard cornering are hard on tires and will shorten their useful life span. Make sure that you don't overload the vehicle or run with incorrect pressure in the tires. Both of these practices will increase tread wear.

➡**For optimum tire life, keep the tires properly inflated, rotate them often and have the wheel alignment checked periodically.**

Inspect your tires frequently. Be especially careful to watch for bubbles in the tread or sidewall, deep cuts or underinflation. Replace any tires with bubbles in the sidewall. If cuts are so deep that they penetrate to the cords, discard the tire. Any cut in the sidewall of a radial tire renders it unsafe. Also look for uneven tread wear patterns that may indicate the front end is out of alignment or that the tires are out of balance.

Unidirectional tires are identifiable by sidewall arrows and/or the word "rotation"

TIRE ROTATION

Tires must be rotated periodically to equalize wear patterns that vary with a tire's position on the vehicle. Tires will also wear in an uneven way as the front steering/suspension system wears to the point where the alignment should be reset.

Rotating the tires will ensure maximum life for the tires as a set, so you will not have to discard a tire early due to wear on only part of the tread. Regular rotation is required to equalize wear.

When rotating "unidirectional tires," make sure that they always roll in the same direction. This means that a tire used on the left side of the vehicle must not be switched to the right side and

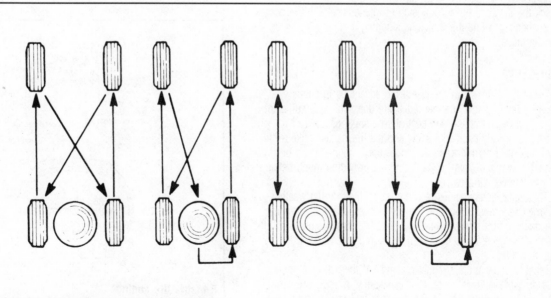

Common tire rotation patterns for 4 and 5-wheel rotations

vice-versa. Such tires should only be rotated front-to-rear or rear-to-front, while always remaining on the same side of the vehicle. These tires are marked on the sidewall as to the direction of rotation; observe the marks when reinstalling the tire(s).

Some styled or "mag" wheels may have different offsets front to rear. In these cases, the rear wheels must not be used up front and vice-versa. Furthermore, if these wheels are equipped with unidirectional tires, they cannot be rotated unless the tire is re-mounted for the proper direction of rotation.

➡**The compact or space-saver spare is strictly for emergency use. It must never be included in the tire rotation or placed on the vehicle for everyday use.**

TIRE DESIGN

For maximum satisfaction, tires should be used in sets of four. Mixing of different types (radial, bias-belted, fiberglass belted) must be avoided. In most cases, the vehicle manufacturer has designated a type of tire on which the vehicle will perform best. Your first choice when replacing tires should be to use the same type of tire that the manufacturer recommends.

When radial tires are used, tire sizes and wheel diameters should be selected to maintain ground clearance and tire load capacity equivalent to the original specified tire. Radial tires should always be used in sets of four.

✳✳ CAUTION

Radial tires should never be used on only the front axle.

When selecting tires, pay attention to the original size as marked on the tire. Most tires are described using an industry size code sometimes referred to as P-Metric. This allows the exact identification of the tire specifications, regardless of the manufacturer. If selecting a different tire size or brand, remember to check the installed tire for any sign of interference with the body or suspension while the vehicle is stopping, turning sharply or heavily loaded.

Snow Tires

Good radial tires can produce a big advantage in slippery weather, but in snow, a street radial tire does not have sufficient tread to provide traction and control. The small grooves of a street tire quickly pack with snow and the tire behaves like a billiard ball on a marble floor. The more open, chunky tread of a snow tire will self-clean as the tire turns, providing much better grip on snowy surfaces.

To satisfy municipalities requiring snow tires during weather emergencies, most snow tires carry either an M + S designation after the tire size stamped on the sidewall, or the designation "all-season." In general, no change in tire size is necessary when buying snow tires.

Most manufacturers strongly recommend the use of 4 snow tires on their vehicles for reasons of stability. If snow tires are fitted only to the drive wheels, the opposite end of the vehicle may become very unstable when braking or turning on slippery surfaces. This instability can lead to unpleasant endings if the driver can't counteract the slide in time.

Note that snow tires, whether 2 or 4, will affect vehicle handling in all non-snow situations. The stiffer, heavier snow tires will noticeably change the turning and braking characteristics of the vehicle. Once the snow tires are installed, you must re-learn the behavior of the vehicle and drive accordingly.

➡**Consider buying extra wheels on which to mount the snow tires. Once done, the "snow wheels" can be installed and removed as needed. This eliminates the potential damage to tires or wheels from seasonal removal and installation. Even if your vehicle has styled wheels, see if inexpensive steel wheels are available. Although the look of the vehicle will change, the expensive wheels will be protected from salt, curb hits and pothole damage.**

TIRE STORAGE

If they are mounted on wheels, store the tires at proper inflation pressure. All tires should be kept in a cool, dry place. If they are stored in the garage or basement, do not let them stand on a concrete floor; set them on strips of wood, a mat or a large stack of newspaper. Keeping them away from direct moisture is of paramount importance. Tires should not be stored upright, but in a flat position.

INFLATION & INSPECTION

The importance of proper tire inflation cannot be overemphasized. A tire employs air as part of its structure. It is designed around the supporting strength of the air at a specified pressure. For this reason, improper inflation drastically reduces the tires's ability to perform as intended. A tire will lose some air in day-to-

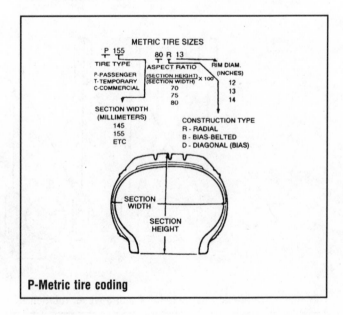

P-Metric tire coding

day use; having to add a few pounds of air periodically is not necessarily a sign of a leaking tire.

Two items should be a permanent fixture in every glove compartment: an accurate tire pressure gauge and a tread depth gauge. Check the tire pressure (including the spare) regularly with a pocket type gauge. Too often, the gauge on the end of the air hose at your corner garage is not accurate because it suffers too much abuse. Always check tire pressure when the tires are cold, as pressure increases with temperature. If you must move the vehicle to check the tire inflation, do not drive more than a mile before checking. A cold tire is generally one that has not been driven for more than three hours.

A plate or sticker is normally provided somewhere in the vehicle (door post, hood, tailgate or trunk lid) which shows the proper pressure for the tires. Never counteract excessive pressure build-up by bleeding off air pressure (letting some air out). This will cause the tire to run hotter and wear quicker.

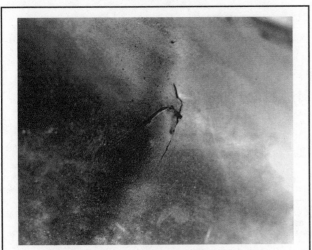

Tires should be checked frequently for any sign of puncture or damage

Tires with deep cuts, or cuts which show bulging should be replaced immediately

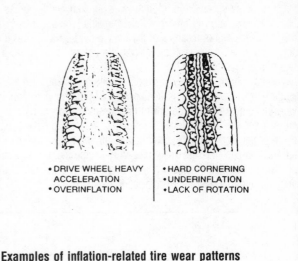

- DRIVE WHEEL HEAVY ACCELERATION
- OVERINFLATION

- HARD CORNERING
- UNDERINFLATION
- LACK OF ROTATION

Examples of inflation-related tire wear patterns

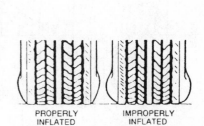

PROPERLY INFLATED   IMPROPERLY INFLATED

RADIAL TIRE

Radial tires have a characteristic sidewall bulge; don't try to measure pressure by looking at the tire. Use a quality air pressure gauge

✳✳ CAUTION

Never exceed the maximum tire pressure embossed on the tire! This is the pressure to be used when the tire is at maximum loading, but it is rarely the correct pressure for everyday driving. Consult the owner's manual or the tire pressure sticker for the correct tire pressure.

Once you've maintained the correct tire pressures for several weeks, you'll be familiar with the vehicle's braking and handling personality. Slight adjustments in tire pressures can fine-tune these characteristics, but never change the cold pressure specification by more than 2 psi. A slightly softer tire pressure will give a softer ride but also yield lower fuel mileage. A slightly harder tire will give crisper dry road handling but can cause skidding on wet surfaces. Unless you're fully attuned to the vehicle, stick to the recommended inflation pressures.

All tires made since 1968 have built-in tread wear indicator bars that show up as ½ in. (13mm) wide smooth bands across the tire when 1/16 in. (1.5mm) of tread remains. The appearance of tread wear indicators means that the tires should be replaced. In fact, many states have laws prohibiting the use of tires with less than this amount of tread.

You can check your own tread depth with an inexpensive gauge or by using a Lincoln head penny. Slip the Lincoln penny (with Lincoln's head upside-down) into several tread grooves. If you can see the top of Lincoln's head in 2 adjacent grooves, the tire has less than 1/16 in. (1.5mm) tread left and should be replaced. You can measure snow tires in the same manner by using the "tails" side of the Lincoln penny. If you can see the top of the Lincoln memorial, it's time to replace the snow tire(s).

CARE OF SPECIAL WHEELS

If you have invested money in magnesium, aluminum alloy or sport wheels, special precautions should be taken to make sure your investment is not wasted and that your special wheels look good for the life of the vehicle.

Special wheels are easily damaged and/or scratched. Occasionally check the rims for cracking, impact damage or air leaks. If any of these are found, replace the wheel. But in order to prevent this type of damage and the costly replacement of a special wheel, observe the following precautions:

• Use extra care not to damage the wheels during removal, installation, balancing, etc. After removal of the wheels from the ve-

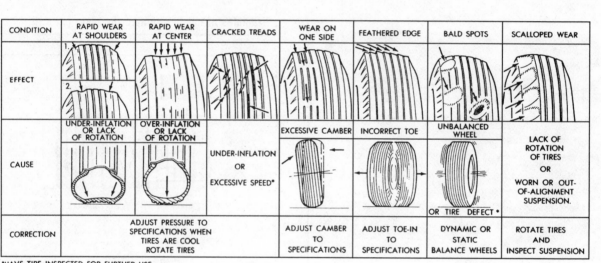

Common tire wear patterns and causes

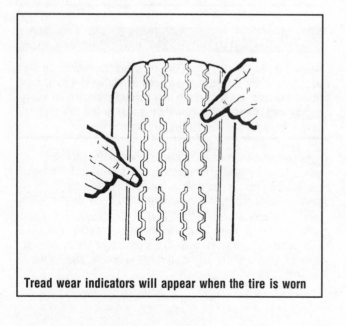

Tread wear indicators will appear when the tire is worn

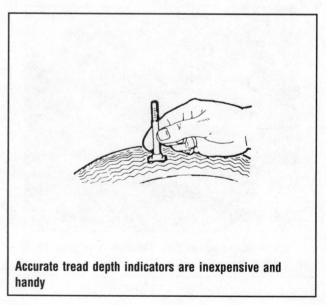

Accurate tread depth indicators are inexpensive and handy

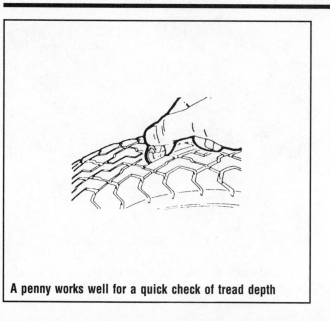

A penny works well for a quick check of tread depth

hicle, place them on a mat or other protective surface. If they are to be stored for any length of time, support them on strips of wood. Never store tires and wheels upright; the tread may develop flat spots.

• When driving, watch for hazards; it doesn't take much to crack a wheel.

• When washing, use a mild soap or non-abrasive dish detergent (keeping in mind that detergent tends to remove wax). Avoid cleansers with abrasives or the use of hard brushes. There are many cleaners and polishes for special wheels.

• If possible, remove the wheels during the winter. Salt and sand used for snow removal can severely damage the finish of a wheel.

• Make certain the recommended lug nut torque is never exceeded or the wheel may crack. Never use snow chains on special wheels; severe scratching will occur.

FLUIDS & LUBRICANTS

Fluid Disposal

Use fluids such as engine oil, transmission fluid, antifreeze and brake fluid are hazardous wastes and must be disposed of properly. Before draining gluids, consult with the authorities; in many areas, waste oil, etc. is being accepted as a part of recycling programs. A number of service stations and auto parts stores are also accepting waste fluids for recycling.

Be sure of the recycling center's policies before draining any fluids, as many will not accept different fluids that have been mixed together, such as oil and antifreeze.

Oil Recommendation

▶ **See Figure 28b**

Use a good quality motor oil of a known brand, which carries the API classification SG or SH. The proper viscosity of the oil depends on the climate and temperature your car is operated in.

✳✳ WARNING

Do not use unlabeled oil or a lower grade of oil which does not meet SH specifications. If 5W, 10W, or 5W-20 oil is used, avoid prolonged high-speed driving.

Change the oil at the intervals recommended. If the vehicle is being used in severe service such as trailer towing, change the oil at more frequent intervals.

It is especially important that the oil be changed at the proper intervals in emission controlled engines, as they run hotter than non-controlled, thus causing the oil to break down faster.

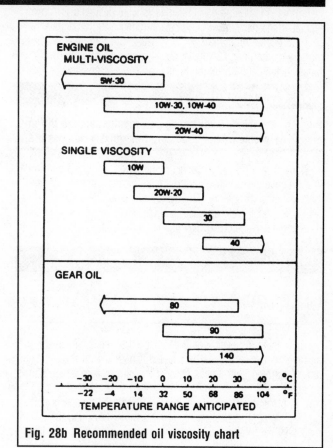

Fig. 28b Recommended oil viscosity chart

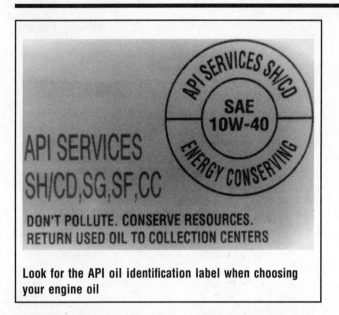

Look for the API oil identification label when choosing your engine oil

When checking the oil, locate and remove the engine oil dipstick

Fuel Recommendations

From 1971 through 1974 all models were designed to run on regular grade gasoline with an octane rating of 90 or higher.

If the engine pings, knocks, or diesels, either the fuel grade is too low or the timing is out of adjustment. Add gasoline of a higher octane and check the timing, as soon as possible.

✳✳ WARNING

Pinging, knocking, or dieseling can rapidly damage the engine. The problem should be cured as quickly as possible.

Starting in 1975 some Toyota models were equipped with a catalytic converter, because lead ruins the catalyst, the use of unleaded fuel is mandatory. All Toyota models equipped with a catalytic converter therefore, must use unleaded gasoline. The others (non-converter equipped) may use leaded gasoline.

Engine

OIL LEVEL CHECK

The engine oil level should be checked at regular intervals; for example, whenever the car is refueled. Check the oil level, if the red oil warning light comes on or if the oil pressure gauge shows an abnormally low reading.

It is preferable to check the oil level when the engine is cold or after the car has been standing for a while. Checking the oil immediately after the engine has been running will result in a false reading. Be sure that the car is on a level surface before checking the oil level.

Remove the dipstick and wipe it with a clean rag. Insert it again (fully) and withdraw it. The oil level should be at the F mark (Full) or between the F and the L (Low) marks. Do not run the engine if the oil level is below the L.

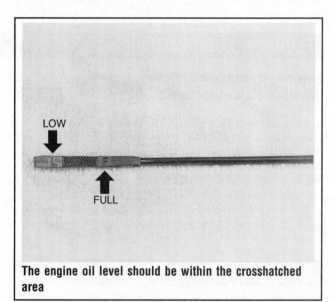

The engine oil level should be within the crosshatched area

✳✳ WARNING

Do not use unlabeled oil or a lower grade of oil which does not meet SH specifications.

Oil Changes

OIL & FILTER CHANGE

▶ See Figures 29 and 30

The oil should be changed at the intervals specified. The amount of oil required for each engine and model may be found in the Capacities chart.

➠**All new cars should have an oil change after the first 1,000 miles. The filter should also be changed at this time.**

When changing the engine oil, remove the oil filler cap from the valve cover

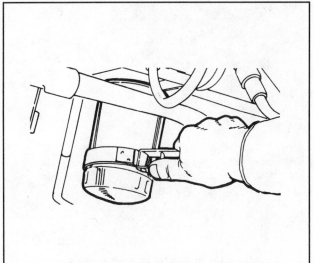

Locate the oil filter and remove it with a filter wrench

Loosen the drain plug from the oil pan

Fig. 29 Use the strap wrench to loosen the filter only

Unthread the drain plug then quickly pull it away

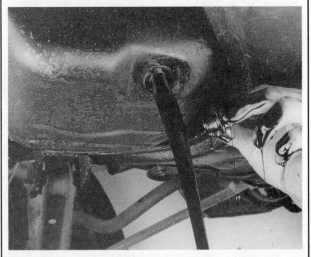

Before installing a new oil filter, lightly coat the rubber gasket with clean oil

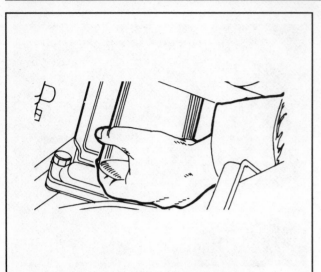

Fig. 30 When installing the oil filter, hand-tighten it only

Use a funnel while adding oil to prevent spills

1. Warm the oil by running the engine for a short period of time; this will make the oil flow more freely from the oil pan.

2. Park on a level surface and put on the parking brake. Stop the engine. Remove the oil filler cap from the top of the valve cover.

3. Place a pan of adequate capacity below the drain plug.

4. Use a wrench of the proper size (not pliers) to remove the drain plug. Loosen the drain plug while maintaining a slight upward force on it to keep the oil from running out around it. Allow the oil to fully drain into the container under the drain hole.

5. Use a band type oil wrench, and remove the oil filter. Turn the filter counter clockwise to remove.

6. Wipe off the filter bracket with a clean rag.

7. Install a new filter and gasket. Lubricate the gasket with clean oil first.

➡**Only hand tighten the oil filter.**

8. Remove the container used to catch the oil and wipe any excess oil from the area around the hole.

9. Install the drain plug, complete with its gasket. Be sure

that the plug is tight enough that the oil does not leak out, but not tight enough to strip the threads.

10. Add clean, new oil of the proper grade and viscosity through the oil filler on the top of the valve cover. Be sure that the oil level registers near the F (full) mark on the dipstick.

Manual Transmission

LEVEL CHECK

♦ **See Figure 31**

The oil in the manual transmission should be checked every 6,000 miles and replaced every 18,000 miles (24,000 miles 1974 models, 25,000 miles 1975–77 models, and 30,000 miles 1978–82 models) or 24 months, whichever occurs first.

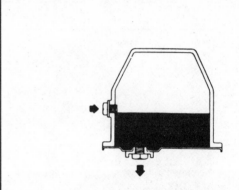

Fig. 31 When checking the level of the manual transmission fluid, it should be up to the bottom of the filler (upper) plug

To check the oil level, remove the transmission filler plug. This is always the upper plug, the lower plug being the drain.

The oil level should reach the bottom of the filler plug. If it is lower than this, add API grade GL-4 oil of the proper viscosity. Use SAE 80 oil in all models, except for 1974–82, which uses SAE 90 oil.

DRAIN & REFILL

The transmission oil should be replaced every 18,000 miles (1970–73), 24,000 miles (1974), 25,000 miles (1975–77), 30,000 miles (1978–82), or 24 months (all years), whichever occurs first.

1. Park the car on a level surface and put on the parking brake.

2. Remove the oil filler (upper) plug.

3. Place a container, of a large enough capacity to catch all of the oil, under the drain (lower) plug. Use the proper size wrench to loosen the drain plug slowly, while maintaining a slight upward force to keep the oil from running out. Once the plug is removed, allow all of the oil to drain from the transmission.

4. Install the drain plug and its gasket, if so equipped.

5. Fill the transmission to capacity. (See the Capacities chart.) Use API grade GL4 SAE 80 oil on all 1970–73 passenger cars. Use SAE 90 in 1974–82 models. Be sure that the oil level reaches the bottom of the filler plug.

6. Remember to install the filler plug when finished.

Automatic Transmission

LEVEL CHECK

♦ **See Figure 32**

Check the level of the transmission fluid every 3,000 miles and replace it every 18,000 miles (24,000 miles 1974 models, 25,000 miles 1975–77 models, and 30,000 miles 1978–82 models). It is important that these figures be adhered to, in order to ensure a long transmission life. The procedures for checking the oil are given as follows:

Start the engine and allow to idle for a few minutes. Set the handbrake and apply the service brakes. Move the gear selector through all ranges.

With the engine still running, the parking brake on and the wheels blocked, place the selector in Neutral. Remove and clean the transmission dipstick. Insert the dipstick fully, remove it and take a reading. The dipstick has two ranges.

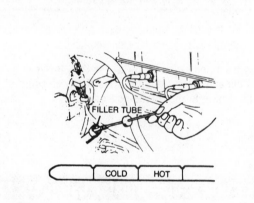

Fig. 32 There are HOT and COLD range markings on the automatic transmission dipstick

1. COLD The fluid level should fall in this range when the engine has been running for only a short time.

2. HOT The fluid level should fall in this range when the engine has reached normal running temperatures.

3. Replenish the fluid through the filler tube with type F fluid for all models. Add fluid to the top of the COLD or HOT range, depending upon engine temperature.

❈❈ WARNING

Do not overfill the transmission.

DRAIN & REFILL

Change the fluid in the automatic transmission every 18,000 (1970–73), 24,000 miles (1974), 25,000 (1975–77), 30,000 miles (1978–82), or 25 months, whichever occurs first.

1. Park the car on a level surface. Set the parking brake.

2. Place a container, which is large enough to catch all of the transmission fluid, under the transmission oil pan drain plug. Unfasten the drain plug and allow all of the fluid to run out into the container.

3. Check the condition of the transmission fluid. If it is burnt, discolored, or has particles in it, the transmission needs to be overhauled. Consult your local Toyota dealer.

To drain the fluid from the automatic transmission, remove the plug to allow the fluid to flow

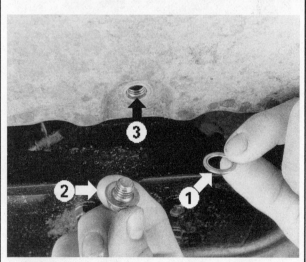

1. Gasket   3. Drain hole
2. Drain plug

There should be a reusable metal gasket when you remove the drain plug

Once the fluid is drained, reinstall the drain plug and fill the transmission with fresh fluid

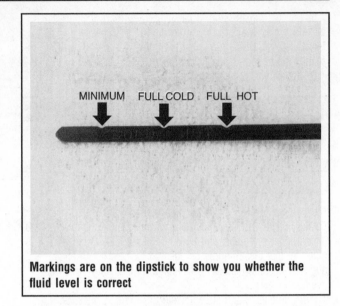

Markings are on the dipstick to show you whether the fluid level is correct

4. Install the drain plug in the transmission oil pan. Be sure that it is tight enough to prevent leakage, but not tight enough to strip the threads.

✳✳ WARNING

Fill the transmission with ATF type F fluid only. Do not use DEXRON®, gear oil or engine oil supplement.

5. Fill the transmission through the filler tube, after removing the dipstick, with ATF type F transmission fluid.

➡ It may be a good idea to fill to less than the recommended capacity (see the Capacities chart) as some of the fluid will remain in the torque converter.

6. Start the engine and check the transmission fluid level, as outlined under Fluid Level Checks. Add fluid, if necessary, but do not overfill.

Brake and Clutch Master Cylinders

LEVEL CHECK

The brake and clutch (manual transmission) master cylinder reservoirs are made of a translucent plastic so that the fluid level can be checked without removing the cap. Check the fluid level frequently.

If the fluid is low, fill the reservoir with DOT 3 fluid, pouring so bubbles do not form in the reservoir. Use care not to spill any fluid on the car's paint, damage may result.

✳✳ WARNING

Do not use a lower grade of brake fluid and never mix different types. Either could result in a brake system failure.

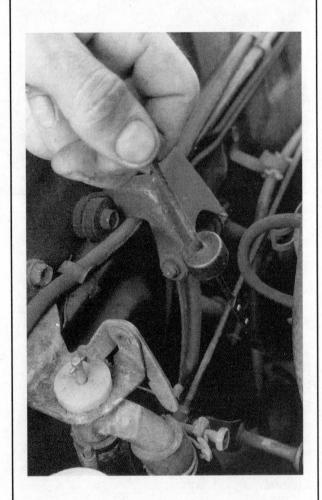

Check the fluid level by removing the dipstick

Remove the brake master cylinder reservoir cap to to top off the fluid level

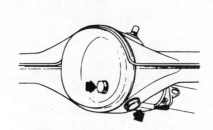

Fig. 33 When checking the fluid level in the differential, the upper plug is for inspection and the lower for draining

Top off the brake master cylinder reservoir with DOT 3 brake fluid to the MAX mark

Drive Axle

LEVEL CHECK

⏷ **See Figure 33**

The oil level in the differential should be checked every 6,000 miles and replaced every 18,000 miles (1974, 24,000 miles; 1975–77, 25,000 miles; 1978–81, 30,000 miles) or 24 months, whichever comes first. The oil should be checked with the car on a level surface. Remove the oil filler and upper plug, located on the back of the differential.

➡**The bottom plug is the drain.**

The oil level should reach to the bottom edge of the filler hole. If low, replenish with API grade GL-5 gear oil of the proper vis-

cosity. The viscosity is determined by the ambient temperature range. If the temperature averages above 10°F, use SAE 90 gear oil. If the temperature averages below 10°F, use SAE 80 oil. Always check for leaks when checking the oil level.

DRAIN & REFILL

All Toyota rear axles use 90 weight, API GL-5 lubricant. Lubricant is changed every 18,000 miles (1970–73), 24,000 miles (1974), 25,000 miles (1975–77), 30,000 miles (1978–82) or 24 months, whichever comes first.

1. Park the vehicle on a level surface. Set the parking brake.
2. Remove the filler (upper) plug. Place a container which is large enough to catch all of the differential oil, under the drain plug.
3. Remove the drain (lower) plug and gasket, if so equipped. Allow all of the oil to drain into the container.
4. Install the drain plug. Tighten it so that it will not leak, but do not overtighten.

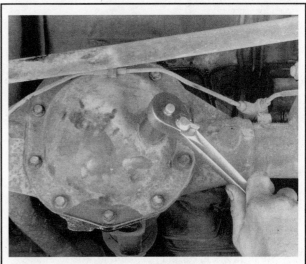

To check the fluid level of the rear axle . . .

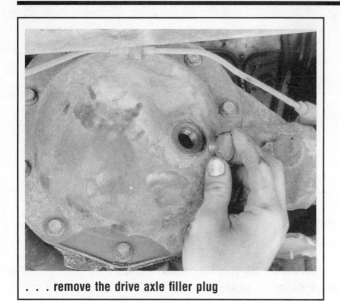

. . . remove the drive axle filler plug

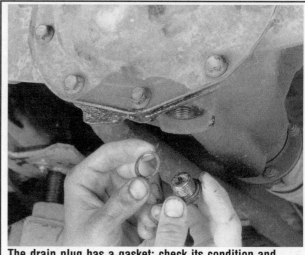

The drain plug has a gasket; check its condition and replace if needed

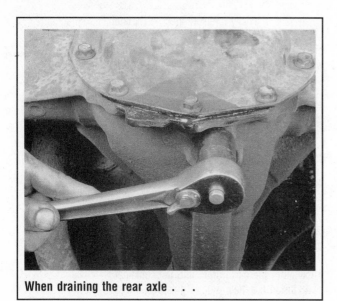

When draining the rear axle . . .

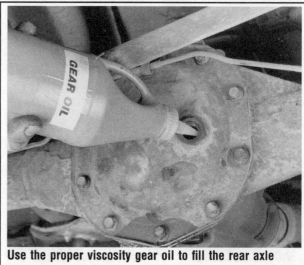

Use the proper viscosity gear oil to fill the rear axle differential

. . . remove the lower plug on the rear axle to allow the fluid to drain

5. Refill with the proper grade and viscosity of axle lubricant. Be sure that the level reaches the bottom of the filler plug.

6. Install the filler plug and check for leakage.

Steering Gear

LEVEL CHECK

Check the steering gear oil level every 12,000 miles. The level should be up to filler plug hole. All pre-1974 models use SAE 80 gear oil. 1974–81 use SAE 90.

Power Steering Reservoir

LEVEL CHECK

All six cylinder and some other models from 1978–81 use power steering. Check the level of the power steering fluid periodically. The fluid level should fall within the crosshatched area of the gauge attached to the reservoir cap. If the fluid level is below this, add DEXRON® fluid. Remember to check for leaks.

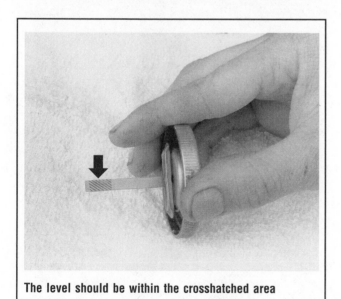

Check the power steering reservoir level while the engine is cold to avoid burns

The level should be within the crosshatched area

If necessary to add fluid, use a funnel to avoid spills

Chassis Greasing

EXCEPT CROWN 4M ENGINE

The chassis lubrication for these models is limited to lubricating the front ball joints every 24,000 miles (1970–74), 25,000 miles (1975–77), or 30,000 miles (1978–82) or 24 months, whichever occurs first.
1. Remove the screw plug from the ball joint. Install a grease nipple.
2. Using a hand-operated grease gun, lubricate the ball joint with NGLI No. 1 molybdenum-disulphide lithium-based grease.

✳✳ WARNING

Do not use multipurpose or chassis grease.

3. Remove the nipple and reinstall the screw plug.
4. Repeat for the other ball joint(s).

CROWN 4M ENGINE

The ball joints on these models do not normally require lubrication. If the dust boots become torn or damaged, however, the boots should be replaced and the ball joint repacked.

Body Lubrication

There is no set period recommended by Toyota for body lubrication. However, it is a good idea to lubricate the following body points at least once a year, especially in the fall before cold weather.

Lubricate with engine oil:
- Door lock latches
- Door lock rollers
- Station wagon tailgate hinges
- Door, hood, and hinge pivots

Lubricate with silicone grease:
- Trunk lid latch and hinge
- Glove box door latch

Lubricate with silicone spray:
- All rubber weather stripping
- Hood stops

When finished lubricating a body part, be sure that all the excess lubricant has been wiped off, especially in the areas of the car which may come in contact with clothing.

Wheel Bearings

The front wheel bearings should be repacked every 24,000 miles on 1970–74 vehicles, 25,000 miles on 1975–77 vehicles, and 30,000 miles on 1978–82 vehicles, or every 24 months, whichever occurs first.

REMOVAL & INSTALLATION

1. Remove the caliper and the disc/hub assembly, as previously detailed.
2. If either the disc or the entire hub assembly is to be replaced, unbolt the hub from the disc.

➡**If only the bearings are to be replaced, do not separate the disc and hub.**

3. Using a brass rod as a drift, tap the inner bearing cone out. Remove the oil seal and the inner bearing.

➡**Throw the old oil seal away.**

4. Drift out the inner bearing cup.
5. Drift out the outer bearing cup.
6. Inspect the bearings and the hub for signs of wear or damage. Replace components, as necessary.

Once the bent ends are cut, grasp the cotter pin and pull or pry it free of the spindle

If difficulty is encountered, gently tap on the pliers with a hammer to help free the cotter pin

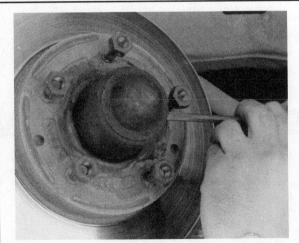

Pry the dust cap from the hub taking care not to distort or damage its flange

Loosen and remove the castellated nut from the spindle

Remove the washer from the spindle

Use a small prytool to remove the old inner bearing seal

With the nut and washer out of the way, the outer bearings may be removed from the hub

With the seal removed, the inner bearing may be withdrawn from the hub

Pull the hub and inner bearing assembly from the spindle

Thoroughly pack the bearing with fresh, high temperature wheel-bearing grease before installation

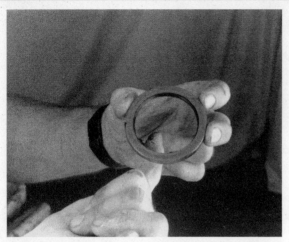

Apply a thin coat of fresh grease to the new inner bearing seal lip

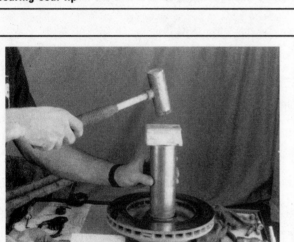

Use a suitably sized driver to install the inner bearing seal to the hub

With new or freshly packed bearings, tighten the nut while gently spinning the wheel, then adjust the bearings

After the bearings are adjusted, install the dust cap by gently tapping on the flange—DO NOT damage the cap by hammering on the center

To install:

7. Install the inner bearing cup and then the outer bearing cup, by drifting them into place.

✳✳ WARNING

Use care not to cock the bearing cups in the hub.

8. Pack the bearings, hub inner well and grease cap with multipurpose grease.
9. Install the inner bearing into the hub.
10. Carefully install a new oil seal with a soft drift.
11. Install the hub on the spindle. Be sure to install all of the washers and nuts which were removed.
12. Adjust the bearing preload, as detailed following.
13. Install the caliper assembly, as previously detailed.

PRELOAD ADJUSTMENT

1. With the front hub/disc assembly installed, tighten the castellated nut to the torque figure specified in the Preload Specifications chart.
2. Rotate the disc back and forth, two or three times, to allow the bearing to seat properly.
3. Loosen the castellated nut until it is only finger-tight.
4. Tighten the nut firmly, using a box wrench.
5. Measure the bearing preload with a spring scale attached to a wheel mounting stud. Check it against the specifications given in the Preload Specifications chart.
6. Install the cotter pin.

➡️If the hole does not align with the nut (or cap) holes, tighten the nut slightly until it does.

7. Finish installing the brake components and the wheel.

TRAILER TOWING

General Recommendations

Your vehicle was primarily designed to carry passengers and cargo. It is important to remember that towing a trailer will place additional loads on your vehicles engine, drivetrain, steering, braking and other systems. However, if you decide to tow a trailer, using the prior equipment is a must.

Local laws may require specific equipment such as trailer brakes or fender mounted mirrors. Check your local laws.

Trailer Weight

The weight of the trailer is the most important factor. A good weight-to-horsepower ratio is about 35:1, 35 lbs. of Gross Combined Weight (GCW) for every horsepower your engine develops. Multiply the engine's rated horsepower by 35 and subtract the weight of the vehicle passengers and luggage. The number remaining is the approximate ideal maximum weight you should tow, although a numerically higher axle ratio can help compensate for heavier weight.

Hitch (Tongue) Weight

Calculate the hitch weight in order to select a proper hitch. The weight of the hitch is usually 9–11% of the trailer gross weight and should be measured with the trailer loaded. Hitches fall into various categories: those that mount on the frame and rear bumper, the bolt-on type, or the weld-on distribution type used for larger trailers. Axle mounted or clamp-on bumper hitches should never be used.

Check the gross weight rating of your trailer. Tongue weight is usually figured as 10% of gross trailer weight. Therefore, a trailer with a maximum gross weight of 2000 lbs. will have a maximum

tongue weight of 200 lbs. Class I trailers fall into this category. Class II trailers are those with a gross weight rating of 2000–3000 lbs., while Class III trailers fall into the 3500–6000 lbs. category. Class IV trailers are those over 6000 lbs. and are for use with fifth wheel trucks, only.

When you've determined the hitch that you'll need, follow the manufacturer's installation instructions, exactly, especially when it comes to fastener torques. The hitch will subjected to a lot of stress and good hitches come with hardened bolts. Never substitute an inferior bolt for a hardened bolt.

Cooling

ENGINE

Overflow Tank

One of the most common, if not THE most common, problems associated with trailer towing is engine overheating. If you have a cooling system without an expansion tank, you'll definitely need to get an aftermarket expansion tank kit, preferably one with at least a 2 quart capacity. These kits are easily installed on the radiator's overflow hose, and come with a pressure cap designed for expansion tanks.

Flex Fan

Another helpful accessory for vehicles using a belt-driven radiator fan is a flex fan. These fans are large diameter units designed to provide more airflow at low speeds, by using fan blades that have deeply cupped surfaces. The blades then flex, or flatten out, at high speed, when less cooling air is needed. These fans are far lighter in weight than stock fans, requiring less horsepower to drive them. Also, they are far quieter than stock fans. If you do decide to replace your stock fan with a flex fan, note that if your vehicle has a fan clutch, a spacer will be needed between the flex fan and water pump hub.

Oil Cooler

Aftermarket engine oil coolers are helpful for prolonging engine oil life and reducing overall engine temperatures. Both of these factors increase engine life. While not absolutely necessary in towing Class I and some Class II trailers, they are recommended for heavier Class II and all Class III towing. Engine oil cooler systems usually consist of an adapter, screwed on in place of the oil filter, a remote filter mounting and a multi-tube, finned heat exchanger, which is mounted in front of the radiator or air conditioning condenser.

TRANSMISSION

An automatic transmission is usually recommended for trailer towing. Modern automatics have proven reliable and, of course,

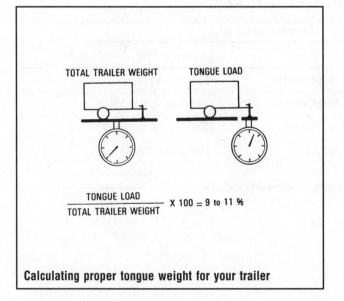

TOTAL TRAILER WEIGHT   TONGUE LOAD

$$\frac{\text{TONGUE LOAD}}{\text{TOTAL TRAILER WEIGHT}} \times 100 = 9 \text{ to } 11 \%$$

Calculating proper tongue weight for your trailer

easy to operate, in trailer towing. The increased load of a trailer, however, causes an increase in the temperature of the automatic transmission fluid. Heat is the worst enemy of an automatic transmission. As the temperature of the fluid increases, the life of the fluid decreases.

It is essential, therefore, that you install an automatic transmission cooler. The cooler, which consists of a multi-tube, finned heat exchanger, is usually installed in front of the radiator or air conditioning compressor, and hooked in-line with the transmission cooler tank inlet line. Follow the cooler manufacturer's installation instructions.

Select a cooler of at least adequate capacity, based upon the combined gross weights of the vehicle and trailer.

Cooler manufacturers recommend that you use an aftermarket cooler in addition to, and not instead of, the present cooling tank in your radiator. If you do want to use it in place of the radiator cooling tank, get a cooler at least two sizes larger than normally necessary.

➡A transmission cooler can, sometimes, cause slow or harsh shifting in the transmission during cold weather, until the fluid has a chance to come up to normal operating temperature. Some coolers can be purchased with or retrofitted with a temperature bypass valve which will allow fluid flow through the cooler only when the fluid has reached above a certain operating temperature.

Handling A Trailer

Towing a trailer with ease and safety requires a certain amount of experience. It's a good idea to learn the feel of a trailer by practicing turning, stopping and backing in an open area such as an empty parking lot.

TOWING THE VEHICLE

For information on towing points for 1970–77 cars, see the chart. On 1978–82 cars, tow using the tie down tabs located under front and rear bumpers.

The following precautions should be observed when towing the vehicle:

1. Always place the transmission in Neutral and release the parking brake.

2. Models equipped with automatic transmissions, except 1974–77 models, may be towed with the transmission in Neutral, but only for short distances at speeds below 20 mph. On 1974–77 models, or if the transmission is inoperative, either tow the car with the rear wheels off the ground or disconnect the drive shaft at the differential end. If you are towing a 1978 or later car with

an automatic transmission, you may tow the car for up to 50 miles and at speeds of up to 30 miles per hour.

3. If the rear axle is defective, the car must be towed with its rear wheels off the ground.

4. Always turn the steering column lock to ON and then return to ACC. This prevents the steering column from locking.

✳✳ WARNING

The steering column lock is not designed to hold the wheels straight while the car is being towed. Therefore, if the car is being towed with its front end down, place a dolly under the front wheels.

Towing Points—1970–77

| Model | Attach the tow line to: | |
	Front	Rear
Corona	Towing hook (front crossmember)	Spring hanger
Mark II/4 (RT)	Towing hook (front crossmember)	Spring hanger
Mark II/6 (MX)	Towing hook (front crossmember)	Differential carrier ② ③
Crown 2300	Front bumper stay ①	Rear bumper stay ① ②
Crown 2600	Front crossmember	Towing hook ②

① Towing hook available from dealer (optional)
② Rear spring hanger–station wagon
③ 1974–77 models—rear towing hooks

JACKING

◆ **See Figure 34**

Your vehicle was supplied with a jack for emergency road repairs. This jack is fine for changing a flat tire or other short term procedures not requiring you to go beneath the vehicle. If it is used in an emergency situation, carefully follow the instructions provided either with the jack or in your owner's manual. Do not attempt to use the jack on any portions of the vehicle other than specified by the vehicle manufacturer. Always block the diagonally opposite wheel when using a jack.

A more convenient way of jacking is the use of a garage or floor jack.

Never place the jack under the radiator, engine or transmission components. Severe and expensive damage will result when the jack is raised. Additionally, never jack under the floorpan or bodywork; the metal will deform.

Whenever you plan to work under the vehicle, you must support it on jackstands or ramps. Never use cinder blocks or stacks of wood to support the vehicle, even if you're only going to be under it for a few minutes. Never crawl under the vehicle when it is supported only by the tire-changing jack or other floor jack.

➡**Always position a block of wood or small rubber pad on top of the jack or jackstand to protect the lifting point's finish when lifting or supporting the vehicle.**

Small hydraulic, screw, or scissors jacks are satisfactory for raising the vehicle. Drive-on trestles or ramps are also a handy

VEHICLE SUPPORT LOCATIONS
JACK POINTS

Front

Rear

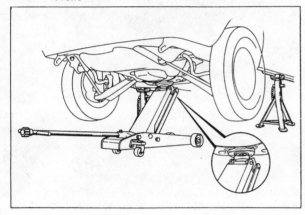
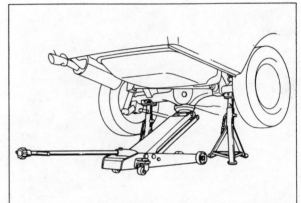

STANDARD SUPPORT LOCATIONS

Front

Rear

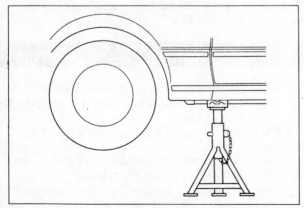
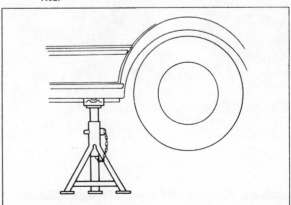

Fig. 34 Common jacking points

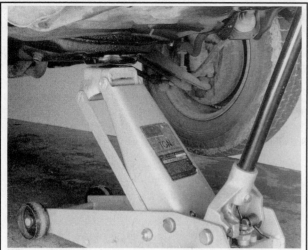

When raising the front of the vehicle, place the jack in the center of the engine support

When raising the rear of the vehicle, place the jack beneath the center of the rear axle

A jackstand may be placed beneath the side frame rail, at the front of the body

Place a jackstand at the rear of the vehicle, beneath the side frame rail

and safe way to both raise and support the vehicle. Be careful though, some ramps may be too steep to drive your vehicle onto without scraping the front bottom panels. Never support the vehicle on any suspension member (unless specifically instructed to do so by a repair manual) or by an underbody panel.

Jacking Precautions

The following safety points cannot be overemphasized:
• Always block the opposite wheel or wheels to keep the vehicle from rolling off the jack.
• When raising the front of the vehicle, firmly apply the parking brake.
• When the drive wheels are to remain on the ground, leave the vehicle in gear to help prevent it from rolling.
• Always use jackstands to support the vehicle when you are working underneath. Place the stands beneath the vehicle's jacking brackets. Before climbing underneath, rock the vehicle a bit to make sure it is firmly supported.

JUMP STARTING A DEAD BATTERY

Whenever a vehicle is jump started, precautions must be followed in order to prevent the possibility of personal injury. Remember that batteries contain a small amount of explosive hydrogen gas which is a by-product of battery charging. Sparks should always be avoided when working around batteries, especially when attaching jumper cables. To minimize the possibility of accidental sparks, follow the procedure carefully.

✳✳ CAUTION

NEVER hook the batteries up in a series circuit or the entire electrical system will go up in smoke, including the starter!

Vehicles equipped with a diesel engine may utilize two 12 volt batteries. If so, the batteries are connected in a parallel circuit (positive terminal to positive terminal, negative terminal to negative terminal). Hooking the batteries up in parallel circuit increases battery cranking power without increasing total battery voltage output. Output remains at 12 volts. On the other hand, hooking two 12 volt batteries up in a series circuit (positive terminal to negative terminal, positive terminal to negative terminal) increases total battery output to 24 volts (12 volts plus 12 volts).

Jump Starting Precautions

- Be sure that both batteries are of the same voltage. Vehicles covered by this manual and most vehicles on the road today utilize a 12 volt charging system.
- Be sure that both batteries are of the same polarity (have the same terminal, in most cases NEGATIVE grounded).
- Be sure that the vehicles are not touching or a short could occur.
- On serviceable batteries, be sure the vent cap holes are not obstructed.
- Do not smoke or allow sparks anywhere near the batteries.
- In cold weather, make sure the battery electrolyte is not frozen. This can occur more readily in a battery that has been in a state of discharge.
- Do not allow electrolyte to contact your skin or clothing.

Jump Starting Procedure

1. Make sure that the voltages of the 2 batteries are the same. Most batteries and charging systems are of the 12 volt variety.
2. Pull the jumping vehicle (with the good battery) into a position so the jumper cables can reach the dead battery and that vehicle's engine. Make sure that the vehicles do NOT touch.
3. Place the transmissions/transaxles of both vehicles in **Neutral** (MT) or **P** (AT), as applicable, then firmly set their parking brakes.

➡**If necessary for safety reasons, the hazard lights on both vehicles may be operated throughout the entire procedure without significantly increasing the difficulty of jumping the dead battery.**

4. Turn all lights and accessories OFF on both vehicles. Make sure the ignition switches on both vehicles are turned to the **OFF** position.
5. Cover the battery cell caps with a rag, but do not cover the terminals.
6. Make sure the terminals on both batteries are clean and free of corrosion or proper electrical connection will be impeded. If necessary, clean the battery terminals before proceeding.
7. Identify the positive (+) and negative (−) terminals on both batteries.
8. Connect the first jumper cable to the positive (+) terminal of the dead battery, then connect the other end of that cable to the positive (+) terminal of the booster (good) battery.
9. Connect one end of the other jumper cable to the negative (−) terminal on the booster battery and the final cable clamp to an engine bolt head, alternator bracket or other solid, metallic point on the engine with the dead battery. Try to pick a ground on the engine that is positioned away from the battery in order to minimize the possibility of the 2 clamps touching should one loosen during the procedure. DO NOT connect this clamp to the negative (−) terminal of the bad battery.

✳✳ CAUTION

Be very careful to keep the jumper cables away from moving parts (cooling fan, belts, etc.) on both engines.

10. Check to make sure that the cables are routed away from any moving parts, then start the donor vehicle's engine. Run the engine at moderate speed for several minutes to allow the dead battery a chance to receive some initial charge.
11. With the donor vehicle's engine still running slightly above idle, try to start the vehicle with the dead battery. Crank the engine for no more than 10 seconds at a time and let the starter cool for at least 20 seconds between tries. If the vehicle does not start in 3 tries, it is likely that something else is also wrong or that the battery needs additional time to charge.

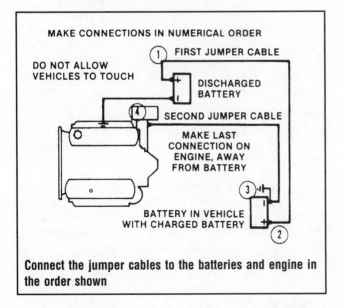

MAKE CONNECTIONS IN NUMERICAL ORDER

DO NOT ALLOW
VEHICLES TO TOUCH

1 — FIRST JUMPER CABLE

DISCHARGED BATTERY

4 — SECOND JUMPER CABLE

MAKE LAST CONNECTION ON ENGINE, AWAY FROM BATTERY

BATTERY IN VEHICLE WITH CHARGED BATTERY

Connect the jumper cables to the batteries and engine in the order shown

12. Once the vehicle is started, allow it to run at idle for a few seconds to make sure that it is operating properly.

13. Turn ON the headlights, heater blower and, if equipped, the rear defroster of both vehicles in order to reduce the severity of voltage spikes and subsequent risk of damage to the vehicles' electrical systems when the cables are disconnected. This step is especially important to any vehicle equipped with computer control modules.

14. Carefully disconnect the cables in the reverse order of connection. Start with the negative cable that is attached to the engine ground, then the negative cable on the donor battery. Disconnect the positive cable from the donor battery and finally, disconnect the positive cable from the formerly dead battery. Be careful when disconnecting the cables from the positive terminals not to allow the alligator clips to touch any metal on either vehicle or a short and sparks will occur.

HOW TO BUY A USED VEHICLE

Many people believe that a two or three year old used car or truck is a better buy than a new vehicle. This may be true as most new vehicles suffer the heaviest depreciation in the first two years and, at three years old, a vehicle is usually not old enough to present a lot of costly repair problems. But keep in mind, when buying a non-warranted automobile, there are no guarantees. Whatever the age of the used vehicle you might want to purchase, this section and a little patience should increase your chances of selecting one that is safe and dependable.

Tips

1. First decide what model you want, and how much you want to spend.

2. Check the used car lots and your local newspaper ads. Privately owned vehicles are usually less expensive, however, you may not get a warranty that, in many cases, comes with a used vehicle purchased from a lot. Of course, some aftermarket warranties may not be worth the extra money, so this is a point you will have to debate and consider based on your priorities.

3. Never shop at night. The glare of the lights make it easy to miss faults on the body caused by accident or rust repair.

4. Try to get the name and phone number of the previous owner. Contact him/her and ask about the vehicle. If the owner of a lot refuses this information, look for a vehicle somewhere else.

A private seller can tell you about the vehicle and maintenance. But remember, there's no law requiring honesty from private citizens selling used vehicles. There is a law that forbids tampering with or turning back the odometer mileage. This includes both the private citizen and the lot owner. The law also requires that the seller or anyone transferring ownership of the vehicle must provide the buyer with a signed statement indicating the mileage on the odometer at the time of transfer.

5. You may wish to contact the National Highway Traffic Safety Administration (NHTSA) to find out if the vehicle has ever been included in a manufacturer's recall. Write down the year, model and serial number before you buy the vehicle, then contact NHTSA (there should be a 1-800 number that your phone company's information line can supply). If the vehicle was listed for a recall, make sure the needed repairs were made.

6. Refer to the Used Vehicle Checklist in this section and check all the items on the vehicle you are considering. Some items are more important than others. Only you know how much money you can afford for repairs, and depending on the price of the vehicle, may consider performing any needed work yourself. Beware, however, of trouble in areas that will affect operation, safety or emission. Problems in the Used Vehicle Checklist break down as follows:

- Numbers 1–8: Two or more problems in these areas indicate a lack of maintenance. You should beware.
- Numbers 9–13: Problems here tend to indicate a lack of proper care, however, these can usually be corrected with a tune-up or relatively simple parts replacement.
- Numbers 14–17: Problems in the engine or transmission can be very expensive. Unless you are looking for a project, walk away from any vehicle with problems in 2 or more of these areas.

7. If you are satisfied with the apparent condition of the vehicle, take it to an independent diagnostic center or mechanic for a complete check. If you have a state inspection program, have it inspected immediately before purchase, or specify on the bill of sale that the sale is conditional on passing state inspection.

8. Road test the vehicle—refer to the Road Test Checklist in this section. If your original evaluation and the road test agree—the rest is up to you.

USED VEHICLE CHECKLIST

➡The numbers on the illustrations refer to the numbers on this checklist.

1. Mileage: Average mileage is about 12,000–15,000 miles per year. More than average mileage may indicate hard usage or could indicate many highway miles (which could be less detrimental than half as many tough around town miles).

2. Paint: Check around the tailpipe, molding and windows for overspray indicating that the vehicle has been repainted.

3. Rust: Check fenders, doors, rocker panels, window moldings, wheelwells, floorboards, under floormats, and in the trunk for signs of rust. Any rust at all will be a problem. There is no way to permanently stop the spread of rust, except to replace the part or panel.

➡If rust repair is suspected, try using a magnet to check for body filler. A magnet should stick to the sheet metal parts of the body, but will not adhere to areas with large amounts of filler.

4. Body appearance: Check the moldings, bumpers, grille, vinyl roof, glass, doors, trunk lid and body panels for general overall condition. Check for misalignment, loose hold-down clips, ripples, scratches in glass, welding in the trunk, severe misalignment of body panels or ripples, any of which may indicate crash work.

5. Leaks: Get down and look under the vehicle. There are no normal leaks, other than water from the air conditioner evaporator.

6. Tires: Check the tire air pressure. One old trick is to pump the tire pressure up to make the vehicle roll easier. Check the

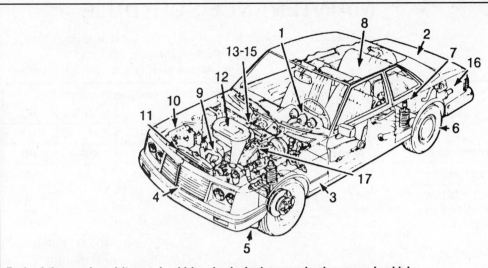

Each of the numbered items should be checked when purchasing a used vehicle

tread wear, then open the trunk and check the spare too. Uneven wear is a clue that the front end may need an alignment.

7. Shock absorbers: Check the shock absorbers by forcing downward sharply on each corner of the vehicle. Good shocks will not allow the vehicle to bounce more than once after you let go.

8. Interior: Check the entire interior. You're looking for an interior condition that agrees with the overall condition of the vehicle. Reasonable wear is expected, but be suspicious of new seat covers on sagging seats, new pedal pads, and worn armrests. These indicate an attempt to cover up hard use. Pull back the carpets and look for evidence of water leaks or flooding. Look for missing hardware, door handles, control knobs, etc. Check lights and signal operations. Make sure all accessories (air conditioner, heater, radio, etc.) work. Check windshield wiper operation.

9. Belts and Hoses: Open the hood, then check all belts and hoses for wear, cracks or weak spots.

10. Battery: Low electrolyte level, corroded terminals and/or cracked case indicate a lack of maintenance.

11. Radiator: Look for corrosion or rust in the coolant indicating a lack of maintenance.

12. Air filter: A severely dirty air filter would indicate a lack of maintenance.

13. Ignition wires: Check the ignition wires for cracks, burned spots, or wear. Worn wires will have to be replaced.

14. Oil level: If the oil level is low, chances are the engine uses oil or leaks. Beware of water in the oil (there is probably a cracked block or bad head gasket), excessively thick oil (which is often used to quiet a noisy engine), or thin, dirty oil with a distinct gasoline smell (this may indicate internal engine problems).

15. Automatic Transmission: Pull the transmission dipstick out when the engine is running. The level should read FULL, and the fluid should be clear or bright red. Dark brown or black fluid that has distinct burnt odor, indicates a transmission in need of repair or overhaul.

16. Exhaust: Check the color of the exhaust smoke. Blue smoke indicates, among other problems, worn rings. Black smoke can indicate burnt valves or carburetor problems. Check the exhaust system for leaks; it can be expensive to replace.

17. Spark Plugs: Remove one or all of the spark plugs (the most accessible will do, though all are preferable). An engine in good condition will show plugs with a light tan or gray deposit on the firing tip.

ROAD TEST CHECKLIST

1. Engine Performance: The vehicle should be peppy whether cold or warm, with adequate power and good pickup. It should respond smoothly through the gears.

2. Brakes: They should provide quick, firm stops with no noise, pulling or brake fade.

3. Steering: Sure control with no binding harshness, or looseness and no shimmy in the wheel should be expected. Noise or vibration from the steering wheel when turning the vehicle means trouble.

4. Clutch (Manual Transmission/Transaxle): Clutch action should give quick, smooth response with easy shifting. The clutch pedal should have free-play before it disengages the clutch. Start the engine, set the parking brake, put the transmission in first gear and slowly release the clutch pedal. The engine should begin to stall when the pedal is $1/2$–$3/4$ of the way up.

5. Automatic Transmission/Transaxle: The transmission should shift rapidly and smoothly, with no noise, hesitation, or slipping.

6. Differential: No noise or thumps should be present. Differentials have no normal leaks.

7. Driveshaft/Universal Joints: Vibration and noise could mean driveshaft problems. Clicking at low speed or coast conditions means worn U-joints.

8. Suspension: Try hitting bumps at different speeds. A vehicle that bounces excessively has weak shock absorbers or struts. Clunks mean worn bushings or ball joints.

9. Frame/Body: Wet the tires and drive in a straight line. Tracks should show two straight lines, not four. Four tire tracks indicate a frame/body bent by collision damage. If the tires can't be wet for this purpose, have a friend drive along behind you and see if the vehicle appears to be traveling in a straight line.

MAINTENANCE SCHEDULE

Maintenance operations: A = Check and/or adjust if necessary;
R = Replace, change or lubricate;
I = Inspect and correct or replace as necessary

System	Maintenance items	Service interval	Miles x 1,000 — 15 / Km x 1,000 — 24 / Months — 12	30 / 48 / 24	45 / 72 / 36	60 / 96 / 48
ENGINE	Valve clearance (2)		A	A	A	A
	Drive belts (including power steering and air conditioner drive belt)	Fed. Canada		R		R
		Calif.		A, (R*)		R
	Engine oil and oil filter (1)		Change every 10,000 miles (16,000 km) or 8 months			
	Engine coolant			R		R
	Cooling and heating systems, hoses and connections					I
	Exhaust pipes and mountings (1)		I	I	I	I
FUEL	Idle speed and fast idle speed (2)		A*	A*		A
	Choke system		I*	I		I
	Fuel filter					R
	Air filter (1)			R		R
	Fuel lines and connections			I		I
	Fuel filler cap			I*		I, (R)(4)
IGNITION	Spark plugs	Fed. Canada	R	R	R	R
		Calif.		R		R
	Ignition wiring (1), (3)	Fed. Canada		I		I
		Calif.				I
EMISSION CONTROL	PCV system	Fed. Canada		I, (R)(5)		I, (R)(5)
		Calif.				I, (R)(5)
	Charcoal canister			I*		I
	Fuel evaporative emission control system, hoses and connections			I*		I
TRANSMISSION	Transmission and differential oil (1)		I	I	I	I
BRAKES	Brake linings and drums (1)		I	I	I	I
	Brake pads and discs (1)		I	I	I	I
	Brake line pipes and hoses		I	I	I	I
CHASSIS	Steering linkage and gear box (1)		I	I	I	I
	Ball joints and dust covers (1)		I	I	I	I
	Wheel bearing and ball joint grease			R		R
	Bolts and nuts on chassis and body (1)		I	I	I	I

* The items marked with an asterisk are recommended maintenance items for California vehicles only, but are required maintenance items for Federal and Canada.

NOTE:

(1) For vehicles normally used under any of the following severe conditions, the applicable items of maintenance should be performed as indicated in the table below.

Maintenance items		Service interval	Severe condition
Engine oil and oil filter	R	Every 3,750 miles (6,000 km) or 3 months	A . . D . F
Exhaust pipes and mountings	I	Every 7,500 miles (12,000 km) or 6 months	A B C . E .
Air filter	I	Every 3,750 miles (6,000 km) or 3 months	. . . D . .
	R	Every 30,000 miles (48,000 km) or 24 months	
Ignition wiring (3)	I	Every 12 months	. . . . E .
Distributor cap (3)	I	Every 12 months	. . . . E .
Brake linings and drums	I	Every 7,500 miles (12,000 km) or 6 months	A B C D . .
Brake pads and discs	I	Every 7,500 miles (12,000 km) or 6 months	A B C D . .
Steering linkage and gear box	I	Every 7,500 miles (12,000 km) or 6 months	. . C . . .
Ball joints and dust covers	I	Every 7,500 miles (12,000 km) or 6 months	. . C D E .
Transmission and differential oil	R	Every 15,000 miles (24,000 km) or 12 months	A . C . . .
Automatic transmission fluid	R	Every 15,000 miles (24,000 km) or 12 months	A . C . . .
Bolts and nuts on chassis and body	I	Every 7,500 miles (12,000 km) or 6 months	. . C . . .

"Severe conditions"

A — Pulling trailers
B — Repeated short trips
C — Driving on rough and/or muddy roads
D — Driving on dusty roads
E — Operating in extremely cold weather and/or driving in areas using road salt
F — Repeated short trips in extremely cold weather

(2) Specifications appear on the information label.

(3) In areas where road salt is used, inspection and cleaning of the distributor cap and ignition wiring should be performed each year just after the snow season.

(4) Replace only the gasket.

(5) Replace only the PCV valve.

Capacities

| Model | Year | Crankcase (qts) | | Transmission (qts) | | Drive Axle (qts) | Fuel Tank (gal) | Cooling System w/heater (qts) |
		w/filter	w/o filter	Manual	Automatic *			
CORONA								
1900	1970–71	5.3	4.4	2.1	3.7	1.4	13.2	7.8
2000	1972–74	5.3	4.2	2.1①	3.7	1.4	13.2②	8.4
2200	1875–80	4.8	4.1	2.9③	2.3④	⑤	14.5⑥	7.4⑦
2400	1981–82	4.8	4.1	2.9③	2.5	⑤	16.1	8.5
MARK II								
1900	1970–71	5.3	4.3	2.1	3.7	1.4	13.7	7.8
2000	1972	5.2	4.2	2.1	3.7	1.4	13.7	7.8
2300	1972	5.5	4.6	3.6	3.7	1.3	15.8⑧	11.6
2600	1973–76	6.2	5.1	2.9	3.0	1.3	15.9⑧	12.3
CROWN								
2300	1970–71	5.5	4.6	2.1	3.4	1.3	18.5⑨	11.6
2600	1972	5.5	4.6	2.1	3.4	1.3	18.5⑨	11.6
CRESSIDA								
2600	1978–80	4.9	4.3	—	2.5	1.5	17.2⑩	11.6
2800	1981–82	4.9	4.3	—	2.5	1.5	17.2⑩	9.5

* Drain and refill
① 4 speed: 2.9
   5 speed: 3.4
② 1974: 14.5 gallons
③ 5 speed: 2.8
④ 1978–80: 2.5

⑤ Unitized type: 1.3
   Banjo type: 1.4
⑥ 1978–79: 15.5 gallons
   1980: 16.1 gallons
⑦ 1979–80: 8.5
⑧ Wagon: 14.5 gallons

⑨ Wagon: 15.8 gallons
⑩ Wagon: 16.2 gallons
⑪ Station wagon: 3.0
   Diesel 4.5 w/Filter; 4.0 w/o
   M.T.: 2.7
   A.T.: 2.1

ENGLISH TO METRIC CONVERSION: MASS (WEIGHT)

Current **mass** measurement is expressed in pounds and ounces (lbs. & ozs.). The metric unit of mass (or weight) is the kilogram (kg). Even although this table does not show conversion of masses (weights) larger than 15 lbs, it is easy to calculate larger units by following the data immediately below.

To convert ounces (oz.) to grams (g): multiply th number of ozs. by 28
To convert grams (g) to ounces (oz.): multiply the number of grams by .035

To convert pounds (lbs.) to kilograms (kg): multiply the number of lbs. by .45
To convert kilograms (kg) to pounds (lbs.): multiply the number of kilograms by 2.2

lbs	kg	lbs	kg	oz	kg	oz	kg
0.1	0.04	0.9	0.41	0.1	0.003	0.9	0.024
0.2	0.09	1	0.4	0.2	0.005	1	0.03
0.3	0.14	2	0.9	0.3	0.008	2	0.06
0.4	0.18	3	1.4	0.4	0.011	3	0.08
0.5	0.23	4	1.8	0.5	0.014	4	0.11
0.6	0.27	5	2.3	0.6	0.017	5	0.14
0.7	0.32	10	4.5	0.7	0.020	10	0.28
0.8	0.36	15	6.8	0.8	0.023	15	0.42

ENGLISH TO METRIC CONVERSION: TEMPERATURE

To convert Fahrenheit (°F) to Celsius (°C): take number of °F and subtract 32; multiply result by 5; divide result by 9

To convert Celsius (°C) to Fahrenheit (°F): take number of °C and multiply by 9; divide result by 5; add 32 to total

| Fahrenheit (F) | Celsius (C) | Celsius (C) | Fahrenheit (F) | Fahrenheit (F) | Celsius (C) | Celsius (C) | Fahrenheit (F) | Fahrenheit (F) | Celsius (C) | Celsius (C) | Fahrenheit (F) |
°F	°C	°C	°F	°F	°C	°C	°F	°F	°C	°C	°F
−40	−40	−38	−36.4	80	26.7	18	64.4	215	101.7	80	176
−35	−37.2	−36	−32.8	85	29.4	20	68	220	104.4	85	185
−30	−34.4	−34	−29.2	90	32.2	22	71.6	225	107.2	90	194
−25	−31.7	−32	−25.6	95	35.0	24	75.2	230	110.0	95	202
−20	−28.9	−30	−22	100	37.8	26	78.8	235	112.8	100	212
−15	−26.1	−28	−18.4	105	40.6	28	82.4	240	115.6	105	221
−10	−23.3	−26	−14.8	110	43.3	30	86	245	118.3	110	230
−5	−20.6	−24	−11.2	115	46.1	32	89.6	250	121.1	115	239
0	−17.8	−22	−7.6	120	48.9	34	93.2	255	123.9	120	248
1	−17.2	−20	−4	125	51.7	36	96.8	260	126.6	125	257
2	−16.7	−18	−0.4	130	54.4	38	100.4	265	129.4	130	266
3	−16.1	−16	3.2	135	57.2	40	104	270	132.2	135	275
4	−15.6	−14	6.8	140	60.0	42	107.6	275	135.0	140	284
5	−15.0	−12	10.4	145	62.8	44	112.2	280	137.8	145	293
10	−12.2	−10	14	150	65.6	46	114.8	285	140.6	150	302
15	−9.4	−8	17.6	155	68.3	48	118.4	290	143.3	155	311
20	−6.7	−6	21.2	160	71.1	50	122	295	146.1	160	320
25	−3.9	−4	24.8	165	73.9	52	125.6	300	148.9	165	329
30	−1.1	−2	28.4	170	76.7	54	129.2	305	151.7	170	338
35	1.7	0	32	175	79.4	56	132.8	310	154.4	175	347
40	4.4	2	35.6	180	82.2	58	136.4	315	157.2	180	356
45	7.2	4	39.2	185	85.0	60	140	320	160.0	185	365
50	10.0	6	42.8	190	87.8	62	143.6	325	162.8	190	374
55	12.8	8	46.4	195	90.6	64	147.2	330	165.6	195	383
60	15.6	10	50	200	93.3	66	150.8	335	168.3	200	392
65	18.3	12	53.6	205	96.1	68	154.4	340	171.1	205	401
70	21.1	14	57.2	210	98.9	70	158	345	173.9	210	410
75	23.9	16	60.8	212	100.0	75	167	350	176.7	215	414

ENGLISH TO METRIC CONVERSION: LENGTH

To convert inches (ins.) to millimeters (mm): multiply number of inches by 25.4

To convert millimeters (mm) to inches (ins.): multiply number of millimeters by .04

Inches		Decimals	Milli-meters	Inches to millimeters inches	mm	Inches		Decimals	Milli-meters	Inches to millimeters inches	mm
	1/64	0.051625	0.3969	0.0001	0.00254		33/64	0.515625	13.0969	0.6	15.24
1/32		0.03125	0.7937	0.0002	0.00508	17/32		0.53125	13.4937	0.7	17.78
	3/64	0.046875	1.1906	0.0003	0.00762		35/64	0.546875	13.8906	0.8	20.32
1/16		0.0625	1.5875	0.0004	0.01016	9/16		0.5625	14.2875	0.9	22.86
	5/64	0.078125	1.9844	0.0005	0.01270		37/64	0.578125	14.6844	1	25.4
3/32		0.09375	2.3812	0.0006	0.01524	19/32		0.59375	15.0812	2	50.8
	7/64	0.109375	2.7781	0.0007	0.01778		39/64	0.609375	15.4781	3	76.2
1/8		0.125	3.1750	0.0008	0.02032	5/8		0.625	15.8750	4	101.6
	9/64	0.140625	3.5719	0.0009	0.02286		41/64	0.640625	16.2719	5	127.0
5/32		0.15625	3.9687	0.001	0.0254	21/32		0.65625	16.6687	6	152.4
	11/64	0.171875	4.3656	0.002	0.0508		43/64	0.671875	17.0656	7	177.8
3/16		0.1875	4.7625	0.003	0.0762	11/16		0.6875	17.4625	8	203.2
	13/64	0.203125	5.1594	0.004	0.1016		45/64	0.703125	17.8594	9	228.6
7/32		0.21875	5.5562	0.005	0.1270	23/32		0.71875	18.2562	10	254.0
	15/64	0.234375	5.9531	0.006	0.1524		47/64	0.734375	18.6531	11	279.4
1/4		0.25	6.3500	0.007	0.1778	3/4		0.75	19.0500	12	304.8
	17/64	0.265625	6.7469	0.008	0.2032		49/64	0.765625	19.4469	13	330.2
9/32		0.28125	7.1437	0.009	0.2286	25/32		0.78125	19.8437	14	355.6
	19/64	0.296875	7.5406	0.01	0.254		51/64	0.796875	20.2406	15	381.0
5/16		0.3125	7.9375	0.02	0.508	13/16		0.8125	20.6375	16	406.4
	21/64	0.328125	8.3344	0.03	0.762		53/64	0.828125	21.0344	17	431.8
11/32		0.34375	8.7312	0.04	1.016	27/32		0.84375	21.4312	18	457.2
	23/64	0.359375	9.1281	0.05	1.270		55/64	0.859375	21.8281	19	482.6
3/8		0.375	9.5250	0.06	1.524	7/8		0.875	22.2250	20	508.0
	25/64	0.390625	9.9219	0.07	1.778		57/64	0.890625	22.6219	21	533.4
13/32		0.40625	10.3187	0.08	2.032	29/32		0.90625	23.0187	22	558.8
	27/64	0.421875	10.7156	0.09	2.286		59/64	0.921875	23.4156	23	584.2
7/16		0.4375	11.1125	0.1	2.54	15/16		0.9375	23.8125	24	609.6
	29/64	0.453125	11.5094	0.2	5.08		61/64	0.953125	24.2094	25	635.0
15/32		0.46875	11.9062	0.3	7.62	31/32		0.96875	24.6062	26	660.4
	31/64	0.484375	12.3031	0.4	10.16		63/64	0.984375	25.0031	27	690.6
1/2		0.5	12.7000	0.5	12.70						

ENGLISH TO METRIC CONVERSION: TORQUE

To convert foot-pounds (ft. lbs.) to Newton-meters: multiply the number of ft. lbs. by 1.3

To convert inch-pounds (in. lbs.) to Newton-meters: multiply the number of in. lbs. by .11

in lbs	N-m	in lbs	N-m	in lbs	N-m	in lbs	N-m	in lbs	N-m
0.1	0.01	1	0.11	10	1.13	19	2.15	28	3.16
0.2	0.02	2	0.23	11	1.24	20	2.26	29	3.28
0.3	0.03	3	0.34	12	1.36	21	2.37	30	3.39
0.4	0.04	4	0.45	13	1.47	22	2.49	31	3.50
0.5	0.06	5	0.56	14	1.58	23	2.60	32	3.62
0.6	0.07	6	0.68	15	1.70	24	2.71	33	3.73
0.7	0.08	7	0.78	16	1.81	25	2.82	34	3.84
0.8	0.09	8	0.90	17	1.92	26	2.94	35	3.95
0.9	0.10	9	1.02	18	2.03	27	3.05	36	4.0

SPARK PLUGS AND WIRES 2-2
SPARK PLUGS 2-3
   SPARK PLUG HEAT RANGE 2-6
   REMOVAL & INSTALLATION 2-6
   INSPECTION & GAPPING 2-7
SPARK PLUG WIRES 2-8
   TESTING 2-8
   REMOVAL & INSTALLATION 2-8
DISTRIBUTOR CAP AND ROTOR 2-9
   REMOVAL & INSTALLATION 2-9
   INSPECTION 2-9
FIRING ORDERS 2-9
POINT TYPE IGNITION 2-10
BREAKER POINTS AND
  CONDENSER 2-10
   OPERATION 2-10
   INSPECTION AND CLEANING 2-10
   REMOVAL & INSTALLATION 2-11
   ADJUSTMENT 2-11
TRANSISTORIZED IGNITION 2-11
DESCRIPTION AND OPERATION 2-11
   SERVICE PRECAUTIONS 2-12
ADJUSTMENTS 2-12
   DWELL 2-12
   PICKUP AIR GAP 2-12
   POINT GAP 2-12
PARTS REPLACEMENT 2-13
   BREAKER POINTS 2-13
IGNITION TIMING 2-13
TIMING 2-13
   INSPECTION & ADJUSTMENT 2-14
OCTANE SELECTOR 2-14
   ADJUSTMENT 2-14
VALVE LASH 2-15
   ADJUSTMENT 2-15
IDLE SPEED AND MIXTURE
  ADJUSTMENT 2-19
CARBURETED VEHICLES 2-19
   IDLE SPEED & MIXTURE 2-19
FUEL INJECTED VEHICLES 2-23
   IDLE ADJUSTMENT 2-23
SPECIFICATION CHARTS
  TUNE-UP SPECIFICATIONS 2-2
  OCTANE SELECTOR TEST
   SPEEDS 2-15
  VACUUM AT IDLE (IN. HG)
   CHART 2-20

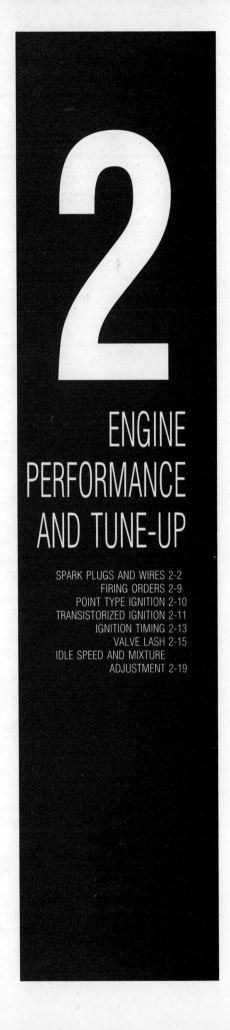

2

ENGINE PERFORMANCE AND TUNE-UP

SPARK PLUGS AND WIRES 2-2
FIRING ORDERS 2-9
POINT TYPE IGNITION 2-10
TRANSISTORIZED IGNITION 2-11
IGNITION TIMING 2-13
VALVE LASH 2-15
IDLE SPEED AND MIXTURE
ADJUSTMENT 2-19

Tune-Up Specifications

Year	Engine Type	Spark Plugs Type	Gap (in.)	Distributor Point Dwell (deg)	Distributor Point Gap (in.)	Ignition Timing (deg) ▲ MT	Ignition Timing (deg) ▲ AT	Compression Pressure (psi) @ 250 rpm**	Fuel Pump Pressure (psi)	Idle Speed (rpm) ▲ MT	Idle Speed (rpm) ▲ AT	Valve Clearance (in.) ‡ Intake	Valve Clearance (in.) ‡ Exhaust
1970	8R-C	W20EP	0.031	52	0.018	TDC	TDC	164	2.8–4.3	650	650	0.008	0.014
	2M	W20EP	0.031	41	0.018	TDC	TDC	156	3.6–5.0	650	650	0.007	0.010
1971	8R-C	W20EP	0.031	52	0.018	10B	10B	164	2.8–4.3	650	650	0.008	0.014
	2M	W20EP	0.031	41	0.018	TDC	TDC	156	3.6–5.0	650	650	0.007	0.010
1972	18R-C	W20EP	0.031	52	0.018	7B	7B	164	2.8–4.3	650	650	0.008	0.014
	2M	W16EP	0.030	41	0.018	7B	7B	149	3.4–4.6	700	600	0.007	0.010
	4M	W14EP	0.031	41	0.018	7B	5B	156	4.2–5.4	700	650	0.007	0.010
1973	18R-C	W20EP	0.031	52	0.018	7B	7B	156	2.8–4.3	650	650	0.008	0.014
	4M	W14EP	0.031	41	0.018	7B	5B	156	4.2–5.4	700	650	0.007	0.010
1974	18R-C	W20EP	0.031	52	0.018	7B	7B	156	2.8–4.3	650	850	0.008	0.014
	4M	W16EP	0.031	41	0.018	5B	5B	156	4.2–5.4	700	750	0.007	0.010
1975–76	20R	W16EP	0.030	52	0.018	8B	8B	156	2.2–4.2	850	850	0.008	0.012
	4M ①	W16EP	0.030	41	0.018	10B	10B	156	4.2–5.4	800	750	0.007	0.010
	4M ②	W16EP	0.030	41	0.018	5B	5B	156	4.2–5.4	800	750	0.007	0.010
1977	20R	W16EP	0.031	52	0.018	8B	8B	156	2.8–4.3	850	800	0.008	0.012
1978–79	20R	BP5EA-L	0.031	Electronic	—	8B	8B	156	2.2–4.2	800	850	0.008	0.012
	4M	BPR5EA-L	0.031	Electronic	—	10B ③	10B ③	156	4.2–5.4	750	750	0.011	0.014
1980–82	20R	BPR5EA-L	0.031	Electronic	—	8B	8B	156	2.2–4.3	800	850	0.008	0.012
	22R	BPR5EA-L	0.031	Electronic	—	8B	8B	156	2.2–4.3	800 ⑤	850 ⑤	0.008	0.012
	4M-E ④	BPR5EA-L	0.031	Electronic	—	—	12B	156	33–38	—	800	0.011	0.014
	5M-E ④	BPR5EA-L	0.031	Electronic	—	—	8B	156	33–38	—	800	0.011	0.014
1983–84	2S-E	BPR5EA-L11	0.043	Electronic	—	5B	5B	156	28–36	700	700	Hyd.	Hyd.
1984	3Y-EC	BPR5EP-11	0.043	Electronic	—	8B	8B	171	33–38	950	950	Hyd.	Hyd.
1984–85	5M-GE	BPR5EP-11	0.043	Electronic	—	10B ⑥	10B ⑥	164	35–38	650	650	Hyd.	Hyd.
1986	5M-GE	BPR5EP-11	0.055	Electronic	—	10B ⑥	10B ⑥	164	33–38	650	650	Hyd.	Hyd.
1985	3Y-EC	BPR5EP-11	0.043	Electronic	—	8B ⑥	8B ⑥	171	33–38	700	750	Hyd.	Hyd.
1986	3Y-EC	BPR5EP-11	0.055	Electronic	—	12B ⑥	12B ⑥	178	33–38	700	750	Hyd.	Hyd.

① USA—except California
② California only
③ Calif.: 8B
④ Electronic fuel injection
⑤ 1982: 700 MT
       750 AT
⑥ Check with connector shorted. See text.

▲ With manual transmission in Neutral and automatic transmission in drive (D).
** Difference between cylinders should not exceed 14 psi. Look for uniformity rather than specific pressures.
‡ Valve clearance checked with engine HOT.
MT—Manual transmission
AT—Automatic transmission
TDC—Top Dead Center
B—Before top dead center
NOTE: *If the information given in this chart disagrees with the information on the engine tune-up decal, use the specifications on the decal—changes may have been made during production.*

SPARK PLUGS AND WIRES

In order to extract the full measure of performance and economy from your engine it is essential that it be properly tuned at regular intervals. A regular tune-up will keep your car's engine running smoothly and will prevent the annoying minor breakdowns and poor performance associated with an untuned engine.

A complete tune-up should be performed every 12,000 miles or twelve months, whichever comes first. This interval should be halved if the car is operated under severe conditions, such as trailer towing, prolonged idling, continual stop and start driving, or if starting or running problems are noticed. It is assumed that the routine maintenance described in Section 1 has been kept up, as this will have a decided effect on the results of a tune-up. All

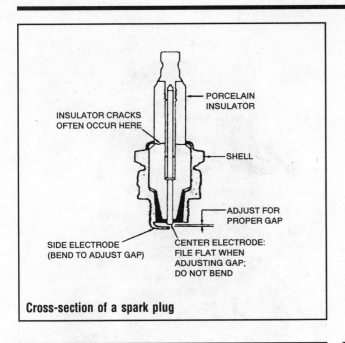

Cross-section of a spark plug

PORCELAIN
INSULATOR

INSULATOR CRACKS
OFTEN OCCUR HERE

SHELL

ADJUST FOR
PROPER GAP

SIDE ELECTRODE
(BEND TO ADJUST GAP)

CENTER ELECTRODE:
FILE FLAT WHEN
ADJUSTING GAP;
DO NOT BEND

of the applicable steps of a tune-up should be followed in order, as the result is a cumulative one.

If the specifications on the tune-up sticker in the engine compartment disagree with the Tune-Up Specifications chart in this chapter, the figures on the sticker must be used. The sticker often reflects changes made during the production run.

Spark Plugs

A typical spark plug consists of a metal shell surrounding a ceramic insulator. A metal electrode extends downward through the center of the insulator and protrudes a small distance. Located at the end of the plug and attached to the side of the outer metal shell is the side electrode. The side electrode bends in at a 90° angle so that its tip is just past and parallel to the tip of the center electrode. The distance between these two electrodes (measured in thousandths of an inch or hundredths of a millimeter) is called the spark plug gap.

The spark plug does not produce a spark but instead provides a gap across which the current can arc. The coil produces any-

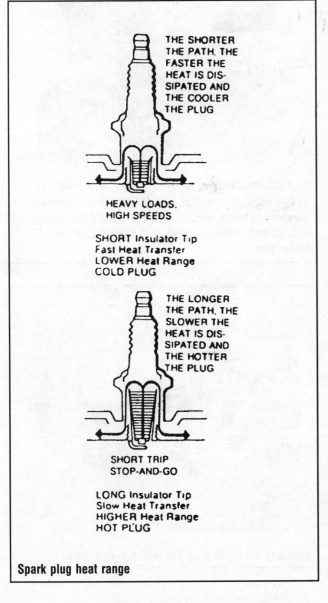

THE SHORTER
THE PATH. THE
FASTER THE
HEAT IS DIS-
SIPATED AND
THE COOLER
THE PLUG

HEAVY LOADS.
HIGH SPEEDS

SHORT Insulator Tip
Fast Heat Transfer
LOWER Heat Range
COLD PLUG

THE LONGER
THE PATH. THE
SLOWER THE
HEAT IS DIS-
SIPATED AND
THE HOTTER
THE PLUG

SHORT TRIP
STOP-AND-GO

LONG Insulator Tip
Slow Heat Transfer
HIGHER Heat Range
HOT PLUG

Spark plug heat range

A normally worn spark plug should have light tan or gray deposits on the firing tip

A carbon fouled plug, identified by soft, sooty, black deposits, may indicate an improperly tuned vehicle. Check the air cleaner, ignition components and engine control system

A physically damaged spark plug may be evidence of severe detonation in that cylinder. Watch that cylinder carefully between services, as a continued detonation will not only damage the plug, but could also damage the engine

A variety of tools and gauges are needed for spark plug service

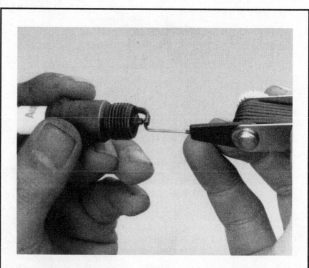

Checking the spark plug gap with a feeler gauge

An oil fouled spark plug indicates an engine with worn piston rings and/or bad valve seals allowing excessive oil to enter the chamber

This spark plug has been left in the engine too long, as evidenced by the extreme gap—Plugs with such an extreme gap can cause misfiring and stumbling accompanied by a noticeable lack of power

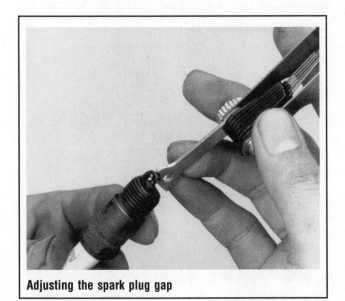

Adjusting the spark plug gap

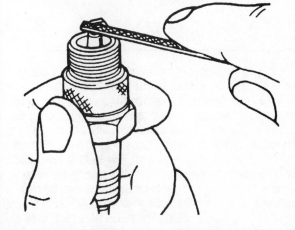

If the standard plug is in good condition, the electrode may be filed flat—CAUTION: do not file platinum plugs

A bridged or almost bridged spark plug, identified by a build-up between the electrodes caused by excessive carbon or oil build-up on the plug

where from 20,000 to 50,000 volts (depending on the type and application) which travels through the wires to the spark plugs. The current passes along the center electrode and jumps the gap to the side electrode, and in doing so, ignites the air/fuel mixture in the combustion chamber.

SPARK PLUG HEAT RANGE

Spark plug heat range is the ability of the plug to dissipate heat. The longer the insulator (or the farther it extends into the engine), the hotter the plug will operate; the shorter the insulator (the closer the electrode is to the block's cooling passages) the cooler it will operate. A plug that absorbs little heat and remains too cool will quickly accumulate deposits of oil and carbon since it is not hot enough to burn them off. This leads to plug fouling and consequently to misfiring. A plug that absorbs too much heat will have no deposits but, due to the excessive heat, the electrodes will burn away quickly and might possibly lead to preignition or other ignition problems. Preignition takes place when plug tips get so hot that they glow sufficiently to ignite the air/fuel mixture before the actual spark occurs. This early ignition will usually cause a pinging during low speeds and heavy loads.

The general rule of thumb for choosing the correct heat range

when picking a spark plug is: if most of your driving is long distance, high speed travel, use a colder plug; if most of your driving is stop and go, use a hotter plug. Original equipment plugs are generally a good compromise between the 2 styles and most people never have the need to change their plugs from the factory-recommended heat range.

REMOVAL & INSTALLATION

A set of spark plugs usually requires replacement after about 20,000–30,000 miles (32,000–48,000 km), depending on your style of driving. In normal operation plug gap increases about 0.001 in. (0.025mm) for every 2500 miles (4000 km). As the gap increases, the plug's voltage requirement also increases. It requires a greater voltage to jump the wider gap and about two to three times as much voltage to fire the plug at high speeds than at idle. The improved air/fuel ratio control of modern fuel injection combined with the higher voltage output of modern ignition systems will often allow an engine to run significantly longer on a

Remove the plug wire from the spark plug

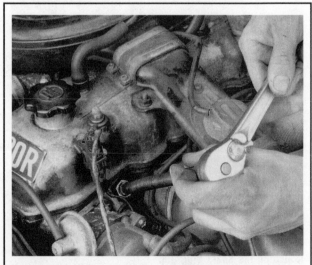

Using a spark plug socket, carefully unscrew the plug

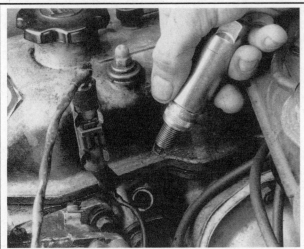

Withdraw the spark plug and inspect it for wear; replace if necessary

set of standard spark plugs, but keep in mind that efficiency will drop as the gap widdens (along with fuel economy and power).

When you're removing spark plugs, work on one at a time. Don't start by removing the plug wires all at once, because, unless you number them, they may become mixed up. Take a minute before you begin and number the wires with tape.

1. Disconnect the negative battery cable, and if the vehicle has been run recently, allow the engine to thoroughly cool.

2. Carefully twist the spark plug wire boot to loosen it, then pull upward and remove the boot from the plug. Be sure to pull on the boot and not on the wire, otherwise the connector located inside the boot may become separated.

3. Using compressed air, blow any water or debris from the spark plug well to assure that no harmful contaminants are allowed to enter the combustion chamber when the spark plug is removed. If compressed air is not available, use a rag or a brush to clean the area.

➡**Remove the spark plugs when the engine is cold, if possible, to prevent damage to the threads. If removal of the plugs is difficult, apply a few drops of penetrating oil or silicone spray to the area around the base of the plug, and allow it a few minutes to work.**

4. Using a spark plug socket that is equipped with a rubber insert to properly hold the plug, turn the spark plug counterclockwise to loosen and remove the spark plug from the bore.

✳✳ WARNING

Be sure not to use a flexible extension on the socket. Use of a flexible extension may allow a shear force to be applied to the plug. A shear force could break the plug off in the cylinder head, leading to costly and frustrating repairs.

To install:

5. Inspect the spark plug boot for tears or damage. If a damaged boot is found, the spark plug wire must be replaced.

6. Using a wire feeler gauge, check and adjust the spark plug gap. When using a gauge, the proper size should pass between the electrodes with a slight drag. The next larger size should not be able to pass while the next smaller size should pass freely.

7. Carefully thread the plug into the bore by hand. If resistance is felt before the plug is almost completely threaded, back the plug out and begin threading again. In small, hard to reach areas, an old spark plug wire and boot could be used as a threading tool. The boot will hold the plug while you twist the end of the wire and the wire is supple enough to twist before it would allow the plug to crossthread.

✳✳ WARNING

Do not use the spark plug socket to thread the plugs. Always carefully thread the plug by hand or using an old plug wire to prevent the possibility of crossthreading and damaging the cylinder head bore.

8. Carefully tighten the spark plug. If the plug you are installing is equipped with a crush washer, seat the plug, then tighten about ¼ turn to crush the washer. If you are installing a tapered seat plug, tighten the plug to specifications provided by the vehicle or plug manufacturer.

9. Apply a small amount of silicone dielectric compound to the end of the spark plug lead or inside the spark plug boot to prevent sticking, then install the boot to the spark plug and push until it clicks into place. The click may be felt or heard, then gently pull back on the boot to assure proper contact.

INSPECTION & GAPPING

Check the plugs for deposits and wear. If they are not going to be replaced, clean the plugs thoroughly. Remember that any kind of deposit will decrease the efficiency of the plug. Plugs can be cleaned on a spark plug cleaning machine, which can sometimes be found in service stations, or you can do an acceptable job of cleaning with a stiff brush. If the plugs are cleaned, the electrodes must be filed flat. Use an ignition points file, not an emery board or the like, which will leave deposits. The electrodes must be filed perfectly flat with sharp edges; rounded edges reduce the spark plug voltage by as much as 50%.

Check spark plug gap before installation. The ground electrode (the L-shaped one connected to the body of the plug) must be parallel to the center electrode and the specified size wire gauge (please refer to the Tune-Up Specifications chart for details) must pass between the electrodes with a slight drag.

➡**NEVER adjust the gap on a used platinum type spark plug.**

Always check the gap on new plugs as they are not always set correctly at the factory. Do not use a flat feeler gauge when measuring the gap on a used plug, because the reading may be inaccurate. A round-wire type gapping tool is the best way to check the gap. The correct gauge should pass through the electrode gap with a slight drag. If you're in doubt, try one size smaller and one larger. The smaller gauge should go through easily, while the larger one shouldn't go through at all. Wire gapping tools usually have a bending tool attached. Use that to adjust the side electrode until the proper distance is obtained. Absolutely never attempt to bend the center electrode. Also, be careful not to bend the side electrode too far or too often as it may weaken and break off within the engine, requiring removal of the cylinder head to retrieve it.

Spark Plug Wires

TESTING

At every tune-up, visually inspect the spark plug cables for burns, cuts, or breaks in the insulation. Check the boots and the nipples on the distributor cap and coil. Replace any damaged wiring.

Every 36,000 miles or so, the resistance of the wires should be checked with an ohmmeter. Wires with excessive resistance will cause misfiring, and may make the engine difficult to start in damp weather. Generally, the useful life of the cables is 36,000–50,000 miles.

To check resistance, remove the distributor cap, leaving the wires attached. Connect one lead of an ohmmeter to an electrode within the cap. Connect the other lead to the corresponding spark plug terminal (remove it from the plug for this test). Replace any wire which shows a resistance over 50,000Ω. Generally speaking, however, resistance should not be over 30,000Ω, and 50,000Ω must be considered the outer limit of acceptability. Test the high tension lead from the coil by connecting the ohmmeter between the center contact in the distributor cap and either of the primary terminals of the coil. If resistance is more than 25,000Ω, remove the cable from the coil and check the resistance of the cable alone. Anything over 15,000Ω is cause for replacement. It should be remembered that resistance is also a function of length; the longer the cable, the greater the resistance. Thus, if the cables on your car are longer than the factory originals, resistance will be higher, quite possibly outside these limits.

When installing new cables, replace them one at a time to avoid mixups. Start by replacing the longest one first. Install the boot firmly over the spark plug. Route the wire over the same path as the original. Insert the nipple firmly into the tower on the cap or the coil.

REMOVAL & INSTALLATION

At every tune-up, visually inspect the spark plug cables for burns, cuts, or breaks in the insulation. Check the boots and the nipples on the distributor cap and coil. Replace any damaged wiring. Always replace spark plug wiring in sets, with a coil wire as well. Length is important; get the correct set for your vehicle.

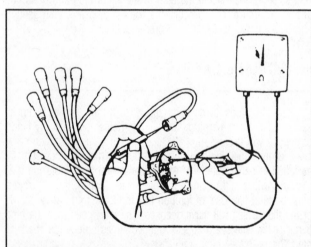

Checking plug wire resistance through the distributor cap with an ohmmeter

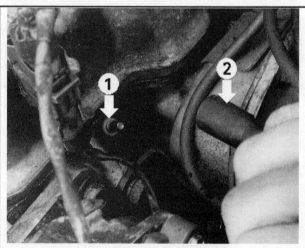

1. Spark plug   2. Plug wire
Grasp the plug wire and separate it from the spark plug

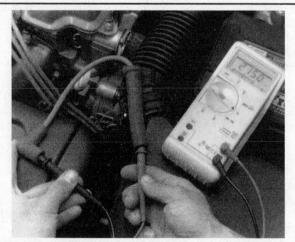

Checking individual plug wire resistance with a digital ohmmeter

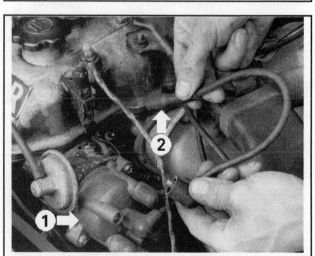

1. Distributor cap   2. Plug wire
Next, remove the plug wire from the distributor cap

When installing new cables, replace them one at a time to avoid mix-ups. Start by replacing the longest one first. Install the boot firmly over the spark plug. Route the wire over the same path as the original. Insert the nipple firmly into the tower on the cap. Replace the wire running between the distributor cap and ignition coil in the same manner.

Distributor Cap and Rotor

REMOVAL & INSTALLATION

1. Disconnect the negative battery cable.
2. If equipped, remove the distributor cap rubber boot.
3. Loosen the screws securing the cap on the distributor.
4. Tag the wires leading to the cap for easy identification upon installation.
5. Lift the cap off the distributor. Pulling from the wire boot, remove the plug wires from the cap.
6. If necessary to remove the rotor, lift it straight off the shaft.

To install:

7. Install the rotor onto the distributor shaft. The rotor only goes on one way, so there should be no mix-up upon replacement.
8. Apply a small amount of dielectric grease on the tip of the rotor and the inside of the cap's carbon button.
9. Attach the tagged wires to their proper locations on the cap.
10. Fit the cap onto the distributor, then tighten the bolts.
11. Make sure all the wires are secure on the cap and at the spark plugs. Connect the negative battery cable.
12. Start the vehicle and check for proper operation.

FIRING ORDERS

▸ See Figures 2, 3 and 4

The firing order is the order in which spark is sent to each cylinder. The spark must arrive at the correct time in the combustion cycle or damage may result. For this reason, connecting the correct plug to the correct distributor terminal is critical.

➡**To avoid confusion, remove and tag the spark plug wires one at a time, for replacement.**

If a distributor is not keyed for installation with only one orientation, it could have been removed previously and rewired. The resultant wiring would hold the correct firing order, but could change the relative placement of the plug towers in relation to the engine. For this reason it is imperative that you label all wires before disconnecting any of them. Also, before removal, compare the current wiring with the accompanying illustrations. If the current wiring does not match, make notes in your book to reflect how your engine is wired.

INSPECTION

▸ See Figure 1

When inspecting a cap and rotor, look for signs of cracks, carbon tracking, burns and wear. The inside of the cap may be burnt or have wear on the carbon ends. On the rotor, look at the tip for burning and excessive wear.

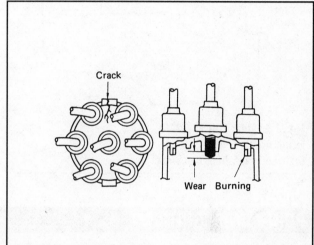

Fig. 1 Inspect the distributor cap for cracks, wear or burning

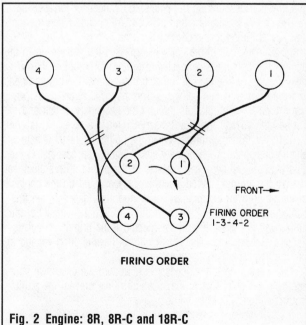

Fig. 2 Engine: 8R, 8R-C and 18R-C
Firing order: 1–3–4–2
Distributor rotation: clockwise

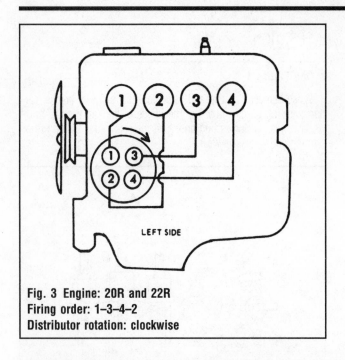

Fig. 3 Engine: 20R and 22R
Firing order: 1–3–4–2
Distributor rotation: clockwise

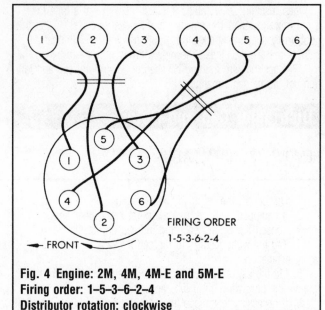

Fig. 4 Engine: 2M, 4M, 4M-E and 5M-E
Firing order: 1–5–3–6–2–4
Distributor rotation: clockwise

POINT TYPE IGNITION

Breaker Points and Condenser

OPERATION

The points and condenser function as a circuit breaker for the primary circuit of the ignition system. The ignition coil must boost the 12 volts (V) of electrical pressure supplied to it by the battery to about 20,000 V in order to fire the spark plugs. To do this, the coil depends on the points and condenser for assistance.

The coil has a primary and a secondary circuit. When the ignition key is turned to the ON position, the battery supplies voltage to the primary side of the coil which passes the voltage on to the points. The points are connected to ground to complete the primary circuit. As the cam in the distributor turns, the points open and the primary circuit collapses. The magnetic force in the primary circuit of the coil cuts through the secondary circuit and increases the voltage in the secondary circuit to a level that is sufficient to fire the spark plugs. When the points open, the electrical charge contained in the primary circuit jumps the gap that is created between the two open contacts of the points. If this electrical charge was not transferred elsewhere, the material on the contacts of the points would melt and that all important gap between the contacts would start to change. If this gap is not maintained, the points will not break the primary circuit. If the primary circuit is not broken, the secondary circuit will not have enough voltage to fire the spark plugs. Enter the condenser.

The function of the condenser is to absorb the excessive voltage from the points when they open and thus prevent the points from becoming pitted or burned.

If you have ever wondered why it is necessary to tune-up your engine occasionally, consider the fact that the ignition system must complete the above cycle each time a spark plug fires. On a four-cylinder, four-cycle engine, two of the four plugs must fire once for every engine revolution. If the idle speed of your engine is 800 revolutions per minute (800 rpm), the breaker points open and close two times for each revolution. For every minute your engine idles, your points open and close 1,600 times (2,800 = 1,600). And that is just at idle. What about at 60 mph?

There are two ways to check breaker point gap: with a feeler gauge or with a dwell meter. Either way you set the points, you are adjusting the amount of time (in degrees of distributor rotation) that the points will remain open. If you adjust the points with a feeler gauge, you are setting the maximum amount the points will open when the rubbing block on the points is on a high point of the distributor cam. When you adjust the points with a dwell meter, you are measuring the number of degrees (of distributor cam rotation) that the points will remain closed before they start to open as a high point of the distributor cam approaches the rubbing block of the points.

If you still do not understand how the points function, take a friend, go outside, and remove the distributor cap from your engine. Have your friend operate the starter (make sure the transmission is not in gear) as you look at the exposed parts of the distributor.

There are two rules that should always be followed when adjusting or replacing points. The points and condenser are a matched set. Never replace one without replacing the other. If you change the point gap or dwell of the engine, you also change the ignition timing. Therefore, if you adjust the points, you must also adjust the timing.

INSPECTION & CLEANING

The breaker points should be inspected and cleaned at 6,000 mile intervals.

1. Disconnect the high tension lead from the coil.
2. Unsnap the two distributor cap retaining clips and lift the

cap straight up. Leave the leads connected to the cap and position it out of the way.

3. Remove the rotor and dust cover by pulling them straight up.

4. Place a screwdriver against the breaker points and pry them open. Examine their condition. If they are excessively worn, burned, or pitted, they should be replaced.

5. Polish the points with a point file. Do not use emery cloth or sandpaper. These may leave particles on the points causing them to arc.

6. Clean the distributor cap and rotor with alcohol. Inspect the cap terminals for looseness and corrosion. Check the rotor tip for excessive burning. Inspect both cap and rotor for cracks. Replace either if they show any of the above signs of wear or damage.

7. Check the operation of the centrifugal advance mechanism by turning the rotor clockwise. Release the rotor. It should return to its original position. If it doesn't, check for binding parts.

8. Check the vacuum advance unit, by removing the plastic cap and pressing on the octane selector. It should return to its original position. Check for binding if it doesn't.

9. If the points do not require replacement, proceed with the adjustment section below. Otherwise perform the point and condenser replacement procedures.

REMOVAL & INSTALLATION

Points

The points should be replaced every 12,000 miles (24,000 miles with transistorized ignition), or if they are badly pitted, worn, or burned.

1. If you have not already done so, perform Steps 1 through 3 of the preceding Inspection and Cleaning procedure.

2. Unfasten the point lead connector.

3. Remove the point retaining clip and unfasten the point hold-down screw(s). It is a good idea to use a magnetic or locking screwdriver to remove the small screws inside the distributor, since they have been dropped.

4. Lift out the point set.

5. Install the new point set in the reverse order of removal. Adjust the points as detailed below, after completing installation.

Condenser

Replace the condenser whenever the points are replaced, or if it is suspected of being defective. On Toyota passenger cars the condenser is located on the outside of the distributor.

1. Carefully remove the nut and washer from the condenser lead terminal.

2. Use a magnetic or locking screwdriver to remove the condenser mounting screw.

3. Remove the condenser.

4. Installation of a new condenser is performed in the reverse order of removal.

ADJUSTMENT

Perform the gap adjustment procedure whenever new points are installed, or as part of routine maintenance. If you are adjusting an old set of points, you must check the dwell as well, since the feeler gauge is only really accurate with a new point set.

1. Rotate the engine by hand or by using a remote starter switch, so that the rubbing block is on the high point of the cam lobe.

2. Insert a 0.45mm feeler gauge between the points. A slight drag should be felt.

3. If no drag is felt or if the feeler gauge cannot be inserted at all, loosen, but do not remove, the point hold-down screw.

4. Insert a screwdriver into the adjustment slot. Rotate the screwdriver until the proper point gap is attained. The point gap is increased by rotating the flat bladed tool counterclockwise and decreased by rotating it clockwise.

5. Tighten the point hold-down screw.

Lubricate the cam lobes, breaker arm, rubbing block, arm pivot, and distributor shaft with special high temperature distributor grease.

TRANSISTORIZED IGNITION

Description and Operation

Transistorized ignition was first used on 1974 4M engines sold in California. With the introduction of 1975 models, usage has been extended to all Toyota vehicles sold in the United States.

The transistorized ignition system employed by Toyota works very much like the conventional system previously described. Regular breaker points are used, but instead of switching primary current to the coil off-and-on, they are used to trigger a switching transistor. The transistor, in turn, switches the coil primary current on and off.

Since only a very small amount of current is needed to operate the transistor, the points will not become burned or pitted, as they would if they had full primary current passing through them. This also allows the primary current to be higher than usual because the use of a higher current would normally cause the points to fail much more rapidly.

As already stated, the condenser is used to absorb any extra high voltage passing through the points. Since, in the transistorized system, there is no high current, no condenser is needed or used.

As a result of the lower stress placed on them, the points only have to be replaced every 24,000 miles instead of the usual 12,000 miles.

The Toyota transistorized ignition system may be quickly identified by the lack of a condenser on the outside of the distributor and by the addition of a control box, which is connected between the distributor and the primary side of the coil.

A fully transistorized ignition system was introduced in 1977. The system, including an ignition signal generating mechanism instead of the normal contact points, became the standard ignition system on all models from 1978.

The mechanism consists of a timing rotor, a magnet and a pick-up coil, all mounted in place of the points inside the distributor. As the signal rotor spins, the teeth on it pass a projection leading form the pick-up coil. When this happens voltage is allowed to pass through the system, firing the spark plugs. There is no physical contact and no electric arcing, hence no need to replace burnt or worn parts.

SERVICE PRECAUTIONS

Basically, the transistorized ignition is serviced just like its conventional counterpart. The points must be checked, adjusted, and replaced in the same manner. Point gap and dwell must be checked and set. The points should also be kept clean and should be replaced at 24,000 mile intervals. Of course, since there is no condenser, it does not have to be replaced when the points are.

However, there are several precautions to observe when servicing the transistorized ignition system.

1. Use only pure alcohol to clean the points. Shop solvent or an oily rag will leave a film on the points which will not allow the low current to pass.

✳✳ WARNING

Hook up a tachometer, dwell meter, or a combination dwell/tachometer to the negative (−) side of the coil, NOT to the distributor or the positive (+) side. Damage to the switching transistor will result if the meter is connected in the usual manner.
See the previous section for point installation and Section 3 for troubleshooting the fully transistorized ignition.

Adjustments

DWELL

1. Connect a dwell meter to the ignition system, according to the manufacturer's instructions.

   a. When checking the dwell on a conventional ignition system, connect meter lead (usually black) to a metallic part of the car to ground the meter. The other lead (usually red) is connected to the coil primary post (the one with the small lead which runs to the distributor body).

   b. When checking dwell on a model with transistorized ignition, ground one meter lead (usually black) to a metallic part of the car. Hook up the other lead (usually red) to the negative (−) coil terminal. Under no circumstances should the meter be connected to the distributor or the positive (+) side of the coil. (See the preceding Service Precautions).

2. If the dwell meter has a set line, adjust the needle until it rests on the line.

3. Start the engine. It should be warmed up and running at the specified idle speed.

➡️**It is not necessary to check the dwell on the fully transistorized system. It is set at the factory and requires no adjustment.**

✳✳ CAUTION

Be sure to keep fingers, tools, clothes, hair, and wires clear of the engine fan. The transmission should be in Neutral (or Park), parking brake set, and the engine running in a well ventilated area.

4. Check the reading on the swell meter. If you have a 4-cylinder engine and your meter doesn't have a 4-cylinder scale, multiply the 8-cylinder reading by two.

5. If the meter reading is within the range specified in the Tune-Up Specifications chart, shut the engine **OFF** and disconnect the dwell meter.

6. If the dwell is not within specifications, shut the engine **OFF** and adjust the point gap as previously outlined. Increasing the point gap decreases the dwell angle and vice versa.

7. Adjust the points until dwell is within specifications, then disconnect the dwell meter. Adjust the timing; see the following section.

PICKUP AIR GAP

1. Remove the distributor cap, rotor, and dust shield.

2. Turn the engine over (you may use a socket wrench on the front pulley bolt to do this) until the projection on the pickup coil is directly opposite the signal rotor tooth.

3. Get a non-ferrous (paper, brass, or plastic) feeler gauge of 0.30mm, and insert it into the pickup air gap. DO NOT USE AN ORDINARY METAL FEELER GAUGE! The gauge should just touch either side of the gap (the permissible range is 0.2–0.4mm).

4. If the gap is either too wide or too narrow, loosen the two Phillips screws mounting the pickup coil onto the distributor base plate. Then, wedge a screwdriver between the notch in the pickup coil assembly and the two dimples on the base plate, and turn the screwdriver back and forth until the pickup gap is correct.

5. Tighten the screws and recheck gap, readjusting if necessary.

POINT GAP

The point set on this ignition system is covered by a piece of protective plastic shielding. Because of this, the gap must be checked between the point rubbing block and the distributor cam lobe instead of between the two points. Do not try to remove the plastic shielding as it will damage the point set.

1. Using your hands, a wrench on the crankshaft pulley nut, or a remote starter switch, rotate the engine so that the rubbing block is resting on the low point (flat side) of the cam lobe.

2. Insert a 0.018 inch (0.46mm) flat feeler gauge between the rubbing block and the cam lobe; a slight drag should be felt.

3. If no drag can be felt or if the feeler gauge cannot be inserted at all, loosen, but do not remove, the point hold-down screw.

4. Insert a flat bladed tool into the point adjustment slot. Rotate the screwdriver until the proper gap is achieved. The gap is

increased by rotating the screwdriver counterclockwise and decreased by rotating it clockwise.

5. Tighten the point hold-down screw. Lubricate the cam lobes, breaker arm, rubbing block, arm pivot and distributor shaft with special high temperature distributor grease.

Parts Replacement

BREAKER POINTS

The points should be replaced every 12,000 miles (19,300 km), or if they are badly pitted, worn, or burned. To replace them, proceed as follows:

1. Disconnect the high tension lead from the coil.

2. Unsnap the two distributor cap retaining clips and lift the cap straight up. Leave the leads connected to the cap and position it out of the way.

3. Remove the rotor and dust cover by pulling them straight up.

4. Unfasten the point lead connector.

5. Remove the point retaining clip and unfasten the point hold-down screw(s). It is a good idea to use a magnetic or locking screwdriver to remove the small screws inside the distributor, since they are almost impossible to find once they have been dropped.

6. Lift out the point set.

7. Install the new point set in the reverse order of removal. Adjust the points as detailed below, after completing installation.

IGNITION TIMING

Timing

▶ **See Figures 4a, 4b and 4c**

Ignition timing is the measurement in degrees of crankshaft rotation of the instant the spark plugs in the cylinders fire, in relation to the location of the piston, while the piston is on its compression stroke.

Ignition timing is adjusted by loosening the distributor locking device and turning the distributor in the engine.

Ideally, the air/fuel mixture in the cylinder will be ignited (by the spark plug) and just beginning its rapid expansion as the piston passes top dead center (TDC) of the compression stroke. If this happens, the piston will be beginning the power stroke just as the compressed (by the movement of the piston) and ignited (by the spark plug) air/fuel mixture starts to expand. The expansion of the air/fuel mixture will then force the piston down on the power stroke and turn the crankshaft.

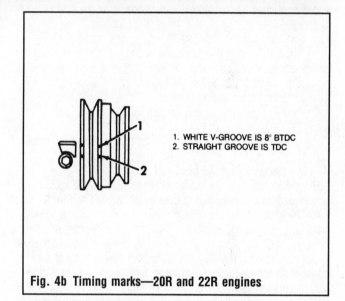

1. WHITE V-GROOVE IS 8° BTDC
2. STRAIGHT GROOVE IS TDC

Fig. 4b Timing marks—20R and 22R engines

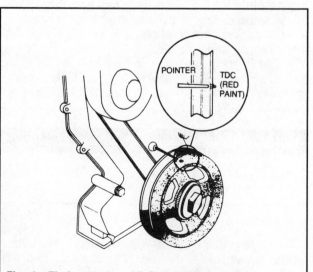

Fig. 4a Timing marks—8R-C and 18R-C engines

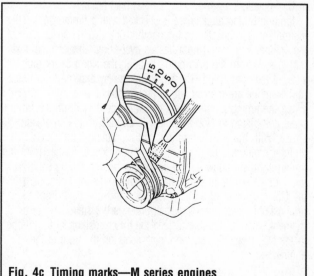

Fig. 4c Timing marks—M series engines

It takes a fraction of a second for the spark from the plug to completely ignite the mixture in the cylinder. Because of this, the spark plug must fire before the piston reaches TDC, if the mixture is to be completely ignited as the piston passes TDC. This measurement is given in degrees of top dead center (BTDC). If the ignition timing setting for your engine is seven degrees (7°) BTDC, this means that the spark plug must fire at a time when the piston for that cylinder is 7° before top dead center of the compression stroke. However, this only holds true while your engine is at idle speed.

As you accelerate from idle, the speed of your engine (rpm) increases. The increase in rpm means that the pistons are now traveling up and down much faster. Because of this, the spark plugs will have to fire even sooner if the mixture is to be completely ignited as the piston passes TDC. To accomplish this, the distributor incorporates means to advance the timing of the spark as engine speed increases.

The distributor in your Toyota has two means of advancing the ignition timing. One is called centrifugal advance and is actuated by weights in the distributor. The other is called vacuum advance and is controlled by that large circular housing on the side of the distributor.

In addition, some distributors have a vacuum-retard mechanism which is contained in the same housing on the side of the distributor as the vacuum advance. The function of this mechanism is to retard the timing of the ignition spark under certain engine conditions. This causes more complete burning of the air/fuel mixture in the cylinder and consequently lowers exhaust emissions.

Because these mechanisms change ignition timing, it is necessary to disconnect and plug the one or two vacuum lines from the distributor when setting the basic ignition timing.

If ignition timing is set too far advanced (BTDC), the ignition and expansion of the air/fuel mixture in the cylinder will try to force the piston down the cylinder while it is still traveling upward. This causes engine ping, a sound which resembles marbles being dropped into an empty tin can. If the ignition timing is too far retarded (after, or ATDC), the piston will have already started down on the power stroke when the air/fuel mixture ignites and expands. This will cause the piston to be forced down only a portion of its travel and will result in poor engine performance and lack of power.

Ignition timing adjustment is checked with a timing light. This instrument is connected to the number one (No. 1) spark plug of the engine. The timing light flashes every time an electrical current is sent from the distributor, through the No. 1 spark plug wire, to the spark plug. The crankshaft pulley and the front cover of the engine are marked with a timing pointer and a timing scale. When the timing pointer is aligned with the 0 mark on the timing scale, the piston in No. 1 cylinder is at TDC of its compression stroke. With the engine running, and the timing light aimed at the timing pointer and timing scale, the stroboscopic flashes from the timing light will allow you to check the ignition timing setting of the engine. The timing light flashes every time the spark plug in the No. 1 cylinder of the engine fires. Since the flash from the timing light makes the crankshaft pulley seem stationary for a moment, you will be able to read the exact position of the piston in the No. 1 cylinder on the timing scale on the front of the engine.

INSPECTION & ADJUSTMENT

1. Warm up the engine. Connect a tachometer and check the engine idle speed to be sure that it is within the specification given in the Tune-Up Specifications chart at the beginning of the chapter.

2. If the timing marks are difficult to see, use a dab of paint or chalk to make them more visible.

3. Connect a timing light according to the manufacturer's instructions. If the light has three wires, one (usually blue or green) must be installed with an adapter between the No. 1 spark plug lead and the spark plug. The other leads are connected to the positive (+) battery terminal (usually a red lead) and the other to the negative (−) battery terminal (usually a black lead).

4. Disconnect the vacuum line(s) from the distributor vacuum unit. Plug it (them) with a pencil or golf tee(s).

5. Be sure that the timing light wires are clear of the fan and start the engine.

✸✸ CAUTION

Keep fingers, clothes, tools, hair, and leads clear of the spinning engine fan. Be sure that you are running the engine in a well ventilated area.

6. Allow the engine to run at the specified idle speed with the gearshift in Neutral with manual transmission and Drive (D) with automatic transmission.

✸✸ WARNING

Be sure that the parking brake is set and that the front wheels are blocked to prevent the car from rolling forward, especially when Drive is selected with an automatic.

7. Point the timing marks at the marks indicated in the chart and illustrations. With the engine at idle, timing should be at the specification given on the Tune-Up Specifications chart at the beginning of the chapter.

8. If the timing is not at the specification, loosen the pinch bolt at the base of the distributor just enough so that the distributor can be turned. Turn the distributor to advance or retard the timing as required. Once the proper marks are seen to align with the timing light, timing is correct.

9. Stop the engine and tighten the pinch bolt. Start the engine and recheck timing. Stop the engine. Disconnect the tachometer and timing light. Connect the vacuum line(s) to the distributor vacuum unit.

Octane Selector

ADJUSTMENT

▶ **See Figure 5**

The octane selector is used as a fine adjustment to match the vehicle's ignition timing to the grade of gasoline being used. It is

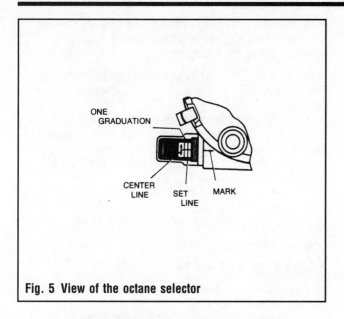

Fig. 5 View of the octane selector

located near the distributor vacuum unit, beneath a plastic dust cover. Normally the octane selector should not require adjustment, however, adjustment is as follows:

1. Align the setting line with the threaded end of the housing and then align the center line with the setting mark on the housing.

2. Drive the car to the speed specified in the Octane Selector Test Speeds chart in High gear on a level road.

3. Depress the accelerator pedal all the way to the floor. A slight pinging sound should be heard. As the car accelerates, the sound should gradually go away. If the pinging sound is loud or if it fails to disappear as the vehicle speed increases, retard the timing by turning the knob toward R (Retard).

4. If there is no pinging sound at all, advance the timing by turning the knob toward A (Advance).

➡**Do not turn the octane selector more than ½ turn toward R. Do not turn it toward A at all.**

5. When the adjustment is completed, replace the plastic dust cover.

➡**One graduation of the octane selector is equal to about ten degrees of crankshaft angle.**

Octane Selector Test Speeds

Engine Type	Test Speed (mph)
8R-C, 20R and 18R-C	16–22
2M and 4M	25

VALVE LASH

Toyota models equipped with mechanical valve lifters should be adjusted at the factory recommended intervals (every 12,000 miles, 15,000 miles for late models).

Valve adjustment is one factor which determines how far the intake and exhaust valves will open into the cylinder.

If the valve clearance is too large, part of the lift of the camshaft will be used up in removing the excessive clearance, thus the valves will not be opened far enough. This condition has two effects, the valve train components will emit a tapping noise as they take up the excessive clearance, and the engine will perform poorly, since the less the intake valves open, the smaller the amount of air/fuel mixture that will be admitted to the cylinders. The less the exhaust valves open, the greater the back-pressure in the cylinder which prevents the proper air/fuel mixture from entering the cylinder.

If the valve clearance is too small, the intake and exhaust valves will not fully seat on the cylinder head when they close. When a valve seats on the cylinder head it does two things. It seals the combustion chamber so none of the gases in the cylinder can escape and it cools itself by transferring some of the heat it absorbed from the combustion process through the cylinder head and into the engine cooling system. Therefore, if the valve clearance is too small, the engine will run poorly (due to gases escaping from the combustion chamber), and the valves will overheat and warp (since they cannot transfer heat unless they are touching the seat in the cylinder head).

While all valve adjustments must be as accurate as possible, it is better to have the valve adjustment slightly loose than slightly tight, as burnt valves may result form overly tight adjustments.

ADJUSTMENT

8R-C and 18R-C Engines
▶ **See Figures 6, 7 and 8**

1. Start the engine and allow it to reach normal operating temperature (above 175°F).

2. Stop the engine. Remove the air cleaner assembly, its hoses, and bracket. Remove any other cables, hoses, wires, etc., which are attached to the valve cover. Remove the valve cover. Be careful, some metal parts get quite hot.

3. Check the torque of the valve rocker shaft bolts and the camshaft bearing bolts. They should be 12–17 ft. lbs.

4. Check the torque specification of the camshaft bearing cap union bolts. They should be torqued to 11–16 ft. lbs.

5. Set the No. 1 cylinder to TDC on its compression stroke. Disconnect the high tension lead from the coil. Remove the spark plug from the No. 1 cylinder and place a screwdriver handle over the hole. Crank the engine until a pressure is felt, then line the V-notch on the crankshaft pulley with the pointer on the timing chain cover. The No. 1 cylinder is now at TDC.

✳✳ CAUTION

Do not cover the spark plug hole with your finger when determining the compression stoke. The cylinder head is hot and a burn could occur.

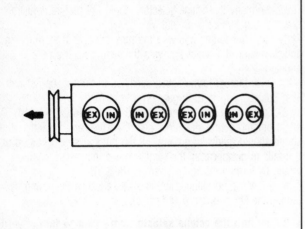

Fig. 6 Valve arrangement for the 8R-C and 18R-C engines

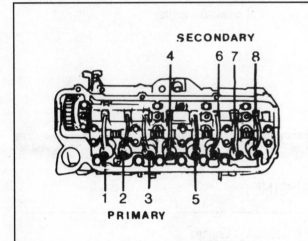

Fig. 7 Valve adjusting sequence—8R-C and 18R-C engines

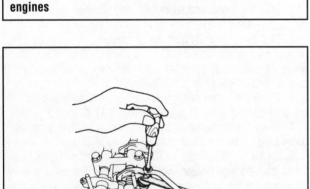

Fig. 8 Measure the clearance between the valve stem and adjusting nut; there should be a slight drag on the feeler gauge when properly installed

➡**Do not start the engine. Valve clearances are checked with the engine stopped to prevent hot oil from being splashed out by the timing chain.**

6. Check the clearances (see the Tune-Up Specifications chart) and adjust valves 1, 2, 3, and 5 to the proper specifications, if necessary.

7. To adjust the valve clearance, loosen the locknut and turn the adjusting screw until the specified clearance is obtained. Tighten the locknut and check the clearance again.

8. Crank the engine one revolution (360 degress) and perform Steps 6 and 7 for valves 4, 6, 7, and 8.

9. Install the spark plug in the No. 1 cylinder. Connect the high tension lead to the coil. Install the valve cover, air cleaner assembly, and any other components which were removed.

20R and 22R Engines
▶ **See Figures 9, 10 and 11**

1. Start the engine and allow it to reach normal operating temperature (above 180°F).

2. Stop the engine. Remove the air cleaner assembly, its hoses, and bracket. Remove any other cables, hoses, wires, etc., which are attached to the valve cover. Remove the valve cover.

3. Set the No. 1 cylinder at top dead center (TDC) of its compression stroke. Remove the high tension lead from the coil. Remove the spark plug from the No. 1 cylinder and place a screwdriver handle over the hole. Crank the engine until pressure is felt and the TDC notch is lined up with the pointer. The No. 1 cylinder is now at TDC.

✳✳ CAUTION

Do not cover the spark plug hole with your finger when determining the compression stroke. The cylinder head is hot and a burn could occur.

4. Measure the clearance between the valve stem and the rocker arm with a feeler gauge for the valves marked FIRST in the illustration. See the Tune-Up Specifications chart for the correct clearance.

5. To adjust the valve clearance, loosen the locknut and turn

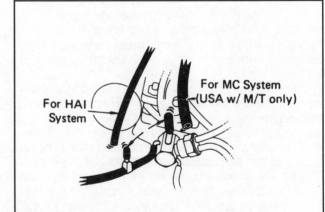

Fig. 9 Disconnect and plug the hot air intake and mixture control hoses before adjusting the valves—20R and 22R engines

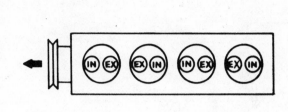

Fig. 10 Valve arrangement—20R and 22R engines

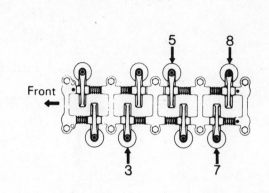

Fig. 12 Turn the crankshaft 360 degrees, then adjust this set of valves—M series engines

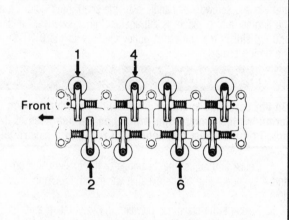

Fig. 11 Adjust this set of valves first—20R and 22R engines

Fig. 13 When adjusting the valves, turn the crankshaft to align the timing marks to TDC of the compression stroke with the pulley in the 0 position

the adjusting screw until the proper clearance is obtained. Tighten the locknut and check the clearance again.

6. Crank the engine one revolution (360°) and perform Steps 4 and 5 for the set of valves marked SECOND in the illustration.

7. Install the spark plug in the No. 1 cylinder and reconnect the coil lead. Install the valve cover, air cleaner, assembly, and any other components which were removed.

M Series Engines
▶ See Figures 12 thru 17

1. Allow the engine to reach normal operating temperature. Stop the engine.

2. Remove the air cleaner assembly, air cleaner bracket, spark plug cable guides, and any other components attached to the valve cover. Remove the valve cover. Be careful, some metal parts get very hot.

3. Disconnect the high tension lead from the coil. Crank the engine until the No. 1 cylinder is at TDC of its compression stroke. To determine this, remove the spark plug from the No. 1 cylinder

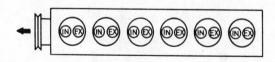

Fig. 14 Valve arrangement for the 4M-E and 5M-E engines

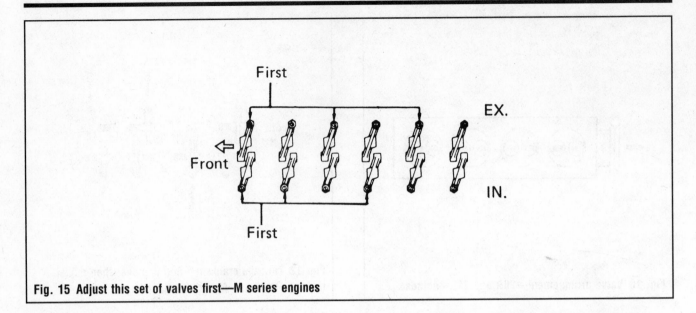

Fig. 15 Adjust this set of valves first—M series engines

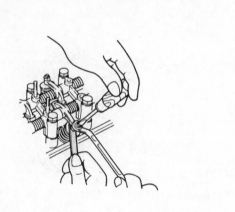

Fig. 16 Using a feeler gauge, measure between the valve stem and the rocker arm, loosen the locknut, then turn the screw to set the clearance

and place a screwdriver handle over the spark plug hole. Crank the engine until pressure is felt against the screwdriver handle and the slot in the crankshaft pulley aligns with the 0 (TDC) on the timing scale.

✳✳ CAUTION

Do not cover the spark plug hole with your finger when determining the compression stroke, as the nearness of the hole to the exhaust manifold could result in a severe burn.

4. Check and adjust the clearance of the intake valve on 1, 2, and 4 cylinders and of the exhaust valves on 1, 3, and 5 cylinders.

5. Measure the clearance between the valve stem and the adjusting screw with a feeler gauge of the proper size. (See the Tune-Up Specifications chart at the beginning of this chapter.)

6. If the valves require adjustment, loosen the locknut and turn the adjusting screw until the proper clearance is obtained. Tighten the locknut. Check the clearance again.

7. Crank the engine one revolution (360°) and repeat Steps 5 and 6 for the remaining valves.

8. Install the cylinder head cover, spark plug cable guides, air cleaner bracket, air cleaner assembly and any other components which were removed. Replace the No. 1 spark plug and reconnect the coil high tension lead, as well.

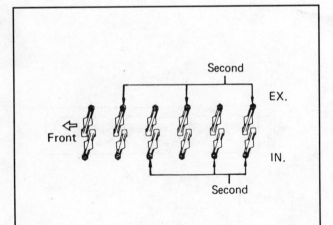

Fig. 17 Turn the crankshaft 360 degrees, then adjust this set of valves—M series engines

IDLE SPEED AND MIXTURE ADJUSTMENT

Carbureted Vehicles

This section contains only carburetor adjustments as they normally apply to engine tune-up. Descriptions of the carburetor and complete adjustment procedures can be found in Section 5.

When the engine in your Toyota is running, air/fuel mixture from the carburetor is being drawn into the engine by a partial vacuum which is created by the downward movement of the pistons on the intake stroke of the four-stroke engine. The amount of air/fuel mixture that enters the engine is controlled by throttle plates in the bottom of the carburetor. When the engine is not running, the throttle plates are closed, completely blocking off the bottom of the carburetor from the inside of the engine. The throttle plates are connected, through the throttle linkage, to the gas pedal in the passenger compartment of the car. After you start the engine and put the transmission in gear, you depress the gas pedal to start the car moving. What you actually are doing when you depress the gas pedal is opening the throttle plates in the carburetor to admit more of the air/fuel mixture to the engine. The further you open the throttle plates in the carburetor, the higher the engine speed becomes.

As previously stated, when the engine is not running, the throttle plates in the carburetor are closed. When the engine is idling, it is necessary to open the throttle plates slightly. To prevent having to keep your foot on the gas pedal. The idle speed adjusting screw was added to the carburetor. This screw has the same effect as keeping your foot slightly depressed on the gas pedal. The idle speed adjusting screw contacts a lever (the throttle lever) on the outside of the carburetor. When the screw is turned in, it opens the throttle plate on the carburetor, raising the idle speed of the engine. This screw is called the curb idle adjusting screw, and the procedures in this section will tell you how to adjust it.

Since it is difficult for the engine to draw the air/fuel mixture from the carburetor with the small amount of throttle plate opening that is present when the engine is idling, an idle mixture passage is provided in the carburetor. This passage delivers air/fuel mixture to the engine from a hole which is located in the bottom of the carburetor below the throttle plates. This idle mixture passage contains an adjusting screw which restricts the amount of air/fuel mixture that enters the engine at idle. The procedures given in this section will tell how to set the idle mixture adjusting screw.

IDLE SPEED & MIXTURE

1970–74 Models
◆ **See Figure 18**

➡**Perform the following adjustments with the air cleaner in place. When adjusting the idle speed and mixture, the gear selector should be placed in Drive (D) on 1970–73 models equipped with an automatic transmission. Be sure to set the parking brake and block the front wheels. On all cars equipped with manual transmissions and all 1974 automatics, adjust the idle speed with the gearshift in Neutral (N).**

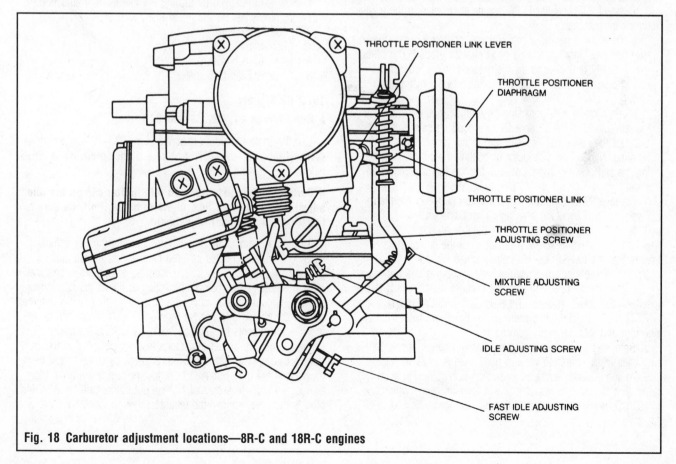

THROTTLE POSITIONER LINK LEVER

THROTTLE POSITIONER DIAPHRAGM

THROTTLE POSITIONER LINK

THROTTLE POSITIONER ADJUSTING SCREW

MIXTURE ADJUSTING SCREW

IDLE ADJUSTING SCREW

FAST IDLE ADJUSTING SCREW

Fig. 18 Carburetor adjustment locations—8R-C and 18R-C engines

Vacuum at Idle (in. Hg)

Year	Engine	Transmission	Minimum Vacuum Gauge Reading
1970–72	8R-C	All	15.7
	18R-C	MT	17.7
		AT	15.7
	2M and 4M	All	15.7
1973	18R-C	MT	17.7
		AT	15.7
	4M	MT	16.3
		AT	13.8
1974	18R-C	All	17.7
	4M	MT	16.3
		AT	13.8
	20R	All	16.5

MT—Manual transmission
AT—Automatic transmission

1. Run the engine until it reaches normal operating temperature. Stop the engine.
2. Connect a tachometer to the engine as detailed in the manufacturer's instructions.
   a. On models having a conventional ignition system, one lead (usually black) goes to a good chassis ground. The other lead (usually red) goes to the distributor primary side of the coil (the terminal with small wire running to the distributor body).
   b. On models with transistorized ignition, connect one lead (usually black) of the tachometer to a good chassis ground. Connect the other lead (usually red) to the negative (−) coil terminal, NOT to the distributor or positive (+) side. Connecting the tach to the wrong side will damage the switching transistor.
3. Remove the plug and install a vacuum gauge in the manifold vacuum port by using a suitable metric adapter.
4. Start the engine and allow it to stabilize at idle.
5. Turn the mixture screw in or out, until the engine runs smoothly at the lowest possible engine speed without stalling.
6. Turn the idle speed screw until the vacuum gauge indicates the highest specified reading (see the Vacuum At Idle chart) at the specified idle speed. (See the Tune-Up Specifications chart).
7. Tighten the idle speed screw to the point just before the engine rpm and vacuum readings drop off.
8. Remove the tachometer and the vacuum gauge. Install the plug back in the manifold vacuum port. Road test the vehicle.
9. In some states, emission inspection is required. In such cases, you should take your car to a diagnostic center which has an HC/CO meter, and have the idle emission level checked to be sure that it is in accordance with state regulations. Starting 1974, CO levels at idle are given on the engine tune-up decal under the hood.

1975–77 Models
◆ See Figures 19 and 20

The idle speed and mixture should be adjusted under the following conditions: the air cleaner must be installed, the choke fully opened, the transmission should be in Neutral (N), all accessories should be turned off, all vacuum lines should be connected, and the ignition timing should be set to specification.

1. Start the engine and allow it to reach normal operating temperature (180°F).
2. Check the float setting. The fuel level should be just about even with the spot on the sight glass. If the fuel level is too high or low, adjust the float level. (See Section 5).
3. Connect a tachometer in accordance with the manufacturer's instructions. However, connect the tachometer positive (+) lead to the coil Negative (−) terminal. Do NOT hook it up to the distributor or positive (+) side; damage to the transistorized ignition will result.
4. Adjust the speed to the highest rpm it will attain with the idle mixture adjusting screw.
5. Set the rpm with the idle speed adjusting screw to:
   20R: 900 rpm
   4M (auto. trans.): 820 rpm
   4M (man. trans.): 870 rpm
6. Repeat steps four and five until the highest rpm can be reached with the mixture screw and then readjust to rpm in Step 5.
7. Now set the speed by turning the idle mixture adjusting screw in (clockwise), to the initial idle speed of:
   20R: 850 + 50 rpm
   4M (man. trans.): 800 rpm
   4M (auto. trans.): 750 rpm
8. Disconnect the tachometer.

1978–82 Models
◆ See Figures 21, 22, 23 and 24

Use the same procedure described for 1975–77 models. However, substitute different idle mixture and idle speeds as specified below:

➡ Certain models may have an idle limiter cap on the idle adjusting screw; if so, use pliers to break it off. Be sure to install a new cap after adjustment.

To meet US emissions regulations, the idle mixture adjusting screw on the later models covered here is preadjusted and plugged by Toyota. When troubleshooting a rough idle, check all other possible causes before attempting to adjust the idle mixture; the plug should not be removed and the adjusting screw tampered with in the course of a normal tune-up. Toyota recommends all mixture adjustments be handled by a professional mechanic equipped with the proper emissions test equipment. If all other trouble causes have been checked, then the carburetor must be removed and the plug removed from the mixture screw hole. Plug all vacuum ports to keep metal chips out before drilling. After the plug is removed, remove the mixture screw to inspect the tip for

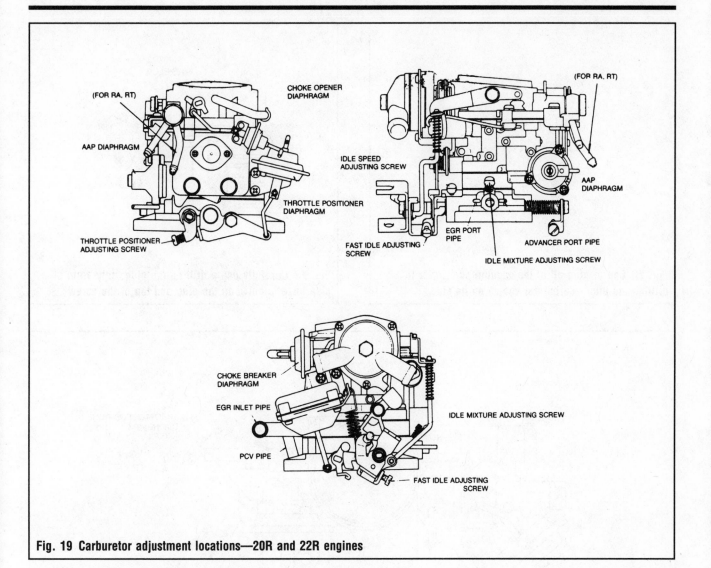

Fig. 19 Carburetor adjustment locations—20R and 22R engines

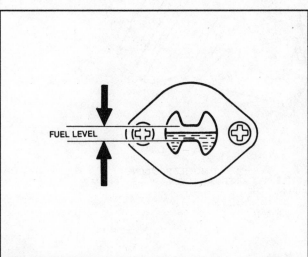

Fig. 20 Checking the fuel level through the sight glass on the carburetor

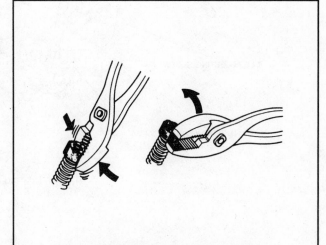

Fig. 21 Break off the idle limiter cap with a pair of pliers (if equipped)—20R and 22R engines

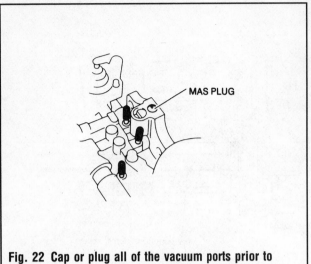

Fig. 22 Cap or plug all of the vacuum ports prior to drilling the plug—carburetor shown on its side

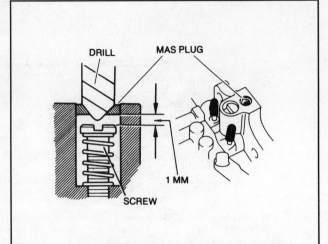

Fig. 23 Carefully use a drill on the plug; only 1mm of clearance is between the plug and top of the screw

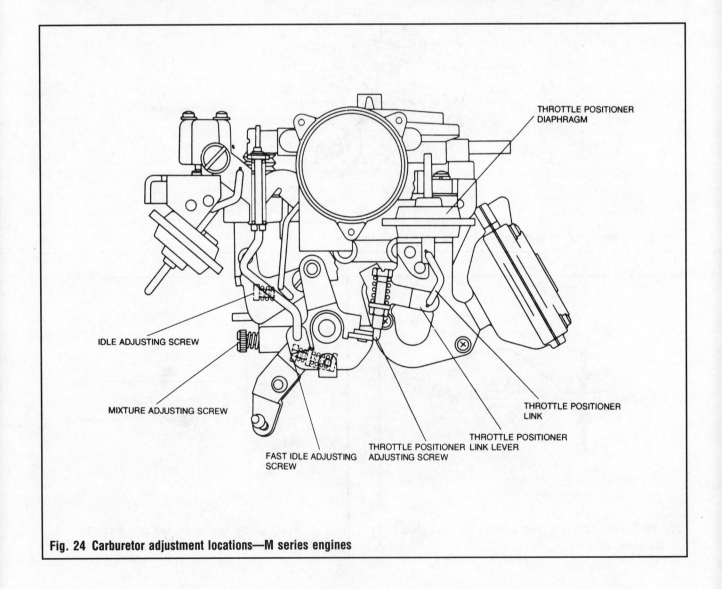

Fig. 24 Carburetor adjustment locations—M series engines

wear, and blow out the hole with compressed air. Reinstall the adjusting screw by screwing it in fully until it just seats, then unscrewing it 2½ full turns. Reinstall the carburetor and proceed with the mixture adjustment, if necessary.

For idle speeds (Step 5), use the following specifications:
1978–79 4M: 820
1978 20R: 850
1979 20R: 870 Manual, 920 Automatic
1980 22R: 750 4 speed Manual
        920 Automatic
1980 22R California models. Idle speed adjusted with idle speed screw only
  800 Manual
  850 Manual
1981–82 22R
  700 Manual
  750 USA-Auto
  850 Canada-Auto
For idle speed adjusted by mixture screw (Step 6), use the following figures:
  1978–79 4M: 750
  1978 20R: 800
  1979 20R: 800 Manual, 850 Automatic
  1980 22R: 700 4 speed Manual
  (exc. Calif.) 800 5 speed Manual
        850 Automatic

Fuel Injected Vehicles

IDLE ADJUSTMENT

▶ **See Figures 25, 26, 27, 28 and 29**

➡In order to complete this procedure, you will need a voltmeter and an EFI idle adjusting wiring harness (Special Service Tool 09842-4010) which is available at your Toyota dealer. If you do not have these tools, which are essential to this procedure, the car should be taken to a competent mechanic or dealership equipped for this procedure.

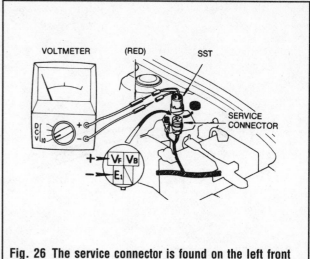

Fig. 26 The service connector is found on the left front fender apron

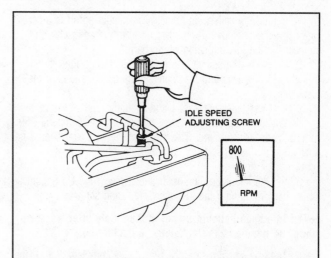

Fig. 27 Idle speed adjustment screw location—4M-E and 5M-E engines

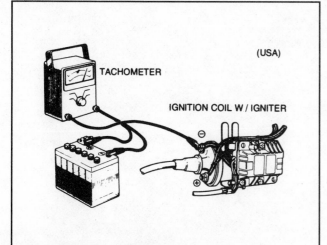

Fig. 25 Tachometer attachment for all US models with electronic ignition

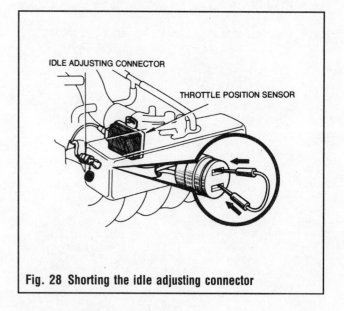

Fig. 28 Shorting the idle adjusting connector

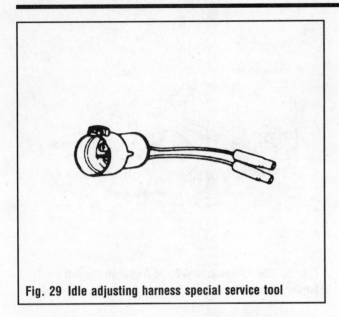

Fig. 29 Idle adjusting harness special service tool

1. Behind the battery on the left front fender apron is a service connector. Remove the rubber cap from the connector and connect the EFI idle adjusting wiring harness.

2. Connect the positive lead of the voltmeter to the red wire of the wiring harness and then connect the negative lead to the black wire.

3. Connect a tachometer as per the manufacturer's instructions.

4. Warm up the oxygen sensor by running the engine at 2500 rpm for about two minutes. The needle of the voltmeter should be fluctuating at this time; if not, turn the idle mixture adjusting screw until it does.

5. Set the idle speed to specifications (see Tune-Up Specifications chart) by turning the idle speed adjusting screw.

➡**The idle speed should be set immediately after warm-up while the needle of the voltmeter is fluctuating.**

6. The idle adjustment procedure is now complete. Follow the remaining steps for the 4M-E and 5M-E engines.

7. Remove the rubber cap from the idle adjusting connector and short both terminals of the connector with a wire

8. While the connector is still shorted, run the engine at 2500 rpm for two more minutes.

9. With the engine at idle and the connector still shorted, read and record the voltage shown on the voltmeter.

10. Remove the short circuit wire from the connector and then race the engine to 2500 rpm once.

11. Adust the idle mixture adjusting screw until the median of the indicated voltage range is the same as the reading taken in Step 8.

12. Replug the idle mixture adjusting screw hole. Disconnect the tachometer, the voltmeter and the special wiring harness. Replace the rubber caps on the service connector and idle adjusting connector.

Dashpot

4M-E AND 5M-E ENGINES

◗ **See Figure 30**

1. Fully open and then release the throttle valve.

2. The throttle valve should return to the idle position in approximately 3.5 seconds.

3. To adjust the return time, loosen the locknut and turn the adjusting bolt.

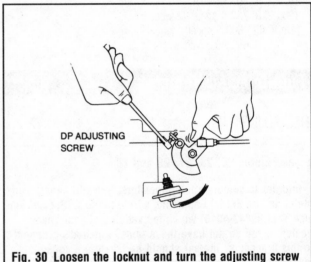

Fig. 30 Loosen the locknut and turn the adjusting screw to set the dashpot

ENGINE ELECTRICAL SYSTEM 3-2
UNDERSTANDING ELECTRICITY 3-2
BASIC CIRCUITS 3-2
TROUBLESHOOTING 3-3
BATTERY, STARTING AND CHARGING
SYSTEMS 3-4
BASIC OPERATING PRINCIPLES 3-4
TRANSISTORIZED IGNITION SYSTEM 3-5
PRECAUTIONS 3-6
TESTING 3-6
REMOVAL & INSTALLATION 3-7
DISTRIBUTOR 3-7
REMOVAL 3-7
INSTALLATION 3-11
ALTERNATOR 3-12
PRECAUTIONS 3-12
REMOVAL & INSTALLATION 3-15
NON-TRANSISTORIZED REGULATOR 3-15
REMOVAL & INSTALLATION 3-15
ADJUSTMENTS 3-15
IC REGULATOR 3-16
REMOVAL & INSTALLATION 3-16
TESTING 3-16
STARTER 3-17
REMOVAL & INSTALLATION 3-17
STARTER OVERHAUL 3-17
BATTERY 3-18
REMOVAL & INSTALLATION 3-19
ENGINE MECHANICAL 3-20
DESCRIPTION 3-21
8R-C AND 18R-C ENGINES 3-21
20R AND 22R ENGINES 3-21
2M, 4M, 4M-E AND 5M-E ENGINES 3-21
ENGINE OVERHAUL TIPS 3-21
TOOLS 3-21
INSPECTION TECHNIQUES 3-21
OVERHAUL TIPS 3-21
REPAIRING DAMAGED THREADS 3-22
COMPRESSION TESTING 3-23
ENGINE 3-26
REMOVAL & INSTALLATION 3-26
CYLINDER HEAD 3-28
REMOVAL & INSTALLATION 3-28
CLEANING & INSPECTION 3-39
RESURFACING 3-40
VALVES AND SPRINGS 3-40
ADJUSTMENT (AFTER ENGINE
SERVICE) 3-40
REMOVAL & INSTALLATION 3-41
INSPECTION 3-42
REFACING 3-44
VALVE LAPPING 3-44
VALVE SEATS 3-45
VALVE GUIDES 3-45
INSPECTION 3-45
REPLACEMENT 3-45
ROCKER SHAFTS 3-45
REMOVAL & INSTALLATION 3-45
ROCKER ARM (VALVE) COVER 3-46
REMOVAL AND INSTALLATION 3-46
ROCKER ARMS 3-48
REMOVAL AND INSTALLATION 3-48
INSPECTION 3-49
INTAKE MANIFOLD 3-50
REMOVAL & INSTALLATION 3-50
EXHAUST MANIFOLD 3-52
REMOVAL & INSTALLATION 3-52
COMBINATION MANIFOLD 3-54
REMOVAL & INSTALLATION 3-54
TIMING GEAR COVER 3-55
REMOVAL & INSTALLATION 3-55

TIMING CHAIN COVER OIL SEAL 3-56
REPLACEMENT 3-56
TIMING CHAIN AND TENSIONER 3-56
REMOVAL & INSTALLATION 3-56
OIL PAN 3-59
REMOVAL & INSTALLATION 3-59
REAR MAIN OIL SEAL 3-59
REMOVAL & INSTALLATION 3-59
OIL PUMP 3-60
REMOVAL & INSTALLATION 3-60
OVERHAUL 3-61
CAMSHAFT AND BEARINGS 3-64
REMOVAL & INSTALLATION 3-64
CAMSHAFT INSPECTION 3-66
PISTONS AND CONNECTING RODS 3-67
REMOVAL & INSTALLATION 3-67
PISTON & CONNECTING ROD
IDENTIFICATION 3-68
CLEANING & INSPECTION 3-69
HONING 3-69
PISTON RING REPLACEMENT 3-70
WRIST PIN REMOVAL &
INSTALLATION 3-71
CYLINDER BORE INSPECTION 3-72
CONNECTING ROD INSPECTION &
BEARING REPLACEMENT 3-72
CRANKSHAFT AND MAIN BEARINGS 3-73
REMOVAL & INSTALLATION 3-73
INSPECTION 3-74
BEARING CLEARANCE CHECK 3-75
BEARING REPLACEMENT 3-75
FREEZE PLUGS 3-76
REMOVAL & INSTALLATION 3-76
BLOCK HEATERS 3-76
REMOVAL & INSTALLATION 3-76
FLYWHEEL AND RING GEAR 3-77
REMOVAL & INSTALLATION 3-77
EXHAUST SYSTEM 3-77
GENERAL INFORMATION 3-77
SAFETY PRECAUTIONS 3-77
CATALYTIC CONVERTER 3-78
REMOVAL & INSTALLATION 3-78
MUFFLER AND/OR TAILPIPE 3-78
REMOVAL & INSTALLATION 3-78
COMPLETE SYSTEM 3-79
REMOVAL & INSTALLATION 3-79
COOLING SYSTEM 3-85
RADIATOR 3-85
REMOVAL & INSTALLATION 3-85
WATER PUMP 3-86
REMOVAL & INSTALLATION 3-86
THERMOSTAT 3-88
REMOVAL & INSTALLATION 3-88
COMPONENT LOCATIONS
ENGINE COMPONENT LOCATIONS—20R
ENGINE 3-20
SPECIFICATION CHARTS
ALTERNATOR AND REGULATOR
SPECIFICATIONS 3-16
GENERAL ENGINE SPECIFICATIONS 3-24
VALVE SPECIFICATIONS 3-24
CRANKSHAFT AND CONNECTING ROD
SPECIFICATIONS 3-25
PISTON AND RING SPECIFICATIONS 3-25
TORQUE SPECIFICATIONS 3-25
TROUBLESHOOTING CHARTS
ENGINE MECHANICAL PROBLEMS 3-90
ENGINE PERFORMANCE 3-93

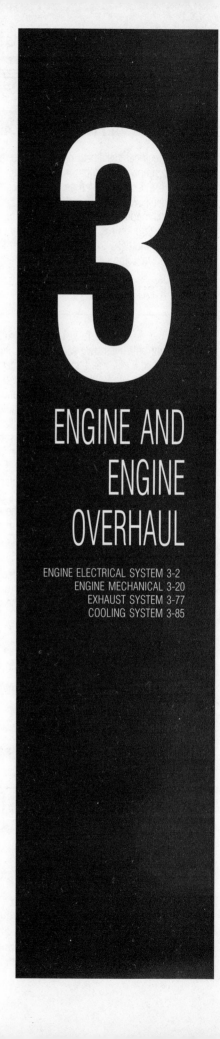

3

ENGINE AND ENGINE OVERHAUL

ENGINE ELECTRICAL SYSTEM 3-2
ENGINE MECHANICAL 3-20
EXHAUST SYSTEM 3-77
COOLING SYSTEM 3-85

ENGINE ELECTRICAL SYSTEM

Understanding Electricity

For any electrical system to operate, there must be a complete circuit. This simply means that the power flow from the battery must make a full circle. When an electrical component is operating, power flows from the battery to the components, passes through the component (load) causing it to function, and returns to the battery through the ground path of the circuit. This ground may be either another wire or a metal part of the vehicle (depending upon how the component is designed).

BASIC CIRCUITS

Perhaps the easiest way to visualize a circuit is to think of connecting a light bulb (with two wires attached to it) to the battery. If one of the two wires was attached to the negative post (−) of the battery and the other wire to the positive post (+), the circuit would be complete and the light bulb would illuminate. Electricity could follow a path from the battery to the bulb and back to the battery. It's not hard to see that with longer wires on our light bulb, it could be mounted anywhere on the vehicle. Further, one wire could be fitted with a switch so that the light could be turned on and off. Various other items could be added to our primitive circuit to make the light flash, become brighter or dimmer under certain conditions, or advise the user that it's burned out.

Ground

Some automotive components are grounded through their mounting points. The electrical current runs through the chassis of the vehicle and returns to the battery through the ground (−) cable; if you look, you'll see that the battery ground cable connects between the battery and the body of the vehicle.

Load

Every complete circuit must include a "load" (something to use the electricity coming from the source). If you were to connect a

Damaged insulation can allow wires to break (causing an open circuit) or touch (causing a short circuit)

wire between the two terminals of the battery (DON'T do this, but take our word for it) without the light bulb, the battery would attempt to deliver its entire power supply from one pole to another almost instantly. This is a short circuit. The electricity is taking a short cut to get to ground and is not being used by any load in the circuit. This sudden and uncontrolled electrical flow can cause great damage to other components in the circuit and can develop a tremendous amount of heat. A short in an automotive wiring harness can develop sufficient heat to melt the insulation on all the surrounding wires and reduce a multiple wire cable to one sad lump of plastic and copper. Two common causes of shorts are broken insulation (thereby exposing the wire to contact with surrounding metal surfaces or other wires) or a failed switch (the pins inside the switch come out of place and touch each other).

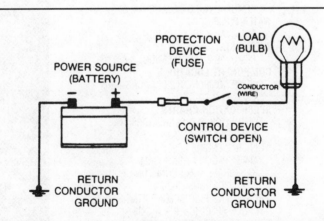

Here is an example of a simple automotive circuit. When the switch is closed, power from the positive battery terminal flows through the fuse, the switch and then the load (light bulb). The light illuminates and the circuit is completed through the return conductor and the vehicle ground. If the light did not work, the tests could be made with a voltmeter or test light at the battery, fuse, switch or bulb socket

Switches and Relays

Some electrical components which require a large amount of current to operate also have a relay in their circuit. Since these circuits carry a large amount of current (amperage or amps), the thickness of the wire in the circuit (wire gauge) is also greater. If this large wire were connected from the load to the control switch on the dash, the switch would have to carry the high amperage load and the dash would be twice as large to accommodate wiring harnesses as thick as your wrist. To prevent these problems, a relay is used. The large wires in the circuit are connected from the battery to one side of the relay and from the opposite side of the relay to the load. The relay is normally open, preventing current from passing through the circuit. An additional, smaller wire is connected from the relay to the control switch for the circuit. When the control switch is turned on, it grounds the smaller wire to the relay and completes its circuit. The main switch inside the relay closes, sending power to the component without routing the main power through the inside of the vehicle. Some common circuits which may use relays are the horn, headlights, starter and rear window defogger systems.

Protective Devices

It is possible for larger surges of current to pass through the electrical system of your vehicle. If this surge of current were to reach the load in the circuit, it could burn it out or severely damage it. To prevent this, fuses, circuit breakers and/or fusible links are connected into the supply wires of the electrical system. These items are nothing more than a built-in weak spot in the system. It's much easier to go to a known location (the fusebox) to see why a circuit is inoperative than to dissect 15 feet of wiring under the dashboard, looking for what happened.

When an electrical current of excessive power passes through the fuse, the fuse blows (the conductor melts) and breaks the circuit, preventing the passage of current and protecting the components.

A circuit breaker is basically a self repairing fuse. It will open the circuit in the same fashion as a fuse, but when either the short is removed or the surge subsides, the circuit breaker resets itself and does not need replacement.

A fuse link (fusible link or main link) is a wire that acts as a fuse. One of these is normally connected between the starter relay and the main wiring harness under the hood. Since the starter is usually the highest electrical draw on the vehicle, an internal short during starting could direct about 130 amps into the wrong places. Consider the damage potential of introducing this current into a system whose wiring is rated at 15 amps and you'll understand the need for protection. Since this link is very early in the electrical path, it's the first place to look if nothing on the vehicle works, but the battery seems to be charged and is properly connected.

TROUBLESHOOTING

Electrical problems generally fall into one of three areas:
• The component that is not functioning is not receiving current.
• The component is receiving power but is not using it or is using it incorrectly (component failure).
• The component is improperly grounded.
The circuit can be can be checked with a test light and a

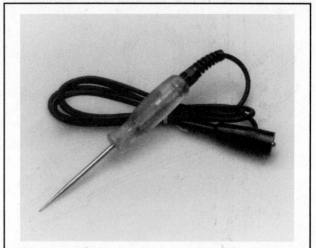

A 12 volt test light is useful when checking parts of a circuit for power

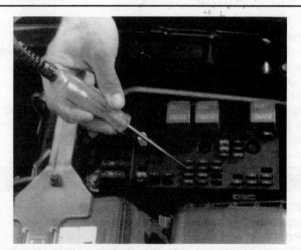

Here, someone is checking a circuit by making sure there is power to the component's fuse

jumper wire. The test light is a device that looks like a pointed screwdriver with a wire on one end and a bulb in its handle. A jumper wire is simply a piece of wire with alligator clips or special terminals on each end. If a component is not working, you must follow a systematic plan to determine which of the three causes is the villain.

1. Turn ON the switch that controls the item not working.

➡**Some items only work when the ignition switch is turned ON.**

2. Disconnect the power supply wire from the component.
3. Attach the ground wire of a test light or a voltmeter to a good metal ground.
4. Touch the end probe of the test light (or the positive lead of the voltmeter) to the power wire; if there is current in the wire, the light in the test light will come on (or the voltmeter will indicate the amount of voltage). You have now established that current is getting to the component.
5. Turn the ignition or dash switch **OFF** and reconnect the wire to the component.

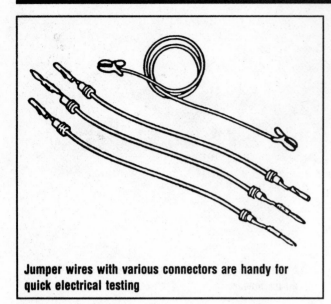

Jumper wires with various connectors are handy for quick electrical testing

If there was no power, then the problem is between the battery and the component. This includes all the switches, fuses, relays and the battery itself. The next place to look is the fusebox; check carefully either by eye or by using the test light across the fuse clips. The easiest way to check is to simply replace the fuse. If the fuse is blown, and upon replacement, immediately blows again, there is a short between the fuse and the component. This is generally (not always) a sign of an internal short in the component. Disconnect the power wire at the component again and replace the fuse; if the fuse holds, the component is the problem.

☼ WARNING

DO NOT test a component by running a jumper wire from the battery UNLESS you are certain that it operates on 12 volts. Many electronic components are designed to operate with less voltage and connecting them to 12 volts could destroy them. Jumper wires are best used to bypass a portion of the circuit (such as a stretch of wire or a switch) that DOES NOT contain a resistor and is suspected to be bad.

If all the fuses are good and the component is not receiving power, find the switch for the circuit. Bypass the switch with the jumper wire. This is done by connecting one end of the jumper to the power wire coming into the switch and the other end to the wire leaving the switch. If the component comes to life, the switch has failed.

☼ WARNING

Never substitute the jumper for the component. The circuit needs the electrical load of the component. If you bypass it, you will cause a short circuit.

Checking the ground for any circuit can mean tracing wires to the body, cleaning connections or tightening mounting bolts for the component itself. If the jumper wire can be connected to the case of the component or the ground connector, you can ground the other end to a piece of clean, solid metal on the vehicle. Again, if the component starts working, you've found the problem.

A systematic search through the fuse, connectors, switches and the component itself will almost always yield an answer. Loose and/or corroded connectors, particularly in ground circuits, are becoming a larger problem in modern vehicles. The computers and on-board electronic (solid state) systems are highly sensitive to improper grounds and will change their function drastically if one occurs.

Remember that for any electrical circuit to work, ALL the connections must be clean and tight.

➡️**For more information on Understanding and Troubleshooting Electrical Systems, please refer to Section 6 of this manual.**

Battery, Starting and Charging Systems

BASIC OPERATING PRINCIPLES

Battery

The battery is the first link in the chain of mechanisms which work together to provide cranking of the automobile engine. In most modern vehicles, the battery is a lead/acid electrochemical device consisting of six 2v subsections (cells) connected in series so the unit is capable of producing approximately 12v of electrical pressure. Each subsection consists of a series of positive and negative plates held a short distance apart in a solution of sulfuric acid and water.

The two types of plates are of dissimilar metals. This sets-up a chemical reaction, and it is this reaction which produces current flow from the battery when its positive and negative terminals are connected to an electrical accessory such as a lamp or motor. The continued transfer of electrons would eventually convert the sulfuric acid to water, and make the two plates identical in chemical composition. As electrical energy is removed from the battery, its voltage output tends to drop. Thus, measuring battery voltage and battery electrolyte composition are two ways of checking the ability of the unit to supply power. During engine cranking, electrical energy is removed from the battery. However, if the charging circuit is in good condition and the operating conditions are normal, the power removed from the battery will be replaced by the alternator which will force electrons back through the battery, reversing the normal flow, and restoring the battery to its original chemical state.

Starting System

The battery and starting motor are linked by very heavy electrical cables designed to minimize resistance to the flow of current. Generally, the major power supply cable that leaves the battery goes directly to the starter, while other electrical system needs are supplied by a smaller cable. During starter operation, power flows from the battery to the starter and is grounded through the vehicle's frame/body or engine and the battery's negative ground strap.

The starter is a specially designed, direct current electric motor capable of producing a great amount of power for its size. One thing that allows the motor to produce a great deal of power is its tremendous rotating speed. It drives the engine through a tiny pinion gear (attached to the starter's armature), which drives the very large flywheel ring gear at a greatly reduced speed. Another factor allowing it to produce so much power is that only intermittent operation is required of it. Thus, little allowance for air circulation is necessary, and the windings can be built into a very small space.

The starter solenoid is a magnetic device which employs the small current supplied by the start circuit of the ignition switch. This magnetic action moves a plunger which mechanically engages the starter and closes the heavy switch connecting it to the battery. The starting switch circuit usually consists of the starting switch contained within the ignition switch, a neutral safety switch or clutch pedal switch, and the wiring necessary to connect these in series with the starter solenoid or relay.

The pinion, a small gear, is mounted to a one way drive clutch. This clutch is splined to the starter armature shaft. When the ignition switch is moved to the **START** position, the solenoid plunger slides the pinion toward the flywheel ring gear via a collar and spring. If the teeth on the pinion and flywheel match properly, the pinion will engage the flywheel immediately. If the gear teeth butt one another, the spring will be compressed and will force the gears to mesh as soon as the starter turns far enough to allow them to do so. As the solenoid plunger reaches the end of its travel, it closes the contacts that connect the battery and starter, then the engine is cranked.

As soon as the engine starts, the flywheel ring gear begins turning fast enough to drive the pinion at an extremely high rate of speed. At this point, the one-way clutch begins allowing the pinion to spin faster than the starter shaft so that the starter will not operate at excessive speed. When the ignition switch is released from the starter position, the solenoid is de-energized, and a spring pulls the gear out of mesh interrupting the current flow to the starter.

Some starters employ a separate relay, mounted away from the starter, to switch the motor and solenoid current on and off. The relay replaces the solenoid electrical switch, but does not eliminate the need for a solenoid mounted on the starter used to mechanically engage the starter drive gears. The relay is used to reduce the amount of current the starting switch must carry.

Charging System

The automobile charging system provides electrical power for operation of the vehicle's ignition system, starting system and all electrical accessories. The battery serves as an electrical surge or storage tank, storing (in chemical form) the energy originally produced by the engine driven generator. The system also provides a means of regulating output to protect the battery from being overcharged and to avoid excessive voltage to the accessories.

The storage battery is a chemical device incorporating parallel lead plates in a tank containing a sulfuric acid/water solution. Adjacent plates are slightly dissimilar, and the chemical reaction of the two dissimilar plates produces electrical energy when the battery is connected to a load such as the starter motor. The chemical reaction is reversible, so that when the generator is producing a voltage (electrical pressure) greater than that produced by the battery, electricity is forced into the battery, and the battery is returned to its fully charged state.

Newer automobiles use alternating current generators or alternators, because they are more efficient, can be rotated at higher speeds, and have fewer brush problems. In an alternator, the field usually rotates while all the current produced passes only through the stator winding. The brushes bear against continuous slip rings. This causes the current produced to periodically reverse the direction of its flow. Diodes (electrical one way valves) block the flow of current from traveling in the wrong direction. A series of diodes is wired together to permit the alternating flow of the stator to be rectified back to 12 volts DC for use by the vehicle's electrical system.

The voltage regulating function is performed by a regulator. The regulator is often built in to the alternator; this system is termed an integrated or internal regulator.

Transistorized Ignition System

▶ See Figures 1 and 2

Troubleshooting the fully transistorized ignition system is easy, but you must have an accurate ohmmeter and voltmeter and take certain precautions as follow.

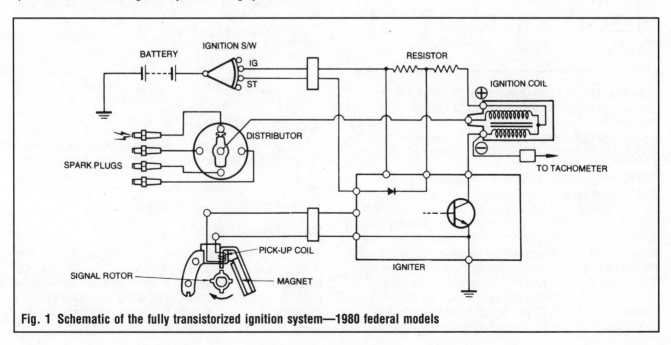

Fig. 1 Schematic of the fully transistorized ignition system—1980 federal models

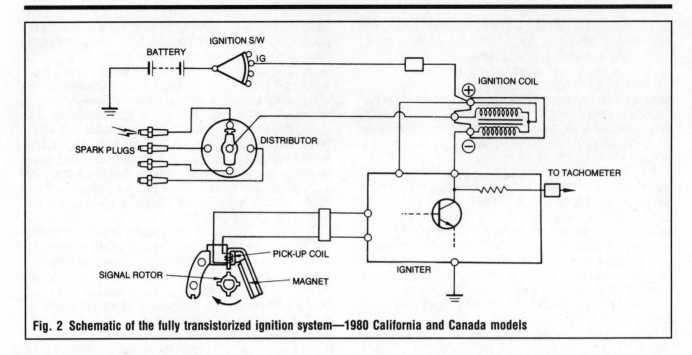

Fig. 2 Schematic of the fully transistorized ignition system—1980 California and Canada models

PRECAUTIONS

1. Do not allow the ignition switch to be ON for more than 10 minutes if the engine will not start.

2. Some tachometers are not compatible with the fully transistorized system. Check the tach's instruction sheet or its manufacturer if there is any doubt in your mind about compatibility.

3. When connecting a tachometer: On USA models, connect the tachometer (plus) terminal to the ignition coil (minus) terminal. On some Canadian models a service wiring connector (covered with a rubber boot) is provided for tachometer connection.

4. Never allow the ignition coil terminals to touch ground. Damage to the ignitor or coil could result if the terminals are grounded.

5. Do not disconnect the battery when the engine is running.

6. Make sure that the ignitor is properly grounded to the body.

TESTING

Before testing the signal generator and the ignitor, several other ignition system components should be checked.

1. Connect a timing light to each plug wire in turn. Crank the engine, if the light flashes it can be assumed that voltage is reaching the plugs. If there is no flash from the timing light, see Step 2.

2. Inspect the spark plug wires. Carefully remove the wires from the spark plugs by twisting the boots. Do not pull or bend the wire, damage to the inside conductor will occur. Inspect the terminals for dirt, looseness and corrosion. If the outside insulation is cracked or broken, replace the wire. Check the resistance of the wire with an ohmmeter. Do not disconnect the wire from the distributor cap. Remove the distributor cap, connect one lead of the ohmmeter to the distributor cap contact and the other to the terminal of the connected plug wire. Replace any wires with excessive resistance, over 8000Ω per foot of cable length (more than 25 kilo-ohms), or any that have no continuity. Inspect the

distributor cap and ignition rotor for cracks, damage or carbon tracking. Replace as necessary.

3. Remove the spark plugs and check for electrode wear, carbon deposits, thread damage and insulator damage. If any problem is found, replace the plugs. If the old plugs are to be reused, clean them with a wire brush or have them cleaned in a spark plug cleaner. (Check your local gas station). After cleaning the plugs, check the gap (see Chapter two) and reinstall.

➡**If the engine still will not start, or the timing light test shows no spark, check the ignition coil resistances.**

Ignition Coil

PRIMARY RESISTANCE

With an ohmmeter, check between the positive (plus) and negative (minus) terminals of the ignition coil. With the coil cold, the resistances should be:

1977–79 All models: 1.3–1.7Ω
1980 Fed. models: 0.5–0.6Ω
1980 Canada & Calif.: 0.8–1.0Ω
1981 22R engine: 0.8–1.0Ω (USA)
1981 Canada: 0.4–0.5Ω
1981 5M-E engine: 0.5–0.6Ω

SECONDARY RESISTANCE

With an ohmmeter, check between the positive (plus) coil terminal and the high tension (coil wire) terminal. Clean the coil wire terminal with a wire brush before testing. The resistance on all models except 1981 and later Canadian models should be 11.5–15.5kΩ; Canadian models (1981 and later): 8.5–11.5kΩ.

Ballast Resistor/Resistor Wire

On models with a coil mounted resistor, connect the ohmmeter leads to the end terminals of the resistor. Resistance should measure 1.2–1.4Ω. On models with a resistor wire, disconnect the plastic connector at the igniter. Connect one ohmmeter lead to the yellow wire and the other to the brown wire. Resistance should measure 1.2–1.4Ω.

➡If the tests on the coil or the resistor show values far from the standard, replace the part or wire, perform the timing light test or attempt to start the engine.

Checking the Air Gap

Remove the distributor cap and ignition rotor. Check the air gap between the timing rotor spoke and the pick up coil. When aligned, the air gap should be 0.2–0.4mm. You will probably have to bump the engine around with the starter to line up the timing rotor. Refer to air gap adjustment in Chapter 2 for adjustment procedure.

Signal Generator (Pickup Coil)

Check the resistance of the signal generator. Unplug the connector to the distributor. Connect one lead of the ohmmeter to the white wire, the other lead to the pink wire. Resistance should be 130–190Ω. If resistance is not correct, replace the signal generator.

Igniter

ALL 1977–80 MODELS AND 1981 CANADIAN

1. Connect the negative (minus) probe of the voltmeter to the negative (minus) terminal of the ignition coil and the positive (plus) probe of the voltmeter to the yellow resistor wire at the connector unplugged from the ignitor. With the ignition switch ON (not start) the voltage should read 12 volts.

2. Check the voltage between the negative (minus) coil terminal and the yellow resistor wire again, but this time use the ohmmeter as resistance. Connect the positive (plus) ohmmeter lead to the pink wire in the plug connector. Connect the negative (minus) ohmmeter lead to the white wire in the connector.

✳✳ WARNING

Do not reverse the connection of the ohmmeter.

Select either the 1Ω or 10Ω range on the ohmmeter. With the voltmeter connected as in Step one and the ignition switch turned ON, the voltage should measure nearly zero. If a problem is found, replace the ignitor.

1981 MODELS (EXCEPT CANADA)

1. Connect the positive (plus) probe of the voltmeter to the positive (plus) terminal of the ignition coil. Connect the negative (minus) probe of the voltmeter to the car body ground. Turn the ignition switch to the ON position. The voltage should read 12 volts.

2. To check the power transistor in the ignitor, connect the positive (plus) probe of the voltmeter to the negative (minus) terminal of the ignition coil and the negative (minus) probe of the voltmeter to the car body ground. Turn the ignition switch to the ON position. The reading should be 12 volts.

3. Unplug the wiring connector from the distributor. With a 1.5 volt dry cell battery in circuit, i.e. connect the positive pole of the battery to the pink terminal of the connector plug, and the negative pole of the battery to the white wire. Connect the voltmeter with the positive (plus) probe connected to the negative (minus) terminal of the ignition coil and the negative (minus) probe of the voltmeter to the car body ground. Turn the ignition switch to the ON position. Voltage should measure 5 volts, less than battery voltage.

✳✳ WARNING

Do not apply voltage for more than five seconds or the power transistor will be destroyed.

If a problem is found, replace the ignitor.

REMOVAL & INSTALLATION

Igniter

The igniter is mounted on either the firewall separately or attached to the ignition coil.
1. Disconnect the negative battery cable.
2. Tag and disconnect the wires attached to the igniter.
3. Unbolt or unscrew the igniter from its mounting place.
To install:
4. Attach the wiring to the igniter.
5. Place the igniter into position and tighten the mounting bolts or screws.
6. Connect the negative battery cable.

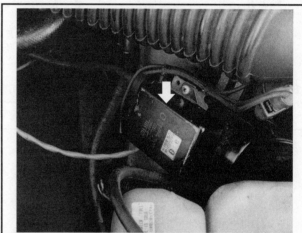

On some models the igniter is attached to the ignition coil on the firewall

Pickup Coil

Remove the distributor cap and ignition rotor. Disconnect the distributor wiring connector. Remove the two screws that mount the signal generator (pickup coil). Install the new signal generator with the two mounting screws, do not completely tighten the screws until you have adjusted the air gap. (See air gap adjustment, Chapter 2). Reconnect the wiring harness, install the rotor and distributor cap. Check for engine starting. If the engine will not start, check the ignitor.

Distributor

REMOVAL

▶ **See Figures 3, 4, 5 and 6**

On all four-cylinder engines, except the 20R and 22R, and the distributor is on the right (passenger's) side. On 20R and 22R en-

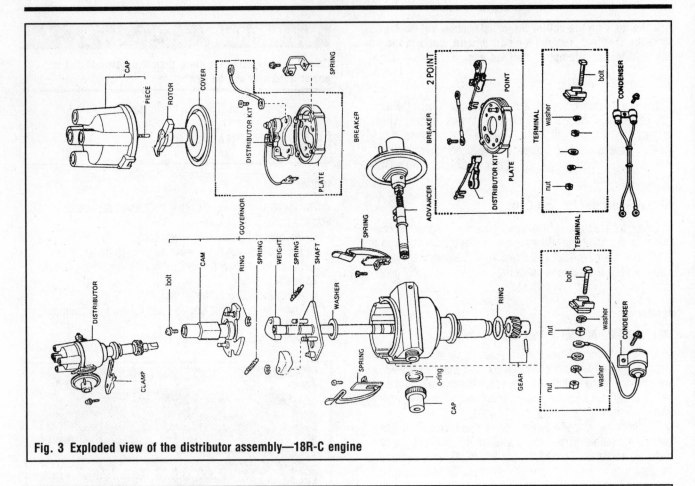

Fig. 3 Exploded view of the distributor assembly—18R-C engine

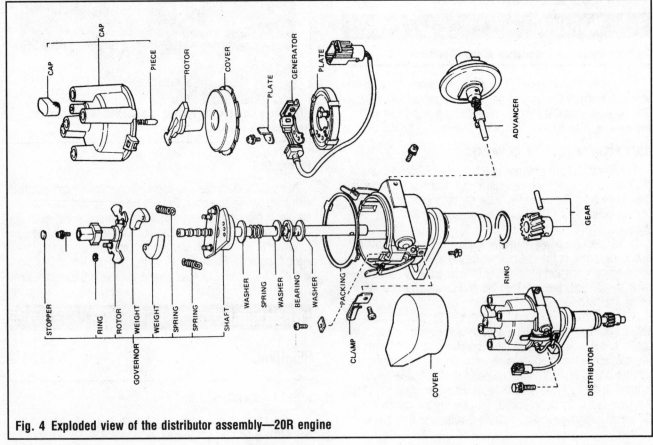

Fig. 4 Exploded view of the distributor assembly—20R engine

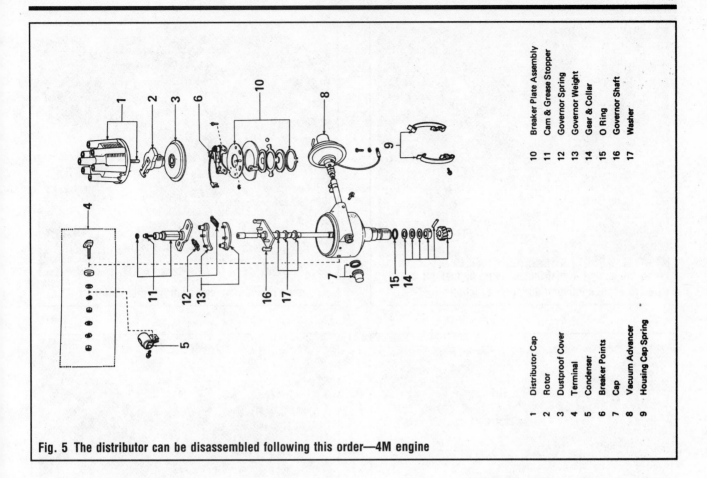

1	Distributor Cap	10	Breaker Plate Assembly
2	Rotor	11	Cam & Grease Stopper
3	Dustproof Cover	12	Governor Spring
4	Terminal	13	Governor Weight
5	Condenser	14	Gear & Collar
6	Breaker Points	15	O Ring
7	Cap	16	Governor Shaft
8	Vacuum Advancer	17	Washer
9	Housing Cap Spring		

Fig. 5 The distributor can be disassembled following this order—4M engine

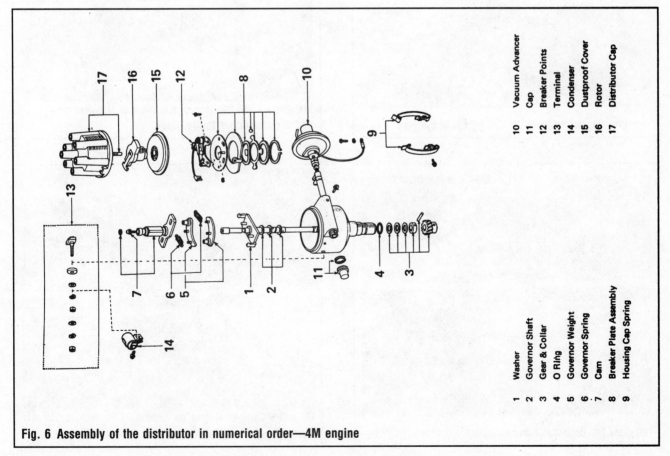

1	Washer	10	Vacuum Advancer
2	Governor Shaft	11	Cap
3	Gear & Collar	12	Breaker Points
4	O Ring	13	Terminal
5	Governor Weight	14	Condenser
6	Governor Spring	15	Dustproof Cover
7	Cam	16	Rotor
8	Breaker Plate Assembly	17	Distributor Cap
9	Housing Cap Spring		

Fig. 6 Assembly of the distributor in numerical order—4M engine

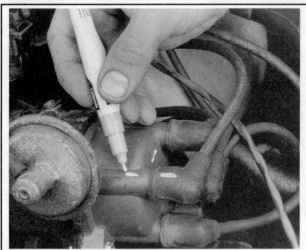

When removing the distributor, begin by marking the wires to avoid confusion during installation

. . . then remove the cap from the distributor

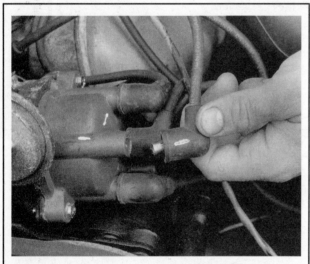

Pull the plug wires from the cap by the boots only

Matchmark the position of the rotor to the distributor, and the distributor to the block

Unscrew the distributor cap retainers . . .

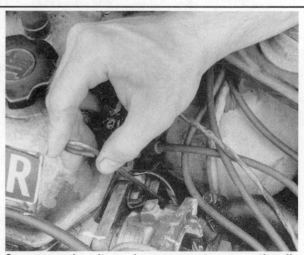

On some engines it may be necessary to remove the oil dipstick—20R engine shown

Disconnect the vacuum line leading to the distributor advance mechanism

. . . then remove the distributor from the engine

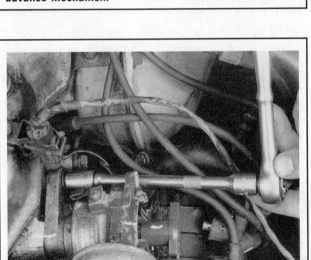

Remove the distributor mounting bolts

Separate any wiring attached to the distributor . . .

gines and all sixes, the distributor is located at the front of the engine on the left driver's side. To remove the distributor, proceed in the following order:

1. Unfasten the retaining clips and lift the distributor cap straight up. It will be easier to install the distributor if the wiring is left connected to the cap. If the wires must be removed from the cap, mark their positions to aid in installation.

2. Remove the dust cover and mark the position of the rotor relative to the distributor body. Then mark the position of the body relative to the block.

3. Disconnect the coil primary wire and the vacuum line(s). If the distributor vacuum unit has two vacuum lines, mark which is which for installation.

4. Remove the pinch bolt and lift the distributor straight up, away from the engine. The rotor and body are marked so that they can be returned to the position from which they were removed. Do not turn or disturb the engine (unless absolutely necessary, such as for engine rebuilding), after the distributor has been removed.

INSTALLATION

Timing Not Disturbed

1. Insert the distributor in the block and align the matchmarks made during removal.

2. Engage the distributor driven gear with the distributor drive.

3. Install the distributor clamp and secure it with the pinch bolt.

4. Install the cap, primary wire, and vacuum line(s).

5. Install the spark plug leads. Consult the marks made during removal to be sure that the proper lead goes to each plug. Install the high tension wire if it was removed.

6. Start the engine. Check the timing and adjust it and the octane selector, as outlined in Chapter 2.

Timing Lost

If the engine has been cranked, dismantled, or the timing otherwise lost, proceed as follows:

1. Determine top dead center (TDC) of the No. 1 cylinder's

compression stroke by removing the spark plug from the No. 1 cylinder and placing your thumb over the spark plug hole. This is important because the timing marks will also line up with the last cylinder in the firing order in its exhaust stroke. Crank the engine until compression pressure starts to build up. Continue cranking the engine until the timing marks indicate TDC (or 0).

2. Next, align the timing marks to the specifications given in the Ignition Timing column of the Tune-Up Specifications chart at the beginning of Chapter 2.

3. Temporarily install the rotor in the distributor without the dust cover. Turn the distributor shaft so that the rotor is pointing toward the No. 1 terminal in the distributor cap. The points should be just about to open.

4. Use a small screwdriver to align the slot on the distributor drive (oil pump driveshaft) with the key on the bottom of the distributor shaft.

5. Align the matchmarks on the distributor body and the blocks which were made during the removal. Install the distributor in the block by rotating it slightly (no more than one gear tooth in either direction) until the driven gear meshes with the drive.

➡**Oil the distributor spiral gear and the oil pump driveshaft end before distributor installation.**

6. Rotate the distributor, once it is installed, so that the points are just about to open or the projection on the pickup coil is almost opposite the signal rotor tooth. Temporarily tighten the pinch bolt.

7. Remove the rotor and install the dust cover. Replace the rotor and the distributor cap.

8. Install the primary wire and the vacuum line(s).

9. Install the No. 1 spark plug. Connect the cables to the spark plugs in the proper order by using the marks made during removal. Install the high tension lead if it was removed.

10. Start the engine. Adjust the ignition timing and the octane selector, as outlined in Chapter 2.

Alternator

◆ **See Figures 7, 8 and 9**

PRECAUTIONS

1. Always observe proper polarity of the battery connections. Be especially careful when jump-starting the car.

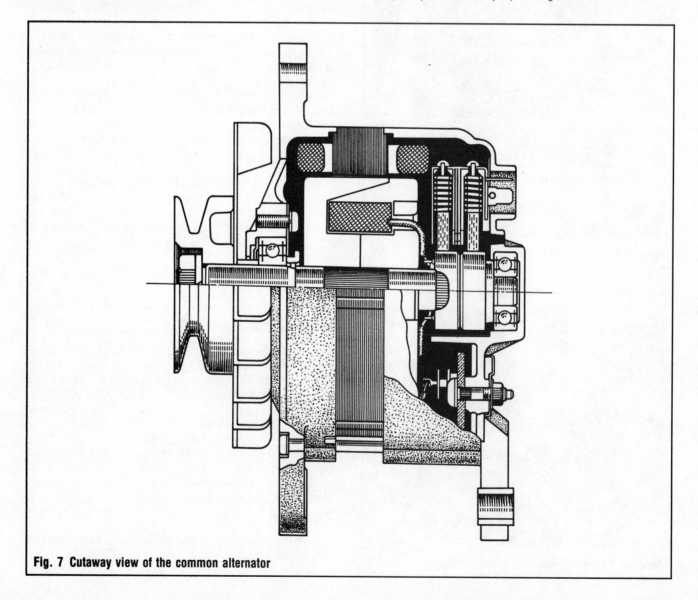

Fig. 7 Cutaway view of the common alternator

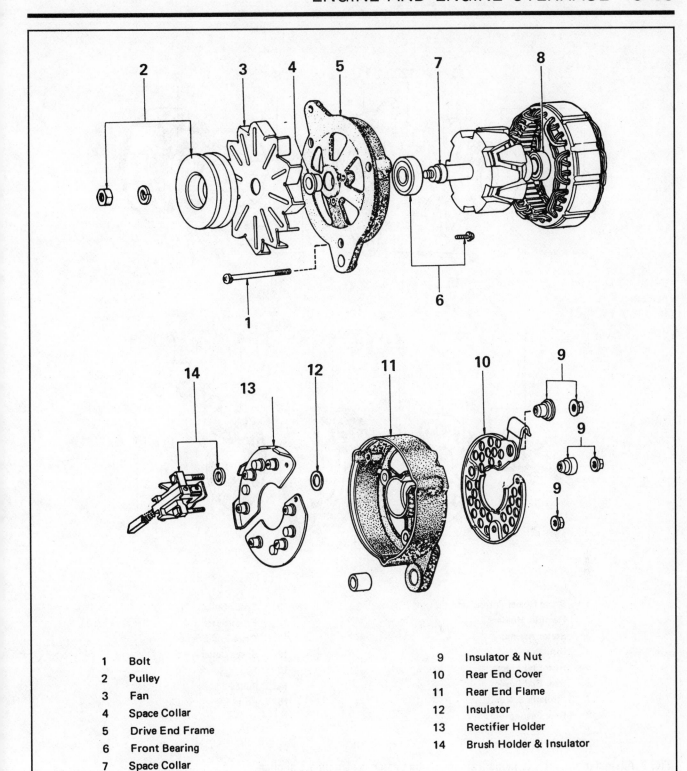

1	Bolt
2	Pulley
3	Fan
4	Space Collar
5	Drive End Frame
6	Front Bearing
7	Space Collar
8	Rear Bearing

9	Insulator & Nut
10	Rear End Cover
11	Rear End Flame
12	Insulator
13	Rectifier Holder
14	Brush Holder & Insulator

Fig. 8 Disassemble the alternator following this order—4M engine shown, others similar

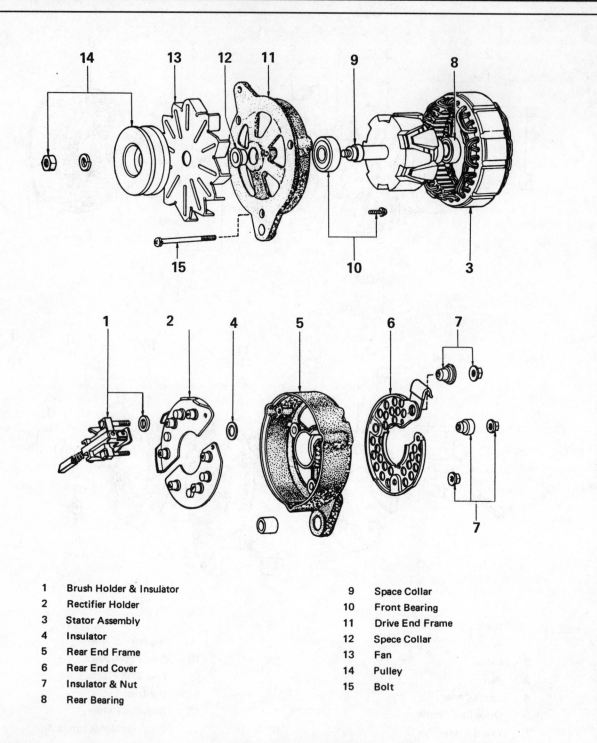

1	Brush Holder & Insulator		9	Space Collar
2	Rectifier Holder		10	Front Bearing
3	Stator Assembly		11	Drive End Frame
4	Insulator		12	Spece Collar
5	Rear End Frame		13	Fan
6	Rear End Cover		14	Pulley
7	Insulator & Nut		15	Bolt
8	Rear Bearing			

Fig. 9 Alternator assembly in numerical order—4M engine shown others similar

2. Never ground or short out any alternator or alternator regulator terminals.

3. Never operate the alternator with any of its or the battery's leads disconnected.

4. Always remove the battery or disconnect both cables (ground cable first) before charging.

5. Always disconnect the ground cable when replacing any electrical components.

6. Never subject the alternator to excessive heat or dampness if the engine is being steam-cleaned.

7. Never use arc welding equipment with the alternator connected.

REMOVAL & INSTALLATION

➡**On some models the alternator is mounted very low in the engine. On these models it may be necessary to remove the gravel shield and work from underneath the car in order to gain access to the alternator.**

1. Disconnect the battery ground (negative) cable. Unfasten the starter-to-battery cable at the battery end.
2. Remove the air cleaner, if necessary, to gain access to the alternator.
3. Unfasten the bolts which attach the adjusting link to the alternator. Remove the alternator drive belt.
4. Unfasten the alternator wiring connections.
5. Remove the alternator attaching bolt and then withdraw the alternator from its bracket.
6. Installation is performed in the reverse order of removal. After installing the alternator, adjust the belt tension as detailed in Chapter 1.

Non-Transistorized Regulator

➡**IC regulators are built onto the alternator. For testing procedures refer to the next section in this chapter.**

REMOVAL & INSTALLATION

1. Remove the cable from the negative (−) battery terminal and then remove the cable from the positive (+) battery terminal.
2. Disconnect the wiring harness connector at the regulator.
3. Unfasten the bolts which secure the regulator. Remove the regulator and its condenser.
4. Installation is the reverse of removal.

ADJUSTMENTS

Voltage

1. Connect a voltmeter up to the battery terminals. Negative (black) lead to the negative (−) terminal; positive (red) lead to positive (+) terminal.
2. Start the engine and gradually increase its speed to about 1,500 rpm.
3. At this speed, the voltage reading should fall within the range specified in the Alternator and Regulator Specifications chart.
4. If the voltage does not fall within the specifications, remove the cover from the regulator and adjust it by bending the adjusting arm.
5. Repeat Steps 2 and 3 if the voltage cannot be brought to specification, proceed with the mechanical adjustments which follow.

Mechanical

➡**Perform the voltage adjustment outlined above, before beginning the mechanical adjustments.**

FIELD RELAY

◗ **See Figure 10**

1. Remove the cover from the regulator assembly.
2. Use a feeler gauge to check the amount that the contact spring is deflected while the armature is being depressed.
3. If the measurement is not within specifications (see the Alternator and Regulator Specifications chart), adjust the regulator by bending point holder P2. (See the illustration.).

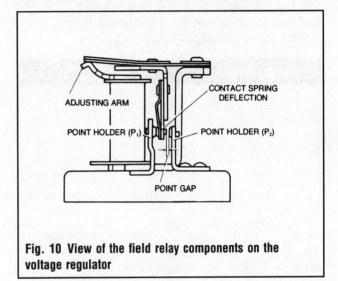

Fig. 10 View of the field relay components on the voltage regulator

4. Check the point gap with a feeler gauge against the specifications in the chart.
5. Adjust the point gap, as required, by bending the point holder P1. (See the illustration).
6. Clean off the points with emery cloth if they are dirty and wash them with solvent.

ARMATURE AND POINT GAPS

◗ **See Figure 11**

1. Use a feeler gauge to measure the air (armature) gap. If it is not within the specifications (see the Alternator and Regulator Specifications chart), adjust it by bending the low speed point holder. (See the illustration).

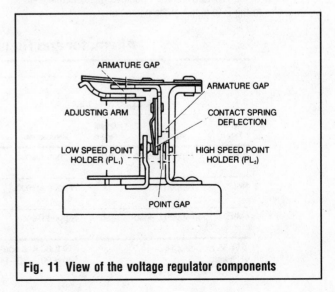

Fig. 11 View of the voltage regulator components

2. Check the point gap with a feeler gauge. If it is not within specifications, adjust it by bending the high speed point holder. (See the illustration.) Clean the points with emery cloth and wash them off with solvent.

3. Check the amount of contact spring deflection while depressing the armature. The specification should be the same as that for the contact spring on the field relay. If the amount of deflection is not within specification, replace, do not adjust, the voltage regulator.

Go back and perform the steps outlined under Voltage Adjustment. If the voltage still fails to come within specifications, the alternator is probably defective and should be replaced.

IC Regulator

The IC regulator is mounted on the alternator housing, is transistorized and is non-adjustable.

REMOVAL & INSTALLATION

1. Disconnect the negative (ground) battery cable from the battery.
2. Remove the end cover of the regulator.
3. Remove the three screws that go through the terminals.
4. Remove the (two) top mounting screws that mount the regulator to the alternator. Remove the regulator.
5. To install the new IC regulator. Place the regulator in position on the alternator. Install and secure the (two) top mounting screws. Install the (three) terminal screws. Install the end cover.
6. Reconnect the battery ground cable.

TESTING

♦ **See Figure 12**

To test the IC regulator you will need a voltmeter and an ammeter.

1. Disconnect the wire connected to the B terminal of the alternator. Connect the wire (that you disconnected) to the negative (minus) terminal of the ammeter.
2. Connect the test lead from the positive (plus) terminal of the ammeter to the B terminal of the alternator.

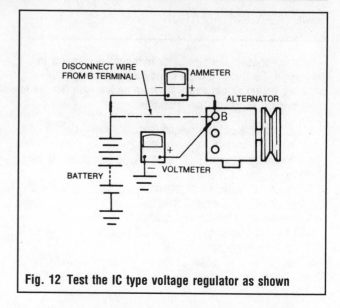

Fig. 12 Test the IC type voltage regulator as shown

3. Connect the positive (plus) lead of the voltmeter to the B terminal of the alternator.
4. Connect the negative (minus) lead of the voltmeter to ground.
5. Start the engine and run at about 2000 rpm. Check the reading on the ammeter and voltmeter. Standard amperage should be less than 10 amps. Standard voltage should be from 14 to 14.7 volts (Temperature 77°F).
6. If the voltage is greater than 15 volts, replace the IC regulator.
7. If the voltage reading is less than 13.5 volts, shut off the engine and check the regulator and alternator as follows.
8. Turn the ignition switch to ON. Check the voltage at the IG terminal of the alternator. If no voltage, check the ENGINE fuse and/or the ignition switch. No problems found, go to next step.
9. Remove the end cover from the IC regulator. Check the voltage reading at the regulator L terminal. If the voltage reading is zero to 2 volts, suspect the alternator.
10. If the voltage is the same as battery voltage, turn off the ignition switch (OFF position) and check for continuity between the regulator L and F terminals.
11. If there is no continuity, suspect the alternator. If there is continuity (approx. 4Ω) replace the IC regulator.

Alternator and Regulator Specifications

| | Alternator | | | Regulator | | | | | |
| | | | | Field Relay | | | Regulator | | |
Engine Type	Manufacturer	Output (amps)	Manufacturer	Contact Spring Deflection (in.)	Point Gap (in.)	Volts to Close	Air Gap (in.)	Point Gap (in.)	Volts
20R ④	Nippon Denso	40 ②	Nippon Denso	0.008–0.024	0.016–0.047 ③	4.5–5.8	0.012	0.010–0.018	13.8–14.8 ①
4M	Nippon Denso	55	Nippon Denso	0.008–0.024	0.016–0.047	4.5–5.8	0.012	0.008–0.024	13.8–14.8
4M-E	Nippon Denso	55	Nippon Denso	————————Not adjustable————————					14.0–14.7 ⑤

① W/55 amp alt.: 14.0–14.7
② Optional: 55
③ 1975–79: 0.0118–0.0177
④ 1980 has non-adjustable regulator
⑤ 1980: 14.3–14.9

Starter

REMOVAL & INSTALLATION

1. Disconnect the negative (ground) cable from the battery.
2. Disconnect the wires/cables connected to the starter motor.
3. On some models it may be necessary to remove the air cleaner, splash shields or linkage that is in the way of easy access to the starter motor.
4. Loosen and remove the starter motor mounting nuts/bolts while supporting the motor.
5. Remove the starter motor.
6. Installation is in the reverse order of removal.

On some engines the starter is not easily accessible

STARTER OVERHAUL

Solenoid and Brush Replacement

DIRECT DRIVE TYPE

▶ See Figure 13

➡ **The starter must be removed from the car in order to perform this operation.**

1. Disconnect the field coil lead from the solenoid terminal.
2. Unfasten the solenoid retaining screws. Remove the solenoid by tilting it upward and withdrawing it.
3. Unfasten the end frame bearing cover screws and remove the cover.
4. Unfasten and withdraw the thru-bolts. Remove the commutator endframe.
5. Withdraw the brushes from their holder if they are to be replaced.
6. Check the brush length against the specification in the Battery and Starter Specifications chart. Replace the brushes with new ones if required.
7. Dress the new brushes with emery cloth so that they will make proper contact.

8. Use a spring scale to check the brush spring tensions against the specification in the chart. Replace the springs if they do not meet specification.
9. Assembly is the reverse order of disassembly. Remember to pack the end bearing cover with multipurpose grease before installing it.

GEAR REDUCTION TYPE

▶ See Figure 14

➡ **The starter must be removed from the car in order to perform this operation.**

1. Disconnect the solenoid lead terminal.
2. Loosen the two bolts on the starter housing and separate the field frame from the solenoid. Remove the O-ring and felt dust seal.
3. Unfasten the two screws and separate the starter drive from the solenoid.
4. Withdraw the clutch and gears. Remove the ball from the clutch shaft bore or solenoid.
5. Remove the brushes from the holder.
6. Measure the brush length and compare it to the figure in the Battery and Starter Specifications chart. Replace the brushes with new ones if they are too short.
7. Replace any worn or chipped gears.
8. Assembly is performed in the reverse order of disassembly. Lubricate all gears and bearings with high temperature grease. Grease the ball before inserting it in the clutch shaft bore. Align the tab on the brush holder with the notch on the field frame. Check the positive (+) brush leads to ensure that they aren't grounded. Align the solenoid marks with the field frame bolt anchors.

Starter Drive Replacement

DIRECT DRIVE STARTER

➡ **The starter must be removed from car.**

1. Loosen the locknut or bolt and remove the connection going to the terminal of the solenoid. Remove the securing screws and remove the solenoid.
2. Remove the front dust cover, E-ring, thrust washers, and the two screws retaining the brush holder assembly. Remove the brush cover thru-bolts and remove the cover assembly.
3. Lift the brushes to free them from the commutator and remove the brush holder.
4. Tap the yoke assembly lightly with a wooden hammer and remove it from the field and case.
5. Remove the nut and bolt which serve as a pin for the shift lever, carefully retaining the associated washers.
6. Remove the armature assembly and shift lever.
7. Push the stop ring (located at the end of the armature shaft) toward the clutch and remove the snapring. Remove the stop ring.
8. Remove the clutch assembly from the armature shaft.
To install:
9. Install the clutch assembly onto the armature shaft.
10. Put the stop ring on and hold it toward the clutch while installing the snapring.
11. Install the armature assembly and shift lever into the yoke.
12. Install the washers, nut and bolt which serve as a shift lever pivot pin.

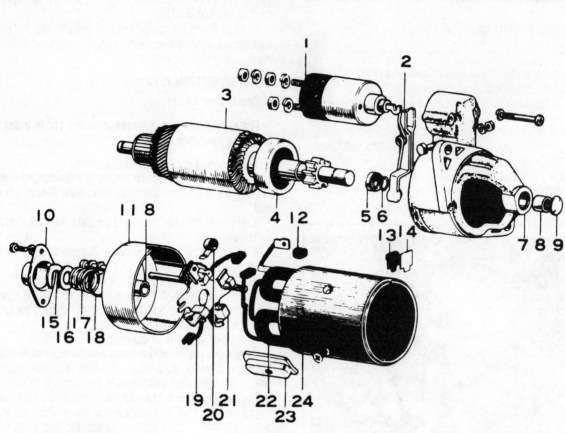

1. Solenoid
2. Engagement lever
3. Armature
4. Overrunning clutch
5. Clutch stop
6. Snap-ring
7. Drive housing
8. Bushing
9. Bearing cover
10. Bearing cover
11. Commutator end frame
12. Rubber bushing
13. Rubber grommet
14. Plate
15. Lockplate
16. Washer
17. Brake spring
18. Gasket
19. Brush
20. Brush spring
21. Brush holder
22. Field coil
23. Pole shoes
24. Field yoke

Fig. 13 Exploded view of the direct drive starter components

13. Install the field back onto the yoke assembly.
14. Lift the brushes and install the brush holder. Install the brush cover and thru-bolts.
15. Replace the brush holder set screws, the thrust washers, E-ring, and the dust cover.
16. Install the solenoid. Reconnect the wire to the terminal of the solenoid.

GEAR REDUCTION TYPE

1. Remove the starter.
2. Remove the solenoid and the shift lever.
3. Remove the bolts securing the center housing to the front cover and separate the parts.
4. Remove the gears and the starter drive.

✳✳ WARNING

Be careful not to lose the steel ball installed in the drive. Remember to reinstall when replacing the drive.

5. Installation is the reverse of removal.

Battery

Refer to Chapter 1 for details on battery maintenance.

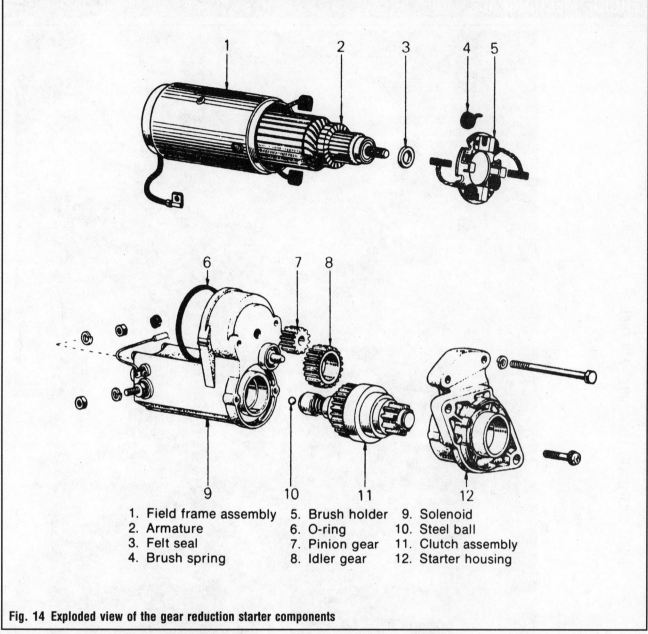

1. Field frame assembly
2. Armature
3. Felt seal
4. Brush spring
5. Brush holder
6. O-ring
7. Pinion gear
8. Idler gear
9. Solenoid
10. Steel ball
11. Clutch assembly
12. Starter housing

Fig. 14 Exploded view of the gear reduction starter components

REMOVAL & INSTALLATION

1. Disconnect the negative (ground) cable from the terminal, and then the positive cable. Special pullers are available to remove the cable clamps.

➡**To avoid sparks, always disconnect the ground cable first, and connect it last.**

2. Remove the battery hold-down clamp.
3. Remove the battery, being careful not to spill the acid.

➡**Spilled acid can be neutralized with a baking soda/water solution. If you somehow get acid into your eyes, flush it out with lots of water and get to a doctor.**

4. Clean the battery posts thoroughly before reinstalling, or when installing a new battery.

5. Clean the cable clamps, using a wire brush, both inside and out.

6. Install the battery and the hold-down clamp or strap. Connect the positive, then the negative cable. Do not hammer them in place. The terminals should be coated lightly (externally) with grease to prevent corrosion. There are also felt washers impregnated with an anti-corrosion substance which are slipped over the battery posts before installing the cables. These are available in auto parts stores.

✳✳ WARNING

Make absolutely sure that the battery is connected properly before you turn on the ignition switch. Reversed polarity can burn out your alternator and regulator within a matter of seconds.

ENGINE MECHANICAL

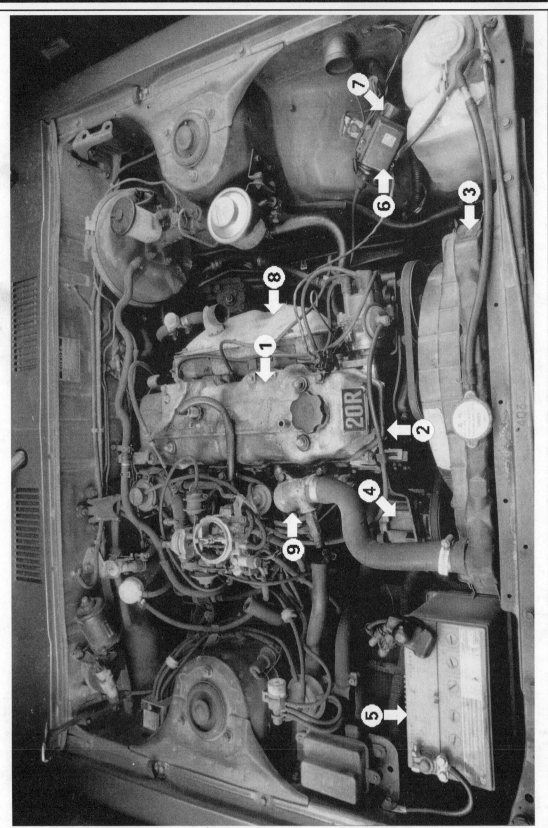

ENGINE COMPONENT LOCATIONS—20R ENGINE

1. Valve cover
2. Cylinder head
3. Radiator
4. Alternator
5. Battery
6. Igniter (on top of coil)
7. Ignition coil
8. Exhaust manifold heat shield
9. Thermostat housing

Description

8R-C AND 18R-C ENGINES

The 8R-C/18R-C family of four cylinder engines was used in the Mark II and the Corona in the early nineteen seventies.

The engine has an overhead cam, and aluminum head and a cast iron block. Displacement of the 8R-C engine is 1,858cc and was enlarged to 1,980cc (in 1972) to become the 18R-C engine.

20R AND 22R ENGINES

The 20R (2,189cc) four cylinder, overhead cam engine was introduced in 1975 and used in the Corona. Features included:

A gear driven oil pump

Single timing chain

Cross-flow head

Hemispherical combustion chambers

With an eye on the future, Toyota designed the engine to help control emissions by casting EGR and air injection passages in the aluminum head.

The 22R engine was introduced in 1981. Based on the 20R, the new engine has a displacement of 2,367cc, a higher compression ratio as well as other refinements which contribute to even better fuel economy than before.

2M, 4M, 4M-E AND 5M-E ENGINES

The M family of engines is the most sophisticated in the Toyota line. Their basic design is similar to that used in some European luxury cars, which they rival in smoothness and power.

These six cylinder, overhead cam engines (featuring cross-flow heads and hemispherical combustion chambers) first appeared in the luxury Crown series. The 2M (2.3 liter) engine was used until 1971. In 1971 the 4M (2.6 liter) engine was introduced and used, in various forms, until 1979. The 4M-E engine, used in the 1980 Cressida, featured electronic fuel injection and was replaced in 1981 by the new 5M-E (2.8 liter) electronic fuel injected engine.

Engine Overhaul Tips

Most engine overhaul procedures are fairly standard. In addition to specific parts replacement procedures and specifications for your individual engine, this section is also a guide to acceptable rebuilding procedures. Examples of standard rebuilding practice are given and should be used along with specific details concerning your particular engine.

Competent and accurate machine shop services will ensure maximum performance, reliability and engine life. In most instances it is more profitable for the do-it-yourself mechanic to remove, clean and inspect the component, buy the necessary parts and deliver these to a shop for actual machine work.

On the other hand, much of the rebuilding work (crankshaft, block, bearings, piston rods, and other components) is well within the scope of the do-it-yourself mechanic's tools and abilities. You will have to decide for yourself the depth of involvement you desire in an engine repair or rebuild.

TOOLS

The tools required for an engine overhaul or parts replacement will depend on the depth of your involvement. With a few exceptions, they will be the tools found in a mechanic's tool kit (see Section 1 of this manual). More in-depth work will require some or all of the following:

• A dial indicator (reading in thousandths) mounted on a universal base

• Micrometers and telescope gauges

• Jaw and screw-type pullers

• Scraper

• Valve spring compressor

• Ring groove cleaner

• Piston ring expander and compressor

• Ridge reamer

• Cylinder hone or glaze breaker

• Plastigage®

• Engine stand

The use of most of these tools is illustrated in this chapter. Many can be rented for a one-time use from a local parts jobber or tool supply house specializing in automotive work.

Occasionally, the use of special tools is called for. See the information on Special Tools and the Safety Notice in the front of this book before substituting another tool.

INSPECTION TECHNIQUES

Procedures and specifications are given in this chapter for inspecting, cleaning and assessing the wear limits of most major components. Other procedures such as Magnaflux® and Zyglo® can be used to locate material flaws and stress cracks. Magnaflux® is a magnetic process applicable only to ferrous materials. The Zyglo® process coats the material with a fluorescent dye penetrant and can be used on any material.

Checking for suspected surface cracks can be more readily made using spot check dye. The dye is sprayed onto the suspected area, wiped off and the area sprayed with a developer. Cracks will show up brightly.

OVERHAUL TIPS

Aluminum has become extremely popular for use in engines, due to its low weight. Observe the following precautions when handling aluminum parts:

• Never hot tank aluminum parts (the caustic hot tank solution will eat the aluminum.

• Remove all aluminum parts (identification tag, etc.) from engine parts prior to the tanking.

• Always coat threads lightly with engine oil or anti-seize compounds before installation, to prevent seizure.

• Never overtorque bolts or spark plugs especially in aluminum threads.

Stripped threads in any component can be repaired using any of several commercial repair kits (Heli-Coil®, Microdot®, Keen-serts®, etc.).

When assembling the engine, any parts that will be exposed to frictional contact must be prelubed to provide lubrication at initial start-up. Any product specifically formulated for this purpose can be used, but engine oil is not recommended as a prelube in most cases.

When semi-permanent (locked, but removable) installation of bolts or nuts is desired, threads should be cleaned and coated with Loctite® or another similar, commercial non-hardening sealant.

REPAIRING DAMAGED THREADS

Several methods of repairing damaged threads are available. Heli-Coil® (shown here), Keenserts® and Microdot® are among

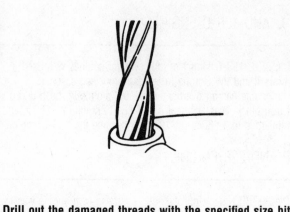

Drill out the damaged threads with the specified size bit. Be sure to drill completely through the hole or to the bottom of a blind hole

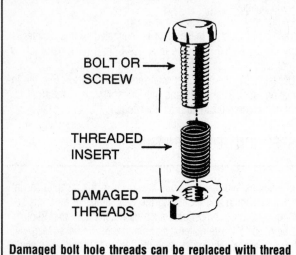

BOLT OR SCREW

THREADED INSERT

DAMAGED THREADS

Damaged bolt hole threads can be replaced with thread repair inserts

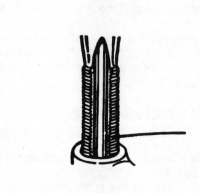

Using the kit, tap the hole in order to receive the thread insert. Keep the tap well oiled and back it out frequently to avoid clogging the threads

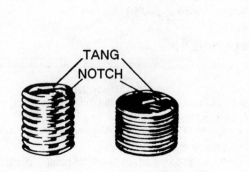

TANG

NOTCH

Standard thread repair insert (left), and spark plug thread insert

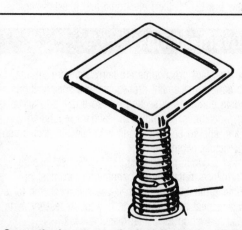

Screw the insert onto the installer tool until the tang engages the slot. Thread the insert into the hole until it is ¼–½ turn below the top surface, then remove the tool and break off the tang using a punch

the most widely used. All involve basically the same principle—drilling out stripped threads, tapping the hole and installing a pre-wound insert—making welding, plugging and oversize fasteners unnecessary.

Two types of thread repair inserts are usually supplied: a standard type for most inch coarse, inch fine, metric course and metric fine thread sizes and a spark lug type to fit most spark plug port sizes. Consult the individual tool manufacturer's catalog to determine exact applications. Typical thread repair kits will contain a selection of prewound threaded inserts, a tap (corresponding to the outside diameter threads of the insert) and an installation tool. Spark plug inserts usually differ because they require a tap equipped with pilot threads and a combined reamer/tap section. Most manufacturers also supply blister-packed thread repair inserts separately in addition to a master kit containing a variety of taps and inserts plus installation tools.

Before attempting to repair a threaded hole, remove any snapped, broken or damaged bolts or studs. Penetrating oil can be used to free frozen threads. The offending item can usually be removed with locking pliers or using a screw/stud extractor. After the hole is clear, the thread can be repaired, as shown in the series of accompanying illustrations and in the kit manufacturer's instructions.

Compression Testing

A noticeable lack of engine power, excessive oil consumption and/or poor fuel mileage measured over an extended period are all indicators of internal engine wear. Worn piston rings, scored or worn cylinder bores, leaking head gaskets, sticking or burnt valves and worn valve seats are all possible culprits here. A check of each cylinder's compression will help you locate the problems.

As mentioned in the Tools and Equipment part of Section 1, a screw-in type compression gauge is more accurate than the type you simply hold against the spark plug hole, although it takes slightly longer to use. It's worth it to obtain a more accurate reading. Follow the procedures below.

A screw-in type compression gauge is more accurate and easier to use without an assistant

1. Warm up the engine to normal operating temperature.
2. Remove all the spark plugs.
3. Disconnect the high tension lead (coil wire) from the ignition coil.
4. Fully open the throttle either by operating the carburetor throttle linkage by hand or by having an assistant floor the accelerator pedal.
5. Screw the compression gauge into the No. 1 spark plug hole until the fitting is snug.

✷✷ WARNING

Be careful not to crossthread the plug hole. On aluminum cylinder heads use extra care, as the threads in these heads are easily ruined.

6. Ask an assistant to depress the accelerator pedal fully on both carbureted and fuel injected vehicles. Then, while you read the compression gauge, ask the assistant to crank the engine two or three times in short bursts using the ignition switch.
7. Read the compression gauge at the end of each series of cranks, and record the highest of these readings. Repeat this procedure for each of the engine's cylinders. As a general rule, new motors will have compression on the order of 150–170 psi (1034–1172 kPa). This number will decrease with age and wear. The number of pounds of pressure that your test shows is not as important as the evenness between all the cylinders. Many engines run very well with all cylinders at 105 psi (724 kPa). The lower number simply shows a general deterioration internally. This motor probably burns a little oil and may be a bit harder to start, but, based on these numbers, doesn't warrant an engine tear-down yet. Compare the highest reading of all the cylinders. Any variation of more than 10% should be considered a sign of potential trouble. For example, on a 4 cylinder engine, if your compression readings for cylinders 1 through 4 were: 135 psi (930 kPa), 125 psi (861 kPa), 90 psi (620 kPa) and 125 psi (861 kPa), it would be fair to say that cylinder number three is not working efficiently and is almost certainly the cause of your oil burning, rough idle or poor fuel mileage.
8. If a cylinder is unusually low, pour a tablespoon of clean engine oil into the cylinder through the spark plug hole and repeat the compression test. If the compression comes up after adding the oil, it appears that the cylinder's piston rings or bore are damaged or worn. (The oil sealed some of the leakage.) If the pressure remains low, the valves may not be seating properly (a valve job is needed), or the head gasket may be blown near that cylinder. If compression in any two adjacent cylinders is low, and if the addition of oil doesn't help the compression, there is leakage past the head gasket. Oil and coolant in the combustion chamber can result from this problem. There may also be evidence of water droplets on the engine oil dipstick when a head gasket has blown.

General Engine Specifications

Year	Engine Type	Engine Cu In. Displacement (cm³/cu in.)	Carburetor Type	Horsepower @ rpm ①	Torque @ rpm (ft. lbs.) ①	Bore x Stroke (in.)	Compression Ratio
1970–71	8R-C	1,858/113.4	2-bbl	108 @ 5,500	113 @ 3,800	3.38 x 3.15	9.0:1
	2M	2,253/137.5	2-bbl	115 @ 5,200	117 @ 3,600	2.96 x 3.35	9.0:1
1972–74	18R-C	1,980/123.0	2-bbl	97 @ 5,500	106 @ 3,600	3.48 x 3.15	8.5:1
	2M ②	2,253/137.5	2-bbl	109 @ 5,200	120 @ 3,600	2.95 x 3.35	8.5:1
	4M	2,563/156.4	2-bbl	122 @ 5,200	141 @ 3,600	3.15 x 3.35	8.5:1
1975–77	20R	2,189/133.6	2-bbl	96 @ 4,800	120 @ 2,800	3.48 x 3.50	8.4:1
	4M	2,563/151.4	2-bbl	108 @ 5,000	130 @ 2,800	3.15 x 3.35	8.5:1
1978–79	4M	2,563/156.4	2-bbl	108 @ 5,000	134 @ 2,800	3.15 x 3.35	8.5:1
	20R	2,189/133.6	2-bbl	95 @ 4,800	122 @ 2,400	3.48 x 3.50	8.4:1
1980	4M-E	2,563/156.4	EFI	110 @ 4,800	136 @ 2,400	3.15 x 3.35	8.5:1
	20R	2,189/133.6	2-bbl	90 @ 4,800	122 @ 2,400	3.48 x 3.50	8.4:1
1981	22R	2,367/144.4	2-bbl	96 @ 4,800	129 @ 2,800	3.62 x 3.50	9.0:1
	5M-E	2,759/168.4	EFI	116 @ 4,800	145 @ 3,600	3.27 x 3.35	8.8:1
1982	5M-E	2,759/168.4	EFI	116 @ 4,800	145 @ 3,600	3.27 x 3.35	8.8:1

① Horsepower and torque ratings given in SAE net figures
② 2M engine not available 1973–74
EFI: Electronic fuel injection

Valve Specifications

Engine Type	Seat Angle (deg)	Face Angle (deg)	Spring Test Pressure (lbs.)		Spring Installed Height (in.)		Stem to Guide Clearance (in.) ▲		Stem Diameter (in.)	
			Inner	Outer	Inner	Outer	Intake	Exhaust	Intake	Exhaust
8R-C and 18R-C	45	45	15.2	50.6	1.480	1.640	0.0010–0.0022	0.0014–0.0030	0.3140	0.3136
2M	45	45	11.9	68.0 ①	1.535	1.654 ②	0.0006–0.0018	0.0014–0.0030	0.3153	0.3121
4M	45	44.5	25.7 ⑥	63.1 ③	1.504	1.642 ④	0.0006–0.0018	0.0010–0.0024	0.3146	0.3140
4M-E	45	44.5	15.6	41.6	1.49	1.63	0.0010–0.0024	0.0014–0.0028	0.3141	0.3137
20R	45	44.5	—	60.0 ⑤	—	1.594	0.0006–0.0024	0.0012–0.0026	0.3141	0.3140

▲ Valve guides are removable
① Exhaust valve spring test pressure: inner—11.5 lbs.; outer—66.6 lbs.
② Exhaust valve installed height: inner—1.535 in.; outer—1.661 in.
③ Exhaust valve spring test pressure: inner—24.6 lbs.; outer—59.4 lbs.
   1978–79 intake and exhaust: 41.9
④ Exhaust valve installed height: inner—1,520 in.; outer—1.657 in.
⑤ 1977–79: 55.1 lbs.
⑥ 1978–79: 15.5

Crankshaft and Connecting Rod Specifications
(All measurements are given in inches)

Engine Type	Crankshaft				Connecting Rod		
	Main Brg Journal Dia	Main Brg Oil Clearance	Shaft End-Play	Thrust on No.	Journal Diameter	Oil Clearance	Side Clearance
8R-C	2.3613–2.3622	0.0008–0.0020	0.0020–0.0100	3	2.0857–2.0866	0.0008–0.0020	0.0043–0.0097
18R-C	2.3613–2.3622	0.0008–0.0020	0.0008–0.0080	3	2.0857–2.0866	0.0010–0.0021	0.0060–0.0100
2M	2.3616–2.3622	0.0007–0.0017	0.0020–0.0170	4	2.0466–2.0472	0.0006–0.0020	0.0040–0.0100
4M, 4M-E	2.3617–2.3627	0.0012–0.0021	0.0020–0.0100	4	2.0463–2.0472	0.0008–0.0021	0.0020–0.0100 ②
20R	2.3614–2.3622	0.0010–0.0022	0.0008–0.0079 ①	3	2.0862–2.0866	0.0010–0.0022	0.0063–0.0100
5M-E	2.3617–2.3627	0.0013–0.0023	0.0020–0.0098	4	2.0463–2.0472	0.0008–0.0021	0.0063–0.0117

Dia—Diameter
Brg—Bearing
① 1978–79: 0.0010–0.0080
② 1978–79: 0.0063–0.0117

Piston and Ring Specifications
(All measurements in inches)

Year	Engine Type	Piston Clearance 68°F	Ring Gap			Ring Side Clearance		
			Top Compression	Bottom Compression	Oil Control	Top Compression	Bottom Compression	Control Oil
All	8R-C	0.0010–0.0020	0.004–0.012	0.004–0.012	0.004–0.012	0.0012–0.0028	0.0012–0.0028	0.0008–0.0028
All	18R-C	0.0020–0.0030	0.004–0.012	0.004–0.012	0.004–0.012	0.0012–0.0028	0.0012–0.0028	0.0008–0.0028
All	2M and 4M	0.0010–0.0020	0.006–0.014	0.006–0.014	0.008–0.020	0.0012–0.0028	0.0008–0.0024	—
1975	4M	0.0020–0.0030	0.004–0.011	0.004–0.011	0.008–0.020	0.0012–0.0028	0.0008–0.0024	—
1976–77	4M	0.0020–0.0030	0.006–0.012	0.003–0.020	0.007–0.040	0.0012–0.0014	0.0008–0.0024	—
1978–79	4M	0.0020–0.0030	0.0039–0.0110	0.0059–0.0110	0.007–0.040	0.0012–0.0014	0.0008–0.0035	—
All	4M-E	0.0020–0.0028	0.0039–0.0110	0.0039–0.0110	0.0079–0.0200	0.0012–0.0028	0.0008–0.0024	NA
All	20R	0.0012–0.0020	0.004–0.012	0.004–0.012	NA	0.008	0.008	NA
All	5M-E	0.0020–0.0028	0.0039–0.0110	0.0039–0.0110	0.0079–0.0200	0.0012–0.0028	0.0008–0.0024	Snug

NA—Not available

Torque Specifications
(All readings in ft. lbs.)

Engine Type	Cylinder Head Bolts	Rod Bearing Bolts	Main Bearing Bolts	Crankshaft Pulley Bolt	Flywheel to Crankshaft Bolts	Manifold	
						Intake	Exhaust
8R-C	75.0–85.0	42.0–48.0	72.0–80.0	43.0–51.0	42.0–49.0	20.0–25.0 ①	
18R-C	72.0–82.0	39.0–48.0	69.0–83.0	43.0–51.0	51.0–58.0	30.0–35.0 ①	
2M	②	25.0–30.0	72.0–79.0	43.0–51.0	41.0–46.0 ③	22.0–29.0 ④	18.0–25.0 ⑤
4M	⑥	30.0–36.0	72.0–78.0	69.0–76.0 ⑧⑪	41.0–46.0 ⑦⑫	17.0–21.0 ④	12.0–17.0 ⑤
4M-E	55–61 ⑥	31–34	72–78	98–119	51–57	10–15	13–16
20R	52.0–64.0	39.0–48.0	69.0–83.0	80.0–94.0 ⑨	62.0–68.0 ⑩	11.0–15.0	29.0–36.0
5M-E	55–61	31–34	72–78	98–119	51–57	10–15	13–16

① Intake and exhaust manifolds combined
② 8 mm bolts—11–14 ft. lbs.
  13 mm bolts—54–61 ft. lbs.
③ Flex-plate (automatic) 14–22 ft. lbs.
④ Intake manifold stud bolt—14–18 ft. lbs.
⑤ Exhaust manifold stud bolt—6–7 ft. lbs.
⑥ 8 mm bolts—7–12 ft. lbs.
⑦ 10 mm bolts—54–61 ft. lbs.
⑧ 1975–76—51–58 ft. lbs.
⑨ 1978–79—102–130
⑩ 1978–79—73–79
⑪ 1978–79—98–119
⑫ 1978–79—51–57

Engine

REMOVAL & INSTALLATION

▶ **See Figure 15**

These instructions provide for removal of the engine and transmission as a unit.

All operations involving hoisting the engine-transmission unit should be done with extreme care and should be carefully planned beforehand. Read the procedure through before beginning. It is best to use fender covers on both fenders and on the firewall cowl to protect the metal and paint form damage or scratches during removal or installation.

✳✳ CAUTION

Be sure to bleed the fuel system on fuel injected engines before disconnecting the fuel lines. (See chapter one, Fuel Filters). Before working underneath the car, be sure it is blocked and supported safely on jackstands.

1. Disconnect the battery cables, negative (ground) cable first. Remove the battery hold-down and the battery.
2. Mark the location of each hood hinge with a scribe, this will help you with alignment when reinstalling the hood.
3. Support the hood so that its weight is not on the hinge bolts. Then, remove the bolts. With the help of an assistant, remove the hood from the car and store in a safe place.
4. Remove the air cleaner assembly and mounting supports.
5. Drain the radiator, the engine crankcase, and the transmission fluid. On some models where splash shields interfere with easy access while working under the car, remove the shields.
6. If your car has an automatic transmission, disconnect and plug the cooler lines from the radiator.
7. Disconnect the radiator hoses from the radiator. On some six cylinder models, an auxiliary engine oil cooler is mounted on the radiator support, disconnect and remove it. Models that have an expansion tank: remove the hose to the radiator and remove the tank.
8. On some four cylinder models, it may be necessary to remove the radiator grille and headlight bezels.
9. Remove the radiator shroud, the hood lock base and support, the upper radiator supports and the condenser (models with air conditioning). Remove the radiator.

➡**On some models it may be possible to remove the radiator and shroud as an assembly.**

10. On some models with air conditioning, loosen the compressor mounting bolts and remove the drive belt. Unbolt the compressor and move it aside, but do not disconnect any of the refrigerant lines. If there is not enough slack in the lines (this may be the case on some older models), the system will have to be discharged and the lines disconnects.

✳✳ CAUTION

Please refer to Section 1 before discharging the compressor or disconnecting air conditioning lines. Damage to the air conditioning system or personal injury could result. Consult your local laws concerning refrigerant discharge and recycling. In many areas it may be illegal for anyone but a certified technician to service the A/C system. Always use an approved recovery station when discharging the air conditioning.

11. On models with power steering, loosen the mounting bolts and remove the drive belt. Remove the mounting bolts and move the pump away from the engine. Do not disconnect the power steering hoses unless there is not enough slack.
12. Disconnect the accelerator linkage on carbureted models.
13. Disconnect and label:
   a. battery ground cable at engine.
   b. starter wiring.
   c. coil to distributor high tension cable.
   d. primary wiring harness to the distributor.
   e. wire to temperature sender.
   f. all other sensor wire connectors.
   g. alternator wiring.
   h. choke heat wire or hoses connecting the choke housing.
   i. fuel lines: on fuel injected systems, bleed line at lower fuel filter hose before disconnecting (see chapter one, Fuel Filter).
   j. EGR solenoid connector wire, if equipped.
   k. all wiring harness and air hoses to the fuel injection.
   l. heater hoses.
   m. vacuum lines to the power brake unit from the intake manifold.
   n. all other wires harnesses and vacuum lines connected to the engine that would interfere with removal.
   o. heater control cable at valve, if equipped.
14. On cars equipped with an hydraulic clutch. Disconnect the line from the master cylinder to the slave cylinder and cap the line.
15. Remove the clutch slave cylinder (manual transmission).
16. Disconnect the speedometer cable from the transmission.
17. Disconnect the transmission control linkage or cross shaft, if equipped (column shift and automatic).
18. Disconnect the wiring to the neutral safety switch, or any other wiring or vacuum lines to the transmission that would interfere with removal.
19. Remove the shift lever (floor mounted controls). On some models it may be necessary to remove the center console.
20. To remove the center console: take out the mounting screws, remove the gear shift knob and the boot. Disconnect the wiring and lift the console off over the shift lever.
21. Remove the shift lever by loosening and removing the four mounting screws and lifting the lever form the shift tower.
22. Automatic transmission models with a floor mounted gear selector: unfasten the connecting rod swivel nut and detach the control rod from the gear selector lever.
23. Disconnect the parking brake lever rod, return spring, intermediate rod and the cable from the equalizer.
24. Disconnect the exhaust pipe from the exhaust manifold. Remove the front splash shield.

➡**On some models, it may be necessary to disconnect and remove the steering relay rod. If so, disconnect the idler arm from the frame, etc.**

25. Mark the driveshaft companion flange and the driveshaft (for installation in the same place). Disconnect the driveshaft at

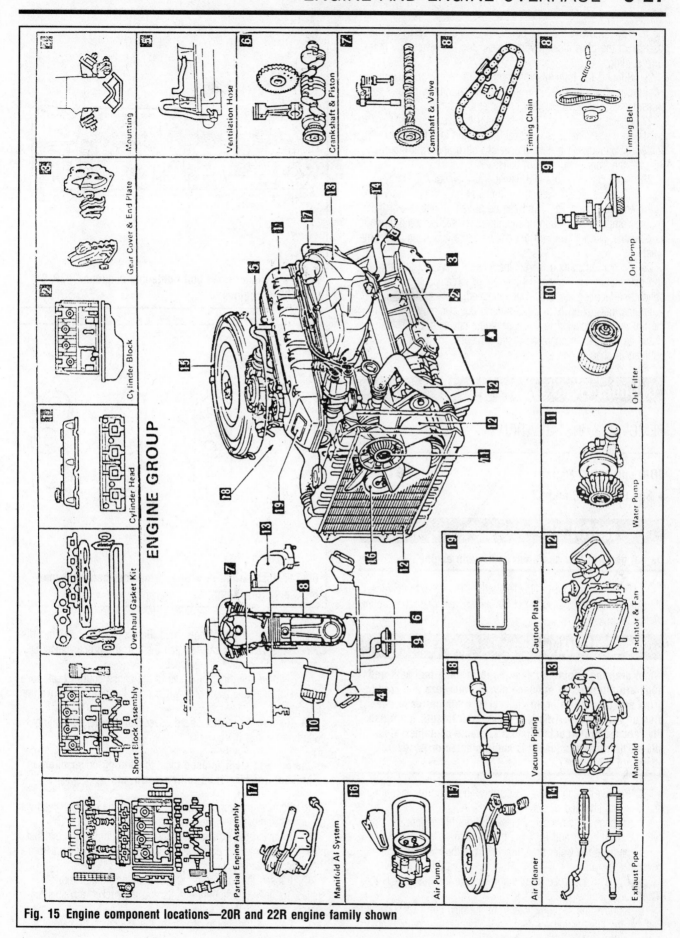

Fig. 15 Engine component locations—20R and 22R engine family shown

the rear by removing the four bolts. Remove the driveshaft. Plug the rear of the transmission with a clean rag to prevent any fluid form spilling.

26. Support the transmission carefully to remove all weight from the rear mounts. Remove the bolts securing the mounts and crossmember. Remove the rear crossmember and the mounts.

27. Attach an adequate cable or chain between the lifting points on the engine. Hook the cable or chain to a hoist and apply just enough lift to take the weight off of the front mounts. Remove the front motor mount bolts.

28. Work carefully to avoid damage to the engine or body parts. Tilt the engine, lowering the transmission as necessary, until the engine/transmission unit can be pulled up and out of the engine compartment. Mount the engine on a secure stand as soon as possible. Do not work on the engine while it is hanging on the hoist.

29. Before reinstalling the engine, carefully inspect the front and rear mounts. If any part of the mount is damaged or if the bonded surface is deteriorated or separated, replace the mount.

Engine installation is in the reverse order of removal. Adjust the linkages as detailed in the appropriate chapters. Bleed the clutch as outlined in chapter six and replenish the fluid levels as outlined in chapter one.

Cylinder Head

REMOVAL & INSTALLATION

8R-C and 18R-C Engines

♦ See Figures 16 and 17

✳✳ WARNING

Do not perform this operation on a warm engine.

1. Bring the engine to No. 1 cylinder TDC. (See the beginning of this chapter.) Disconnect the battery and drain the cooling system.

✳✳ CAUTION

When draining engine coolant, keep in mind that cats and dogs are attracted to ethylene glycol antifreeze and could drink any that is left in an uncovered container or in puddles on the ground. This will prove fatal in sufficient quantity. Always drain coolant into a sealable container. Coolant should be reused unless it is contaminated or is several years old.

2. Remove the air cleaner assembly, including the mounting brackets and attached hoses.

3. Disconnect the accelerator cable from the support on the cylinder head cover and from the throttle arm.

4. Remove the water hose bracket from the cylinder head cover.

5. Unfasten the hose clamps and remove the hoses from the water pump and water valve.

6. Remove the vacuum lines from the distributor vacuum unit. Remove the lines which run from various emission control compo-

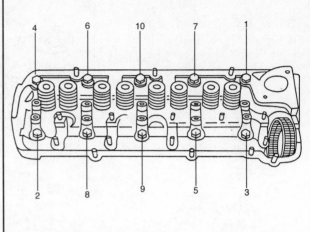

Fig. 16 Cylinder head bolt tightening sequence—8R-C and 18R-C engines

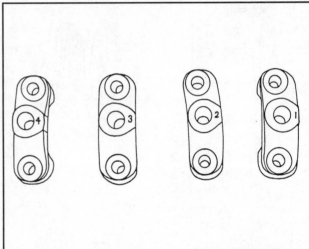

Fig. 17 Installation direction of the cam bearing caps—8R-C and 18R-C engines

nents mounted on the cylinder head. Be sure to label all lines disconnected so that you can reinstall them in the proper place. Disconnect the EGR valve, if equipped.

7. Remove the piper or hoses to the choke control heat stove.

8. Unfasten the spark plug wires from the plugs. Remove the spark plugs.

9. Remove the cylinder head cover (valve cover) mounting bolts and remove the cover.

➡Use a clean cloth, placed over the timing cover opening, to prevent anything from falling down into it.

10. Remove the upper radiator hose from the cylinder head water outlet. Remove the water outlet and the thermostat.

11. Unfasten the exhaust pipe mounting clamp at the exhaust manifold. Remove the combination intake/exhaust manifold from the cylinder head.

12. Loosen the rocker arm shaft mounting bolts, evenly in stages. Remove the mounting bolts and the rocker arm shaft assembly and oil delivery tube.

13. Remove the timing gear from the camshaft. Be careful to

support the gear and chain so they do not fall down into the timing cover.

14. Remove the camshaft bearing caps and the camshaft. Mark the bearing caps as to direction and position.

15. Remove the cam bearings from the head. Place them, in order, with the caps you just removed.

16. Separate the timing gear and chain. Fasten the chain so that it will not fall into the timing cover.

17. Loosen the head bolts in two or three stages (see sequence illustration). Remove the bolts, keep them in order of removal, they are different lengths and must be installed in the proper direction.

18. Lift the cylinder head from the engine block.

➡ **The head is positioned on dowels, do not try to slide it from the engine.**

To install:

Prior to installation, thoroughly clean the cylinder block and head mating surfaces. Refer to the Engine Rebuilding section (in this chapter) for details on checking the head and block for flatness, and other services that may be necessary.

19. Blow out the mounting bolt holes in the cylinder block, if air is available. If not, be sure the holes are clean and free of water.

20. Use a liquid sealer around the oil and water holes on both the head and block. Be careful not to get sealer in the passages or in the mounting bolt holes.

21. Place a new head gasket on the engine block and lower the cylinder head into position.

❋❋ WARNING

Do not slide the cylinder head across the block; lower it into position.

22. Tighten the cylinder head mounting bolts in proper sequence (see illustration) and in three or four stages. Tighten the bolts to the specifications given in the Torque Specifications chart.

23. Install the lower camshaft bearings into the seat from which they were removed. Install the camshaft and the bearing caps, numbers facing forward. Tighten the cap nuts to 12–17 ft. lb.

➡ **Cam bearings may be checked the same way as engine main and connecting rod bearings for oil clearance. Refer to the Engine Rebuilding section on how to use Plastigage®. The oil clearance should be 0.025–0.050mm; the end-play should be 0.043–0.167mm.**

24. If you did not have the engine at TDC when the cylinder head was removed or if the engine has been turned from TDC, realign the engine to No. 1 piston TDC (see beginning of this chapter).

25. Align the mark on the timing chain with the dowel hole on the camshaft timing gear and the stamped mark on the camshaft. All three marks should be aligned so that they are facing upward.

26. Install the chain and gear on the camshaft.

27. Install the rocker arm assembly. Tighten the mounting bolts to 12–17 ft. lb., in sequence and in two or three stages.

28. Attach the oil delivery tube to the rocker arm assembly and the camshaft bearing caps. Tighten the mounting bolts to 11–16 ft. lb.

29. Adjust the valve clearance as outlined in chapter two, to the following cold specifications:
Intake: 0.1778mm
Exhaust: 0.3302mm

30. The rest of the cylinder head installation is in the reverse order of removal. Change the engine oil before starting the engine because it could be contaminated by the coolant when the cylinder head was removed.

20R and 22R Engines

◆ **See Figures 18 thru 34 (p. 30–35)**

❋❋ WARNING

Do not perform this operation on a warm engine.

➡ **The cylinder head removal procedure that follows allows the intake and exhaust manifold to remain on the head. If you wish to remove them before the cylinder head, refer to the manifold removal section contained in this chapter.**

1. Disconnect the battery.

2. Remove the three exhaust pipe flange nuts and separate the pipe from the manifold.

3. Drain the cooling system (both radiator and block). If the coolant is to be reused, place a large, clean container underneath the drains.

❋❋ CAUTION

When draining engine coolant, keep in mind that cats and dogs are attracted to ethylene glycol antifreeze and could drink any that is left in an uncovered container or in puddles on the ground. This will prove fatal in sufficient quantity. Always drain coolant into a sealable container. Coolant should be reused unless it is contaminated or is several years old.

4. Remove the air cleaner assembly, complete with hoses, from the carburetor.

➡ **Cover the carburetor with a clean shop cloth so that nothing can fall into it.**

5. Mark all vacuum hoses to aid installation and disconnect them. Remove all linkages, fuel lines, etc., from the carburetor, cylinder head, and manifolds. Remove the wire supports.

6. Mark the spark plug leads and disconnect them from the plugs.

7. Matchmark the distributor housing and block. Disconnect the primary lead and remove the distributor. Installation will be easier if you leave the cap and leads in place.

8. Unfasten the four 14mm nuts which secure the valve cover.

9. Remove the rubber camshaft seals. Use a 19mm wrench to remove the cam sprocket bolt. Slide the distributor drive gear off the cam and wire the cam sprocket in place.

10. Remove the 14mm bolt at the front of the head that connects the head to the timing cover. This must be done before the head bolts are removed.

11. Remove the cylinder head bolts in the order shown. Improper removal could cause head damage.

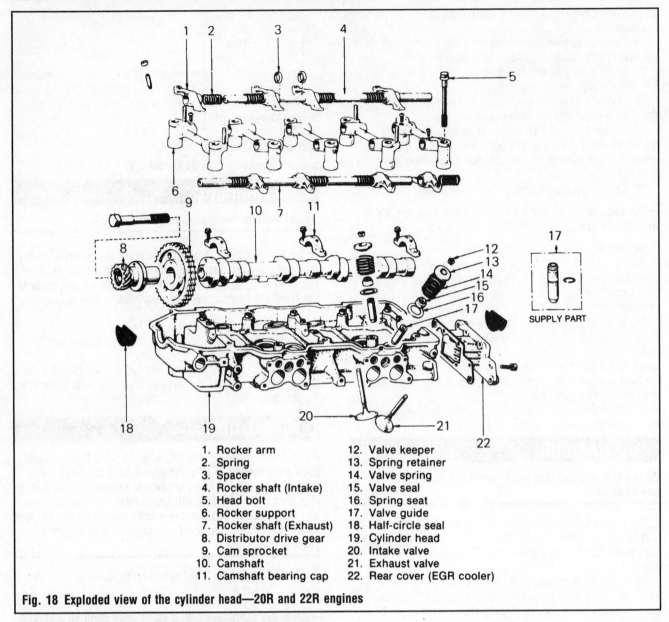

1. Rocker arm
2. Spring
3. Spacer
4. Rocker shaft (Intake)
5. Head bolt
6. Rocker support
7. Rocker shaft (Exhaust)
8. Distributor drive gear
9. Cam sprocket
10. Camshaft
11. Camshaft bearing cap
12. Valve keeper
13. Spring retainer
14. Valve spring
15. Valve seal
16. Spring seat
17. Valve guide
18. Half-circle seal
19. Cylinder head
20. Intake valve
21. Exhaust valve
22. Rear cover (EGR cooler)

Fig. 18 Exploded view of the cylinder head—20R and 22R engines

To remove the cylinder head, begin by removing the distributor from the engine

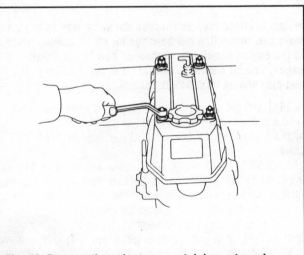

Fig. 19 Remove the valve cover retaining nuts and washers—20R and 22R engines

Remove the valve cover and gasket from the cylinder head

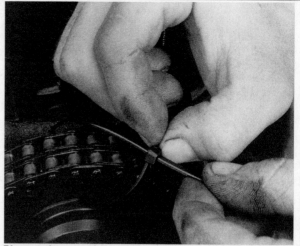

Place a tie around the chain to keep it in place during camshaft sprocket removal

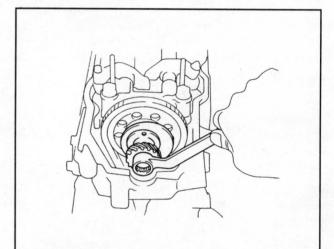

Fig. 21 Place a wrench on the camshaft sprocket bolt— 20R and 22R engines

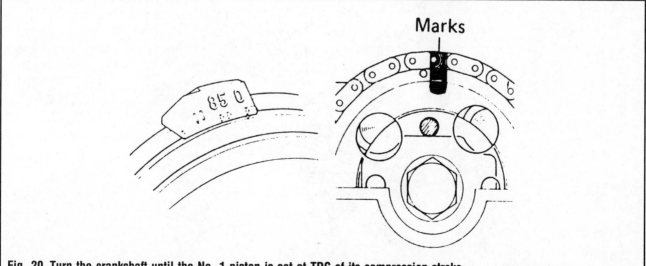

Fig. 20 Turn the crankshaft until the No. 1 piston is set at TDC of its compression stroke

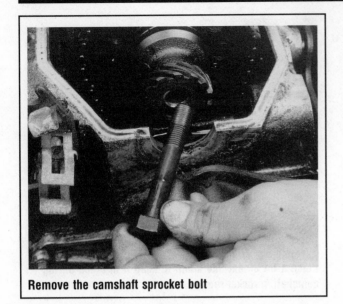

Remove the camshaft sprocket bolt

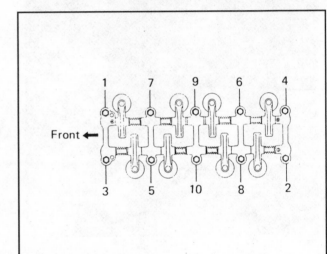

Fig. 24 Remove the bolt at the front of the cylinder head first—20R and 22R engines

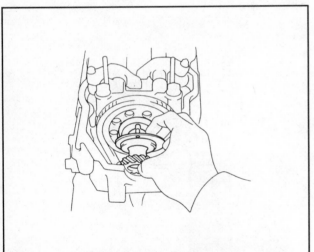

Fig. 22 Remove the distributor drive gear and camshaft thrust plate—20R and 22R engines

Fig. 25 Remove the cylinder head bolts in this sequence—20R and 22R engines

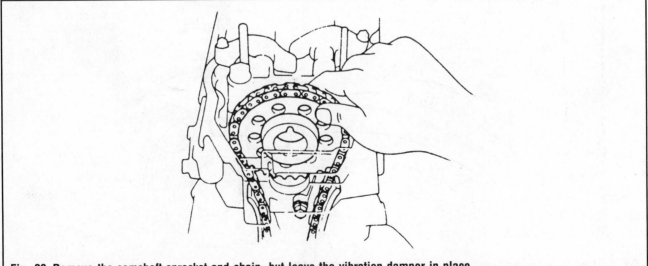

Fig. 23 Remove the camshaft sprocket and chain, but leave the vibration damper in place

Lift the rocker arm assembly out of the cylinder head—20R engine shown

Place rags in each cylinder to prevent gasket material from falling in

Remove the head gasket . . .

The cylinder head can now be removed from the engine block

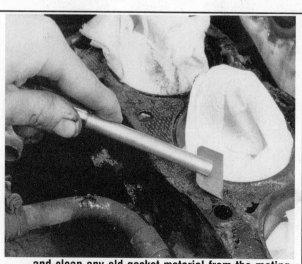

. . . and clean any old gasket material from the mating surface of the cylinder block

Use a torque wrench to tighten the cylinder head bolts

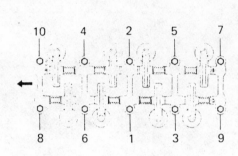

Fig. 27 Tighten the cylinder head bolts in three passes using this sequence—20R and 22R engines

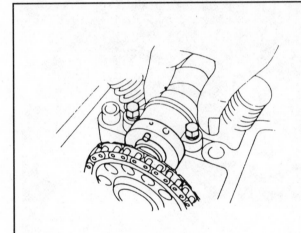

Fig. 28 Turn the camshaft to position the dowel pin at the top—20R and 22R engine

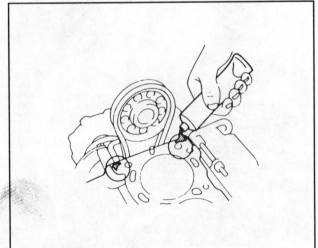

Fig. 26 Apply sealer to the two spots on the block as shown

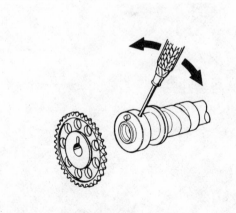

Fig. 29 If the chain is not long enough, turn the camshaft back and forth while pulling up on the chain and sprocket

Fig. 30 Set the No. 1 piston to TDC of its compression stroke—20R and 22R engines

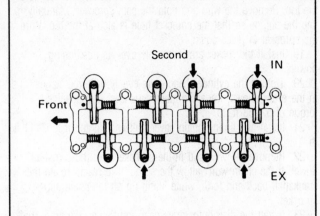

Fig. 33 Turn the crankshaft one revolution, then adjust the other valves

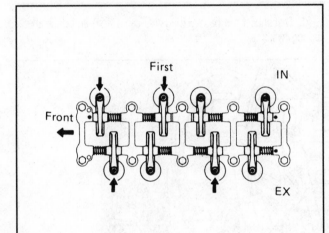

Fig. 31 Adjust the valve clearance, beginning with the valves indicated

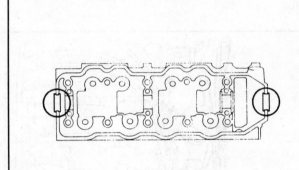

Fig. 34 Install the half moon seals on the ends of the cylinder head—20R and 22R engines

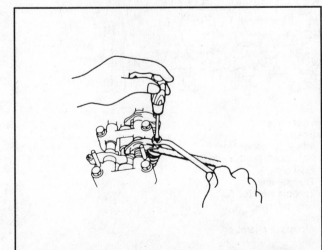

Fig. 32 Loosen the locknut and turn the adjusting screw to set the proper clearance—20R and 22R engines

12. Remove the rocker arm shaft assembly. It may be necessary to pry it from the mounting dowel. Using prybars applied evenly at the front and the rear of the valve rocker assembly, pry the assembly off its mounting dowels.

13. Lift the head off its dowels. Do NOT pry it off.

14. Support the head solidly on a work bench and remove the intake and exhaust manifolds.

15. Drain the engine oil from the crankcase after the head has been removed, because the oil will become contaminated with coolant while the head is being removed.

Prior to installation, thoroughly clean the cylinder block and head mating surfaces. Refer to the Engine Rebuilding section (in this chapter) for details on checking the head and block for flatness, and other services that may be necessary.

To install:

16. Apply liquid sealer to the front corners of the block and install the head gasket.

17. Lower the head over the locating dowels. Do not attempt to slide it into place.

18. Rotate the camshaft so that the sprocket aligning pin is at the top. Remove the wire and hold the cam sprocket. Manually rotate the engine so that the sprocket hole is also at the top. Wire the sprocket in place again.

19. Install the rocker arm assembly over its positioning dowels.

20. Tighten the cylinder head bolts evenly, in three stages, and in the order shown, under Torque Sequences, to a specified torque of 52–63 ft. lb.

21. Install the timing chain cover bolt and tighten it to 7–11 ft. lb.

22. Remove the wire and fit the sprocket over the camshaft dowel. If the chain won't allow the sprocket to reach, rotate the crankshaft back and forth, while lifting up on the chain and sprocket.

23. Install the distributor drive gear and tighten the crankshaft bolt to 51–65 ft. lb.

24. Set the No. 1 piston to TDC of its compression stroke and adjust the valves as outlined in Chapter 2.

25. After completing valve adjustments, rotate the crankshaft 352 degrees, so that the 8 degree BTDC mark on the pulley aligns with the pointer.

26. Install the distributor, as outlined in the beginning of this chapter.

27. Install the spark plugs and leads.

28. Make sure that the oil drain plug is installed. Fill the engine with oil after installing the rubber cam seals. Pour the oil over the distributor drive gear and the valve rockers.

29. Install the rocker cover and tighten the bolts to 8–11 ft. lb.

30. Connect all the vacuum hoses and electrical leads which were removed during disassembly. Install the spark plug lead supports. Fill the cooling system. Install the air cleaner.

31. Tighten the exhaust pipe-to-manifold flange bolts to 25–33 ft. lb.

32. Reconnect the battery. Start the engine and allow it to reach normal operating temperature. Check and adjust the timing and valve clearance. Adjust the idle speed and mixture. Road test the vehicle.

M Series

▶ See Figures 35 thru 43

✷✷ WARNING

Do not perform this operation on a warm engine.

1. Disconnect the battery (negative cable first) and drain the cooling system.

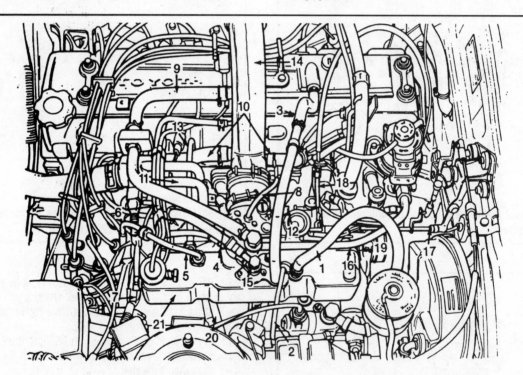

1. Hose	12. Water hose
2. Hose	13. Hose
3. Hose (for PCV)	14. Intake air connector
4. Hose	15. Cold start injector w/gasket
5. Hose	16. EGR pipe
6. Hose (for Idle-up)	17. Throttle link
7. Wiring	18. Throttle wire for A/T
8. Hose	19. Ground wire
9. Hose	20. Hose
10. Hose	21. Air intake chamber
11. Water hose	

Fig. 35 Before removing the air intake chamber, remove the hoses in numerical order (as per this diagram)—4M-E and 5M-E engines

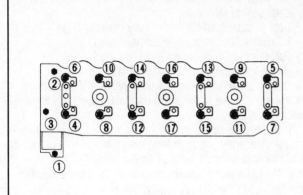

Fig. 36 Cylinder head bolt removal sequence—2M engine

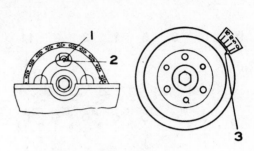

1. Valve timing mark (5/32 in. hole)
2. V-notch—camshaft flange
3. V-notch—crankshaft pulley

Fig. 39 Crankshaft and camshaft timing marks—4M-E and 5M-E engines

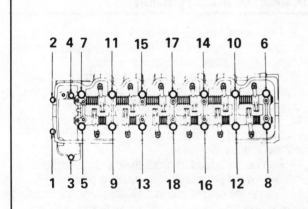

Fig. 37 Cylinder head bolt removal sequence—4M engine

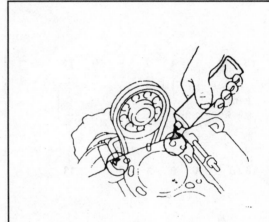

Fig. 40 Apply sealer to the two spots on the block as shown

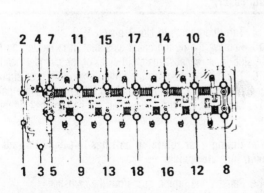

Fig. 38 Cylinder head bolt removal sequence—4M-E and 5M-E engines

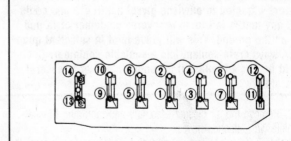

Fig. 41 Cylinder head bolt tightening sequence—2M engine

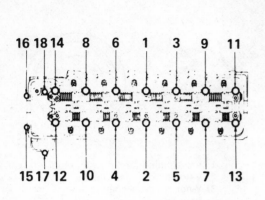

Fig. 42 Cylinder head bolt tightening sequence—4M-E engine

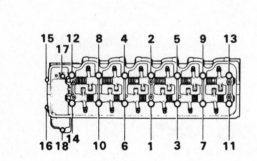

Fig. 43 Cylinder head bolt tightening sequence—5M-E engine

✳✳ CAUTION

When draining engine coolant, keep in mind that cats and dogs are attracted to ethylene glycol antifreeze and could drink any that is left in an uncovered container or in puddles on the ground. This will prove fatal in sufficient quantity. Always drain coolant into a sealable container. Coolant should be reused unless it is contaminated or is several years old.

2. Remove the air cleaner assembly and mounting brackets, complete with attached hoses.

3. Mark (for identification) and disconnect the hoses from the air injection system and the vacuum switching valve (if equipped).

4. Disconnect the following:
• Accelerator cable from both the support on the cylinder head and the throttle arm.
• The automatic transmission linkage connected to the carburetor and intake manifold.

• The water hoses, upper and lower, from the engine, and from the heater control valve.
• Control cable from the heater valve control.
• PCV valve hose to the cylinder head cover.
• Fuel lines to the carburetor.
• Choke lines and/or hoses to the choke.
• Disconnect all other vacuum lines, hoses and wire connectors that are attached to the intake manifold. Label them for identification.

5. Remove the intake manifold mounting nuts/bolts starting from the outer ends and alternating toward the center. Remove the intake manifold and carburetor as an assembly.

6. On fuel injected models, disconnect the battery (negative cable first) and drain the cooling system. Remove the radiator hoses and heater hoses attached to the cylinder head or manifolds.

7. On fuel injected models, refer to the illustration provided and disconnect or remove the parts in the numerical order shown.

✳✳ WARNING

The fuel system is under pressure. Refer to chapter one, Fuel Filters, for bleeding procedure.

8. Remove the intake air chamber (manifold) mounting nuts/bolts starting from the outer ends and alternating toward the center. Remove the chamber and injector as a unit.

9. Remove the spark plug wires from the spark plugs and from the wire supports that are mounted on the cylinder head cover. Remove the spark plugs from the cylinder head.

10. Disconnect the various lines/hoses to, or that would interfere, with removing the exhaust manifold. Once again label any hoses/lines that are removed.

11. Remove the exhaust manifold shield (if equipped) and loosen and remove the exhaust pipe mounting bolts/nuts.

12. Remove the exhaust manifold by unfastening the mounting bolts/nuts. Start from the outer ends and work your way toward the center, alternating as you go.

13. Unfasten the retaining bolts that hold the cylinder head cover (valve cover) to the head. Remove the valve cover.

✳✳ WARNING

Take care not to drop any bolts, nuts, etc. into the timing chain cover.

14. Turn the engine to No. 1 piston TDC.

15. Remove the timing chain tensioner. It is located on the right side front (exhaust manifold side) of the cylinder head.

16. The match marks on the timing chain and gear should be aligned. It might be helpful to highlight them with some paint.

17. Straighten out the locking tab on the camshaft timing gear retaining bolt. Remove the bolt.

➡**The timing gear retaining bolt has left-hand threads. To loosen turn clockwise.**

18. Remove the timing gear from the camshaft.

19. Loosen and remove the rocker arm shaft mounting bolts. Follow the sequence shown, uniformly loosening them in two or three passes.

20. Remove the rocker arm shaft assembly.

21. Remove the camshaft bearing caps, keep them in order (mark the caps so they cannot get mixed up). Remove the camshaft.

22. Loosen and remove the cylinder head mounting bolts. Follow the sequence shown, uniformly loosening them in two or three passes.

23. Lift the cylinder head from the engine block. Locating dowel pins are installed in the front and the rear of the engine, making it impossible to slide off the head.

Prior to installation, thoroughly clean the cylinder block and head mating surfaces.

To install:

24. Blow out the mounting bolt holes in the cylinder block, if air is available. If not, be sure the holes are clean and free of water.

25. Use a liquid sealer around the oil and water holes on both the head and the block and on the timing cover upper surfaces. Be careful not to get sealer in the passages or in the mounting holes.

26. Place a new head gasket on the engine block and lower the cylinder head into position.

27. Tighten the cylinder head mounting bolts in proper sequence (see illustration) and in three or four stages. Tighten the bolts to the specifications given in the Torque Specifications chart.

28. Install the lower camshaft bearings if removed. Install the camshaft and bearing caps. Tighten the cap nuts to 12–17 ft. lb.

➡**Cam bearings may be checked the same way as engine main and connecting rod bearings for oil clearance. Refer to the Engine Rebuilding section on how to use Plastigage®. Oil clearance limit is 0.099mm; end-play limit is 0.304mm.**

29. Install the rocker arm shaft assembly. Tighten the mounting bolts to 12–17 ft. lb., in sequence and in two or three stages.

30. Make sure that the engine has not been turned from No. 1 piston TDC. The crankshaft pulley should have its V notch aligned with the zero mark on the timing cover scale.

31. Align the V-notch on the camshaft with the 4mm hole on the No. 1 camshaft bearing cap, or the pin on the camshaft flange with the embossed pointer on the No. 1 rocker shaft support.

32. Install the timing chain (marked link up) on the camshaft gear (mark on gear aligned with marked link) and install on the end of the camshaft. Align the pin on the camshaft flange with the hole in the cam gear.

33. Install the timing gear bolt (left-hand thread) with the locking tab. Bolt torque is 47–54 ft. lb.

34. Install the timing chain tensioner. Tighten to 22–29 ft. lb.

35. Turn the crankshaft two complete revolutions. If, at the end of the two revolutions, the timing marks do not align, repeat steps 30 through 34. If they still will not align, see step 37.

36. Adjust the timing chain tensioner. Turn the crankshaft in the regular direction until there is a maximum amount of slack in the chain. Loosen the locknut on the tensioner and turn the screw clockwise until resistance is felt. Loosen the screw two turns and tighten the locknut.

➡**If the timing marks do not align after once again turning the engine two complete revolutions the chain could be stretched. Toyota has provided other pin holes in the cam gear to correct this problem.**

37. If the crankshaft pulley notch will not align with the zero mark while the cam gear and chain are aligned with the rocker arm support, remove and reposition the cam gear to the second pin hole position. Recheck crankshaft timing marks.

38. Adjust the valve clearance, as outlined in chapter two, to the following cold specifications:
Intake: 0.15mm
Exhaust: 0.20mm

39. The rest of the cylinder head installation is in the reverse order of removal.

➡**Before starting the engine, change the motor oil. The old oil could be contaminated from coolant.**

CLEANING & INSPECTION

When the rocker assembly and valve train have been removed from the cylinder head (see Valves and Springs, later in this section), set the head on two wooden blocks on the bench, combustion chamber side up. Using a scraper or putty knife, carefully

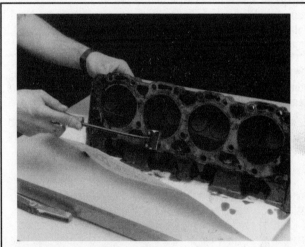

Use a gasket scraper to remove the bulk of the old head gasket from the mating surface

An electric drill equipped with a wire wheel will expedite complete gasket removal

scrape away any gasket material that may have stuck to the head-to-block mating surface when the head was removed. Make sure you DO NOT gouge the mating surface with the tool.

Only use a wire brush on cast iron heads. Using a wire brush chucked into your electric drill, remove the carbon in each combustion chamber. Make sure the brush is actually removing the carbon and not merely burnishing it.

Clean all the valve guides using a valve guide brush (available at most auto parts or auto tool shops) and solvent. A fine-bristled rifle bore cleaning brush also works here.

Inspect the threads of each spark plug hole by screwing a plug into each, making sure it screws down completely. Heli-coil® any plug hole this is damaged.

✳✳ WARNING

DO NOT hot tank the cylinder head! The head material on most Toyota engines is aluminum, which is ruined if subjected to the hot tank solution. Some of the early 8R-C and 18-R engines were equipped with cast iron heads, which can be hot-tanked (a service performed by most machine shops in which the head is immersed in a hot, caustic solution for cleaning). To be sure your engine's cylinder head is aluminum, check around its perimeter with a magnet. Your engine has an iron head if the magnet sticks.

➡**Before hot-tanking any overhead cam head, check with the machine shop doing the work. Some cam bearings are easily damaged by the hot tank solution.**

Finally, go over the entire head with a clean shop rag soaked in solvent to remove any grit, old gasket particles, etc. Blow out the bolt holes, coolant galleys, intake and exhaust ports, valve guides and plug holes with compressed air.

While the cylinder head is removed, the top of the cylinder block and pistons should also be cleaned. Before you begin, rotate the crankshaft until one or more pistons are flush with the top of the block (on the four cylinder engines, you will either have Nos. 1 and 4 up, or Nos. 2 and 3 up). Carefully stuff clean rags into the cylinders in which the pistons are down. This will help keep grit and carbon chips out during cleaning. Using care not to gouge or scratch the block-to-head mating surface and the piston top(s), clean away any old gasket material with a wire brush and/or scraper. On the piston tops, make sure you are actually removing the carbon and not merely burnishing it.

Remove the rags from the down cylinders after you have wiped the top of the block with a solvent soaked rag. Rotate the crankshaft until the other pistons come up flush with the top of the block, and clean those pistons.

➡**Because you have rotated the crankshaft, you will have to re-time the engine following the procedure listed under the Timing Chain/Timing Belt removal. Make sure you wipe out each cylinder thoroughly with a solvent-soaked rag, to remove all traces of grit, before the cylinder head is reassembled to the block.**

RESURFACING

While the head is removed, check the head-to-block mating surface for straightness. If the engine has overheated and blown a head gasket, this must be done as a matter of course. A warped

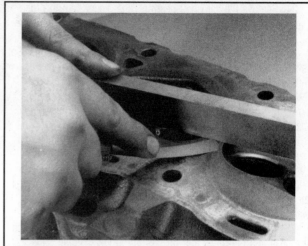

Check the cylinder head for flatness across the head surface

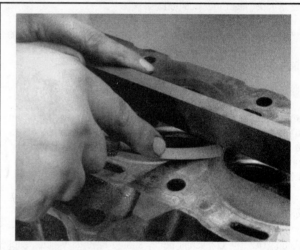

Checks should be made both straight across the cylinder head and at both diagonals

mating surface must be resurfaced (milled); this is done on a milling machine and is quite similar to planing a piece of wood.

Using a precision steel straightedge and a blade-type feeler gauge, check the surface of the head across its length, width and diagonal length as shown in the illustrations. Also check the intake and exhaust manifold mating surfaces and valve cover (all) mating surfaces. If warpage exceed 0.003 inch (0.076mm) in a 6 inch (152mm) span, or 0.006 inch (0.152mm) over the total length, the head must be milled. If warpage is highly excessive, the head must be replaced. Again, consult the machine shop operator on head milling limitations.

Valves and Springs

ADJUSTMENT (AFTER ENGINE SERVICE)

The valves on all engines covered and must be adjusted following any valve train disassembly. Follow the procedure given in Section 2 for Valve Lash adjustment.

REMOVAL & INSTALLATION

A valve spring compressor is needed to remove the valves and springs; these are available at most auto parts and auto tool shops. A small magnet is very helpful for removing the keepers and spring seats.

Set the head on its side on the bench. Install the spring compressor so that the fixed side of the tool is flat against the valve head in the combustion chamber, and the screw side is against the retainer. Slowly turn the screw in towards the head, compressing the spring. As the spring compresses, the keepers will be revealed; pick them off of the valve stem with the magnet as they are easily fumbled and lost. When the keepers are removed, back the screw out and remove the retainers and springs. Remove the compressor and pull the valves out of the head from the other

A magnet may be helpful in removing the valve keepers

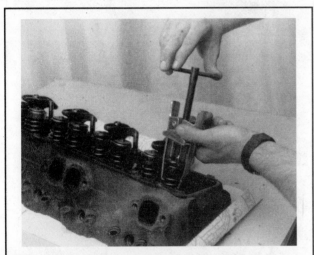

Use a valve spring compressor tool to relieve spring tension from the valve caps

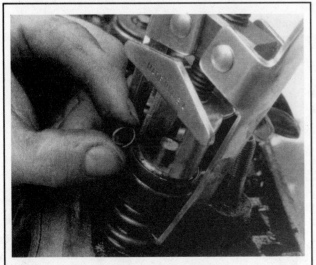

Be careful not to lose the valve keepers

side. Remove the valve seals by hand and remove the spring seats with the magnet.

Since it is very important that each valve and its spring, retainer, spring seat and keepers is reassembled in its original location, you must keep these parts in order. The best way to do this to to cut either eight (four cylinder) or twelve (six cylinder) holes in a piece of heavy cardboard or wood. Label each hole with the cylinder number and either IN or EX, corresponding to the location of each valve in the head. As you remove each valve, insert it into the holder, and assemble the seats, springs, keepers and retainers to the stem on the labeled side of the holder. This way each valve and its attending parts are kept together, and can be put back into the head in their proper locations.

After lapping each valve into its seat (see Valve Lapping below), oil each valve stem, and install each valve into the head in the reverse order of removal, so that all parts except the keepers

Remove the spring from the valve stem in order to access the seal

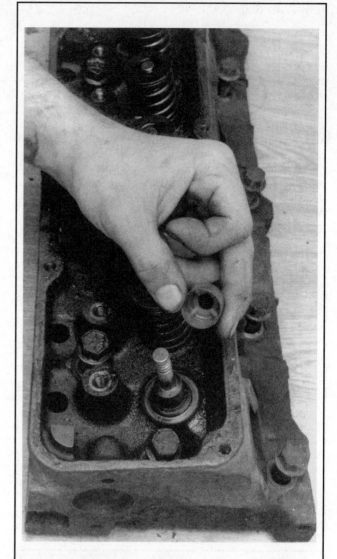

Remove the valve stem seal from the cylinder head

are assembled on the stem. Always use new valve stem seals. Install the spring compressor, and compress the retainer and spring until the keeper groove on the valve stem is fully revealed. Coat the groove with a wipe of grease (to hold the keepers until the retainer is released) and install both keepers, wide end up. Slowly back the screw of the compressor out until the spring retainer covers the keepers. Remove the tool. Lightly tap the end of each valve stem with a rubber hammer to ensure proper fit of the retainers and keepers.

INSPECTION

▶ **See Figures 44 and 45**

Before the valves can be properly inspected, the stem, lower end of the stem and the entire valve face and head must be cleaned. An old valve works well for chipping carbon from the valve head, and a wire brush, gasket scraper or putty knife can be used for cleaning the valve face and the area between the face

Invert the cylinder head and withdraw the valve from the cylinder head bore

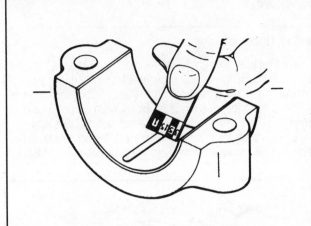

Fig. 44 Carefully scrape the carbon from the valve's head during inspection

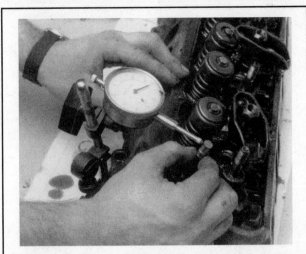

A dial gauge may be used to check valve stem-to-guide clearance

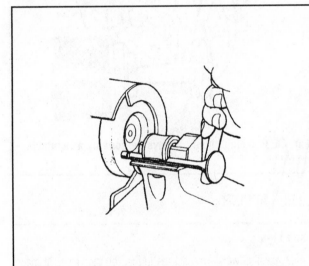

Fig. 45 The valve stem tip can be ground if necessary

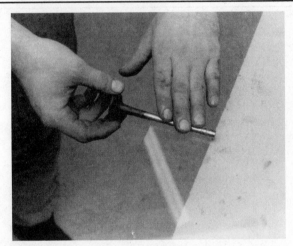

Valve stems may be rolled on a flat surface to check for bends

and lower stem. Do not scratch the valve face during cleaning. Clean the entire stem with a rag soaked in thinners to remove all varnish and gum.

Thorough inspection of the valves requires the use of a micrometer, and a dial indicator is needed to measure the inside diameter of the valve guides. If there instruments are not available to you, the valves and head can be taken to a reputable machine ship for inspection. Refer to the Valve Specifications chart for valve stem and stem-to-guide specifications.

If the above instruments are at your disposal, measure the diameter of each valve stem at the locations illustrated. Jot these measurements down. Using the dial indicator, measure the inside diameter of the valve guides at their bottom, top and midpoint 90° apart. Jot these measurements down also. Subtract the valve stem measurement from the valve guide inside measurement; if the clearance exceed that listed in the specifications chart under Stem-to-Guide Clearance, replace the valve(s). Stem-to-guide clearance can also be checked at a machine shop, where a dial indicator would be used.

Check the top of each valve stem for pitting and unusual wear

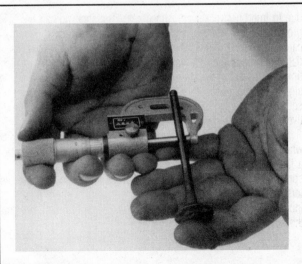

Use a micrometer to check the valve stem diameter

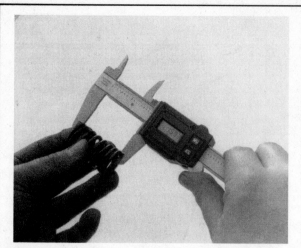

Use a caliper gauge to check the valve spring free-length

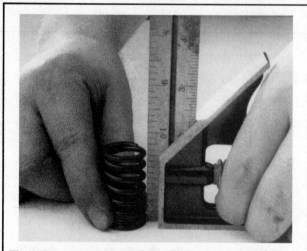

The valve spring should be straight up and down when placed like this

due to improper rocker adjustment, etc. The stem tip can be ground flat if it is worn, but no more than 0.020 inch (0.50mm) can be removed; if this limit must be exceeded to make the tip flat and square, then the valve must be replaced. If the valve stem tips are ground, make sure you fix the valve securely into a jig designed for this purpose, so the tip contacts the grinding wheel squarely at exactly 90°. Most machine shops that handle automotive work are equipped for this job.

Valve spring squareness, length and tension should be checked while the valve train is disassembled. Place each valve spring on a flat surface next to a steel square. Measure the length of the spring, and rotate it against the edge of the square to measure distortion. If spring length varies (by comparison) by more than 1/16 inch (1.5mm) or if distortion exceeds 1/16 inch (1.5mm), replace the spring.

Spring tension must be checked on a spring tester.

REFACING

◆ See Figure 46

Valve refacing should only be handled by a reputable machine shop, as the experience and equipment needed to do the job are beyond that of the average owner/mechanic. During the course of a normal valve job, refacing is necessary when simply lapping the valves into their seats will not correct the seat and face wear. When the valves are reground (resurfaced), the valve seats must also be recut, again requiring special equipment and experience.

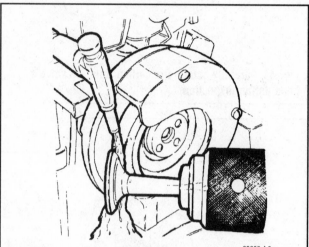

Fig. 46 Refacing should always be done by a reputable machine shop

VALVE LAPPING

◆ See Figure 47

After machine work has been performed on the valves, it may be necessary to lap the valves to assure proper contact with their seats. You should first contact your machine shop to determine if lapping is necessary. Some machine shops will perform this as

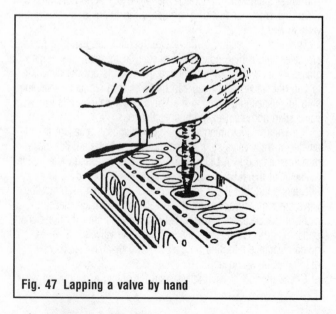

Fig. 47 Lapping a valve by hand

part of their service, but the precision machining which is available today often makes lapping unnecessary. Additionally, the hardened valves and seats used in modern automobiles may make lapping difficult or impossible. If your machine shop does recommend that you lap the valves, proceed as follows:

1. Set the cylinder head on the workbench, combustion chamber side up. Rest the head on wooden blocks on either end, so there are two or three inches between the tops of the valve guides and the bench.

2. Lightly lube the valve stem with clean engine oil. Coat the valve seat completely with valve grinding compound. Use just enough compound that the full width and circumference of the seat are covered.

3. Install the valve in its proper location in the head. Attach the suction cup end of the valve lapping tool to the valve head. It usually helps to put a small amount of saliva into the suction cup to aid it sticking to the valve.

4. Rotate the tool between the palms, changing position and lifting the tool often to prevent grooving. Lap the valve in until a smooth, evenly polished seat and valve face are evident.

5. Remove the valve from the head. Wipe away all traces of grinding compound from the valve face and seat. Wipe out the port with a solvent soaked rag, and swab out the valve guide with a piece of solvent soaked rag to make sure there are no traces of compound grit inside the guide. This cleaning is important.

6. Proceed through the remaining valves, one at a time. Make sure the valve faces, seats, cylinder ports and valve guides are clean before reassembling the valve train.

Valve Seats

The valve seats in the engines covered in this guide are all non-replaceable, and must be recut when service is required. Seat recutting requires a special tool and experience, and should be handled at a reputable machine shop. Seat concentricity should also be checked by a machinist.

Valve Guides

INSPECTION

Valve guides should be cleaned as outlined earlier, and checked when valve stem diameter and stem-to-guide clearance is checked. Generally, if the engine is using oil through the guides (assuming the valve seals are OK) and the valve stem diameter is within specification, it is the guides that are worn and need replacing.

Valve guides which are not excessively worn or distorted may, in some cases, are knurled rather than replaced. Knurling is a process in which metal inside the valve guide bore is displaced and raised (forming a very fine cross-hatch pattern), thereby reducing clearance. Knurling also provides for excellent oil control. The possibility of knurling rather than replacing the guides should be discussed with a machinist.

REPLACEMENT

1. Heat the cylinder head to 176–212°F, evenly, before beginning the replacement procedure.

2. Use a brass rod to break the valve guide off above its snapring. (See the illustration).

3. Drive out the valve guide, toward the combustion chamber. Use a tool fabricated as described in the Engine Rebuilding section.

4. Install a snapring on the new valve guide. Apply liquid sealer. Drive in the valve guide until the snapring contacts the head. Use the tool previously described.

5. Measure the guide bore. If the stem-to-guide clearance is below specification, ream it out, using a valve guide reamer.

Rocker Shafts

REMOVAL & INSTALLATION

▶ **See Figures 47a, 47b, 47c**

Valve rocker shaft removal and installation is given as part of the various Cylinder Head Removal and Installation procedures. Perform only the steps of the appropriate Cylinder Head Re-

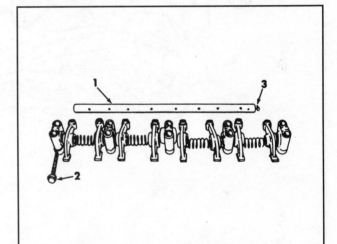

Fig. 47a Single rocker shaft assembly. Note the attaching bolts (2) and shaft retaining screw (3)

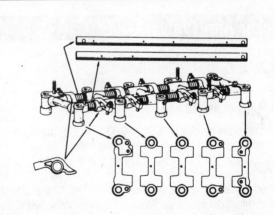

Fig. 47b Double rocker shaft assembly used on 20R and 22R engines; the rocker arms must be assembled in their original positions

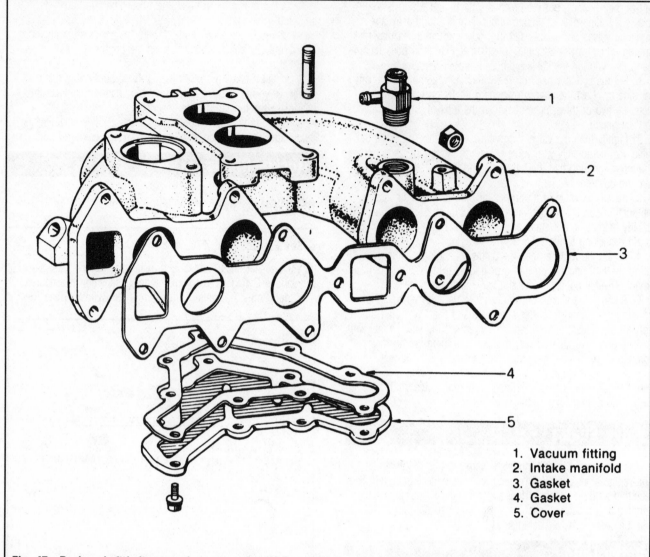

1. Vacuum fitting
2. Intake manifold
3. Gasket
4. Gasket
5. Cover

Fig. 47c Rocker shaft bolt removal sequence for 4M-E and 5M-E engines; first remove oil union bolt A, then union B

moval and Installation procedures necessary to remove and install the rocker shafts.

Rocker Arm (Valve) Cover

REMOVAL & INSTALLATION

◆ **See Figures 48, 49 and 50**

1. Remove the air cleaner assembly. On some of the M engines, disconnect and remove the air intake hose.
2. Disconnect the PCV hose(s) from the valve cover.
3. Remove the acorn nuts and washers. Lift the valve cover off the cylinder head. Cover the oil return hole in the head to prevent dirt or objects from falling in. Remove the valve cover gasket.

To install:

4. Install a new valve cover gasket to the valve cover
5. Place the valve cover on the cylinder head, then install the new washers to the cover if used.

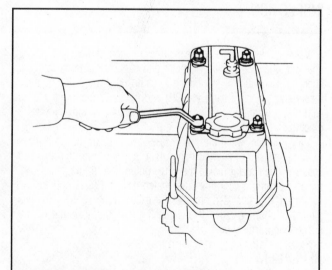

Fig. 48 Some of the valve covers have the mounting bolts on top—22R engine shown

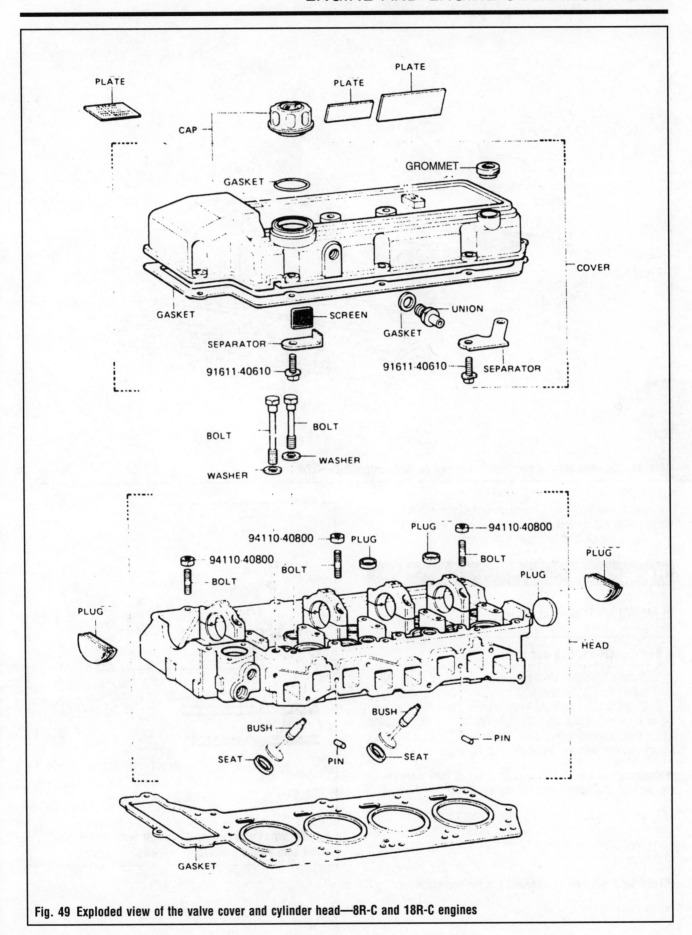

Fig. 49 Exploded view of the valve cover and cylinder head—8R-C and 18R-C engines

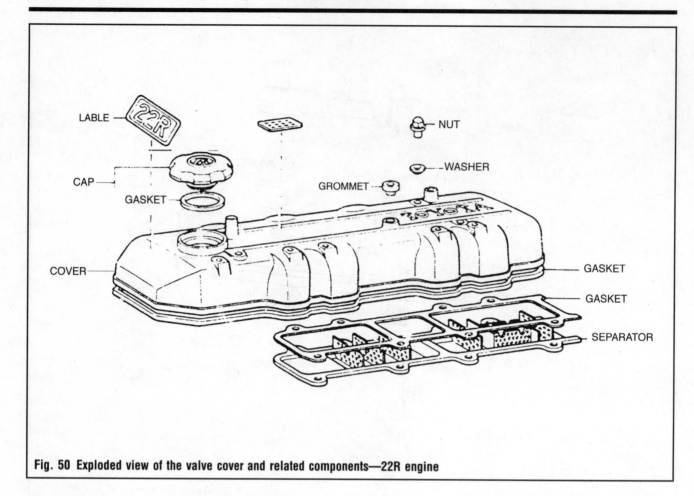

Fig. 50 Exploded view of the valve cover and related components—22R engine

6. Tighten the acorn nuts evenly, reconnect the PCV hose and install the air cleaner assembly.

7. Check the oil level and top off if necessary.

Rocker Arms

REMOVAL AND INSTALLATION

◆ **See Figures 51, 51A and 51B**

1. Remove the rocker shaft assemblies, as detailed in the Cylinder Head portion of this section.

2. On the single rocker shaft engines (8R-C and 18R), remove the rocker shaft support attaching bolts (#2 in illustration) and the rocker shaft retaining screw (#3 in illustration). Slide the tension springs, rocker arms and supports off of the shafts.

➡**Make sure you keep the parts in order as they were removed from the shaft—this is very important.**

3. On the double rocker shaft engines, remove the rocker shaft assemblies. Remove the three retaining screws and slide the rocker supports, springs and rocker arms off of the shafts. Keep all parts in order;

➡**The shafts must be reassembled in the correct order.**

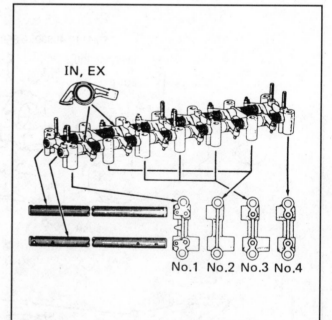

Fig. 51 When assembling the rocker arms on the shaft, make sure they are in order—4M engine shown

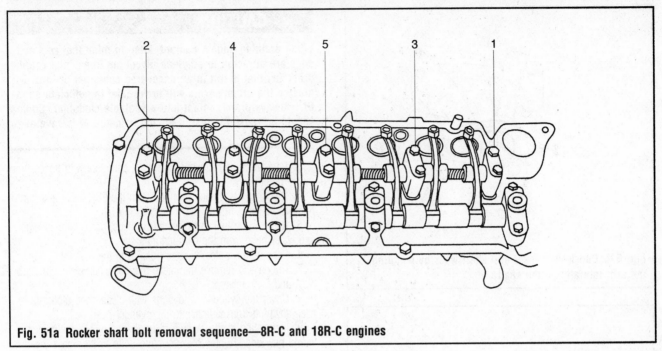

Fig. 51a Rocker shaft bolt removal sequence—8R-C and 18R-C engines

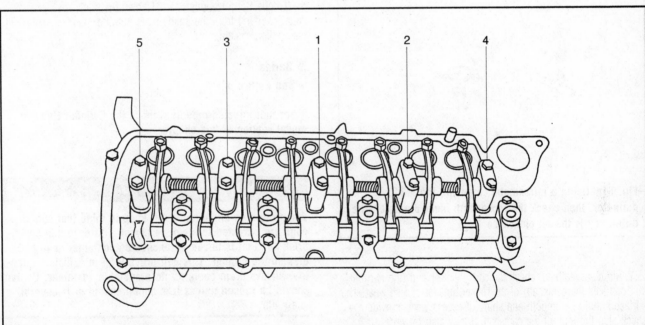

Fig. 51b Rocker shaft bolt tightening sequence—8R-C and 18R-C engines

4. Assembly is in the opposite order of removal; make sure all components are reassembled in their original positions. Adjust the valves.

5. Check the oil level and top off if necessary.

INSPECTION

▶ **See Figures 51c and 51d**

The oil clearance between the rocker arm and shaft is measured in two steps. Measure the outside diameter of the rocker shaft with a micrometer. Measure the inside diameter of the rocker arms with a dial indicator. The difference between the rocker arm inner diameter and the shaft outer diameter is the oil clearance. Clearance specs are as follows:

- 8R-C—0.0012–0.015 in. (0.030–0.381mm)
- 18R—0.00067–0.00201 in. (0.017–0.051mm)
- 20R—0.0004–0.0020 in. (0.010–0.050mm)
- 22R—0.0031 in. (0.078mm)
- 4M, 4M-E and 5M-E—0.0005–0.0013 in. (0.0127–0.0330mm)

If specs are not within these ranges, replace either the rocker shaft or rocker arm. Clearance can also be checked by moving the rocker arm laterally on the shaft when assembled. There should be little or no movement.

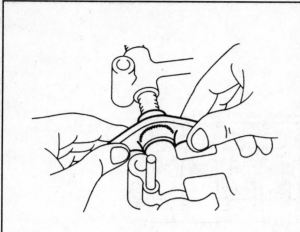

Fig. 51c Check the rocker arm shaft wear by wiggling the arm laterally on the shaft

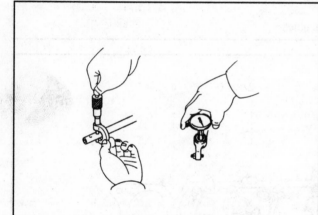

Fig. 51d Using a micrometer, measure the shaft diameter, then check the rocker arm inner diameter; the difference is the oil clearance

While disassembled, check the cam follower end (the flat end that contacts the camshaft) of the rocker arm for excess wear. The surface should be smooth and shiny. If excess wear is evident, check also the lobe of the camshaft, it may also be worn.

Reassemble the rocker shaft assemblies in the exact opposite order or removal. Accelerated camshaft wear and/or sloppy valve action will result if rocker arms are mixed and end up operating against the wrong cam lobes.

Intake Manifold

REMOVAL & INSTALLATION

20R and 22R Engines
▶ See Figure 52

1. Disconnect the battery.
2. Drain the cooling system.

✳✳ CAUTION

When draining engine coolant, keep in mind that cats and dogs are attracted to ethylene glycol antifreeze and could drink any that is left in an uncovered container or in puddles on the ground. This will prove fatal in sufficient quantity. Always drain coolant into a sealable container. Coolant should be reused unless it is contaminated or is several years old.

3. Remove the air cleaner assembly, complete with hoses, from the carburetor.
4. Disconnect the vacuum lines from the EGR valve and carburetor. Mark them first to aid in installation.
5. Remove the fuel lines, electrical leads, accelerator linkage, and water hose from the carburetor.
6. Remove the water by-pass hose from the manifold.
7. Unbolt and remove the intake manifold, complete with carburetor and EGR valve.
8. Cover the cylinder head ports with clean shop cloths to keep anything from falling into the cylinder head or block.
9. Installation is the reverse of removal. Replace the gasket with a new one. Tighten the mounting bolts to the figure given in the Torque Specifications chart. Tighten the bolts in several stages working from the inside bolts outward. Remember to refill the cooling system.

M Series
▶ See Figure 53

➡For fuel injected models refer to the Cylinder Head removal section of this chapter.

1. Drain the cooling system.

✳✳ CAUTION

When draining engine coolant, keep in mind that cats and dogs are attracted to ethylene glycol antifreeze and could drink any that is left in an uncovered container or in puddles on the ground. This will prove fatal in sufficient quantity. Always drain coolant into a sealable container. Coolant should be reused unless it is contaminated or is several years old.

2. Remove the air cleaner assembly, complete with hoses, from its mounting bracket.
3. Remove the distributor cap.
4. Remove the upper radiator hose from the elbow.
5. Remove the wiring from the temperature gauge sender.
6. Remove the following from the carburetor: fuel lines; vacuum line; choke stove hoses, emission control system hoses (and wires); accelerator torque rod; and automatic transmission linkage (if so equipped).
7. Remove the emission control system lines and wiring from the manifold when equipped with a vacuum switching valve on engines with EGR, remove the EGR lines and fittings.
8. Remove the water by-pass hose from the manifold.
9. Unbolt and remove the manifold, complete with the carburetor.
10. Installation is in the reverse order of removal. Remember

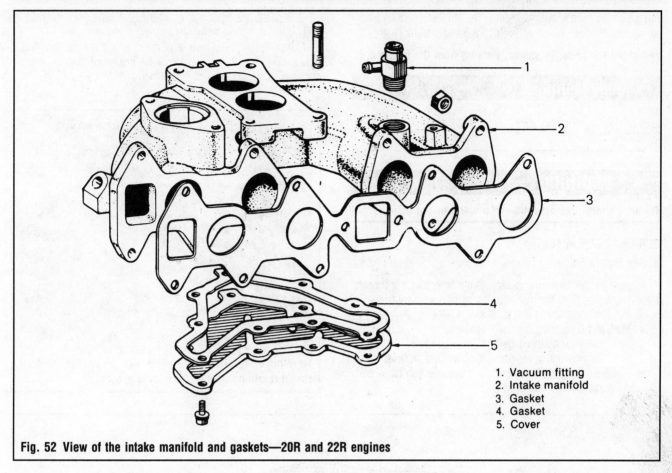

1. Vacuum fitting
2. Intake manifold
3. Gasket
4. Gasket
5. Cover

Fig. 52 View of the intake manifold and gaskets—20R and 22R engines

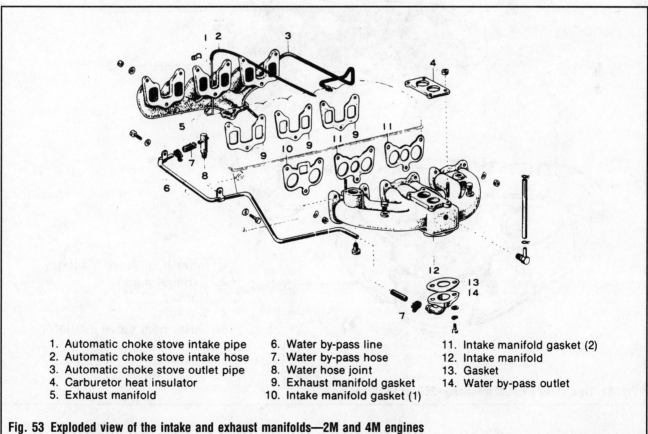

1. Automatic choke stove intake pipe
2. Automatic choke stove intake hose
3. Automatic choke stove outlet pipe
4. Carburetor heat insulator
5. Exhaust manifold

6. Water by-pass line
7. Water by-pass hose
8. Water hose joint
9. Exhaust manifold gasket
10. Intake manifold gasket (1)

11. Intake manifold gasket (2)
12. Intake manifold
13. Gasket
14. Water by-pass outlet

Fig. 53 Exploded view of the intake and exhaust manifolds—2M and 4M engines

to replace the gaskets with new ones. Tighten the mounting bolts to the specifications given in the Torque Specifications chart.

➡**Tighten the bolts, in stages, working from the inside out.**

Exhaust Manifold

REMOVAL & INSTALLATION

✳✳ WARNING

Do not perform this operation on a warm or hot engine.

20R and 22R Engines

▶ **See Figure 54**

1. Remove the three exhaust pipe flange bolts and disconnect the exhaust pipe from the manifold. It may be necessary to remove the outer heat shield first on some models.
2. Mark and disconnect the spark plug leads.
3. Remove the air cleaner tube from the heat stove.
4. Use a 14mm wrench to remove the manifold securing nuts.
5. Remove the manifold, complete with air injection tubes and the inner portion of the heat stove.

6. Separate the inner portion of the heat stove from the manifold.

7. Installation is the reverse of removal. Tighten the retaining nuts to 29–36 ft. lb., working from the inside out, and in several stages. Tighten the exhaust pipe flange nuts to 25–32 ft. lb.

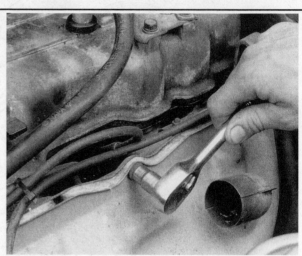

To remove the exhaust manifold, first disengage the heat shield retaining nuts—20R engine shown

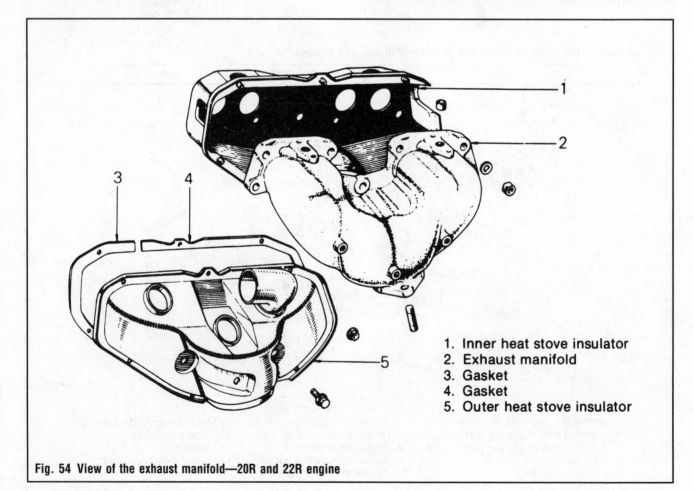

1. Inner heat stove insulator
2. Exhaust manifold
3. Gasket
4. Gasket
5. Outer heat stove insulator

Fig. 54 View of the exhaust manifold—20R and 22R engine

1. Outer heat shield
2. Inner heat shield
3. Exhaust manifold
4. Heat shield gasket

Now, remove the outer heat shield from the manifold

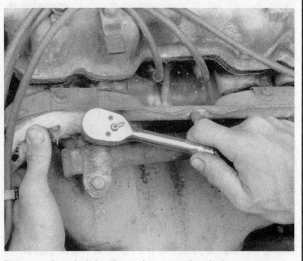

Remove the air injection tube mounting bolts . . .

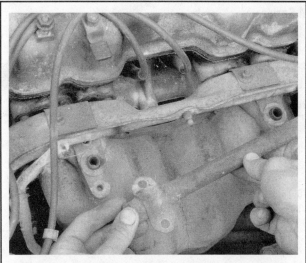

. . . and separate the injection tube from the manifold

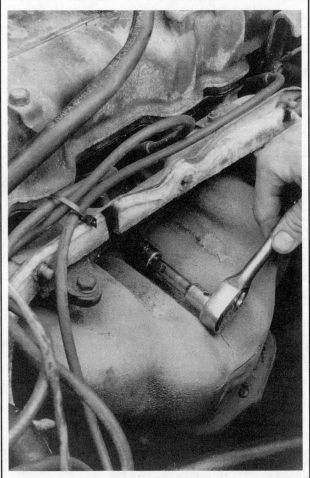

Loosen and remove the exhaust manifold mounting bolts

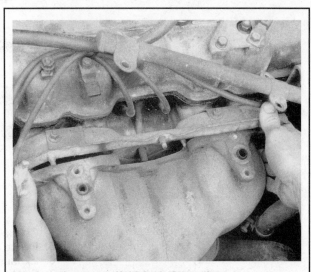

Lift the exhaust manifold from the engine

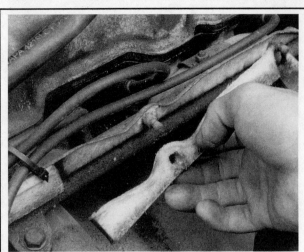

During installation, remove the old heat shield gasket and replace it with a new one

M Series

1. Raise the front and the rear of the car and support it with jackstands.

✳✳ CAUTION

Be sure that the car is securely supported.

2. Remove the right-hand gravel shield from beneath the engine.

3. Remove the downpipe support bracket.

4. Unfasten the bolts from the flange and detach the downpipe from the manifold. It may be necessary to remove the outer heat shield first.

5. Remove the automatic choke and air cleaner stove hoses from the exhaust manifold.

6. Remove or move aside, any of the air injection system components which may be in the way when removing the manifold. Unfasten the EGR valve and pipes.

7. In order to remove the manifold, unfasten the manifold retaining bolts.

✳✳ WARNING

Remove and tighten the bolts in two or three stages and, starting from the inside, working out.

8. Installation is performed in the reverse order of removal. Always use a new gasket. Tighten the retaining bolts to the specifications given in two or three stages.

Combination Manifold

REMOVAL & INSTALLATION

✳✳ WARNING

Do not perform this procedure on a warm engine.

8R-C and 18R-C Engines
▶ **See Figure 55**

1. Remove the air cleaner assembly, complete with hoses, from its mounting bracket.

2. Remove the fuel line, vacuum lines, automatic choke stove hoses, PCV hose, and accelerator linkage from the carburetor.

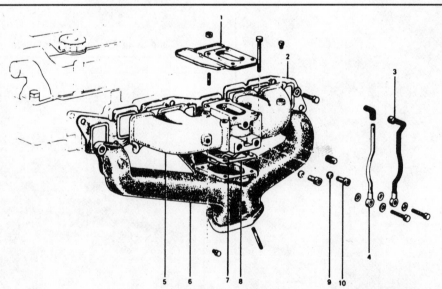

1. Heat insulator
2. Manifold gasket (manifold-to-head)
3. Choke stove outlet pipe
4. Choke stove intake pipe
5. Intake manifold
6. Exhaust manifold
7. Choke stove pipe
8. Manifold gasket (intake-to-exhaust)
9. Sleeve
10. Union

Fig. 55 View of the combination manifold—8R-C and 18R-C engines

3. Unfasten the carburetor securing nuts. Remove the torque rod support, carburetor, and heat insulator.

4. Use a jack to raise the front of the car. Support the car with jackstands.

✳✳ CAUTION

Be sure that the car is securely supported.

5. Unfasten the bolts which attach the downpipe flange to the exhaust manifold.

6. In order to remove the manifold assembly, unfasten the manifold retaining bolts. On 1974 California engines, remove the EGR valve and tubes first.

✳✳ WARNING

Remove and tighten the bolts in two or three stages, starting from the inside and working out.

7. Installation is performed in the reverse order of removal. Always use new gaskets. Tighten the manifold securing bolts to the figure shown in the Torque Specifications chart, in the reverse sequence of removal.

Timing Gear Cover

REMOVAL & INSTALLATION

◆ **See Figure 56**

1. Perform the Cylinder Head Removal procedure as detailed in the appropriate previous sections.

2. Remove the radiator.

3. Remove the alternator.

4. On engines equipped with air pumps, unfasten the adjusting link bolts and the drive belt. Remove the hoses from the pump. Remove the pump and bracket from the engine.

➡ **If the car is equipped with power steering, see Chapter 8 for its pump removal procedure.**

5. Remove the fan and water pump as a complete assembly.

✳✳ WARNING

To prevent the fluid from running out of the fan coupling, do not tip the assembly over on its side.

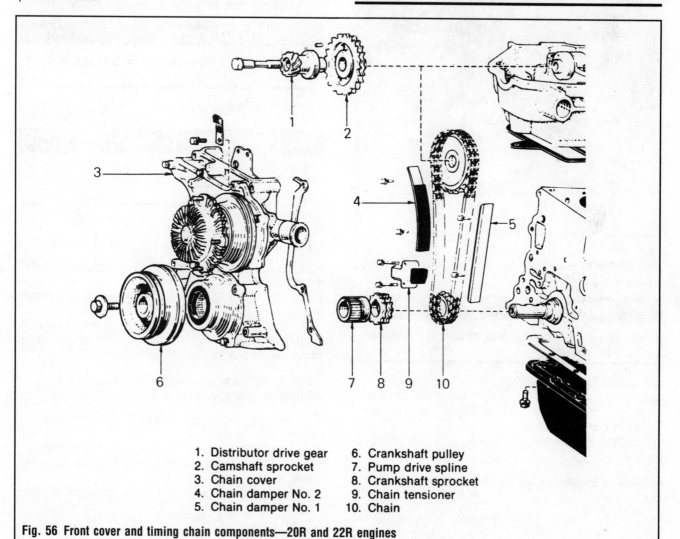

1. Distributor drive gear	6. Crankshaft pulley
2. Camshaft sprocket	7. Pump drive spline
3. Chain cover	8. Crankshaft sprocket
4. Chain damper No. 2	9. Chain tensioner
5. Chain damper No. 1	10. Chain

Fig. 56 Front cover and timing chain components—20R and 22R engines

To remove the timing cover, loosen and remove the bolts . . .

. . . and separate it from the front of the engine—20R engine shown others similar

6. Unfasten the crankshaft pulley securing bolt and remove the pulley with a gear puller.

✳✳ WARNING

Do not remove the 10mm bolt from its hole, if installed as it is used for balancing.

7. Loosen the bolts securing the front of the oil pan, after draining the engine oil. Lower the front of the oil pan. It may be necessary to loosen the front motor mounts and jack up the engine slightly on some models.
8. Remove the bolts securing the timing chain cover. Withdraw the cover.

➡**The M series engines use two gaskets on the timing chain cover.**

9. Tighten the timing chain cover bolts to the specifications below:
　8R-C and 18R-C engines, all bolts: 11–15 ft. lb.
　20R and 22R engines, all bolts: 7–12 ft. lb.
　M Series 6 cylinder Engines
　　8mm bolts: 7–12 ft. lb.
　　10mm bolts: 14–22 ft. lb.

Timing Chain Cover Oil Seal

REPLACEMENT

1. Remove the timing chain cover, as previously detailed in the appropriate section.
2. Inspect the oil seal for signs of wear, leakage, or damage.
3. If worn, pry the old oil seal out, using a small prybar. Remove it toward the front of the cover.

➡**Once the oil seal has been removed, it must be replaced with a new one.**

4. Use a socket, pipe, or block of wood and a hammer to drift the oil seal into place. Work from the front of the cover.

✳✳ CAUTION

Be extremely careful not to damage the seal or else it will leak.

5. Install the timing chain cover as previously outlined.

Timing Chain and Tensioner

REMOVAL & INSTALLATION

8R-C and 18R-C Engines
◆ **See Figure 57**

1. Remove the cylinder head and timing chain cover as previously detailed.
2. Remove the timing chain (front) together with the camshaft drive sprocket.
3. Remove the crankshaft sprocket and oil pump jack shaft, complete with the pump jack shaft, complete with the pump drive chain (rear). Remove the chain vibration damper.

➡**Both timing chains are identical. Tag them for proper identification during installation.**

4. Inspect the chains and sprockets for wear or damage. Clean the chains with solvent.
5. Use a vernier caliper to measure the amount of stretch of both chains. Measure any 17 links while pulling the chain which is being measured taut.
6. Repeat Step 5 at two other places on each chain. Replace

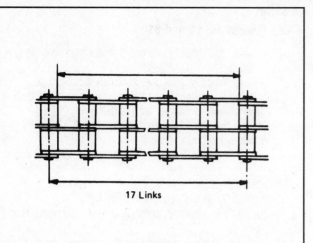

Fig. 57 Timing chain stretch measurement—8R-C and 18R-C engines

either of the chains if any of the 17 link measurements exceed 147mm or if the difference between the minimum and maximum readings is more than 2mm, on any one chain.

7. Remove the plunger and spring from one of the chain tensioners. Inspect all of the parts of the tensioner for wear or damage. Fill it with oil and assemble it if it is not defective.

8. Repeat Step 7 for the other tensioner.

❊❊ WARNING

Do not mix the parts of the two chain tensioners together.

To install:

9. Position the No. 1 piston at TDC by having the crankshaft keyway point straight up (perpendicular to) toward the cylinder head.

10. Align the oil pump jack shaft, with the keyway pointing straight up as well.

11. Align the marks on the timing sprocket and the oil pump drive sprocket with each of the marks on the chain.

12. Install the chain and sprocket assembly over the keyways, while retaining alignment of the chain/sprocket timing marks.

❊❊ WARNING

Use care not to disengage the welch plug at the rear of the oil pump driveshaft by forcing the sprocket over the keyway.

13. Install the gasket for the timing chain cover.

➡**Use liquid sealer on the gasket before installation.**

14. Install both of the chain tensioners in their respective places, being careful not to mix them up. Tighten their securing bolts to 12–17 ft. lb.

❊❊ WARNING

Use care when installing the chain tensioner bolts; they have oil holes tapped in them.

15. Fit the camshaft drive sprocket over the keyway on the oil pump driveshaft. Tighten its securing nut to 58–72 ft. lb.

16. Install the camshaft drive chain over the camshaft drive sprocket. Align the mating marks on the chain and sprocket.

17. Apply tension to the chain by tying it to the chain tensioner. This will prevent it from falling back into the timing chain cover once it is installed.

20R and 22R Engines
▶ **See Figure 58**

1. Remove the cylinder head and timing chain cover as previously outlined.

2. Separate the chain from the damper, and remove the chain, complete with the camshaft sprocket.

3. Remove the crankshaft sprocket and the oil pump drive with a puller.

4. Inspect the chain for wear or damage. Replace it if necessary.

5. Inspect the chain tensioner for wear. If it measures less than 11mm, replace it.

6. Check the dampers for wear. If their measurements are below the following specifications, replace them:
Upper damper: 5mm
Lower damper: 4.5mm

To install:

7. Rotate the crankshaft until its key is at TDC. Slide the sprocket in place over the key.

8. Place the chain over the sprocket so that its single bright link aligns with the mark on the camshaft sprocket.

9. Install the cam sprocket so that the timing mark falls between the two bright links on the chain.

10. Fit the oil pump drive spline over the crankshaft key.

11. Install the timing cover gasket on the front of the block.

12. Rotate the camshaft sprocket counterclockwise to remove the slack from the chain.

13. Install the timing chain cover and cylinder head as previously outlined.

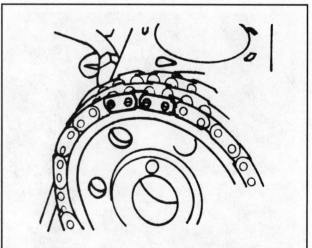

Fig. 58 Timing chain alignment marking—20R and 22R engines

1. Timing chain
2. Camshaft sprocket

View of the timing chain and camshaft sprocket

1. Chain tensioner   3. Timing chain
2. Chain damper

On the lower end of the engine, the chain is surrounded by a tensioner and two dampers

M Series

▶ **See Figures 59, 60 and 61**

1. Remove the cylinder head and timing chain cover as previously outlined.
2. Remove the chain tensioner assembly (arm and gear).
3. Unfasten the bolts retaining the chain damper and damper guide and withdraw the damper and guide.
4. Remove the oil slinger from the crankshaft.
5. Withdraw the timing chain.
6. Inspect the chain for wear or damage. Replace it if necessary.

To install:

7. Position the No. 1 cylinder at TDC.
8. Position the crankshaft sprocket 0 mark downward, facing the oil pan.
9. Align the Toyota trademarks on the sprockets as illustrated.
10. Fit the tensioner gear assembly on the block.

➡**Its dowel pin should be positioned 38mm from the surface of the block.**

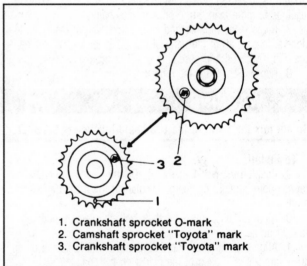

1. Crankshaft sprocket O-mark
2. Camshaft sprocket "Toyota" mark
3. Crankshaft sprocket "Toyota" mark

Fig. 59 Timing marks—M series engines

Fig. 60 Timing mark alignment—M series engines

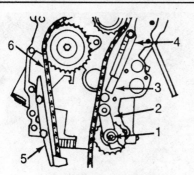

1. Timing chain tensioner gear
2. Timing chain tensioner arm
3. Damper guide
4. Vibration damper
5. Vibration damper
6. Crankshaft oil slinger

Fig. 61 View of the timing chain components—M series engine

11. Install the chain over the two gears while maintaining tension.

12. Install both of the vibration dampers and the damper guide.

13. Fit the oil slinger to the crankshaft.

14. Tie the chain to the upper vibration damper, to keep it from falling into the chain cover, once the cover is installed.

15. Install the timing chain cover as previously detailed.

16. Perform the cylinder head installation procedure as detailed previously.

➡**If proper valve timing cannot be obtained, it is possible to adjust it by placing the camshaft slotted pin in the second or third hole on the camshaft timing gear, as required. If the timing is out by more than 15 degrees, replace the chain and both of the sprockets.**

Oil Pan

REMOVAL & INSTALLATION

➡**It may be easier to remove the engine, on some models (Crown 2300 and 2600), in order to remove the oil pan. However, with a little patience it is possible to remove the pan with the engine installed in the car.**

1. Open the hood. Drain the coolant from the radiator and disconnect the upper and lower hoses from the radiator connections. Disconnect the negative battery cable.

✳✳ CAUTION

When draining engine coolant, keep in mind that cats and dogs are attracted to ethylene glycol antifreeze and could drink any that is left in an uncovered container or in puddles on the ground. This will prove fatal in sufficient quantity. Always drain coolant into a sealable container. Coolant should be reused unless it is contaminated or is several years old.

2. Loosen the front wheel lugs slightly. Raise the front of the car and support with jackstands. Remove the front wheels.

✳✳ CAUTION

Be sure the car is supported securely. Remember, you will be working underneath it.

3. Drain the engine oil.

4. Detach the steering relay rod and the tie rod ends from the idler arm, pitman arm and the steering knuckles. (Refer to Chapter eight).

5. Remove the splash shields. Remove the engine stiffening plates (supports between the engine and transmission—if equipped).

6. Support the front of the engine with a jack and remove the front motor mount bolts.

7. Raise the engine and place blocks between the mount and the frame. Lower the engine on the blocks, make sure it is supported securely.

8. Check the clearance between the oil pan and the crossmember. It may be necessary to raise the rear of the engine as well.

9. To raise the rear of the engine, place a jack under the bell housing (between the engine and transmission) remove the rear motor mount bolts and raise the rear of the engine. Place blocks between the rear mounts and the crossmember. Slowly lower the engine onto the blocks. Make sure it is secure.

10. Remove the oil pan mounting bolts and remove the oil pan.

➡**If you still do not have enough room to remove the oil pan it may be necessary to place thicker blocks under the front or rear of the engine. Do so carefully.**

11. Installation is the reverse of removal. Apply liquid sealer to the corners of the oil pan and install a new pan gasket.

Rear Main Oil Seal

REMOVAL & INSTALLATION

➡**This procedure applies only to those models with manual transmissions. If your car has an automatic transmission, leave removal of the oil seal to your dealer.**

1. Remove the transmission as detailed in Chapter 6.

2. Remove the clutch cover assembly and flywheel. See Chapter 6 also.

3. Remove the oil seal retaining plate, complete with the oil seal.

4. Use a screwdriver to pry the oil seal from the retaining plate. Be careful not to damage the plate.

5. Install the new seal, carefully, by using a block of wood to drift it into place.

✳✳ WARNING

Do not damage the seal. A leak will result.

6. Lubricate the lips of the seal with multi-purpose grease.

7. Installation is performed in the reverse order from removal.

Oil Pump

REMOVAL & INSTALLATION

➡ It may be necessary to remove the radiator on some models, to gain the necessary room.

All Engines Except 20R and 22R

1. Remove the oil pan, as outlined in the appropriate preceding section.
2. Unbolt the oil pump securing bolts and remove it as an assembly.
3. Installation is the reverse of removal.

20R and 22R Engines

1. Remove the oil pan as previously outlined.
2. Unfasten the three bolts which secure the oil strainer.

. . . then remove the outer pulley bolts

To separate the oil pump from the engine, you must remove the crankshaft pulley

This will allow the pulley to come off the front of the engine—20R engine shown, others similar

Remove the center damper bolt . . .

Place a gear puller on the front of the dampner pulley . . .

. . . and remove the dampner from the engine

Loosen and remove the bolts securing the pump . . .

. . . then remove the pump from the engine

Always remove and replace the O-ring from the oil pump mating surface

3. Remove the drive belts, the pulley bolt, and the crankshaft pulley.

4. Unfasten the bolts which secure the oil pump housing to the timing chain cover, and remove the pump assembly.

5. Remove the oil pump drive spline and the rubber O-ring.

6. Installation is performed in the reverse order of removal. Apply sealer to the top oil pump housing bolt. Use a new oil strainer gasket.

OVERHAUL

There are three types of oil pumps. The 4M-E and 5M-E engines use a geared impeller type pump. The 20R and 22R series use an automatic transmission type gear pump. The 8R-C and 18R-C use a trochoid rotary type pump. In both gear types, there is a drive gear and a driven gear; pump inspection procedures are very similar on both types. Inspection of the trochoid pumps is similar to the gear types.

8R-C and 18R-C Engines
▶ **See Figure 62**

1. Remove the oil pump.

2. Disassemble the pump by removing the oil strainer, relief valve plug, gasket, spring, and relief valve from the pump cover. Remove the cover, drive shaft and driven rotor from the pump body.

3. Clean all parts in solvent and inspect for unusual wear and/or damage. Replace any parts if necessary. Pay special attention to the pump shaft, drive and driven rotors.

4. Check drive-to-driven rotor tip clearance, using a feeler gauge. If clearance exceed 0.008 inches (0.203mm), replace the rotors as a set.

5. Using the feeler gauge and a steel square or steel block, check side clearance between the rotor and pump cover surface. Replace the rotor and/or body if clearance exceeds 0.006 inches (0.152mm).

6. Measure the clearance between the driven rotor and pump body; clearance should be less than 0.008 inches (0.203mm). Re-

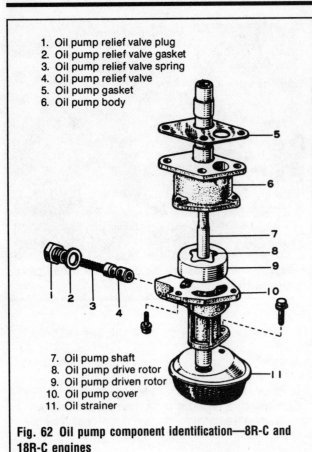

1. Oil pump relief valve plug
2. Oil pump relief valve gasket
3. Oil pump relief valve spring
4. Oil pump relief valve
5. Oil pump gasket
6. Oil pump body

7. Oil pump shaft
8. Oil pump drive rotor
9. Oil pump driven rotor
10. Oil pump cover
11. Oil strainer

Fig. 62 Oil pump component identification—8R-C and 18R-C engines

place the body and/or rotors as a set if clearance exceeds this figure.

7. Reassemble the pump in the reverse order of disassembly. Stamped marks are provided on the drive rotor and driven rotor, and should face toward the pump cover side (toward the underneath of the engine when installed).

8. Check pump operation by immersing the suction end of the pump in clean engine oil and turning the shaft counterclockwise by hand. Oil should come out of the discharge hole. Close the discharge hole with your thumb, and turn the shaft. The shaft should be difficult to turn. Use a flat bladed tool to rotate the rotor shaft.

20R and 22R Engines
▶ **See Figures 63, 64, 65 and 66**

1. Remove the oil pump.
2. Matchmark the drive and driven gears before disassembling the pump.
3. Disassemble the pump by unscrewing the relief valve plug and removing the spring and relief valve piston. Remove the drive and driven gears, and clean all parts in solvent. Inspect all parts for unusual wear and replace if necessary.
4. Align the matchmarks and assemble the gears into the pump body. Using a feeler gauge, measure the clearance between inches (0.203mm), replace the gear and/or body.
5. Measure the clearance between both gear tips and the crescent with a feeler gauge. If clearance exceeds 0.012 inches (0.304mm), replace the gears and/or body.
6. Using a feeler gauge and steel square or flat steel block, measure the gear side clearance as shown. If the clearance is

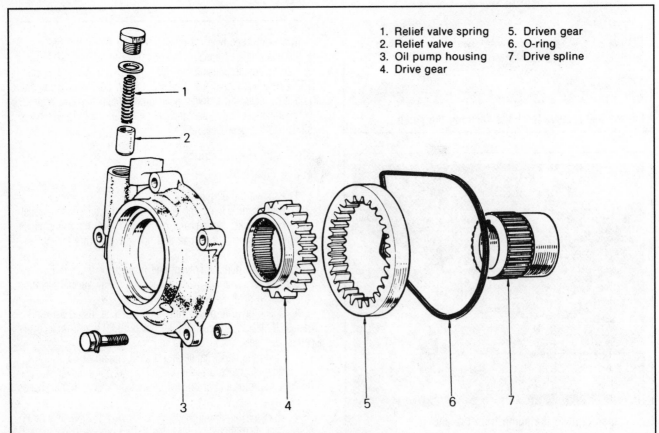

1. Relief valve spring
2. Relief valve
3. Oil pump housing
4. Drive gear
5. Driven gear
6. O-ring
7. Drive spline

Fig. 63 Exploded view of oil pump components—20R engine shown

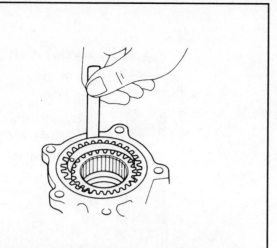

Fig. 64 Checking the driven gear-to-body clearance on the 20R engine's oil pump

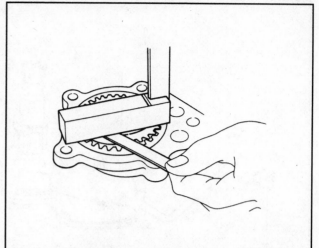

Fig. 66 Checking the side clearance on the 20R engine's oil pump

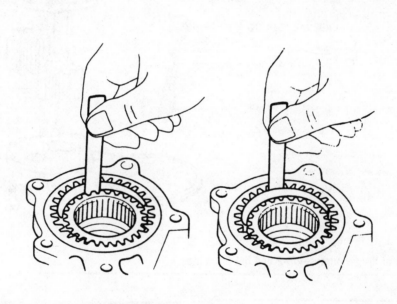

Fig. 65 Measuring the gear tip-to-crescent clearance

greater than 0.15 inches (3.81mm), replace the gears and/or body.

7. Assemble the pump in the reverse order of disassembly.

M Series Engines

▶ **See Figures 67 and 68**

1. Remove the oil pump.

2. Disassemble the pump by removing the relief valve plug, spring and relief valve. Remove the pump cover and driven gear. Using needlenose pliers, remove the snapring and remove the spacer, drive shaft gear, key and shaft sub-assembly.

3. Clean all parts in solvent, and inspect for scoring or other unusual wear. Replace any part that looks worn or damaged.

4. Measure driven gear-to-body clearance with a feeler gauge;

if clearance exceeds 0.008 inches (0.203mm), replace the gear and/or body.

5. Insert a feeler gauge between the meshing faces of the two gears (gear backlash measurement). If the backlash is greater than 0.035 inches (0.889mm), replace the shaft sub-assembly and/or driven gear.

6. Using a feeler gauge and steel square or flat steel block, measure the side clearance. If clearance is greater than 0.0059 inches (0.149mm), replace the gears and/or pump body.

7. Reassemble the pump in the reverse order of disassembly. Check pump operation by immersing the suction end of the pump in clean engine oil and turning the shaft counterclockwise by hand. Oil should come out of the discharge hole. Close the discharge hole with your thumb, and turn the shaft. The shaft should be difficult to turn.

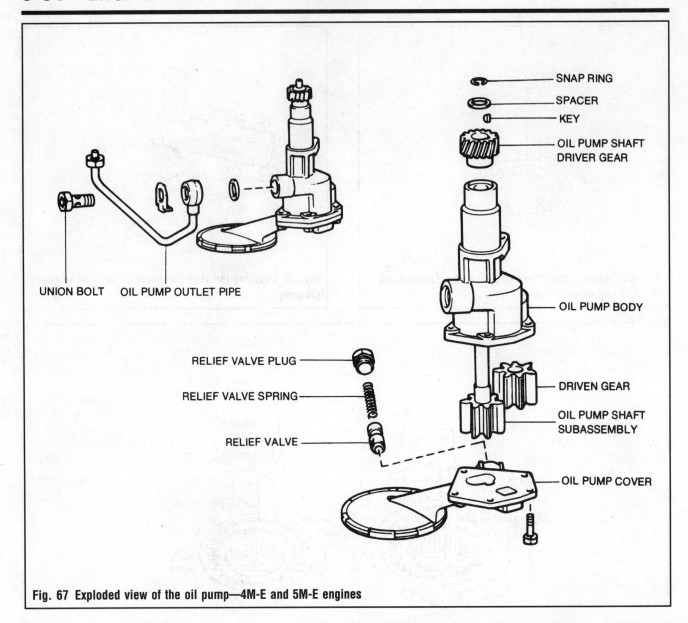

UNION BOLT   OIL PUMP OUTLET PIPE

SNAP RING
SPACER
KEY
OIL PUMP SHAFT DRIVER GEAR

OIL PUMP BODY

RELIEF VALVE PLUG

RELIEF VALVE SPRING

RELIEF VALVE

DRIVEN GEAR

OIL PUMP SHAFT SUBASSEMBLY

OIL PUMP COVER

Fig. 67 Exploded view of the oil pump—4M-E and 5M-E engines

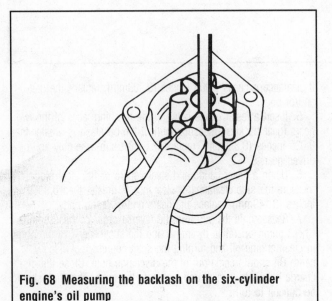

Fig. 68 Measuring the backlash on the six-cylinder engine's oil pump

Camshaft and Bearings

REMOVAL & INSTALLATION

1. Perform the Cylinder Head Removal procedure (for your engine) far enough to gain access to the camshaft bearing cap bolts. If you are going to remove the head anyway, remove the cam after removing the cylinder head.

2. Prior to removing the camshaft, measure its end-play with a feeler gauge. The end-play limit is 0.0098 inch (0.248mm) for the 8R-C, 18R-C, 20R and 22R engines; 0.01 inch (0.254mm) for the 4M-E and 5M-E engines. If the end-play is beyond this, replace the head.

3. Use a 12mm wrench to remove the bearing cap bolts. Remove the caps. Keep them in order, or mark them.

4. Measure the bearing oil clearance by placing a piece of Plastigage® on each journal. Replace the caps and tighten their bolts to 13–16 ft. lbs. (17–22 Nm).

View of the camshaft with the rocker shafts removed—
20R engine shown

. . . and lift the cap off of the cylinder head

Each cap is marked as to installation direction and
journal number

Remove the bearing cap bolts . . .

Lift the camshaft out of the cylinder head

5. Remove the caps and measure each piece of Plastigage®. If the clearance is greater than 0.004 inch (0.101mm), replace the head and cam.

6. Lift the camshaft out of the head.

To install:

7. Coat all of the camshaft bearing journals with engine oil.

8. Lay the camshaft in the head.

9. Install the bearing caps in numerical order with their arrows pointing forward (toward the front of the engine).

10. Install the cap bolts and tighten them to 13–16 ft. lbs. (17–21 Nm).

11. Complete the cylinder head installation procedure as previously outlined.

CAMSHAFT INSPECTION

♦ **See Figures 69 thru 75**

A dial indicator, micrometer and inside micrometer are all needed to properly measure the camshaft and camshaft housing.

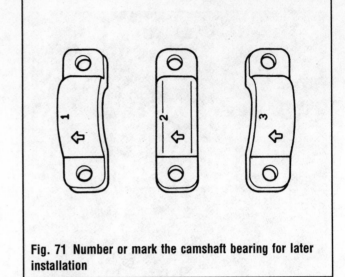

Fig. 71 Number or mark the camshaft bearing for later installation

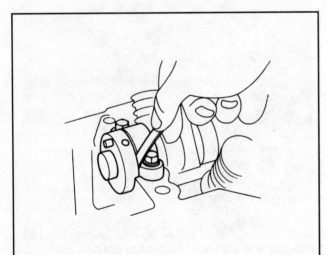

Fig. 69 Use a flat feeler gauge to measure the camshaft end-play

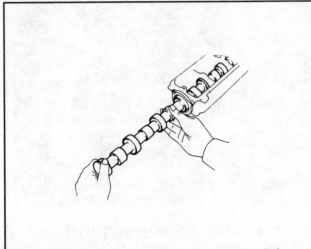

Fig. 72 Slowly turn the camshaft as you remove it from the back of the housing

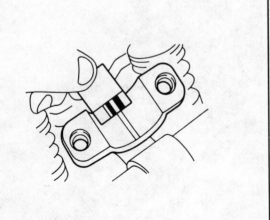

Fig. 70 Use a piece of Plastigage® to measure the camshaft bearing clearance

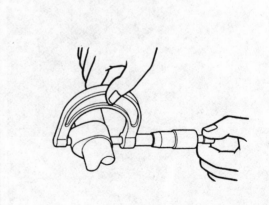

Fig. 73 Measure the lobe height (shown) and journal diameter with a micrometer

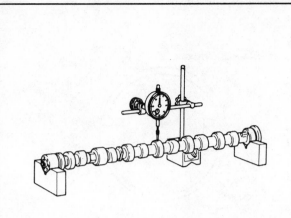

Fig. 74 The camshaft run-out must be measured with a dial indicator

Fig. 75 Use an inside micrometer to measure the camshaft housing bore diameter

If these instruments are available to you, proceed; if they are not available, have the parts checked at a reputable machine shop. Camshaft specifications are included in a chart in this section.

1. Using the micrometer, measure the height of each cam lobe. If a lobe height is less than the minimum specified, the lobe is worn and the camshaft must be replaced. Minimum intake and exhaust lobe heights are as follows:
- 8R-C—1.721 inch (43.71mm) Intake; 1.724 inch (43.78mm) Exhaust
- 18R—1.7206 inch (43.70mm) Intake; 1.7245 inch (43.80mm) Exhaust
- 20R—1.6783–1.6819 inch (42.62–42.72mm) Intake; 1.6806–1.6841 inch (42.68–42.77mm) Exhaust
- 22R—1.6783–1.6819 inch (42.62–42.72mm) Intake; 1.6807–1.6842 inch (40.84–42.77mm) Exhaust
- 4M and 4M-E—1.6797–1.6822 inch (42.66–42.72mm) Intake; 1.664–1.666 inch (42.26–42.31mm) Exhaust
- 5M-E—1.6961 inch (43.08mm) Intake; 1.6988 inch (43.14mm) Exhaust

2. Place the camshaft in V-blocks and measure its run-out at the center journal with a dial indicator. On all but the 4M, 4M-E and 5M-E engines, replace the camshaft if run-out exceeds 0.008 inch (0.203mm). On the 4M engine, replace the camshaft if run-out exceeds 0.0012 inch (0.03mm). On the 4M-E and 5M-E engines, replace the camshaft if run-out exceeds 0.002 inch (0.05mm).

3. Using the micrometer, measure journal diameter, jot down the readings and compare the readings with those listed in the Camshaft Specifications chart. Measure the housing bore inside diameter with the inside micrometer, and jot down the measurements. Subtract the journal diameter measurement from the housing bore measurement. If the clearance is greater than the maximum listed under Bearing Clearance in the chart, replace the camshaft and/or the housing.

Pistons and Connecting Rods

REMOVAL & INSTALLATION

1. Remove the cylinder head as outlined in the appropriate preceding section.
2. Remove the oil pan and pump.
3. Ream the ridges from the top of the cylinder bores, as detailed in Engine Rebuilding, at the end of this chapter. Remove the oil strainer if it is in the way.
4. Unbolt the connecting rod caps. Mark the caps with the number of the cylinder from which they were removed.
5. Remove the connecting rod and piston through the top of the cylinder bore.

✳✳ WARNING

Use care not to scratch the journals or the cylinder walls.

6. Mark the pistons and connecting rods with the numbers of the cylinders from which they were removed.
   To install:
7. Apply a light coating of engine oil to the pistons, rings, and wrist pins.
8. Examine the piston to ensure that it has been assembled with its parts positioned correctly. (See the illustrations.) Be sure that the ring gaps are not pointed toward the thrust face of the piston and that they do not overlap.
9. Install the pistons, using a ring compressor, into the cylinder bore. Be sure that the appropriate marks on the piston are facing the front of the cylinder.

✳✳ WARNING

It is important that the pistons, rods, bearings, etc., be returned to the same cylinder bore from which they were removed.

10. Install the connecting rod bearing caps and tighten them to the torque figures given in the Torque Specifications chart.

✱✱ WARNING

Be sure that the mating marks on the connecting rods and rod bearing caps are aligned.

11. The rest of the removal procedure is performed in the reverse order of installation.

PISTON & CONNECTING ROD IDENTIFICATION

◆ **See Figures 76 thru 82**

The pistons are marked with a notch in the piston head. When installed in the engine, the notch markings must be facing towards the front of the engine.

The connecting rods should be installed in the engine with the forged marks on the bearing caps and on the bottom of the rod facing toward the front of the engine also.

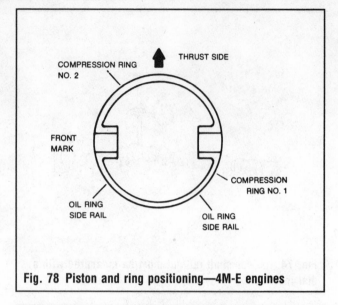

Fig. 78 Piston and ring positioning—4M-E engines

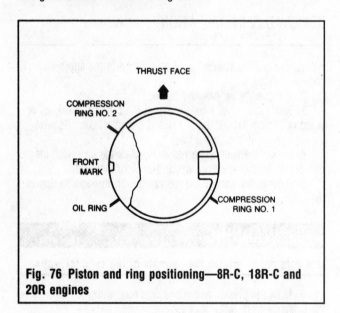

Fig. 76 Piston and ring positioning—8R-C, 18R-C and 20R engines

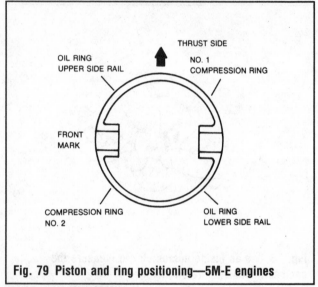

Fig. 79 Piston and ring positioning—5M-E engines

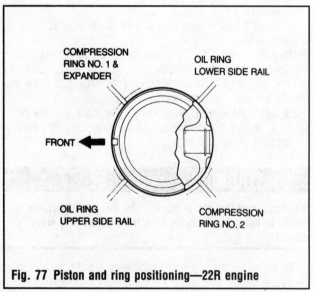

Fig. 77 Piston and ring positioning—22R engine

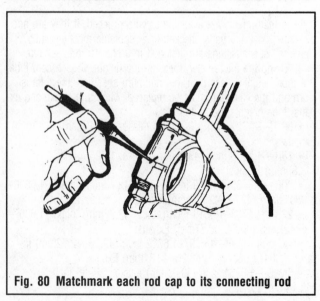

Fig. 80 Matchmark each rod cap to its connecting rod

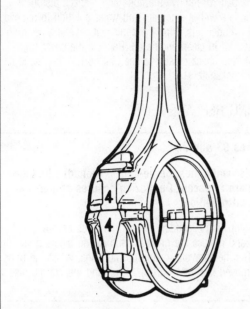

Fig. 81 Match each rod and cap with its cylinder number for correct assembly

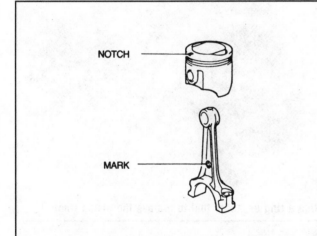

Fig. 82 Identification marks can be found on the pistons and connecting rods in all engines

➡️It is advisable to number the pistons, connecting rods and bearing caps in some manner so that they can be reinstalled in the same cylinder, facing the same direction, from which they were removed.

The piston rings must be installed with their gaps in the same position as shown in the accompanying illustrations.

CLEANING & INSPECTION

Clean the piston after removing the rings, by first scraping any carbon from the piston top. Do not scratch the piston in any way during cleaning. Use a broken piston ring or ring cleaning tool to clean out the ring grooves. Clean the entire piston with solvent and a brush (NOT a wire brush).

Clean the piston grooves using a ring groove cleaner

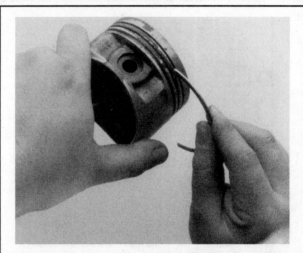

You can use a piece of an old ring to clean the piston grooves, BUT be careful, the ring is sharp

Once the piston is thoroughly cleaned, insert the side of a good piston ring (both No. 1 and No. 2 compression on each piston) into its respective groove. Using a feeler gauge, measure the clearance between the ring and its groove. If clearance is greater than the maximum listed under Ring Side Clearance in the Piston and Ring chart, replace the ring(s) and if necessary, the piston.

To check ring end-gap, insert a compression ring into the cylinder. Lightly oil the cylinder bore and push the ring down into the cylinder with a piston, to the bottom of its travel. Measure the ring end-gap with a feeler gauge. If the gap is not within specification, replace the ring; DO NOT file the ring ends.

HONING

Most inspection and service work on the cylinder block should be handled by a machinist or professional engine rebuilding shop. Included in this work are bearing alignment checks, line boring, deck resurfacing, hot-tanking and cylinder honing or boring. A block that has been checked and properly serviced will last much

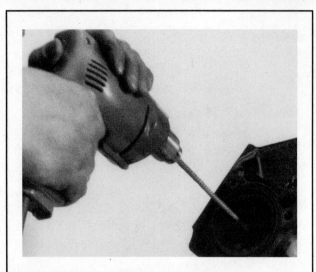
Removing cylinder glazing using a flexible hone

A properly cross-hatched cylinder bore

longer than one which has not had the proper attention when the opportunity was there for it.

Cylinder de-glazing (honing) can, however, be performed by the owner/mechanic who is careful and takes his or her time. The cylinder bores become glazed during normal operation as the rings continually ride up and down against them. This shiny glaze must be removed in order for a new set of piston rings to be able to properly seat themselves.

Cylinder hones are available at most auto tool stores and parts jobbers. With the piston and rod assemblies removed from the block, cover the crankshaft completely with a rag or cover to keep grit from the hone and cylinder material off of it. Chuck a hone into a variable speed power drill (preferable here to a constant speed drill), and insert it into the cylinder.

➡**Make sure the drill and hone are kept square to the cylinder bore throughout the entire honing operation.**

Start the hone and move it up and down in the cylinder at a rate which will produce approximately a 60 degrees cross-hatch pattern. DO NOT extend the hone below the cylinder bore! After

developing the pattern, remove the hone and recheck piston fit. Wash the cylinders with a detergent and water solution to remove the hone and cylinder grit. Wipe the bores out several times with a clean rag soaked in clean engine oil. Remove the cover from the crankshaft, and check closely to see that no grit has found its way onto the crankshaft.

PISTON RING REPLACEMENT

♦ **See Figures 83 and 84**

➡**The cylinder walls must be de-glazed (honed) when the piston rings are replaced. De-glazing ensures proper ring seating and oil retention.**

Using a piston ring expander, remove the rings one by one. Always remove and replace the rings of each piston before going on to the next. This helps avoid mixing up the rings. When the rings have been removed from each piston, clean and inspect the pis-

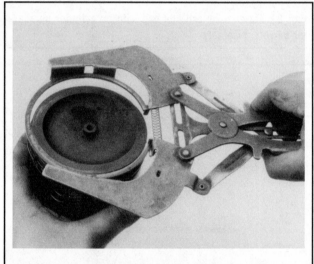
Use a ring expander tool to remove the piston rings

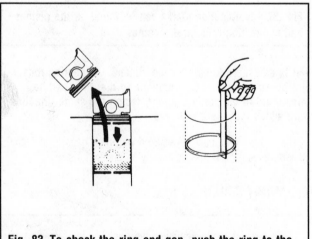
Fig. 83 To check the ring end-gap, push the ring to the bottom of its travel, then check the gap with a feeler gauge

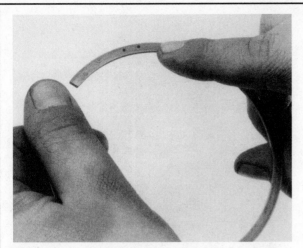

Most rings are marked to show which side should face upward

Fig. 85 Rock the piston at a right angle to check wrist pin-to-check pin wear and small end bushing wear

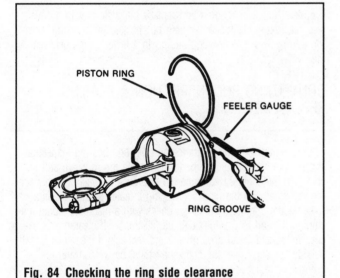

PISTON RING

FEELER GAUGE

RING GROOVE

Fig. 84 Checking the ring side clearance

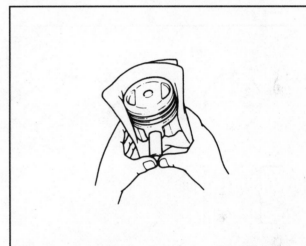

Fig. 86 When fully heated, the wrist pin should be able to be pushed into place by hand

ton, as described later in this section. The rings are marked on one side, the mark denoting the up side for installation.

Install the rings using the ring expander, starting with the top compression ring and working down. Make sure the marks are facing up on each ring. Position the rings so that the ring and gaps are set as in the illustrations. Never align the end gaps!

WRIST PIN REMOVAL & INSTALLATION

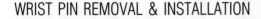

▶ See Figures 85 and 86

Wrist pin and/or connecting rod small-end bushing wear can be checked by rocking the piston at a right angle to the wrist pin by hand. If more than very slight movement is felt, the pin and/or rod busing must be replaced.

The pistons on the engines covered here must be heated in hot water to expand them before the wrist pins can be removed and installed. The four cylinder pistons must be heated to 176 degrees F (80 degrees C), and all six cylinder pistons must be heated to

140 degrees F (60 degrees C). This job can be performed at a machine shop if the idea of boiling pistons in the kitchen doesn't appeal to you. If you decide to do it, however, remember that each piston, pin and connecting rod assembly is a matched set and must be kept together until reassembly.

1. Using needlenose or snapring pliers, remove the snaprings from the piston.

2. Heat the piston(s) in hot water (as noted above depending on engine).

3. Using a plastic-faced hammer and driver, lightly tap the wrist pin out of the piston. Remove the piston from the connecting rod.

4. Assembly is in the opposite order of disassembly. The piston must again be heated to install the wrist pin and rod; it should be able to be pushed into place with your thumb when heated. When assembling, make sure the marks on the piston and connecting rod are aligned on the same side as shown.

CYLINDER BORE INSPECTION

▶ **See Figure 87**

Place a rag over the crankshaft journals. Wipe out each cylinder with a clean, solvent-soaked rag. Visually inspect the cylinder bores for roughness, scoring or scuffing; also check the bores by feel. Measure the cylinder bore diameter with an inside micrometer, or a telescope gauge and micrometer. Measure the bore at points parallel and perpendicular to the engine centerline at the top (below the ridge) and bottom of the bore. Subtract the bottom measurements from the top to determine cylinder taper.

Measure the piston diameter with a micrometer; since this micrometer may not be part of your tool kit (as it is necessarily large), you may need to have the pistons "miked" at a machine shop. Take the measurements at right angles to the wrist pin center line, about an inch down the piston skirt from the top. Compare this measurement to the bore diameter of each cylinder. The difference is the piston clearance. If the clearance is greater than that specified in the Piston and Ring Specifications chart, have the

Measure the piston's outer diameter using a micrometer

cylinders honed or rebored and replace the pistons with an oversize set. Piston clearance can also be checked by inverting a piston into a oiled cylinder, and sliding in a feeler gauge between the two.

CONNECTING ROD INSPECTION & BEARING REPLACEMENT

Connecting rod side clearance and big-end bearing inspection and replacement should be performed while the rods are still installed in the engine. Determine the clearance between the connecting rod sides and the crankshaft using a feeler gauge. If clearance is below the minimum tolerance, check with a machinist about machining the rod to provide adequate clearance. If clearance is excessive, substitute an unworn rod and recheck; if clearance is still outside specifications, the crankshaft must be welded and reground, or replaced.

To check connecting rod big-end bearing clearances, remove the rod bearing caps one at a time. Using a clean, dry shop rag, thoroughly clean all oil from the crank journal and bearing insert in the cap.

➡ **The Plastigage® gauging material you will be using to check clearances which is soluble in oil; therefore any oil on the journal or bearing could result in an incorrect reading.**

Lay a strip of Plastigage® along the full length of the bearing insert (along the crank journal if the engine is out of the car and inverted). Reinstall the cap and tighten to specifications listed in the Torque Specifications chart.

Remove the rod cap and determine the bearing clearance by comparing the width of the now flattened Plastigage® to the scale on the Plastigage® envelope. Journal taper is determined by comparing the width of the Plastigage® strip near its ends. Rotate the crankshaft 90 degrees and retest, to determine journal eccentricity.

➡ **Do not rotate the crankshaft with the Plastigage® installed.**

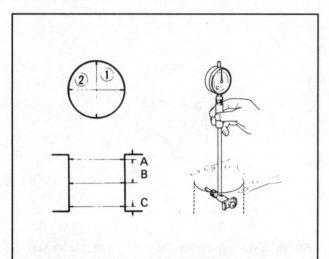
Fig. 87 Use a dial indicator to check the cylinder bore and piston clearance

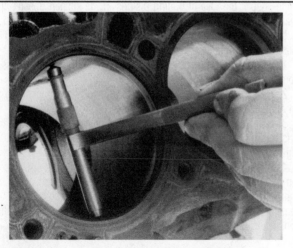
A telescoping gauge may be used to measure the cylinder bore diameter

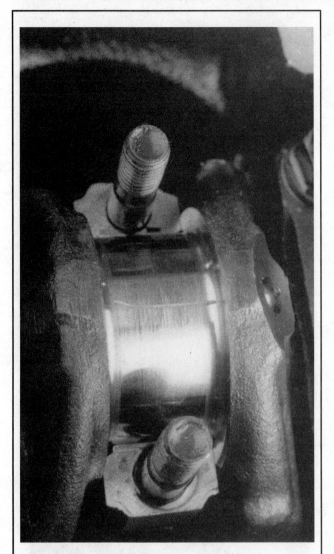

Apply a strip of gauging material to the bearing journal, then install and torque the cap

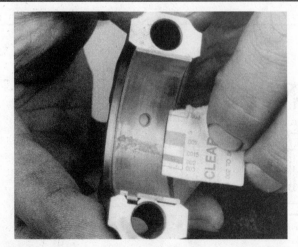

After the cap is removed again, use the scale supplied with the gauge material to check clearances

The notch on the the side of the bearing cap matches the groove on the bearing insert

If the bearing insert and crank journal appear intact and are within tolerances, no further service is required and the bearing caps can be reinstalled (remove Plastigage® before installation). If clearances are not within tolerances, the bearing inserts in both the connecting rod and rod cap must be replaced with undersize inserts, and/or the crankshaft must be reground. To install the bearing insert halves, press them into the bearing caps and connecting rods. Make sure the tab in each insert fits into the notch in each rod and cap. Lubricate the face of each insert with engine oil prior to installing each rod into the engine.

The connecting rods can be further inspected when they are removed form the engine and separated from their pistons. Rod alignment (straightness and squareness) must be checked by a machinist, as the rod must be set in a special fixture. Many machine shops also perform a Magnafluxing service, which is a process that shows up any tiny cracks that you may be unable to see.

Crankshaft and Main Bearings

REMOVAL & INSTALLATION

◗ **See Figures 88 and 89**

➡**Before removing the crankshaft, check main bearing clearances as described under Main Bearing Clearance Check below.**

1. Remove the piston and connecting rod assemblies following the procedure in this section.
2. Check crankshaft thrust clearance (end play) before removing the crank from the block. Using a prybar, pry the crankshaft the extent of its travel forward, and measure thrust clearance at the center main bearing (No. 4 bearing on 6 cylinder engines, No. 3 on 4 cylinder engines) with a feeler gauge. Pry the crankshaft the extent of its rearward travel, and measure the other side of the bearing. If clearance is greater than that specified, the thrust washers must be replaced (see main bearing installation, below).

3. Using a punch, mark the corresponding main bearing caps and saddles according to position: one punch on the front main cap and saddle, two on the second, three on the third, etc. This ensures correct reassembly.

4. Remove the main bearing caps after they have been marked.

5. Remove the crankshaft form the block.

6. Follow the crankshaft inspection, main bearing clearance checking and replacement procedures below before reinstalling the crankshaft.

INSPECTION

Crankshaft inspection and servicing should be handled exclusively by a reputable machinist, as most of the necessary procedures require a dial indicator and fixing jig, a large micrometer, and machine tools such as a crankshaft grinder. While at the machine shop, the crankshaft should be thoroughly cleaned (especially the oil passages). Magnafluxed (to check for minute cracks) and the following checks made: main journal diameter, crank pin

A dial gauge may be used to check crankshaft end-play

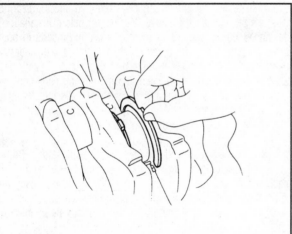

Fig. 88 Install the thrust washers with the oil grooves facing out

Carefully pry the shaft back and forth while reading the dial gauge for play

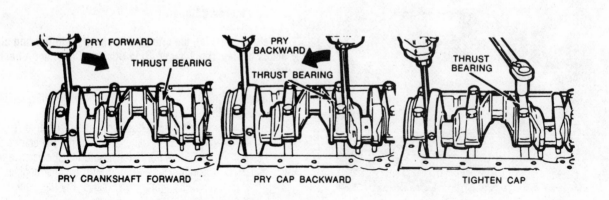

Fig. 89 Aligning the crankshaft thrust bearing

(connecting rod journal) diameter, taper and out-of-round, and run-out. Wear, beyond specification limits, in any of these areas means the crankshaft must be reground or replaced.

BEARING CLEARANCE CHECK

Checking main bearing clearances is done in the same manner as checking connecting rod big-end clearances.

1. With the crankshaft installed, remove the main bearing cap. Clean all oil form the bearing insert in the cap and from the crankshaft journal, as the Plastigage® material is oil-soluble.

2. Lay a strip of Plastigage® along the full width of the bearing cap (or along the width of the crank journal if the engine is out of the car and inverted).

3. Install the bearing cap and tighten to specification.

➡ **Do not rotate the crankshaft with the Plastigage® installed.**

4. Remove the bearing cap and determine bearing clearance by comparing the width of the now-flattened Plastigage® with the scale on the Plastigage® envelope. Journal taper is determined by comparing the width of the Plastigage® strip near its ends. Rotate the crankshaft 90 degrees and retest, to determine journal eccentricity.

5. Repeat the above for the remaining bearings. If the bearing journal and insert appear in good shape (with not unusual wear visible) and are within tolerances, no further main bearing service is required. If unusual wear is evident and/or the clearances are outside specifications, the bearings must be replaced and the cause of their wear found.

BEARING REPLACEMENT

Main bearings can be replaced with the crankshaft both in the engine (with the engine still in the car) and out of the engine (with the engine on a work stand or bench). Both procedures are covered here. The main bearings must be replaced if the crankshaft has been reground; the replacement bearing being available in various undersize increments from most auto parts jobbers or your local Toyota dealer.

Engine Out of Car

1. Remove the crankshaft from the engine block.

2. Remove the main bearing inserts from the bearing caps and from the main bearing saddles. Remove the thrust washers from the No. 3 (4-cylinder engine) or No. 4 (6-cylinder engine) crankshaft journal.

3. Thoroughly clean the saddles, bearing caps, and crankshaft.

4. Make sure the crankshaft has been fully checked and is ready for reassembly. Place the upper main bearings in the block saddles so that the oil grooves and/or oil holes are correctly aligned with their corresponding grooves or holes in the saddles.

5. Install the thrust washers on the center main bearing, with the oil grooves facing out.

6. Lubricate the faces of all bearings with clean engine oil, and place the crankshaft in the block.

7. Install the main bearing caps in numbered order with the arrows or any other orientation marks facing forward. Tighten all

Mounting a dial gauge to read crankshaft run-out

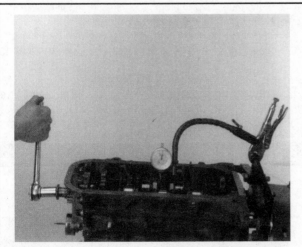

Turn the crankshaft slowly by hand while checking the gauge

bolts except the center cap bolts in sequence in two or three passes to the specified torque. Rotate the crankshaft after each pass to ensure even tightness.

8. Align the thrust bearing by prying the crankshaft the extent of its axial travel several times with a prybar. On last movement hold the crankshaft toward the front of the engine and tighten the thrust bearing cap to specifications. Measure the crankshaft thrust clearance (end play) as previously described in this section. If clearance is outside specifications (too sloppy), install a new set of oversize thrust washers and check clearance again.

Engine and Crankshaft Installed

1. Remove the main bearing caps and keep them in order.
2. Make a bearing roll-out pin from a cotter pin as shown.
3. Carefully roll out the old inserts from the upper side of the crankshaft journal, noting the positions of the oil grooves and/or oil holes so the new inserts can be correctly installed.
4. Roll each new insert into its saddle after lightly oiling the crankshaft-side face of each. Make sure the notches and/or oil holes are correctly positioned.
5. Replace the bearing inserts in the caps with new inserts. Oil the face of each, and install the caps in numbered order with the arrows or other orientation marks facing forward. Tighten the bolts to the specified torque in two or three passes in the sequence shown.

Freeze Plugs

REMOVAL & INSTALLATION

1. Raise and safely support the vehicle, as required.

✳✳ CAUTION

When draining coolant, keep in mind that cats and dogs are attracted by ethylene glycol antifreeze, and are quite likely to drink any that is left in an uncovered container or in puddles on the ground. This will prove fatal in sufficient quantity. Always drain coolant into a sealable container. Coolant may be reused unless it is contaminated or several years old.

2. Drain the cooling system. If the freeze plug is located in the cylinder block, it will be necessary to remove the drain plug from the side of the block to make sure all coolant is drained.
3. Drill a 1/2 in. (13mm) hole in the center of the plug. Remove the plug with a slide hammer or pry it out with a prybar.

➡**Be careful to stop drilling as soon as the bit breaks through the plug to prevent damaging the engine.**

4. Clean all dirt and corrosion from the freeze plug bore. Check the freeze plug bore for damage that would interfere with sealing. If the bore is damaged, the bore will have to be machined for an oversize plug.

To install:

5. Coat the plug bore and the freeze plug sealing surface with water proof sealer.
6. Install cup-type freeze plugs with the flanged edge outward. The plug must be driven in with a tool that does not contact the

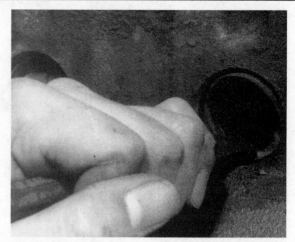

Using a punch and hammer, the freeze plug can be loosened in the block

Once the freeze plug has been loosened, it can be removed from the block

flange of the plug. If an improper tool is used, the plug sealing edge will be damaged and leakage will result.

7. Expansion-type freeze plugs are installed with the flanged edge inward. The plug must be driven in with a tool that does not contact the crowned portion of the plug. If an improper tool is used, the plug and/or plug bore will be damaged.
8. Replace any drain plugs that were removed and lower the vehicle.
9. Fill the cooling system, start the engine and check for leaks.

Block Heaters

REMOVAL & INSTALLATION

There are two basic types, one for oil and one for coolant. The oil heater usually just slips into the dipstick tube or replaces the oil drain plug. The following procedure is for the coolant type.

1. Remove the negative battery cable.
2. Drain the cooling system.

When draining coolant, keep in mind that cats and dogs are attracted by ethylene glycol antifreeze, and are quite likely to drink any that is left in an uncovered container or in puddles on the ground. This will prove fatal in sufficient quantity. Always drain coolant into a sealable container. Coolant may be reused unless it is contaminated or several years old.

3. Remove the block heater in the same way as the freeze plugs. Some heater units have a bolt that must be loosened or a V-clamp that must be unsecured to remove the heating element.

4. Disconnect the heater wire and remove the heater element.

To install:

5. Coat the new heater with sealant reinstall into the engine.

6. Fill the engine with a coolant and water mixture.

7. Start the engine, check for leaks and top off the coolant.

Flywheel and Ring Gear

REMOVAL & INSTALLATION

1. Remove the transmission, if the engine is installed in the car.

2. Remove the clutch assembly, if equipped.

3. Remove the flywheel.

4. To install, use new flywheel bolts. Tighten the bolts in a crisscross pattern to the torque specified in the chart in this section.

EXHAUST SYSTEM

General Information

➡**Safety glasses should be worn at all times when working on or near the exhaust system. Older exhaust systems will almost always be covered with loose rust particles which will shower you when disturbed. These particles are more than a nuisance and could injure your eye.**

Whenever working on the exhaust system always keep the following in mind:

• Check the complete exhaust system for open seams, holes loose connections, or other deterioration which could permit exhaust fumes to seep into the passenger compartment.

• The exhaust system is usually supported by free-hanging rubber mountings which permit some movement of the exhaust system, but does not permit transfer of noise and vibration into the passenger compartment. Do not replace the rubber mounts with solid ones.

• Before removing any component of the exhaust system, ALWAYS squirt a liquid rust dissolving agent onto the fasteners for ease of removal. A lot of knuckle skin will be saved by following this rule. It may even be wise to spray the fasteners and allow them to sit overnight.

Allow the exhaust system to cool sufficiently before spraying a solvent exhaust fasteners. Some solvents are highly flammable and could ignite when sprayed on hot exhaust components.

• Annoying rattles and noise vibrations in the exhaust system are usually caused by misalignment of the parts. When aligning the system, leave all bolts and nuts loose until all parts are properly aligned, then tighten, working from front to rear.

• When installing exhaust system parts, make sure there is enough clearance between the hot exhaust parts and pipes and hoses that would be adversely affected by excessive heat. Also make sure there is adequate clearance from the floor pan to avoid possible overheating of the floor.

Safety Precautions

• For a number of reasons, exhaust system work can be the most dangerous type of work you can do on your car. Always observe the following precautions:

• Support the car extra securely. Not only will you often be working directly under it, but you'll frequently be using a lot of force, such as heavy hammer blows, to dislodge rusted parts. This can cause a vehicle that's improperly supported to shift and possibly fall.

• Wear goggles. Exhaust system parts are always rusty. Metal chips can be dislodged, even when you're only turning rusted bolts. Attempting to pry pipes apart with a chisel makes the chips fly even more frequently.

• If you're using a cutting torch, keep it a great distance from either the fuel tank or lines. Stop what you're doing and feel the temperature of the fuel pipes on the tank frequently. Even slight heat can expand and/or vaporize fuel, resulting in accumulated vapor (or even a liquid leak) near your torch.

• Watch where your hammer blows fall and make sure you hit squarely. You could easily tap a brake or fuel line when you hit an exhaust system part with a glancing blow. Inspect all lines and hoses in the area where you've been working.

Be very careful when working on or near the catalytic converter. External temperatures can reach 1,500 degrees F (816 degrees C) and more, causing severe burns. Removal or installation should be performed only on a cold exhaust system.

A number of special exhaust system tools can be rented from auto supply houses or local stores that rent special equipment. A common one is a tail pipe expander, designed to enable you to join pipes of identical diameter.

The exhaust system of these Toyota models consist of several pieces. At the front of the vehicle, the first section of pipe connects the exhaust manifold to the catalytic converter. The in-line 6-cylinder uses a Y-pipe to connect the two outputs from the exhaust manifold. The catalytic converter is a sealed, non-service-able unit which can be easily unbolted from the system and re-placed if necessary.

The exhaust system is attached to the body by several hooks and flexible rubber hangers; these hangers absorb exhaust vibra-tions and isolate the system from the body of the car. A series of metal heat shields runs along the exhaust piping, protecting the underbody from excess heat.

When inspecting or replacing exhaust system parts, make sure there is adequate clearance from all points on the body to avoid possible overheating of the floorpan. Check the complete system for broken damaged, missing or poorly positioned parts. Rattles and vibrations in the exhaust system are usually caused by mis-alignment of parts. When aligning the system, leave all the nuts and bolts loose until everything is in its proper place, then tighten the hardware working from the front to the rear. Remember that what appears to be proper clearance during repair may change as the truck moves down the road. The motion of the engine, body and suspension must be considered when replacing parts.

Catalytic Converter

REMOVAL & INSTALLATION

✳✳ CAUTION

Do NOT perform exhaust repairs with the engine or exhaust hot. Allow the system to cool completely before attempting any work. Exhaust systems are noted for sharp edges, flak-ing metal and rusted bolts. Gloves and eye protection are required. A healthy supply of penetrating oil and rags is highly recommended.

1. Raise and support the vehicle on jackstands.
2. Remove the heat shield.
3. Some models have rubber O-ring supports; that may be in the way of removal, detach them, ensuring there is another sup-port for the converter once removed.
4. On some models you will need to remove the oxygen sen-sor. Unbolt the oxygen sensor and remove it. Protect the tip of the sensor from damage and do not place it on or near any petro-leum based solvents. This includes putting it on a greasy rag.
5. Remove the bolts at the front and rear of the converter.

➡**Always support the pipe running to the manifold, either by the normal clamps/hangers or by using string, stiff wire, etc. If left loose, the pipe can develop enough leverage to crack the manifold.**

6. Remove the converter and gaskets.
To install:
7. Check the rubber supports that hang the exhaust, they have a tendency to stretch and crack with age, replace if necessary.
8. Using new gaskets, attach the converter to the exhaust pipes. Tighten the bolts to 29–32 ft. lbs. (39–43 Nm).

➡**ALWAYS use a new gasket at each pipe joint whenever the joint is disassembled. Use new nuts and bolts to hold the joint properly. These two low-cost items will serve to prevent future leaks as the system ages.**

9. On models with the oxygen sensor in the catalyst, tighten the nuts to 14 ft. lbs. (20 Nm). Don't forget to connect the wire harness.

Muffler and/or Tailpipe

REMOVAL & INSTALLATION

✳✳ CAUTION

Do NOT perform exhaust repairs with the engine or exhaust hot. Allow the system to cool completely before attempting any work. Exhaust systems are noted for sharp edges, flak-ing metal and rusted bolts. Gloves and eye protection are required. A healthy supply of penetrating oil and rags is highly recommended.

The muffler and tailpipe on most Toyotas are one piece and should be replaced as a unit. The muffler includes a lead-in pipe to the muffler. All Toyota exhaust components bolt together with gaskets at the joints; no welding is involved.

1. Elevate and firmly support the rear of the vehicle.
2. On some models you will need to remove the oxygen sen-sor. Unbolt the oxygen sensor and remove it. Protect the tip of the sensor from damage and do not place it on or near any petro-leum based solvents. This includes putting it on a greasy rag.
3. Disconnect the nuts holding the muffler and/or tailpipe to the adjacent pipes.
4. Remove or disconnect the clamps and supports holding the pipe at either end. Leave the supports closest to the center in place until last.
5. Remove the last supports or hangers and lower the unit to the ground. At NO TIME should the muffler be allowed to hang partially supported; the leverage can break the next component in line.

➡**If the muffler or tailpipe is being replaced due to rust or corrosion, adjacent pipes should be checked for the same condition. The pieces tend to age at about the same rate.**

To install:
6. Check the rubber supports that hang the exhaust, they have a tendency to stretch and crack with age, replace if necessary.
7. Lift the new unit into place and loosely attach the hangers or supports to hold it in place. Allow some play to adjust the muf-fler.
8. Using new gaskets, connect each end to the adjoining pipe. Tighten the joint bolts and nuts to 29–32 ft. lbs. (39–43 Nm).

➡**ALWAYS use a new gasket at each pipe joint whenever the joint is disassembled. Use new nuts and bolts to hold the joint properly. These two low-cost items will serve to prevent future leaks as the system ages.**

9. Tighten the supports and hangers. Make certain the rubber hangers are securely attached to their mounts.

Complete System

REMOVAL & INSTALLATION

◆ **See Figures 90 thru 100 (p. 79–84)**

✴✴ CAUTION

Do NOT perform exhaust repairs with the engine or exhaust hot. Allow the system to cool completely before attempting any work. Exhaust systems are noted for sharp edges, flak-ing metal and rusted bolts. Gloves and eye protection are required. A healthy supply of penetrating oil and rags is highly recommended.

If the entire exhaust system is to be replaced, it is much easier to remove the system as a unit than remove each individual piece. Disconnect the first pipe at the manifold joint and work towards the rear removing brackets and hangers as you go. Separate the rear pipe at the catalytic converter. Remove any retaining brackets and O-rings from the center of exhaust system and back. Then, slide the rear section of the exhaust system out from the back the vehicle. Once removed from the vehicle, you can detach the cata-

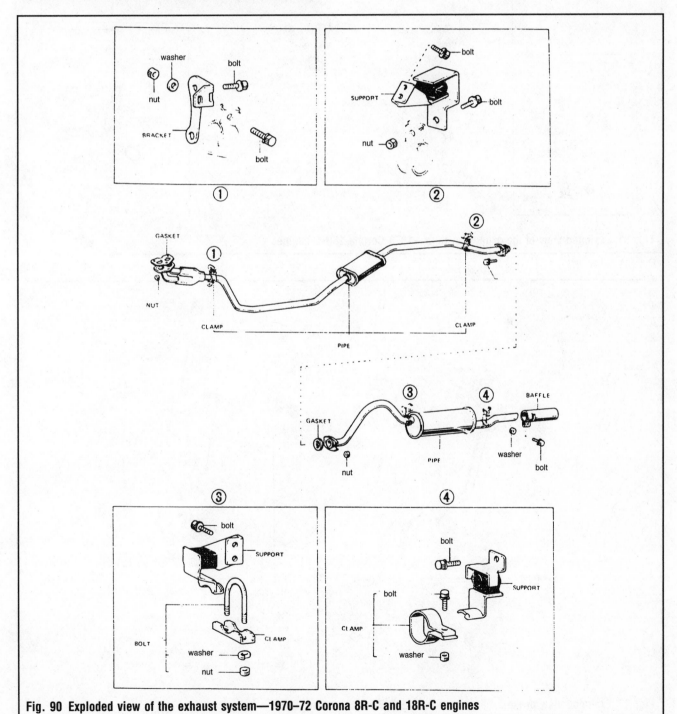

Fig. 90 Exploded view of the exhaust system—1970–72 Corona 8R-C and 18R-C engines

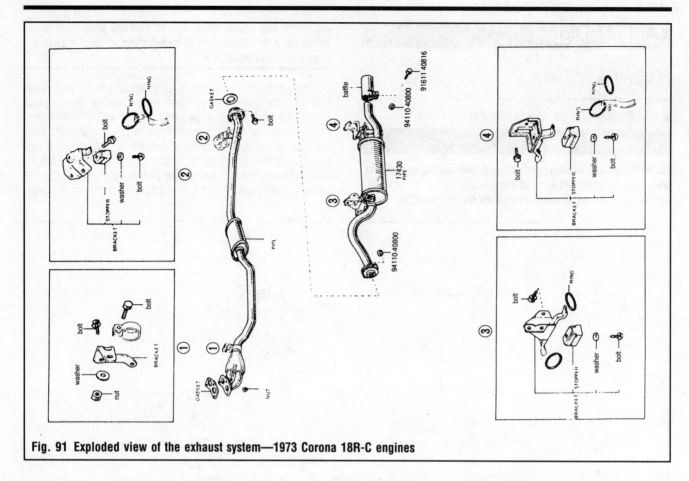

Fig. 91 Exploded view of the exhaust system—1973 Corona 18R-C engines

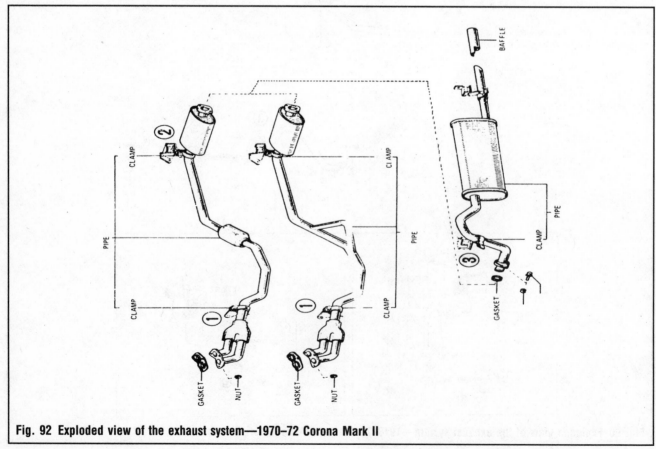

Fig. 92 Exploded view of the exhaust system—1970–72 Corona Mark II

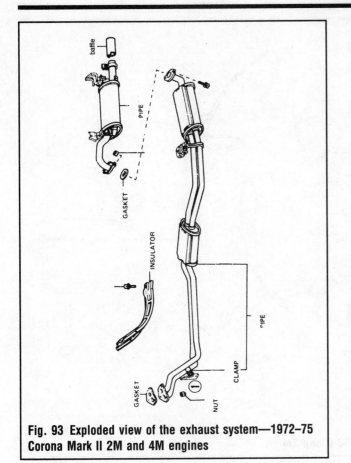

Fig. 93 Exploded view of the exhaust system—1972–75 Corona Mark II 2M and 4M engines

Fig. 94 Exploded view of the exhaust system—1975–77 Corona Mark II sedan 4M engine

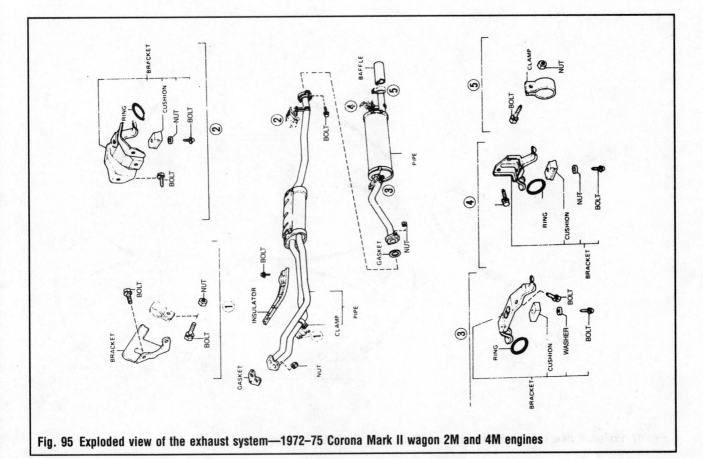

Fig. 95 Exploded view of the exhaust system—1972–75 Corona Mark II wagon 2M and 4M engines

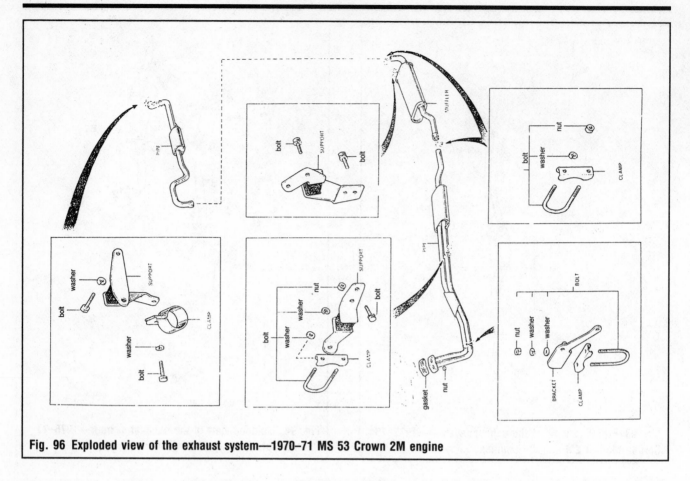

Fig. 96 Exploded view of the exhaust system—1970–71 MS 53 Crown 2M engine

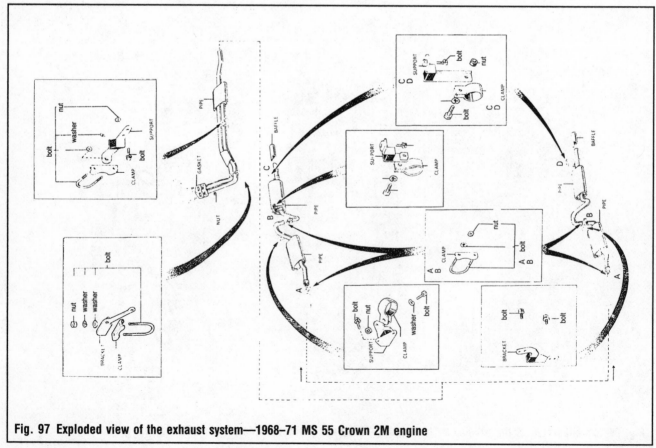

Fig. 97 Exploded view of the exhaust system—1968–71 MS 55 Crown 2M engine

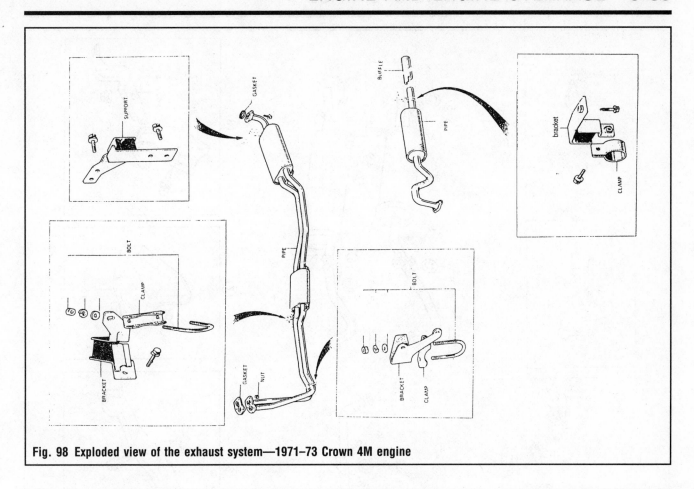

Fig. 98 Exploded view of the exhaust system—1971–73 Crown 4M engine

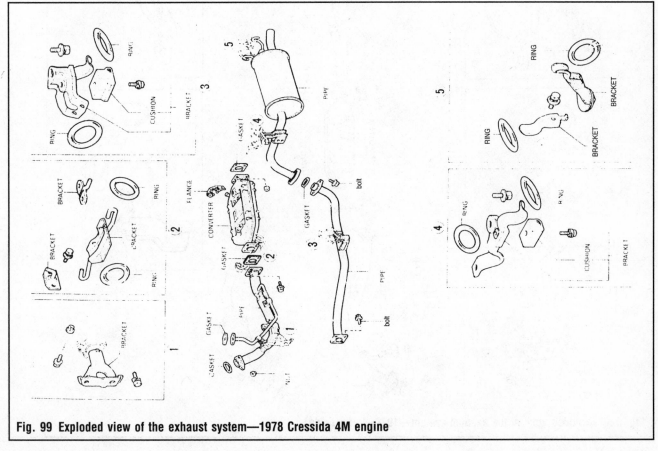

Fig. 99 Exploded view of the exhaust system—1978 Cressida 4M engine

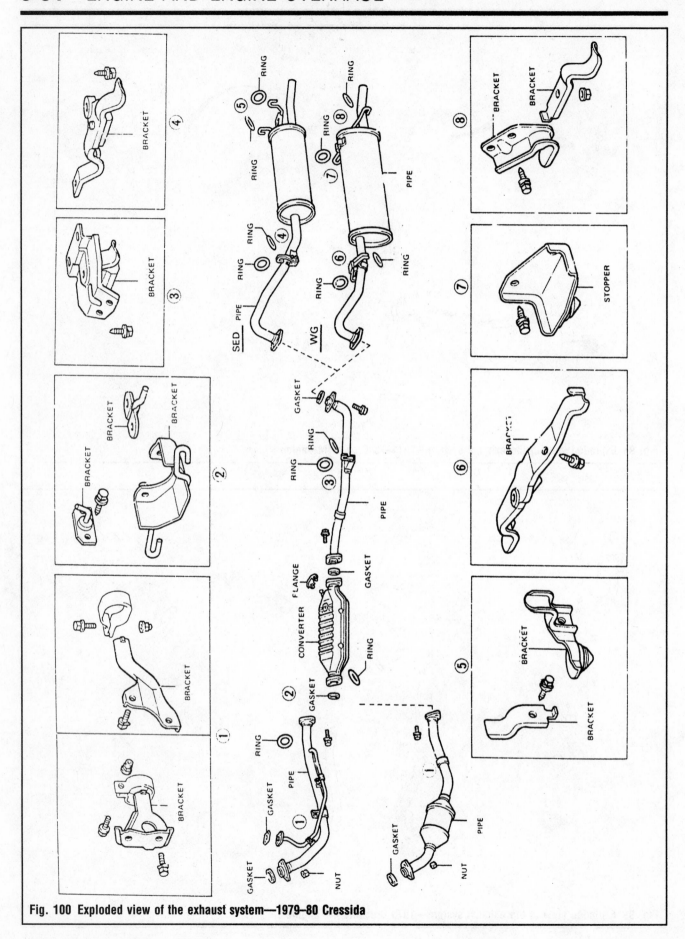

Fig. 100 Exploded view of the exhaust system—1979–80 Cressida

lytic converter from the system, as it is usually good enough to reuse.

The new system can then be bolted up on the workbench and easily checked for proper tightness and gasket integrity. When installing the new assembly, suspend it from the flexible hangers first, then attach the fixed (solid) brackets. Check the clearance to the body and suspension and install the manifold joint bolts, tightening them correctly.

COOLING SYSTEM

Radiator

REMOVAL & INSTALLATION

1. Drain the cooling system.

✳✳ CAUTION

When draining engine coolant, keep in mind that cats and dogs are attracted to ethylene glycol antifreeze and could drink any that is left in an uncovered container or in puddles on the ground. This will prove fatal in sufficient quantity. Always drain coolant into a sealable container. Coolant should be reused unless it is contaminated or is several years old.

2. Unfasten the clamps and remove the radiator upper and lower hoses. If equipped with an automatic transmission, remove the oil cooler lines.
3. Detach the hood lock cable and remove the hood lock from the radiator upper support.

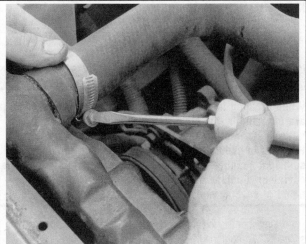

To remove the radiator, drain the system and remove the hose clamps . . .

Dont forget to detach the overflow hose from the cap, if equipped

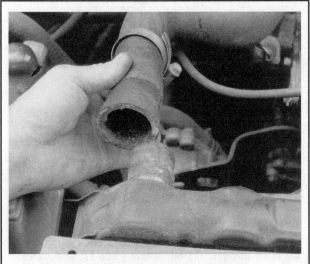

. . . and separate the hoses from the radiator

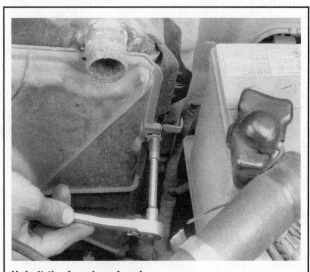

Unbolt the fan shroud and . . .

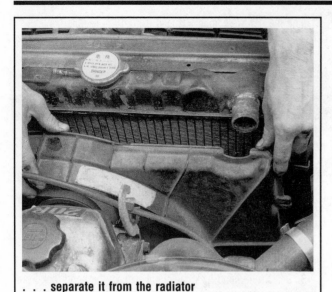

... **separate it from the radiator**

Unbolt the radiator from the supports

Carefully lift the unit from the engine compartment

➡It may be necessary to remove the grille in order to gain access to the hood lock/radiator support assembly.

4. Remove the fan shroud, if so equipped.
5. On models equipped with a coolant recovery system, disconnect the hose from the thermal expansion tank and remove the tank from its bracket.
6. Unbolt and remove the radiator upper support.
7. Unfasten the bolts and remove the radiator.

❊❊ WARNING

Use care not to damage the radiator fins on the cooling fan.

8. Installation is performed in the reverse order of removal. Remember to check the transmission fluid level on cars with automatic transmissions. Fill the radiator to the specified level, as detailed under Fluid Level Checks, in Chapter 1. Remember to check for leaks after installation is completed.

Water Pump

REMOVAL & INSTALLATION

1. Drain the cooling system.

❊❊ CAUTION

When draining the coolant, keep in mind that cats and dogs are attracted by the ethylene glycol antifreeze, and are quite likely to drink any that is left in an uncovered container or in puddles on the ground. This will prove fatal in sufficient quantity. Always drain the coolant into a sealable container. Coolant should be reused unless it is contaminated or several years old.

2. Unfasten the fan shroud securing bolts and remove the fan shroud, if so equipped.
3. Loosen the alternator adjusting link bolt and remove the drive belt.

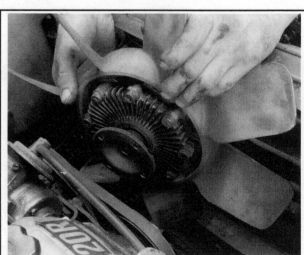

On some engines, the fan coupling and blade must be removed to access the water pump

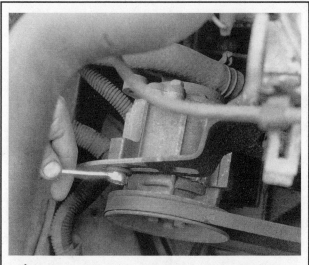

Loosen the tension on the drive belt, then remove it

. . . and separate the pump from the engine

Remove the pulley off the front of the water pump

Scrape all of the old gasket from the engine surface and water pump

Unbolt the water pump . . .

4. Repeat Step 3 for the air and/or power steering pump drive belt, if so equipped.

5. Detach the by-pass hose from the water pump. On the 5M-GE, remove the air cleaner case.

6. Unfasten the water pump retaining bolts and remove the water pump and fan assembly, using care not to damage the radiator with the fan.

➡ Some engines require fan coupling and blade removal.

✳✳ WARNING

If the fan is equipped with a fluid coupling, do not tip the fan/pump assembly on its side, as the fluid will run out.

7. Installation is performed in the reverse order of removal. Always use a new gasket between the pump body and its mounting.

Thermostat

REMOVAL & INSTALLATION

1. Drain the cooling system.

✳✳ CAUTION

When draining the coolant, keep in mind that cats and dogs are attracted by the ethylene glycol antifreeze, and are quite likely to drink any that is left in an uncovered container or in puddles on the ground. This will prove fatal in sufficient quantity. Always drain the coolant into a sealable container. Coolant should be reused unless it is contaminated or several years old.

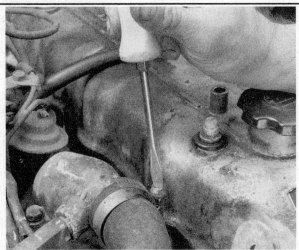

On thermostat removal, unfasten the clamps from the radiator hose attached to the housing

Use an extension to help reach the attaching bolts

Lift the housing off the engine to access the thermostat

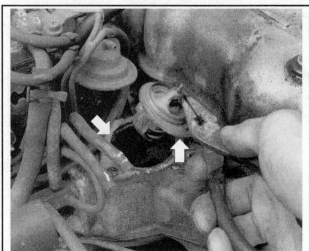

Remove the thermostat and scrape the old gasket material off the mating surfaces

2. Unfasten the clamp and remove the supper radiator hose from the water outlet elbow.
3. Unbolt and remove the water outlet (thermostat housing).
4. Withdraw the thermostat.
5. Installation is performed in the reverse order of the removal procedure. Use a new gasket on the water outlet.

✳✳ WARNING

Be sure that the thermostat is installed with the spring pointing down.

USING A VACUUM GAUGE

White needle = steady needle   *Dark needle = drifting needle*

The vacuum gauge is one of the most useful and easy-to-use diagnostic tools. It is inexpensive, easy to hook up, and provides valuable information about the condition of your engine.

Indication: Normal engine in good condition

Gauge reading: Steady, from 17–22 in./Hg.

Indication: Sticking valve or ignition miss

Gauge reading: Needle fluctuates from 15–20 in./Hg. at idle

Indication: Late ignition or valve timing, low compression, stuck throttle valve, leaking carburetor or manifold gasket.

Gauge reading: Low (15–20 in./Hg.) but steady

Indication: Improper carburetor adjustment, or minor intake leak at carburetor or manifold

NOTE: Bad fuel injector O-rings may also cause this reading.

Gauge reading: Drifting needle

Indication: Weak valve springs, worn valve stem guides, or leaky cylinder head gasket (vibrating excessively at all speeds).

NOTE: A plugged catalytic converter may also cause this reading.

Gauge reading: Needle fluctuates as engine speed increases

Indication: Burnt valve or improper valve clearance. The needle will drop when the defective valve operates.

Gauge reading: Steady needle, but drops regularly

Indication: Choked muffler or obstruction in system. Speed up the engine. Choked muffler will exhibit a slow drop of vacuum to zero.

Gauge reading: Gradual drop in reading at idle

Indication: Worn valve guides

Gauge reading: Needle vibrates excessively at idle, but steadies as engine speed increases

Troubleshooting Engine Mechanical Problems

Problem	Cause	Solution
External oil leaks	• Cylinder head cover RTV sealant broken or improperly seated	• Replace sealant; inspect cylinder head cover sealant flange and cylinder head sealant surface for distortion and cracks
	• Oil filler cap leaking or missing	• Replace cap
	• Oil filter gasket broken or improperly seated	• Replace oil filter
	• Oil pan side gasket broken, improperly seated or opening in RTV sealant	• Replace gasket or repair opening in sealant; inspect oil pan gasket flange for distortion
	• Oil pan front oil seal broken or improperly seated	• Replace seal; inspect timing case cover and oil pan seal flange for distortion
	• Oil pan rear oil seal broken or improperly seated	• Replace seal; inspect oil pan rear oil seal flange; inspect rear main bearing cap for cracks, plugged oil return channels, or distortion in seal groove
	• Timing case cover oil seal broken or improperly seated	• Replace seal
	• Excess oil pressure because of restricted PCV valve	• Replace PCV valve
	• Oil pan drain plug loose or has stripped threads	• Repair as necessary and tighten
	• Rear oil gallery plug loose	• Use appropriate sealant on gallery plug and tighten
	• Rear camshaft plug loose or improperly seated	• Seat camshaft plug or replace and seal, as necessary
Excessive oil consumption	• Oil level too high	• Drain oil to specified level
	• Oil with wrong viscosity being used	• Replace with specified oil
	• PCV valve stuck closed	• Replace PCV valve
	• Valve stem oil deflectors (or seals) are damaged, missing, or incorrect type	• Replace valve stem oil deflectors
	• Valve stems or valve guides worn	• Measure stem-to-guide clearance and repair as necessary
	• Poorly fitted or missing valve cover baffles	• Replace valve cover
	• Piston rings broken or missing	• Replace broken or missing rings
	• Scuffed piston	• Replace piston
	• Incorrect piston ring gap	• Measure ring gap, repair as necessary
	• Piston rings sticking or excessively loose in grooves	• Measure ring side clearance, repair as necessary
	• Compression rings installed upside down	• Repair as necessary
	• Cylinder walls worn, scored, or glazed	• Repair as necessary

Troubleshooting Engine Mechanical Problems

Problem	Cause	Solution
Excessive oil consumption (cont.)	• Piston ring gaps not properly staggered	• Repair as necessary
	• Excessive main or connecting rod bearing clearance	• Measure bearing clearance, repair as necessary
No oil pressure	• Low oil level	• Add oil to correct level
	• Oil pressure gauge, warning lamp or sending unit inaccurate	• Replace oil pressure gauge or warning lamp
	• Oil pump malfunction	• Replace oil pump
	• Oil pressure relief valve sticking	• Remove and inspect oil pressure relief valve assembly
	• Oil passages on pressure side of pump obstructed	• Inspect oil passages for obstruction
	• Oil pickup screen or tube obstructed	• Inspect oil pickup for obstruction
	• Loose oil inlet tube	• Tighten or seal inlet tube
Low oil pressure	• Low oil level	• Add oil to correct level
	• Inaccurate gauge, warning lamp or sending unit	• Replace oil pressure gauge or warning lamp
	• Oil excessively thin because of dilution, poor quality, or improper grade	• Drain and refill crankcase with recommended oil
	• Excessive oil temperature	• Correct cause of overheating engine
	• Oil pressure relief spring weak or sticking	• Remove and inspect oil pressure relief valve assembly
	• Oil inlet tube and screen assembly has restriction or air leak	• Remove and inspect oil inlet tube and screen assembly. (Fill inlet tube with lacquer thinner to locate leaks.)
	• Excessive oil pump clearance	• Measure clearances
	• Excessive main, rod, or camshaft bearing clearance	• Measure bearing clearances, repair as necessary
High oil pressure	• Improper oil viscosity	• Drain and refill crankcase with correct viscosity oil
	• Oil pressure gauge or sending unit inaccurate	• Replace oil pressure gauge
	• Oil pressure relief valve sticking closed	• Remove and inspect oil pressure relief valve assembly
Main bearing noise	• Insufficient oil supply	• Inspect for low oil level and low oil pressure
	• Main bearing clearance excessive	• Measure main bearing clearance, repair as necessary
	• Bearing insert missing	• Replace missing insert
	• Crankshaft end-play excessive	• Measure end-play, repair as necessary
	• Improperly tightened main bearing cap bolts	• Tighten bolts with specified torque
	• Loose flywheel or drive plate	• Tighten flywheel or drive plate attaching bolts
	• Loose or damaged vibration damper	• Repair as necessary

Troubleshooting Engine Mechanical Problems

Problem	Cause	Solution
Connecting rod bearing noise	• Insufficient oil supply	• Inspect for low oil level and low oil pressure
	• Carbon build-up on piston	• Remove carbon from piston crown
	• Bearing clearance excessive or bearing missing	• Measure clearance, repair as necessary
	• Crankshaft connecting rod journal out-of-round	• Measure journal dimensions, repair or replace as necessary
	• Misaligned connecting rod or cap	• Repair as necessary
	• Connecting rod bolts tightened improperly	• Tighten bolts with specified torque
Piston noise	• Piston-to-cylinder wall clearance excessive (scuffed piston)	• Measure clearance and examine piston
	• Cylinder walls excessively tapered or out-of-round	• Measure cylinder wall dimensions, rebore cylinder
	• Piston ring broken	• Replace all rings on piston
	• Loose or seized piston pin	• Measure piston-to-pin clearance, repair as necessary
	• Connecting rods misaligned	• Measure rod alignment, straighten or replace
	• Piston ring side clearance excessively loose or tight	• Measure ring side clearance, repair as necessary
	• Carbon build-up on piston is excessive	• Remove carbon from piston
Valve actuating component noise	• Insufficient oil supply	• Check for: (a) Low oil level (b) Low oil pressure (c) Wrong hydraulic tappets (d) Restricted oil gallery (e) Excessive tappet to bore clearance
	• Rocker arms or pivots worn	• Replace worn rocker arms or pivots
	• Foreign objects or chips in hydraulic tappets	• Clean tappets
	• Excessive tappet leak-down	• Replace valve tappet
	• Tappet face worn	• Replace tappet; inspect corresponding cam lobe for wear
	• Broken or cocked valve springs	• Properly seat cocked springs; replace broken springs
	• Stem-to-guide clearance excessive	• Measure stem-to-guide clearance, repair as required
	• Valve bent	• Replace valve
	• Loose rocker arms	• Check and repair as necessary
	• Valve seat runout excessive	• Regrind valve seat/valves
	• Missing valve lock	• Install valve lock
	• Excessive engine oil	• Correct oil level

Troubleshooting Engine Performance

Problem	Cause	Solution
Hard starting (engine cranks normally)	• Faulty engine control system component	• Repair or replace as necessary
	• Faulty fuel pump	• Replace fuel pump
	• Faulty fuel system component	• Repair or replace as necessary
	• Faulty ignition coil	• Test and replace as necessary
	• Improper spark plug gap	• Adjust gap
	• Incorrect ignition timing	• Adjust timing
	• Incorrect valve timing	• Check valve timing; repair as necessary
Rough idle or stalling	• Incorrect curb or fast idle speed	• Adjust curb or fast idle speed (If possible)
	• Incorrect ignition timing	• Adjust timing to specification
	• Improper feedback system operation	• Refer to Chapter 4
	• Faulty EGR valve operation	• Test EGR system and replace as necessary
	• Faulty PCV valve air flow	• Test PCV valve and replace as necessary
	• Faulty TAC vacuum motor or valve	• Repair as necessary
	• Air leak into manifold vacuum	• Inspect manifold vacuum connections and repair as necessary
	• Faulty distributor rotor or cap	• Replace rotor or cap (Distributor systems only)
	• Improperly seated valves	• Test cylinder compression, repair as necessary
	• Incorrect ignition wiring	• Inspect wiring and correct as necessary
	• Faulty ignition coil	• Test coil and replace as necessary
	• Restricted air vent or idle passages	• Clean passages
	• Restricted air cleaner	• Clean or replace air cleaner filter element
Faulty low-speed operation	• Restricted idle air vents and passages	• Clean air vents and passages
	• Restricted air cleaner	• Clean or replace air cleaner filter element
	• Faulty spark plugs	• Clean or replace spark plugs
	• Dirty, corroded, or loose ignition secondary circuit wire connections	• Clean or tighten secondary circuit wire connections
	• Improper feedback system operation	• Refer to Chapter 4
	• Faulty ignition coil high voltage wire	• Replace ignition coil high voltage wire (Distributor systems only)
	• Faulty distributor cap	• Replace cap (Distributor systems only)
Faulty acceleration	• Incorrect ignition timing	• Adjust timing
	• Faulty fuel system component	• Repair or replace as necessary
	• Faulty spark plug(s)	• Clean or replace spark plug(s)
	• Improperly seated valves	• Test cylinder compression, repair as necessary
	• Faulty ignition coil	• Test coil and replace as necessary

Troubleshooting Engine Performance

Problem	Cause	Solution
Faulty acceleration (cont.)	• Improper feedback system operation	• Refer to Chapter 4
Faulty high speed operation	• Incorrect ignition timing • Faulty advance mechanism	• Adjust timing (if possible) • Check advance mechanism and repair as necessary (Distributor systems only)
	• Low fuel pump volume • Wrong spark plug air gap or wrong plug • Partially restricted exhaust manifold, exhaust pipe, catalytic converter, muffler, or tailpipe	• Replace fuel pump • Adjust air gap or install correct plug • Eliminate restriction
	• Restricted vacuum passages • Restricted air cleaner	• Clean passages • Cleaner or replace filter element as necessary
	• Faulty distributor rotor or cap	• Replace rotor or cap (Distributor systems only)
	• Faulty ignition coil • Improperly seated valve(s)	• Test coil and replace as necessary • Test cylinder compression, repair as necessary
	• Faulty valve spring(s)	• Inspect and test valve spring tension, replace as necessary
	• Incorrect valve timing	• Check valve timing and repair as necessary
	• Intake manifold restricted	• Remove restriction or replace manifold
	• Worn distributor shaft	• Replace shaft (Distributor systems only)
	• Improper feedback system operation	• Refer to Chapter 4
Misfire at all speeds	• Faulty spark plug(s) • Faulty spark plug wire(s) • Faulty distributor cap or rotor	• Clean or relace spark plug(s) • Replace as necessary • Replace cap or rotor (Distributor systems only)
	• Faulty ignition coil • Primary ignition circuit shorted or open intermittently • Improperly seated valve(s)	• Test coil and replace as necessary • Troubleshoot primary circuit and repair as necessary • Test cylinder compression, repair as necessary
	• Faulty hydraulic tappet(s) • Improper feedback system operation • Faulty valve spring(s)	• Clean or replace tappet(s) • Refer to Chapter 4 • Inspect and test valve spring tension, repair as necessary
	• Worn camshaft lobes • Air leak into manifold	• Replace camshaft • Check manifold vacuum and repair as necessary
	• Fuel pump volume or pressure low • Blown cylinder head gasket • Intake or exhaust manifold passage(s) restricted	• Replace fuel pump • Replace gasket • Pass chain through passage(s) and repair as necessary
Power not up to normal	• Incorrect ignition timing • Faulty distributor rotor	• Adjust timing • Replace rotor (Distributor systems only)

Troubleshooting Engine Performance

Problem	Cause	Solution
Power not up to normal (cont.)	• Incorrect spark plug gap	• Adjust gap
	• Faulty fuel pump	• Replace fuel pump
	• Faulty fuel pump	• Replace fuel pump
	• Incorrect valve timing	• Check valve timing and repair as necessary
	• Faulty ignition coil	• Test coil and replace as necessary
	• Faulty ignition wires	• Test wires and replace as necessary
	• Improperly seated valves	• Test cylinder compression and repair as necessary
	• Blown cylinder head gasket	• Replace gasket
	• Leaking piston rings	• Test compression and repair as necessary
	• Improper feedback system operation	• Refer to Chapter 4
Intake backfire	• Improper ignition timing	• Adjust timing
	• Defective EGR component	• Repair as necessary
	• Defective TAC vacuum motor or valve	• Repair as necessary
Exhaust backfire	• Air leak into manifold vacuum	• Check manifold vacuum and repair as necessary
	• Faulty air injection diverter valve	• Test diverter valve and replace as necessary
	• Exhaust leak	• Locate and eliminate leak
Ping or spark knock	• Incorrect ignition timing	• Adjust timing
	• Distributor advance malfunction	• Inspect advance mechanism and repair as necessary (Distributor systems only)
	• Excessive combustion chamber deposits	• Remove with combustion chamber cleaner
	• Air leak into manifold vacuum	• Check manifold vacuum and repair as necessary
	• Excessively high compression	• Test compression and repair as necessary
	• Fuel octane rating excessively low	• Try alternate fuel source
	• Sharp edges in combustion chamber	• Grind smooth
	• EGR valve not functioning properly	• Test EGR system and replace as necessary
Surging (at cruising to top speeds)	• Low fuel pump pressure or volume	• Replace fuel pump
	• Improper PCV valve air flow	• Test PCV valve and replace as necessary
	• Air leak into manifold vacuum	• Check manifold vacuum and repair as necessary
	• Incorrect spark advance	• Test and replace as necessary
	• Restricted fuel filter	• Replace fuel filter
	• Restricted air cleaner	• Clean or replace air cleaner filter element
	• EGR valve not functioning properly	• Test EGR system and replace as necessary
	• Improper feedback system operation	• Refer to Chapter 4

Troubleshooting the Serpentine Drive Belt

Problem	Cause	Solution
Tension sheeting fabric failure (woven fabric on outside circumference of belt has cracked or separated from body of belt)	• Grooved or backside idler pulley diameters are less than minimum recommended • Tension sheeting contacting (rubbing) stationary object • Excessive heat causing woven fabric to age • Tension sheeting splice has fractured	• Replace pulley(s) not conforming to specification • Correct rubbing condition • Replace belt • Replace belt
Noise (objectional squeal, squeak, or rumble is heard or felt while drive belt is in operation)	• Belt slippage • Bearing noise • Belt misalignment • Belt-to-pulley mismatch • Driven component inducing vibration • System resonant frequency inducing vibration	• Adjust belt • Locate and repair • Align belt/pulley(s) • Install correct belt • Locate defective driven component and repair • Vary belt tension within specifications. Replace belt.
Rib chunking (one or more ribs has separated from belt body)	• Foreign objects imbedded in pulley grooves • Installation damage • Drive loads in excess of design specifications • Insufficient internal belt adhesion	• Remove foreign objects from pulley grooves • Replace belt • Adjust belt tension • Replace belt
Rib or belt wear (belt ribs contact bottom of pulley grooves)	• Pulley(s) misaligned • Mismatch of belt and pulley groove widths • Abrasive environment • Rusted pulley(s) • Sharp or jagged pulley groove tips • Rubber deteriorated	• Align pulley(s) • Replace belt • Replace belt • Clean rust from pulley(s) • Replace pulley • Replace belt
Longitudinal belt cracking (cracks between two ribs)	• Belt has mistracked from pulley groove • Pulley groove tip has worn away rubber-to-tensile member	• Replace belt • Replace belt
Belt slips	• Belt slipping because of insufficient tension • Belt or pulley subjected to substance (belt dressing, oil, ethylene glycol) that has reduced friction • Driven component bearing failure • Belt glazed and hardened from heat and excessive slippage	• Adjust tension • Replace belt and clean pulleys • Replace faulty component bearing • Replace belt
"Groove jumping" (belt does not maintain correct position on pulley, or turns over and/or runs off pulleys)	• Insufficient belt tension • Pulley(s) not within design tolerance • Foreign object(s) in grooves	• Adjust belt tension • Replace pulley(s) • Remove foreign objects from grooves

AIR POLLUTION 4-2
NATURAL POLLUTANTS 4-2
INDUSTRIAL POLLUTANTS 4-2
AUTOMOTIVE POLLUTANTS 4-2
    TEMPERATURE INVERSION 4-2
    HEAT TRANSFER 4-3
AUTOMOTIVE EMISSIONS 4-3
EXHAUST GASES 4-3
    HYDROCARBONS 4-3
    CARBON MONOXIDE 4-4
    NITROGEN 4-4
    OXIDES OF SULFUR 4-4
    PARTICULATE MATTER 4-4
CRANKCASE EMISSIONS 4-5
EVAPORATIVE EMISSIONS 4-5
EMISSION CONTROLS 4-5
CRANKCASE VENTILATION
  SYSTEM 4-5
    OPERATION 4-5
    REMOVAL & INSTALLATION 4-7
    TESTING 4-7
AIR INJECTION SYSTEM 4-8
    OPERATION 4-8
    REMOVAL & INSTALLATION 4-14
    TESTING 4-15
EVAPORATIVE EMISSION CONTROL
  SYSTEM 4-17
    OPERATION 4-17
    REMOVAL & INSTALLATION 4-21
    TESTING 4-21
CARBURETOR AUXILIARY SLOW
  SYSTEM 4-23
    OPERATION 4-23
    REMOVAL & INSTALLATION 4-23
    TESTING 4-23
THROTTLE POSITIONER 4-23
    OPERATION 4-23
    ADJUSTMENT 4-25
MIXTURE CONTROL VALVE 4-25
    REMOVAL & INSTALLATION 4-27
    TESTING 4-27
AUXILIARY ACCELERATION PUMP
  SYSTEM 4-27
    OPERATION 4-27
    TESTING 4-28
AUXILIARY ENRICHMENT SYSTEM 4-29
    TESTING 4-30
SPARK DELAY VALVE 4-30
    TESTING 4-30
DUAL DIAPHRAGM DISTRIBUTOR 4-30
    TESTING 4-30
ENGINE MODIFICATIONS SYSTEM 4-31
    OPERATION 4-31
    INSPECTION 4-32
CHOKE OPENER SYSTEM 4-32
    OPERATION 4-32
FAST IDLE CAM BREAKER 4-33
    TESTING 4-33
CHOKE BREAKER SYSTEM 4-34
    ADJUSTMENT 4-34
HOT IDLE COMPENSATION VALVE 4-35

TESTING 4-35
SECONDARY SLOW CIRCUIT FUEL CUT
  SYSTEM 4-35
    TESTING 4-35
DECELERATION FUEL CUT
  SYSTEM 4-35
    TESTING 4-35
HIGH ALTITUDE COMPENSATION
  SYSTEM 4-35
BI-METAL VACUUM SWITCHING
  VALVE 4-35
    TESTING 4-35
HOT AIR INTAKE SYSTEM 4-36
EXHAUST GAS RECIRCULATION (EGR)
  SYSTEM 4-36
    OPERATION 4-36
    TESTING 4-38
    SYSTEM CHECKS 4-40
CATALYTIC CONVERTERS 4-40
    PRECAUTIONS 4-40
    WARNING LIGHT CHECKS 4-42
    REMOVAL & INSTALLATION 4-42
VACUUM DIAGRAMS 4-43
COMPONENT LOCATIONS
  TYPICAL EMISSION COMPONENT
    LOCATIONS—20R ENGINE 4-13
TROUBLESHOOTING CHARTS
  AIR INJECTION SYSTEM DIAGNOSIS
    CHART 4-16
  THROTTLE POSITIONER SETTINGS
    (RPM) 4-25

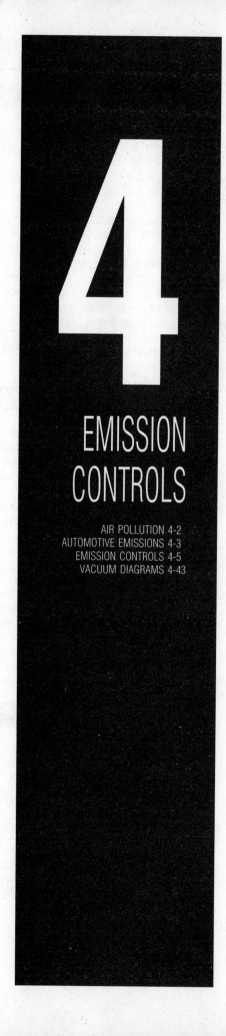

4
EMISSION CONTROLS

AIR POLLUTION 4-2
AUTOMOTIVE EMISSIONS 4-3
EMISSION CONTROLS 4-5
VACUUM DIAGRAMS 4-43

AIR POLLUTION

The earth's atmosphere, at or near sea level, consists approximately of 78 percent nitrogen, 21 percent oxygen and 1 percent other gases. If it were possible to remain in this state, 100 percent clean air would result. However, many varied sources allow other gases and particulates to mix with the clean air, causing our atmosphere to become unclean or polluted.

Some of these pollutants are visible while others are invisible, with each having the capability of causing distress to the eyes, ears, throat, skin and respiratory system. Should these pollutants become concentrated in a specific area and under certain conditions, death could result due to the displacement or chemical change of the oxygen content in the air. These pollutants can also cause great damage to the environment and to the many man made objects that are exposed to the elements.

To better understand the causes of air pollution, the pollutants can be categorized into 3 separate types, natural, industrial and automotive.

Natural Pollutants

Natural pollution has been present on earth since before man appeared and continues to be a factor when discussing air pollution, although it causes only a small percentage of the overall pollution problem. It is the direct result of decaying organic matter, wind born smoke and particulates from such natural events as plain and forest fires (ignited by heat or lightning), volcanic ash, sand and dust which can spread over a large area of the countryside.

Such a phenomenon of natural pollution has been seen in the form of volcanic eruptions, with the resulting plume of smoke, steam and volcanic ash blotting out the sun's rays as it spreads and rises higher into the atmosphere. As it travels into the atmosphere the upper air currents catch and carry the smoke and ash, while condensing the steam back into water vapor. As the water vapor, smoke and ash travel on their journey, the smoke dissipates into the atmosphere while the ash and moisture settle back to earth in a trail hundreds of miles long. In some cases, lives are lost and millions of dollars of property damage result.

Industrial Pollutants

Industrial pollution is caused primarily by industrial processes, the burning of coal, oil and natural gas, which in turn produce smoke and fumes. Because the burning fuels contain large amounts of sulfur, the principal ingredients of smoke and fumes are sulfur dioxide and particulate matter. This type of pollutant occurs most severely during still, damp and cool weather, such as at night. Even in its less severe form, this pollutant is not confined to just cities. Because of air movements, the pollutants move for miles over the surrounding countryside, leaving in its path a barren and unhealthy environment for all living things.

Working with Federal, State and Local mandated regulations and by carefully monitoring emissions, big business has greatly reduced the amount of pollutant introduced from its industrial sources, striving to obtain an acceptable level. Because of the mandated industrial emission clean up, many land areas and streams in and around the cities that were formerly barren of vegetation and life, have now begun to move back in the direction of nature's intended balance.

Automotive Pollutants

The third major source of air pollution is automotive emissions. The emissions from the internal combustion engines were not an appreciable problem years ago because of the small number of registered vehicles and the nation's small highway system. However, during the early 1950's, the trend of the American people was to move from the cities to the surrounding suburbs. This caused an immediate problem in transportation because the majority of suburbs were not afforded mass transit conveniences. This lack of transportation created an attractive market for the automobile manufacturers, which resulted in a dramatic increase in the number of vehicles produced and sold, along with a marked increase in highway construction between cities and the suburbs. Multi-vehicle families emerged with a growing emphasis placed on an individual vehicle per family member. As the increase in vehicle ownership and usage occurred, so did pollutant levels in and around the cities, as suburbanites drove daily to their businesses and employment, returning at the end of the day to their homes in the suburbs.

It was noted that a smoke and fog type haze was being formed and at times, remained in suspension over the cities, taking time to dissipate. At first this "smog," derived from the words "smoke" and "fog," was thought to result from industrial pollution but it was determined that automobile emissions shared the blame. It was discovered that when normal automobile emissions were exposed to sunlight for a period of time, complex chemical reactions would take place.

It is now known that smog is a photo chemical layer which develops when certain oxides of nitrogen (NOx) and unburned hydrocarbons (HC) from automobile emissions are exposed to sunlight. Pollution was more severe when smog would become stagnant over an area in which a warm layer of air settled over the top of the cooler air mass, trapping and holding the cooler mass at ground level. The trapped cooler air would keep the emissions from being dispersed and diluted through normal air flows. This type of air stagnation was given the name "Temperature Inversion."

TEMPERATURE INVERSION

In normal weather situations, surface air is warmed by heat radiating from the earth's surface and the sun's rays. This causes it to rise upward, into the atmosphere. Upon rising it will cool through a convection type heat exchange with the cooler upper air. As warm air rises, the surface pollutants are carried upward and dissipated into the atmosphere.

When a temperature inversion occurs, we find the higher air is no longer cooler, but is warmer than the surface air, causing the cooler surface air to become trapped. This warm air blanket can extend from above ground level to a few hundred or even a few thousand feet into the air. As the surface air is trapped, so are the pollutants, causing a severe smog condition. Should this stagnant air mass extend to a few thousand feet high, enough air movement with the inversion takes place to allow the smog layer to rise above ground level but the pollutants still cannot dissipate. This inversion can remain for days over an area, with the smog level only rising or lowering from ground level to a few hundred feet high. Meanwhile, the pollutant levels increase, causing eye irritation, respiratory problems, reduced visibility, plant damage and in some cases, even disease.

This inversion phenomenon was first noted in the Los Angeles, California area. The city lies in terrain resembling a basin and with certain weather conditions, a cold air mass is held in the basin while a warmer air mass covers it like a lid.

Because this type of condition was first documented as prevalent in the Los Angeles area, this type of trapped pollution was named Los Angeles Smog, although it occurs in other areas where a large concentration of automobiles are used and the air remains stagnant for any length of time.

HEAT TRANSFER

Consider the internal combustion engine as a machine in which raw materials must be placed so a finished product comes out. As in any machine operation, a certain amount of wasted material is formed. When we relate this to the internal combustion engine, we find that through the input of air and fuel, we obtain power during the combustion process to drive the vehicle. The by-product or waste of this power is, in part, heat and exhaust gases with which we must dispose.

AUTOMOTIVE EMISSIONS

Before emission controls were mandated on internal combustion engines, other sources of engine pollutants were discovered along with the exhaust emissions. It was determined that engine combustion exhaust produced approximately 60 percent of the total emission pollutants, fuel evaporation from the fuel tank and carburetor vents produced 20 percent, with the final 20 percent being produced through the crankcase as a by-product of the combustion process.

Exhaust Gases

The exhaust gases emitted into the atmosphere are a combination of burned and unburned fuel. To understand the exhaust emission and its composition, we must review some basic chemistry.

When the air/fuel mixture is introduced into the engine, we are mixing air, composed of nitrogen (78 percent), oxygen (21 percent) and other gases (1 percent) with the fuel, which is 100 percent hydrocarbons (HC), in a semi-controlled ratio. As the combustion process is accomplished, power is produced to move the vehicle while the heat of combustion is transferred to the cooling system. The exhaust gases are then composed of nitrogen, a diatomic gas (N_2), the same as was introduced in the engine, carbon dioxide (CO_2), the same gas that is used in beverage carbonation, and water vapor (H_2O). The nitrogen (N_2), for the most part, passes through the engine unchanged, while the oxygen (O_2) reacts (burns) with the hydrocarbons (HC) and produces the carbon dioxide (CO_2) and the water vapors (H_2O). If this chemical process would be the only process to take place, the exhaust emis-

The heat from the combustion process can rise to over 4000°F (2204°C). The dissipation of this heat is controlled by a ram air effect, the use of cooling fans to cause air flow and a liquid coolant solution surrounding the combustion area to transfer the heat of combustion through the cylinder walls and into the coolant. The coolant is then directed to a thin-finned, multi-tubed radiator, from which the excess heat is transferred to the atmosphere by 1 of the 3 heat transfer methods, conduction, convection or radiation.

The cooling of the combustion area is an important part in the control of exhaust emissions. To understand the behavior of the combustion and transfer of its heat, consider the air/fuel charge. It is ignited and the flame front burns progressively across the combustion chamber until the burning charge reaches the cylinder walls. Some of the fuel in contact with the walls is not hot enough to burn, thereby snuffing out or quenching the combustion process. This leaves unburned fuel in the combustion chamber. This unburned fuel is then forced out of the cylinder and into the exhaust system, along with the exhaust gases.

Many attempts have been made to minimize the amount of unburned fuel in the combustion chambers due to quenching, by increasing the coolant temperature and lessening the contact area of the coolant around the combustion area. However, design limitations within the combustion chambers prevent the complete burning of the air/fuel charge, so a certain amount of the unburned fuel is still expelled into the exhaust system, regardless of modifications to the engine.

sions would be harmless. However, during the combustion process, other compounds are formed which are considered dangerous. These pollutants are hydrocarbons (HC), carbon monoxide (CO), oxides of nitrogen (NOx) oxides of sulfur (SOx) and engine particulates.

HYDROCARBONS

Hydrocarbons (HC) are essentially fuel which was not burned during the combustion process or which has escaped into the atmosphere through fuel evaporation. The main sources of incomplete combustion are rich air/fuel mixtures, low engine temperatures and improper spark timing. The main sources of hydrocarbon emission through fuel evaporation on most vehicles used to be the vehicle's fuel tank and carburetor float bowl.

To reduce combustion hydrocarbon emission, engine modifications were made to minimize dead space and surface area in the combustion chamber. In addition, the air/fuel mixture was made more lean through the improved control which feedback carburetion and fuel injection offers and by the addition of external controls to aid in further combustion of the hydrocarbons outside the engine. Two such methods were the addition of air injection systems, to inject fresh air into the exhaust manifolds and the installation of catalytic converters, units that are able to burn traces of hydrocarbons without affecting the internal combustion process or fuel economy.

To control hydrocarbon emissions through fuel evaporation,

modifications were made to the fuel tank to allow storage of the fuel vapors during periods of engine shut-down. Modifications were also made to the air intake system so that at specific times during engine operation, these vapors may be purged and burned by blending them with the air/fuel mixture.

CARBON MONOXIDE

Carbon monoxide is formed when not enough oxygen is present during the combustion process to convert carbon (C) to carbon dioxide (CO_2). An increase in the carbon monoxide (CO) emission is normally accompanied by an increase in the hydrocarbon (HC) emission because of the lack of oxygen to completely burn all of the fuel mixture.

Carbon monoxide (CO) also increases the rate at which the photo chemical smog is formed by speeding up the conversion of nitric oxide (NO) to nitrogen dioxide (NO_2). To accomplish this, carbon monoxide (CO) combines with oxygen (O_2) and nitric oxide (NO) to produce carbon dioxide (CO_2) and nitrogen dioxide (NO_2). ($CO + O_2 + NO$ $CO_2 + NO_2$).

The dangers of carbon monoxide, which is an odorless and colorless toxic gas are many. When carbon monoxide is inhaled into the lungs and passed into the blood stream, oxygen is replaced by the carbon monoxide in the red blood cells, causing a reduction in the amount of oxygen supplied to the many parts of the body. This lack of oxygen causes headaches, lack of coordination, reduced mental alertness and, should the carbon monoxide concentration be high enough, death could result.

NITROGEN

Normally, nitrogen is an inert gas. When heated to approximately 2500°F (1371°C) through the combustion process, this gas becomes active and causes an increase in the nitric oxide (NO) emission.

Oxides of nitrogen (NOx) are composed of approximately 97–98 percent nitric oxide (NO). Nitric oxide is a colorless gas but when it is passed into the atmosphere, it combines with oxygen and forms nitrogen dioxide (NO_2). The nitrogen dioxide then combines with chemically active hydrocarbons (HC) and when in the presence of sunlight, causes the formation of photo-chemical smog.

Ozone

To further complicate matters, some of the nitrogen dioxide (NO_2) is broken apart by the sunlight to form nitric oxide and oxygen. (NO_2 + sunlight NO + O). This single atom of oxygen then combines with diatomic (meaning 2 atoms) oxygen (O_2) to form ozone (O_3). Ozone is one of the smells associated with smog. It has a pungent and offensive odor, irritates the eyes and lung tissues, affects the growth of plant life and causes rapid deterioration of rubber products. Ozone can be formed by sunlight as well as electrical discharge into the air.

The most common discharge area on the automobile engine is the secondary ignition electrical system, especially when inferior quality spark plug cables are used. As the surge of high voltage is routed through the secondary cable, the circuit builds up an electrical field around the wire, which acts upon the oxygen in the surrounding air to form the ozone. The faint glow along the cable

with the engine running that may be visible on a dark night, is called the "corona discharge." It is the result of the electrical field passing from a high along the cable, to a low in the surrounding air, which forms the ozone gas. The combination of corona and ozone has been a major cause of cable deterioration. Recently, different and better quality insulating materials have lengthened the life of the electrical cables.

Although ozone at ground level can be harmful, ozone is beneficial to the earth's inhabitants. By having a concentrated ozone layer called the "ozonosphere," between 10 and 20 miles (16–32 km) up in the atmosphere, much of the ultra violet radiation from the sun's rays are absorbed and screened. If this ozone layer were not present, much of the earth's surface would be burned, dried and unfit for human life.

OXIDES OF SULFUR

Oxides of sulfur (SOx) were initially ignored in the exhaust system emissions, since the sulfur content of gasoline as a fuel is less than $\frac{1}{10}$ of 1 percent. Because of this small amount, it was felt that it contributed very little to the overall pollution problem. However, because of the difficulty in solving the sulfur emissions in industrial pollutions and the introduction of catalytic converter to the automobile exhaust systems, a change was mandated. The automobile exhaust system, when equipped with a catalytic converter, changes the sulfur dioxide (SO_2) into sulfur trioxide (SO_3).

When this combines with water vapors (H_2O), a sulfuric acid mist (H_2SO_4) is formed and is a very difficult pollutant to handle since it is extremely corrosive. This sulfuric acid mist that is formed, is the same mist that rises from the vents of an automobile battery when an active chemical reaction takes place within the battery cells.

When a large concentration of vehicles equipped with catalytic converters are operating in an area, this acid mist may rise and be distributed over a large ground area causing land, plant, crop, paint and building damage.

PARTICULATE MATTER

A certain amount of particulate matter is present in the burning of any fuel, with carbon constituting the largest percentage of the particulates. In gasoline, the remaining particulates are the burned remains of the various other compounds used in its manufacture. When a gasoline engine is in good internal condition, the particulate emissions are low but as the engine wears internally, the particulate emissions increase. By visually inspecting the tail pipe emissions, a determination can be made as to where an engine defect may exist. An engine with light gray or blue smoke emitting from the tail pipe normally indicates an increase in the oil consumption through burning due to internal engine wear. Black smoke would indicate a defective fuel delivery system, causing the engine to operate in a rich mode. Regardless of the color of the smoke, the internal part of the engine or the fuel delivery system should be repaired to prevent excess particulate emissions.

Diesel and turbine engines emit a darkened plume of smoke from the exhaust system because of the type of fuel used. Emission control regulations are mandated for this type of emission and more stringent measures are being used to prevent excess emission of the particulate matter. Electronic components are being introduced to control the injection of the fuel at precisely the proper time of piston travel, to achieve the optimum in fuel ignition and fuel usage. Other particulate after-burning components are being tested to achieve a cleaner emission.

Good grades of engine lubricating oils should be used, which meet the manufacturers specification. Cut-rate oils can contribute to the particulate emission problem because of their low flash or ignition temperature point. Such oils burn prematurely during the combustion process causing emission of particulate matter.

The cooling system is an important factor in the reduction of particulate matter. The optimum combustion will occur, with the cooling system operating at a temperature specified by the manufacturer. The cooling system must be maintained in the same manner as the engine oiling system, as each system is required to perform properly in order for the engine to operate efficiently for a long time.

Crankcase Emissions

Crankcase emissions are made up of water, acids, unburned fuel, oil fumes and particulates. These emissions are classified as hydrocarbons (HC) and are formed by the small amount of unburned, compressed air/fuel mixture entering the crankcase from the combustion area (between the cylinder walls and piston rings) during the compression and power strokes. The head of the compression and combustion help to form the remaining crankcase emissions.

Since the first engines, crankcase emissions were allowed into the atmosphere through a road draft tube, mounted on the lower side of the engine block. Fresh air came in through an open oil filler cap or breather. The air passed through the crankcase mixing with blow-by gases. The motion of the vehicle and the air blowing past the open end of the road draft tube caused a low pressure area (vacuum) at the end of the tube. Crankcase emissions were simply drawn out of the road draft tube into the air.

To control the crankcase emission, the road draft tube was deleted. A hose and/or tubing was routed from the crankcase to the intake manifold so the blow-by emission could be burned with the air/fuel mixture. However, it was found that intake manifold vacuum, used to draw the crankcase emissions into the manifold, would vary in strength at the wrong time and not allow the proper emission flow. A regulating valve was needed to control the flow of air through the crankcase.

Testing, showed the removal of the blow-by gases from the crankcase as quickly as possible, was most important to the longevity of the engine. Should large accumulations of blow-by gases remain and condense, dilution of the engine oil would occur to form water, soots, resins, acids and lead salts, resulting in the formation of sludge and varnishes. This condensation of the blow-by gases occurs more frequently on vehicles used in numerous starting and stopping conditions, excessive idling and when the engine is not allowed to attain normal operating temperature through short runs.

Evaporative Emissions

Gasoline fuel is a major source of pollution, before and after it is burned in the automobile engine. From the time the fuel is refined, stored, pumped and transported, again stored until it is pumped into the fuel tank of the vehicle, the gasoline gives off unburned hydrocarbons (HC) into the atmosphere. Through the redesign of storage areas and venting systems, the pollution factor was diminished, but not eliminated, from the refinery standpoint. However, the automobile still remained the primary source of vaporized, unburned hydrocarbon (HC) emissions.

Fuel pumped from an underground storage tank is cool but when exposed to a warmer ambient temperature, will expand. Before controls were mandated, an owner might fill the fuel tank with fuel from an underground storage tank and park the vehicle for some time in warm area, such as a parking lot. As the fuel would warm, it would expand and should no provisions or area be provided for the expansion, the fuel would spill out of the filler neck and onto the ground, causing hydrocarbon (HC) pollution and creating a severe fire hazard. To correct this condition, the vehicle manufacturers added overflow plumbing and/or gasoline tanks with built in expansion areas or domes.

However, this did not control the fuel vapor emission from the fuel tank. It was determined that most of the fuel evaporation occurred when the vehicle was stationary and the engine not operating. Most vehicles carry 5–25 gallons (19–95 liters) of gasoline. Should a large concentration of vehicles be parked in one area, such as a large parking lot, excessive fuel vapor emissions would take place, increasing as the temperature increases.

To prevent the vapor emission from escaping into the atmosphere, the fuel systems were designed to trap the vapors while the vehicle is stationary, by sealing the system from the atmosphere. A storage system is used to collect and hold the fuel vapors from the carburetor (if equipped) and the fuel tank when the engine is not operating. When the engine is started, the storage system is then purged of the fuel vapors, which are drawn into the engine and burned with the air/fuel mixture.

EMISSION CONTROLS

Crankcase Ventilation System

OPERATION

▶ **See Figures 1, 2 and 3**

A positive crankcase ventilation (PCV) system is used on all Toyotas sold in the United States. Blow-by gases are routed from the crankcase to the carburetor, where they are combined with the fuel/air mixture and burned during combustion.

A valve (PCV) is used in the line to prevent the gases in the crankcase from being ignited in case of a backfire. The amount of blow-by gases entering the mixture is also regulated by the PCV Valve, which is spring-loaded and has a variable orifice.

On Toyotas, the valve is either mounted on the valve cover or in the line which runs from the intake manifold to the crankcase. The valve should be replaced at the following intervals:
- 1970–71 models—12,000mi/12mo
- 1972–74 models—24,000mi/24mo
- 1975–77 models—25,000mi/24mo
- 1978–82 models—30,000mi/24mo
- 1980–82 Calif.—69,000mi/48mo

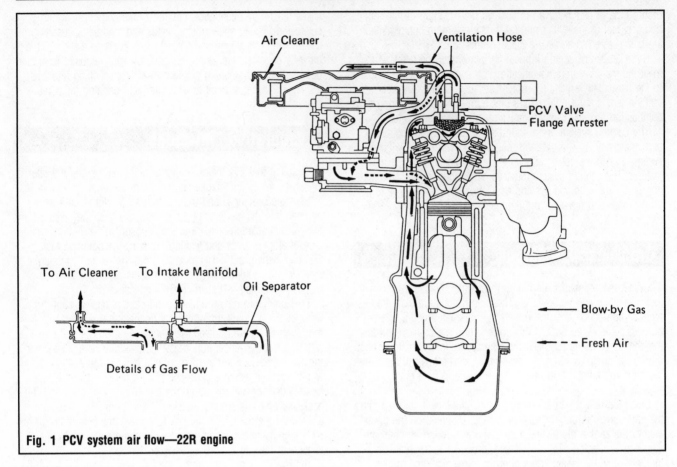

Fig. 1 PCV system air flow—22R engine

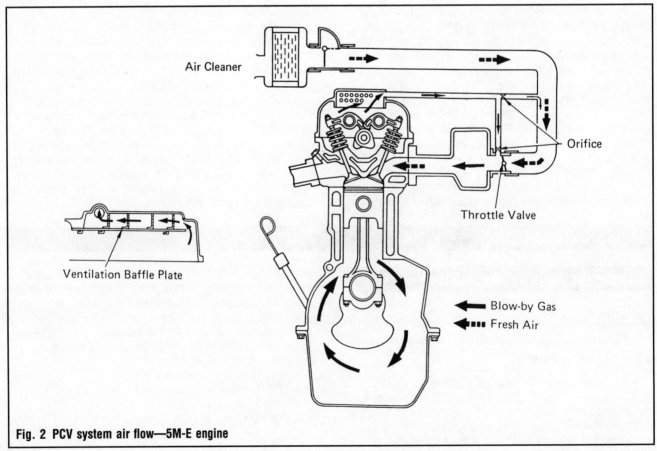

Fig. 2 PCV system air flow—5M-E engine

Engine not Running or if Backfiring

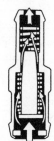

Intake Manifold Side

○ PCV VALVE IS CLOSED.

Cylinder Head Side

Normal Operation

○ PCV VALVE IS OPEN.

○ VACUUM PASSAGE IS LARGE.

Idling or Decelerating

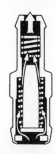

○ PCV VALVE IS OPEN.

○ VACUUM PASSAGE IS SMALL.

Acceleration or High Load

○ PCV VALVE IS FULLY OPEN.

Fig. 3 The PCV valve functions differently according to engine operating conditions

REMOVAL & INSTALLATION

Remove the PCV valve from the cylinder head cover or from the manifold-to-crankcase hose. Check the attaching hoses for cracks or clogs. Install a new PCV valve into the hoses, or reinstall in the cylinder head cover.

1. PCV valve   2. Grommet   3. Ventilation hose
The PCV valve seats into a grommet located in the valve cover

TESTING

◗ See Figures 4, 5 and 6

Check the PCV system hoses and connections, to ensure that there are no leaks, then replace or tighten, as necessary.

To check the valve, remove it and blow through both of its ends. When blowing from the side which goes toward the intake manifold, very little air should pass through. When blowing from the crankcase (valve cover) side, air should pass through freely.

Replace the valve with a new one, if the valve fails to function as outlined.

➡**Do not attempt to clean or adjust the valve. Replace it with a new one.**

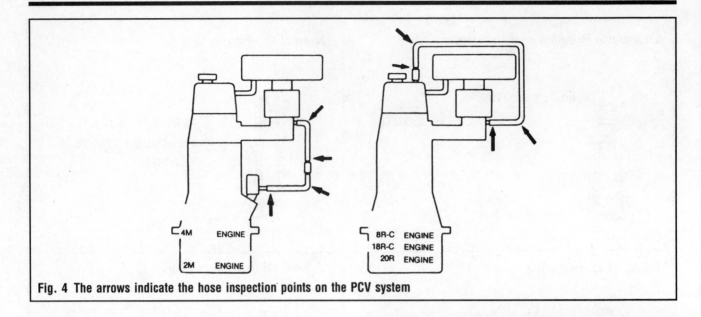

Fig. 4 The arrows indicate the hose inspection points on the PCV system

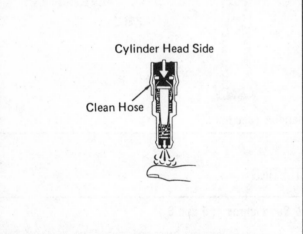

Fig. 5 When testing the PCV valve, blow air into the cylinder head side and check for good flow

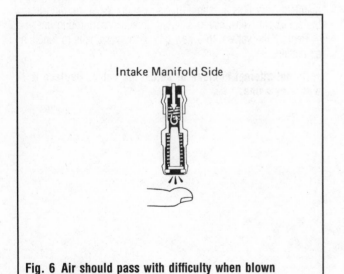

Fig. 6 Air should pass with difficulty when blown through the intake side

Air Injection System

OPERATION

▶ **See Figures 7, 8, 9, 10 and 11 (p. 9–12)**

A belt-driven pump supplies air to an injection manifold which has nozzles in each exhaust port. Injection of air at this point causes combustion of unburned hydrocarbons in the exhaust manifold rather than allowing them to escape into the atmosphere. An anti-backfire valve controls the flow of air from the pump to prevent backfiring which results from an overly rich mixture under closed throttle conditions. There are two types of antibackfire valve used on Toyota models: 1970–71 models use gulp valves; 1972–82 models air bypass valves.

A check valve prevents hot exhaust gas backflow into the pump and hoses, in case of a pump failure, or when the antibackfire valve is not working.

In addition, all 1975–82 engines have an Air Switching Valve (ASV). On engines without catalytic converters, the ASV is used to stop air injection under a constant heavy engine load condition.

On engines with catalytic converters, the ASV is also used to protect the catalyst from overheating, by blocking the injector air necessary for the operation of the converter.

Since 1975 on most passenger car engines, the pump relief valve is built into the ASV.

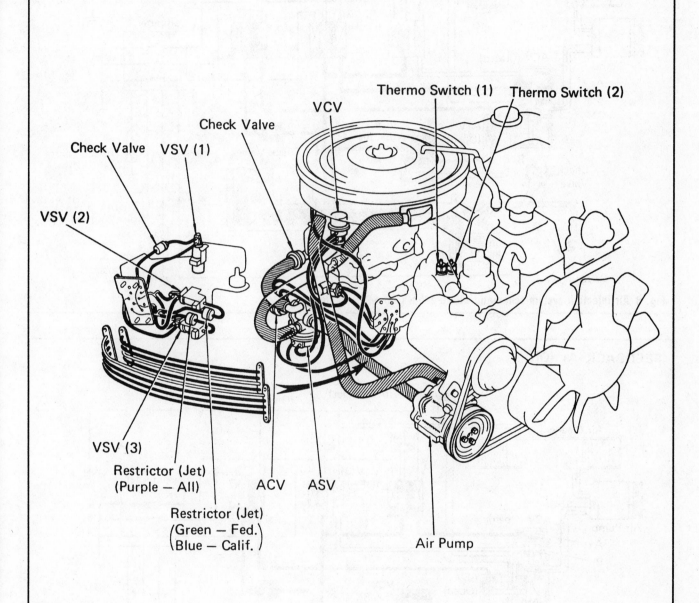

Check Valve

Check Valve   VSV (1)

VSV (2)

VCV

Thermo Switch (1)   Thermo Switch (2)

VSV (3)

Restrictor (Jet)
(Purple — All)

ACV   ASV

Restrictor (Jet)
(Green — Fed.)
(Blue — Calif.)

Air Pump

Fig. 7 Air injection system components—22R engine

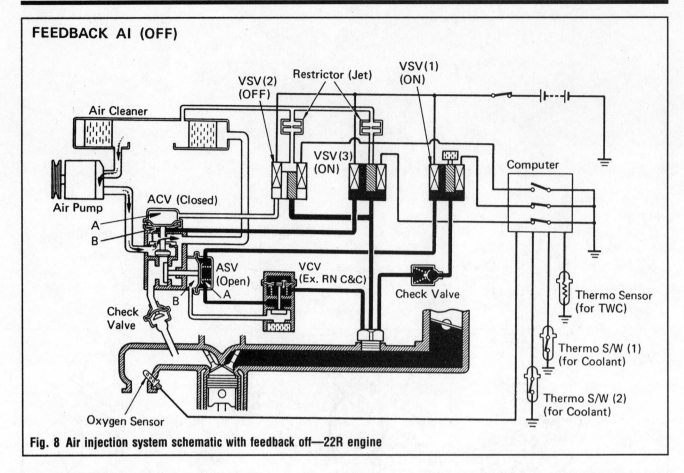

Fig. 8 Air injection system schematic with feedback off—22R engine

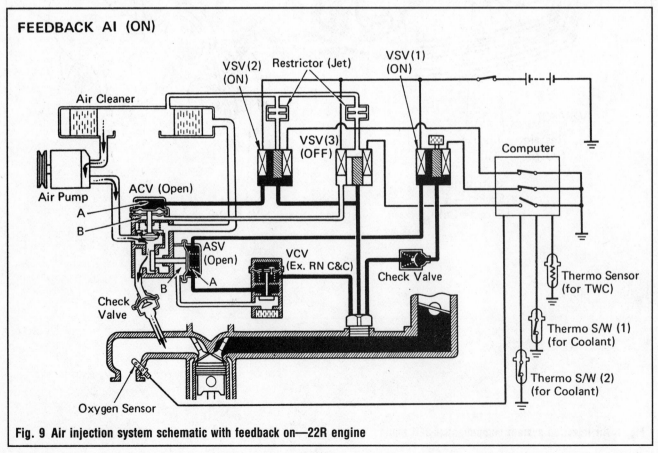

Fig. 9 Air injection system schematic with feedback on—22R engine

To oxidize and reduce HC, CO and NOx emissions efficiently in the TWC, this system maintains the air-fuel ratio of the inlet gas for the TWC stoichiometric by switching the compressed air from the air pump to either the exhaust ports or the air cleaner in response to the oxygen (O_2) concentration in the exhaust manifold.

AI Control by ASV

TWC Temp.	Coolant Temp.	Vehicle Condition	Vacuum in VCV Chamber A and B	VSV (1)	ASV Chambers		ASV	AI
					Chamber A	Chamber B		
Below 600°C (1,110°F)	Below 6°C (43°F)	—	—	OFF	Atmosphere	Atmosphere	CLOSED	Always OFF
	Between 18 – 98°C (64 – 208°F)	Except following condition	Same	ON	Vacuum	Atmosphere	OPEN	Controlled by ACV
		Sudden deceleration	High vacuum acts on chamber A	ON	Vacuum	Vacuum	CLOSED	Momentarily OFF
	Above 110°C (230°F)	—	—	OFF	Atmosphere	Atmosphere	CLOSED	Always OFF
Above 785°C (1,445°F)	—	—	—	OFF	Atmosphere	Atmosphere	CLOSED	Always OFF

AI Control by ACV

Coolant Temp.	Air-fuel Ratio for TWC	(1) O_2 Sensor Signal	VSV (2)	VSV (3)	ACV Chambers		ACV	AI (2) Feedback
					Chamber A	Chamber B		
Below 43°C (109°F)	—	—	ON	OFF	Vacuum	Atmosphere	OPEN	Always ON
Above 55°C (131°F)	RICH	RICH	ON	OFF	Vacuum	Atmosphere	OPEN	ON
	LEAN	LEAN	OFF	ON	Atmosphere	Vacuum	CLOSED	OFF

Remarks: 1) Signal of air-fuel ratio of the inlet gas for TWC.
2) By means of O_2 sensor, detects oxygen concentration in exhaust manifold after combustion. If air-fuel ratio is rich for TWC, turns AI ON. If lean, turns AI OFF.

Air-fuel ratio RICH → Air Injection ON → Air-fuel ratio LEAN → Air Injection OFF ┐
└ Air-fuel ratio RICH → Air Injection ON → Air-fuel ratio LEAN → Air Injection OFF ┘

Fig. 10 Air injection system operating conditions

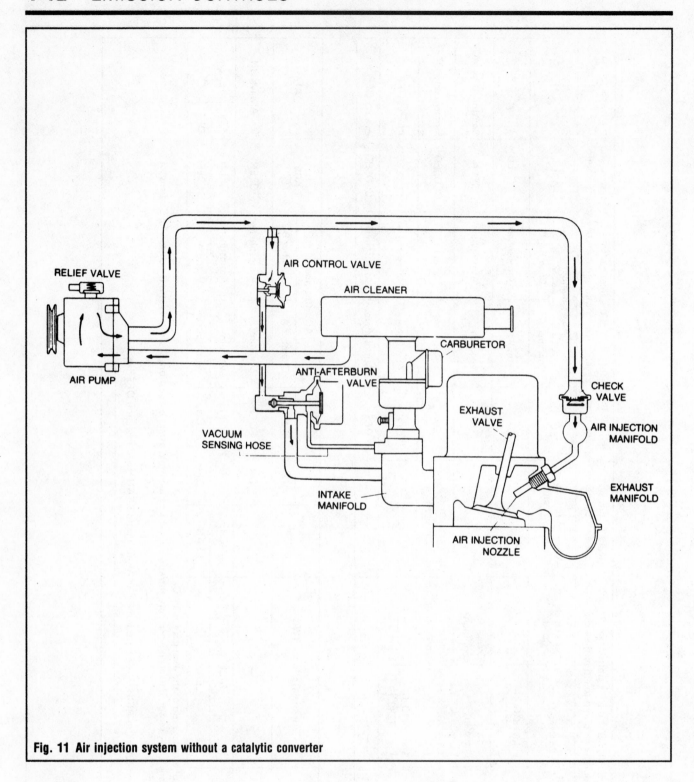

Fig. 11 Air injection system without a catalytic converter

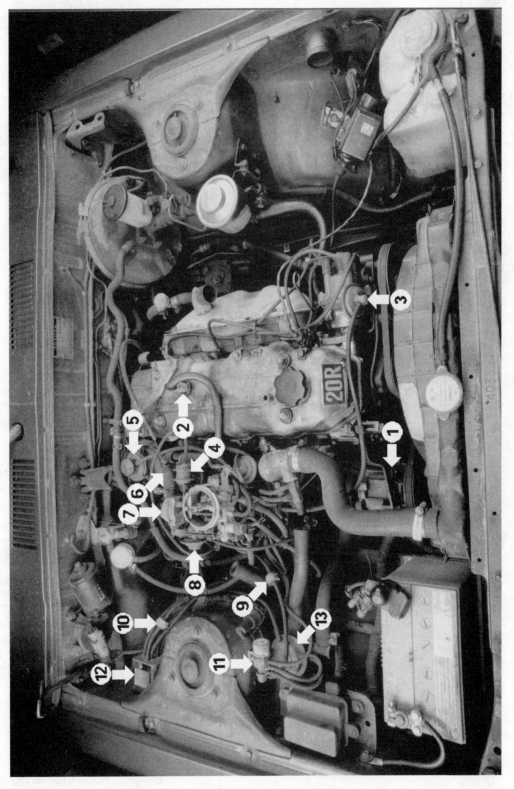

TYPICAL EMISSION COMPONENT LOCATIONS—20R ENGINE SHOWN

1. Air pump
2. PCV valve
3. Vacuum advance
4. Idle-up diaphragm
5. EGR vacuum modulator

6. EGR valve (under modulator)
7. Electric choke
8. Choke opener diaphragm
9. Vacuum Transmitting Valve (VTV)
10. Vacuum Transmitting Valve (VTV)

11. Vacuum Control Valve (VCV)
12. Vacuum Switching Valve (VSV)
13. Air Switching Valve (ASV)

REMOVAL & INSTALLATION

Air Pump

1. Disconnect the air hoses from the pump.
2. Loosen the bolt on the adjusting link and remove the drive belt.
3. Remove the mounting bolts and withdraw the pump.

✴✴ WARNING

Do not pry on the pump housing. It may be distorted.

4. Installation is in the reverse order of removal. Adjust the drive belt tension after installation. Belt deflection should be ½–¾ inch with 22 lbs. pressure.

Loosen the air pump mounting bolts . . .

. . . and slide the bolts out to remove the air pump

Anti-backfire Valve and Air Switching Valve

1. Detach the air hoses from the valve, and electrical leads (if equipped).
2. Remove the valve securing bolt.
3. Withdraw the valve.
4. Installation is performed in the reverse order of removal.

Check Valve

1. Detach the intake hose from the valve.
2. Use an open-end wrench to remove the valve from its mounting.
3. Installation is the reverse of removal.

Relief Valve

➡**From 1975 on models with ASV-mounted relief valves, replace the entire ASV/relief valve as an assembly.**

1. Remove the air pump from the car.
2. Support the pump so that it cannot rotate.

✴✴ WARNING

Never clamp the pump in a vise. The aluminum case will be distorted.

3. Use a bridge to remove the relief valve from the top of the pump.
4. Position the new relief valve over the opening in the pump.

➡**The air outlet should be pointing toward the left.**

5. Gently tap the relief valve home, using a block of wood and a hammer.
6. Install the pump on the engine, as outlined above.

Air Injection Manifold

1. Remove the check valve, as previously outlined.
2. Loosen the air injection manifold attachment nuts and withdraw the manifold.

→**On some engines it may be necessary to remove the exhaust manifold first.**

3. Installation is in the reverse order of removal.

Air Injection Nozzles

1. Remove the air injection manifold as previously outlined.
2. Remove the cylinder head, as detailed in Section 3.
3. Place a new nozzle on the cylinder head.
4. Install the air injection manifold over it.
5. Install the cylinder head on the engine block.

TESTING

Air Pump

✳✳ WARNING

Do not hammer, pry, or bend the pump housing while tightening the drive belt or testing the pump.

BELT TENSION AND AIR LEAKS

1. Before proceeding with the tests, check the pump drive belt tension to ensure that it is within specifications.
2. Turn the engine. If the pump has seized, the belt will slip, making a noise. Disregard any chirping, squealing, or rolling sounds from inside the pump. These are normal when it is turned by hand.
3. Check the hoses and connections for leaks. Hissing or a blast of air indicates a leak. Soapy water, applied lightly around the area in question, is a good method for detecting leaks.

AIR OUTPUT
▶ **See Figure 12**

1. Disconnect the air supply hose at the anti-backfire valve.
2. Connect a vacuum gauge, using a suitable adaptor, to the air supply hose.

→**If there are two hoses, plug the second one.**

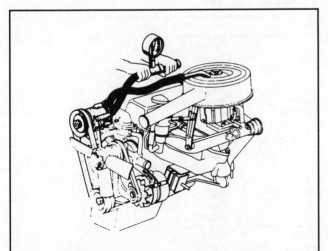

Fig. 12 Attach a vacuum gauge to the supply hose of the anti-backfire valve to test the air pump output

3. With the engine at normal operating temperature, increase the idle speed and watch the vacuum gauge.
4. The airflow from the pump should be steady (between 2 and 6 psi). If it is unsteady or falls below specs, the pump is defective and must be replaced.

Pump Noise

The air pump is normally noisy. As engine speed increases, the noise of the pump will rise in pitch. The rolling sound the pump bearings make is normal. But if this sound becomes objectionable at certain speeds, the pump is defective and will have to be replaced.

A continual hissing sound from the air pump pressure relief valve at idle, indicates a defective valve. Replace the relief valve.

If the pump rear bearing fails, a continual knocking sound will be heard. Since the rear bearing is not separately replaceable, the pump will have to be replaced as an assembly.

Anti-backfire Valve

There are two different types of anti-backfire valve used with air injection systems. A bypass valve is used on 1971–82 engines, while 1970–71 engines use a gulp type anti-backfire valve. Test procedures for both types are given below.

GULP VALVE

1. Detach the air supply hose which runs between the pump and the gulp valve.
2. Connect a tachometer and run the engine to 1,500–2,000 rpm.
3. Allow the throttle to snap shut. This should produce a loud sucking sound from the gulp valve.
4. Repeat this operation several times. If no sound is present, the valve is not working or else the vacuum connections are loose.
5. Check the vacuum connections. If they are secure, replace the gulp valve.

BYPASS VALVE

1. Detach the hose, which runs from the bypass valve to the check valve, at the bypass valve hose connection.
2. Connect a tachometer to the engine. With the engine running at normal idle speed, check to see that air is flowing from the by-pass valve hose connection.
3. Speed up the engine so that it is running at 1,500–2,000 rpm. Allow the throttle to snap shut. The flow of air from the bypass valve at the check valve hose connection should stop momentarily and air should then flow from the exhaust port on the valve body or the silencer assembly.
4. Repeat Step 3 several times. If the flow of air is not diverted into the atmosphere from the valve exhaust port or if it fails to stop flowing from the hose connection, check the vacuum lines and connections. If these are tight, the valve is defective and requires replacement.
5. A leaking diaphragm will cause the air to flow out both the hose connection and the exhaust port at the same time. If this happens, replace the valve.

Check Valve

1. Before starting the test, check all of the hoses and connections for leaks.
2. Insert a suitable probe into the check valve and depress the

plate. Release it. The plate should return to its original position against the valve seat. If binding is evident, replace the valve.

3. With the engine running at normal operating temperature, gradually increase its speed to 1,500 rpm. Check for exhaust gas leakage. If any is present, replace the valve assembly.

➡Vibration and flutter of the check valve at idle speed is a normal condition and does not mean that the valve should be replaced.

Air Switching Valve (ASV)

1975–82 20R and 22R ENGINES

1. Start the engine and allow it to reach normal operating temperature and speed.

2. At curb idle, the air from the by-pass valve should be discharged through the hose which runs to the ASV.

3. When the vacuum line to the ASV is disconnected, the air from the by-pass valve should be diverted out through the ASV to-air cleaner hose. Reconnect the vacuum line.

4. Disconnect the ASV-to-check valve hose and connect a pressure gauge to it.

5. Increase the engine speed. The relief valve should open when the pressure gauge registers 2.7–6.5 psi.

6. If the ASV fails any of the above tests, replace it. Reconnect all hoses.

1975–79 M SERIES ENGINES

▶ See Figure 13

1. Start the engine and allow it to reach normal operating temperature and speed.

2. At curb idle, air from the pump should be discharged through the hose which runs to the check valve.

3. Race the engine and allow the throttle valve to snap shut. The air from the pump should be discharged into the air cleaner.

4. Disconnect the ASV-to-check valve hose and connect a pressure gauge to it.

5. Increase the engine speed gradually. The relief valve should open when the gauge registers 3.7–7.7 psi. Reconnect the check valve hose.

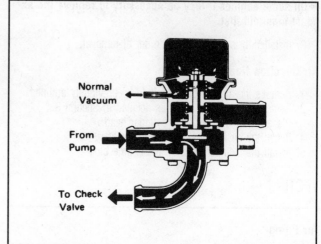

Fig. 13 Testing the Air Switching Valve (ASV) on the 4M engine

6. Unfasten the wiring connector and the hoses from the solenoid valve, which is attached to the ASV. Air should pass through the solenoid valve when either the top or bottom port is blown into.

7. Connect a 12v power source to the terminals on the valve. No air should flow through the valve when either port is blown into.

8. If the solenoid valve or the ASV fail any of the above tests, replace either or both of them, as necessary.

Vacuum Delay Valve

1975–82 20R and 22R ENGINES

The vacuum delay valve is located in the line which runs from the intake manifold to the vacuum surge tank.

1. Remove the vacuum delay valve from the vacuum lines. Be sure to note which end points toward the intake manifold.

2. When air is blown in from the ASV (surge tank) side, it should pass through the valve freely.

Air Injection System Diagnosis Chart

Problem	Cause	Cure
1. Noisy drive belt	Loose belt	Tighten belt
	Seized pump	Replace
2. Noisy pump	Leaking hose	Trace and fix leak
	Loose hose	Tighten hose clamp
	Hose contacting other parts	Reposition hose
	Diverter or check valve failure	Replace
	Pump mounting loose	Tighten securing bolts
	Defective pump	Replace
3. No air supply	Loose belt	Tighten belt
	Leak in hose or at fitting	Trace and fix leak
	Defective antibackfire valve	Replace
	Defective check valve	Replace
	Defective pump	Replace
	Defective ASV	Replace
4. Exhaust backfire	Vacuum or air leaks	Trace and fix leak
	Defective antibackfire valve	Replace
	Sticking choke	Service choke
	Choke setting rich	Adjust choke

3. When air is blown in from the intake manifold side, a resistance should be felt.

4. Replace the valve if it fails either of the above tests.

5. Install the valve in the vacuum line, being careful not to install it backward.

Evaporative Emission Control System

OPERATION

◆ See Figures 14 thru 22 (p. 17–21)

To prevent hydrocarbon emissions from entering the atmosphere, Toyota vehicles use Evaporative Emission Control (EEC) systems. Models produced between 1970 and 1971 use a case storage system, while later models use a charcoal canister storage system.

The major components of the case storage system are a purge control or vacuum switching valve, a fuel vapor storage case, an air filter, a thermal expansion tank, and a special fuel tank.

When the vehicle is stopped or the engine is running at a low speed, the purge control or vacuum switching valve is closed. Fuel vapor travels only as far as the case where it is stored.

When the engine is running at a high speed (cruising speed), the purge control valve is opened by pressure from the air pump or else the vacuum switching valve opens, depending upon the type of emission control system used (see the Evaporative Emission Control System Usage chart). This allows the vapor stored in the case to be drawn into the intake manifold along with fresh air which is drawn in from the filter.

The charcoal canister storage system functions in a similar

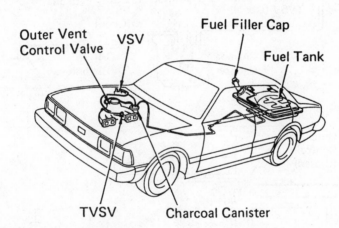

(Ex. Station Wagon)

Outer Vent Control Valve — VSV — Fuel Filler Cap — Fuel Tank — TVSV — Charcoal Canister

Fig. 14 EVAP system components—Corona except wagon

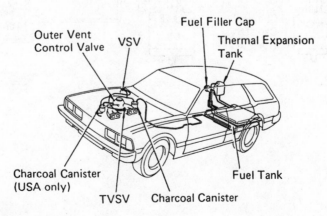

(Station Wagon)

Outer Vent Control Valve — VSV — Fuel Filler Cap — Thermal Expansion Tank — Charcoal Canister (USA only) — TVSV — Charcoal Canister — Fuel Tank

Fig. 15 EVAP system components—Corona wagon

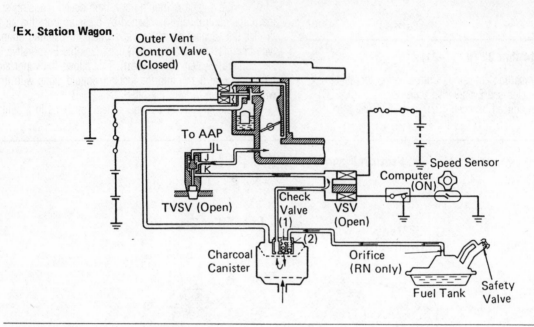

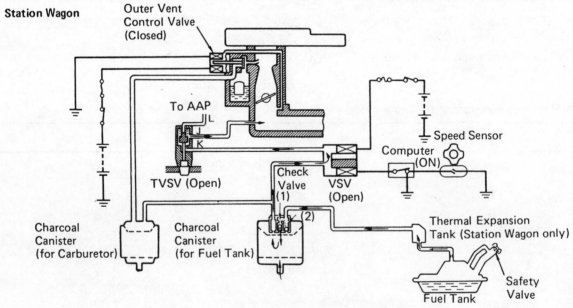

Fig. 16 EVAP system schematic—Corona

To reduce HC emissions, evaporated fuel from fuel tank and float chamber is routed through the charcoal canister to the intake manifold for combustion in the cylinders.

IG S/W	Engine	*Outer Vent Control Valve	Coolant Temp.	TVSV	Vehicle Speed	Com-puter	VSV	Check Valve (1)	(2)	Safety Valve in Cap	Evaporated Fuel (HC)
OFF	Not running	OPEN	—	—	—	—	—	—	—	—	HC from tank and float chamber is absorbed into the canister.
ON	Running	CLOSED	Below 60°C (140°F)	CLOSED (J—K)	—	—	—	—	—	—	HC from tank is absorbed into the canister.
			Above 75°C (167°F)	OPEN (J—K)	Below 7 mph (11 km/h)	OFF	CLOSED	—	—	—	
					Above 16 mph (26 km/h)	ON	OPEN	—	—	—	HC from canister is led into the intake manifold.
High pressure in tank	—	—	—	—	—	—	—	OPEN	CLOSED	CLOSED	HC from tank is absorbed into the canister.
High vacuum in tank	—	—	—	—	—	—	—	CLOSED	OPEN	OPEN	(Air is led into the tank.)

REMARKS: *The outer vent control valve is pulled by intake manifold vacuum and held by the solenoid. The solenoid itself cannot pull the valve.

Fig. 17 EVAP system operating conditions—Corona

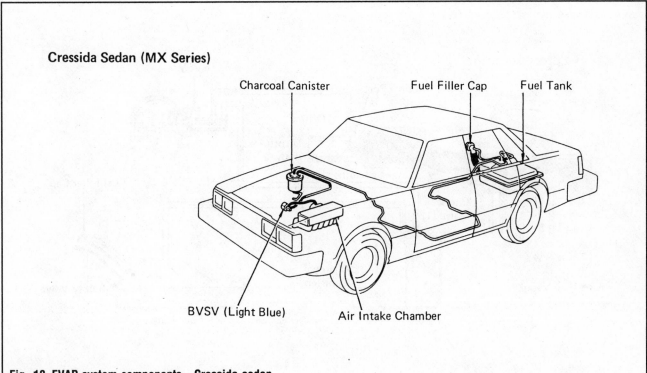

Cressida Sedan (MX Series)

Charcoal Canister   Fuel Filler Cap   Fuel Tank

BVSV (Light Blue)   Air Intake Chamber

Fig. 18 EVAP system components—Cressida sedan

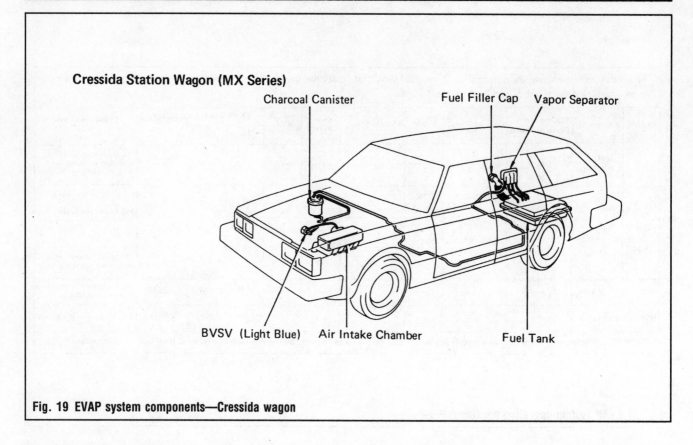

Fig. 19 EVAP system components—Cressida wagon

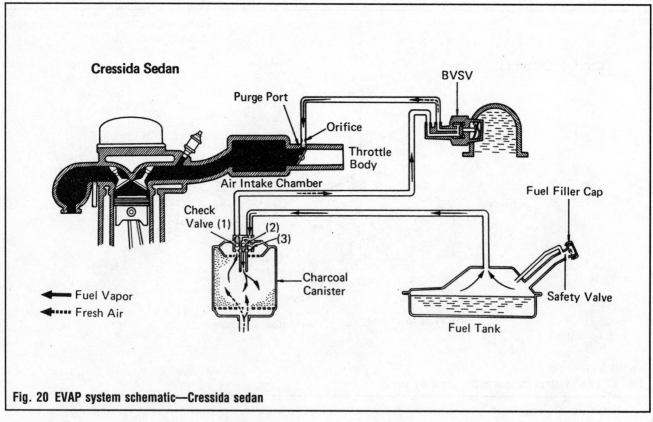

Fig. 20 EVAP system schematic—Cressida sedan

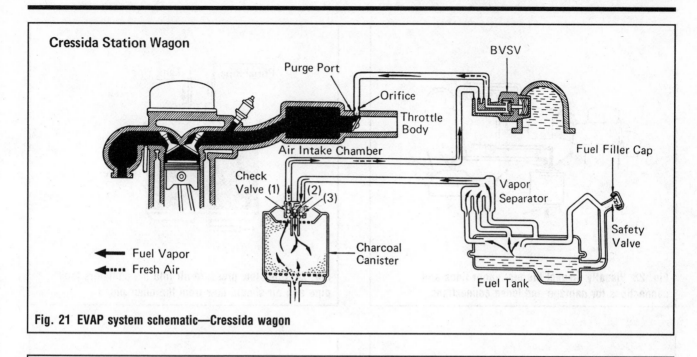

Fig. 21 EVAP system schematic—Cressida wagon

To reduce HC emission, evaporated fuel from fuel tank is routed through the charcoal canister to the intake manifold for combustion in the cylinders.

Coolant Temp.	BVSV	Throttle Valve Opening	Check Valve			Safety Valve in Cap	Evaporated Fuel (HC)
			(1)	(2)	(3)		
Below 35°C (95°F)	CLOSED	—	—	—	—	—	HC from tank is absorbed in the canister
Above 54°C (129°F)	OPEN	Positioned below purge port	CLOSED	—	—	—	HC from tank is absorbed in the canister
		Positioned above purge port	OPEN	—	—	—	HC from canister is led into air intake chamber
High pressure in tank	—	—	—	OPEN	CLOSED	CLOSED	HC from tank is absorbed in the canister
High vacuum in tank	—	—	—	CLOSED	OPEN	OPEN	(Air is led into the fuel tank.

Fig. 22 EVAP system operating conditions—Cressida

manner to the case system, except that the fuel vapors are stored in a canister filled with activated charcoal, rather than in a case, and that all models use a vacuum switching valve to purge the system. The air filter is not external as it is on the case system. Rather, it is an integral part of the charcoal canister.

REMOVAL & INSTALLATION

Removal and installation of the various evaporative emission control system components consists of unfastening hoses, loosening securing screws, and removing the part which is to be replaced from its mounting bracket. Installation is the reverse of removal.

➡**When replacing any EEC system hoses, always use hoses that are fuel-resistant or are marked "EVAP".**

TESTING

EEC System Troubleshooting
◆ **See Figures 23, 24, 25, 26 and 27**

There are several things which may be checked if a malfunction of the evaporative emission control system is suspected.

1. Leaks may be traced by using a hydrocarbon tests. Run the test probe along the lines and connections. The meter will indicate the presence of a leak by a high hydrocarbon (HC) reading.

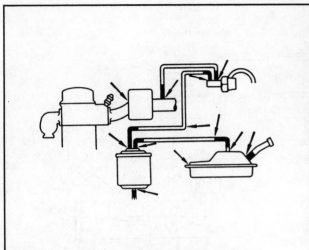

Fig. 23 Visually inspect the fuel vapor lines and connections for damage and loose connections

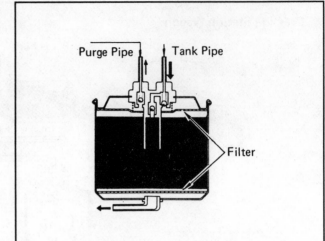

Fig. 26 Blow low pressure air into the canisters tank pipe and air should flow from the other pipes

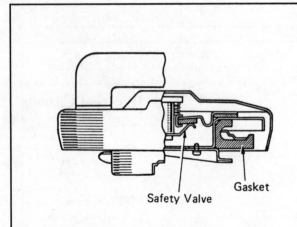

Fig. 24 Check the gas cap for a damaged gasket or a stuck safety valve, and replace if necessary

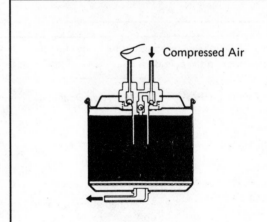

Fig. 27 To clean the carbon canister, blow air into the tank pipe, while holding the other pipes closed

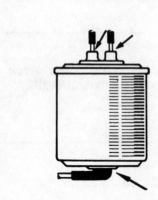

Fig. 25 The charcoal canister connections should be inspected for cracks

This method is much more accurate than visual inspection which would only indicate the presence of a leak large enough to pass liquid.

2. Leaks may be caused by any of the following:
   a. Defective or worn hoses
   b. Disconnected or pinched hoses
   c. Improperly routed hoses
   d. A defective filler cap or safety valve (sealed cap system)

➡**If it becomes necessary to replace any of the hoses used in the evaporative emission control system, use only hoses which are fuel-resistant or are marked "EVAP."**

3. If the fuel tank, storage case or thermal expansion tank collapses, it may be the fault of clogged or pinched vent lines, a defective vapor separator, or a plugged or incorrect filler cap.

4. To test the filler cap (if it is the safety valve type), clean it and place it against your mouth. Blow into the relief valve housing. If the cap passes pressure with light blowing, or fails to release with hard blowing, it is defective and must be replaced.

→Use the proper cap for the type of system in your car. Either a sealed cap or safety valve cap is required.

Purge Control Valve

1970–71 MODELS WITH AIR INJECTION

1. Disconnect the line which runs from the storage case to the valve, at the valve.
2. Connect a tachometer to the engine, according to the manufacturer's instructions.
3. Start the engine, set the parking brake, place the transmission in neutral and slowly increase engine speed to 2,500 rpm.
4. Place your finger over the hose fitting on the valve.
5. If there is no vacuum felt, the air pump is probably defective. If the air pump is good, replace the valve.

Purge Control Valve

1974–82 MODELS

The purge control valve is connected to a carburetor port, which is located above the throttle control valve. When the engine is stopped or at idle, there is no vacuum signal at the purge control valve, so, it remains closed.

When the throttle valve opens, the carburetor port is uncovered and a vacuum signal is sent to the purge control valve, which opens and allows vapors stored in the canister to be pulled into the carburetor.

1. Note the routing of the vacuum lines and remove the canister from the car.
2. Place your finger over the purge control valve opening, located at the center of the canister on its top side.
3. Gently blow through the vapor intake. No resistance should be felt.
4. Uncover the purge control valve opening and blow through it. No air should come out of the vapor intake or the bottom of the canister.
5. If the purge control valve fails either test, replace the canister. If the valve is okay, put the canister back in the car.
6. If the valve once again, appears to be malfunctioning after installation, you have either defective vacuum lines or a clogged carburetor port.

Check Valve

The check valve is located in the line which runs from the fuel tank or vapor separator, to the canister. On all 1973 models, it is located in the trunk. On all other models, it is in the engine compartment, near the canister.

1. Remove the check valve from the fuel tank-to-canister line.
2. Blow into the fuel tank end. A slight resistance should be felt at first.
3. Blow through the canister end. No resistance should be felt.
4. If the check valve is defective, replace it.

Carburetor Auxiliary Slow System

OPERATION

A carburetor auxiliary slow system is used on 1970–71 2M engines. It provides uniform combustion during deceleration. The components of the auxiliary slow system consist of a vacuum op-

erated valve, a fresh air intake, and a fuel line which is connected to the carburetor float chamber.

During deceleration, manifold vacuum acts on the valve which opens it causing additional air/fuel mixture to flow into the intake manifold.

REMOVAL & INSTALLATION

1. Remove the hoses from the auxiliary slow system.
2. Unfasten the recessed screws and remove the system as a unit.
3. Installation is the reverse of removal.

TESTING

♦ See Figure 28

1. Start the engine and run it to normal operating temperature.
2. Remove the rubber cap from the diaphragm and place your finger over the opening. There should be no vacuum at idle speed. If there is, the diaphragm must be replaced.
3. Pinch the air intake hose which runs from the air cleaner to the auxiliary slow system. There should be no change in the engine idle with the hose pinched.
4. Disconnect the air intake hose at the auxiliary slow system. Race the engine. Place your finger over the air intake. Release the throttle. Suction should be felt at the air intake.
5. If any of the tests indicate a failed component, replace the system as a unit.

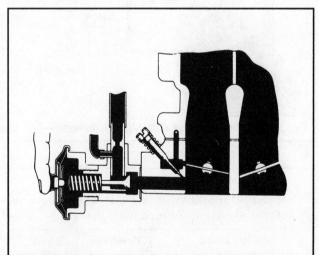

Fig. 28 Testing the carburetor auxiliary slow system diaphragm

Throttle Positioner

OPERATION

♦ See Figures 29, 30 and 31

The throttle positioner reduces emissions during deceleration. It prevents the throttle from closing completely. Vacuum is reduced

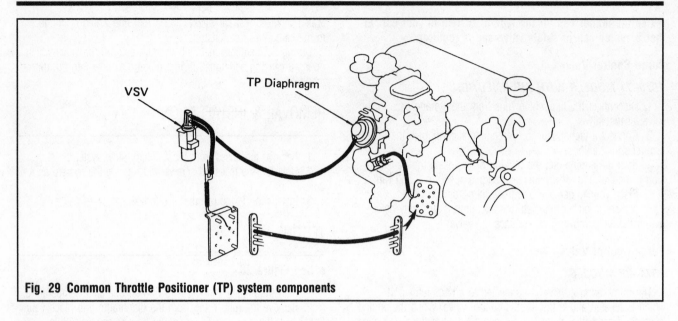

Fig. 29 Common Throttle Positioner (TP) system components

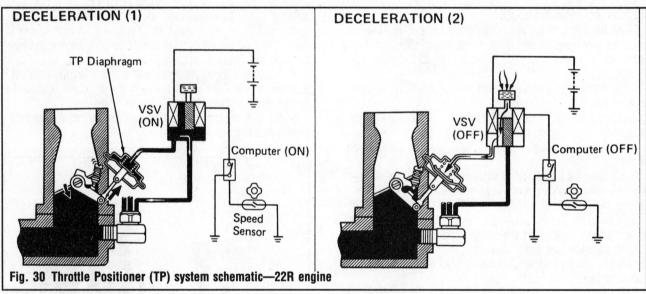

Fig. 30 Throttle Positioner (TP) system schematic—22R engine

To reduce HC and CO emissions, the TP opens the throttle valve slightly more than at idle position when decelerating. This causes the air-fuel mixture to burn completely.

Vehicle Speed	Computer	VSV	Throttle Positioner	Throttle Valve
Medium or high speeds above 16 mph (26 km/h)	ON	ON	TP IS SET. (Intake manifold vacuum acts on TP diaphragm.)	Medium or high speed position
Deceleration (1) above 7 mph (11 km/h)				Throttle valve is held in a position that is slightly more opened than at idle.
Deceleration (2) below 7 mph (11 km/h)	OFF	OFF	TP IS RELEASED. (Atmospheric pressure acts on TP diaphragm.)	Throttle valve is returned to the idle position.

Fig. 31 Throttle Positioner (TP) system operating conditions—22R engine; others similar

under the throttle which, in turn, acts on the retard chamber of the distributor vacuum unit. This compensates for the loss of engine braking caused by the partially opened throttle.

Once the vehicle speed drops below a predetermined value, the vacuum switching valve provides vacuum to the throttle positioner diaphragm. The throttle positioner retracts, allowing the throttle valve to close completely.

ADJUSTMENT

◆ **See Figure 32**

1. Start the engine and run it to normal operating temperature.
2. Adjust the idle speed as described in Section 1.

➡**Leave the tachometer connected after completing the idle adjustments.**

3. Detach the vacuum line from the positioner diaphragm unit and plug the line up.
4. Accelerate the engine slightly to set the throttle positioner in place.
5. Check the engine speed with a tachometer when the throttle positioner is set.
6. If necessary, adjust the engine speed, with the throttle positioner adjusting screw, to the specifications given in the Throttle Positioner Settings chart.
7. Connect the vacuum hose to the positioner diaphragm.
8. The throttle lever should be freed from the positioner as soon as the vacuum hose is connected. Engine idle should return to normal.
9. If the throttle positioner fails to function properly, check its linkage, and vacuum diaphragm. If there are no defects in either of these, the fault probably lies in the vacuum switching valve or the speed marker unit.

Throttle Positioner Settings (rpm)

Year	Engine	Engine rpm (positioner set)
1970	8R-C	1,400
1971	8R-C	1,400
1972–74	18R-C	1,400
	2M, 4M	1,300 MT 1,400 AT
1975–77	20R	1,400 MT 1,050 AT
	4M	1,200 AT
1978–80	20R/22R	1,050
	4M	950

MT—Manual transmission
AT—Automatic transmission

➡**Due to the complexity of these two components, and also because they require special test equipment, their service is best left to an authorized facility.**

Mixture Control Valve

◆ **See Figures 33, 34 and 35**

The mixture control valve, used on some models with manual transmissions, aids in combustion of unburned fuel during periods of deceleration. The mixture control valve is operated by the vacuum switching valve during periods of deceleration to admit additional fresh air into the intake manifold. The extra air allows more complete combustion of the fuel, thus reducing hydrocarbon emissions.

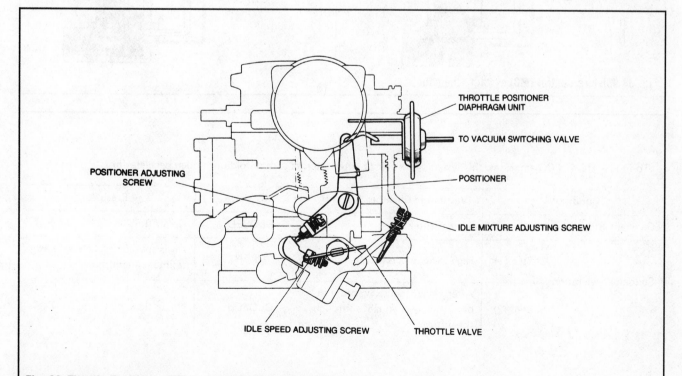

THROTTLE POSITIONER DIAPHRAGM UNIT

TO VACUUM SWITCHING VALVE

POSITIONER

IDLE MIXTURE ADJUSTING SCREW

POSITIONER ADJUSTING SCREW

IDLE SPEED ADJUSTING SCREW

THROTTLE VALVE

Fig. 32 Throttle Positioner (TP) system adjusting component locations

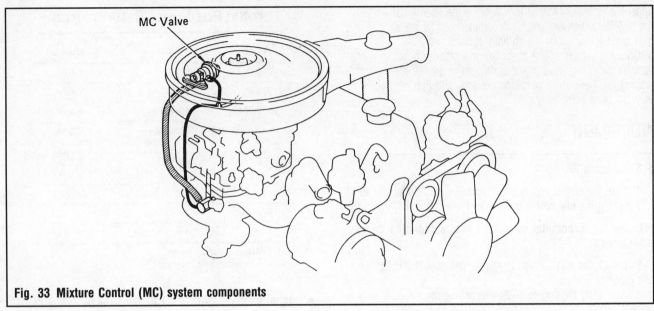

Fig. 33 Mixture Control (MC) system components

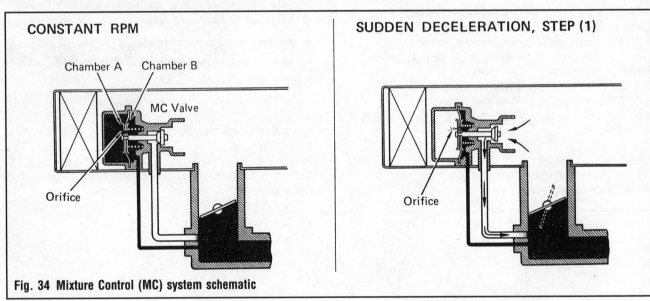

CONSTANT RPM

SUDDEN DECELERATION, STEP (1)

Fig. 34 Mixture Control (MC) system schematic

To reduce HC and CO emissions, this system allows air to enter the intake manifold on sudden deceleration.

Condition		Vacuum in Chamber A and B	MC Valve	Fresh Air
Constant RPM		Same vacuum	CLOSED	No air flow
Sudden deceleration	Step (1)	High vacuum acts on chamber B.	OPEN	Air is routed through MC valve to intake manifold.
	Step (2)	After a few seconds, vacuum in both chambers equalize through the orifice.	CLOSED	No air flow

Fig. 35 Mixture Control (MC) system operating conditions

REMOVAL & INSTALLATION

1. Unfasten the vacuum switching valve line from the mixture control valve.
2. Remove the intake manifold hose from the valve.
3. Remove the valve from its engine mounting.
4. Installation is performed in the reverse order of removal.

TESTING

▶ **See Figure 36**

1. Start the engine and allow it to idle (warmed up).
2. Place your hand over the air intake at the bottom of the valve.

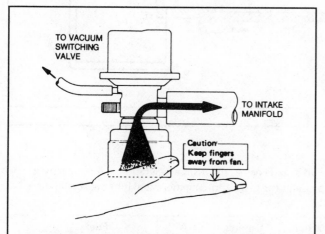

Fig. 36 When testing the MC valve, place your hand over the bottom of the valve with your fingers away from the fan

Keep your fingers clear of the engine fan.

3. Increase the engine speed and then release the throttle.
4. Suction should be felt at the air intake only while the engine is decelerating. Once the engine has returned to idle, no suction should be felt.

If the above test indicates a malfunction, proceed with the next step. If not, the mixture control valve is functioning properly and requires no further adjustment.

5. Disconnect the vacuum line from the mixture control valve. If suction can be felt underneath the valve with the engine at idle, the valve seat is defective and must be replaced.
6. Reconnect the vacuum line to the valve. Disconnect the other end of the line from the vacuum switching valve and place it in your mouth.
7. With the engine idling, suck on the end of the vacuum line to duplicate the action of the vacuum switching valve.
8. Suction at the valve air intake should only be felt for an instant. If air cannot be drawn into the valve at all, or if it is continually drawn in, replace the mixture control valve.

If the mixture control valve is functioning properly, and all of the hose and connections are in good working order, the vacuum switching valve is probably at fault.

Auxiliary Acceleration Pump System

OPERATION

▶ **See Figures 37, 38 and 39**

When the engine is cold, an Auxiliary Acceleration Pump (AAP) system unit in the carburetor is operated to squirt extra fuel into

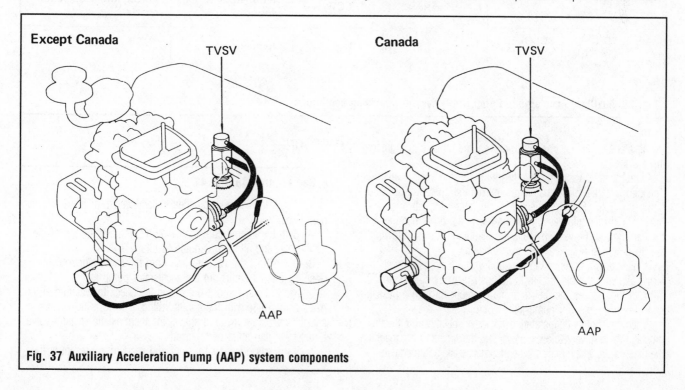

Fig. 37 Auxiliary Acceleration Pump (AAP) system components

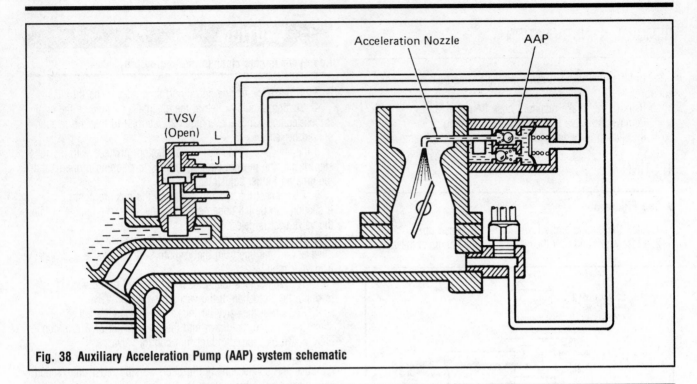

Fig. 38 Auxiliary Acceleration Pump (AAP) system schematic

The carburetor air-fuel mixture is very lean. When accelerating with a cold engine, the main acceleration pump capacity is insufficient to provide good acceleration. The AAP system compensates for this by forcing more fuel into the acceleration nozzle to obtain better cold engine performance.

Coolant Temp.	TVSV	Engine	Intake Vacuum	Diaphragm in AAP	Fuel
Below 60°C (140°F)	OPEN (J–L)	Constant RPM	HIGH	Pulled by vacuum	Drawn into AAP chamber
		Acceleration	LOW	Returned by spring tension	Forced into acceleration nozzle
Above 75°C (167°F)	CLOSED (J–L)	—	—	No operation	—

Fig. 39 Auxiliary Acceleration Pump (AAP) system operating conditions

the acceleration circuit in order to prevent the mixture from becoming too lean.

A thermostatic vacuum valve (warmup-sensing valve), which is threaded into the intake manifold, controls the operation of the enrichment circuit. Below a specified temperature, the valve is opened and manifold vacuum is allowed to act on a diaphragm in the carburetor. The vacuum pulls the diaphragm down, allowing fuel to flow into a special chamber above it.

Under sudden acceleration manifold vacuum drops momentarily, allowing the diaphragm to be pushed up by spring tension. This, in turn, forces the fuel from the chamber through a passage and out the accelerator pump jet.

When the coolant temperature goes above specification, the thermostatic vacuum valve closes, preventing the vacuum from reaching the diaphragm, which makes the enrichment system inoperative.

TESTING

▶ **See Figures 40 and 41**

1. Check for clogged, pinched, disconnected, or misrouted vacuum lines.

2. With the engine cold (below 75°F), remove the top of the air cleaner, and allow the engine to idle.

3. Disconnect the vacuum line from the carburetor AAP unit. Gasoline should squirt out the accelerator pump jet.

4. If gas doesn't squirt out of the jet, check for vacuum at the AAP vacuum line with the engine idling. If there is no vacuum and the hoses are in good shape, the thermostatic vacuum valve is defective and must be replaced.

5. If the gas doesn't squirt out and vacuum is present at the

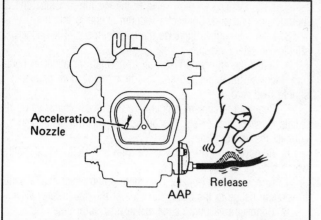

Fig. 40 Test the AAP system when the engine is cold—pinch the AAP hose, release, and check for fuel spurts from the nozzle

vacuum line in Step 4, the AAP unit is defective and must be replaced.

➡**On later models, a diaphragm kit is available.**

6. Repeat Step 3 with the engine at normal operating temperature. If gasoline squirts out of the pump jet, the thermostatic vacuum valve is defective and must be replaced.

7. Reconnect all of the vacuum lines and install the top of the air cleaner.

Auxiliary Enrichment System

◆ **See Figures 42, 43 and 44**

This system is used on the 4M engine to improve driveability. It cuts air supplied to the main nozzle of the carburetor under certain conditions to improve performance.

If the system is suspected to be operating improperly, test the Vacuum Control Valve (VCV) as described below. If any of the tests are failed, replace the valve.

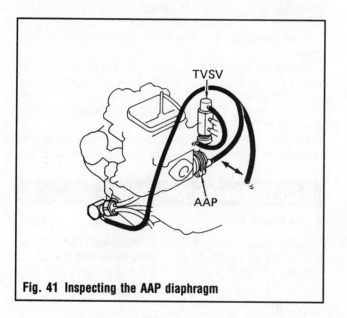

Fig. 41 Inspecting the AAP diaphragm

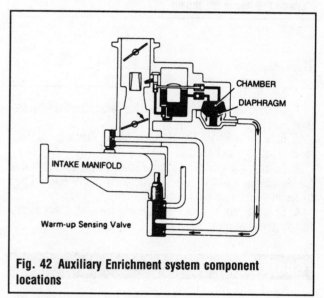

Fig. 42 Auxiliary Enrichment system component locations

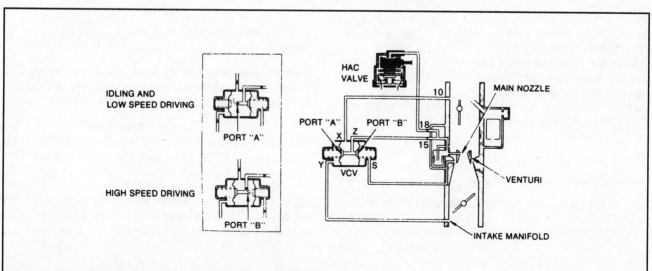

Fig. 43 Auxiliary Enrichment system schematic—1978–79 models

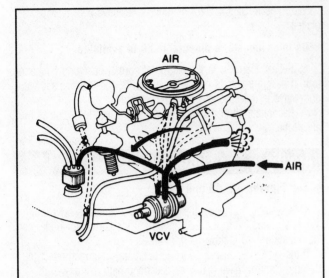

Fig. 44 When testing the Vacuum Control Valve (VCV), attach the hoses as shown

TESTING

1. Disconnect hoses 10 and 15 at the carburetor. Start the engine.
2. Blow air into hose No. 10 at idle speed. Check to see that air is expelled from hose 15.
3. Connect the VCV S pipe to the intake manifold as shown in the illustration. Again, blow air into hoses 10 at idle speed. Check to see that air comes out of hose 15.
4. Stop the engine. Again blow air into hose 10. Check to see that air does not come out of hose.

Spark Delay Valve

The Spark Delay Valve (SDV) is located in the distributor vacuum line. The valve has a small orifice in it, which slows down the vacuum flow to the vacuum advance unit on the distributor. By delaying the vacuum to the distributor, a reduction in HC and CO emissions is possible.

When the coolant temperature is below 95°F, a coolant temperature operated vacuum control valve is opened, allowing the distributor to receive undelayed, ported vacuum through a separate vacuum line. Above 95°F, this line is blocked and all ported vacuum must go through the spark delay valve.

TESTING

1. Allow the engine to cool, so that the coolant temperature is below 95°F.
2. Disconnect the vacuum line which runs from the coolant

temperature operated vacuum valve to the vacuum advance unit at the advance unit end. Connect a vacuum gauge to this line.

3. Start the engine. Increase the engine speed. The gauge should indicate a vacuum.
4. Allow the engine to warm-up to normal operating temperature. Increase the engine speed. This time the vacuum gauge should read zero.
5. Replace the coolant temperature operated vacuum valve, if it fails either of these tests. Disconnect the vacuum gauge and reconnect the vacuum lines.
6. Remove the spark delay valve from the vacuum line, noting which side faces the distributor.
7. Connect a hand-operated vacuum pump which has a built-in vacuum gauge to the carburetor side of the spark delay valve.
8. Connect a vacuum gauge to the distributor side of the valve.
9. Operate the hand pump to create a vacuum. The vacuum gauge on the distributor side should show a hesitation before registering.
10. The gauge reading on the pump side should drop slightly, taking several seconds for it to balance with the reading on the other gauge.
11. If Steps 9 and 10 are negative, replace the spark delay valve.
12. Remove the vacuum gauge from the distributor side of the valve. Cover the distributor side of the valve with your finger and operate the pump to create a vacuum of 15 in. Hg.
13. The reading on the pump gauge should remain steady. If the gauge reading drops, replace the valve.
14. Remove your finger. The reading of the gauge should drop slowly. If the reading goes to zero rapidly, replace the valve.

Dual Diaphragm Distributor

▶ **See Figure 45**

Some Toyota models are equipped with a dual diaphragm distributor unit. This distributor has a retard diaphragm, as well as a diaphragm for advance.

TESTING

1. Connect a timing light to the engine. Check the ignition timing.

➡**Before proceeding with the tests, disconnect any spark control devices, distributor vacuum valves, etc. If these are left connected, inaccurate results may be obtained.**

2. Remove the retard hose from the distributor and plug it. Increase the engine speed. The timing should advance. If it fails to do so, then the vacuum unit is faulty and must be replaced.
3. Check the timing with the engine at normal idle speed. Unplug the retard hose and connect it to the vacuum unit. The timing should instantly be retarded from 4 to 10 degrees. If this does not occur, the retard diaphragm has a leak and the vacuum unit must be replaced.

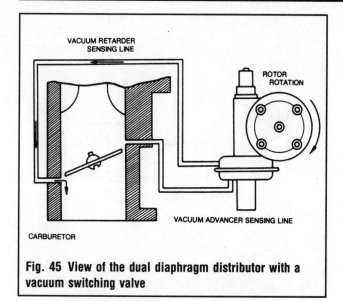

Fig. 45 View of the dual diaphragm distributor with a vacuum switching valve

Engine Modifications System

OPERATION

▶ **See Figure 46**

Toyota also uses an assortment of engine modifications to regulate exhaust emissions. Most of these devices fall into the category of engine vacuum controls. There are three principal components used on the engine modifications system, as well as a number of smaller parts. The three major components are: a

speed sensor, a computer (speed marker), and a vacuum switching valve.

The vacuum switching valve and computer circuit operate most of the emission control components. Depending upon year and engine usage, the vacuum switching valve and computer may operate the pure control for the evaporative emission control system, the Transmission Controlled Spark (TCS) or Speed Controlled Spark (SCS), the dual diaphragm distributor, the throttle positioner systems, the EGR system, the catalyst protection system, etc.

The functions of the evaporative emission control system, the throttle positioner, and the dual diaphragm distributor are described in detail in the preceding sections. However, a word is necessary about the functions of the TCS and SCS systems before discussing the operation of the vacuum switching valve/computer circuit.

The major difference between the transmission controlled spark and speed controlled spark systems is the manner in which system operation is determined. Toyota TCS systems use a speed sensor built into the speedometer cable.

Below a predetermined speed, or any gear other than fourth, the vacuum advance unit on the distributor is rendered inoperative or the timing retarded. By changing the distributor advance curve in this manner, it is possible to reduce emissions of oxides of nitrogen (NOx).

➡ **Some engines are equipped with a thermo-sensor so that the TCS or SCS system only operates when the coolant temperature is 140°–212°F.**

Aside from determining the preceding conditions, the vacuum switching valve computer circuit operates other devices in the emission control system (EGR, catalytic converter, etc.)

The computer acts as a speed marker. At certain speeds it sends a signal to the vacuum switching valve which acts as a

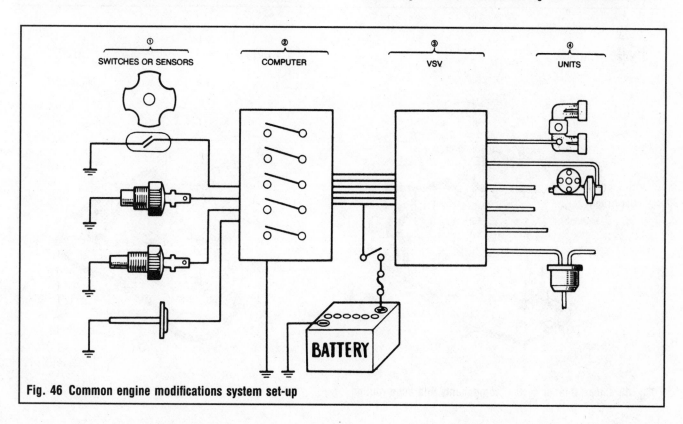

Fig. 46 Common engine modifications system set-up

gate, opening and closing the emission control system vacuum circuits.

The vacuum switching valve on all 1970 and some 1971 engines is a simple affair. A single solenoid operates a valve which uncovers certain vacuum ports at the same time others are covered.

The valve used on all 1972–82 and some 1971 engines contains several solenoid and valve assemblies so that different combinations of opened and closed vacuum ports are possible. This allows greater flexibility of operation for the emission control system.

INSPECTION

◆ **See Figure 47**

Due to the complexity of the components involved, about the only engine modifications system checks which can be made, are the following:

1. Examine the vacuum lines to ensure that they are not clogged, pinched, or loose.

2. Check the electrical connections for tightness and corrosion.

3. Be sure that the vacuum sources for the vacuum switching valve are not plugged.

4. On models equipped with speed controlled spark, a broken speedometer cable could also render the system inoperative.

Beyond these checks, servicing the engine modifications system is best left to an authorized service facility.

➡**A faulty vacuum switching valve or computer could cause more than one of the emission control systems to fail. Therefore, if several systems are out, these two units (and the speedometer cable) would be the first things to check.**

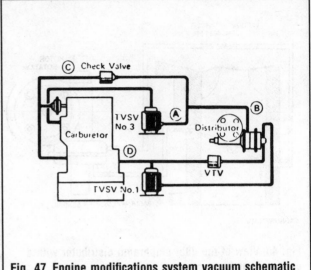

Fig. 47 Engine modifications system vacuum schematic

Choke Opener System

OPERATION

◆ **See Figures 48, 49 and 50**

This system holds the choke open during warmup to prevent an overly rich mixture from emitting pollutants above acceptable limits. When the coolant temperature rises above 140°F, a thermostatic vacuum switching valve allows vacuum from the manifold to

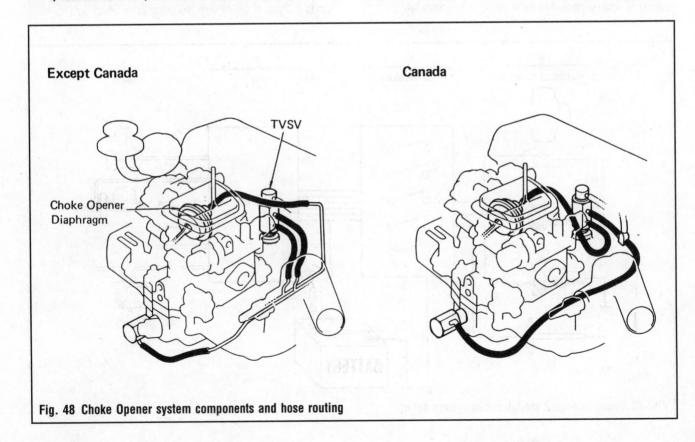

Fig. 48 Choke Opener system components and hose routing

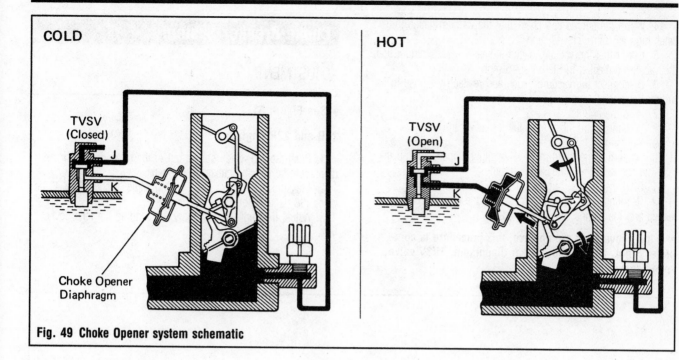

Fig. 49 Choke Opener system schematic

After warm-up, this system forcibly holds the choke valve open to prevent an over-rich mixture and release the fast idle to the 4th step to lower the engine rpm.

Coolant Temp.	TVSV	Diaphragm	Choke Valve	Fast Idle Cam	Engine RPM
Below 60°C (140°F)	CLOSED (J–K)	Released by spring tension	Closed by automatic choke	Set at 1st or 2nd step	HIGH
Above 75°C (167°F)	OPEN (J–K)	Pulled by manifold vacuum	OPEN	Released to 4th step	LOW

Fig. 50 Choke Opener system operating conditions

pull in on the choke opener diaphragm which is connected to the choke valve. Thus the choke valve is opened sooner than if just the automatic choke was operating it. When the coolant is below 95°F, the choke opener works with the automatic choke to close the choke valve and permit the choke to close until the engine is warm. Some models use two thermosensor switches and a speed sensor to trigger a miniature computer, which in turn triggers the vacuum switching valve.

Fast Idle Cam Breaker

After warm-up, this system forcibly releases the fast idle cam, which lowers the engine speed.

TESTING

1. Use a 3-way connector to attach a vacuum gauge to the fast idle cam breaker.
2. Use enough vacuum line to bring the gauge into the vehicle and set it on the drivers seat.
3. Perform a road test observing the speedometer and vacuum gauge.

➡**With the coolant temperature below (122°F) check that the gauge reads zero regardless of engine speed.**

4. Warm the engine and check that the vacuum gauge indicates high vacuum below 7 mph.

5. Check that the vacuum gauge indicates lower vacuum than the vacuum indicated in Step 4 at 16 mph.

6. Disconnect the vacuum gauge and reattach the hose to its proper location.

7. Stop the engine.

8. Disconnect the hose from the fast idle cam breaker.

9. Set the fast idle cam.

10. While holding the throttle valve slightly open, pull up the fast idle cam and then release the throttle.

11. Start the engine, but do not touch the accelerator.

12. Reconnect the hose and check that the fast idle cam is released and the engine rpm is lowered.

→**If the above tests are positive, this procedure is complete. If not, inspect the breaker diaphragm, TVSV valve, speed sensor or VSV.**

Choke Breaker System

ADJUSTMENT

▶ **See Figure 51**

20R and 22R Engines

1. Push the rod which comes out of the upper (choke break) diaphragm so that the choke valve opens.

2. Measure the choke valve opening angle. It should be 40 degrees (38 degrees for 1976–79 models).

3. Adjust the angle, if necessary, by bending the relief lever link.

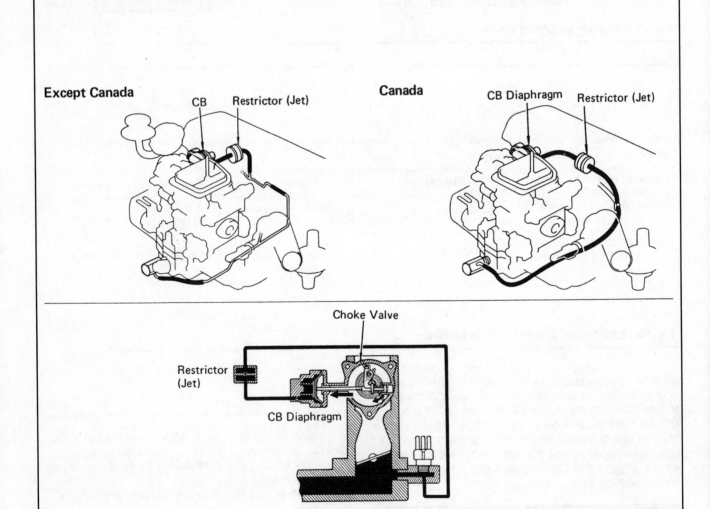

Fig. 51 Choke Breaker system components and schematic

Hot Idle Compensation Valve

This system allows the air controlled by the Hot Idle Compensation (HIC) valve to enter the intake manifold to maintain proper air fuel mixture during high temperatures at idle.

TESTING

1. Close the pipe to the intake manifold with your finger.
2. Blow air into the open end. The passage should be closed at temperatures below 86°F.
3. Heat the valve in hot water.

✸✸ WARNING

Do not allow water to get in the valve.

4. Blow air into the valve again. As the temperature nears 104°F the passage should open.
5. A small amount of air should flow through the valve when the temperature of the valve is 104°F to 158°F.
6. A large amount of air should flow through the valve when the temperature is above 176°F.
7. If air does not flow through the valve replace it.

Secondary Slow Circuit Fuel Cut System

This system cuts off part of the fuel in the secondary slow circuit of the carburetor to prevent dieseling.

TESTING

1. Completely open and close the throttle valve.
2. Measure the stroke of the valve. (1.5–2.0mm).
3. If necessary adjust the stroke.

➡**The stroke should be set to specifications before the secondary throttle valve opens.**

Deceleration Fuel Cut System

This system cuts off part of the fuel in the slow circuit of the carburetor to prevent overheating and afterburning in the exhaust system.

TESTING

1. Start the engine.
2. Check that the engine runs normally.
3. Pinch the vacuum hose to the vacuum switch.
4. Gradually increase the engine speed to 2,500 rpm. Check that the engine misfires between 2,000–2,500 rpm.

✸✸ WARNING

Perform this procedure quickly to prevent overheating of the catalytic converter.

5. Release the pinched hose and see that the engine returns to normal operation.
6. Unplug the solenoid valve until the engine misfires or stalls.
7. Stop the engine and reconnect the wire.

➡**If the above tests are positive the procedure is complete. If not, inspect the solenoid valve and vacuum switch.**

Fuel Solenoid

1. Remove the solenoid.
2. Using two test wires, hook one to the positive and the other to the negative battery terminals.
3. Touch these two wires to the solenoid to determine if it clicks.
4. If it does click, it is operational. If not, discard it and replace it with a new one.

Vacuum Switch

1. Use a ohmmeter to check the continuity between the switch and the terminal body.
2. Start the engine.
3. Check that there is no continuity between the switch and the terminal body. If there is, replace the switch.

High Altitude Compensation System

For all engines to be sold in areas over 4000 ft. in altitude, a system has been installed to automatically lean out the fuel mixture by supplying additional air. This also results in lower emissions.

Low atmospheric pressure allows the bellows in the system to expand the close a port, allowing more air to enter from different sources.

In the 20R and 22R engines, this also results in a timing advance to improve driveability.

All parts in this system must be replaced. The only adjustment available is in the timing.

Bi-Metal Vacuum Switching Valve

TESTING

1. Drain the engine coolant.
2. Remove the vacuum hoses and remove the BVSV.
3. Cool the BVSV to 86°F.
4. Blow air through the valve. At this time the valve should be closed and not allow air to pass.
5. Heat the valve to 111°F. The valve should open and allow air to pass through.
6. Repeat Step 4.

7. If the valve is inoperative it must be replaced.
8. Apply a liquid sealer to the threads and replace the valve.
9. Reconnect the vacuum lines.
10. Refill the coolant.

Hot Air Intake System

In order to keep the temperature of the air drawn into the carburetor as constant as possible, all engines are equipped with a Hot Air Intake (HAI) System.

In all engines, the system depends on a thermo valve to control the temperature.

At normal temperatures the air is drawn into the inlet in the air filter. When the temperature drops, the valve switches position, opening the way for air to be drawn from around the exhaust manifold.

When inspecting, check all hoses for poor connections or damage and visually check the air control valve in the air duct.

➡**When checking valve movement, do not push too strongly on the control face.**

Should there be a malfunction, replace the part involved.

Exhaust Gas Recirculation (EGR) System

OPERATION

◆ **See Figures 52 thru 58 (p. 36–39)**

Starting with 1974 models, exhaust gas recirculation (EGR) was used on 18R-C, and 4M engines sold in California. All engines, since 1975 use EGR.

In all cases, the EGR valve is controlled by the same computer and vacuum switching valve which is used to operate other emission control system components.

On four cylinder engines, the EGR valve is operated by vacuum supplied from a port above the throttle blades and fed through the vacuum switching valve.

On M engines, vacuum from the carburetor vacuum advance port flows through the vacuum switching valve to an EGR vacuum control valve. The vacuum from the advance port opens the vacuum control valve which then allows venturi vacuum to act on the chamber above the EGR valve diaphragm, causing the EGR valve

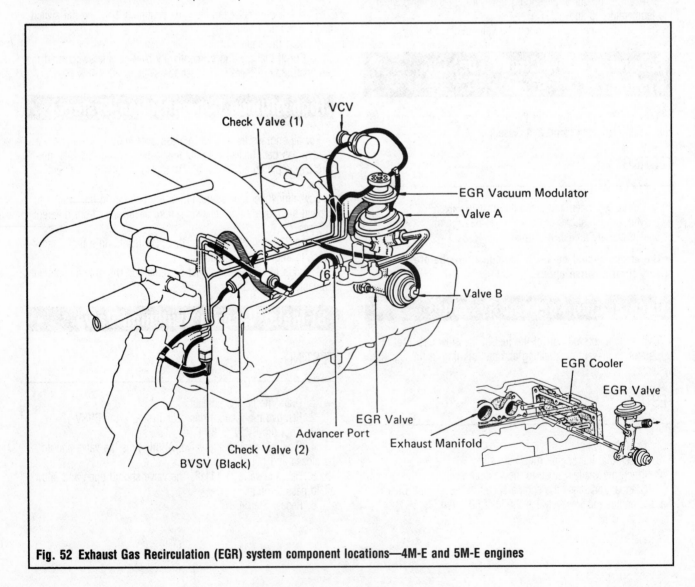

Fig. 52 Exhaust Gas Recirculation (EGR) system component locations—4M-E and 5M-E engines

To reduce NOx emission, part of the exhaust gas is recirculated through the EGR valve to the intake manifold in order to lower the maximum combustion temperature.

Coolant Temp.	BVSV	Throttle Valve Opening Angle	Condition	VCV	Pressure in the EGR Valve Pressure Chamber	EGR Vacuum Modulator	EGR Valve Valve A	Valve B	Exhaust Gas
Below 50°C (122°F)	CLOSED	—	—	—	—	—	CLOSED	—	NOT RECIRCULATED
Above 64°C (147°F)	OPEN	Positioned below advancer port	Idling	—	—	—	CLOSED	OPEN	NOT RECIRCULATED
		Positioned above advancer port	Normal driving	CLOSED	LOW (1)	OPENS passage to atmosphere	CLOSED	OPEN	RECIRCULATED
					*Pressure constantly alternating between low and high				
					HIGH (2)	CLOSED passage to atmosphere	OPEN	OPEN	RECIRCULATED
			Deceleration (3)	Momentarily OPEN	—	—	Momentarily CLOSED	OPEN	Momentarily NOT RECIRCULATED
			Intake vacuum above 600 mmHg (23.62 in.Hg)	—	—	—	CLOSED	CLOSED	NOT RECIRCULATED

Remarks * Pressure increase → Modulator closes → EGR valve opens → Pressure drops
Pressure decrease → Modulator opens → EGR valve closed → Modulator opens
** EGR valve B controls EGR gas volume; if intake manifold vacuum is high, it decreases the gas volume, if intake manifold vacuum is low, it decreases volume.

Fig. 55 Exhaust Gas Recirculation (EGR) system operating conditions— 4M-E and 5M-E engines

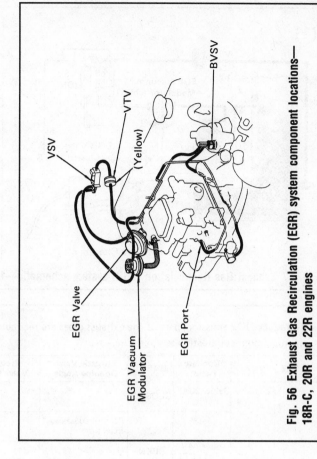

Fig. 56 Exhaust Gas Recirculation (EGR) system component locations— 18R-C, 20R and 22R engines

(1)

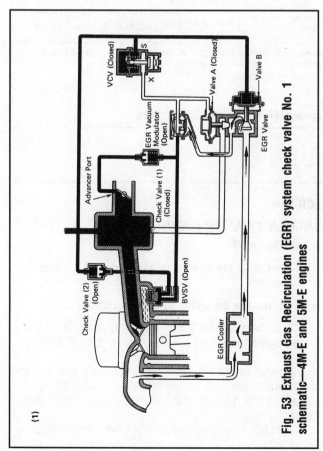

Fig. 53 Exhaust Gas Recirculation (EGR) system check valve No. 1 schematic—4M-E and 5M-E engines

(2)

(3) Deceleration

Fig. 54 Exhaust Gas Recirculation (EGR) system check valves No. 2 and 3 schematic—4M-E and 5M-E engines

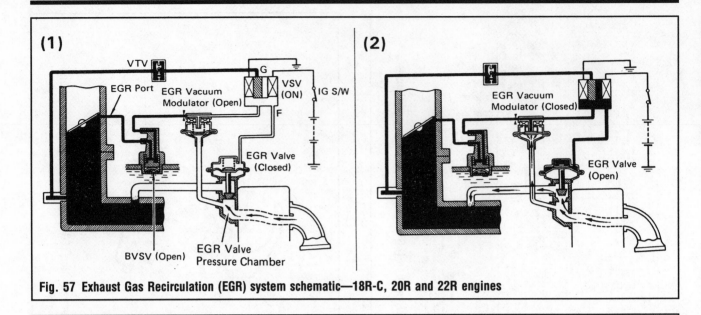

Fig. 57 Exhaust Gas Recirculation (EGR) system schematic—18R-C, 20R and 22R engines

To reduce NOx emission, part of the exhaust gases are recirculated through the EGR valve to the intake manifold to lower the maximum combustion temperature.

IG S/W	*VSV	Coolant Temp.	BVSV	Throttle Valve Opening Angle	Pressure in the EGR Valve Pressure Chamber		EGR Vacuum Modulator	EGR Valve	Exhaust Gas
		Below 30°C (86°F)	CLOSED	—	—		—	CLOSED	Not recirculated
ON	ON	Above 44°C (111°F)	OPEN	Positioned below EGR port	—		—	CLOSED	Not recirculated
				Positioned above EGR port	(1) LOW	**Pressure constantly alternating between low and high	OPENS passage to atmosphere	CLOSED	Not recirculated
					(2) HIGH		CLOSES passage to atmosphere	OPEN	Recirculated

Remarks: * For prevention of dieseling, the VSV opens (Port F to G) when the ignition is turned off so the EGR valve opens by intake manifold vacuum, allowing the flow of EGR gas to the intake manifold and insuring smooth engine shutdown.

** Pressure increase → Modulator closes → EGR valve opens → Pressure drops

EGR valve closes ← Modulator opens ←

Fig. 58 Exhaust Gas Recirculation (EGR) system operating conditions—18R-C, 20R and 22R engines

to open. When exhaust gas recirculation is not required, the vacuum switching valve stops sending the advance port vacuum signal to the EGR vacuum control valve which closes, sending intake manifold vacuum to the chamber below the EGR valve diaphragm. This closes the EGR valve, blocking the flow of exhaust gases to the intake manifold.

On all engines there are several conditions, determined by the computer and vacuum switching valve, which permit exhaust gas recirculation to take place:
1. Vehicle speed.
2. Engine coolant temperature.
3. EGR valve temperature (4 cylinder).
4. Carburetor flange temperature (4 cylinder).

On 4-cylinder engines equipped with EGR, the exhaust gases are carried from the exhaust manifold to the EGR valve and from the EGR valve to the carburetor, via external tubing. Some later engines have an exhaust gas cooler mounted on the back of the cylinder head.

On M series engines, the EGR valve is mounted on the exhaust manifold and exhaust gases from it are carried through external tubing to the intake manifold.

TESTING

EGR Valve

18R-C, 20R AND 22R ENGINES

◆ **See Figure 59**

1. Allow the engine to warm up and remove the top from the air cleaner.

➡**Do not remove the entire air cleaner assembly.**

2. Disconnect the hose (white tape coded), which runs from the vacuum switching valve to the EGR valve, at its EGR valve end.

3. Remove the intake manifold hose (red coded) from the vacuum switching valve and connect it to the EGR valve. When the engine is at idle, a hollow sound should be heard coming from the air cleaner.

4. Disconnect the hose from the EGR valve. The hollow sound should disappear.

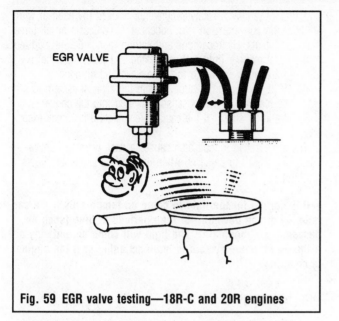

Fig. 59 EGR valve testing—18R-C and 20R engines

5. If the sound doesn't vary, the EGR valve is defective and must be replaced.

6. Reconnect the vacuum hoses as they were originally found. Install the top on the air cleaner.

M SERIES ENGINES

▶ **See Figure 60**

1. Warm up the engine and allow it to idle.

2. Disconnect the vacuum sensing line from the upper vacuum chamber of the EGR valve.

3. Disconnect the sensing line from the lower chamber of the EGR valve.

4. Now, take the hose which was disconnected from the lower chamber and connect it to the upper EGR valve chamber.

➡**Leave the lower chamber vented to the atmosphere.**

5. The engine idle should become rough or the engine should stall with the hoses connected in this manner. If the engine runs normally, check the EGR vacuum control valve (see below). If the

vacuum control valve is in good working order, then replace the EGR valve.

6. Reconnect the vacuum sensing lines as they were originally found.

EGR Valve Thermo-Sensor

18R-C, 20R AND 22R ENGINES

1. Disconnect the electrical lead which runs to the EGR valve thermo-sensor.

2. Remove the thermo-sensor from the side of the EGR valve.

3. Heat the thermo-sensor in a pan of water to 260°F.

4. Connect an ohmmeter, in series with a 10 ohm resistor, between the thermo-sensor terminal and case.

5. With the ohmmeter set on the $K\Omega$ scale, the reading should be 2.55 $K\Omega$.

6. Replace the thermo-sensor if the ohmmeter readings vary considerably from those specified.

7. To install the thermo-sensor on the EGR valve, tighten it to 15–21 ft. lbs.

✳✳ WARNING

Do not tighten the thermo-sensor with an impact wrench.

EGR Vacuum Control Valve

M SERIES ENGINES

▶ **See Figure 61**

1. Connect the EGR vacuum control valve hoses up, so that carburetor advance port vacuum operates directly on its diaphragm (top hose connection).

2. Disconnect the two hoses from the EGR vacuum control valve which run to the upper and lower diaphragm chambers of the EGR valve.

3. Take two vacuum gauges and connect one to each of the ports from which you removed a hose in Step 2.

4. Race the engine. The vacuum gauges should indicate the following:

Upper chamber port—Venturi vacuum
Lower chamber port—Atmospheric pressure

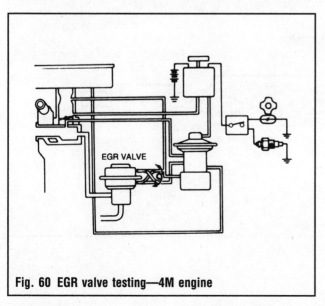

Fig. 60 EGR valve testing—4M engine

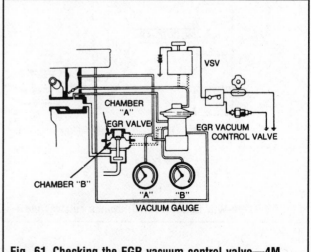

Fig. 61 Checking the EGR vacuum control valve—4M engine

5. Disconnect the sensing hose from the carburetor advance port.

6. The vacuum gauges should now show the following:
Upper chamber port—Atmospheric pressure
Lower chamber port—Intake manifold vacuum.

➡**The atmospheric pressure reading should be nearly equal to that obtained in Step 4.**

7. Replace the EGR vacuum control valve if the readings on the vacuum gauges are incorrect.

8. Hook up the vacuum lines as they were originally found.

SYSTEM CHECKS

If, after having completed the above tests, the EGR system still doesn't work right and everything else checks out OK, the fault probably lies in the computer or the vacuum switching valve systems. If this is the case, it is best to have the car checked out by test facility which has the necessary Toyota emission system test equipment.

➡**A good indication that the fault doesn't lie in the EGR system, but rather in the vacuum supply system, would be if several emission control systems were not working properly.**

Catalytic Converters

All Mark II and all California models were equipped with catalytic converters in 1975. Since 1975, stricter emission level standards have made it necessary for all Toyota models to utilize one or another (or both) type(s) of catalytic converter(s).

Earlier models and today's Canadian models use an oxidation converter. That is, one that converts carbon monoxide and hydrocarbons into carbon dioxide and water.

A three-way (TWC) catalytic converter is used (by itself or with an oxidation converter) on late models. The TWC acts on all three major pollutants. Hydrocarbons and carbon monoxide are oxidized in the usual manner (into carbon dioxide and water) and the oxides of nitrogen are reduced to free oxygen and nitrogen.

An air pump is used to supply air to the exhaust system to aid in the reaction. A thermosensor, inserted into the converter, shuts off the air supply if the catalyst temperature becomes excessive.

The same sensor circuit also causes a dash warning light labeled EXH TEMP to come on when the catalyst temperature gets too high.

➡**It is normal for the light to come on temporarily if the car is being driven downhill for long periods of time (such as descending a mountain). The light will come on and stay on if the air injection system is malfunctioning or if the engine is misfiring.**

PRECAUTIONS

▸ **See Figures 62 thru 67**

• Use only unleaded fuel.
• Avoid prolonged idling. The engine should run no longer than 20 minutes at curb idle, nor longer than 10 minutes at fast idle.
• Reduce the fast idle speed, by quickly depressing and releasing the accelerator pedal, as soon as the coolant temperature reaches 120°F.
• Do not disconnect any spark plug leads while the engine is running.
• Make engine compression checks as quickly as possible.
• Do not dispose of the catalyst in a place where anything coated with grease, gas, or oil is present. Spontaneous combustion could result.

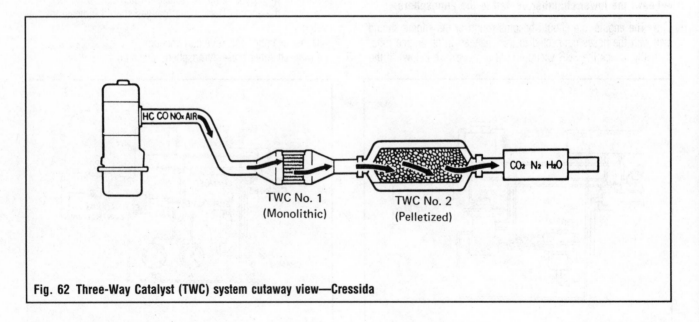

Fig. 62 Three-Way Catalyst (TWC) system cutaway view—Cressida

To reduce CO, HC and NOx emissions, they are oxidized, reduced and converted to dinitrogen (N_2), carbon dioxide (CO_2) and water (H_2O) in the catalyst.

Exhaust Port		TWC No. 1		TWC No. 2		Exhaust Gas
CO, HC, NOx AND AIR (Proper Temperature)	⇒	OXIDATION AND REDUCTION (Temperature is increased.)	⇒	OXIDATION AND REDUCTION (Temperature is increased.)	⇒	CO_2 H_2O N_2

Fig. 63 Three-Way Catalyst (TWC) system operating conditions—Cressida

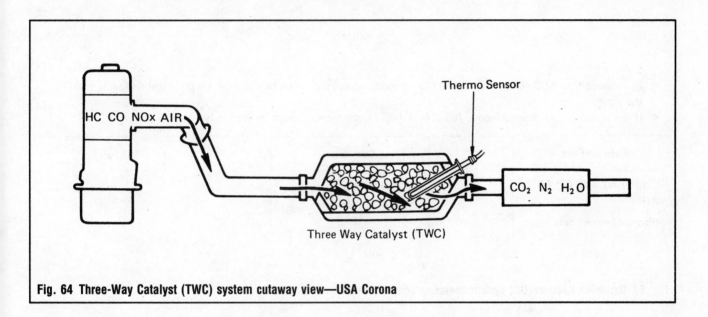

Fig. 64 Three-Way Catalyst (TWC) system cutaway view—USA Corona

- To reduce HC, CO and NOx emissions, they are oxidized and converted to dinitrogen (N_2), carbon dioxide (CO_2) and water (H_2O) in the catalyst.
- If the catalyst is overheated (above 785°C or 1,445°F), the thermo sensor in the catalyst turns the AI system OFF.

Exhaust Port		Converter		Exhaust Gas
UNBURNT HC, CO, NOx AND AIR (Proper Temperature)	⇒	OXIDATION AND REDUCTION (Temperature is increased.)	⇒	CO_2 H_2O N_2

Fig. 65 Three-Way Catalyst (TWC) system operating conditions—Corona

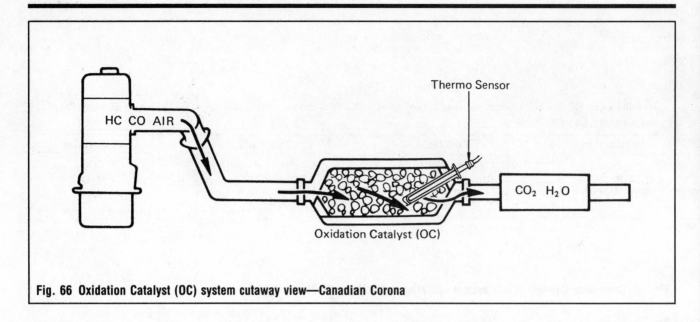

Fig. 66 Oxidation Catalyst (OC) system cutaway view—Canadian Corona

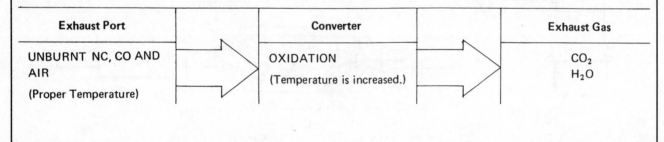

- To reduce HC and CO emissions, HC and CO are oxidized and converted to water (H_2O) and carbon dioxide (CO_2) in the catalyst.
- If the catalyst is overheated (above 785°C or 1,445°F), the thermo sensor in the catalyst turns AS system OFF.

Exhaust Port		Converter		Exhaust Gas
UNBURNT NC, CO AND AIR (Proper Temperature)	⟹	OXIDATION (Temperature is increased.)	⟹	CO_2 H_2O

Fig. 67 Oxidation Catalyst (OC) system operating conditions—Canadian Corona

WARNING LIGHT CHECKS

➡**The warning light comes on while the engine is being cranked, to test its operation, just like any of the other warning lights.**

1. If the warning light comes on and stays on, check the components of the air injection system as previously outlined. If these are not defective, check the ignition system for faulty leads, plugs, points, or control box.
2. If no problems can be found in Step 1, check the wiring for the light for shorts or opened circuits.
3. If nothing else can be found wrong in Steps 1 and 2, check the operation of the emission control system vacuum switching valve or computer, either by substitution of a new unit, or by taking it to a service facility which has Toyota's special emission control system checker.

REMOVAL & INSTALLATION

▸ **See Figure 68**

✳✳ CAUTION

Do not perform this operation on a hot (or even warm) engine. Catalyst temperatures may go as high as 1,700°F, so any contact with the catalyst could cause severe burns.

1. Disconnect the lead from the converter thermosensor.
2. Remove the wiring shield.
3. Unfasten the pipe clamp securing bolts at either end of the converter. Remove the clamps.
4. Push the tailpipe rearward and remove the converter, complete with thermosensor.

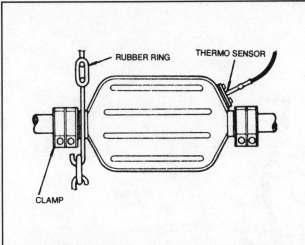

Fig. 68 When installing a catalytic converter, be sure the clamps are secure and the O-rings are in place

5. Carry the converter with the thermo-sensor upward to prevent the catalyst from falling out.

6. Unfasten the screws and withdraw the thermosensor and gasket.

To install:

7. Place a new gasket on the thermosensor. Push the thermosensor into the converter and secure it with its two bolts. Be careful not to drop the thermosensor.

➡**Service replacement converters are provided with a plastic thermosensor guide. Slide the sensor into the guide to install it. Do not remove the guide.**

8. Install new gaskets on the converter mounting flanges.

9. Secure the converter with its mounting clamps.

10. If the converter is attached to the body with rubber O-rings, install the O-rings over the body and converter mounting hooks.

11. Install the wire protector and connect the lead to the thermosensor.

VACUUM DIAGRAMS

Following are vacuum diagrams for most of the engine and emissions package combinations covered by this manual. Because vacuum circuits will vary based on various engine and vehicle options, always refer first to the vehicle emission control information label, if present. Should the label be missing, or should vehicle be equipped with a different engine from the vehicle's original equipment, refer to the diagrams below for the same or similar configuration.

If you wish to obtain a replacement emissions label, most manufacturers make the labels available for purchase. The labels can usually be ordered from a local dealer.

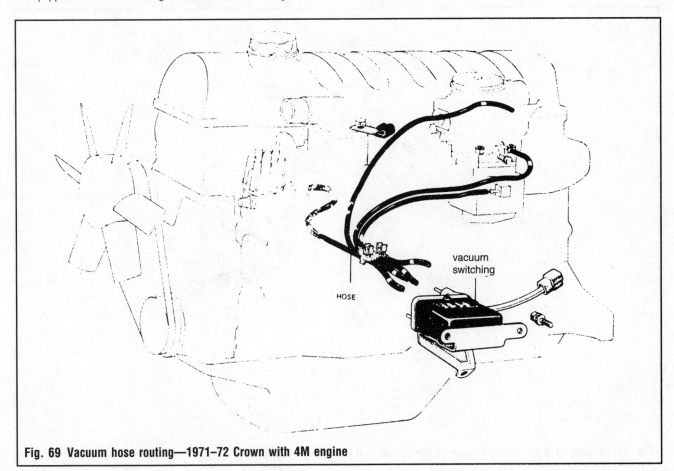

Fig. 69 Vacuum hose routing—1971–72 Crown with 4M engine

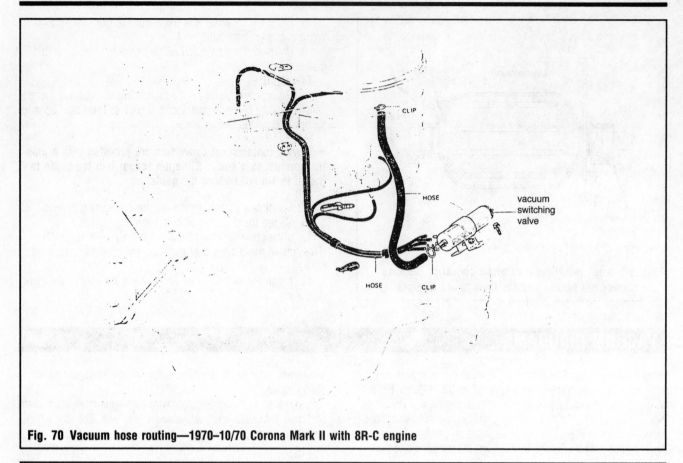

Fig. 70 Vacuum hose routing—1970–10/70 Corona Mark II with 8R-C engine

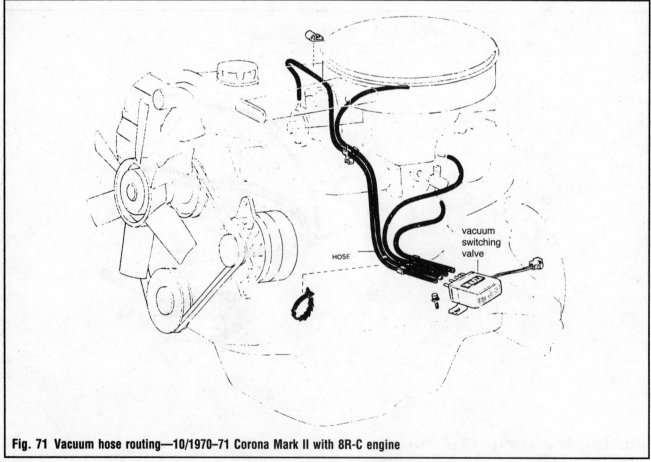

Fig. 71 Vacuum hose routing—10/1970–71 Corona Mark II with 8R-C engine

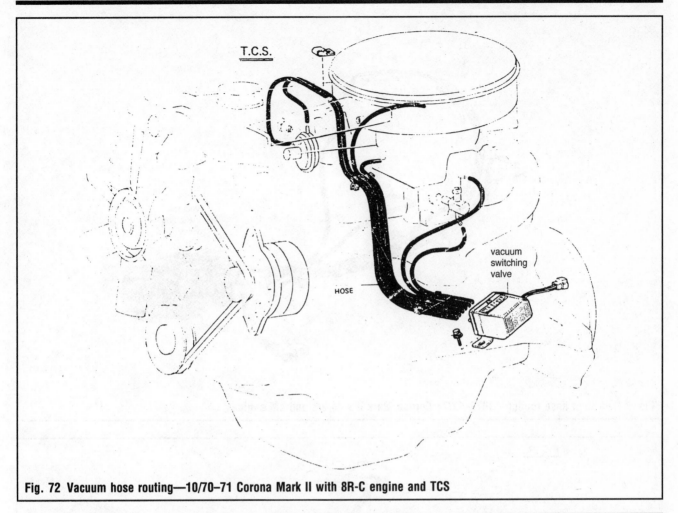

Fig. 72 Vacuum hose routing—10/70–71 Corona Mark II with 8R-C engine and TCS

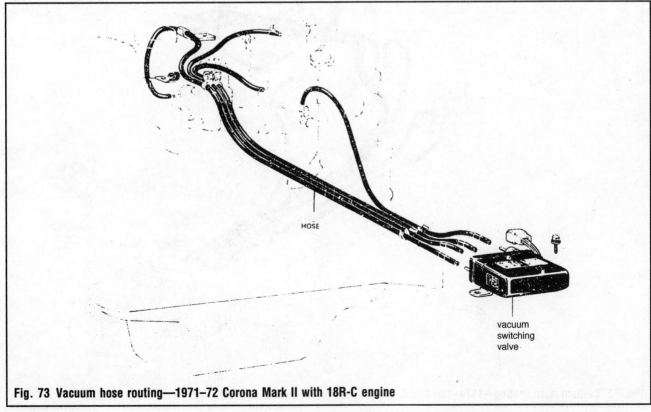

Fig. 73 Vacuum hose routing—1971–72 Corona Mark II with 18R-C engine

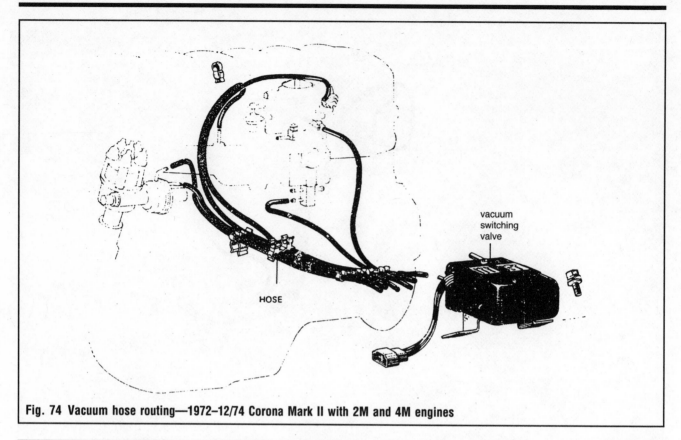

Fig. 74 Vacuum hose routing—1972–12/74 Corona Mark II with 2M and 4M engines

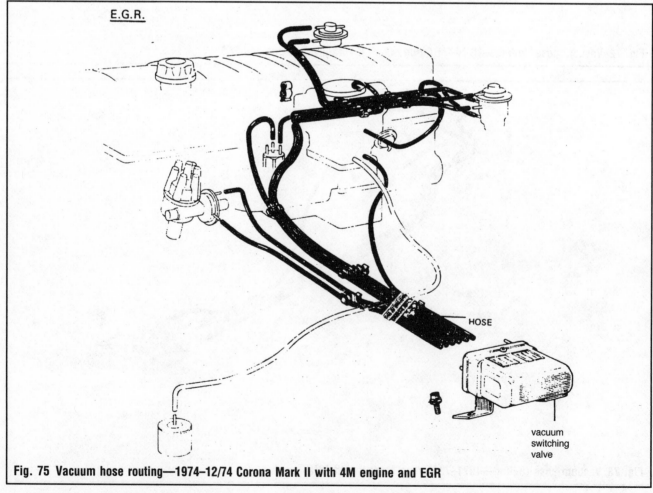

Fig. 75 Vacuum hose routing—1974–12/74 Corona Mark II with 4M engine and EGR

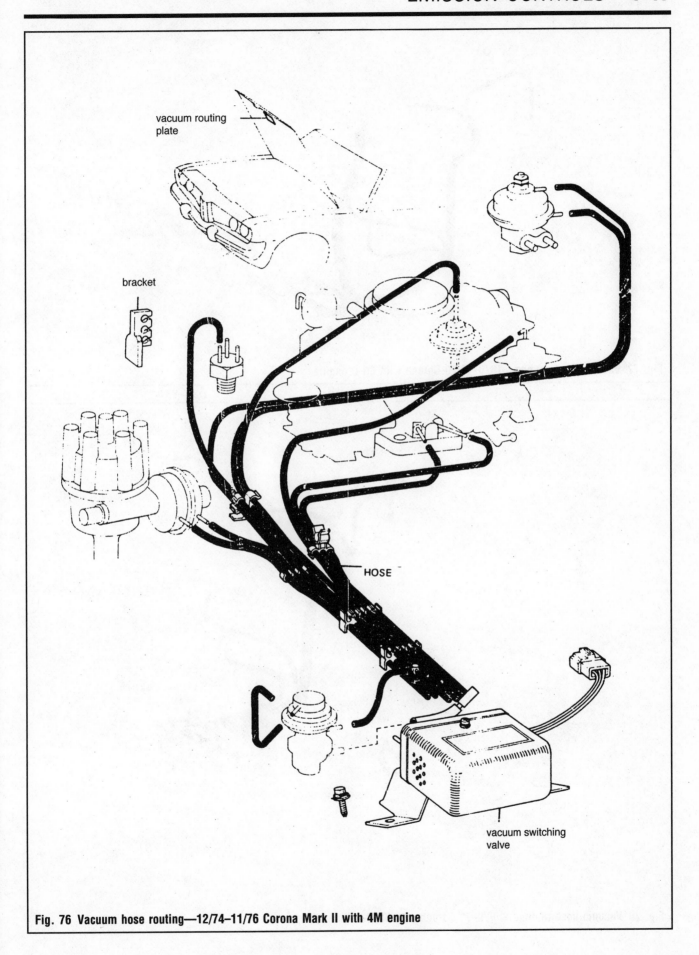

vacuum routing plate

bracket

HOSE

vacuum switching valve

Fig. 76 Vacuum hose routing—12/74–11/76 Corona Mark II with 4M engine

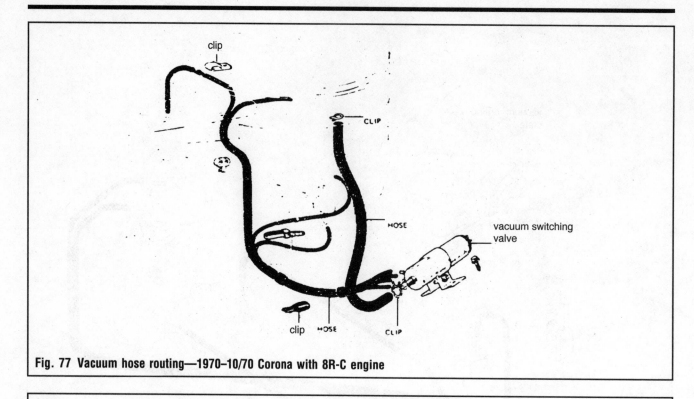

Fig. 77 Vacuum hose routing—1970–10/70 Corona with 8R-C engine

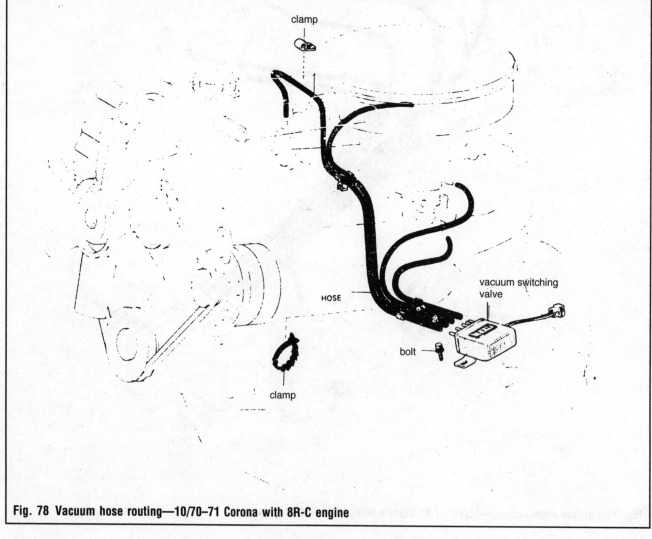

Fig. 78 Vacuum hose routing—10/70–71 Corona with 8R-C engine

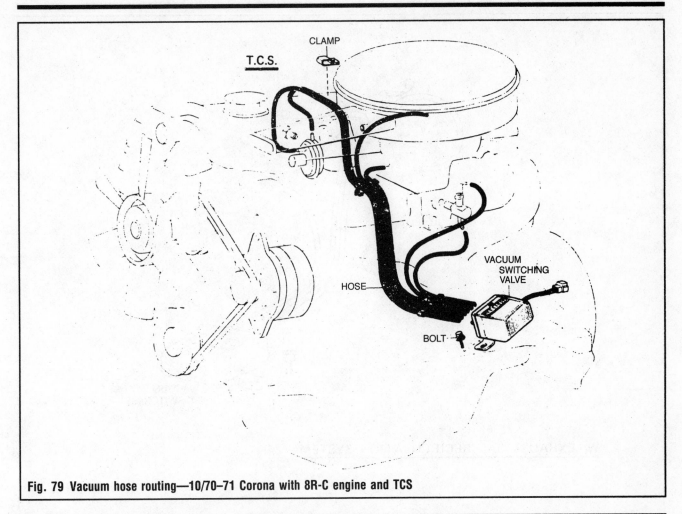

Fig. 79 Vacuum hose routing—10/70–71 Corona with 8R-C engine and TCS

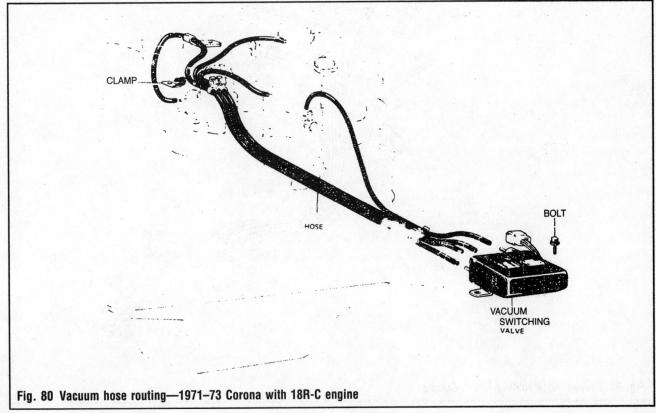

Fig. 80 Vacuum hose routing—1971–73 Corona with 18R-C engine

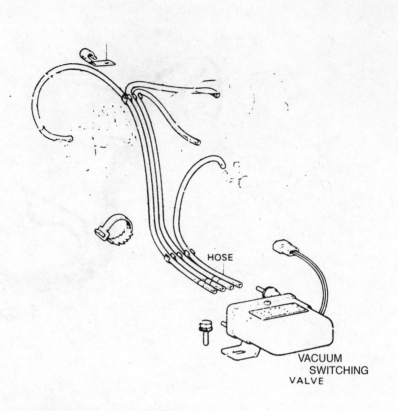

HOSE

VACUUM
SWITCHING
VALVE

W/ EXHAUST GAS RECIRCULATION SYSTEM

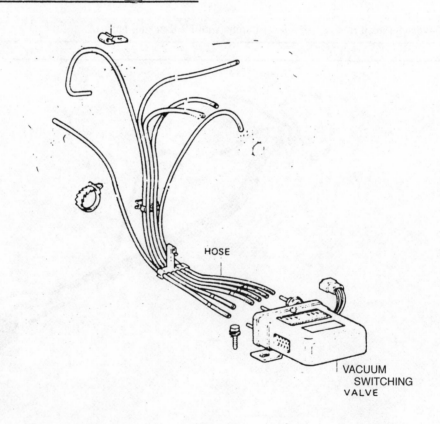

HOSE

VACUUM
SWITCHING
VALVE

Fig. 81 Vacuum hose routing—1974 Corona

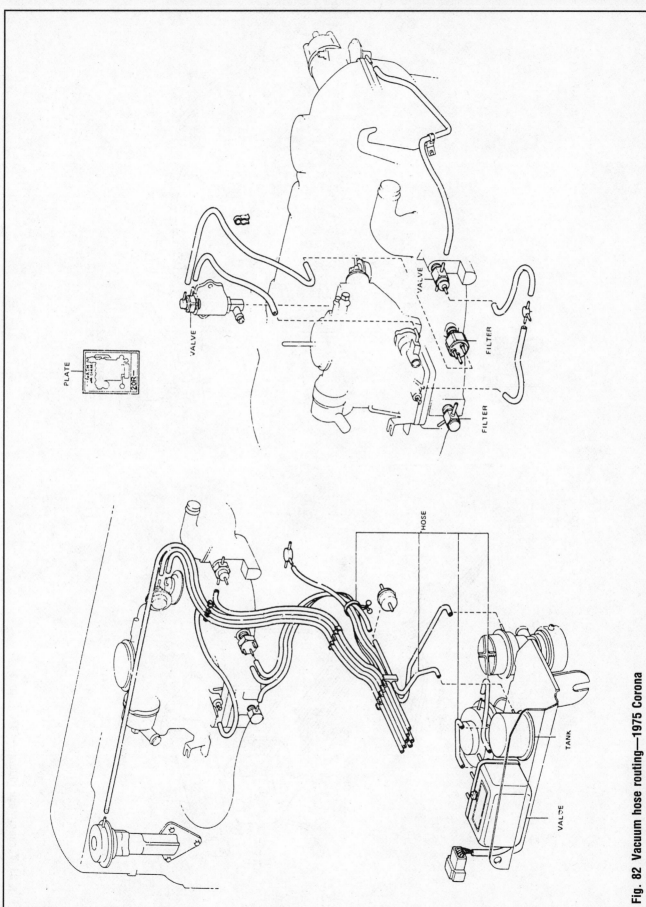

Fig. 82 Vacuum hose routing—1975 Corona

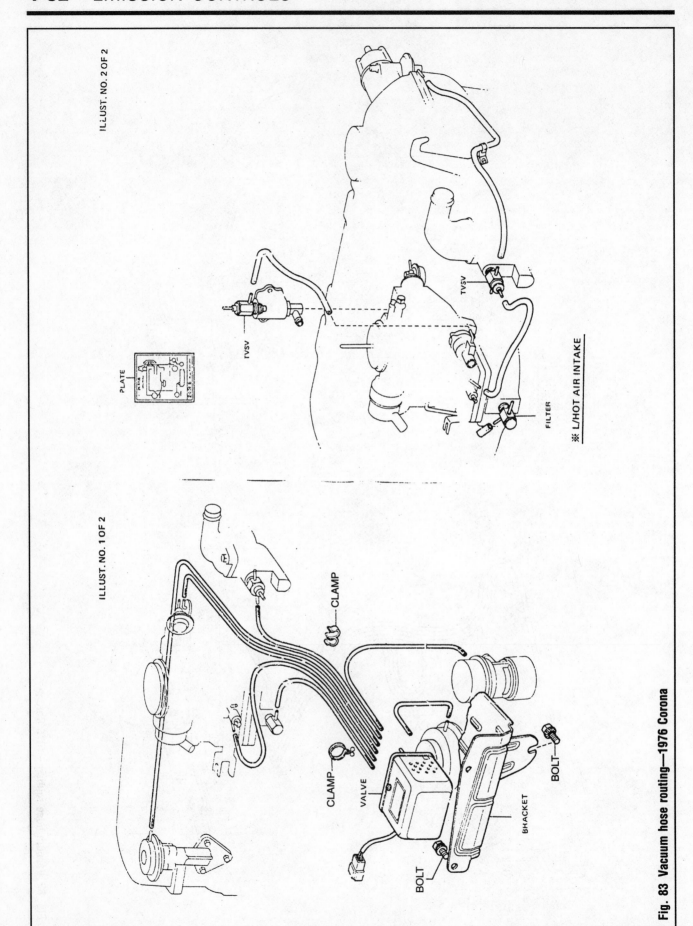

PLATE

TVSV

TVSV

FILTER

※ L/HOT AIR INTAKE

CLAMP

CLAMP

VALVE

BOLT

BRACKET

BOLT

BOLT

Fig. 83 Vacuum hose routing—1976 Corona

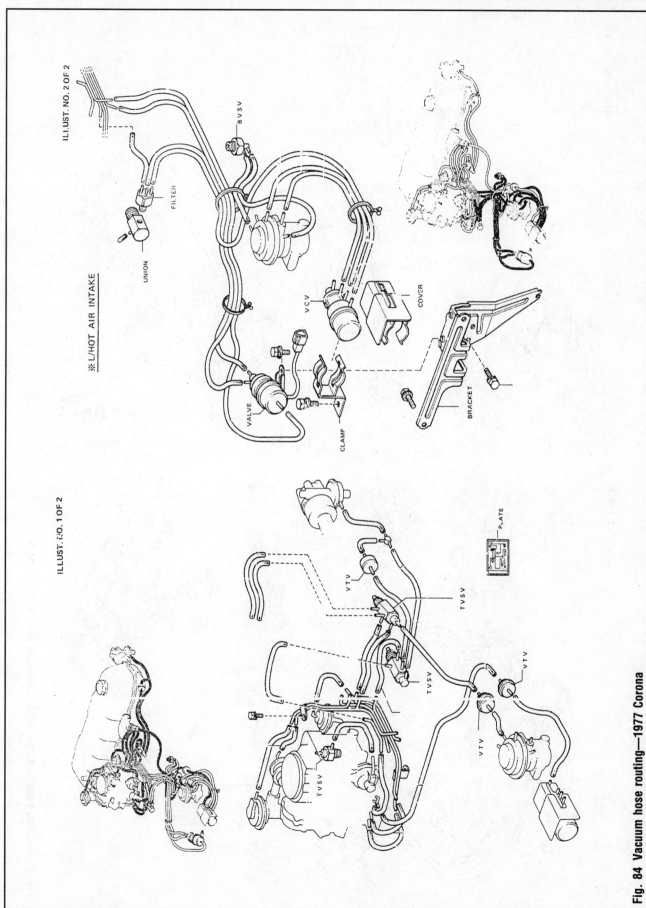

Fig. 84 Vacuum hose routing—1977 Corona

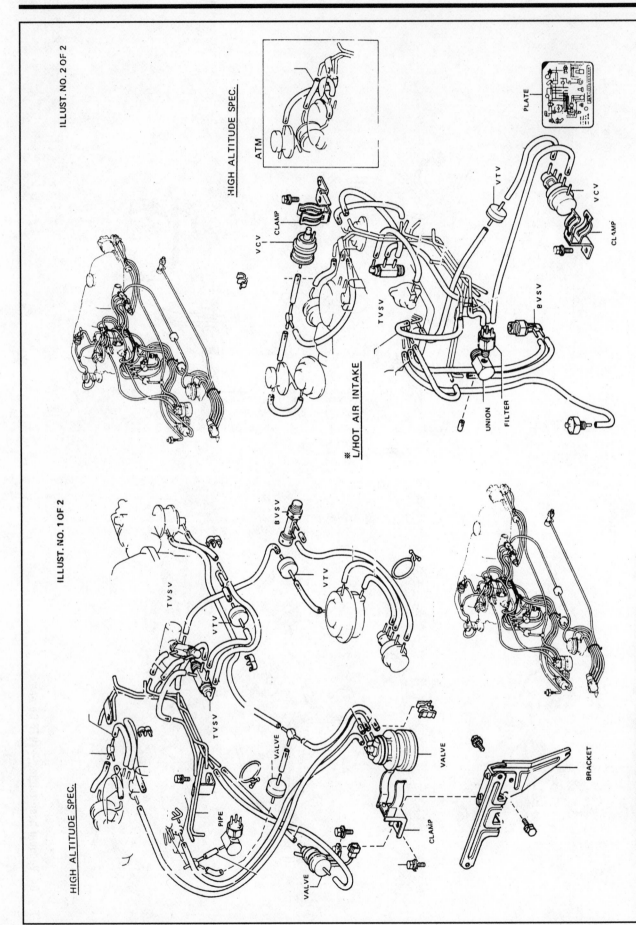

HIGH ALTITUDE SPEC.

ATM

PLATE

VCV

CLAMP

VCV

VTV

VCV

CLAMP

BVSV

TVSV

UNION

FILTER

※ L/HOT AIR INTAKE

HIGH ALTITUDE SPEC.

TVSV

VTV

TVSV

BVSV

VTV

VALVE

VALVE

VALVE

PIPE

CLAMP

BRACKET

VALVE

Fig. 85 Vacuum hose routing—1978 Corona (High Altitude models)

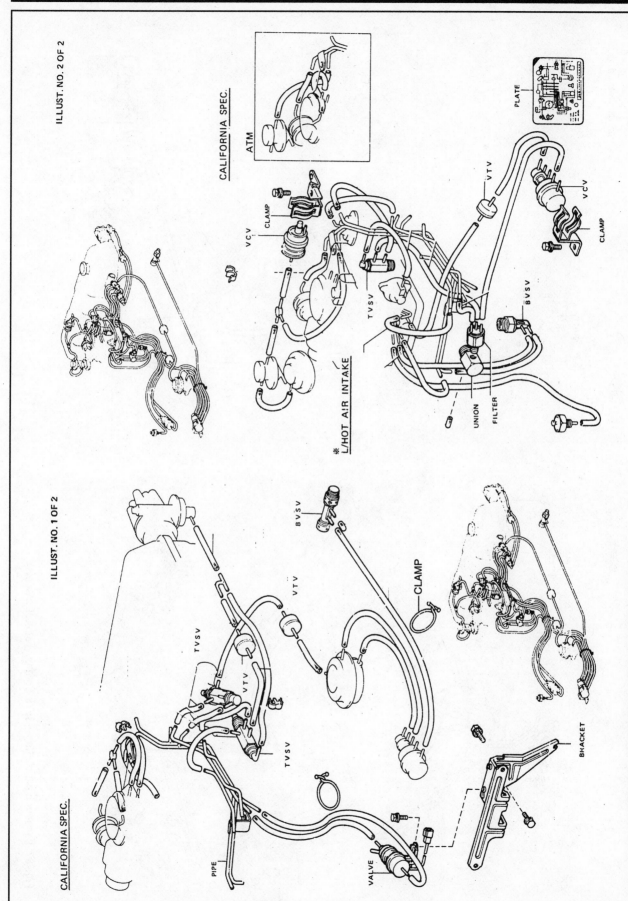

ILLUST. NO. 2 OF 2

CALIFORNIA SPEC.

ATM

PLATE

VCV

CLAMP

VCV

CLAMP

VTV

VCV

TVSV

BVSV

※L/HOT AIR INTAKE

UNION

FILTER

ILLUST. NO. 1 OF 2

BVSV

VTV

CLAMP

TVSV

VTV

TVSV

BRACKET

CALIFORNIA SPEC.

PIPE

VALVE

Fig. 86 Vacuum hose routing—1978 Corona (California models)

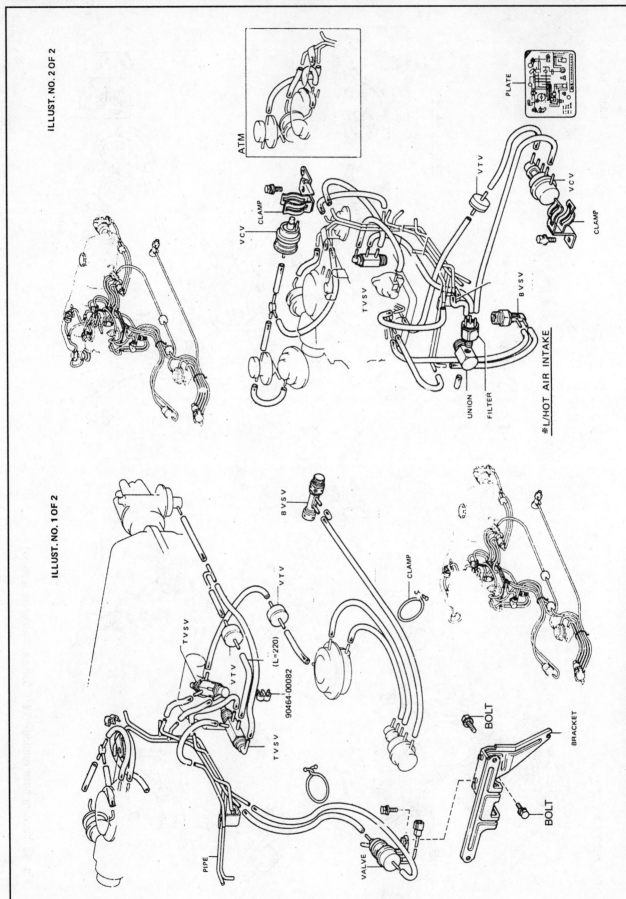

Fig. 87 Vacuum hose routing—1978 Corona (Federal models)

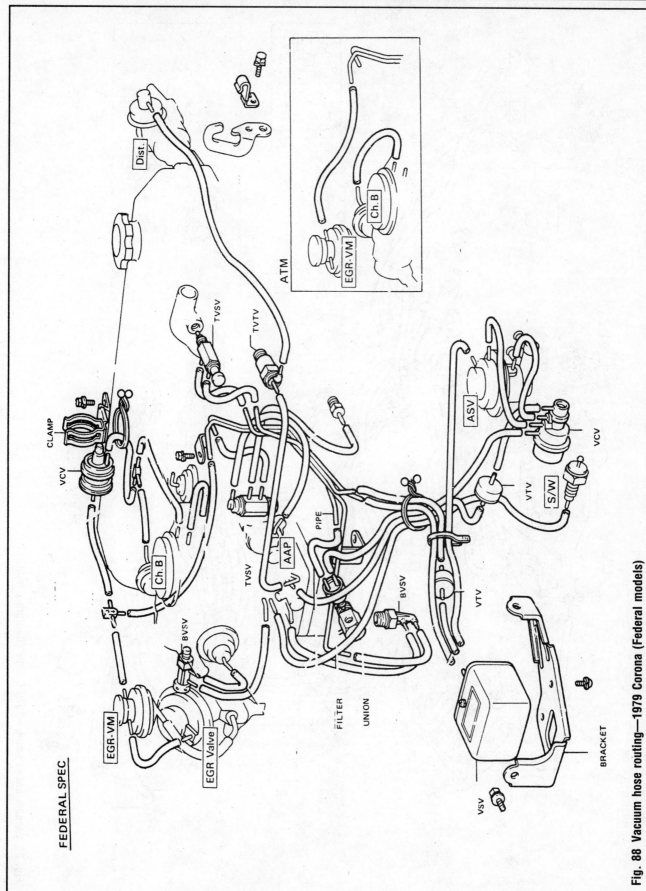

Fig. 88 Vacuum hose routing—1979 Corona (Federal models)

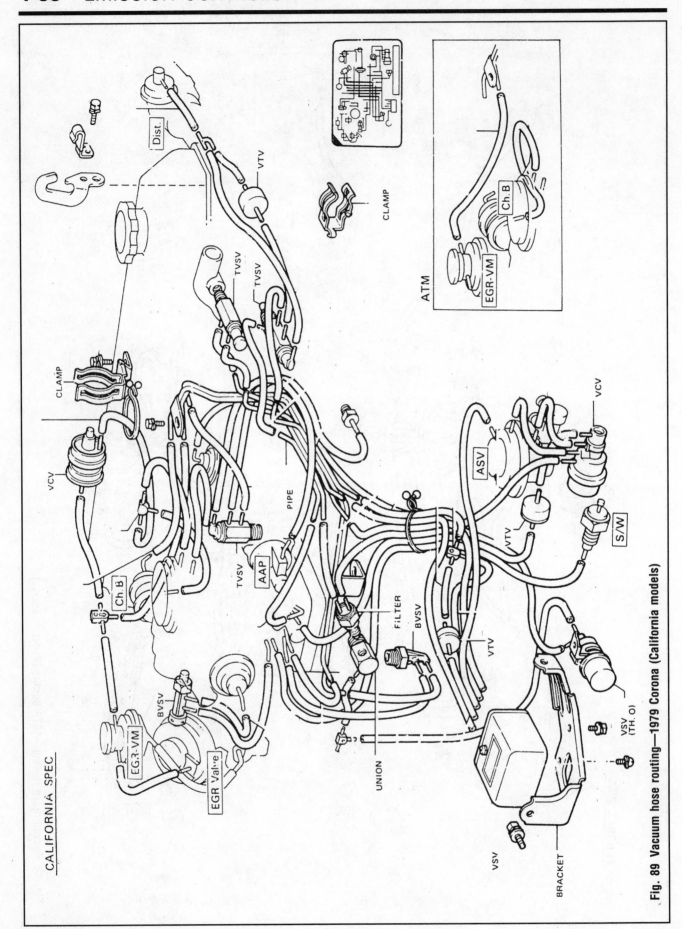

Fig. 89 Vacuum hose routing—1979 Corona (California models)

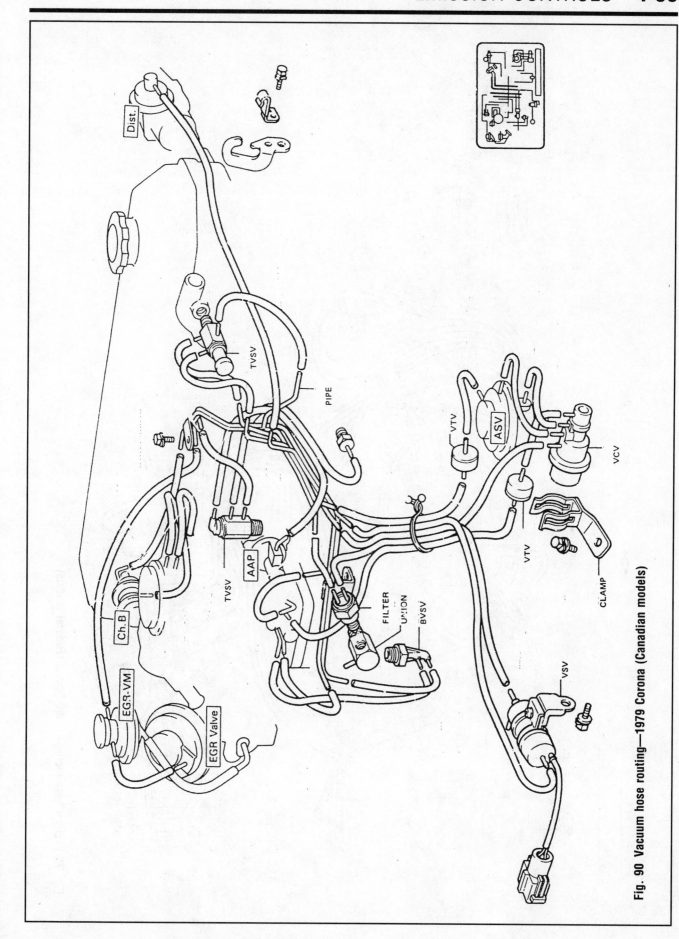

Fig. 90 Vacuum hose routing—1979 Corona (Canadian models)

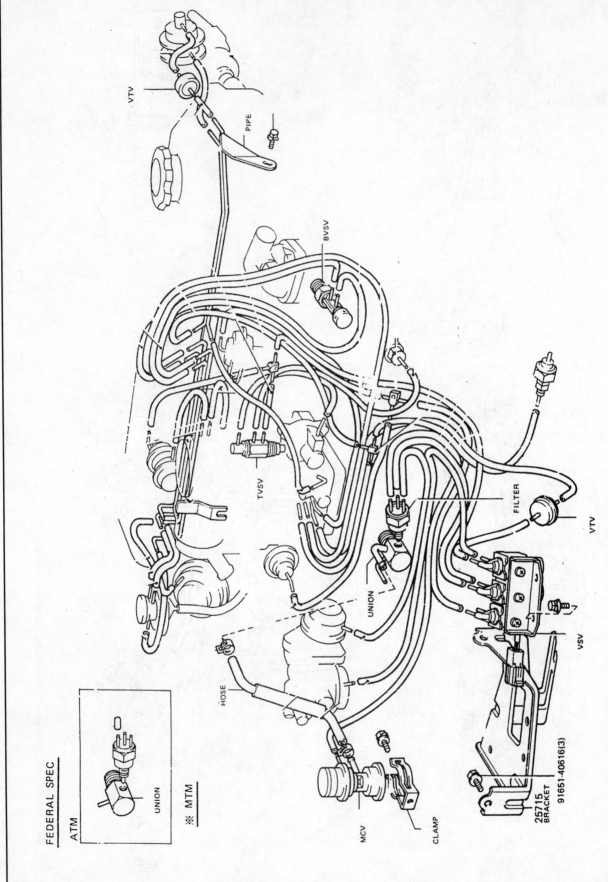

Fig. 91 Vacuum hose routing—1980 Corona (Federal models)

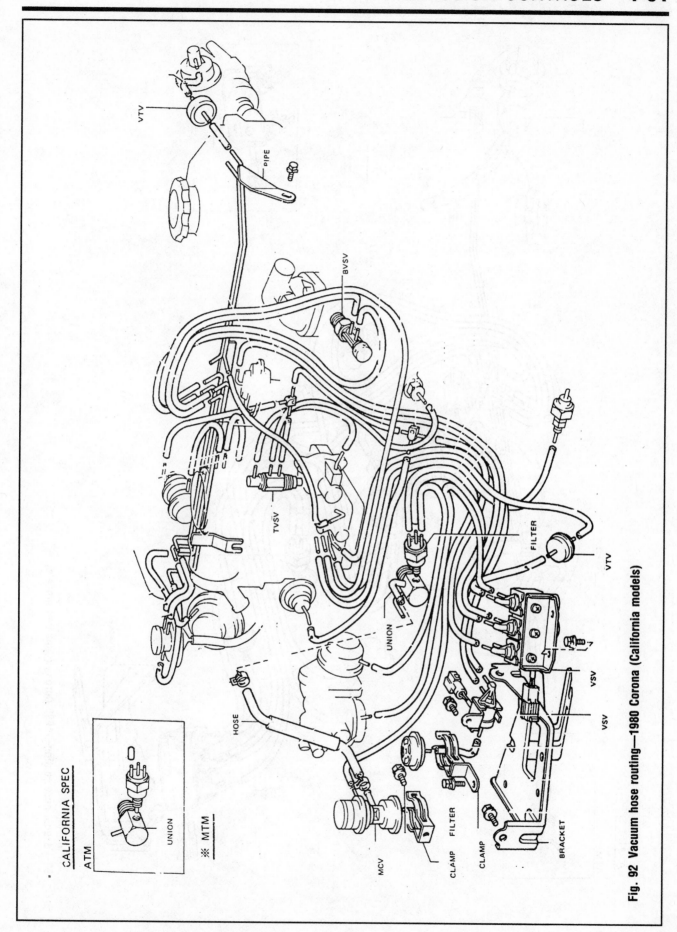

Fig. 92 Vacuum hose routing—1980 Corona (California models)

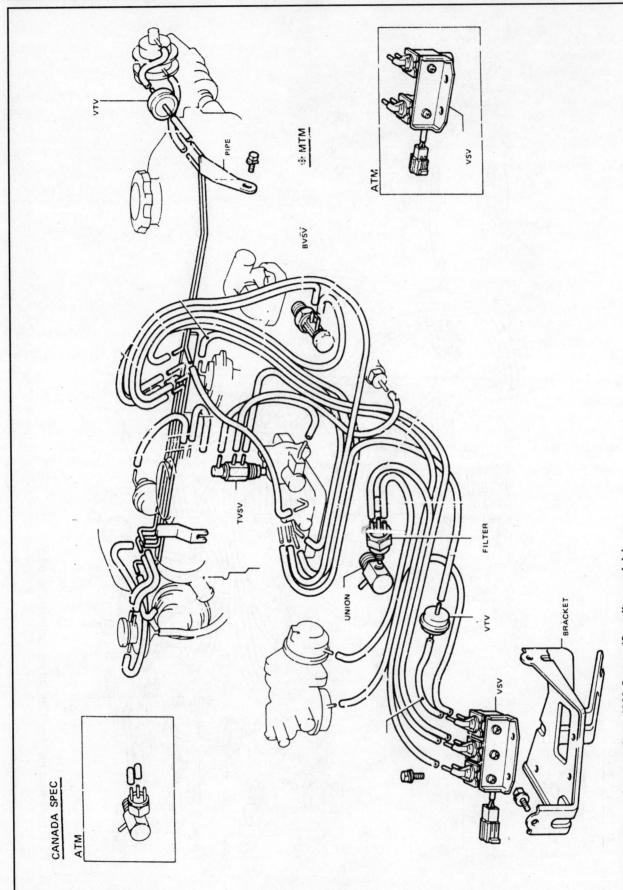

Fig. 93 Vacuum hose routing—1980 Corona (Canadian models)

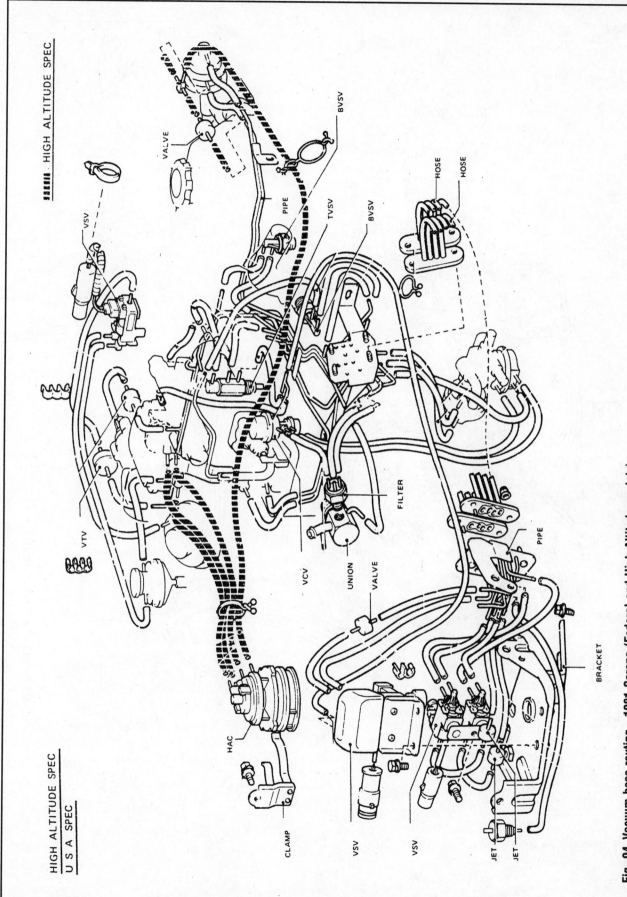

Fig. 94 Vacuum hose routing—1981 Corona (Federal and High Altitude models)

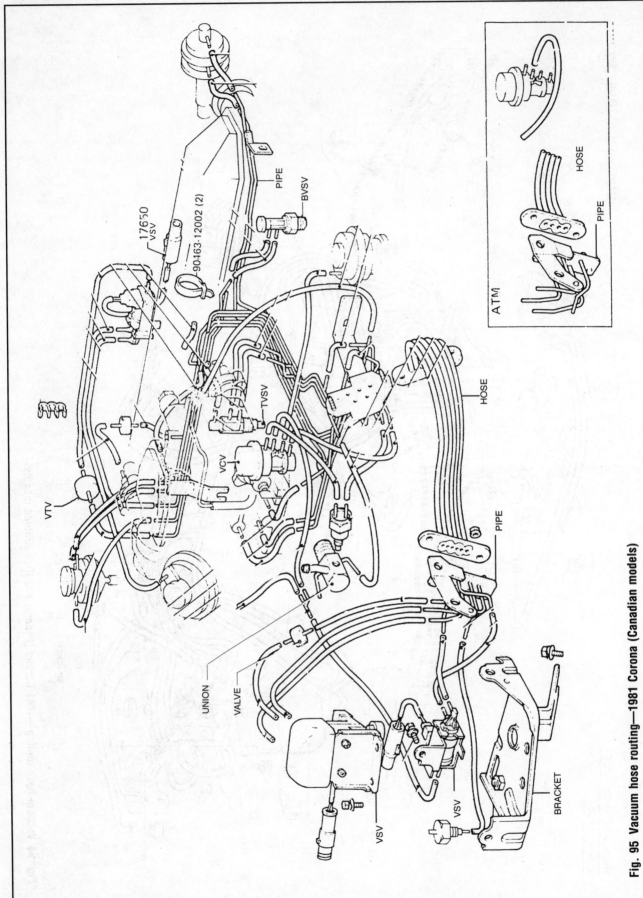

Fig. 95 Vacuum hose routing—1981 Corona (Canadian models)

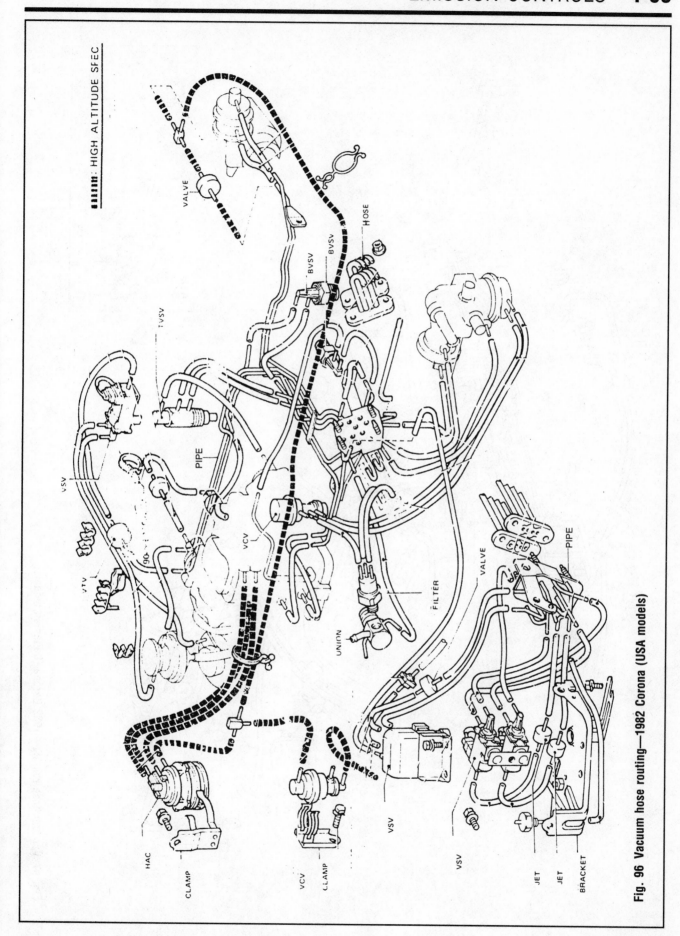

Fig. 96 Vacuum hose routing—1982 Corona (USA models)

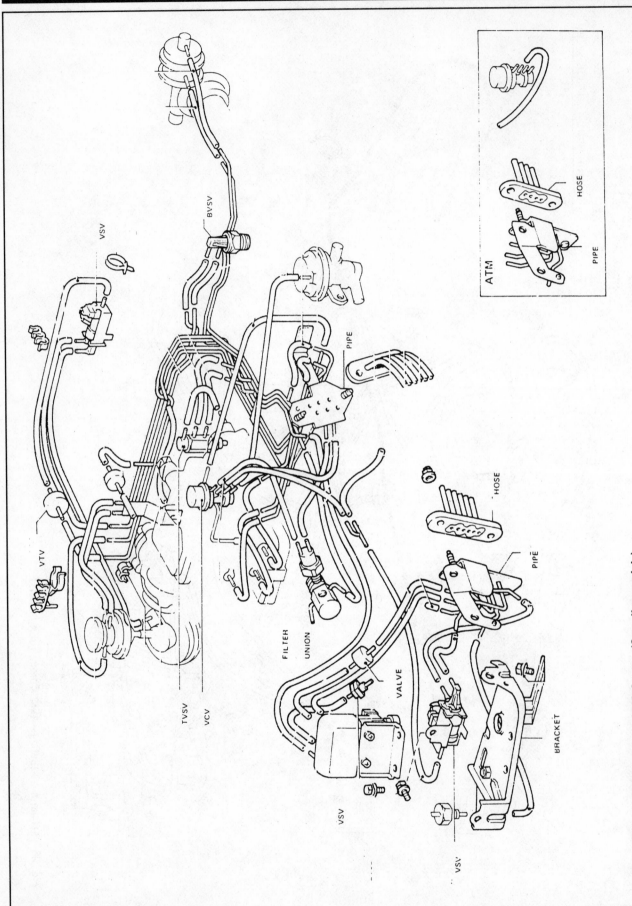

Fig. 97 Vacuum hose routing—1982 Corona (Canadian models)

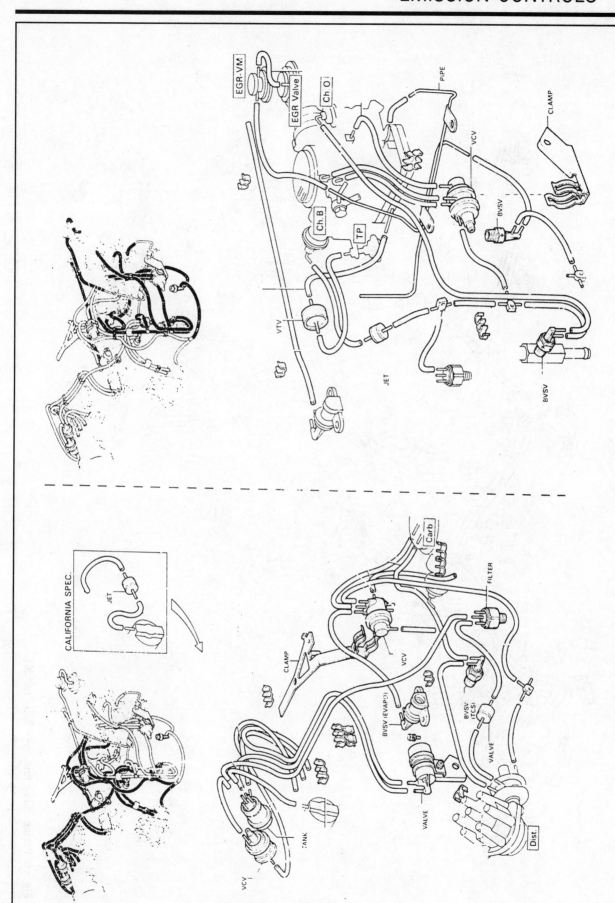

Fig. 98 Vacuum hose routing—1978 Cressida

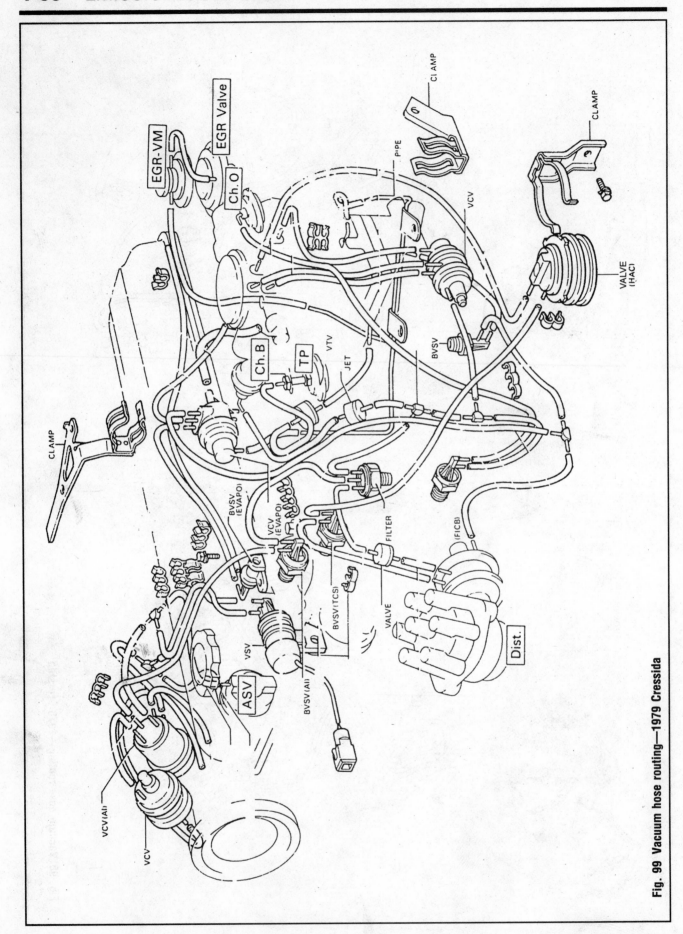

Fig. 99 Vacuum hose routing—1979 Cressida

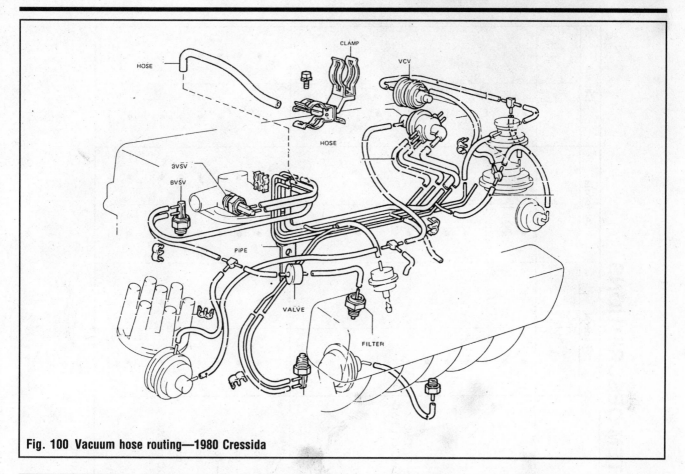

Fig. 100 Vacuum hose routing—1980 Cressida

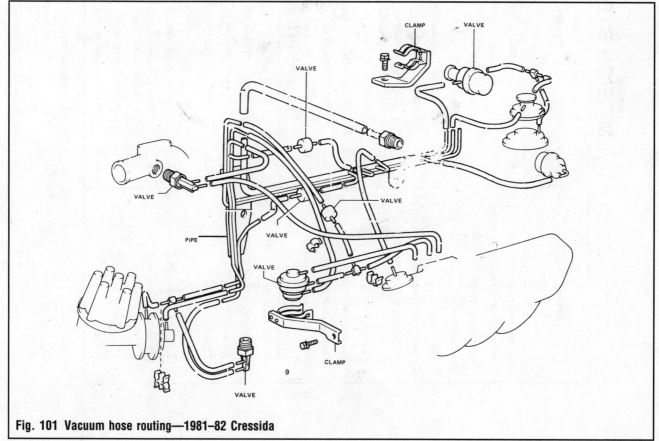

Fig. 101 Vacuum hose routing—1981–82 Cressida

EMISSION SYSTEM DESCRIPTIONS

System	Abbreviation	Purpose	Federal		California		Canada	
Positive crankcase ventilation	PCV	Reduces blow-by gas (HC)	•		•			•
Fuel evaporative emission control	EVAP	Reduces evaporative HC	•*1		•*1			•
Throttle positioner	TP	Reduces HC & CO						
Mixture control	MC	Reduces HC & CO	•*2		•*2			
Spark control	SC	Reduces NOx & HC	•		•			•
Exhaust gas recirculation	EGR	Reduces NOx	•		•			
Air injection with feedback	AI	Maintains air-fuel ratio for TWC and reduces HC, CO & NOx in TWC	•		•			
Air suction	AS	Reduces HC & CO						•
Three-way catalyst	TWC	Reduces HC, CO & NOx	•		•			
Oxidation catalyst	OC	Reduces HC & CO						•
High altitude compensation	HAC	Insures air-fuel mixture at high altitude	(OPT)					
Auxiliary system:								
Automatic hot air intake	HAI	Improves driveability – cold	•	•	•	•	•	•
Automatic choke	–	Improves driveability – cold	•	•	•	•	•	•
Choke breaker	CB	Improves driveability – cold	•	•	•	•	•	•
Choke opener	–	Improves driveability – hot	•	•	•	•	•	•
Auxiliary acceleration pump	AAP	Improves driveability – cold	•	•	•	•	•	•
Deceleration fuel cut	–	Prevents overheating OC or TWC, and after burning	•	•	•	•		•
Idle advance	–	Improves fuel economy at idle	•	•	•	•	•	•
Air bleed	–	Prevents overheating TWC						

REMARKS: *1 Only RT station wagon equipped with two canisters.
          *2 M/T vehicle only

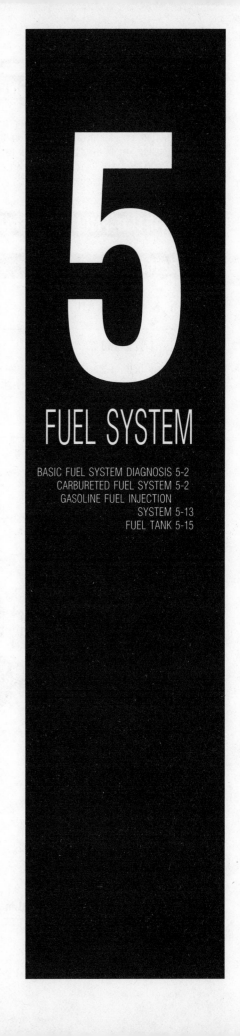

**BASIC FUEL SYSTEM
DIAGNOSIS 5-2**
CARBURETED FUEL SYSTEM 5-2
MECHANICAL FUEL PUMP 5-2
REMOVAL & INSTALLATION 5-2
ELECTRIC FUEL PUMP 5-4
REMOVAL & INSTALLATION 5-4
TESTING 5-5
CARBURETOR 5-5
REMOVAL & INSTALLATION 5-5
OVERHAUL NOTES 5-7
ADJUSTMENTS 5-7
VACUUM LIMITER SYSTEM 5-13
REMOVAL & INSTALLATION 5-13
TESTING 5-13
**GASOLINE FUEL INJECTION
SYSTEM 5-13**
DESCRIPTION OF SYSTEM 5-13
ELECTRIC FUEL PUMP 5-13
REMOVAL & INSTALLATION 5-13
TESTING 5-13
THROTTLE BODY 5-14
REMOVAL & INSTALLATION 5-14
AIR VALVE 5-14
REMOVAL & INSTALLATION 5-14
TESTING 5-14
PRESSURE REGULATOR 5-14
REMOVAL & INSTALLATION 5-14
CIRCUIT OPENING RELAY 5-15
TESTING 5-15
WATER THERMO SENSOR 5-15
TESTING 5-15
FUEL TANK 5-15
TANK ASSEMBLY 5-15
REMOVAL & INSTALLATION 5-15
SPECIFICATION CHARTS
FLOAT LEVEL ADJUSTMENTS
CHART 5-8
FAST IDLE ADJUSTMENT CHART 5-9
FAST IDLE SPEED CHART 5-10
CHOKE UNLOADER ADJUSTMENT
CHART 5-10
KICK-UP ADJUSTMENT CHART 5-12

5

FUEL SYSTEM

BASIC FUEL SYSTEM DIAGNOSIS 5-2
CARBURETED FUEL SYSTEM 5-2
GASOLINE FUEL INJECTION
SYSTEM 5-13
FUEL TANK 5-15

BASIC FUEL SYSTEM DIAGNOSIS

When there is a problem starting or driving a vehicle, two of the most important checks involve the ignition and the fuel systems. The questions most mechanics attempt to answer first, "is there spark?" and "is there fuel?" will often lead to solving most basic problems. For ignition system diagnosis and testing, please refer to the information on engine electrical components and ignition systems found earlier in this manual. If the ignition system checks out (there is spark), then you must determine if the fuel system is operating properly (is there fuel?).

CARBURETED FUEL SYSTEM

Mechanical Fuel Pump

REMOVAL & INSTALLATION

▶ **See Figures 1, 2 and 3**

1. Disconnect both of the fuel lines from the pump.
2. Unfasten the bolts which attach the fuel pump to the cylinder block.
3. Withdraw the pump assembly.

4. Installation is performed in the reverse order of removal. Always use a new gasket when installing the fuel pump. After the pump is installed check its discharge rate against the Tune-Up Specifications chart in Section 2.

Some pumps are equipped with a fuel return cut valve installed. This valve is designed to vary the amount of fuel returned to the gas tank according to the engine load. It helps to avoid gas percolation when the engine is hot and lightly loaded.

➡**Failure to use a gasket of the correct thickness could result in an improper pump discharge rate.**

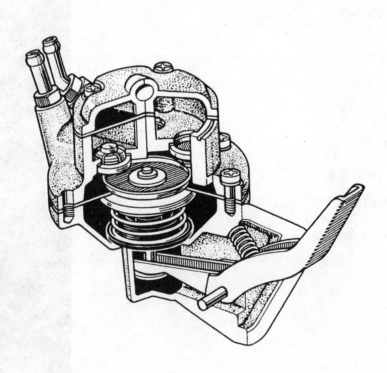

Fig. 1 Cutaway view of the mechanical fuel pump on 1970–72 models

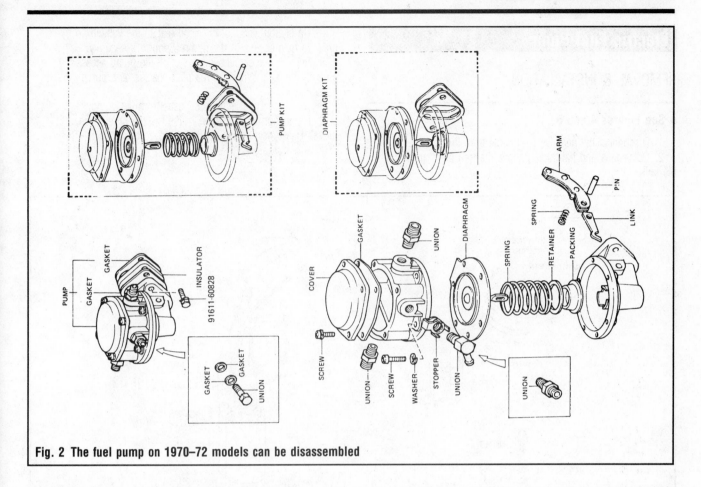

Fig. 2 The fuel pump on 1970–72 models can be disassembled

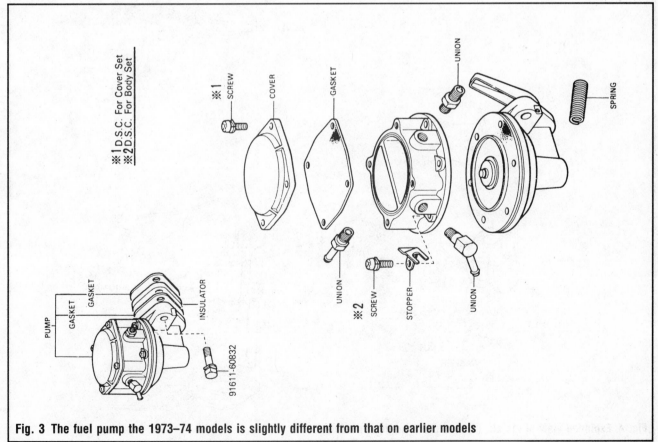

Fig. 3 The fuel pump the 1973–74 models is slightly different from that on earlier models

Electric Fuel Pump

REMOVAL & INSTALLATION

▶ **See Figures 4 and 5**

1. Disconnect the negative (−) cable from the battery.
2. On sedans and hardtops, remove the trim panel from inside the tank.

3. On station wagons, raise the rear of the vehicle, in order to gain access to the pump. Support it securely.
4. Remove the screws which secure the pump access plate to the tank. Withdraw the plate, gasket, and pump assembly.
5. Disconnect the leads and hoses from the pump.
6. Installation is performed in the reverse order of removal. Use a new gasket on the pump access plate.

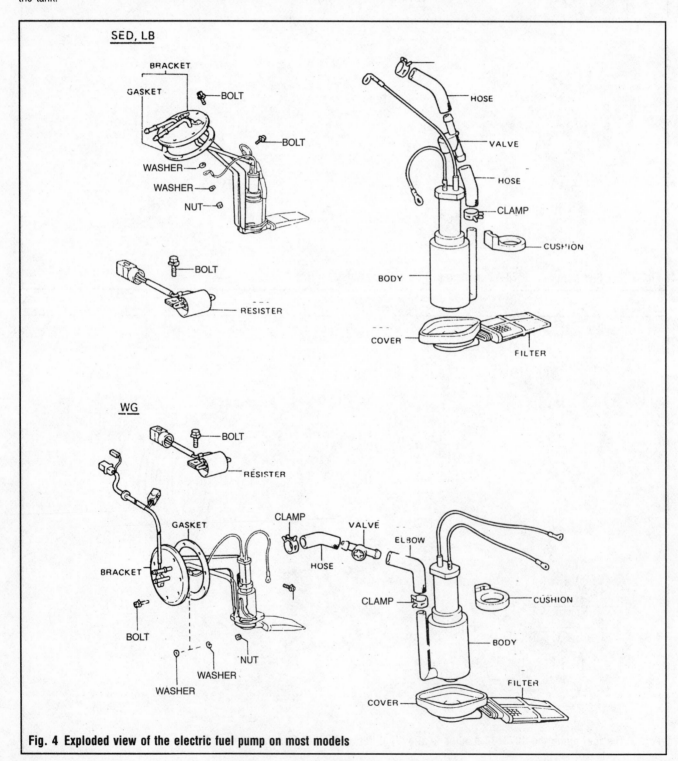

Fig. 4 Exploded view of the electric fuel pump on most models

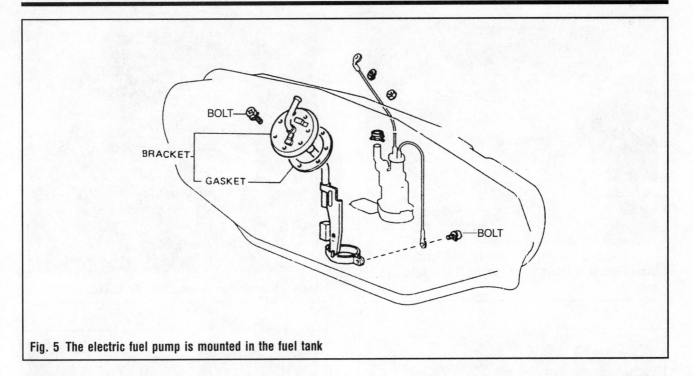

Fig. 5 The electric fuel pump is mounted in the fuel tank

TESTING

1. Disconnect the lead from the oil pressure warning light sender.
2. Unfasten the line from the outlet side of the fuel filter.
3. Connect a pressure gauge to the filter outlet with a length of rubber hose.
4. Turn the ignition switch to the **ON** position, but do not start the engine.
5. Check the pressure gauge reading against the figure given in the Tune-Up Specifications chart in Section 2.
6. Check for a clogged filter or pinched lines if the pressure is not up to specification.
7. If there is nothing wrong with the filter or lines, replace the fuel pump.
8. Turn the ignition **OFF** and reconnect the fuel line to the filter. Connect the lead to the oil pressure sender also.

Carburetor

The carburetors used on Toyota models are conventional two-barrel, downdraft types similar to domestic carburetors. The main circuits are: primary, for normal operational requirements; secondary, to supply high speed fuel needs; float, to supply fuel to the primary and secondary circuits; accelerator, to supply fuel for quick and safe acceleration; choke, for reliable starting in cold weather; and power valve, for fuel economy. Although slight differences in appearance may be noted, these carburetors are basically alike. Of course, different jets and settings are demanded by the different engines to which they are fitted.

REMOVAL & INSTALLATION

1. Remove the air filter housing, disconnect all air hoses from the filter base, and disconnect the battery ground cable.

➡**On 20R and 22R engines, drain the cooling system to prevent coolant from running into the intake manifold.**

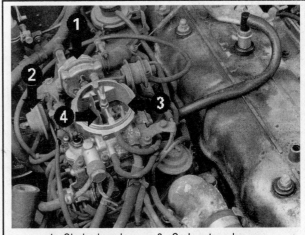

1. Choke housing   3. Carburetor plenum
2. Choke opener   4. Choke plate

View of the carburetor—1979 Corona with a 20R engine

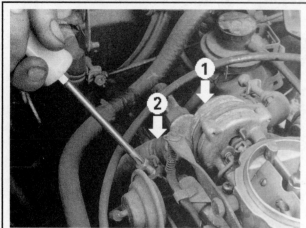

1. Choke housing   2. Coolant hose for choke

Disconnect the coolant hoses leading to the choke housing

Separate the throttle linkage from the throttle lever

Remove the hose clamps, then slide the fuel lines from the carburetor

Remove the carburetor base mounting bolts

Pull the hairpin clip from the throttle linkage

Once all components are separated from the unit, remove the carburetor from the engine

2. Disconnect the fuel line, choke pipe, and distributor vacuum line. On 20R and 22R engines, disconnect the choke coolant hose. Disconnect any electrical leads which run to the carburetor.

3. Remove the accelerator linkage. (With an automatic transmission, also remove the throttle rod to the transmission).

4. Remove the four nuts which secure the carburetor to the manifold and lift off the carburetor and gasket.

5. Cover the open manifold with a clean rag to prevent small objects from dropping into the engine.

6. Installation is performed in the reverse order of removal. After the engine is warmed up, check for fuel leaks and float level settings.

OVERHAUL NOTES

Efficient carburetion depends greatly on careful cleaning and inspection during overhaul since dirt, gum, water, or varnish in or on the carburetor parts are often responsible for poor performance.

Overhaul your carburetor in a clean, dust-free area. Carefully disassemble the carburetor, referring often to the exploded views. Keep all similar and lookalike parts segregated during disassembly and cleaning to avoid accidental interchange during assembly. Make a note of all jet sizes.

When the carburetor is disassembled, wash all parts (except diaphragms, electrical choke units, pump plunger, and any other plastic, leather, fiber, or rubber parts) in clean carburetor solvent. Do not leave parts in the solvent any longer than is necessary to sufficiently loosen the deposits. Excessive cleaning may remove the special finish from the float bowl and choke valve bodies, leaving these parts unfit for service. Rinse all parts in clean solvent and blow them dry with compressed air or allow them to air dry. Wipe clean all cork, plastic, leather, and fiber parts with a clean, lint-free cloth.

Blow out all passages and jets with compressed air and be sure that there are no restrictions or blockages. Never use wire or similar tools to clean jets, fuel passages, or air bleeds. Clean all jets and valves separately to avoid accidental interchange.

Check all parts for wear or damage. If wear or damage is found, replace the defective parts. Especially check the following:

1. Check the float needle and seat for wear. If wear is found, replace the complete assembly.

2. Check the flat hinge pin for wear. If wear is found, replace the complete assembly.

3. Check the throttle and choke shaft bores for wear or an out-of-round condition. Damage or wear to the throttle arm, shaft, or shaft bore will often require replacement of the throttle body. These parts require a close tolerance of fit. Wear may allow air leakage, which could affect starting and idling.

➡**Throttle shafts and bushings are not included in overhaul kits. They can be purchased separately.**

4. Inspect the idle mixture adjusting needles for burrs or grooves. Any such condition requires replacement of the needle, since you will not be able to obtain a satisfactory idle.

5. Test the accelerator pump check valves. They should pass air one way but not the other. Test for proper seating by blowing and sucking on the valve. Replace the valve if necessary. If the valve is satisfactory, wash the valve again to remove breath moisture.

6. Check the bowl cover for warped surfaces with a straight-edge.

7. Closely inspect the valves and seats for wear and damage, replacing as necessary.

8. After the carburetor is assembled, check the choke valve for freedom of operation.

Carburetor overhaul kits are recommended for each overhaul. These kits contain all gaskets and new parts to replace those that deteriorate most rapidly and complete instructions for rebuilding. Failure to replace all parts supplied with the kit (especially gaskets) can result in poor performance later.

Some carburetor manufacturers supply overhaul kits of 3 basic types: minor repair, major repair, and gasket kits. Basically, they contain the following:

Minor Repair Kits
• All gaskets
• Float needle valve
• Volume control screw
• All diaphragms

Major Repair Kits
• All jets and gaskets
• All diaphragms
• Float needle valve
• Volume control screw
• Pump ball valve
• Float
• Complete intermediate rod
• Intermediate pump lever
• Some cover hold-down screws and washers

Gasket Kits
• All gaskets

After cleaning and checking all components, reassemble the carburetor, using new parts and referring to the exploded views. When reassembling, make sure that all screws and jets are tight in their seats, but do not overtighten, as the tips will be distorted. Tighten all screws gradually, in rotation. Do not tighten needle valves into their seats. Uneven jetting will result. Always use new gaskets. Be sure to adjust the float level when reassembling.

ADJUSTMENTS

Float Level
◗ **See Figures 6, 7 and 8**

Float level adjustments are unnecessary on models equipped with a carburetor sight glass, if the fuel level falls within the lines when the engine is running.

There are two float level adjustments which may be made on Toyota carburetors. One is with the air horn inverted, so that the float is in a fully raised position. The other is with the air horn in an upright position, so that the float falls to the bottom of its travel.

The float level is either measured with a special carburetor float level gauge, which comes with a rebuilding kit, or with a standard wire gauge. For the proper type of gauge, as well as the points to be measured, see the Float Level Adjustments chart.

1. Turn the air horn upside down and let the float hang down by its own weight.

2. Using a special float gauge (available at your local dealer), check the clearance between the tip of the float and the flat surface of the air horn. The clearance should be:

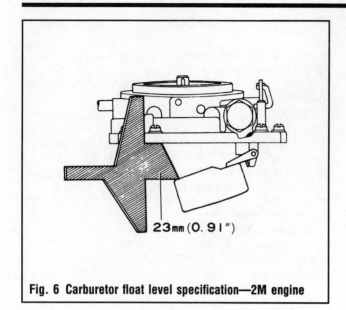

Fig. 6 Carburetor float level specification—2M engine

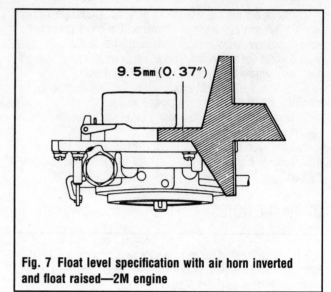

Fig. 7 Float level specification with air horn inverted and float raised—2M engine

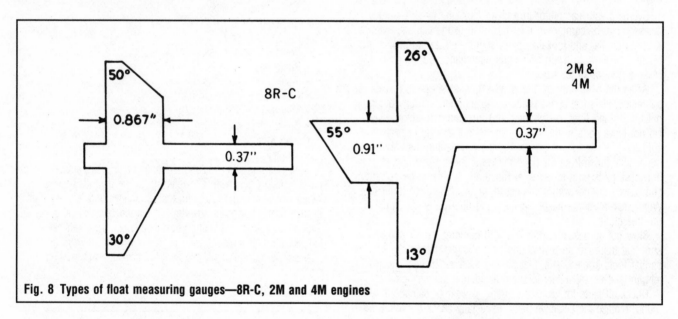

Fig. 8 Types of float measuring gauges—8R-C, 2M and 4M engines

Float Level Adjustments

Engine	Gauge Type	Float Raised Machine Distance Between:	Gap (in.)	Gauge Type	Float Lowered Measure Distance Between:	Gap (in.)
8R-C	Special	Float and air horn	0.370	Wire	Needle valve bushing pin and float tab	0.039
18R-C	Special	Float and air horn	0.200 ①	Wire	Needle valve bushing pin and float tab	0.039
20R	Special	Float and air horn	0.197 ②	Special	Needle valve bushing pin and float tab	0.039
2M and 4M	Special	Float end and air horn	0.370 ③	Special	Float end and air horn	0.910 ④

① 1976–77—0.236 in.
② 1978–79—0.276 in.
③ 1975–76—0.394 in.
④ 1975–76—0.039 in.

- 2M and 4M (1971–74) 0.370 in. (9mm)
- 4M (1975–76) 0.394 in. (10mm)
- 8R-C—0.370 in. (9mm)
- 18R-C—0.200 in. (5mm)
- 20R (1975–77)—0.197 in. (5mm)
- 20R (1978–80)—0.276 in. (7mm)
- 22R (1981)—0.386 in. (9mm)
- 22R (1982)—0.413 inch (10mm)

➡**This measurement should be made without the gasket on the air horn.**

3. If the float clearance is not within specifications, adjust it by bending the upper (center) float tab.

4. Lift up the float and check the clearance between the needle valve plunger and the float lip. Clearance on the 8R-C and 18R-C engines may be checked with a special float gauge or with a standard wire feeler gauge. 20R and 22R engines must only use the special float gauge. The clearance should be 0.039 in. (0.99mm) on all engines.

5. If the clearance is not within specifications, adjust it by bending the lower float tabs.

Fast Idle Adjustment

OFF VEHICLE

◆ **See Figure 9**

The fast idle adjustment is performed with the choke valve fully closed. Adjust the gap between the throttle valve edge and bore to the specifications, where given, in the Fast Idle Adjustment chart. Use a wire gauge to determine the gap.

The chart also gives the proper primary throttle valve opening angle, where necessary, and the proper means of fast idle adjustment.

➡**The throttle valve opening angle is measured with a gauge supplied in the carburetor rebuilding kit. It is also possible to make one out of cardboard by using a protractor to obtain the correct angle.**

ON VEHICLE

➡**Disconnect the EGR valve vacuum line on 20R and 22R engines.**

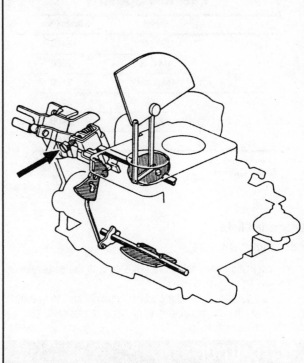

Fig. 9 To adjust the fast idle, turn the screw to set the first throttle valve angle to specification

1. Perform the idle speed/mixture adjustments as outlined in Section 2. Leave the tachometer connected.

2. Remove the top of the air cleaner.

3. Open the throttle valve slightly and close the choke valve. Next, hold the choke valve with your finger and close the throttle valve. The choke valve is now fully closed.

4. Without depressing the accelerator pedal, start the engine.

5. Check the engine fast idle speed against the following chart.

6. If the reading on the tachometer is not within specifications, adjust the fast idle speed by turning the fast idle screw.

7. Disconnect the tachometer, install the air cleaner cover, and connect the EGR valve vacuum line if it was disconnected.

Fast Idle Adjustment

Engine	Throttle Valve to Bore Clearance (in.)	Primary Throttle Angle (deg)	To Adjust Fast Idle:
8R-C	0.029	11—from closed	Turn the fast idle adjusting screw
18R-C	0.041	13—from closed	Turn the fast idle adjusting screw
20R	0.047	—	Turn the fast idle screw
2M	—	24—from closed	Turn the fast idle adjusting screw
4M	—	16—from closed ①	Turn the fast idle adjusting screw

—Not available
① 1977   9°

Fast Idle Speed

	Engine	Speed (rpm)
1975–77	20R (All)	2400
	4M (US)	2600
	4M (Calif)	2400
1978–81	20R	2400
	22R	2400
	4M	2500

US—United States
Calif—California

Automatic Choke
♦ **See Figure 10**

The automatic choke should be adjusted with the carburetor installed and the engine running.

1. Check to ensure that the choke valve will close from fully opened when the coil housing is turned counterclockwise (2M and 4M engines clockwise).

✳✳ CAUTION

On models equipped with a 20R or 22R engine, do not loosen the center bolt or coolant will run out.

2. Align the mark on the coil housing with the center line on the thermostat case. In this position, the choke valve should be fully closed when the ambient temperature is 77°F.
3. If necessary, adjust the mixture by turning the coil housing. If the mixture is too rich, rotate the housing clockwise. If too lean, rotate the housing counterclockwise. On models equipped with the

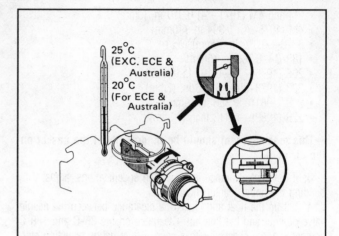

Fig. 10 The automatic choke valve becomes fully closed when the atmospheric temperature reaches the indicated values—4M engine

2M and 4M engines, rotate the housing in exactly the reverse direction of the above.

➡**Each graduation on the thermostat case is equivalent to 9°F.**

Unloader
♦ **See Figure 11**

Make the unloader adjustment with the primary valve fully opened. Adjust by performing the procedure indicated on the Choke Unloader Adjustment chart. The total angle of choke valve opening, in the chart, is measured with either a special gauge, supplied in the carburetor rebuilding kit, or a gauge of the proper angle fabricated from cardboard.

Choke Unloader Adjustment

		Choke Valve Angle (deg)			
Year	Engine	Throttle Valve Fully Closed (deg)	From Closed to Fully Open (deg)	Throttle Valve Open (total) (deg)	To Adjust Bend:
1970–75	20R	30	—	50	Fast idle lever
	8R-C	32	19	51	Fast idle cam follower or choke shaft tab
	18R-C	—	27	47	Fast idle cam follower or choke shaft tab
	4M	20	15	35 ①	Fast idle lever
1976–82	20R	—	50	90	Fast idle lever, follower or choke shaft tab
	4M	20	15	90	Fast idle lever

—Not available
① 1975—50°

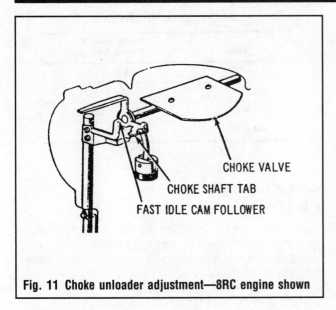

Fig. 11 Choke unloader adjustment—8RC engine shown

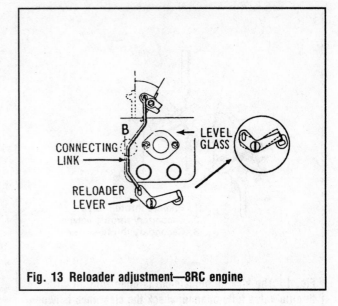

Fig. 13 Reloader adjustment—8RC engine

Reloader
▶ See Figures 12 and 13

A reloader is used on the 8R-C engine to prevent the throttle valve from opening during automatic choke operation.

1. When the choke valve is opened 45° from the closed position, the reloader lever should disengage from its stop.

➡**Angle A, in the illustration, should be 20 degrees when measured with a gauge.**

2. To adjust, bend the portion of the linkage where angle A was measured.

3. When the primary throttle valve is fully opened, with the reloader in operating position, the clearance between the secondary throttle valve edge and bore should be 0.35–0.76mm. Measure the clearance with a wire gauge and bend the reloader tab to adjust it.

4. Fully open the choke valve by hand. The reloader lever should be disengaged from its stop by the weight on its link.

Choke Breaker
▶ See Figure 14

1. Push the rod which comes out of the upper (choke breaker) diaphragm so that the choke valve opens.

2. Measure the choke valve opening angle. It should be 40°.

3. Adjust the angle, if necessary, by bending the relief lever link.

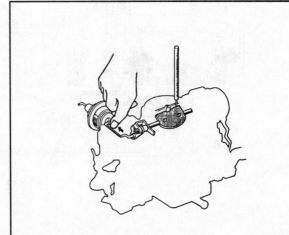

Fig. 14 Push the choke breaker rod to open the choke valve, then check the clearance between the valve and carburetor body

Fig. 12 Check the choke valve opening angle with a gauge

Kick-Up
▶ See Figure 15

1. Open the primary throttle valve the amount specified in the Kick-Up Adjustment chart.

2. Measure the secondary throttle valve-to-bore clearance with a 0.2mm (0.2–0.4mm—1970–74 2M/4M engines) gauge.

3. Adjust the clearance by bending the secondary throttle lever.

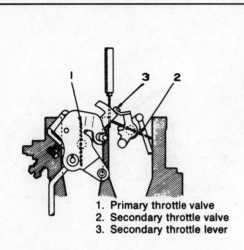

1. Primary throttle valve
2. Secondary throttle valve
3. Secondary throttle lever

Fig. 15 The kick-up adjustment is done with the primary throttle valve fully opened; check the clearance between the secondary throttle valve and carburetor body

Kick-Up Adjustment

Engine	Primary Throttle Valve Opening Angle (deg)
18R-C	64 from bore
20R	fully opened
2M/4M	55 from closed
4M (1975–79)	64–90 from closed

Initial Idle Mixture Screw
♦ **See Figure 16**

When assembling the carburetor, turn the idle mixture screw the number of turns specified below. After the carburetor is installed, perform the appropriate idle speed/mixture adjustment as outlined in Section 2.
- 8R-C engine—2 turns from seating
- 18R-C engine—2½ turns from fully closed
- 20R, 22R engine—1¾ turns from fully closed
- 2M/4M engines—1½ turns out

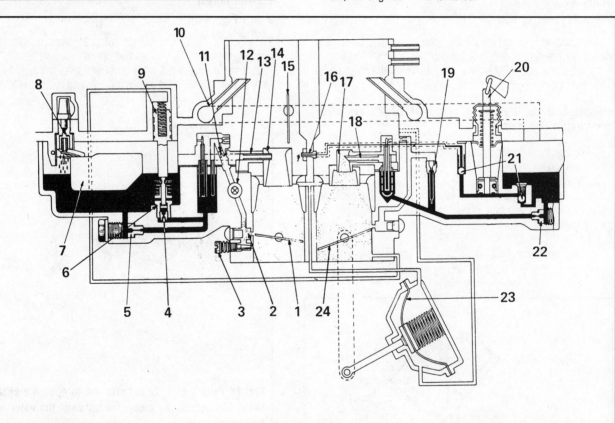

1.	First Throttle Valve	9. Power Piston	17. Second Small Venturi
2.	First Slow Port	10. Air Vent	18. Second Main Nozzle
3.	Idle Mixture Adjusting Screw	11. Economizer Jet	19. Second Slow Jet
4.	Power Jet	12. Solenoid Valve	20. Pump Plunger
5.	First Main Jet	13. First Main Nozzle	21. Steel Ball
6.	Power Valve	14. First Small Venturi	22. Second Main Jet
7.	Float	15. Choke Valve	23. Diaphragm
8.	Needle Valve	16. Pump Jet	24. Second Throttle Valve

Fig. 16 Cutaway view of a carburetor—4M engine shown

✳✳ WARNING

Seat the idle mixture screw lightly. Overtightening will damage its tip.

Choke Return System

Some engines have a choke return system to protect the catalytic converter. Because of the chance of overheating the exhaust system and damaging the catalytic converter by running with the choke out, a thermoswitch and return spring system automatically close the choke when the coolant temperature reaches 104°F.

A holding coil and holding plate surround the choke cable and retain it when the temperature is low enough. When the temperature reaches 104°F the thermoswitch opens, freeing the return spring to pull in the choke. There are no adjustments on the system. If a malfunction occurs, trace the loss and replace that segment of the unit.

Vacuum Limiter System

This system allows fresh air to enter the air intake chamber upon sudden deceleration to reduce hydrocarbons and carbon dioxide emissions. This system is used on the 1980–81 4M and 4-ME engines only.

REMOVAL & INSTALLATION

1. Remove the two vacuum lines.
2. Remove the intake chamber line.
3. Remove the valve from its mounting.
4. Installation is the reverse of removal.

TESTING

1. Disconnect the air inlet hose of the vacuum limiter from the air connector and plug the air connector port.
2. Start the engine.
3. Close the inlet of the vacuum limiter with your finger.
4. Increase the speed of the engine and then release the throttle.
5. When the throttle valve is opened and closed you should momentarily feel vacuum. If not the vacuum limiter is defective and must be replaced.

GASOLINE FUEL INJECTION SYSTEM

Description of System

▶ **See Figure 17**

The 4M-E and 5M-E engines are equipped with electronic fuel injection. The EFI system precisely controls fuel injection to match engine requirements, reducing emissions and increasing driveability.

The electric fuel pump pumps fuel through a damper and filter to the pressure regulator. The six fuel injectors are electric solenoid valves which open and close by signals from the control unit.

The EFI computer receives input from various sensors to determine engine operating condition.

- Air flow meter—measures the amount of intake air.
- Ignition coil—engine RPM.
- Throttle valve switch—amount of throttle opening.
- Water temperature sensor or cylinder head temperature sensor—temperature of coolant or engine.
- Air temperature sensor—temperature of intake air (ambient temperature).
- Thermotime switch—signal used to control cold start valve fuel enrichment when the engine is cold.
- Starting switch—signals that the starter is operating.
- Altitude switch used to signal changes in atmospheric pressure.
- Exhaust gas sensor used to measure the oxygen content of the exhaust gas. The sensors provide the input to the control unit, which determines the amount of fuel to be injected by its preset program.

The fuel injection system is a highly complex unit. All repair or adjustment should be left to an expert Toyota technician.

Electric Fuel Pump

REMOVAL & INSTALLATION

The electric pump used on fuel injected models is removed by simply disconnecting the fuel lines and electrical connector from the pump and dismounting the pump.

TESTING

1. Turn the ignition switch to the ON position, but do not start the engine.
2. Remove the rubber cap from the fuel pump check connector and short both terminals.
3. Check that there is pressure in the hose to the cold start injector.

➡ **At this time, you should be able to hear the fuel return noise from the pressure regulator.**

4. If no pressure can be felt in the line, check the fuses and all other related electrical connections. If everything is all right, the fuel pump will probably require replacement.
5. Remove the service wire, reinstall the rubber cap and turn **OFF** the ignition switch.

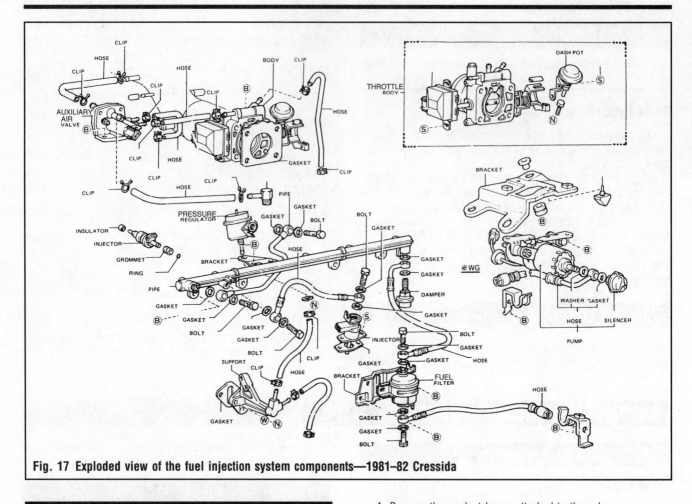

Fig. 17 Exploded view of the fuel injection system components—1981–82 Cressida

Throttle Body

REMOVAL & INSTALLATION

1. Drain the cooling system.
2. Disconnect the negative battery cable.
3. Disconnect the air valve and PCV hoses.
4. Remove the coolant hoses in the area.
5. Label and disconnect all vacuum hoses and wiring leading to or around the throttle body.
6. Remove the air intake connector and hose.
7. Unbolt and remove the throttle body and discard the gasket.
8. Install the parts in the reverse order of removal. Make sure to use a new throttle body gasket. Tighten the throttle body bolts 8–11 ft. lbs. Fill the cooling system and connect the negative battery cable.
9. Check the system for leaks.

Air Valve

REMOVAL & INSTALLATION

1. Disconnect the negative battery cable.
2. Drain the cooling system.
3. Remove the air hoses attached to the air valve.

4. Remove the coolant hoses attached to the valve.
5. Unplug the connector from the valve.
6. Remove the valve.
7. Install the parts in the reverse sequence of removal. Fill the cooling system and connect the negative battery cable.
8. Check the system for leaks.

TESTING

1. Check the engine RPM by pinching shut the air hose on the valve.
   a. At low temperatures, below 60° C (140° F), the RPM should drop.
   b. After warm-up, the RPM should not drop more than 150 RPM.
2. Check the opening condition of the air valve.
3. Disconnect the air hose and check that the valve opens slightly when the temperature is about 20° C (68° F).

Pressure Regulator

REMOVAL & INSTALLATION

1. Drain the cooling system.
2. Disconnect the negative battery cable.

3. Remove the air hose to the pressure regulator and PCV valve hose.

4. Remove the coolant hose leading to the pressure regulator.

5. Tag and disconnect all vacuum hoses around the pressure regulator.

6. Unplug the air intake connector.

7. Remove the throttle body and gasket. Discard the gasket.

8. Separate the fuel pipe.

9. Disconnect the fuel return hose.

10. Remove the pressure regulator.

11. Install the parts in the reverse order of disassembly. Install the throttle body using a new gasket. Tighten the fuel pipe bolts 19–25 ft. lbs. Tighten the throttle body bolts 8–11 ft. lbs.

Circuit Opening Relay

TESTING

➡This relay is on Cressida models only.

1. Remove the left kick panel or glove box.

2. Using a voltmeter, check that the meter indicates voltage at Fp terminal during engine cranking and running.

FUEL TANK

Tank Assembly

REMOVAL & INSTALLATION

Carbureted Vehicles
▶ See Figures 18, 19, 20, 21 and 22 (p. 16–18)

1. Disconnect the negative battery cable.

2. Remove the drain plug and drain all fuel from the tank.

3. Remove mat and access cover from the luggage compartment. Disconnect the gauge unit electrical wiring. Disconnect

3. Stop the engine.

4. Disconnect the wiring harness leading to the relay.

5. Measure the resistance between each terminal. The correct values are:
- Terminals STA-E1: 30–60 ohms
- Terminals B-Fc: 80–120 ohms
- Terminals B-Fp: Infinity

6. Plug the wiring harness into the relay.

7. Install the kick panel or glove box.

Water Thermo Sensor

TESTING

1. Unplug the wiring leading to the sensor.

2. Using an ohmmeter, measure the resistance between both terminals. Check the chart.

the outlet or outlet and return hose(s) at the tank. Label the wires.

4. Remove the nuts from the two tank securing bands and lower the tank slightly.

5. Disconnect and label the three ventilation hoses used on models with evaporative emission control. Disconnect the fuel tank filler pipe. Remove the tank.

6. The tank should be checked carefully for dents or cracks which might cause leaks. Replace the tank as necessary.

7. Installation is the reverse of removal. Be sure to connect the filler hose after the tank has been mounted, to prevent leakage at the connection. Be careful not to kink hoses or overtighten fittings when reconnecting.

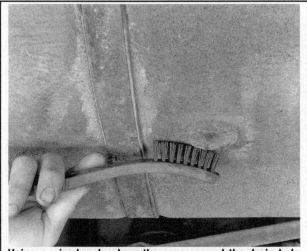

Using a wire brush, clean the area around the drain hole in the fuel tank . . .

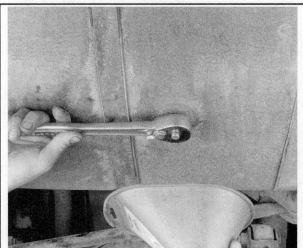

. . . then, place a container and funnel under the tank and remove the plug to allow the fuel to flow

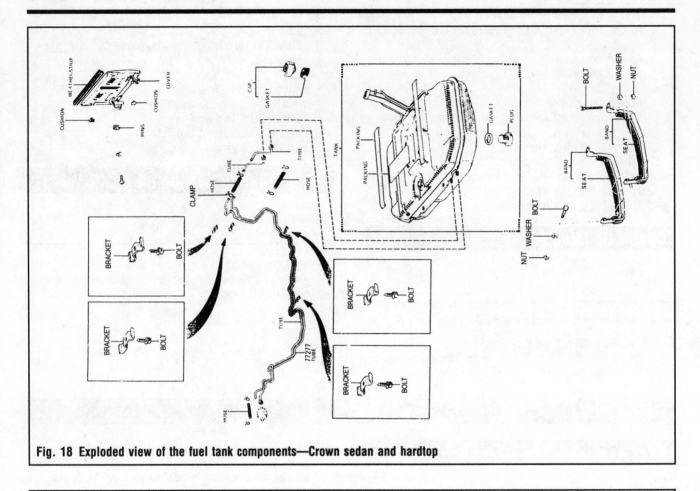

Fig. 18 Exploded view of the fuel tank components—Crown sedan and hardtop

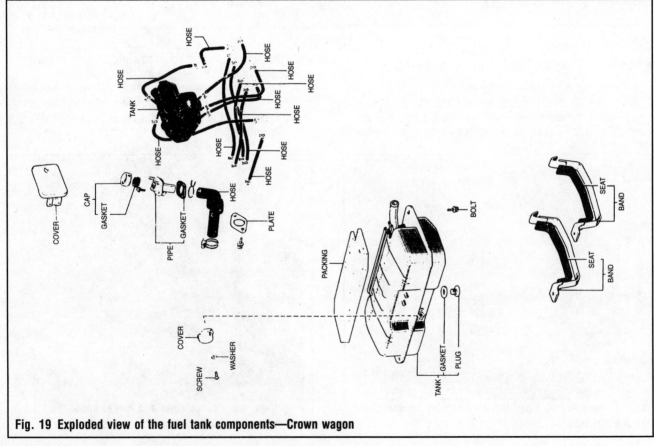

Fig. 19 Exploded view of the fuel tank components—Crown wagon

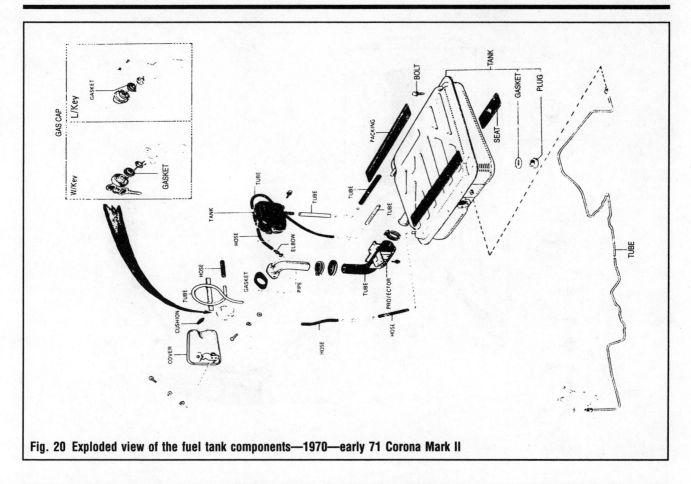

Fig. 20 Exploded view of the fuel tank components—1970—early 71 Corona Mark II

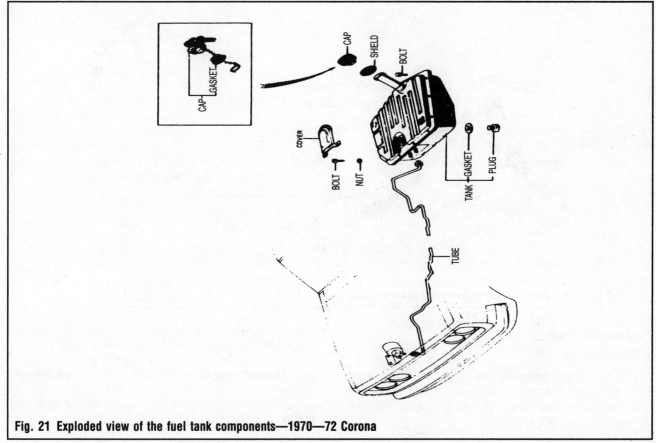

Fig. 21 Exploded view of the fuel tank components—1970—72 Corona

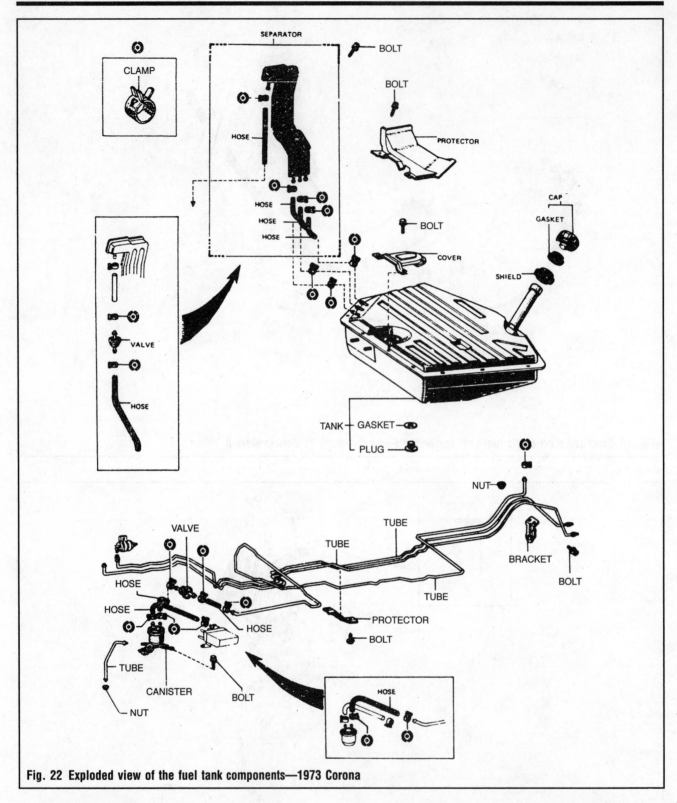

Fig. 22 Exploded view of the fuel tank components—1973 Corona

Fuel Injected Vehicles
▶ **See Figure 23**

1. Reduce the fuel pressure to zero. See Section 1 under Fuel Filters for the correct procedure.

2. Disconnect the fuel outlet hose from the fuel pipe and drain the tank if no drain plug is provided.

3. Remove the luggage compartment mat. Remove the cover over the tank sending unit and hose connections. Disconnect the gauge electrical harness, ventilation, fuel feed and fuel return hoses.

4. Remove the nut and the fuel tank retaining straps. Remove the tank.

5. Installation is the reverse of removal. Be careful not to twist or kink any of the hoses.

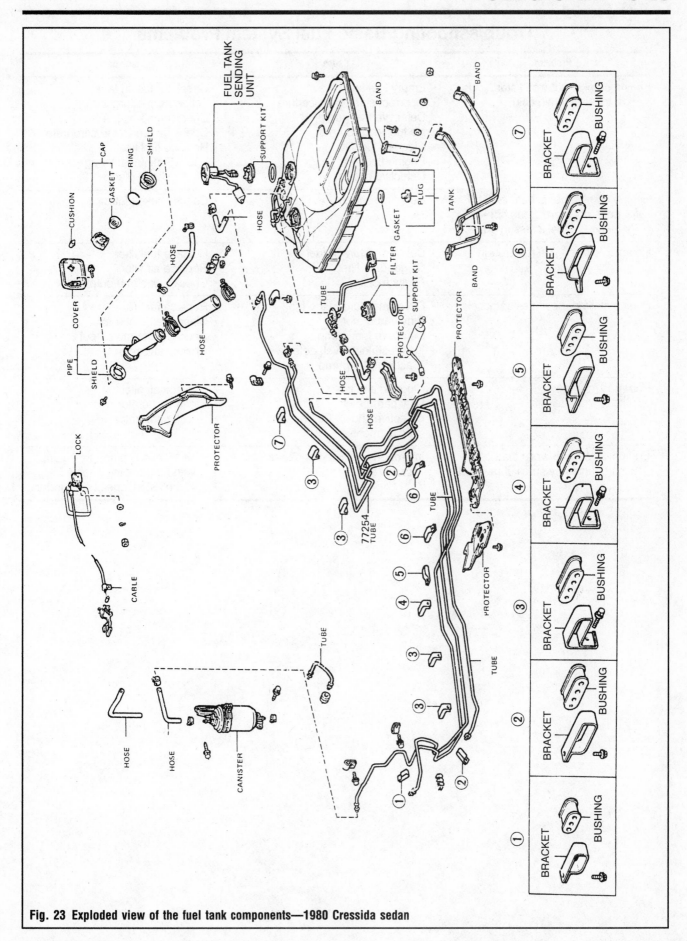

Fig. 23 Exploded view of the fuel tank components—1980 Cressida sedan

Troubleshooting Basic Fuel System Problems

Problem	Cause	Solution
Engine cranks, but won't start (or is hard to start) when cold	• Empty fuel tank • Incorrect starting procedure • Defective fuel pump • No fuel in carburetor • Clogged fuel filter • Engine flooded • Defective choke	• Check for fuel in tank • Follow correct procedure • Check pump output • Check for fuel in the carburetor • Replace fuel filter • Wait 15 minutes; try again • Check choke plate
Engine cranks, but is hard to start (or does not start) when hot— (presence of fuel is assumed)	• Defective choke	• Check choke plate
Rough idle or engine runs rough	• Dirt or moisture in fuel • Clogged air filter • Faulty fuel pump	• Replace fuel filter • Replace air filter • Check fuel pump output
Engine stalls or hesitates on acceleration	• Dirt or moisture in the fuel • Dirty carburetor • Defective fuel pump • Incorrect float level, defective accelerator pump	• Replace fuel filter • Clean the carburetor • Check fuel pump output • Check carburetor
Poor gas mileage	• Clogged air filter • Dirty carburetor • Defective choke, faulty carburetor adjustment	• Replace air filter • Clean carburetor • Check carburetor
Engine is flooded (won't start accompanied by smell of raw fuel)	• Improperly adjusted choke or carburetor	• Wait 15 minutes and try again, without pumping gas pedal • If it won't start, check carburetor

**UNDERSTANDING AND
TROUBLESHOOTING ELECTRICAL
SYSTEMS 6-2**
SAFETY PRECAUTIONS 6-2
UNDERSTANDING BASIC
  ELECTRICITY 6-2
    THE WATER ANALOGY 6-2
    CIRCUITS 6-2
    AUTOMOTIVE CIRCUITS 6-3
    SHORT CIRCUITS 6-3
TROUBLESHOOTING 6-3
    BASIC TROUBLESHOOTING
      THEORY 6-4
    TEST EQUIPMENT 6-4
    TESTING 6-6
WIRING HARNESSES 6-8
    WIRING REPAIR 6-8
ADD-ON ELECTRICAL EQUIPMENT 6-10
HEATER 6-12
BLOWER MOTOR 6-12
    REMOVAL & INSTALLATION 6-12
HEATER CORE 6-14
    REMOVAL & INSTALLATION 6-14
HEATER CONTROL VALVE 6-15
    REMOVAL & INSTALLATION 6-15
CONTROL ASSEMBLY 6-15
    REMOVAL & INSTALLATION 6-15
CONTROL CABLES 6-15
    REMOVAL & INSTALLATION 6-15
ENTERTAINMENT SYSTEM 6-17
RADIO 6-17
    REMOVAL & INSTALLATION 6-17
SPEAKERS 6-19
    REMOVAL & INSTALLATION 6-19
**WINDSHIELD WIPERS AND
  WASHERS 6-21**
WINDSHIELD WIPER BLADE AND
  ARM 6-21
    REMOVAL & INSTALLATION 6-21
WINDSHIELD WIPER MOTOR 6-22
    REMOVAL & INSTALLATION 6-22
WIPER LINKAGE 6-22
    REMOVAL & INSTALLATION 6-22
WASHER FLUID RESERVOIR 6-24
    REMOVAL & INSTALLATION 6-24
WASHER PUMP 6-27
    REMOVAL & INSTALLATION 6-27
**INSTRUMENTS AND
  SWITCHES 6-27**
INSTRUMENT CLUSTER 6-27
    REMOVAL & INSTALLATION 6-27
SPEEDOMETER, TACHOMETER, AND
  GAUGES 6-32
    REMOVAL & INSTALLATION 6-32
PRINTED CIRCUIT BOARD 6-32
    REMOVAL & INSTALLATION 6-32
SPEEDOMETER CABLE 6-32
    REMOVAL & INSTALLATION 6-32
IGNITION SWITCH 6-32
LIGHTING 6-34
HEADLIGHTS 6-34

REMOVAL & INSTALLATION 6-34
SIGNAL AND MARKER LIGHTS 6-37
    REMOVAL & INSTALLATION 6-37
DOME LAMPS 6-44
    REMOVAL & INSTALLATION 6-44
TRAILER WIRING 6-46
CIRCUIT PROTECTION 6-47
TURN SIGNALS AND FLASHERS 6-47
    REMOVAL & INSTALLATION 6-47
FUSES AND FUSIBLE LINK 6-48
    REPLACEMENT 6-48
CIRCUIT BREAKERS 6-48
WIRING DIAGRAMS 6-51
COMPONENT LOCATIONS
  WINDSHIELD WIPER
    COMPONENTS 6-21

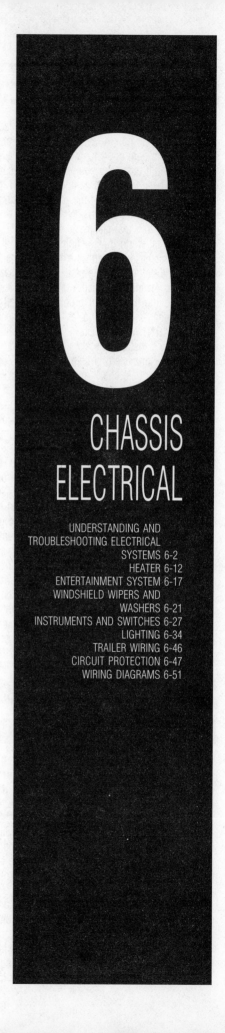

6

CHASSIS
ELECTRICAL

UNDERSTANDING AND
TROUBLESHOOTING ELECTRICAL
SYSTEMS 6-2
HEATER 6-12
ENTERTAINMENT SYSTEM 6-17
WINDSHIELD WIPERS AND
WASHERS 6-21
INSTRUMENTS AND SWITCHES 6-27
LIGHTING 6-34
TRAILER WIRING 6-46
CIRCUIT PROTECTION 6-47
WIRING DIAGRAMS 6-51

UNDERSTANDING AND TROUBLESHOOTING ELECTRICAL SYSTEMS

Over the years import and domestic manufacturers have incorporated electronic control systems into their production lines. In fact, electronic control systems are so prevalent that all new cars and trucks built today are equipped with at least one on-board computer. These electronic components (with no moving parts) should theoretically last the life of the vehicle, provided that nothing external happens to damage the circuits or memory chips.

While it is true that electronic components should never wear out, in the real world malfunctions do occur. It is also true that any computer-based system is extremely sensitive to electrical voltages and cannot tolerate careless or haphazard testing/service procedures. An inexperienced individual can literally cause major damage looking for a minor problem by using the wrong kind of test equipment or connecting test leads/connectors with the ignition switch **ON**. When selecting test equipment, make sure the manufacturer's instructions state that the tester is compatible with whatever type of system is being serviced. Read all instructions carefully and double check all test points before installing probes or making any test connections.

The following section outlines basic diagnosis techniques for dealing with automotive electrical systems. Along with a general explanation of the various types of test equipment available to aid in servicing modern automotive systems, basic repair techniques for wiring harnesses and connectors are also given. Read the basic information before attempting any repairs or testing. This will provide the background of information necessary to avoid the most common and obvious mistakes that can cost both time and money. Although the replacement and testing procedures are simple in themselves, the systems are not, and unless one has a thorough understanding of all components and their function within a particular system, the logical test sequence these systems demand cannot be followed. Minor malfunctions can make a big difference, so it is important to know how each component affects the operation of the overall system in order to find the ultimate cause of a problem without replacing good components unnecessarily. It is not enough to use the correct test equipment; the test equipment must be used correctly.

Safety Precautions

❊❊ CAUTION

Whenever working on or around any electrical or electronic systems, always observe these general precautions to prevent the possibility of personal injury or damage to electronic components.

• Never install or remove battery cables with the key **ON** or the engine running. Jumper cables should be connected with the key **OFF** to avoid power surges that can damage electronic control units. Engines equipped with computer controlled systems should avoid both giving and getting jump starts due to the possibility of serious damage to components from arcing in the engine compartment if connections are made with the ignition **ON**.

• Always remove the battery cables before charging the battery. Never use a high output charger on an installed battery or attempt to use any type of "hot shot" (24 volt) starting aid.

• Exercise care when inserting test probes into connectors to in-sure good contact without damaging the connector or spreading the pins. Always probe connectors from the rear (wire) side, NOT the pin side, to avoid accidental shorting of terminals during test procedures.

• Never remove or attach wiring harness connectors with the ignition switch **ON**, especially to an electronic control unit.

• Do not drop any components during service procedures and never apply 12 volts directly to any component (like a solenoid or relay) unless instructed specifically to do so. Some component electrical windings are designed to safely handle only 4 or 5 volts and can be destroyed in seconds if 12 volts are applied directly to the connector.

• Remove the electronic control unit if the vehicle is to be placed in an environment where temperatures exceed approximately 176°F (80°C), such as a paint spray booth or when arc/gas welding near the control unit location.

Understanding Basic Electricity

Understanding the basic theory of electricity makes electrical troubleshooting much easier. Several gauges are used in electrical troubleshooting to see inside the circuit being tested. Without a basic understanding, it will be difficult to understand testing procedures.

THE WATER ANALOGY

Electricity is the flow of electrons—hypothetical particles thought to constitute the basic stuff of electricity. Many people have been taught electrical theory using an analogy with water. In a comparison with water flowing in a pipe, the electrons would be the water. As the flow of water can be measured, the flow of electricity can be measured. The unit of measurement is amperes, frequently abbreviated amps. An ammeter will measure the actual amount of current flowing in the circuit.

Just as the water pressure is measured in units such as pounds per square inch, electrical pressure is measured in volts. When a voltmeter's two probes are placed on two live portions of an electrical circuit with different electrical pressures, current will flow through the voltmeter and produce a reading which indicates the difference in electrical pressure between the two parts of the circuit.

While increasing the voltage in a circuit will increase the flow of current, the actual flow depends not only on voltage, but on the resistance of the circuit. The standard unit for measuring circuit resistance is an ohm, measured by an ohmmeter. The ohmmeter is somewhat similar to an ammeter, but incorporates its own source of power so that a standard voltage is always present.

CIRCUITS

An actual electric circuit consists of four basic parts. These are: the power source, such as a generator or battery; a hot wire, which conducts the electricity under a relatively high voltage to the component supplied by the circuit; the load, such as a lamp, motor, resistor or relay coil; and the ground wire, which carries the current back to the source under very low voltage. In such a circuit the bulk of the resistance exists between the point where the hot wire is connected to the load, and the point where the load is grounded. In an automobile, the vehicle's frame or body, which is made of steel, is used as a part of the ground circuit for many of the electrical devices.

Remember that, in electrical testing, the voltmeter is connected in parallel with the circuit being tested (without disconnecting any wires) and measures the difference in voltage between the locations of the two probes; that the ammeter is connected in series with the load (the circuit is separated at one point and the ammeter inserted so it becomes a part of the circuit); and the ohmmeter is self-powered, so that all the power in the circuit should be off and the portion of the circuit to be measured contacted at either end by one of the probes of the meter.

For any electrical system to operate, it must make a complete circuit. This simply means that the power flow from the battery must make a complete circle. When an electrical component is operating, power flows from the battery to the component, passes through the component causing it to perform it to function (such as lighting a light bulb) and then returns to the battery through the ground of the circuit. This ground is usually (but not always) the metal part of the vehicle on which the electrical component is mounted.

Perhaps the easiest way to visualize this is to think of connecting a light bulb with two wires attached to it to your vehicle's battery. The battery in your vehicle has two posts (negative and positive). If one of the two wires attached to the light bulb was attached to the negative post of the battery and the other wire was attached to the positive post of the battery, you would have a complete circuit. Current from the battery would flow out one post, through the wire attached to it and then to the light bulb, where it would pass through causing it to light. It would then leave the light bulb, travel through the other wire, and return to the other post of the battery.

AUTOMOTIVE CIRCUITS

The normal automotive circuit differs from this simple example in two ways. First, instead of having a return wire from the bulb to the battery, the light bulb return the current to the battery through the chassis of the vehicle. Since the negative battery cable is attached to the chassis and the chassis is made of electrically conductive metal, the chassis of the vehicle can serve as a ground wire to complete the circuit. Secondly, most automotive circuits contain switches to turn components on and off.

Some electrical components which require a large amount of current to operate also have a relay in their circuit. Since these circuits carry a large amount of current, the thickness of the wire in the circuit (gauge size) is also greater. If this large wire were connected from the component to the control switch on the instrument panel, and then back to the component, a voltage drop would occur in the circuit. To prevent this potential drop in voltage, an electromagnetic switch (relay) is used. The large wires in the circuit are connected from the vehicle battery to one side of the relay, and from the opposite side of the relay to the component. The relay is normally open, preventing current from passing through the circuit. An additional, smaller wire is connected from the relay to the control switch for the circuit. When the control

switch is turned on, it grounds the smaller wire from the relay and completes the circuit.

SHORT CIRCUITS

If you were to disconnect the light bulb (from the previous example of a light-bulb being connected to the battery by two wires) from the wires and touch the two wires together (please take our word for this; don't try it), the result will be a shower of sparks. A similar thing happens (on a smaller scale) when the power supply wire to a component or the electrical component itself becomes grounded before the normal ground connection for the circuit. To prevent damage to the system, the fuse for the circuit blows to interrupt the circuit—protecting the components from damage. Because grounding a wire from a power source makes a complete circuit—less the required component to use the power—the phenomenon is called a short circuit. The most common causes of short circuits are: the rubber insulation on a wire breaking or rubbing through to expose the current carrying core of the wire to a metal part of the car, or a shorted switch.

Some electrical systems on the vehicle are protected by a circuit breaker which is, basically, a self-repairing fuse. When either of the described events takes place in a system which is protected by a circuit breaker, the circuit breaker opens the circuit the same way a fuse does. However, when either the short is removed from the circuit or the surge subsides, the circuit breaker resets itself and does not have to be replaced as a fuse does.

Troubleshooting

When diagnosing a specific problem, organized troubleshooting is a must. The complexity of a modern automobile demands that you approach any problem in a logical, organized manner. There are certain troubleshooting techniques that are standard:

1. Establish when the problem occurs. Does the problem appear only under certain conditions? Were there any noises, odors, or other unusual symptoms?

2. Isolate the problem area. To do this, make some simple tests and observations; then eliminate the systems that are working properly. Check for obvious problems such as broken wires, dirty connections or split/disconnected vacuum hoses. Always check the obvious before assuming something complicated is the cause.

3. Test for problems systematically to determine the cause once the problem area is isolated. Are all the components functioning properly? Is there power going to electrical switches and motors? Is there vacuum at vacuum switches and/or actuators? Is there a mechanical problem such as bent linkage or loose mounting screws? Performing careful, systematic checks will often turn up most causes on the first inspection without wasting time checking components that have little or no relationship to the problem.

4. Test all repairs after the work is done to make sure that the problem is fixed. Some causes can be traced to more than one component, so a careful verification of repair work is important in order to pick up additional malfunctions that may cause a problem to reappear or a different problem to arise. A blown fuse, for example, is a simple problem that may require more than another fuse to repair. If you don't look for a problem that caused a fuse to blow, a shorted wire (for example) may go undetected.

Experience has shown that most problems tend to be the result of a fairly simple and obvious cause, such as loose or corroded connectors or air leaks in the intake system. This makes careful inspection of components during testing essential to quick and accurate troubleshooting.

BASIC TROUBLESHOOTING THEORY

Electrical problems generally fall into one of three areas:
• The component that is not functioning is not receiving current.
• The component itself is not functioning.
• The component is not properly grounded.

Problems that fall into the first category are by far the most complicated. It is the current supply system to the component which contains all the switches, relay, fuses, etc.

The electrical system can be checked with a test light and a jumper wire. A test light is a device that looks like a pointed screwdriver with a wire attached to it. It has a light bulb in its handle. A jumper wire is a piece of insulated wire with an alligator clip attached to each end.

If a light bulb is not working, you must follow a systematic plan to determine which of the three causes is the villain.

1. Turn on the switch that controls the inoperable bulb.
2. Disconnect the power supply wire from the bulb.
3. Attach the ground wire to the test light to a good metal ground.
4. Touch the probe end of the test light to the end of the power supply wire that was disconnected from the bulb. If the bulb is receiving current, the test light will go on.

➡**If the bulb is one which works only when the ignition key is turned on (turn signal), make sure the key is turned on.**

If the test light does not go on, then the problem is in the circuit between the battery and the bulb. As mentioned before, this includes all the switches, fuses, and relays in the system. Turn to a wiring diagram and find the bulb on the diagram. Follow the wire that runs back to the battery. The problem is an open circuit between the battery and the bulb. If the fuse is blown and, when replaced, immediately blows again, there is a short circuit in the system which must be located and repaired. If there is a switch in the system, bypass it with a jumper wire. This is done by connecting one end of the jumper wire to the power supply wire into the switch and the other end of the jumper wire to the wire coming out of the switch. If the test light illuminates with the jumper wire installed, the switch or whatever was bypassed is defective.

➡**Never substitute the jumper wire for the bulb, as the bulb is the component required to use the power from the power source.**

5. If the bulb in the test light goes on, then the current is getting to the bulb that is not working in the car. This eliminates the first of the three possible causes. Connect the power supply wire and connect a jumper wire from the bulb to a good metal ground. Do this with the switch which controls the bulb works with jumper wire installed, then it has a bad ground. This is usually caused by the metal area on which the bulb mounts to the vehicle being coated with some type of foreign matter.

6. If neither test located the source of the trouble, then the light bulb itself is defective.

The above test procedure can be applied to any of the compo-

nents of the chassis electrical system by substituting the component that is not working for the light bulb. Remember that for any electrical system to work, all connections must be clean and tight.

TEST EQUIPMENT

➡**Pinpointing the exact cause of trouble in an electrical system can sometimes only be accomplished by the use of special test equipment. The following describes different types of commonly used test equipment and explains how to use them in diagnosis. In addition to the information covered below, the tool manufacturer's instructions booklet (provided with the tester) should be read and clearly understood before attempting any test procedures.**

Jumper Wires

Jumper wires are simple, yet extremely valuable, pieces of test equipment. They are basically test wires which are used to bypass sections of a circuit. The simplest type of jumper wire is a length of multi-strand wire with an alligator clip at each end. Jumper wires are usually fabricated from lengths of standard automotive wire and whatever type of connector (alligator clip, spade connector or pin connector) that is required for the particular vehicle being tested. The well equipped tool box will have several different styles of jumper wires in several different lengths. Some jumper wires are made with three or more terminals coming from a common splice for special purpose testing. In cramped, hard-to-reach areas it is advisable to have insulated boots over the jumper wire terminals in order to prevent accidental grounding, sparks, and possible fire, especially when testing fuel system components.

Jumper wires are used primarily to locate open electrical circuits, on either the ground (−) side of the circuit or on the hot (+) side. If an electrical component fails to operate, connect the jumper wire between the component and a good ground. If the component operates only with the jumper installed, the ground circuit is open. If the ground circuit is good, but the component does not operate, the circuit between the power feed and component may be open. By moving the jumper wire successively back from the lamp toward the power source, you can isolate the area

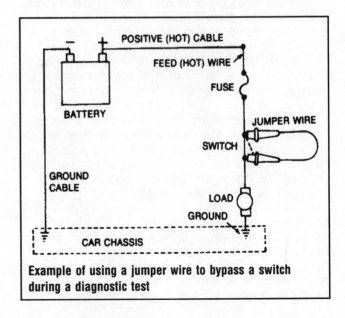

Example of using a jumper wire to bypass a switch during a diagnostic test

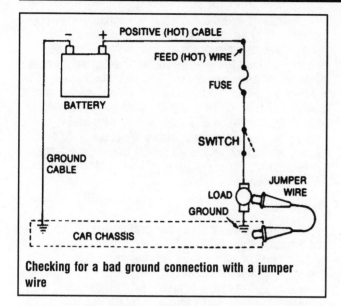

Checking for a bad ground connection with a jumper wire

of the circuit where the open is located. When the component stops functioning, or the power is cut off, the open is in the segment of wire between the jumper and the point previously tested.

You can sometimes connect the jumper wire directly from the battery to the hot terminal of the component, but first make sure the component uses 12 volts in operation. Some electrical components, such as fuel injectors, are designed to operate on about 4 volts and running 12 volts directly to the injector terminals can cause damage.

By inserting an in-line fuse holder between a set of test leads, a fused jumper wire can be used for bypassing open circuits. Use a 5 amp fuse to provide protection against voltage spikes. When in doubt, use a voltmeter to check the voltage input to the component and measure how much voltage is normally being applied.

❊❊ CAUTION

Never use jumpers made from wire that is of lighter gauge than that which is used in the circuit under test. If the jumper wire is of too small a gauge, it may overheat and possibly melt. Never use jumpers to bypass high resistance loads in a circuit. Bypassing resistances, in effect, creates a short circuit. This may, in turn, cause damage and fire. Jumper wires should only be used to bypass lengths of wire.

Unpowered Test Lights

The 12 volt test light is used to check circuits and components while electrical current is flowing through them. It is used for voltage and ground tests. Twelve volt test lights come in different styles but all have three main parts; a ground clip, a probe, and a light. The most commonly used 12 volt test lights have pick-type probes. To use a 12 volt test light, connect the ground clip to a good ground and probe wherever necessary with the pick. The pick should be sharp so that it can be probed into tight spaces.

❊❊ CAUTION

Do not use a test light to probe electronic ignition spark plug or coil wires. Never use a pick-type test light to probe

wiring on computer controlled systems unless specifically instructed to do so. Any wire insulation that is pierced by the test light probe should be taped and sealed with silicone after testing.

Like the jumper wire, the 12 volt test light is used to isolate opens in circuits. But, whereas the jumper wire is used to bypass the open to operate the load, the 12 volt test light is used to locate the presence of voltage in a circuit. If the test light glows, you know that there is power up to that point; if the 12 volt test light does not glow when its probe is inserted into the wire or connector, you know that there is an open circuit (no power). Move the test light in successive steps back toward the power source until the light in the handle does glow. When it glows, the open is between the probe and point which was probed previously.

➡**The test light does not detect that 12 volts (or any particular amount of voltage) is present; it only detects that some voltage is present. It is advisable before using the test light to touch its terminals across the battery posts to make sure the light is operating properly.**

Self-Powered Test Lights

The self-powered test light usually contains a 1.5 volt penlight battery. One type of self-powered test light is similar in design to the 12 volt unit. This type has both the battery and the light in the handle, along with a pick-type probe tip. The second type has the light toward the open tip, so that the light illuminates the contact point. The self-powered test light is a dual purpose piece of test equipment. It can be used to test for either open or short circuits when power is isolated from the circuit (continuity test). A powered test light should not be used on any computer controlled system or component unless specifically instructed to do so. Many engine sensors can be destroyed by even this small amount of voltage applied directly to the terminals.

Voltmeters

A voltmeter is used to measure voltage at any point in a circuit, or to measure the voltage drop across any part of a circuit. It can also be used to check continuity in a wire or circuit by indicating current flow from one end to the other. Analog voltmeters usually have various scales on the meter dial and a selector switch to allow the selection of different voltages. The voltmeter has a positive and a negative lead. To avoid damage to the meter, always connect the negative lead to the negative (−) side of the circuit (to ground or nearest the ground side of the circuit) and connect the positive lead to the positive (+) side of the circuit (to the power source or the nearest power source). Note that the negative voltmeter lead will always be black and that the positive voltmeter will always be some color other than black (usually red).

Depending on how the voltmeter is connected into the circuit, it has several uses. A voltmeter can be connected either in parallel or in series with a circuit and it has a very high resistance to current flow. When connected in parallel, only a small amount of current will flow through the voltmeter current path; the rest will flow through the normal circuit current path and the circuit will work normally. When the voltmeter is connected in series with a circuit, only a small amount of current can flow through the circuit. The circuit will not work properly, but the voltmeter reading will show if the circuit is complete or not.

Ohmmeters

The ohmmeter is designed to read resistance (which is measured in ohms or Ω) in a circuit or component. Although there are several different styles of ohmmeters, all analog meters will usually have a selector switch which permits the measurement of different ranges of resistance (usually the selector switch allows the multiplication of the meter reading by 10, 100, 1000, and 10,000). A calibration knob allows the meter to be set at zero for accurate measurement. Since all ohmmeters are powered by an internal battery, the ohmmeter can be used as a self-powered test light. When the ohmmeter is connected, current from the ohmmeter flows through the circuit or component being tested. Since the ohmmeter's internal resistance and voltage are known values, the amount of current flow through the meter depends on the resistance of the circuit or component being tested.

The ohmmeter can be used to perform a continuity test for opens or shorts (either by observation of the meter needle or as a self-powered test light), and to read actual resistance in a circuit. It should be noted that the ohmmeter is used to check the resistance of a component or wire while there is no voltage applied to the circuit. Current flow from an outside voltage source (such as the vehicle battery) can damage the ohmmeter, so the circuit or component should be isolated from the vehicle electrical system before any testing is done. Since the ohmmeter uses its own voltage source, either lead can be connected to any test point.

➡**When checking diodes or other solid state components, the ohmmeter leads can only be connected one way in order to measure current flow in a single direction. Make sure the positive (+) and negative (−) terminal connections are as described in the test procedures to verify the one-way diode operation.**

In using the meter for making continuity checks, do not be concerned with the actual resistance readings. Zero resistance, or any ohm reading, indicates continuity in the circuit. Infinite resistance indicates an open in the circuit. A high resistance reading where there should be none indicates a problem in the circuit. Checks for short circuits are made in the same manner as checks for open circuits except that the circuit must be isolated from both power and normal ground. Infinite resistance indicates no continuity to ground, while zero resistance indicates a dead short to ground.

Ammeters

An ammeter measures the amount of current flowing through a circuit in units called amperes or amps. Amperes are units of electron flow which indicate how fast the electrons are flowing through the circuit. Since Ohms Law dictates that current flow in a circuit is equal to the circuit voltage divided by the total circuit resistance, increasing voltage also increases the current level (amps). Likewise, any decrease in resistance will increase the amount of amps in a circuit. At normal operating voltage, most circuits have a characteristic amount of amperes, called "current draw" which can be measured using an ammeter. By referring to a specified current draw rating, measuring the amperes, and comparing the two values, one can determine what is happening within the circuit to aid in diagnosis. An open circuit, for example, will not allow any current to flow so the ammeter reading will be zero. More current flows through a heavily loaded circuit or when the charging system is operating.

An ammeter is always connected in series with the circuit being tested. All of the current that normally flows through the circuit must also flow through the ammeter; if there is any other path for the current to follow, the ammeter reading will not be accurate. The ammeter itself has very little resistance to current flow and therefore will not affect the circuit, but it will measure current draw only when the circuit is closed and electricity is flowing. Excessive current draw can blow fuses and drain the battery, while a reduced current draw can cause motors to run slowly, lights to dim and other components to not operate properly. The ammeter can help diagnose these conditions by locating the cause of the high or low reading.

Multimeters

Different combinations of test meters can be built into a single unit designed for specific tests. Some of the more common combination test devices are known as Volt/Amp testers, Tach/Dwell meters, or Digital Multimeters. The Volt/Amp tester is used for charging system, starting system or battery tests and consists of a voltmeter, an ammeter and a variable resistance carbon pile. The voltmeter will usually have at least two ranges for use with 6, 12 and/or 24 volt systems. The ammeter also has more than one range for testing various levels of battery loads and starter current draw. The carbon pile can be adjusted to offer different amounts of resistance. The Volt/Amp tester has heavy leads to carry large amounts of current and many later models have an inductive ammeter pickup that clamps around the wire to simplify test connections. On some models, the ammeter also has a zero-center scale to allow testing of charging and starting systems without switching leads or polarity. A digital multimeter is a voltmeter, ammeter and ohmmeter combined in an instrument which gives a digital readout. These are often used when testing solid state circuits because of their high input impedance (usually 10 megohms or more).

The tach/dwell meter that combines a tachometer and a dwell (cam angle) meter is a specialized kind of voltmeter. The tachometer scale is marked to show engine speed in rpm and the dwell scale is marked to show degrees of distributor shaft rotation. In most electronic ignition systems, dwell is determined by the control unit, but the dwell meter can also be used to check the duty cycle (operation) of some electronic engine control systems. Some tach/dwell meters are powered by an internal battery, while others take their power from the vehicle battery in use. The battery powered testers usually require calibration (much like an ohmmeter) before testing.

TESTING

Open Circuits

To use the self-powered test light or a multimeter to check for open circuits, first isolate the circuit from the vehicle's 12 volt power source by disconnecting the battery or wiring harness connector. Connect the test light or ohmmeter ground clip to a good ground and probe sections of the circuit sequentially with the test light. (start from either end of the circuit). If the light is out/or there is infinite resistance, the open is between the probe and the circuit ground. If the light is on/or the meter shows continuity, the open is between the probe and end of the circuit toward the power source.

Short Circuits

By isolating the circuit both from power and from ground, and using a self-powered test light or multimeter, you can check for shorts to ground in the circuit. Isolate the circuit from power and ground. Connect the test light or ohmmeter ground clip to a good ground and probe any easy-to-reach test point in the circuit. If the light comes on or there is continuity, there is a short somewhere in the circuit. To isolate the short, probe a test point at either end of the isolated circuit (the light should be on/there should be continuity). Leave the test light probe engaged and open connectors, switches, remove parts, etc., sequentially, until the light goes out/continuity is broken. When the light goes out, the short is between the last circuit component opened and the previous circuit opened.

➡The battery in the test light and does not provide much current. A weak battery may not provide enough power to illuminate the test light even when a complete circuit is made (especially if there are high resistances in the circuit). Always make sure that the test battery is strong. To check the battery, briefly touch the ground clip to the probe; if the light glows brightly the battery is strong enough for testing. Never use a self-powered test light to perform checks for opens or shorts when power is applied to the electrical system under test. The 12 volt vehicle power will quickly burn out the light bulb in the test light.

Available Voltage Measurement

Set the voltmeter selector switch to the 20V position and connect the meter negative lead to the negative post of the battery. Connect the positive meter lead to the positive post of the battery and turn the ignition switch **ON** to provide a load. Read the voltage on the meter or digital display. A well charged battery should register over 12 volts. If the meter reads below 11.5 volts, the battery power may be insufficient to operate the electrical system properly. This test determines voltage available from the battery and should be the first step in any electrical trouble diagnosis procedure. Many electrical problems, especially on computer controlled systems, can be caused by a low state of charge in the battery. Excessive corrosion at the battery cable terminals can cause a poor contact that will prevent proper charging and full battery current flow.

Normal battery voltage is 12 volts when fully charged. When the battery is supplying current to one or more circuits it is said to be "under load." When everything is off the electrical system is under a "no-load" condition. A fully charged battery may show about 12.5 volts at no load; will drop to 12 volts under medium load; and will drop even lower under heavy load. If the battery is partially discharged the voltage decrease under heavy load may be excessive, even though the battery shows 12 volts or more at no load. When allowed to discharge further, the battery's available voltage under load will decrease more severely. For this reason, it is important that the battery be fully charged during all testing procedures to avoid errors in diagnosis and incorrect test results.

Voltage Drop

When current flows through a resistance, the voltage beyond the resistance is reduced (the larger the current, the greater the reduction in voltage). When no current is flowing, there is no voltage drop because there is no current flow. All points in the circuit which are connected to the power source are at the same voltage as the power source. The total voltage drop always equals the total source voltage. In a long circuit with many connectors, a series of small, unwanted voltage drops due to corrosion at the connectors can add up to a total loss of voltage which impairs the operation of the normal loads in the circuit. The maximum allowable voltage drop under load is critical, especially if there is more than one high resistance problem in a circuit because all voltage drops are cumulative. A small drop is normal due to the resistance of the conductors.

INDIRECT COMPUTATION OF VOLTAGE DROPS

1. Set the voltmeter selector switch to the 20 volt position.
2. Connect the meter negative lead to a good ground.
3. While operating the circuit, probe all loads in the circuit with the positive meter lead and observe the voltage readings. A drop should be noticed after the first load. But, there should be little or no voltage drop before the first load.

DIRECT MEASUREMENT OF VOLTAGE DROPS

1. Set the voltmeter switch to the 20 volt position.
2. Connect the voltmeter negative lead to the ground side of the load to be measured.
3. Connect the positive lead to the positive side of the resistance or load to be measured.
4. Read the voltage drop directly on the 20 volt scale.

Too high a voltage indicates too high a resistance. If, for example, a blower motor runs too slowly, you can determine if perhaps there is too high a resistance in the resistor pack. By taking voltage drop readings in all parts of the circuit, you can isolate the problem. Too low a voltage drop indicates too low a resistance. Take the blower motor for example again. If a blower motor runs too fast in the MED and/or LOW position, the problem might be isolated in the resistor pack by taking voltage drop readings in all parts of the circuit to locate a possibly shorted resistor.

HIGH RESISTANCE TESTING

1. Set the voltmeter selector switch to the 4 volt position.
2. Connect the voltmeter positive lead to the positive post of the battery.
3. Turn on the headlights and heater blower to provide a load.
4. Probe various points in the circuit with the negative voltmeter lead.
5. Read the voltage drop on the 4 volt scale. Some average maximum allowable voltage drops are:
- FUSE PANEL: 0.7 volts
- IGNITION SWITCH: 0.5 volts
- HEADLIGHT SWITCH: 0.7 volts
- IGNITION COIL (+): 0.5 volts
- ANY OTHER LOAD: 1.3 volts

➡Voltage drops are all measured while a load is operating; without current flow, there will be no voltage drop.

Resistance Measurement

The batteries in an ohmmeter will weaken with age and temperature, so the ohmmeter must be calibrated or "zeroed" before taking measurements. To zero the meter, place the selector switch in its lowest range and touch the two ohmmeter leads together. Turn the calibration knob until the meter needle is exactly on zero.

➡All analog (needle) type ohmmeters must be zeroed before use, but some digital ohmmeter models are automatically calibrated when the switch is turned on. Self-calibrating digital ohmmeters do not have an adjusting knob, but its a good idea to check for a zero readout before use by touching the leads together. All computer controlled systems require the use of a digital ohmmeter with at least 10 megohms impedance for testing. Before any test procedures are attempted, make sure the ohmmeter used is compatible with the electrical system or damage to the on-board computer could result.

To measure resistance, first isolate the circuit from the vehicle power source by disconnecting the battery cables or the harness connector. Make sure the key is **OFF** when disconnecting any components or the battery. Where necessary, also isolate at least one side of the circuit to be checked in order to avoid reading parallel resistances. Parallel circuit resistances will always give a lower reading than the actual resistance of either of the branches. When measuring the resistance of parallel circuits, the total resistance will always be lower than the smallest resistance in the circuit. Connect the meter leads to both sides of the circuit (wire or component) and read the actual measured ohms on the meter scale. Make sure the selector switch is set to the proper ohm scale for the circuit being tested to avoid misreading the ohmmeter test value.

❄❄ WARNING

Never use an ohmmeter with power applied to the circuit. Like the self-powered test light, the ohmmeter is designed to operate on its own power supply. The normal 12 volt automotive electrical system current could damage the meter!

Wiring Harnesses

The average automobile contains about ½ mile of wiring, with hundreds of individual connections. To protect the many wires from damage and to keep them from becoming a confusing tangle, they are organized into bundles, enclosed in plastic or taped together and called wiring harnesses. Different harnesses serve different parts of the vehicle. Individual wires are color coded to help trace them through a harness where sections are hidden from view.

Automotive wiring or circuit conductors can be in any one of three forms:
1. Single strand wire
2. Multi-strand wire
3. Printed circuitry

Single strand wire has a solid metal core and is usually used inside such components as alternators, motors, relays and other devices. Multi-strand wire has a core made of many small strands of wire twisted together into a single conductor. Most of the wiring in an automotive electrical system is made up of multi-strand wire, either as a single conductor or grouped together in a harness. All wiring is color coded on the insulator, either as a solid color or as a colored wire with an identification stripe. A printed circuit is a thin film of copper or other conductor that is printed on an insulator backing. Occasionally, a printed circuit is sandwiched between two sheets of plastic for more protection and flexibility. A complete printed circuit, consisting of conductors, insulat-

ing material and connectors for lamps or other components is called a printed circuit board. Printed circuitry is used in place of individual wires or harnesses in places where space is limited, such as behind instrument panels.

Since automotive electrical systems are very sensitive to changes in resistance, the selection of properly sized wires is critical when systems are repaired. A loose or corroded connection or a replacement wire that is too small for the circuit will add extra resistance and an additional voltage drop to the circuit. A ten percent voltage drop can result in slow or erratic motor operation, for example, even though the circuit is complete. The wire gauge number is an expression of the cross-section area of the conductor. The most common system for expressing wire size is the American Wire Gauge (AWG) system.

Gauge numbers are assigned to conductors of various cross-section areas. As gauge number increases, area decreases and the conductor becomes smaller. A 5 gauge conductor is smaller than a 1 gauge conductor and a 10 gauge is smaller than a 5 gauge. As the cross-section area of a conductor decreases, resistance increases and so does the gauge number. A conductor with a higher gauge number will carry less current than a conductor with a lower gauge number.

➡Gauge wire size refers to the size of the conductor, not the size of the complete wire. It is possible to have two wires of the same gauge with different diameters because one may have thicker insulation than the other.

12 volt automotive electrical systems generally use 10, 12, 14, 16 and 18 gauge wire. Main power distribution circuits and larger accessories usually use 10 and 12 gauge wire. Battery cables are usually 4 or 6 gauge, although 1 and 2 gauge wires are occasionally used. Wire length must also be considered when making repairs to a circuit. As conductor length increases, so does resistance. An 18 gauge wire, for example, can carry a 10 amp load for 10 feet without excessive voltage drop; however if a 15 foot wire is required for the same 10 amp load, it must be a 16 gauge wire.

An electrical schematic shows the electrical current paths when a circuit is operating properly. It is essential to understand how a circuit works before trying to figure out why it doesn't. Schematics break the entire electrical system down into individual circuits and show only one particular circuit. In a schematic, no attempt is made to represent wiring and components as they physically appear on the vehicle; switches and other components are shown as simply as possible. Face views of harness connectors show the cavity or terminal locations in all multi-pin connectors to help locate test points.

If you need to backprobe a connector while it is on the component, the order of the terminals must be mentally reversed. The wire color code can help in this situation, as well as a keyway, lock tab or other reference mark.

WIRING REPAIR

Soldering is a quick, efficient method of joining metals permanently. Everyone who has the occasion to make wiring repairs should know how to solder. Electrical connections that are soldered are far less likely to come apart and will conduct electricity much better than connections that are only "pig-tailed" together. The most popular (and preferred) method of soldering is with an electrical soldering gun. Soldering irons are available in many sizes and wattage ratings. Irons with higher wattage ratings deliver higher temperatures and recover lost heat faster. A small soldering iron rated for no more than 50 watts is recommended, especially on electrical systems where excess heat can damage the components being soldered.

There are three ingredients necessary for successful soldering; proper flux, good solder and sufficient heat. A soldering flux is necessary to clean the metal of tarnish, prepare it for soldering and to enable the solder to spread into tiny crevices. When soldering, always use a rosin core solder which is non-corrosive and will not attract moisture once the job is finished. Other types of flux (acid core) will leave a residue that will attract moisture and cause the wires to corrode. Tin is a unique metal with a low melting point. In a molten state, it dissolves and alloys easily with many metals. Solder is made by mixing tin with lead. The most common proportions are 40/60, 50/50 and 60/40, with the percentage of tin listed first. Low priced solders usually contain less tin, making them very difficult for a beginner to use because more heat is required to melt the solder. A common solder is 40/60 which is well suited for all-around general use, but 60/40 melts easier and is preferred for electrical work.

Soldering Techniques

Successful soldering requires that the metals to be joined be heated to a temperature that will melt the solder, usually 360–460°F (182–238°C). Contrary to popular belief, the purpose of the soldering iron is not to melt the solder itself, but to heat the parts being soldered to a temperature high enough to melt the solder when it is touched to the work. Melting flux-cored solder on the soldering iron will usually destroy the effectiveness of the flux.

→**Soldering tips are made of copper for good heat conductivity, but must be "tinned" regularly for quick transference of heat to the project and to prevent the solder from sticking to the iron. To "tin" the iron, simply heat it and touch the flux-cored solder to the tip; the solder will flow over the hot tip. Wipe the excess off with a clean rag, but be careful as the iron will be hot.**

After some use, the tip may become pitted. If so, simply dress the tip smooth with a smooth file and "tin" the tip again. Flux-cored solder will remove oxides but rust, bits of insulation and oil or grease must be removed with a wire brush or emery cloth. For maximum strength in soldered parts, the joint must start off clean and tight. Weak joints will result in gaps too wide for the solder to bridge.

If a separate soldering flux is used, it should be brushed or swabbed on only those areas that are to be soldered. Most solders contain a core of flux and separate fluxing is unnecessary. Hold the work to be soldered firmly. It is best to solder on a wooden board, because a metal vise will only rob the piece to be soldered of heat and make it difficult to melt the solder. Hold the soldering tip with the broadest face against the work to be soldered. Apply solder under the tip close to the work, using enough solder to give a heavy film between the iron and the piece being soldered, while moving slowly and making sure the solder melts properly. Keep the work level or the solder will run to the lowest part and favor the thicker parts, because these require more heat to melt the solder. If the soldering tip overheats (the solder coating on the face of the tip burns up), it should be retinned. Once the soldering is completed, let the soldered joint stand until cool. Tape and seal all soldered wire splices after the repair has cooled.

Wire Harness Connectors

Most connectors in the engine compartment or that are otherwise exposed to the elements are protected against moisture and dirt which could create oxidation and deposits on the terminals.

These special connectors are weather-proof. All repairs require the use of a special terminal and the tool required to service it. This tool is used to remove the pin and sleeve terminals. If removal is attempted with an ordinary pick, there is a good chance that the terminal will be bent or deformed. Unlike standard blade type terminals, these weather-proof terminals cannot be straightened once they are bent. Make certain that the connectors are properly seated and all of the sealing rings are in place when connecting leads. On some models, a hinge-type flap provides a backup or secondary locking feature for the terminals. Most secondary locks are used to improve connector reliability by retaining the terminals if the small terminal lock tangs are not positioned properly.

Molded-on connectors require complete replacement of the connection. This means splicing a new connector assembly into the harness. All splices should be soldered to insure proper contact. Use care when probing the connections or replacing terminals in them as it is possible to short between opposite terminals. If this happens to the wrong terminal pair, it is possible to damage certain components. Always use jumper wires between connectors for circuit checking and never probe through weatherproof seals.

Open circuits are often difficult to locate by sight because corrosion or terminal misalignment are hidden by the connectors. Merely wiggling a connector on a sensor or in the wiring harness may correct the open circuit condition. This should always be considered when an open circuit or a failed sensor is indicated. Intermittent problems may also be caused by oxidized or loose connections. When using a circuit tester for diagnosis, always probe connections from the wire side. Be careful not to damage sealed connectors with test probes.

All wiring harnesses should be replaced with identical parts, using the same gauge wire and connectors. When signal wires are spliced into a harness, use wire with high temperature insulation only. It is seldom necessary to replace a complete harness. If replacement is necessary, pay close attention to insure proper harness routing. Secure the harness with suitable plastic wire clamps to prevent vibrations from causing the harness to wear in spots or contact any hot components.

→**Weatherproof connectors cannot be replaced with standard connectors. Instructions are provided with replacement connector and terminal packages. Some wire harnesses have mounting indicators (usually pieces of colored tape) to mark where the harness is to be secured.**

In making wiring repairs, its important that you always replace damaged wires with wiring of the same gauge as the wire being replaced. The heavier the wire, the smaller the gauge number. Wires are color-coded to aid in identification and whenever possible the same color coded wire should be used for replacement. A wire stripping and crimping tool is necessary to install solderless terminal connectors. Test all crimps by pulling on the wires; it should not be possible to pull the wires out of a good crimp.

Wires which are open, exposed or otherwise damaged are repaired by simple splicing. Where possible, if the wiring harness is accessible and the damaged place in the wire can be located, it is best to open the harness and check for all possible damage. In an inaccessible harness, the wire must be bypassed with a new insert, usually taped to the outside of the old harness.

When replacing fusible links, be sure to use fusible link wire, NOT ordinary automotive wire. Make sure the fusible segment is of the same gauge and construction as the one being replaced and double the stripped end when crimping the terminal connector for a good contact. The melted (open) fusible link segment of the wiring harness should be cut off as close to the harness as possible, then a new segment spliced in as described. In the case of a damaged fusible link that feeds two harness wires, the harness connections should be replaced with two fusible link wires so that each circuit will have its own separate protection.

➡**Most of the problems caused in the wiring harness are due to bad ground connections. Always check all vehicle ground connections for corrosion or looseness before performing any power feed checks to eliminate the chance of a bad ground affecting the circuit.**

Hard-Shell Connectors

Unlike molded connectors, the terminal contacts in hard-shell connectors can be replaced. Weatherproof hard-shell connectors with the leads molded into the shell have non-replaceable terminal ends. Replacement usually involves the use of a special terminal removal tool that depresses the locking tangs (barbs) on the connector terminal and allows the connector to be removed from the rear of the shell. The connector shell should be replaced if it shows any evidence of burning, melting, cracks, or breaks. Replace individual terminals that are burnt, corroded, distorted or loose.

➡**The insulation crimp must be tight to prevent the insulation from sliding back on the wire when the wire is pulled. The insulation must be visibly compressed under the crimp tabs, and the ends of the crimp should be turned in for a firm grip on the insulation.**

The wire crimp must be made with all wire strands inside the crimp. The terminal must be fully compressed on the wire strands with the ends of the crimp tabs turned in to make a firm grip on the wire. Check all connections with an ohmmeter to insure a good contact. There should be no measurable resistance between the wire and the terminal when connected.

Fusible Links

The fuse link is a short length of special, Hypalon (high temperature) insulated wire, integral with the engine compartment wiring harness and should not be confused with standard wire. It is several wire gauges smaller than the circuit which it protects. Under no circumstances should a fuse link replacement repair be made using a length of standard wire cut from bulk stock or from another wiring harness.

To repair any blown fuse link use the following procedure:

1. Determine which circuit is damaged, its location and the cause of the open fuse link. If the damaged fuse link is one of three fed by a common No. 10 or 12 gauge feed wire, determine the specific affected circuit.
2. Disconnect the negative battery cable.
3. Cut the damaged fuse link from the wiring harness and discard it. If the fuse link is one of three circuits fed by a single feed wire, cut it out of the harness at each splice end and discard it.
4. Identify and procure the proper fuse link with butt connectors for attaching the fuse link to the harness.

➡**Heat shrink tubing must be slipped over the wire before crimping and soldering the connection.**

5. To repair any fuse link in a 3-link group with one feed:
   a. After cutting the open link out of the harness, cut each of the remaining undamaged fuse links close to the feed wire weld.
   b. Strip approximately ½ in. (13mm) of insulation from the detached ends of the two good fuse links. Insert two wire ends into one end of a butt connector, then carefully push one stripped end of the replacement fuse link into the same end of the butt connector and crimp all three firmly together.

➡**Care must be taken when fitting the three fuse links into the butt connector as the internal diameter is a snug fit for three wires. Make sure to use a proper crimping tool. Pliers, side cutters, etc. will not apply the proper crimp to retain the wires and withstand a pull test.**

   c. After crimping the butt connector to the three fuse links, cut the weld portion from the feed wire and strip approximately ½ in. (13mm) of insulation from the cut end. Insert the stripped end into the open end of the butt connector and crimp very firmly.
   d. To attach the remaining end of the replacement fuse link, strip approximately ½ in. (13mm) of insulation from the wire end of the circuit from which the blown fuse link was removed, and firmly crimp a butt connector or equivalent to the stripped wire. Then, insert the end of the replacement link into the other end of the butt connector and crimp firmly.
   e. Using rosin core solder with a consistency of 60 percent tin and 40 percent lead, solder the connectors and the wires at the repairs then insulate with electrical tape or heat shrink tubing.
6. To replace any fuse link on a single circuit in a harness, cut out the damaged portion, strip approximately ½ in. (13mm) of insulation from the two wire ends and attach the appropriate replacement fuse link to the stripped wire ends with two proper size butt connectors. Solder the connectors and wires, then insulate.
7. To repair any fuse link which has an eyelet terminal on one end such as the charging circuit, cut off the open fuse link behind the weld, strip approximately ½ in. (13mm) of insulation from the cut end and attach the appropriate new eyelet fuse link to the cut stripped wire with an appropriate size butt connector. Solder the connectors and wires at the repair, then insulate.
8. Connect the negative battery cable to the battery and test the system for proper operation.

➡**Do not mistake a resistor wire for a fuse link. The resistor wire is generally longer and has print stating, "Resistor-don't cut or splice."**

When attaching a single No. 16, 17, 18 or 20 gauge fuse link to a heavy gauge wire, always double the stripped wire end of the fuse link before inserting and crimping it into the butt connector for positive wire retention.

Add-On Electrical Equipment

The electrical system in your vehicle is designed to perform under reasonable operating conditions without interference between components. Before any additional electrical equipment is installed, it is recommended that you consult your dealer or a reputable repair facility that is familiar with the vehicle and its systems.

If the vehicle is equipped with mobile radio equipment and/or

REMOVE EXISTING VINYL TUBE SHIELDING
REINSTALL OVER FUSE LINK BEFORE CRIMPING
FUSE LINK TO WIRE ENDS

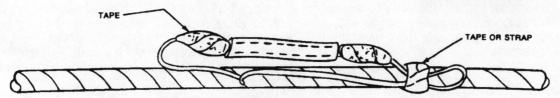

TAPE

TAPE OR STRAP

TYPICAL REPAIR USING THE SPECIAL #17 GA. (9.00" LONG-YELLOW) FUSE LINK REQUIRED FOR THE AIR/COND.
CIRCUITS (2) #687E and #261A LOCATED IN THE ENGINE COMPARTMENT

FUSE LINK

TAPE OR STRAP

TYPICAL REPAIR FOR ANY IN-LINE FUSE LINK USING THE SPECIFIED GAUGE FUSE LINK FOR THE SPECIFIC CIRCUIT

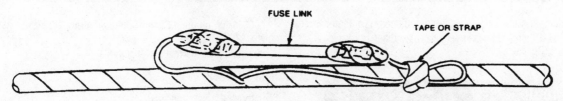

TAPE

TYPICAL REPAIR USING THE EYELET TERMINAL FUSE LINK OF THE SPECIFIED GAUGE FOR ATTACHMENT TO A CIRCUIT WIRE END

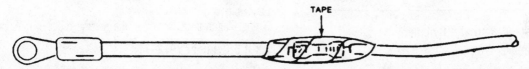

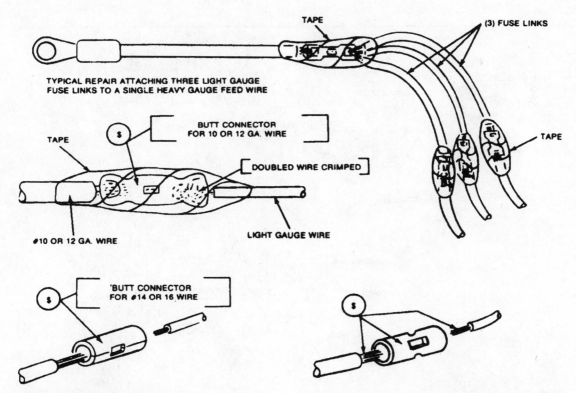

TAPE

(3) FUSE LINKS

TYPICAL REPAIR ATTACHING THREE LIGHT GAUGE
FUSE LINKS TO A SINGLE HEAVY GAUGE FEED WIRE

TAPE

Ⓢ   BUTT CONNECTOR
FOR 10 OR 12 GA. WIRE

DOUBLED WIRE CRIMPED

TAPE

#10 OR 12 GA. WIRE

LIGHT GAUGE WIRE

Ⓢ   'BUTT CONNECTOR
FOR #14 OR 16 WIRE

Ⓢ

FUSIBLE LINK REPAIR PROCEDURE

General fusible link repair—never replace a fusible link with regular wire or a fusible link rated at a higher amperage than the one being replaced

mobile telephone, it may have an effect upon the operation of any on-board computer control modules. Radio Frequency Interference (RFI) from the communications system can be picked up by the vehicle's wiring harnesses and conducted into the control module, giving it the wrong messages at the wrong time. Although well shielded against RFI, the computer should be further protected by taking the following measures:

• Install the antenna as far as possible from the control module. For instance, if the module is located behind the center console area, then the antenna should be mounted at the rear of the vehicle.

• Keep the antenna wiring a minimum of eight inches away from any wiring running to control modules and from the module itself. NEVER wind the antenna wire around any other wiring.

• Mount the equipment as far from the control module as possible. Be very careful during installation not to drill through any wires or short a wire harness with a mounting screw.

• Insure that the electrical feed wire(s) to the equipment are properly and tightly connected. Loose connectors can cause interference.

• Make certain that the equipment is properly grounded to the vehicle. Poor grounding can damage expensive equipment.

HEATER

On some models the air conditioner, if so equipped, is integral with the heater, and therefore, heater removal may differ from the procedures detailed below.

Blower Motor

REMOVAL & INSTALLATION

Corona (1970–73) and Mark II 4 Cylinder
▶ **See Figures 1 and 2**

1. Working from under the instrument panel, unfasten the defroster hoses from the heater box.
2. Unplug the multiconnector.

3. Loosen the mounting screws and withdraw the blower assembly.
4. Installation is the reverse of removal.

Corona 1974–82

1. Remove the package tray.
2. Remove the trim panel.
3. Disconnect the heater blower motor wiring harness.
4. Loosen the three screws which secure the motor to the housing and remove the motor blower assembly.
5. Installation is performed in the reverse order of removal.

Mark II 6 Cylinder 1972–77

1. Remove the center console, if equipped, by removing the shift knob (manual), unfastening the wiring, connector, and undoing the console securing screws.

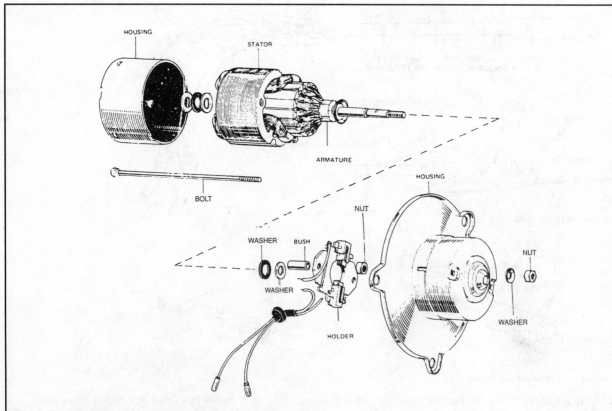

Fig. 1 Exploded view of a common heater blower motor

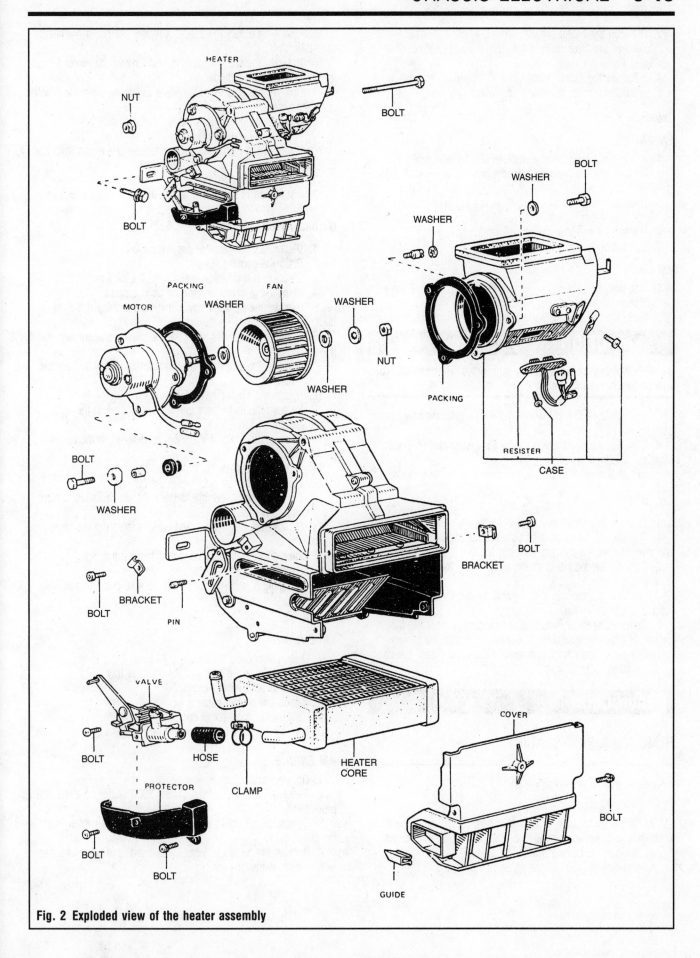

Fig. 2 Exploded view of the heater assembly

2. Unfasten the heater blower wiring connector.

3. Remove the three bolts which secure the blower motor to the heater box.

4. Withdraw the motor, complete with fan, from the box.

5. Installation is the reverse of removal.

Crown

2M ENGINE

1. Remove the air cleaner, complete with its attendant hoses.

2. Remove the left-hand front fender and the wheel arch. (Both are bolted in place).

3. Unfasten the three bolts which secure the heater blower motor to the heater box.

4. Withdraw the motor, complete with the fan.

5. Installation is the reverse of removal.

4M ENGINE

1. Unfasten the cables and remove the battery. Next remove the ignition coil and fuel filter.

2. Raise the front of the car and support it with jackstands.

✳✳ CAUTION

Be sure that the car is securely supported. Remember, you will be working underneath it.

3. Remove the left-hand wheel arch by unfastening its retaining bolts.

4. Unfasten the bolts which secure the heater blower motor; withdraw it, complete with the fan.

5. Installation is performed in the reverse order of removal.

Cressida

1. Remove the parcel tray located under the dash.

2. Remove the two discharge duct bracket mounting screens, and then remove the two brackets and the duct.

3. Remove the mounting screw, and remove the right side forward console cover.

4. Unscrew the mounting screw and remove the relay bracket located under the motor.

5. Remove the three mounting screws, and remove the motor, gasket, and blower assembly. If necessary, remove the blower mounting nut and washers, and remove the blower from the shaft.

6. Install in reverse order.

Heater Core

REMOVAL & INSTALLATION

Corona (1970–73) and Mark II

1. Drain the cooling system.

2. Remove the console, if so equipped, by removing the shift knob (manual), wiring connector, and console attaching screws.

3. Remove the carpeting from the tunnel.

4. If necessary, remove the cigarette lighter and ash tray.

5. Remove the package tray, if it makes access to the heater core difficult.

6. Unfasten the securing screws and remove the center air outlet on the Mark II 6 cylinder.

7. Remove the bottom cover/intake assembly screws and withdraw the assembly.

8. Remove the cover from the water valve.

9. Remove the water valve.

10. Unfasten the hose clamps and remove the hoses from the core.

11. Withdraw the core.

12. Installation is performed in the reverse order of removal.

Corona 74–82

1. Disconnect the negative battery cable.

2. Drain the cooling system.

3. Disconnect the heater hoses from the engine.

4. Remove the center console, if so equipped.

5. Remove the package tray and disconnect the heater air duct.

6. Unfasten the screws and take the glove compartment out of the dash.

7. Working through the glove compartment opening, remove the rear duct.

8. Detach the fresh air ventilation duct.

9. Remove the instrument cluster, as detailed in the appropriate section.

10. Remove the radio, if installed, as detailed in the appropriate section.

11. Remove the heater control assembly.

12. Take the defroster duct assembly out.

13. Tilt the heater assembly to the right and withdraw it from the package tray side.

14. Remove the water valve and outlet hose from the heater assembly.

15. Take off the retaining band and remove the bolt.

16. Remove the core.

17. Installation is performed in the reverse order of removal.

Crown

2M ENGINE

1. Drain the cooling system.

2. Remove the glove box and the package tray.

3. Unfasten both water hoses.

4. Detach the control cable.

5. Remove the dash panel ducts.

6. Remove the core from beneath the heater.

4M ENGINE

1. Disconnect the fusible link.

2. Perform Steps 1–3 of the Crown 2300 heater core removal procedure.

3. Detach the air intake door and heater control cables from the core.

4. Remove the air ducts, center, left-hand, and right-hand, as well as both defroster hoses.

5. Remove the heater core from the top of the heater box.

6. Installation is performed in the reverse of removal.

Cressida

1. Disconnect the battery ground and drain the radiator. Remove parts as described in steps 1–4 in the blower motor removal procedure above.

2. Remove the console.

3. Remove the two remaining air ducts.

4. Remove:

    a. Right and left side cowl trim panels

    b. Fuse box and steering column covers

    c. Glove box

    d. Radio (see below)

5. Remove the center air discharge panel.

6. Remove the instrument cluster.

7. Disengage damper operating cables and spring.

8. Remove the lower duct plenum by lifting it up at the rear.

9. Remove the heater valve and disconnect the two core hoses.

10. Remove the two heater unit retaining bolts and the mounting nuts, and pull the unit out on the passenger's side. Pull the heater core upward out of the unit.

11. Installation is the reverse of removal.

Heater Control Valve

The heater control valve is usually located under the hood near the firewall. On some models it is located under the dash on the passenger's side. It is operated by a cable connected to the dashboard temperature control lever. The valve is opened to admit hot coolant into the heater core when the operator moves the lever into the warm or hot range.

REMOVAL & INSTALLATION

1. Drain the engine coolant.

❊❊ CAUTION

When draining engine coolant, keep in mind that cats and dogs are attracted to ethylene glycol antifreeze and could drink any that is left in an uncovered container or in puddles on the ground. This will prove fatal in sufficient quantity. Always drain coolant into a sealable container. Coolant should be reused unless it is contaminated or is several years old.

2. Disconnect the control cable from the valve.

3. Disconnect the inlet and outlet hoses from the valve.

4. If equipped, remove the harness connector.

5. If the valve is held by a retaining bolt, remove it, then remove the valve.

To install:

6. Reinstall in reverse order. Use new hose clamps.

7. Move the temperature selector lever to HOT. Adjust the valve lever to the corresponding position and connect the cable. Lift the spring clip and adjust the cable so that the valve achieves full travel to the closed position.

8. Refill the coolant.

Control Assembly

REMOVAL & INSTALLATION

◗ See Figure 3 (p.16)

➡**These procedures allow the control unit to be pulled forward out of the dash. Generally, this is sufficient to allow inspection of the lever functions, etc. If the control head is to be removed, the cables must be disconnected from each lever. In some cases, it may be easier to disconnect the cable at the heater linkage and pull the cable through the dash.**

1. Remove the trim panel surrounding the controls.

2. Remove the knobs from the control levers. These knobs do pull off, although often with great effort. Don't damage anything when exerting force on the knob.

3. If equipped with air conditioning, remove the A/C switch.

4. Use a thin, flat bladed tool with a protected or taped edge. Carefully work the blade into the area at the bottom of the control unit and pry it out.

5. Gently pull the unit forward. If equipped with a clock in the housing, disconnect the clock. Disconnect the lighting harness and pull the control unit forward.

To install:

6. Install in reverse order, making sure the electrical connectors are engaged before installing the unit. Install the knobs securely and install the trim panel.

Control Cables

REMOVAL & INSTALLATION

◗ See Figure 4 (p.17)

1. Remove the control assembly from the dash.

2. Tag and remove the cables from the back of the control assembly.

3. Disconnect the cable from the component it is attached to,

To install:

4. Attach the cable to its appropriate location in the back of the control assembly. Then route it to the appropriate component. Adjust the able is necessary.

5. Check for proper operation.

How the heater and vent controls work

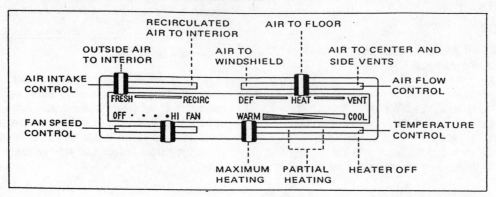

How the air conditioner works

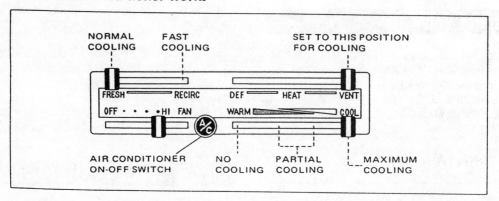

Automatic air conditioner

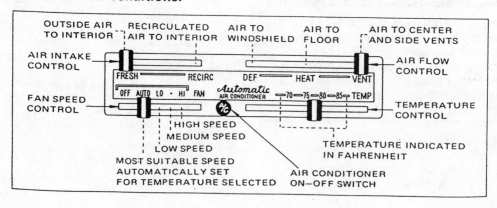

Fig. 3 Common heater control panels used on models covered by this manual

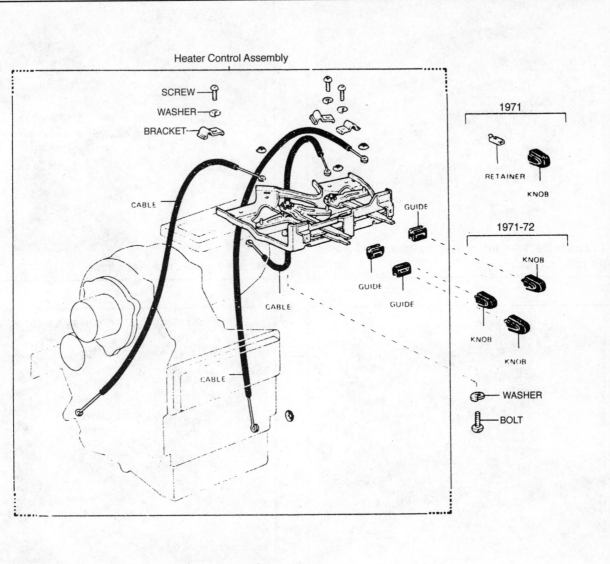

Fig. 4 Common heater control cable routing—1971–72 Corona shown

ENTERTAINMENT SYSTEM

Radio

➡**Never operate the radio without a speaker. Severe damage to the output transistors will result. If the speaker must be replaced, use a speaker of the correct impedance (ohms) or else the output transistors will be damaged and require replacement.**

REMOVAL & INSTALLATION

Corona 1970–73

1. Remove the center air outlet from under the dash.
2. Unfasten the radio control mounting bracket.
3. Remove the radio control knobs and then the retaining nuts from the control shafts.

4. Detach the speaker, and the power and antenna leads from the radio.
5. Withdraw the radio from underneath the dashboard.
6. Unfasten the speaker retaining nuts and remove the speaker.
7. Installation is performed in the reverse order of removal.

Corona 1974–82

INSTRUMENT PANEL MOUNTED

1. Remove the ashtray from the dash.
2. Remove the two screws securing the instrument cluster trim panel and remove the trim panel.
3. Remove the knobs from the heater controls and the heater control face if necessary.
4. Remove the four screws which secure the center trim panel (two are behind the heater control opening).
5. Remove the radio knobs and remove the center trim panel.

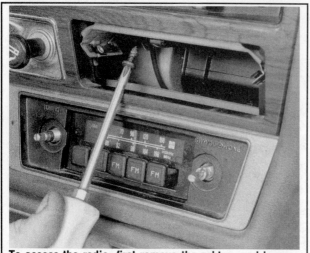

To access the radio, first remove the ashtray and loosen the panel screws

Remove the radio mounting screws . . .

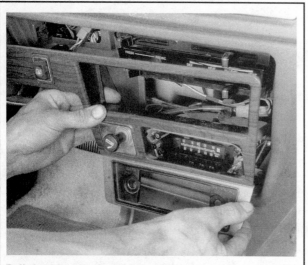

Pull the trim panel off of the dash

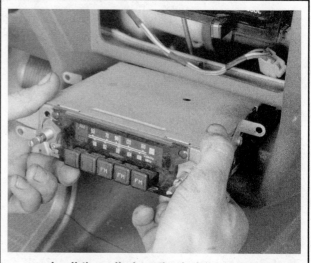

. . . and pull the radio from the dash

Separate the lighter and rear defroster switch from the trim panel wire connectors

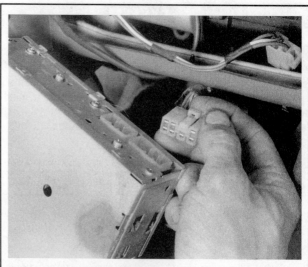

Disconnect all wiring from the back of the radio unit

6. Remove the screws which secure the radio bracket.

7. Pull the radio far enough out to remove the antenna, power, and speaker leads.

8. Remove the radio.

9. Installation is performed in the reverse order of removal.

CONSOLE MOUNTED

1. Remove the screws which secure the console, and remove the console by lowering the armrest and lifting up on the center of the console.

2. Unplug the multiconnector from the radio and disconnect the antenna lead.

3. Remove the radio knobs.

4. Remove the radio bracket, then remove the radio.

5. Installation is performed in the reverse order of removal.

Mark II

4 CYLINDER

1. Disconnect the battery.

2. Remove the left and right instrument panel moldings.

3. Remove the heater control knobs, unfasten the screws, and remove the heater control trim panel.

4. Remove the five screws and withdraw the center crash pad from the instrument panel area around the heater controls.

5. Working from beneath the dash, disconnect the radio and clock leads.

6. Unfasten the screws securing the radio and clock trim panel.

7. Remove the radio bracket attaching screws. Remove the trim panel, radio and clock.

8. Remove the knobs and unfasten the nuts which secure the radio to the face plate.

9. Installation is the reverse of removal.

6 CYLINDER

1. Remove the instrument cluster housing.

2. Remove the heater control panel.

3. Remove the two radio attaching bolts.

4. Disconnect all radio leads.

5. Remove the radio.

6. Installation is the reverse of removal.

Crown

2M ENGINE

1. Remove the glove compartment.

2. Remove all leads from the radio.

3. Remove the radio control knobs.

4. Remove the radio shaft nuts.

5. Slide the radio sideways, and out through the glove compartment opening.

6. Installation is the reverse of removal.

Crown

4M ENGINE

1. Remove the center and right side heater ducts.

2. Disconnect all leads from the radio.

3. Remove the control knobs, and the nuts from the top of the radio trim panel.

4. Remove the trim panel.

5. Remove the tape deck mounting screws and remove the tape deck.

6. Unfasten the radio mounting bracket and remove the radio.

7. Installation is the reverse of removal.

Cressida

1. Remove the radio knobs and face plate.

2. Remove the bezel nuts from the control shafts and remove the bezel from the dash.

3. Remove the driver's side forward console trim board.

4. Remove the radio forward mounting bolt, disconnect the wiring, and remove the radio.

5. Installation is the reverse of removal.

Speakers

REMOVAL & INSTALLATION

➡**Always disconnect the negative battery cable before attempting to remove the speakers.**

Dash Mounted

▶ **See Figure 5**

Dash mounted speakers can be accessed after removing the appropriate trim panel. These panels are usually retained by screws and clips. Be sure you have removed all of the attaching screws before prying the panel from the dash. Do not use excessive force on the panel as this will only lead to damage. Once the panel has been removed, loosen the speaker attaching bolts/screws, then pull the speaker from the dash and unplug the electrical connection.

Door Mounted

▶ **See Figure 6**

Door mounted speakers can be accessed after removing the door panel. These panels are usually retained by screws and clips. Be sure you have removed all of the attaching screws before prying the panel from the door. A special tool can be purchased for this purchase. Do not use excessive force on the panel as this will only lead to damage. Once the panel has been removed, loosen the speaker attaching bolts/screws, then pull the speaker from its mount and unplug the electrical connection.

REAR SPEAKERS

Removing the rear speakers involves basically the same procedure as the front speakers. Remove the appropriate trim panel, then remove the speaker. The rear speakers on some models can be assessed from inside the rear hatch.

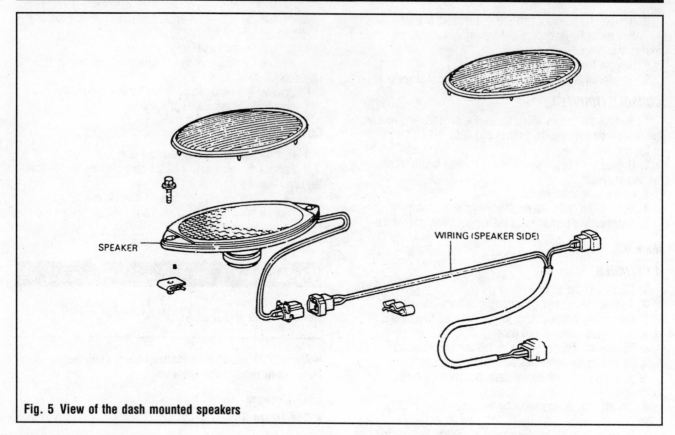

Fig. 5 View of the dash mounted speakers

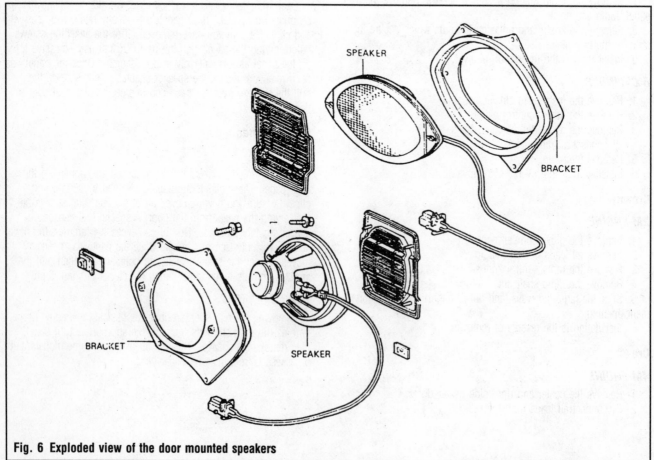

Fig. 6 Exploded view of the door mounted speakers

WINDSHIELD WIPERS AND WASHERS

WINDSHIELD WIPER COMPONENTS

1. Washer fluid reservoir   2. Wiper motor   3. Wiper arms

Windshield Wiper Blade and Arm

REMOVAL & INSTALLATION

1. To remove the wiper blades, lift up on the spring release tab on the wiper blade-to-arm connector.

2. Pull the blade assembly off the wiper arm.

3. There are two types of replacements for Toyotas:

   a. Pre-1973, replace the entire wiper blade as an assembly. Simply snap the replacement into place on the arm.

   b. Post-1973, press the old blade insert down, away from the blade assembly to free it from the retaining clips on the blade ends. Slide the insert out of the blade carrier, slide the new insert in and bend the insert upwards slightly to engage the retaining clips.

4. To replace a wiper arm, unscrew the acorn nut which secures it to the pivot and carefully pull the arm upwards and off of the pivot. Installation is the reverse of removal.

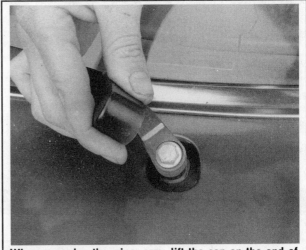

When removing the wiper arm, lift the cap on the end of the arm

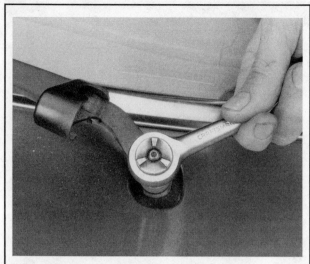

Remove the nut retaining the arm to the shaft

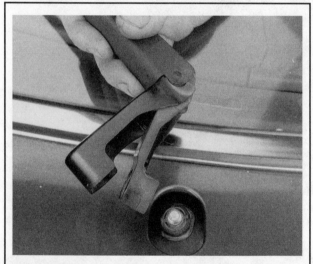

Pulling straight up, lift the arm off the shaft

Windshield Wiper Motor

REMOVAL & INSTALLATION

Corona and Crown
▶ See Figure 7

1. Disconnect the wiper motor multiconnector.
2. Remove the service cover and loosen the motor mounting bolts.
3. Use a screwdriver to separate the wiper link-to-motor connection.

✳✳ WARNING

Be careful not to bend the linkage.

4. Remove the wiper motor.
5. Installation is the reverse of removal.

Mark II 4 Cylinder

1. Remove the access hole cover.
2. Separate the wiper link from the motor by prying gently.
3. Remove the left and right cowl ventilators by lifting the retaining clips.
4. Remove the wiper arms and linage retaining nuts. Push the pivots into the ventilators.
5. Loosen the wiper link connectors at their ends.
6. Start the wiper motor and turn the ignition key **OFF** when the motor crank is at the position illustrated.

➡**The wiper motor is difficult to remove when it is in the PARK position.**

7. Unplug the multiconnector at the motor.
8. Remove the motor mounting bolts and lift out the motor.
9. Installation is the reverse of removal. Assemble the crank as illustrated.

1972–76 Mark II 6 Cylinder and Cressida

1. Remove the cover from the service hole.
2. Set the wiper crank 180° from the PARK position by turning the ignition switch **OFF** at that point.
3. Separate the link from the motor crank.
4. Unplug the multiconnector at the motor.
5. Remove the mounting nuts and lift out the motor.
6. Installation is the reverse of removal.

Wiper Linkage

REMOVAL & INSTALLATION

Corona

1. Remove the wiper motor.
2. Loosen the wiper arm retaining nuts and remove the arms.
3. Remove the wiper pivot nuts and lift out the linkage through the access hole.
4. Installation is the reverse of removal.

Mark II 4 Cylinder

The linkage is removed along with the motor.

Mark II 6 Cylinder and Cressida

1. Remove the wiper arms.
2. Remove the left and right cowl ventilators.
3. Remove the ventilator service hole cover.
4. Remove the linkage attaching screws.
5. Remove the wiper motor access cover.
6. Unfasten the wiper linkage from the motor crank. (See the wiper motor removal procedures).
7. Withdraw the linkage through the access hole.
8. Installation is performed in the reverse order of removal.

Crown

1. Perform Steps 1–5 of the Mark II 6 Cylinder Linkage Removal procedure.
2. Remove both of the pivots and the connecting linkage. Be careful not to damage the windshield washer nozzle.
3. Installation is performed in the reverse order of removal.

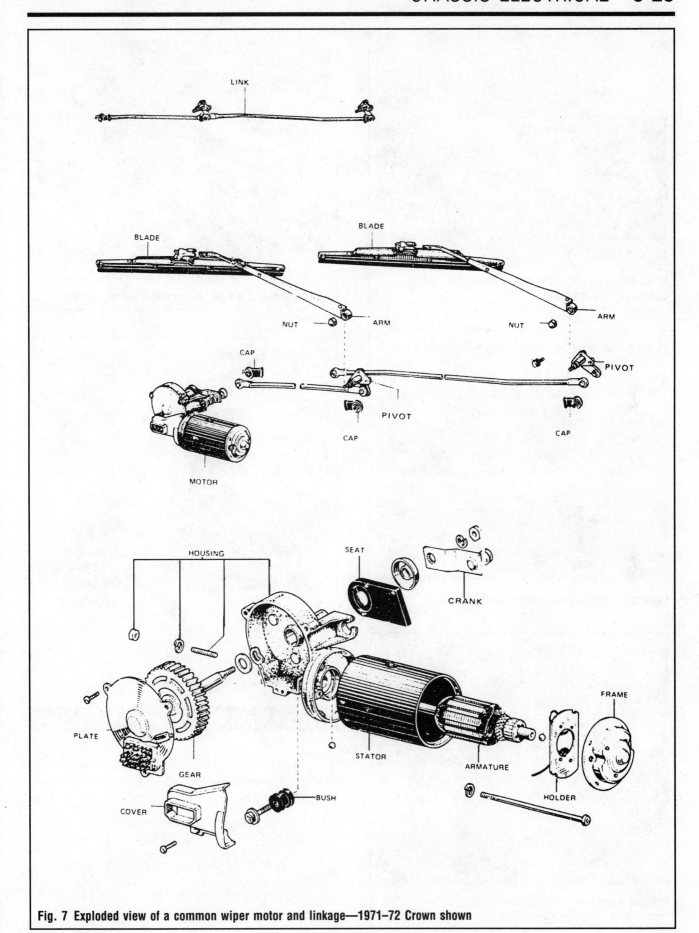

Fig. 7 Exploded view of a common wiper motor and linkage—1971–72 Crown shown

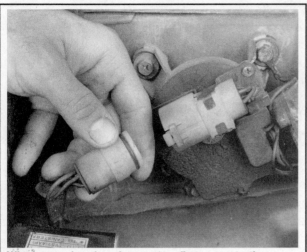

When removing the wiper motor, first separate the connector from the motor

. . . separate the wiper linkage-to-motor connection

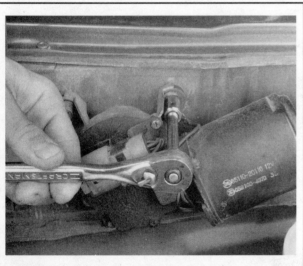

Loosen and remove the motor mounting nuts

1. Wiper motor
2. Wiper linkage
3. Motor electrical connection
4. Motor drive linkage
5. Mounting bolts

View of the wiper motor

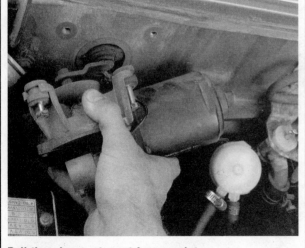

Pull the wiper motor out far enough to . . .

Washer Fluid Reservoir

REMOVAL & INSTALLATION

▶ **See Figures 8 and 9**

1. Unbolt the washer reservoir from the upper radiator support.
2. Lift the unit from the engine compartment or trunk, then slide the hose from the unit.
3. Unhook the wiring harness for the pump from the side of the reservoir.
4. Disconnect the wiring harness from the pump, then remove

the pump from the reservoir. Check the condition of the grommet that the pump sits into.

To install:

5. Install the pump into the reservoir, ensure the grommet is in good condition.

6. Attach the wiring to the pump, then run the hose for the pump along the side of the reservoir.

7. Seat the reservoir into position and secure with the mounting bolt.

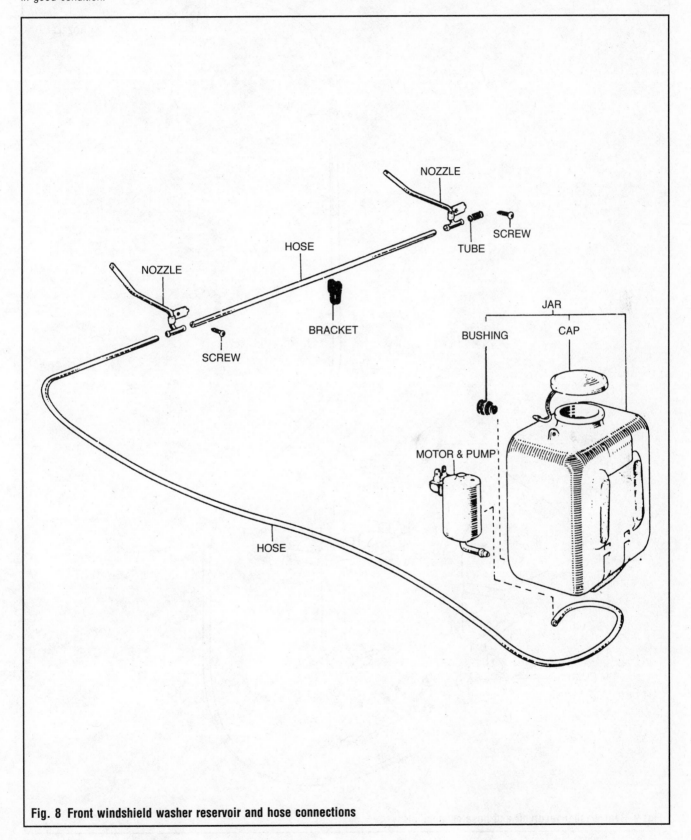

Fig. 8 Front windshield washer reservoir and hose connections

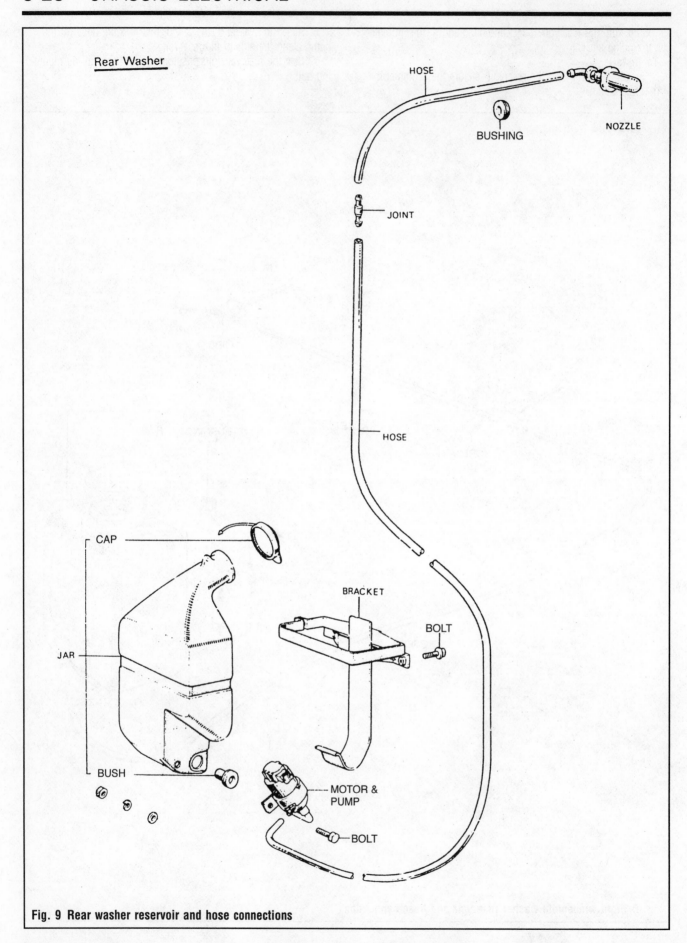

Rear Washer

HOSE

BUSHING

NOZZLE

JOINT

HOSE

CAP

JAR

BUSH

BRACKET

BOLT

MOTOR & PUMP

BOLT

Fig. 9 Rear washer reservoir and hose connections

Washer Pump

REMOVAL & INSTALLATION

1. Remove the washer reservoir from the vehicle.
2. Unhook the wiring harness for the pump.
3. Disconnect the wiring harness from the pump, then remove the pump from the reservoir. Check the grommet.

INSTRUMENTS AND SWITCHES

Instrument Cluster

REMOVAL & INSTALLATION

Corona

1970–73 MODELS

▶ **See Figure 10**

1. Disconnect the battery.
2. Remove the fuse box block attachment bolts.
3. Remove the parking brake bracket.
4. Detach the fuel gauge/warning light pod wiring harness and remove its mounting screws. Pull out the pod.
5. Perform Step 4 for the clock.
6. Disconnect the speedometer wiring harness and cable.
7. Unfasten the wiring harness clamp then push the harness toward the front.
8. Loosen the speedometer attaching screws and remove the speedometer.

➡**Cover the lens with a cloth during removal.**

9. Installation is performed in the reverse order of removal.

1974–82 MODELS

1. Disconnect the negative (−) battery cable.
2. Remove the two instrument cluster surround securing screws. One is located above the speedometer lens and the other above the fuel gauge on hardtops. On sedans and wagons the screws are above the combination gauge and clock.
3. Remove the side air outlet control knob and the clock setting knob.
4. Lift off the trim panel.
5. Unfasten the five screws which secure the instrument cluster to the instrument panel support.
6. Disconnect the speedometer cable and the instrument cluster wiring harness.
7. Lift out the cluster assembly.
8. Installation is performed in the reverse order of removal.

To install:
4. Install the pump into the reservoir.
5. Connect the wiring for the pump.
6. Install the reservoir.
7. Attach the wiring to the pump, then run the hose for the pump along the side of the reservoir.
8. Seat the reservoir into the engine compartment. Secure with the mounting bolt.

Mark II

4 CYLINDER

▶ **See Figure 11 (p. 30)**

1. Disconnect the battery.
2. Remove the package shelf from beneath the dashboard.
3. Remove the fuse block bracket.
4. Remove the lower left side crash pad and the left-hand trim molding.
5. Unfasten the instrument cluster securing screws and tip the cluster slightly forward.
6. Detach the cluster wiring harness and the speedometer cable. Remove the cluster.

➡**If the car is not equipped with a radio, it is much easier to remove the glove box and then remove the instrument cluster through the opening.**

7. Installation is performed in the reverse order of removal.

6 CYLINDER

▶ **See Figure 11 (p. 30)**

1. Remove the housing from the steering column.
2. Remove the control knobs from the heater and radio.
3. Loosen the heater control floodlight and pull it out slightly.
4. Remove the nine screws which attach the cluster surround.
5. Push the upper crash pad away from the trim panel and slightly pull out the panel.
6. Remove the heater control floodlight from the trim panel.
7. Remove the trim panel toward the right.
8. Remove the instrument panel lower garnish moldings. Remove the ash tray.
9. Remove the heater control assembly.
10. Unfasten the dash side ventilator mounting screws.
11. Remove the radio and tape deck, if so equipped.
12. Remove the heater control bracket.
13. Remove the six cluster securing bolts and lift it out slightly.
14. Detach the speedometer cable and all of the wiring harnesses. Remove the cluster.
15. Installation is performed in the reverse order of removal.

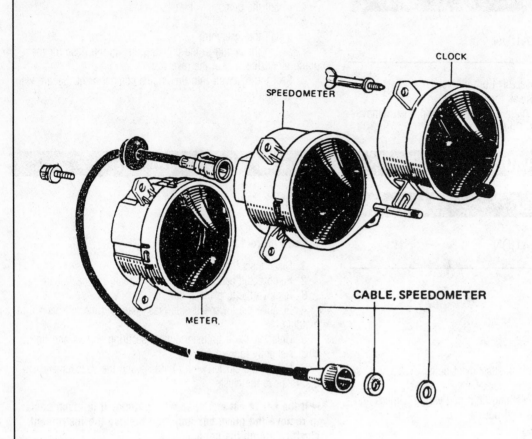

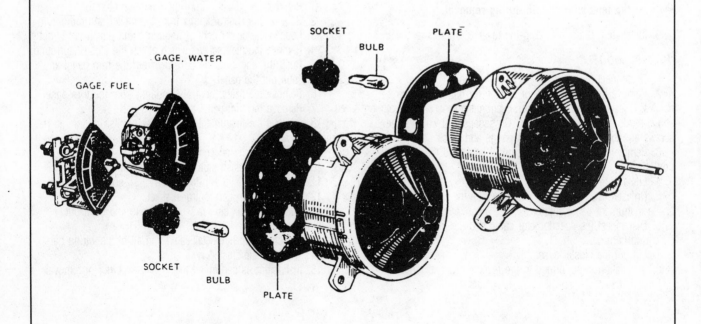

Fig. 10 View of the combination meter gauges—1970—73 Corona

View of the dash instrument cluster—1979 Corona

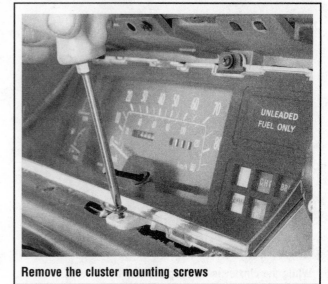

Remove the cluster mounting screws

Remove the trim screws located around the cluster

Pull the cluster from the dash far enough to . . .

Carefully pry the trim panel off the dash after all the retainers have been removed

. . . separate the wiring from the back of it

While the cluster is out, replace any burnt bulbs

➡Have the heater control floodlight installed in the cluster surround prior to its installation.

Crown 2M Engine

▸ See Figure 12

1. Disconnect the battery.
2. Detach the heater control cables at the heater box.
3. Loosen the steering column clamping nuts and lower the column.

✳✳ WARNING

Be careful when handling the column. It is the collapsible type. Cover the column shroud with a cloth to protect it.

4. Loosen the instrument panel screws and tilt the panel forward.
5. Detach the speedometer cable and wiring connectors. Remove the entire panel assembly.

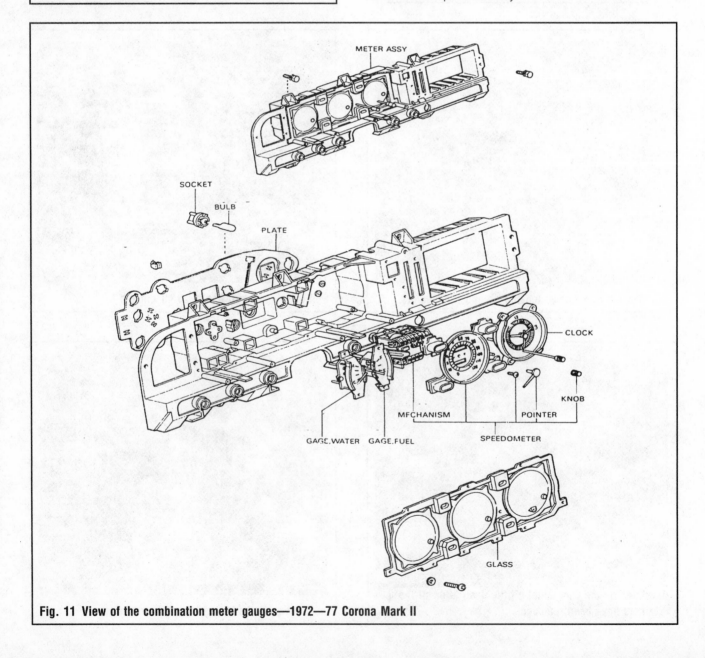

Fig. 11 View of the combination meter gauges—1972—77 Corona Mark II

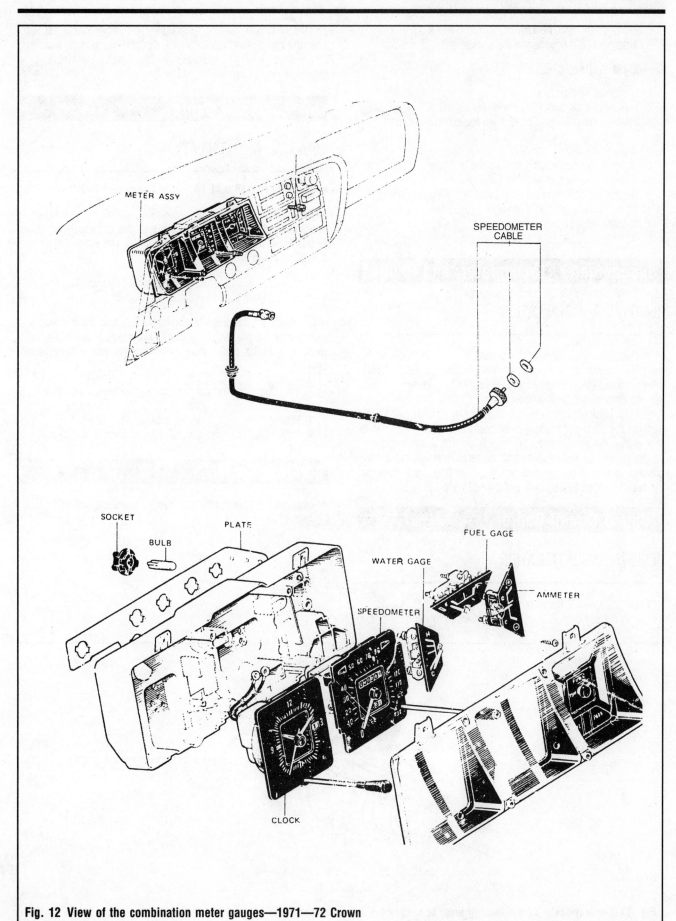

Fig. 12 View of the combination meter gauges—1971—72 Crown

6. Remove the instruments from the panel as required.

7. Installation is performed in the reverse order of removal.

Crown 4M Engine, Cressida

1. Disconnect the battery.

2. Remove the air duct from the center air outlet.

3. Remove the radio trim panel from the center instrument panel.

4. Remove the radio.

5. Unfasten the screws and remove the instrument cluster trim panel. Remove the cluster housing.

6. Detach the speedometer drive cable and wiring connectors by reaching through the radio opening.

7. Withdraw the instrument cluster.

8. Installation is performed in the reverse order of removal.

Speedometer, Tachometer, and Gauges

REMOVAL & INSTALLATION

The gauges on all the models covered here can be replaced in the same basic manner. First, remove the instrument cluster and the front lens. Then, remove the gauge's attaching screws on either the front or the back of the cluster.

When replacing a speedometer or odometer assembly, the law requires the odometer reading of the replacement unit to be set to register the same mileage as the prior odometer. If the mileage cannot be set, the law requires that the replacement be set at zero and a proper label be installed on the drivers door frame to show the previous odometer reading and date of replacement.

Printed Circuit Board

REMOVAL & INSTALLATION

The printed circuit board on all models covered here are removed in the same basic manner. It is attached to the back of the instrument cluster, making it necessary to remove the cluster first. After the cluster has been removed, disconnect the bulb sockets and remove the attaching screws or clips. Handle the circuit board with care to prevent damage.

Speedometer Cable

REMOVAL & INSTALLATION

▶ **See Figures 13 and 14**

➡**Depending on the particular model, there are two types of methods for attaching the cable to the speedometer. One is the conventional screw-in type, while the other employs a locking lever to secure the cable.**

1. Remove the instrument cluster and disconnect the cable from the speedometer.

➡**On some models, cable disconnection can be accomplished by simply reaching under the dash. If possible, this method is much easier than removing the entire instrument cluster.**

2. Feed the cable through its hold in the firewall and then trace it down to where it connects to the transmission.

3. Unscrew the cable from the transmission end.

4. Installation is in the reverse order of removal.

Ignition Switch

Information on removing and installing ignition switches can be found in Section 8.

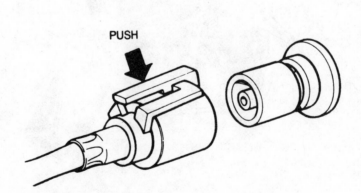

PUSH

Fig. 13 Some models have a locking lever to secure the speedometer cable

WITHOUT TRANSDUCER

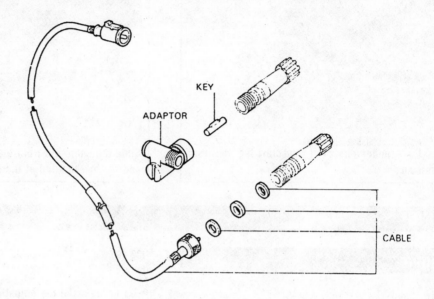

KEY

ADAPTOR

CABLE

WITH TRANSDUCER

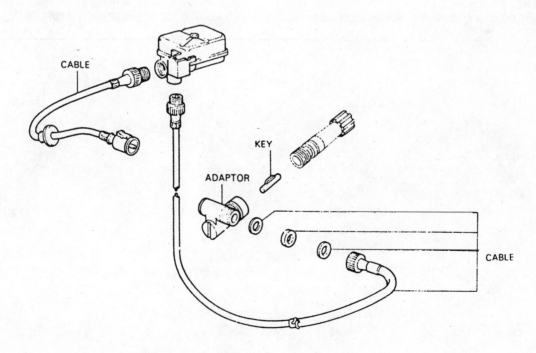

CABLE

KEY

ADAPTOR

CABLE

Fig. 14 Speedometer cable and adapter—1972–77 models shown others similar

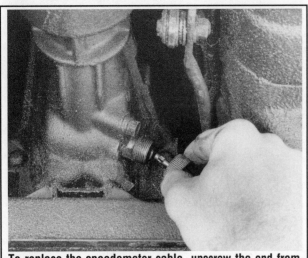

To replace the speedometer cable, unscrew the end from the transmission

Slide the cable out from the underneath of the vehicle and remove the end at the speedometer head

LIGHTING

Headlights

REMOVAL & INSTALLATION

▶ See Figures 15, 16 and 17 (p. 34–36)

1. Unscrew the headlight bezel or headlight grille retaining screws. Remove the bezel or grille.
2. Loosen, but do not remove, the three headlight retaining ring screws, on some models, rotate the ring counterclockwise to remove it.

➡Do not mistake the adjusting screws for the retaining ring screws. There are only two adjusting screws for each headlight. They are located right next to the top and the side retaining ring screws. Turning these screws will result in improper headlight adjustment.

3. On models with square headlights, remove the four headlight retaining ring screws and then remove the ring.

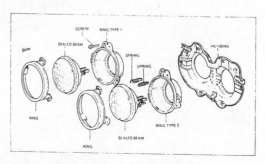

Fig. 15 Exploded view of the headlamp assembly—1972–77 Corona shown

HEADLAMP BULBS

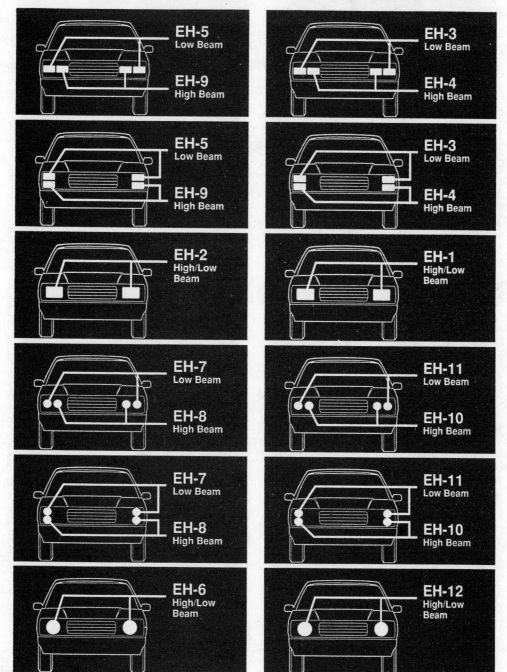

Bulb/Headlamp Number	Customer I.D.#		Bulb/Headlamp Number	Customer I.D.#		Bulb/Headlamp Number	Customer I.D.#
89	EB-6		13050	EB-10		H4651	EH-4
158	EB-8		4000	EH-7		H4656	EH-3
194	EB-7		4001/5001	EH-8		H5001	EH-10
1034	EB-4		4651	EH-9		H5006	EH-11
1073	EB-5		4652	EH-5		H6024	EH-12
1156	EB-3		6014	EH-6		H6054	EH-1
1157	EB-2		6052	EH-2		H6545	EH-13
12100	EB-9					H9004	EB-1

Fig. 16 Headlamp identification

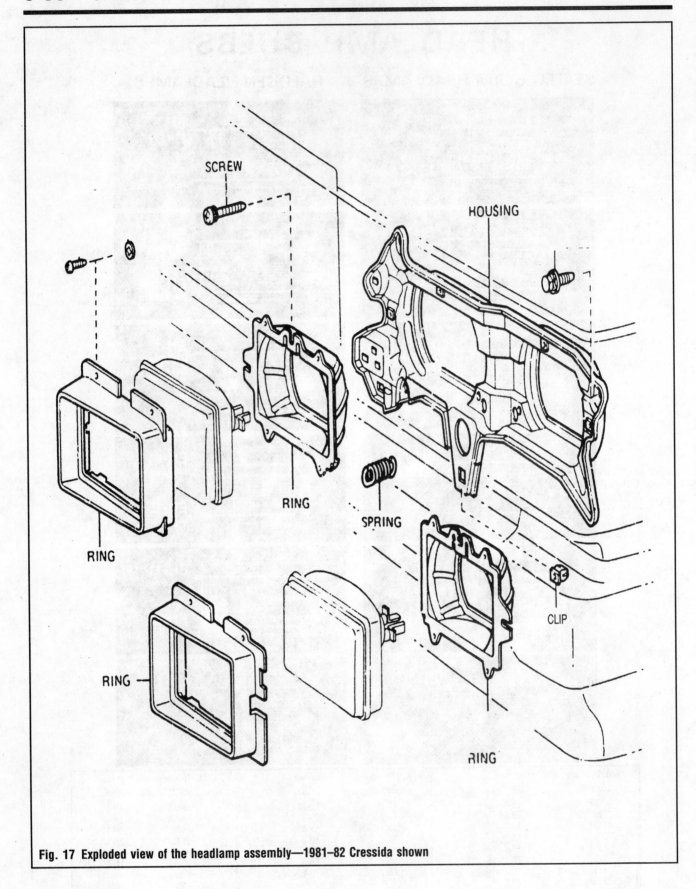

Fig. 17 Exploded view of the headlamp assembly—1981–82 Cressida shown

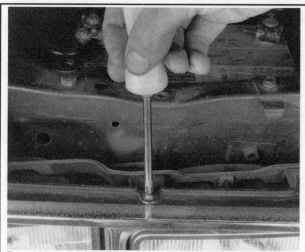

To replace the headlamp, remove the screws retaining the headlight bezel

. . . then separate the trim from the headlamp

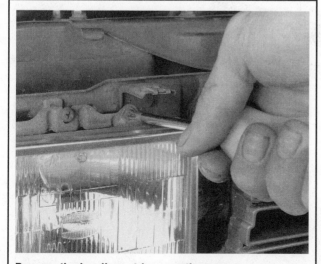

Pull the bezel off the front of the vehicle

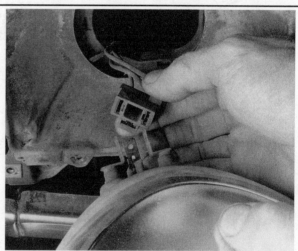

Pull the bulb from the vehicle and separate the electrical connection

4. Pull the headlight away from its positioning ring slightly and unplug the electrical connection at its rear.
5. Remove the headlight.
6. Installation is in the reverse order of removal.

➡**Do not interchange the inner and outer headlights.**

Signal and Marker Lights

REMOVAL & INSTALLATION

Front Turn Signal, Parking and Marker Lights
♦ **See Figures 18 and 19**

The lens is removed to allow access to the bulb. External lenses usually have a rubber gasket around them to keep dust and water out of the housing; the gasket must be present and in

Remove the headlamp trim mounting screws . . .

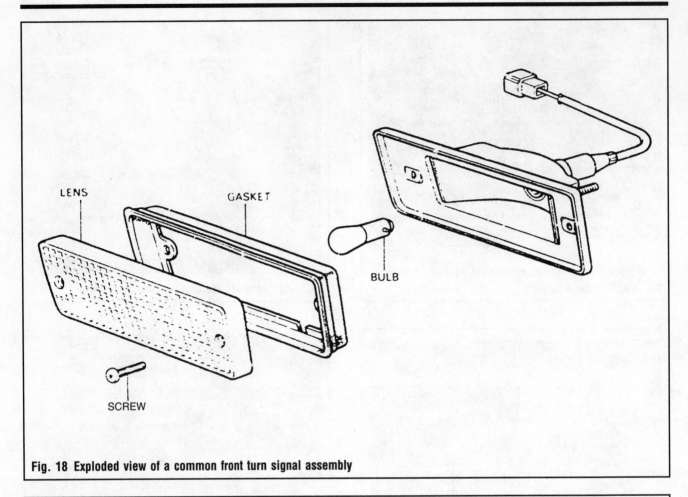

Fig. 18 Exploded view of a common front turn signal assembly

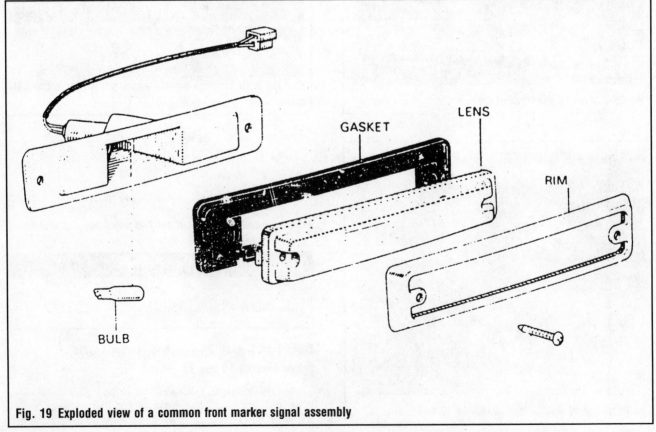

Fig. 19 Exploded view of a common front marker signal assembly

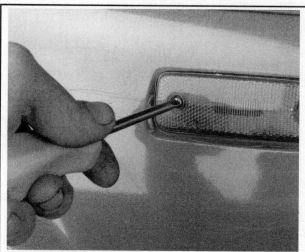

To remove the lens on a side marker light, remove the mounting screws

. . . and lift the lens off

Then pull out the bulb and replace if it is burnt out

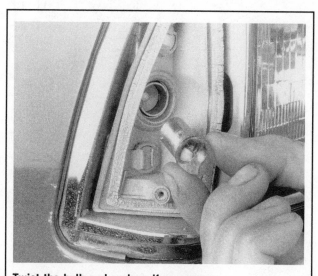

Twist the bulb and replace if necessary

Remove the clearance lens screws . . .

good condition at reinstallation. Exterior lenses are held by one or more screws which must be removed. Once the lens is removed from the body, the bulb is removed from the socket and replaced. For some front marker lamps and front turn signals, the socket and bulb is removed from the lens with a counterclockwise turn.

The bulbs used on Toyotas are all US stardard and may be purchased at any auto store or dealer. Because of the variety of lamps used on any vehicle, take the old one with you when shopping for the replacement.

On some models the lens can be replaced separately. On others, you have to replace the lens with the plastic backing attached.

Rear Turn Signal, Brake and Parking Lights
▶ **See Figures 20 and 21**

Most rear lenses are fastened in place from inside the luggage compartment. A stud is attached to the lens and passes through the sheet metal at the rear of the body. Remove the attaching nuts

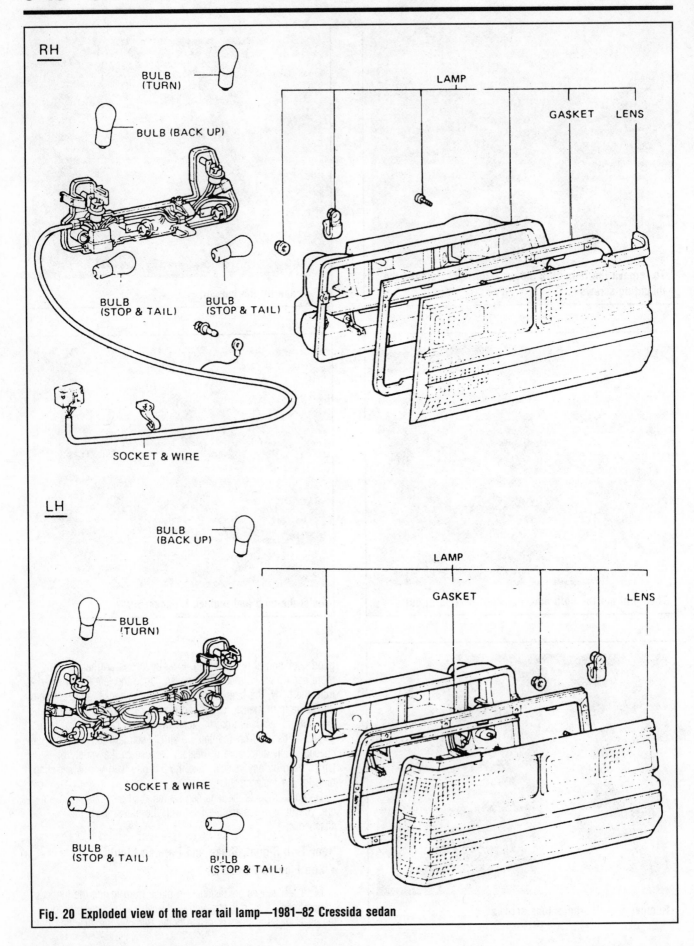

Fig. 20 Exploded view of the rear tail lamp—1981–82 Cressida sedan

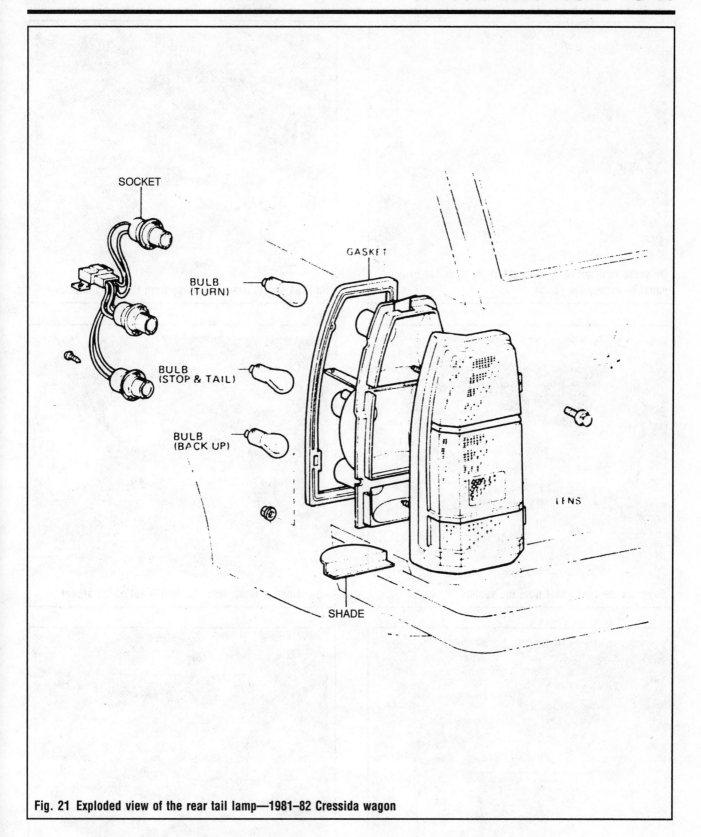

Fig. 21 Exploded view of the rear tail lamp—1981–82 Cressida wagon

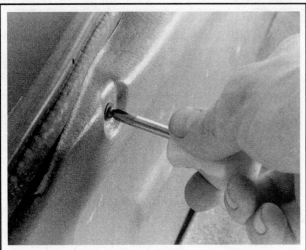

On some rear tail lamp assemblies, remove the trim panel to access the lamps

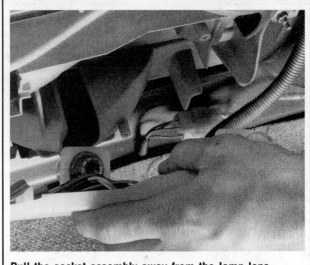

Pull the socket assembly away from the lamp lens

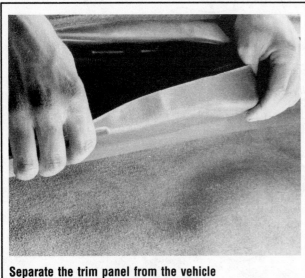

Separate the trim panel from the vehicle

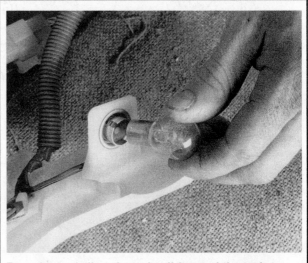

To replace a bulb, twist and pull it out of the socket

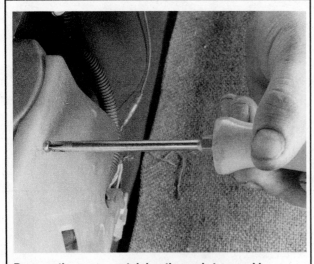

Remove the screws retaining the socket assembly

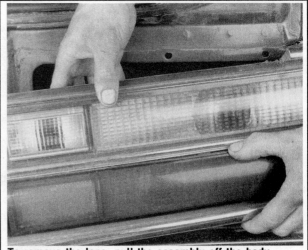

To remove the lens, pull the assembly off the body panel

from inside the luggage compartment and pull the lens off. a few small lenses may be attached with screws that are accessible from the rear. To remove these, the outer chrome trim may need to be removed. Then simply remove the screws and remove the lens.

Once the lens is removed, the bulb can be replaced simply by depressing it, turning it counterclockwise, and removing it. Install in reverse order.

License Plate Lights
♦ **See Figure 22**

1. Remove the lamp attaching bolts or screws.
2. Remove the lamp socket then remove the bulb.
3. Installation is the reverse of removal.

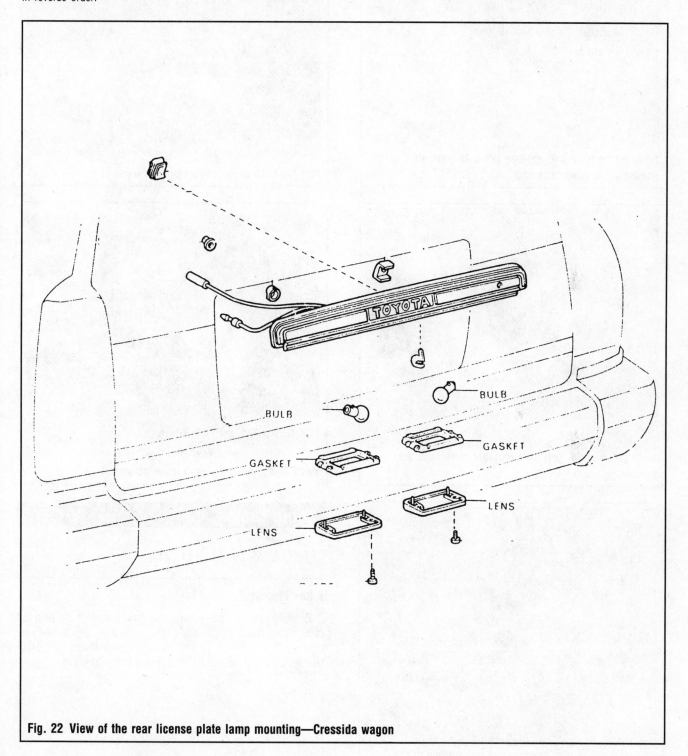

Fig. 22 View of the rear license plate lamp mounting—Cressida wagon

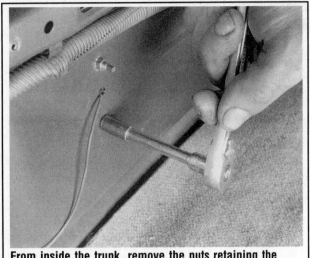

From inside the trunk, remove the nuts retaining the license plate lamp assembly

From the outside, pull the assembly away from the vehicle

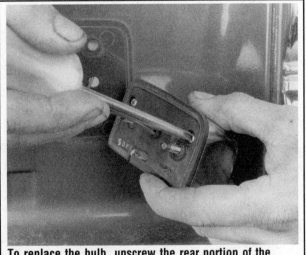

To replace the bulb, unscrew the rear portion of the lamp

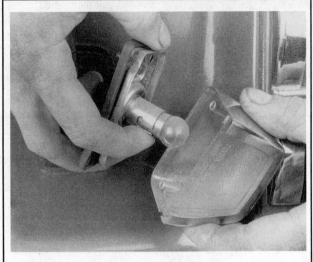

Pull the back of the lamp from the lens

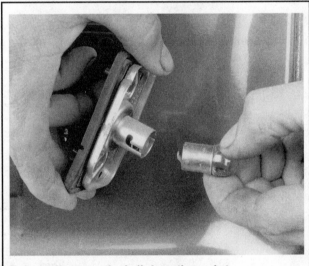

Twist and remove the bulb from the socket

Dome Lamps

REMOVAL & INSTALLATION

♦ **See Figures 23 and 23a**

Carefully pry or unscrew the dome lamp lens. Pull the bulb out of its socket and inspect the element for damage. Replace the bulb is necessary. Test the bulb to make sure it is operating properly. If the unit is OK, snap or screw the lens into place.

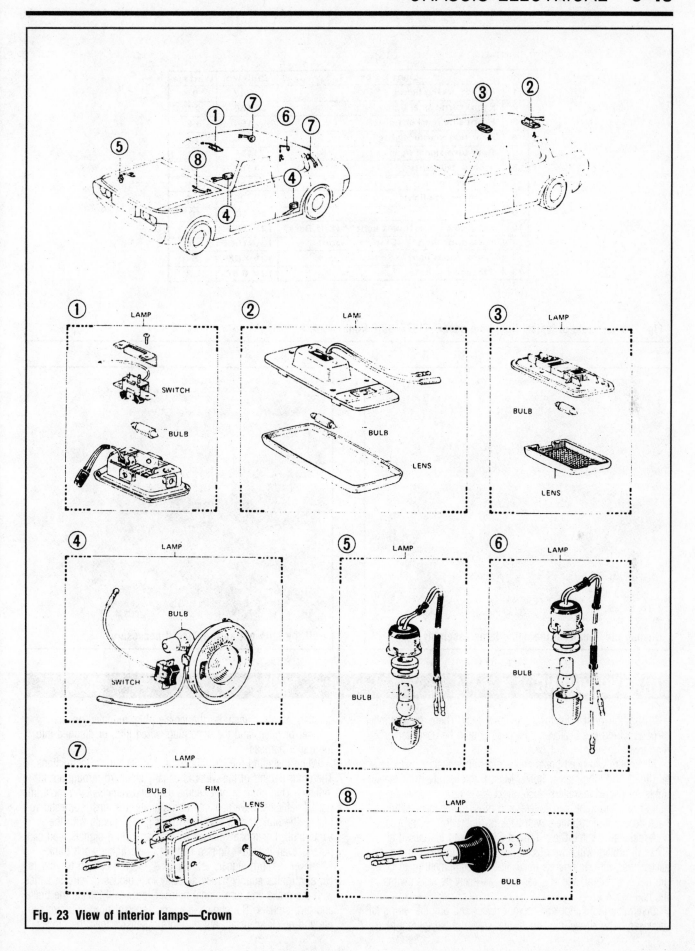

Fig. 23 View of interior lamps—Crown

No.	Light Bulbs	Bulb No.	Wattage
1	Front parking lights	87	8
2	Front turn signal lights	1156	27
3	Front side marker lights*	194	3.8
4	Rear side marker lights*	194	3.8
5	Rear turn signal lights	1156	27
6	Stop & tail lights	1157	27/8
7	Back-up lights	1156	27
8	License plate lights	89	7.5
9	Interior light**	12V-10CP	10
10	Luggage compartment light** (Lift Back)	12V-3CP	5
11	Back door light** (Station Wagon)	12V-10CP	10
12	Trunk room light* (Sedan)	12V-4CP	5
13	Glovebox light*	12V-0.6CP	1.2

Fig. 23a Example of typical light bulb usage—1975–80 Corona shown

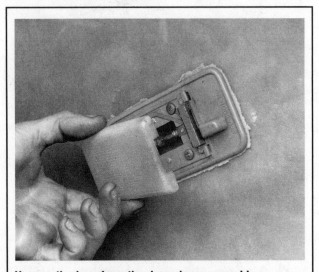

Unsnap the lens from the dome lamp assembly

Pull the bulb out and replace if necessary

TRAILER WIRING

Wiring the vehicle for towing is fairly easy. There are a number of good wiring kits available and these should be used, rather than trying to design your own.

All trailers will need brake lights and turn signals as well as tail lights and side marker lights. Most areas require extra marker lights for overwide trailers. Also, most areas have recently required back-up lights for trailers, and most trailer manufacturers have been building trailers with back-up lights for several years.

Additionally, some Class I, most Class II and just about all Class III trailers will have electric brakes. Add to this number an accessories wire, to operate trailer internal equipment or to charge the trailer's battery, and you can have as many as seven wires in the harness.

Determine the equipment on your trailer and buy the wiring kit necessary. The kit will contain all the wires needed, plus a plug

adapter set which includes the female plug, mounted on the bumper or hitch, and the male plug, wired into, or plugged into the trailer harness.

When installing the kit, follow the manufacturer's instructions. The color coding of the wires is usually standard throughout the industry. One point to note: some domestic vehicles, and most imported vehicles, have separate turn signals. On most domestic vehicles, the brake lights and rear turn signals operate with the same bulb. For those vehicles with separate turn signals, you can purchase an isolation unit so that the brake lights won't blink whenever the turn signals are operated, or, you can go to your local electronics supply house and buy four diodes to wire in series with the brake and turn signal bulbs. Diodes will isolate the brake and turn signals. The choice is yours. The isolation units are simple and quick to install, but far more expensive than the diodes.

The diodes, however, require more work to install properly, since they require the cutting of each bulb's wire and soldering in place of the diode.

One, final point, the best kits are those with a spring loaded cover on the vehicle mounted socket. This cover prevents dirt and moisture from corroding the terminals. Never let the vehicle socket hang loosely; always mount it securely to the bumper or hitch.

CIRCUIT PROTECTION

Turn Signals and Flashers

REMOVAL & INSTALLATION

Except Crown
♦ See Figure 24

These models' turn signals and hazard warning flashers are combined in a single unit. It is located on the left-hand side, underneath the dashboard, next to the fuse block.

➡**On some models it may be necessary to remove the fuse block bracket in order to gain access to the flasher.**

Crown

2M ENGINE

The turn signal and hazard warning flasher is located on a bracket next to the parking brake handle.

4M ENGINE

The turn signal/hazard flasher is located behind the left-hand (driver's) ash tray. In order to remove the flasher, first take out the ash tray.

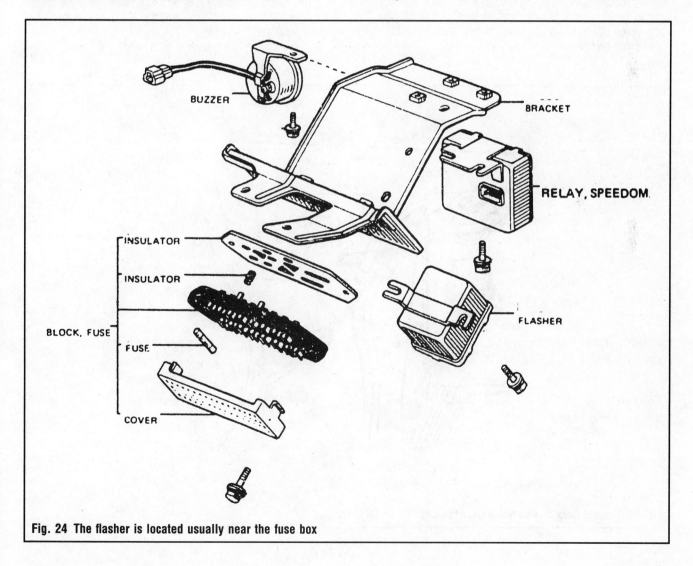

Fig. 24 The flasher is located usually near the fuse box

Fuses and Fusible Link

REPLACEMENT

1970–78 Models

▶ **See Figures 25 and 25a**

The fuse box is located on the left-hand side, underneath the dashboard, on all models except the Crown 2600. On the Crown 2600, the fuse box is located behind a door on the driver's side kick panel.

All models are equipped with fusible links on the battery cables running from the positive (+) battery terminal.

On all Mark II 6 cylinder models, and on all other passenger cars made in 1974 and later, the headlights are protected by a relay and the fusible link, rather than by individual fuses.

1979–81 Models

These models have two fuse blocks. One is located behind a panel in the dash, while the other can be found on the left front fender apron. There may be on some models, separate fusible links located behind the left and right kick panels.

1982 Models

A single fuse block unit is located under the hood (driver's side) on these models. Fusible links may also be located in the left and right kick panels.

Circuit Breakers

On 1980–81 models, a circuit breaker is used in place of a fuse for the rear window defogger. It is located under the left or right side of the instrument panel, behind the kick panel. Circuit breakers may also be used for air conditioning, power windows, magnetic door locks and power sun roof on 1982 models.

If the circuit breaker cuts off:

1. Remove the left or right kick panel.

2. Unplug the wiring connector from the circuit breaker and then remove the circuit breaker assembly.

3. Unlock the stopper and pull out the circuit breaker.

4. To reset the circuit breakers, insert a needle into the reset hole and push it.

5. Using an ohmmeter, check for continuity between the two circuit breaker terminals. If there isn't any, the circuit breaker will require replacement.

6. Installation is in the reverse order of removal.

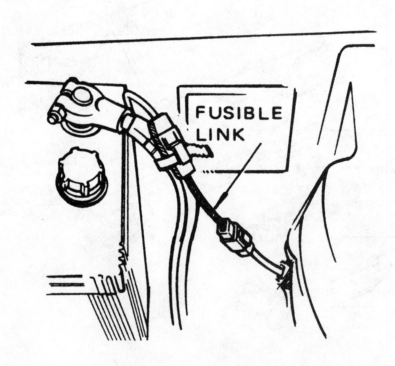

Fig. 25 Fusible links can be found near the positive battery terminal

WIPER (20A): Windshield wiper and washer, and rear window wiper and washer

ENGINE (10A): Alternator voltage regulator (IG terminal)

HORN-HAZ. (10A): Horns and emergency flashers

CHARGE (5A)

Instrument panel fuses

PANEL L. (5A): Heater panel lights, clock light, cigarette lighter light, meter and gauge lights, automatic transmission indicator light and glovebox light

TAIL (RH) (5A): Right tail lights, right front parking light, right front side marker light and license plate lights

TAIL (LH) (5A): Left tail lights, left front parking light and left front side marker light

CIG. L (15A): Cigarette lighter, digital

STOP (15A): Stop lights
clock display, light reminder control relay and power antenna

TURN SIG. (10A): Turn signal lights

GAUGES (10A): Back-up lights, discharge warning light, low oil pressure warning light, seat belt warning light and buzzer, key reminder buzzer, low fuel level warning light, brake system warning light, engine temperature gauge and fuel gauge

RADIO (5A): Radio and stereo tape player

DOME, CLK. (5A): Interior light, interior light retainer relay, open door warning light, clock, luggage compartment light and back door light

HEATER-A/C (20A): Heater or air conditioner blower motor and compressor magnetic clutch

ENGINE (10A): Ignition relay[1], main relay[2], emission control computer and outer vent control valve

[1]: The ignition relay, if activated, supplies voltage from the battery to the "WIPER" and "ENGINE" fuses in the engine room.

[2]: The main relay, if activated, supplies voltage from the battery to the "TURN", "GAUGES" and "DEFOG" fuses.

NOTE: The **rear window defogger circuit** is protected by a circuit breaker. It is located in left side kick panel.

Fig. 25a Example of typical fuse usage—1975–80 Corona shown

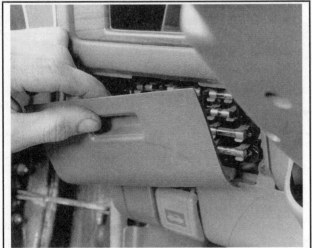

Remove the fuse box cover inside the vehicle under the dash—1979 Corona shown

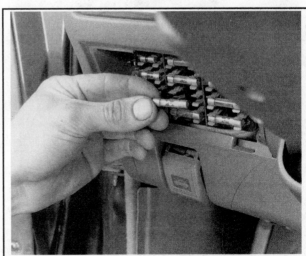

Remove the fuse and replace it with the correct amperage fuse

On the fuse box in the engine compartment, remove the cover retaining screws—1979 Corona shown

Lift the fuses out of the box and replace them with the same amperage fuse

Next, lift the cover off the fuse box

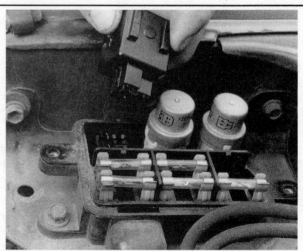

Relays are also located in this fuse block and can be pulled out and replaced if necessary

WIRING DIAGRAMS

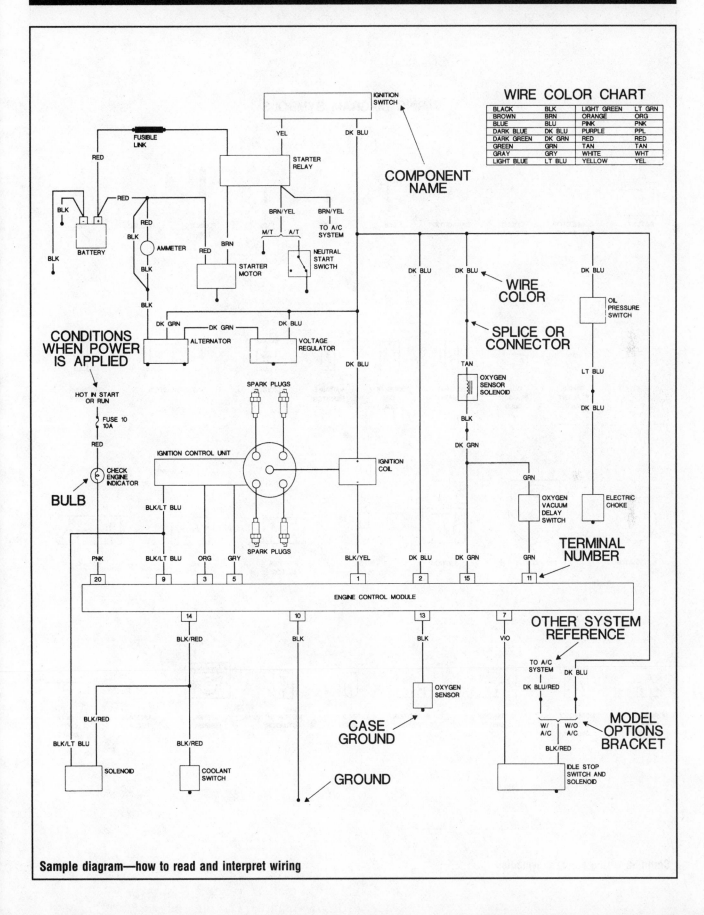

WIRE COLOR CHART

BLACK	BLK	LIGHT GREEN	LT GRN
BROWN	BRN	ORANGE	ORG
BLUE	BLU	PINK	PNK
DARK BLUE	DK BLU	PURPLE	PPL
DARK GREEN	DK GRN	RED	RED
GREEN	GRN	TAN	TAN
GRAY	GRY	WHITE	WHT
LIGHT BLUE	LT BLU	YELLOW	YEL

Sample diagram—how to read and interpret wiring

WIRING DIAGRAM SYMBOLS

BATTERY	CONNECTOR OR SPLICE	CIRCUIT BREAKER	CAPACITOR	COIL	DIODE	FUSE	FUSIBLE LINK	GROUND	LED

RESISTOR	SINGLE FILAMENT BULB	DUAL FILAMENT BULB	HEATING ELEMENT	SOLENOID OR COIL	VARIABLE RESISTOR	CRYSTAL	POTENTIOMETER	HORN OR SPEAKER

ALTERNATOR	DISTRIBUTOR ASSEMBLY	IGNITION COIL	SPARK PLUG	STEPPER MOTOR	HEAT ACTIVATED SWITCH	RELAY

NORMALLY OPEN SWITCH	NORMALLY CLOSED SWITCH	GANGED SWITCH	3-POSITION SWITCH	REED SWITCH	MOTOR OR ACTUATOR	SPEED SENSOR	JUNCTION BLOCK	MODEL OPTIONS BRACKET

Common wiring diagram symbols

1972-77 CORONA MK MARK II, MX MARK II, AND MARK II 6 CYL

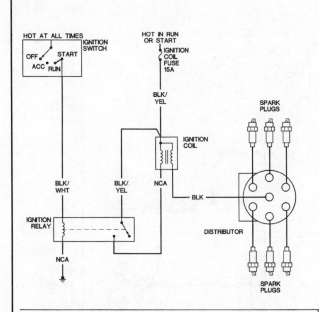

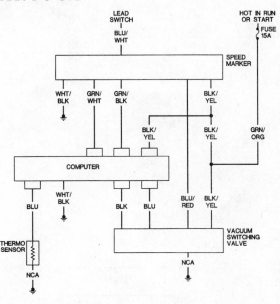

1970-72 CORONA MARK II AND MK II 4 CYL

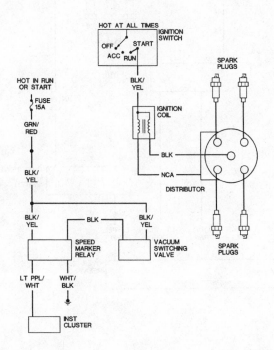

1970-73 CORONA 4 CYL

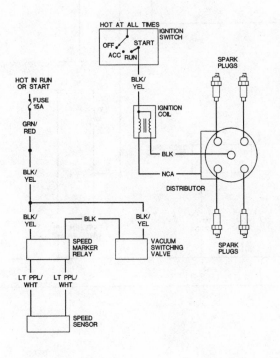

Fig. 26 Engine wiring—1970–76 Corona Mark II and 1970–73 Corona

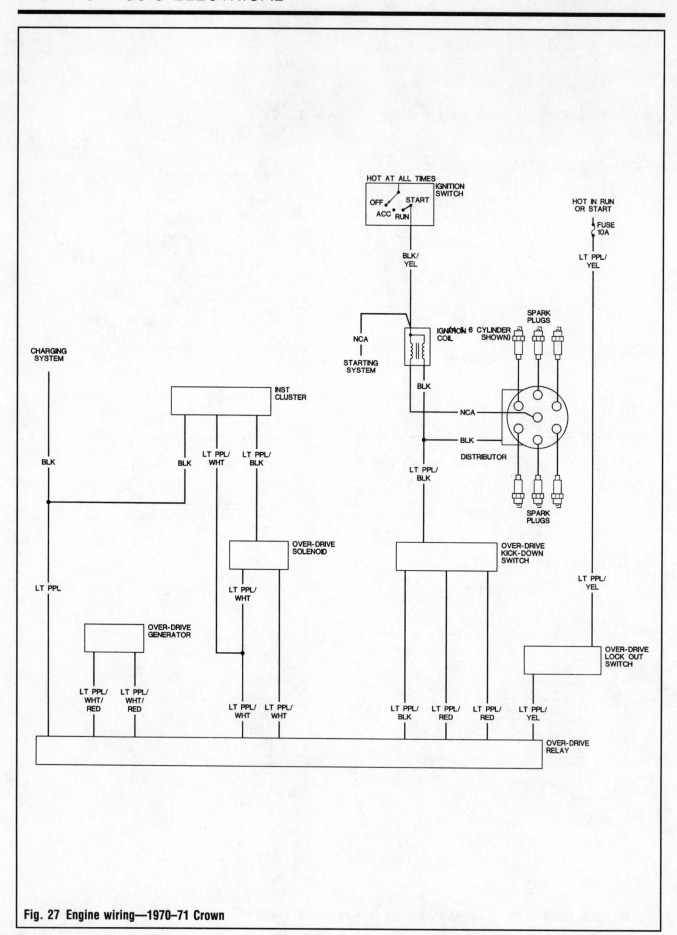

Fig. 27 Engine wiring—1970-71 Crown

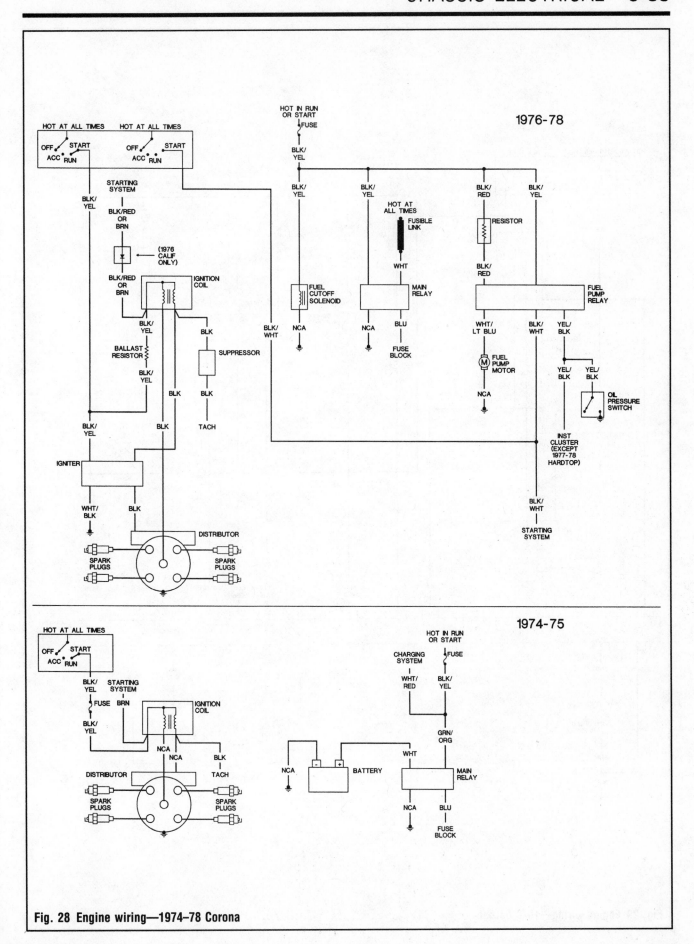

Fig. 28 Engine wiring—1974–78 Corona

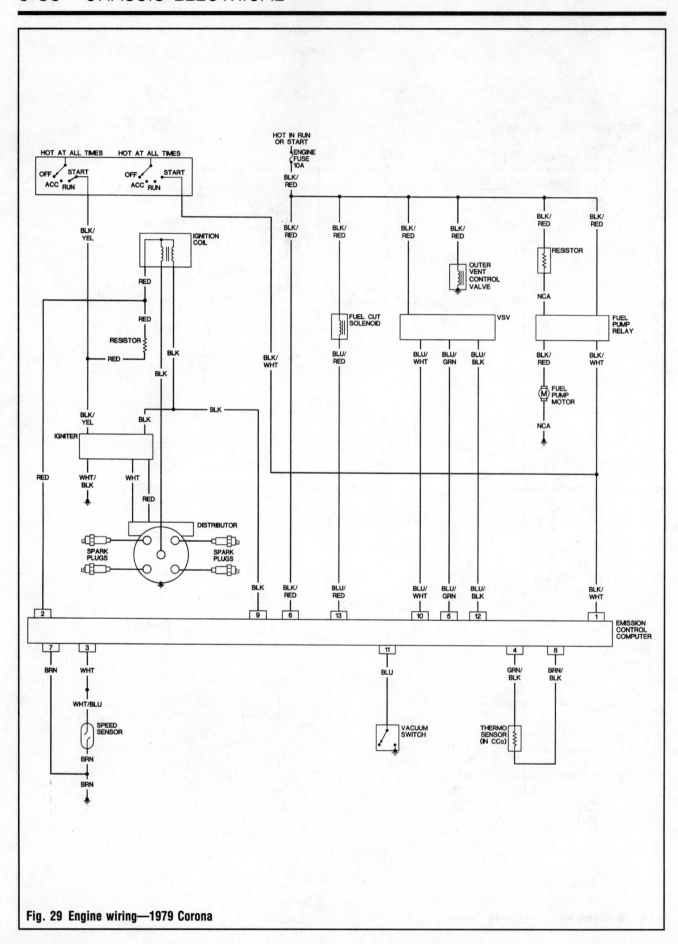

Fig. 29 Engine wiring—1979 Corona

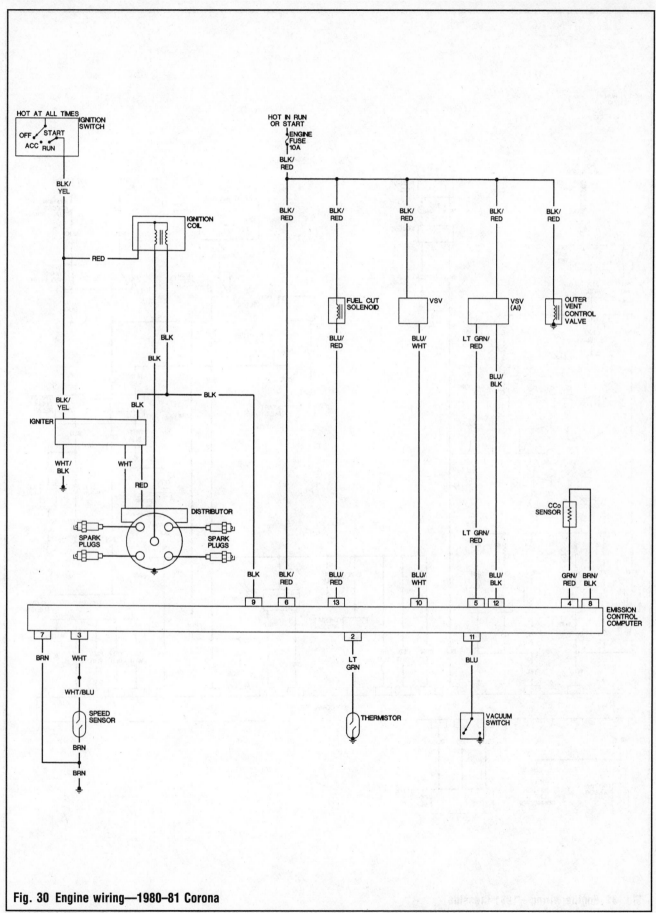

Fig. 30 Engine wiring—1980–81 Corona

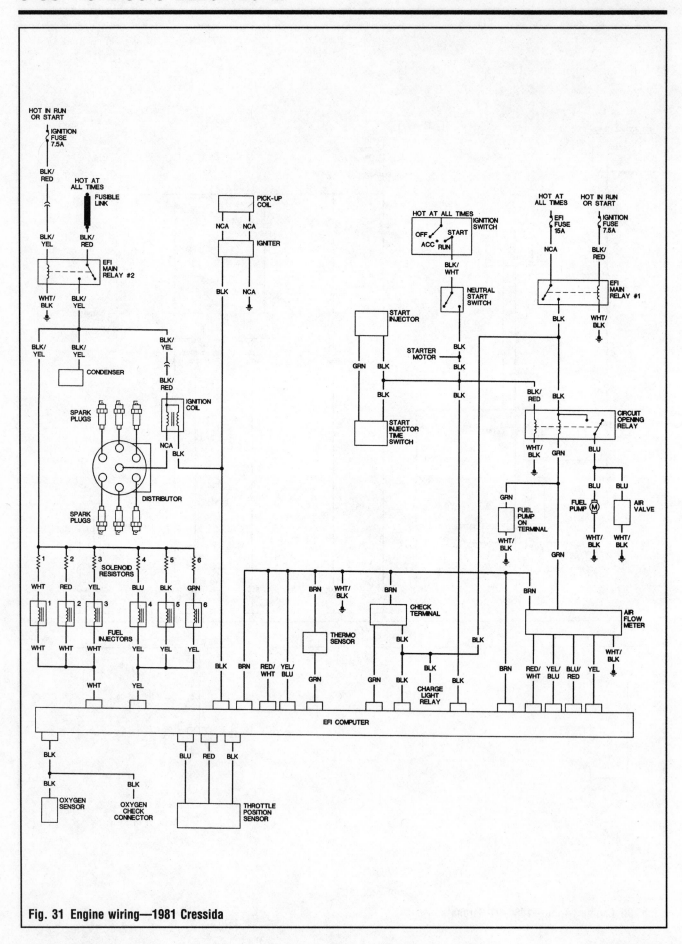

Fig. 31 Engine wiring—1981 Cressida

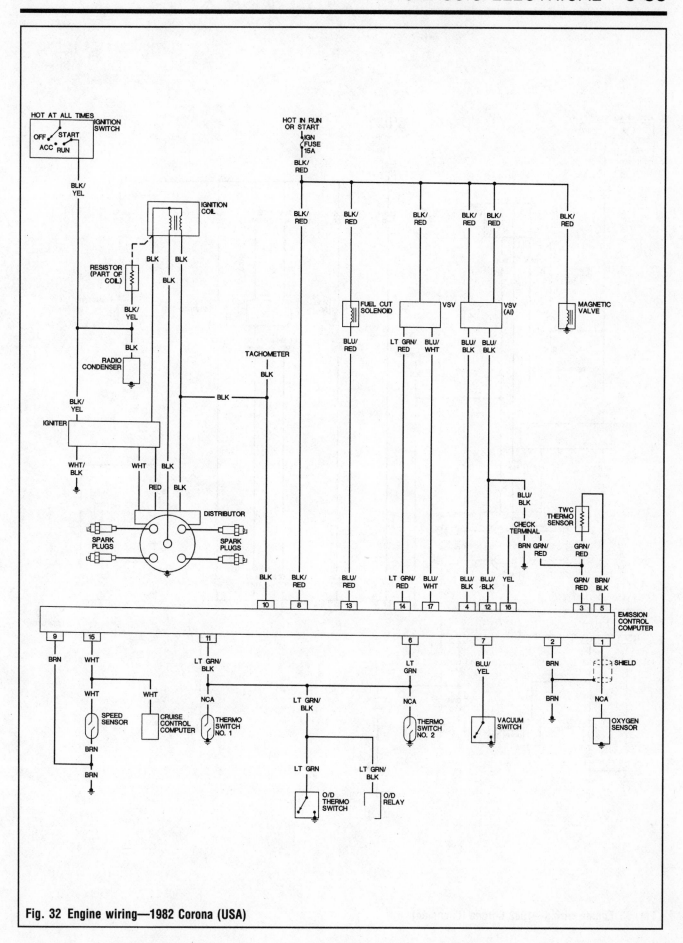

Fig. 32 Engine wiring—1982 Corona (USA)

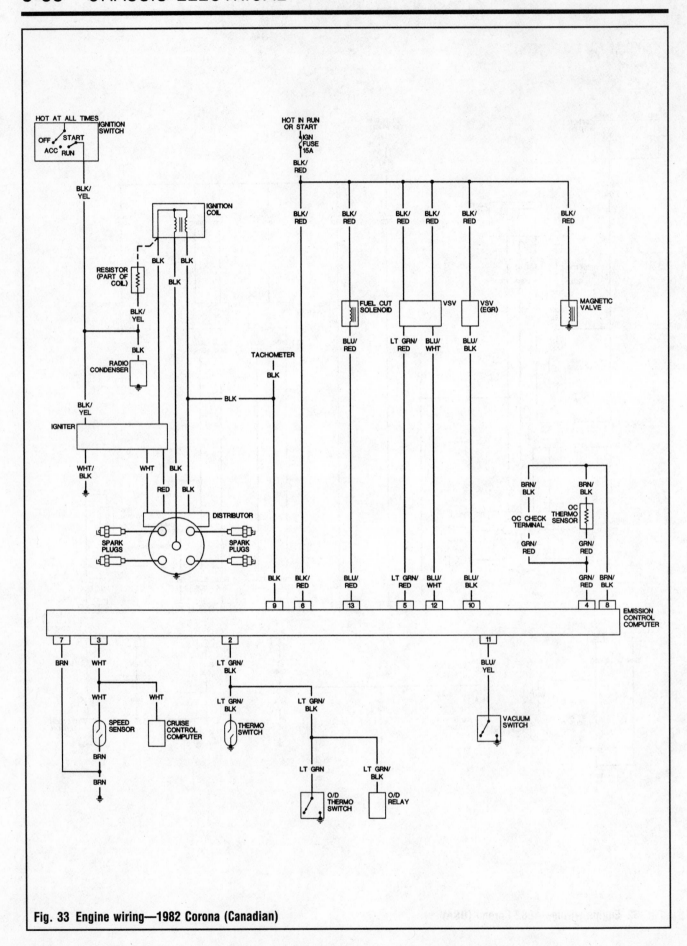

Fig. 33 Engine wiring—1982 Corona (Canadian)

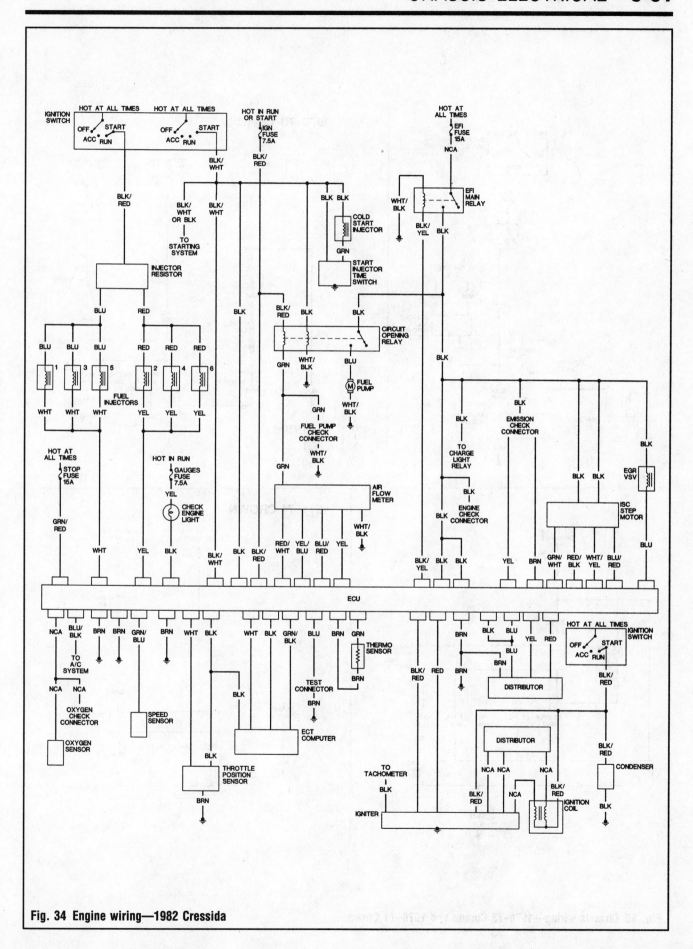

Fig. 34 Engine wiring—1982 Cressida

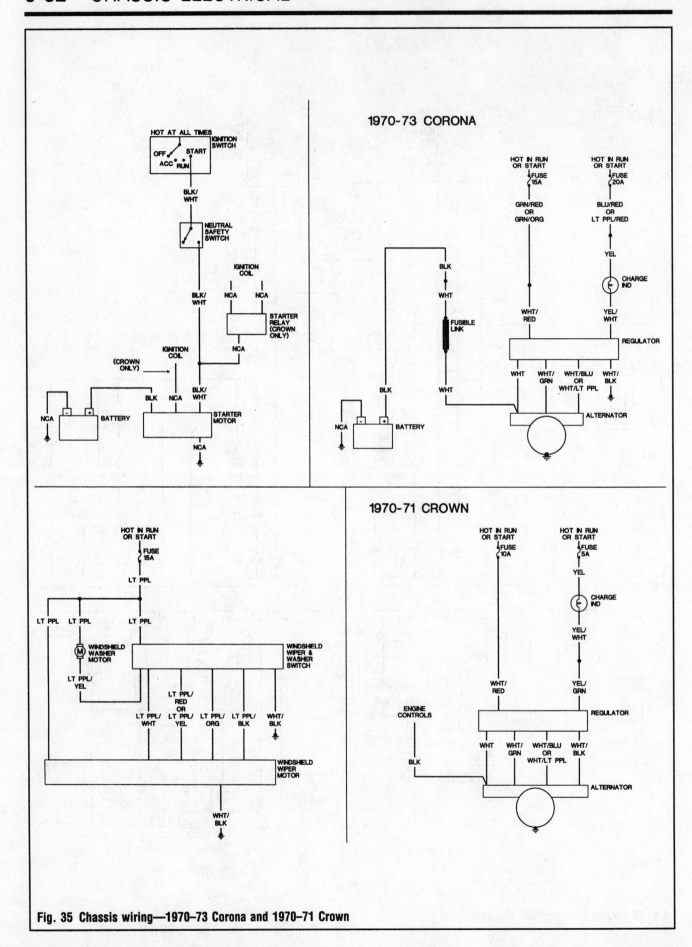

Fig. 35 Chassis wiring—1970–73 Corona and 1970–71 Crown

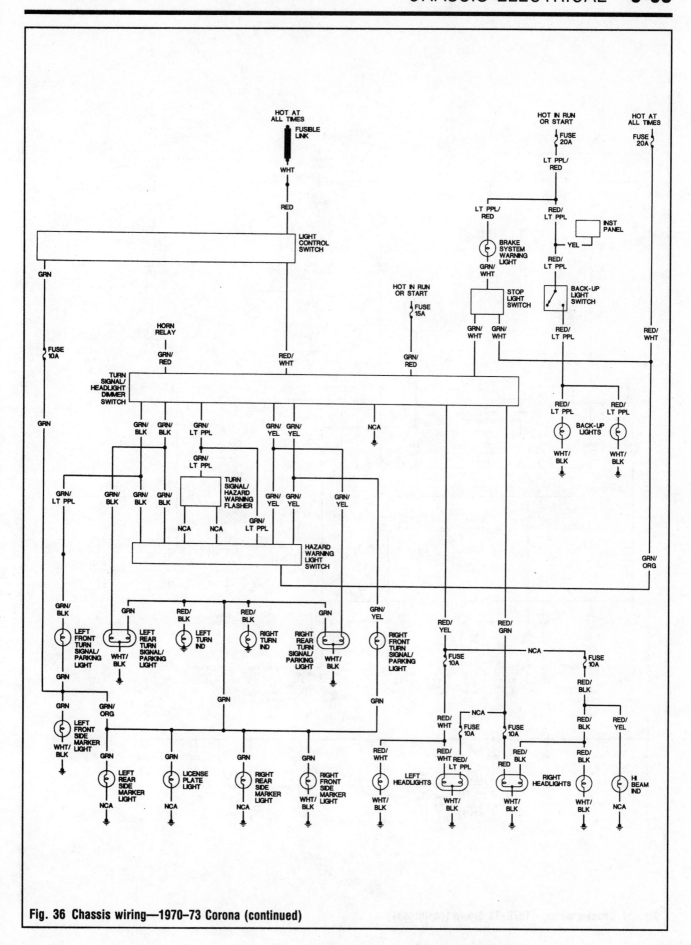

Fig. 36 Chassis wiring—1970-73 Corona (continued)

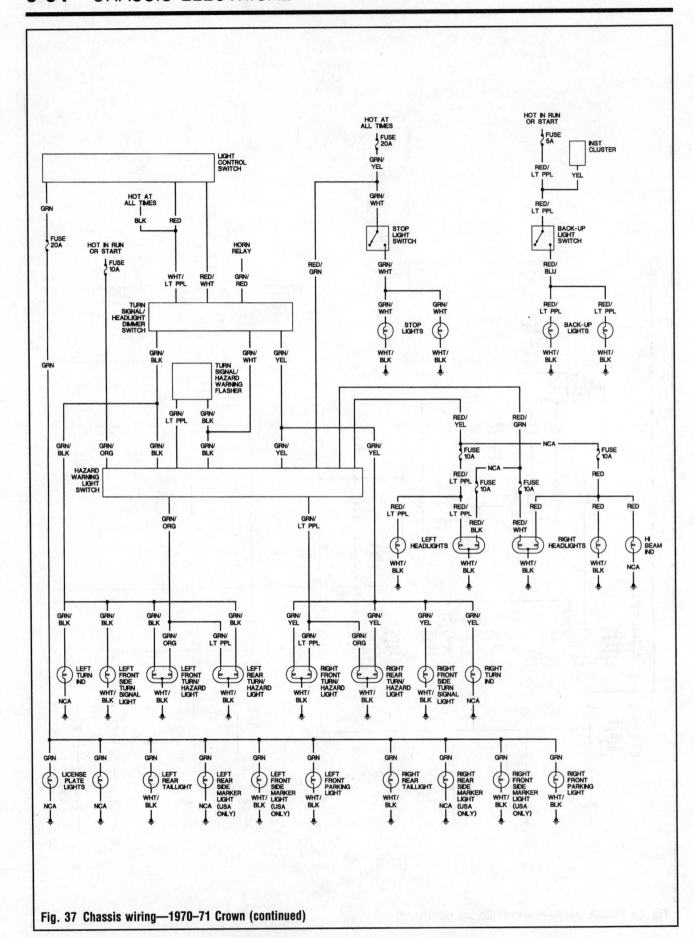

Fig. 37 Chassis wiring—1970–71 Crown (continued)

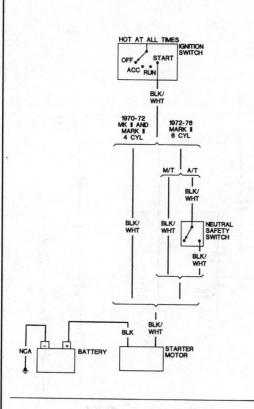

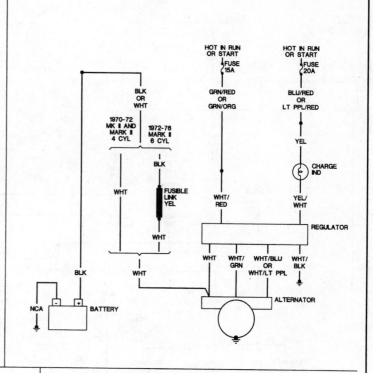

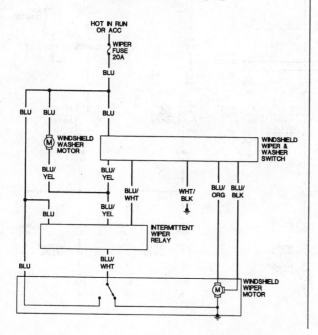

1972-76 MARK II 6 CYL

1970-72 MK II AND MARK II 4 CYL

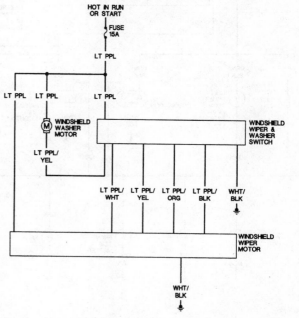

Fig. 38 Chassis wiring—1970–76 Corona Mark II

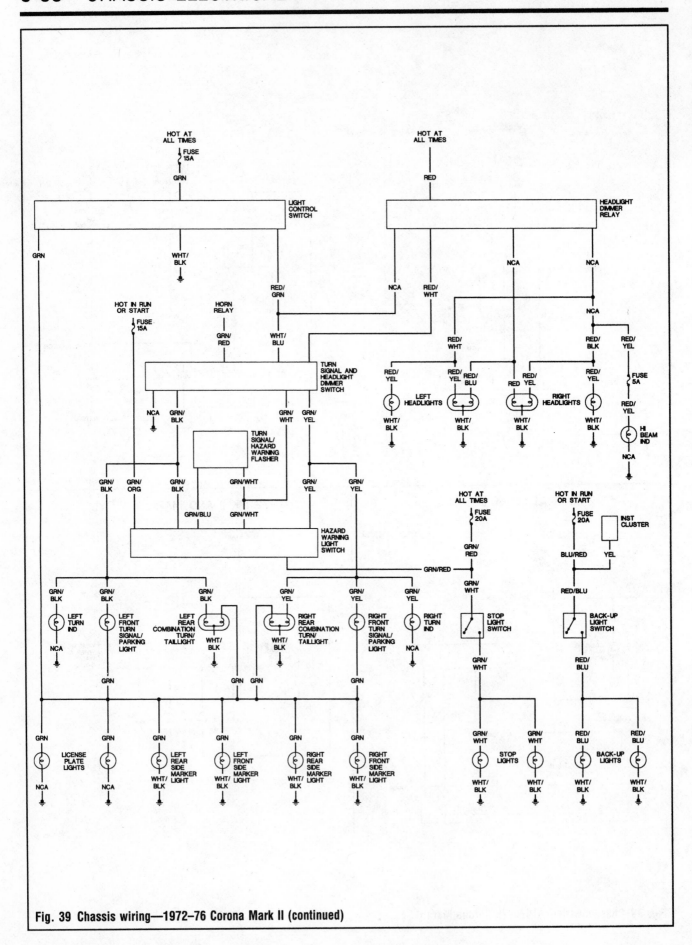

Fig. 39 Chassis wiring—1972–76 Corona Mark II (continued)

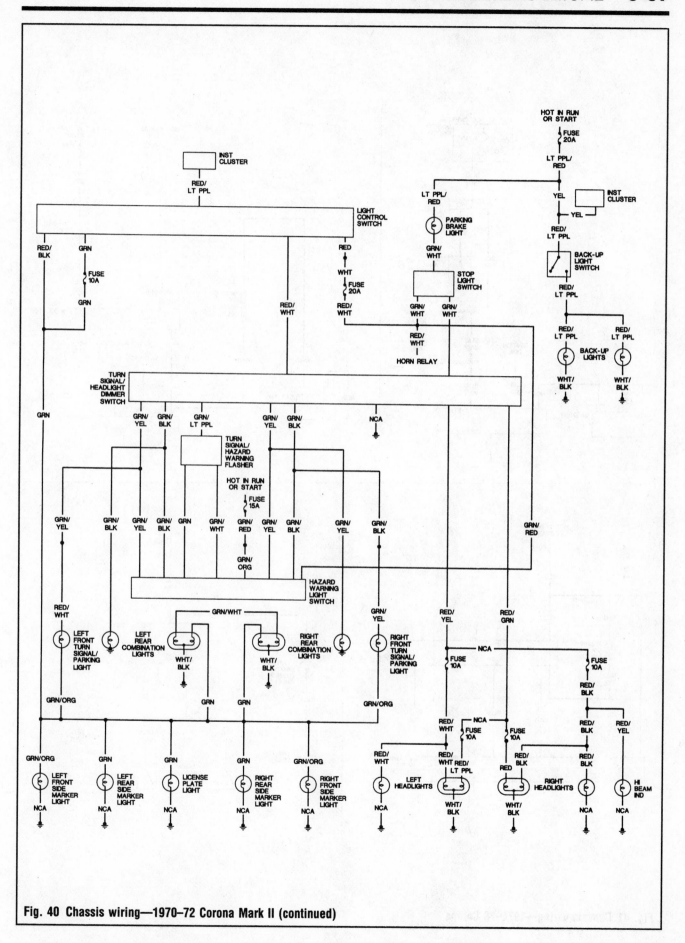

Fig. 40 Chassis wiring—1970-72 Corona Mark II (continued)

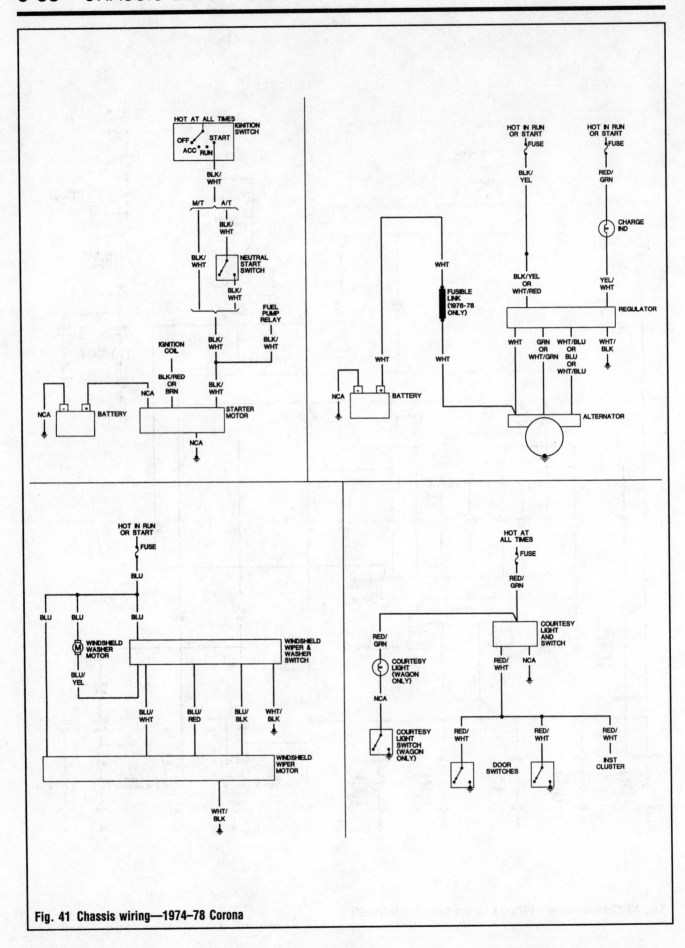

Fig. 41 Chassis wiring—1974-78 Corona

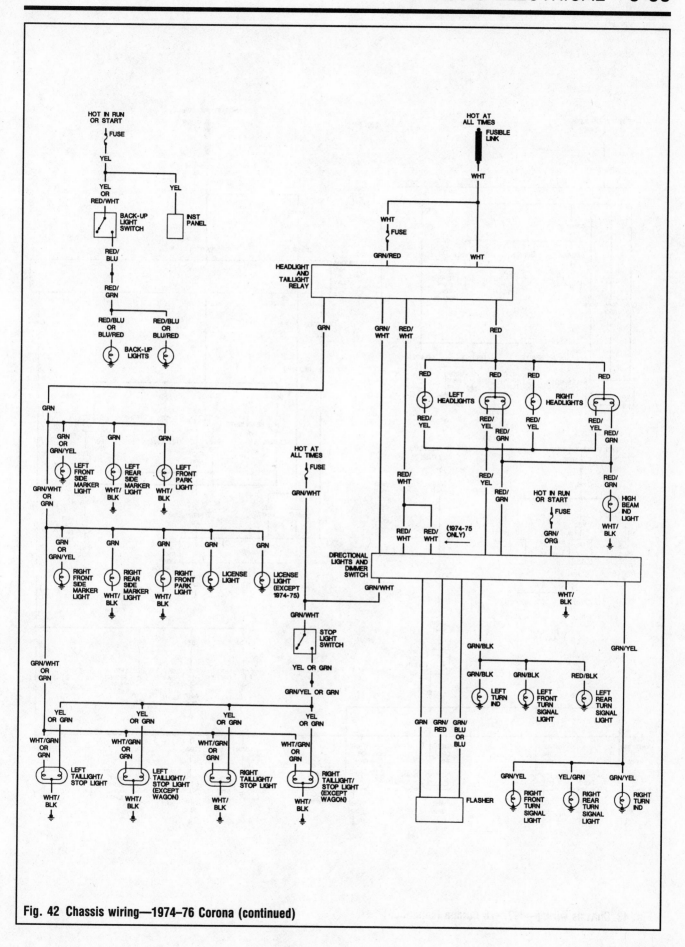

Fig. 42 Chassis wiring—1974-76 Corona (continued)

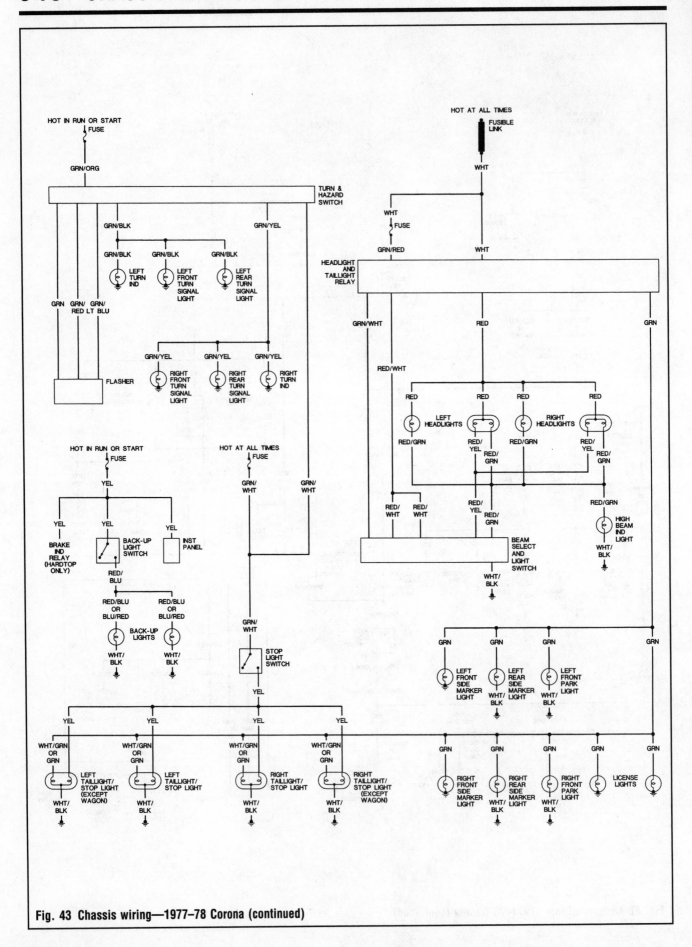

Fig. 43 Chassis wiring—1977-78 Corona (continued)

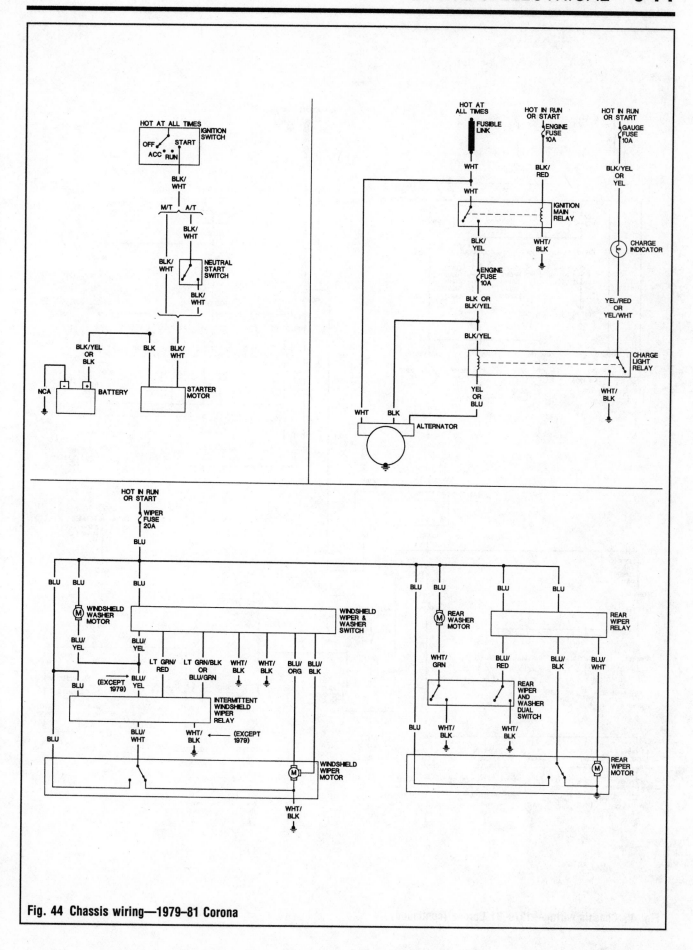

Fig. 44 Chassis wiring—1979-81 Corona

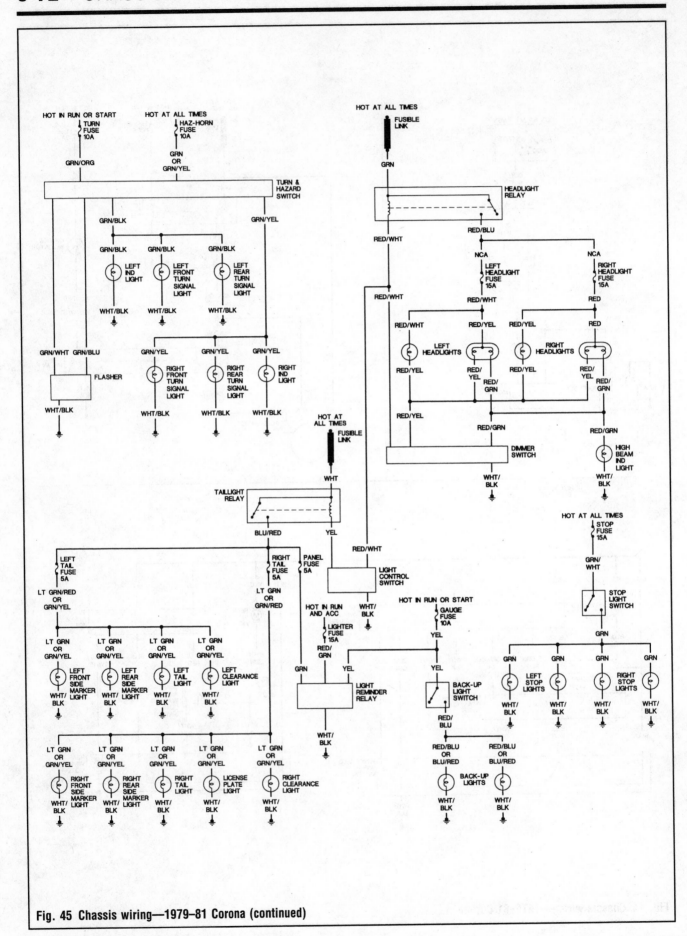

Fig. 45 Chassis wiring—1979–81 Corona (continued)

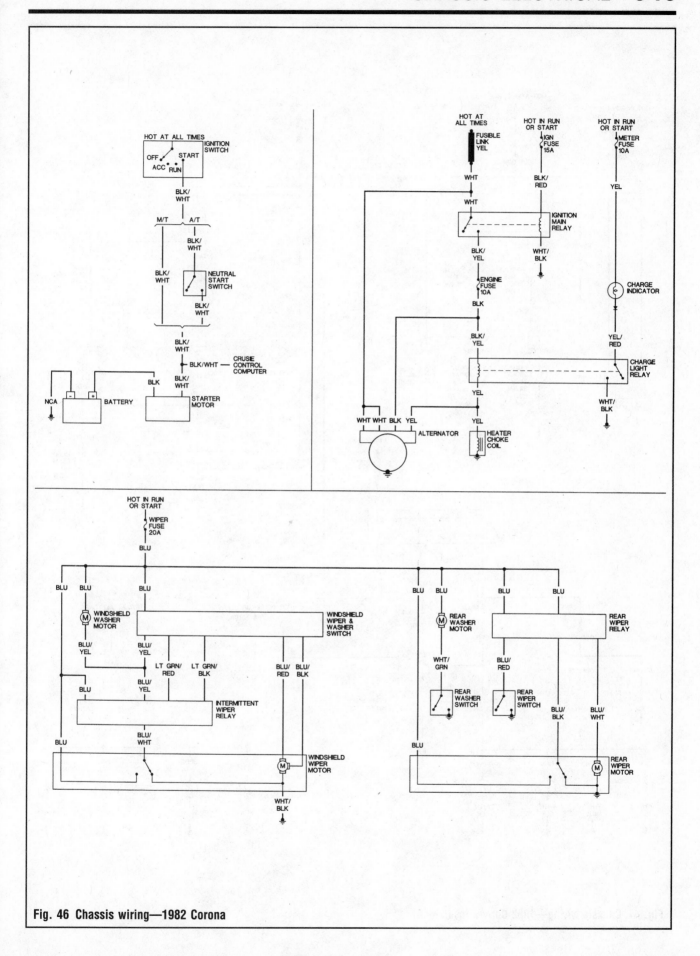

Fig. 46 Chassis wiring—1982 Corona

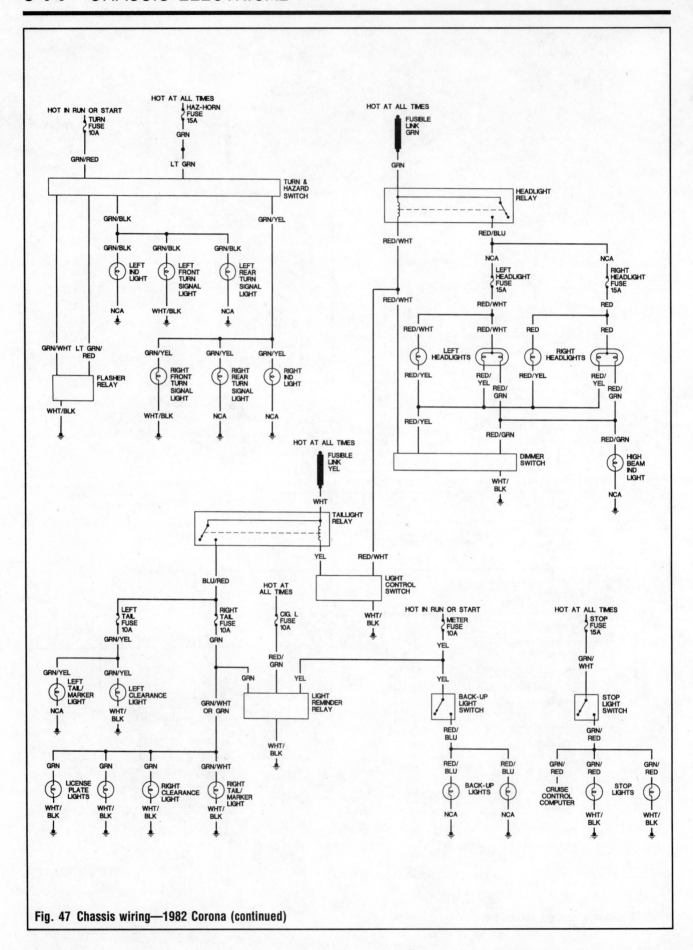

Fig. 47 Chassis wiring—1982 Corona (continued)

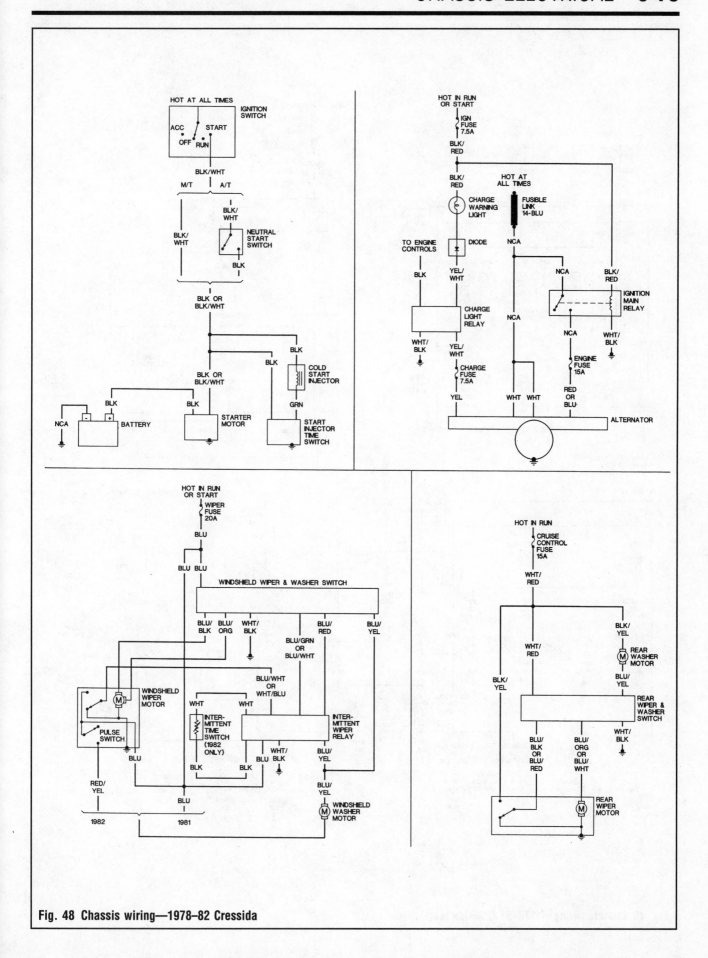

Fig. 48 Chassis wiring—1978–82 Cressida

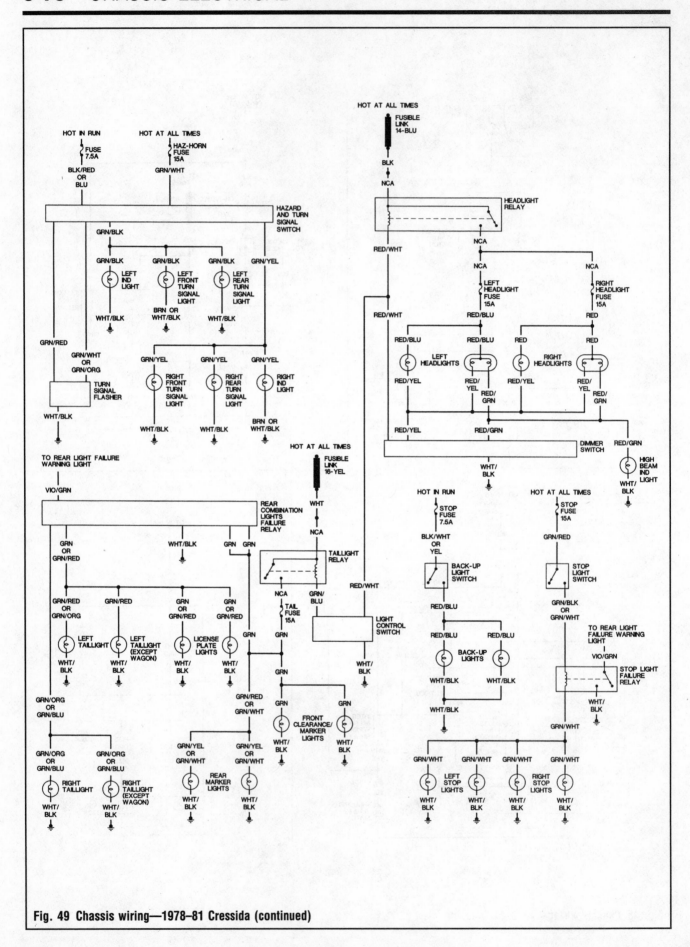

Fig. 49 Chassis wiring—1978-81 Cressida (continued)

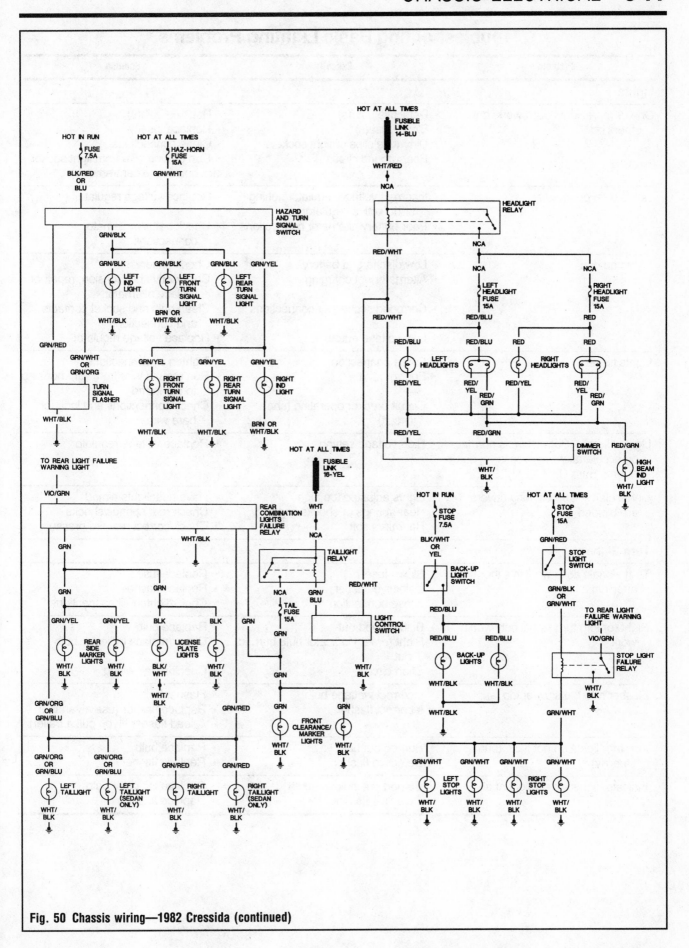

Fig. 50 Chassis wiring—1982 Cressida (continued)

Troubleshooting Basic Lighting Problems

Problem	Cause	Solution
Lights		
One or more lights don't work, but others do	• Defective bulb(s) • Blown fuse(s) • Dirty fuse clips or light sockets • Poor ground circuit	• Replace bulb(s) • Replace fuse(s) • Clean connections • Run ground wire from light socket housing to car frame
Lights burn out quickly	• Incorrect voltage regulator setting or defective regulator • Poor battery/alternator connections	• Replace voltage regulator • Check battery/alternator connections
Lights go dim	• Low/discharged battery • Alternator not charging • Corroded sockets or connections • Low voltage output	• Check battery • Check drive belt tension; repair or replace alternator • Clean bulb and socket contacts and connections • Replace voltage regulator
Lights flicker	• Loose connection • Poor ground • Circuit breaker operating (short circuit)	• Tighten all connections • Run ground wire from light housing to car frame • Check connections and look for bare wires
Lights "flare"—Some flare is normal on acceleration—if excessive, see "Lights Burn Out Quickly"	• High voltage setting	• Replace voltage regulator
Lights glare—approaching drivers are blinded	• Lights adjusted too high • Rear springs or shocks sagging • Rear tires soft	• Have headlights aimed • Check rear springs/shocks • Check/correct rear tire pressure
Turn Signals		
Turn signals don't work in either direction	• Blown fuse • Defective flasher • Loose connection	• Replace fuse • Replace flasher • Check/tighten all connections
Right (or left) turn signal only won't work	• Bulb burned out • Right (or left) indicator bulb burned out • Short circuit	• Replace bulb • Check/replace indicator bulb • Check/repair wiring
Flasher rate too slow or too fast	• Incorrect wattage bulb • Incorrect flasher	• Flasher bulb • Replace flasher (use a variable load flasher if you pull a trailer)
Indicator lights do not flash (burn steadily)	• Burned out bulb • Defective flasher	• Replace bulb • Replace flasher
Indicator lights do not light at all	• Burned out indicator bulb • Defective flasher	• Replace indicator bulb • Replace flasher

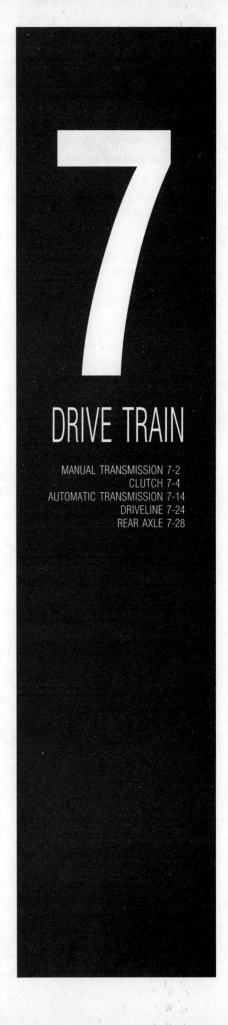

MANUAL TRANSMISSION 7-2
UNDERSTANDING THE MANUAL
  TRANSMISSION 7-2
ADJUSTMENT 7-2
  LINKAGE 7-2
TRANSMISSION ASSEMBLY 7-2
  REMOVAL & INSTALLATION 7-2
CLUTCH 7-4
UNDERSTANDING THE CLUTCH 7-4
ADJUSTMENTS 7-5
  PEDAL HEIGHT 7-5
  FREE-PLAY 7-6
DRIVEN DISC AND PRESSURE
  PLATE 7-6
  REMOVAL & INSTALLATION 7-6
MASTER CYLINDER 7-12
  REMOVAL & INSTALLATION 7-12
  OVERHAUL 7-12
SLAVE CYLINDER 7-12
  REMOVAL & INSTALLATION 7-12
  OVERHAUL 7-12
  HYDRAULIC SYSTEM
    BLEEDING 7-12
AUTOMATIC TRANSMISSION 7-14
UNDERSTANDING AUTOMATIC
  TRANSMISSIONS 7-14
  TORQUE CONVERTER 7-14
  PLANETARY GEARBOX 7-15
  SERVOS AND
    ACCUMULATORS 7-15
  HYDRAULIC CONTROL
    SYSTEM 7-16
IDENTIFICATION 7-16
TRANSMISSION ASSEMBLY 7-16
  REMOVAL & INSTALLATION 7-16
PAN AND FILTER 7-18
  REMOVAL & INSTALLATION 7-18
ADJUSTMENTS 7-21
  FRONT BAND 7-21
  SHIFT LINKAGE 7-22
  THROTTLE LINKAGE 7-22
NEUTRAL SAFETY SWITCH 7-23
  REMOVAL & INSTALLATION 7-23
  ADJUSTMENT 7-23
DRIVELINE 7-24
DRIVESHAFT AND U-JOINTS 7-24
  REMOVAL & INSTALLATION 7-24
  U-JOINT OVERHAUL 7-27
REAR AXLE 7-28
DETERMINING AXLE RATIO 7-28
AXLE SHAFT 7-28
  REMOVAL & INSTALLATION 7-28
COMPONENT LOCATIONS
  DRIVELINE COMPONENTS 7-27
SPECIFICATION CHARTS
  PEDAL HEIGHT SPECIFICATIONS 7-5
  CLUTCH PEDAL FREE-PLAY
    ADJUSTMENTS CHART 7-6
  CLUTCH TORQUE SPECIFICATIONS
    (FT. LBS.) 7-11
TROUBLESHOOTING CHARTS

BASIC DRIVESHAFT AND REAR AXLE
  PROBLEMS 7-30

7

DRIVE TRAIN

MANUAL TRANSMISSION 7-2
CLUTCH 7-4
AUTOMATIC TRANSMISSION 7-14
DRIVELINE 7-24
REAR AXLE 7-28

MANUAL TRANSMISSION

Understanding the Manual Transmission

Because of the way an internal combustion engine breathes, it can produce torque (or twisting force) only within a narrow speed range. Most overhead valve pushrod engines must turn at about 2500 rpm to produce their peak torque. Often by 4500 rpm, they are producing so little torque that continued increases in engine speed produce no power increases.

The torque peak on overhead camshaft engines is, generally, much higher, but much narrower.

The manual transmission and clutch are employed to vary the relationship between engine RPM and the speed of the wheels so that adequate power can be produced under all circumstances. The clutch allows engine torque to be applied to the transmission input shaft gradually, due to mechanical slippage. The vehicle can, consequently, be started smoothly from a full stop.

The transmission changes the ratio between the rotating speeds of the engine and the wheels by the use of gears. 4-speed or 5-speed transmissions are most common. The lower gears allow full engine power to be applied to the rear wheels during acceleration at low speeds.

The clutch driveplate is a thin disc, the center of which is splined to the transmission input shaft. Both sides of the disc are covered with a layer of material which is similar to brake lining and which is capable of allowing slippage without roughness or excessive noise.

The clutch cover is bolted to the engine flywheel and incorporates a diaphragm spring which provides the pressure to engage the clutch. The cover also houses the pressure plate. When the clutch pedal is released, the driven disc is sandwiched between the pressure plate and the smooth surface of the flywheel, thus forcing the disc to turn at the same speed as the engine crankshaft.

The transmission contains a mainshaft which passes all the way through the transmission, from the clutch to the driveshaft. This shaft is separated at one point, so that front and rear portions can turn at different speeds.

Power is transmitted by a countershaft in the lower gears and reverse. The gears of the countershaft mesh with gears on the mainshaft, allowing power to be carried from one to the other. Countershaft gears are often integral with that shaft, while several of the mainshaft gears can either rotate independently of the shaft or be locked to it. Shifting from one gear to the next causes one of the gears to be freed from rotating with the shaft and locks another to it. Gears are locked and unlocked by internal dog clutches which slide between the center of the gear and the shaft. The forward gears usually employ synchronizers; friction members which smoothly bring gear and shaft to the same speed before the toothed dog clutches are engaged.

Adjustment

LINKAGE

All Toyota passenger cars equipped with floor mounted shifters have internally mounted shift linkage. On some older models, the linkage is contained in the side cover which is bolted on the transmission case. All of the other models have the linkage mounted inside the top of the transmission case, itself.

No external adjustments are needed or possible.

Transmission Assembly

REMOVAL & INSTALLATION

Corona (1970–73) and Mark II 4-Cylinder
◆ See Figure 1

1. Unfasten the cable from the negative battery terminal.
2. Remove the accelerator torque rod from its valve cover mounting.
3. Separate the downpipe from the flange and remove the flange. Remove the exhaust pipe bracket.
4. Raise the car with a jack and support it with jackstands.

✳✳ CAUTION

Be sure that the car is securely supported. Remember, you will be working underneath it.

4. Remove the parking brake equalizer support bracket.
5. Unfasten the speedometer cable and back up lamp wiring harness from the transmission.
6. Remove the control shaft lever retainer.
7. Remove the clutch release cylinder from the transmission and set it up, out of the way.

➡**Do not disconnect the hydraulic line from the release cylinder.**

8. Drain the transmission oil.
9. Remove the driveshaft.

➡**To prevent oil from draining out of the transmission, cover the opening with a plastic bag secured by a rubber band.**

10. Support the transmission with a jack.

➡**Place a support under the engine to prevent the total weight from being supported by the front mounts. Be careful of oil pan damage.**

11. Unfasten the rear engine mounts and remove the engine rear support crossmember (see Section 3).
12. Lower the jack.
13. Unfasten the bolts securing the clutch housing to the cylinder block.
14. Remove the transmission toward the rear of the car.
15. Installation is the reverse of removal. However, before installing the transmission apply a light coating of multipurpose grease to the input shaft end, input shaft spline, clutch release bearing and the driveshaft end. After installation, fill the transmission and the cooling system. Adjust the clutch.

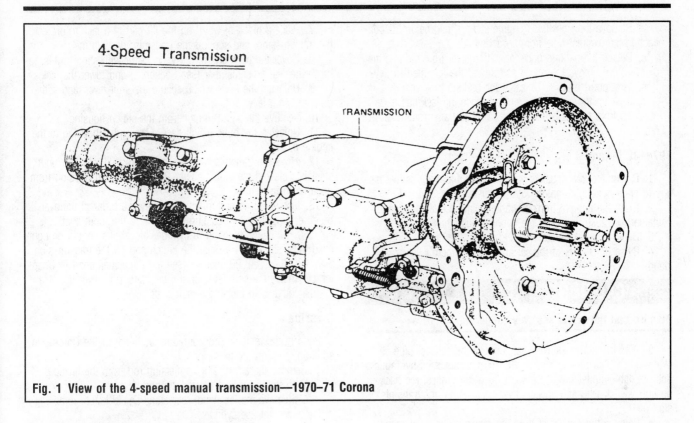

4-Speed Transmission

TRANSMISSION

Fig. 1 View of the 4-speed manual transmission—1970–71 Corona

Mark II 6-Cylinder and Crown 2600

Working from inside of the car, perform the following:

1. Place the gear selector in Neutral. Remove the center console, if so equipped.
2. Remove the trim boot at the base of the shift lever and the boot underneath it on the shift tower.
3. Unfasten the four shift lever plate returning screws.
4. Withdraw the shift lever assembly.
5. Remove the gasket.

➡ **Cover the hole with a clean cloth to prevent anything from falling into the transmission case.**

Working in the engine compartment perform the following:

6. Drain the cooling system and disconnect the cable from the negative side of the battery.
7. Remove the radiator hoses.
8. Separate the downpipe from the flange and remove the flange. Remove the exhaust pipe bracket.
9. Raise the car with a jack and support it with jackstands.

✳✳ CAUTION

Be sure that the car is securely supported with jackstands. Remember, you will be working underneath it.

10. Drain the transmission oil.
11. Detach the exhaust pipe from the manifold and remove the exhaust pipe support bracket.
12. Remove the driveshaft.

➡ **It will be necessary to plug the opening in the end of the transmission with an old yoke or, if none is available, cover it with a plastic bag secured by a rubber band.**

13. Unfasten the speedometer cable from the right side of the transmission.
14. Remove the clutch release cylinder assembly from the transmission and tie it aside, so that it is out of the way.
15. Unplug the back-up lamp switch connector.
16. Support the transmission with a jack.
17. Unfasten the engine rear mounts. (See Section 3). Remove the rear crossmember.

➡ **Be sure to support the engine so that total weight will not be on the front mounts. Be careful of oil pan damage.**

18. Unbolt the clutch housing from the engine and withdraw the transmission assembly.
19. Installation is performed in the reverse order of removal, but remember to perform the following during installation.

Apply a light coating of multipurpose grease to the input shaft end, input shaft spline, clutch release bearing, and driveshaft end.

After installation, fill the transmission and the cooling system. Adjust the clutch.

Crown 2300

Perform the removal procedure as previously outlined for the Corona (1970–73) and Mark II 4-cylinder. In addition, perform the following steps:

1. Working under the hood:
   a. Disconnect the radiator hoses after draining the cooling system.
   b. Remove the air cleaner assembly complete with hoses.
   c. Detach the connecting rod from the accelerator linkage, before removing the torque rod.
2. With car jacked up and supported, perform the following:
   a. Disconnect the starter wiring and remove the starter.

b. Remove the right-hand engine stone shield before disconnecting the exhaust pipe from the manifold.

c. Detach the parking brake operating lever from the intermediate lever. Remove the return spring and the intermediate lever from its support bracket. Unfasten the parking brake cable.

d. Jack up the front of the engine, once the jack has been removed from the transmission, to facilitate transmission removal.

1974–82 Corona

1. Disconnect the negative battery cable, then the positive battery-to-starter cable, complete with the fusible link.

2. Drain the coolant from the radiator into a suitable clean container for reuse. Unfasten the upper radiator hose.

3. Detach the accelerator rod and link at the firewall side.

4. Raise both ends of the car and support them with jackstands.

❊❊ CAUTION

Be sure that the car is securely supported.

5. Working underneath the car, remove the exhaust pipe clamp and clutch release cylinder (Don't disconnect its hydraulic line, set the cylinder out of the way). Next, disconnect the backup light switch lead and speedometer cable. Drain the transmission oil.

6. Remove the driveshaft from the transmission, after matchmarking it and the companion flange for assembly.

➡**To prevent oil from draining out of the transmission, cover the opening with a plastic bag secured with a rubber band.**

7. Place a block of wood on the lift pad of a jack to protect the transmission, and support the transmission with the jack.

8. Cover the back end of the valve cover with shop towels, remove the rear crossmember (see Section 3) and lower the jack.

9. Unfasten the bolts which secure the shift lever, and withdraw the shift lever.

10. Remove the starter motor from the clutch housing.

11. Unfasten the bolts which secure the clutch housing to the engine block.

12. Move the transmission and jack rearward, until the input shaft has cleared the clutch cover. Remove the transmission from underneath the car.

13. Installation is performed in the reverse order of removal. Be sure to apply a thin coating of grease to the input shaft splines. The clutch housing-to-cylinder blockbolts should be tightened to 37–58 ft. lbs. Adjust the clutch and fill the transmission with API GL-4 SAE 90 gear oil (see the Capacities chart in Chapter 1). Grease the shift lever spring seat and shift lever tip. Use the matchmarks to install the driveshaft.

Cressida

Perform the removal procedures as outlined for the Corona. In addition, perform the following:

1. Remove the accelerator connecting rod from the linkage.

2. With the car jacked up and supported:

a. Remove the left-hand, rear stone shield before removing the clutch release cylinder.

b. Remove the flywheel housing lower cover and its braces.

3. Installation is the reverse or removal.

➡**Use a clutch guide tool, during installation, to locate the clutch disc.**

CLUTCH

Understanding the Clutch

The purpose of the clutch is to disconnect and connect engine power at the transmission. A vehicle at rest requires a lot of engine torque to get all that weight moving. An internal combustion engine does not develop a high starting torque (unlike steam engines) so it must be allowed to operate without any load until it builds up enough torque to move the vehicle. To a point, torque increases with engine rpm. The clutch allows the engine to build up torque by physically disconnecting the engine from the transmission, relieving the engine of any load or resistance.

The transfer of engine power to the transmission (the load) must be smooth and gradual; if it weren't, drive line components would wear out or break quickly. This gradual power transfer is made possible by gradually releasing the clutch pedal. The clutch disc and pressure plate are the connecting link between the engine and transmission. When the clutch pedal is released, the disc and plate contact each other (the clutch is engaged) physically joining the engine and transmission. When the pedal is pushed in, the disc and plate separate (the clutch is disengaged) disconnecting the engine from the transmission.

Most clutch assemblies consists of the flywheel, the clutch disc, the clutch pressure plate, the throw out bearing and fork, the actuating linkage and the pedal. The flywheel and clutch pressure plate (driving members) are connected to the engine crankshaft and rotate with it. The clutch disc is located between the flywheel and pressure plate, and is splined to the transmission shaft. A driving member is one that is attached to the engine and transfers engine power to a driven member (clutch disc) on the transmission shaft. A driving member (pressure plate) rotates (drives) a driven member (clutch disc) on contact and, in so doing, turns the transmission shaft.

There is a circular diaphragm spring within the pressure plate cover (transmission side). In a relaxed state (when the clutch pedal is fully released) this spring is convex; that is, it is dished outward toward the transmission. Pushing in the clutch pedal actuates the attached linkage. Connected to the other end of this is the throw out fork, which hold the throw out bearing. When the clutch pedal is depressed, the clutch linkage pushes the fork and bearing forward to contact the diaphragm spring of the pressure plate. The outer edges of the spring are secured to the pressure plate and are pivoted on rings so that when the center of the spring is compressed by the throw out bearing, the outer edges bow outward and, by so doing, pull the pressure plate in the same direction away from the clutch disc. This action separates the disc from the plate, disengaging the clutch and allowing the transmission to be shifted into another gear. A coil type clutch return spring attached to the clutch pedal arm permits full release of the pedal. Releasing the pedal pulls the throw out bearing away from the diaphragm spring resulting in a reversal of spring position. As bearing pressure is gradually released from the spring center, the outer edges of the spring bow outward, pushing the pressure plate into closer contact with the clutch disc. As the disc and plate move closer together, friction between the two increases and slippage is reduced until, when full spring pressure is applied (by fully releasing the pedal) the speed of the disc and plate are the same. This stops all slipping, creating a direct connection between the plate and disc which results in the transfer of power from the engine to the transmission. The clutch disc is now rotating with the pressure plate at engine speed and, because it is splined to the transmission shaft, the shaft now turns at the same engine speed.

The clutch is operating properly if:

1. It will stall the engine when released with the vehicle held stationary.

2. The shift lever can be moved freely between 1st and reverse gears when the vehicle is stationary and the clutch disengaged.

Adjustments

PEDAL HEIGHT

♦ **See Figures 2 and 3**

Adjust the pedal height to the specification given in the following chart, by rotating the pedal stop (nut).

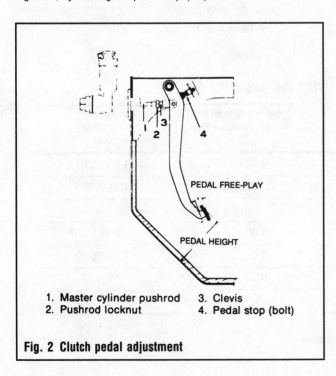

1. Master cylinder pushrod
2. Pushrod locknut
3. Clevis
4. Pedal stop (bolt)

Fig. 2 Clutch pedal adjustment

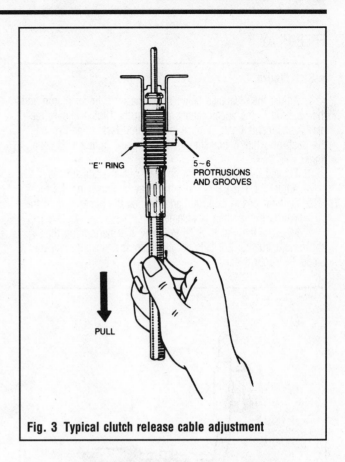

Fig. 3 Typical clutch release cable adjustment

Pedal Height Specifications

Model	Height (In.)	Measure Between:
Corona ('70–'73)	5.7–6.1	Pedal pad and floor mat
Corona ('74–'77)	6.3–6.7	Pedal pad and top of asphalt
Corona ('78–'82)	6.5–6.9	Pedal pad and floor mat
Mark II 4-cylinder	6.0–6.2	Pedal pad and top of floor panel
Mark II 6-cylinder	6.2–6.6 ①	Pedal pad and asphalt seat
Crown 2300	5.7	Pedal pad and floor
Crown 2600	6.8	Pedal pad and asphalt seat
Cressida	6.1–6.5	From floor mat
Camry	7.6–8.0	Pedal pad and kickpanel

① 1976—6–6.4

FREE-PLAY

◆ **See Figure 4**

1. Adjust the clearance between the master cylinder piston and the pushrod to the specifications given in the Clutch Pedal Free-play Adjustments chart. Loosen the pushrod locknut and rotate the pushrod while depressing the clutch pedal lightly with your finger.

2. Tighten the locknut when finished with the adjustment.

3. Adjust the release cylinder free-play by loosening the release cylinder pushrod locknut and rotating the pushrod until the specification in the chart is obtained.

4. Measure the clutch pedal free-play after performing the above adjustments. If it fails to fall within specifications, repeat Steps 1–3 until it does.

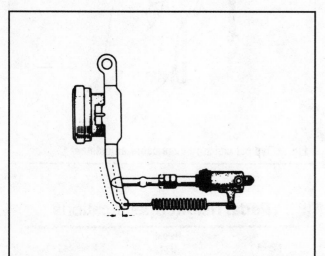

Fig. 4 Release (slave) cylinder free-play is the distance between the arrows

Driven Disc and Pressure Plate

REMOVAL & INSTALLATION

◆ **See Figure 5**

✳✳ WARNING

Do not drain the transmission oil and do not allow grease or oil to get on any part of the clutch disc, pressure plate or flywheel surfaces.

1. Remove the transmission from the car as previously detailed.

2. Loosen the set bolts one turn at a time until the spring tension is relieved.

3. Remove the set bolts and then pull off the clutch assembly.

4. Unfasten the release fork bearing clips. Withdraw the release bearing hub, complete with the release bearing.

5. Remove the tension spring from the clutch linkage.

6. Remove the release fork and support.

7. Punch matchmarks on the clutch cover and the pressure plate so that the pressure plate can be returned to its original position during installation.

✳✳ CAUTION

If the screws are released too fast, the clutch assembly will fly apart, causing possible injury or loss of parts.

8. Slowly unfasten the screws which attach the retracting springs.

9. Separate the clutch cover and pressure plate from the clutch disc/spring assembly.

Clutch Pedal Free-Play Adjustments

Model	Master Cylinder Piston to Pushrod Clearance (in.)	Release Cylinder to Release Fork Free-Play (in.)	Pedal Free-Play (in.)
Corona 2000	0.02–0.12	0.08–0.14	1.00–1.75
Corona 2000/2200 ④	—	0.08–0.12 ⑥	0.04–0.28 ⑤
Corona 1978–80	Not adj	Not adj	0.51–0.91
Mark II 4-cylinder	①	0.08–0.14	0.79–1.58 ⑦
Mark II 6-cylinder	0.02–0.12	0.08–0.12	1.20–1.80
Crown 2300	0.02–0.10 ②	0.08–0.14	1.40–2.00
Crown 2600	0.02–0.12	0.08–0.14 ③	1.40–2.20

① Not adjustable
② Measured at clutch pedal
③ Adjustable type only
④ 1975–79
⑤ 1978–79: 0.2–0.6
⑥ 1978–79: Not adjustable
⑦ 1976—0.04–0.28

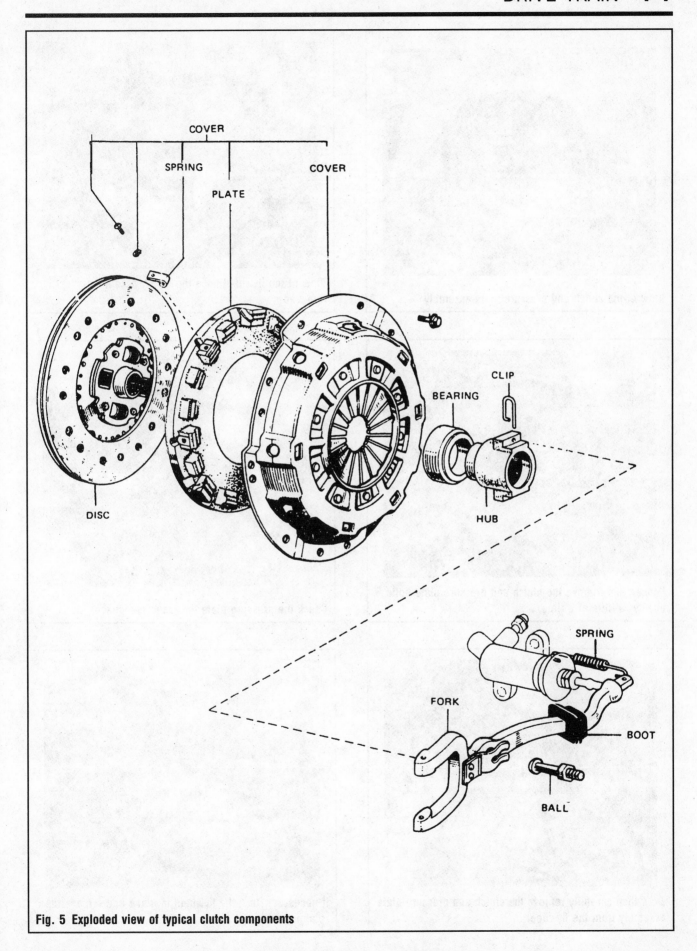

Fig. 5 Exploded view of typical clutch components

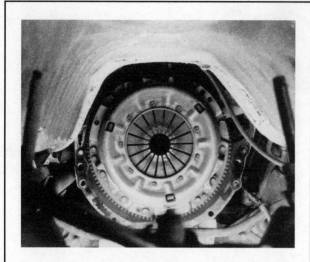

View of the clutch and pressure plate assembly

View of the flywheel once the clutch assembly is removed

Loosen and remove the clutch and pressure plate bolts evenly, a little at a time . . .

Check the pressure plate for excessive wear

. . . then carefully remove the clutch and pressure plate assembly from the flywheel

If necessary, lock the flywheel in place and remove the retaining bolts . . .

. . . then remove the flywheel from the crankshaft in order replace it or have it machined

Install a clutch alignment arbor, to align the clutch assembly during installation

Upon installation, it is usually a good idea to apply a thread-locking compound to the flywheel bolts

Clutch plate installed with the arbor in place

Be sure that the flywheel surface is clean, before installing the clutch

Pressure plate-to-flywheel bolt holes should align

You may want to use a thread locking compound on the clutch assembly bolts

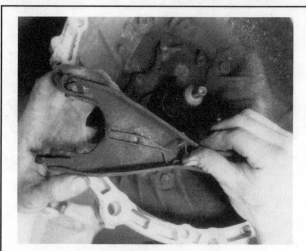

View of the clutch release fork, check this for signs of damage

Be sure to use a torque wrench to tighten all bolts

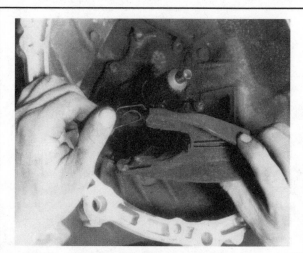

View of the clutch release fork bearing clips, make sure these are not bent or broken

Grease the clutch release fork ball

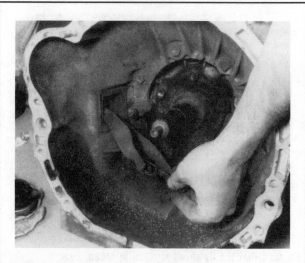

Removing the clutch release fork bearing clips

Grease the throwout bearing assembly at the outer contact points

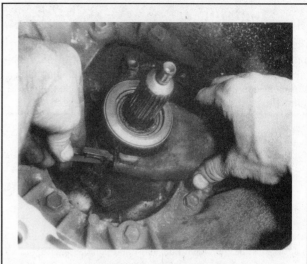

Installing the clutch release fork bearing clip

Grease the throwout bearing assembly at the inner contact points

View of the clutch release fork assembly installed, be sure all parts move freely

Clutch Torque Specifications (ft. lbs.)

Model	Release Fork	Retracting Spring Bolts	Clutch Cover-to-Flywheel Bolts
Corona	13.7–22.4	10.9–15.9	7.2–11.6 ②
Mark II/4	14–22	—	11
Mark II/6	—	2.9–5.1	10.8–15.9
Crown 2300	—	3–5	6–9.5
Crown 2600	—	2.9–5.1	7.2–11.6

① 1975 Corolla—15–16 ft. lbs.; 1976 and later—10.9–15.9 ft. lbs.
② 1976 and later—10.9–15.9 ft. lbs.

✳✳ CAUTION

The clutch driven disc may contain asbestos, which has been determined to be a cancer causing agent. Avoid inhaling any dust from any clutch surface! When cleaning clutch surfaces, use a commercially available brake cleaning fluid. Never clean clutch surfaces with compressed air.

10. Inspect the parts for wear or deterioration. Replace parts as required.

11. Installation is performed in the reverse order of removal. Several points should be noted, however.

 a. Be sure to align the matchmarks on the clutch cover and pressure plate which were made during disassembly.

 b. Apply a thin coating of multi-purpose grease to the release bearing hub and release fork contact points. Pack the groove inside the clutch hub with multi-purpose grease.

 c. Center the clutch disc by using a clutch pilot tool or an old input shaft. Insert the pilot into the end of the input shaft front bearing and bolt the clutch to the flywheel.

➡ **Bolt the clutch assembly to the flywheel in two or three stages, evenly to 15–22 ft. lbs. (20–29 Nm).**

12. Adjust the clutch as outlined earlier in this section.

Master Cylinder

REMOVAL & INSTALLATION

▶ **See Figure 6**

1. Remove the clevis pin.
2. Detach the hydraulic line from the tube.

✳✳ WARNING

Do not spill brake fluid on the painted surfaces of the vehicle.

3. Unfasten the bolts which secure the master cylinder to the firewall. Withdraw the assembly.

4. Installation is the reverse of removal. Bleed the system as detailed following. Adjust the clutch pedal height and free-play as previously detailed.

OVERHAUL

1. Clamp the master cylinder body in a vise with soft jaws.
2. Separate the reservoir assembly from the master cylinder.
3. Remove the snapring and remove the pushrod/piston assembly.
4. Inspect all of the parts and replace any which are worn or defective.

➡ **Honing of the cylinder may be necessary to smooth pitting.**

To install:

5. Coat all parts with clean brake fluid, prior to assembly.
6. Install the piston assembly in the cylinder bore.

7. Fit the pushrod over the washer and secure them with the snapring.
8. Install the reservoir.

Slave Cylinder

REMOVAL & INSTALLATION

▶ **See Figure 7 (p. 14)**

✳✳ WARNING

Avoid spilling brake fluid on any painted surface.

1. Raise and support the front end on jackstands.
2. Remove the gravel shield to gain access to the slave cylinder.
3. Remove the clutch fork return spring.
4. Disconnect the hydraulic line from the slave cylinder.
5. Screw the threaded end of the pushrod in.
6. Remove the cylinder attaching nuts and pull out the cylinder.
7. Installation is the reverse of removal.

OVERHAUL

1. Remove the pushrod and rubber boot.
2. Remove the piston, with cup. Don't remove the cup unless you are replacing it.
3. Wash all parts in clean brake fluid. Inspect all parts for wear or damage. The bore can be honed to remove minor imperfections. If it is severely pitted or scored, the cylinder must be replaced. If piston-to-bore clearance is greater than 0.006 inches, replace the unit.
4. Assembly is the reverse of disassembly. Coat all parts with clean brake fluid prior to assembly.

HYDRAULIC SYSTEM BLEEDING

➡ **This operation must be performed any time the clutch master or slave cylinder has been removed, or if any of the hydraulic lines have been opened.**

1. Fill the master cylinder reservoir with brake fluid.

✳✳ WARNING

Do not spill brake fluid on the painted surfaces of the vehicle. If fluid is spilt, immediately wash the surface with plenty of clean water.

2. Remove the cap and loosen the bleeder plug. Block the outlet hole with your finger.

3. Pump the clutch pedal several times, then take your finger from the hole while depressing the clutch pedal. Allow the air to flow out. Place your finger back over the hole and release the pedal.

4. After fluid pressure can be felt (with your finger), tighten the bleeder plug.

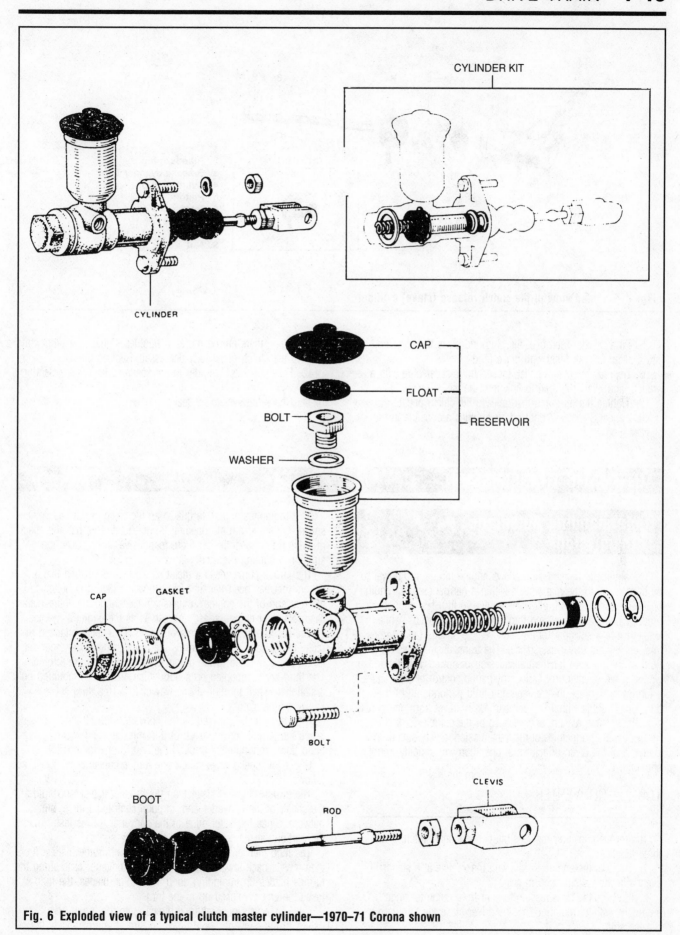

CYLINDER KIT

CYLINDER

CAP

FLOAT

BOLT

WASHER

RESERVOIR

CAP GASKET

BOLT

BOOT ROD CLEVIS

Fig. 6 Exploded view of a typical clutch master cylinder—1970–71 Corona shown

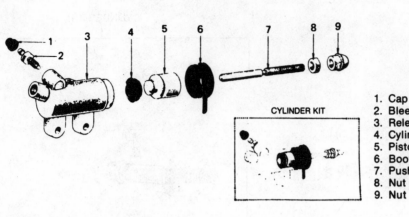

1. Cap
2. Bleeder plug
3. Release cylinder body
4. Cylinder cup
5. Piston
6. Boot
7. Pushrod
8. Nut
9. Nut

Fig. 7 Exploded view of the clutch release (slave) cylinder

5. Fit a bleeder tube over the plug and place the other end into a clean jar half filled with brake fluid.

6. Depress the clutch pedal, loosen the bleeder plug with a wrench, and allow the fluid to flow into the jar.

7. Tighten the plug and then release the clutch pedal.

8. Repeat Steps 6–7 until no air bubbles are visible in the bleeder tube.

9. When there are no more air bubbles, tighten the plug while keeping the clutch pedal fully depressed. Replace the cap.

10. Fill the master cylinder to the specified level. (See Section 1).

11. Check the system for leaks.

AUTOMATIC TRANSMISSION

Understanding Automatic Transmissions

The automatic transmission allows engine torque and power to be transmitted to the rear wheels within a narrow range of engine operating speeds. It will allow the engine to turn fast enough to produce plenty of power and torque at very low speeds, while keeping it at a sensible rpm at high vehicle speeds (and it does this job without driver assistance). The transmission uses a light fluid as the medium for the transmission of power. This fluid also works in the operation of various hydraulic control circuits and as a lubricant. Because the transmission fluid performs all of these functions, trouble within the unit can easily travel from one part to another. For this reason, and because of the complexity and unusual operating principles of the transmission, a very sound understanding of the basic principles of operation will simplify troubleshooting.

TORQUE CONVERTER

The torque converter replaces the conventional clutch. It has three functions:

1. It allows the engine to idle with the vehicle at a standstill, even with the transmission in gear.

2. It allows the transmission to shift from range-to-range smoothly, without requiring that the driver close the throttle during the shift.

3. It multiplies engine torque to an increasing extent as vehicle speed drops and throttle opening is increased. This has the effect of making the transmission more responsive and reduces the amount of shifting required.

The torque converter is a metal case which is shaped like a sphere that has been flattened on opposite sides. It is bolted to the rear end of the engine's crankshaft. Generally, the entire metal case rotates at engine speed and serves as the engine's flywheel.

The case contains three sets of blades. One set is attached directly to the case. This set forms the torus or pump. Another set is directly connected to the output shaft, and forms the turbine. The third set is mounted on a hub which, in turn, is mounted on a stationary shaft through a one-way clutch. This third set is known as the stator.

A pump, which is driven by the converter hub at engine speed, keeps the torque converter full of transmission fluid at all times. Fluid flows continuously through the unit to provide cooling.

Under low speed acceleration, the torque converter functions as follows:

The torus is turning faster than the turbine. It picks up fluid at the center of the converter and, through centrifugal force, slings it outward. Since the outer edge of the converter moves faster than the portions at the center, the fluid picks up speed.

The fluid then enters the outer edge of the turbine blades. It then travels back toward the center of the converter case along the turbine blades. In impinging upon the turbine blades, the fluid loses the energy picked up in the torus.

If the fluid was now returned directly into the torus, both halves of the converter would have to turn at approximately the same speed at all times, and torque input and output would both be the same.

In flowing through the torus and turbine, the fluid picks up two types of flow, or flow in two separate directions. It flows through the turbine blades, and it spins with the engine. The stator, whose blades are stationary when the vehicle is being accelerated at low speeds, converts one type of flow into another. Instead of allowing the fluid to flow straight back into the torus, the stator's curved blades turn the fluid almost 90° toward the direction of rotation of the engine. Thus the fluid does not flow as fast toward the torus, but is already spinning when the torus picks it up. This has the effect of allowing the torus to turn much faster than the turbine. This difference in speed may be compared to the difference in speed between the smaller and larger gears in any gear train. The result is that engine power output is higher, and engine torque is multiplied.

As the speed of the turbine increases, the fluid spins faster and faster in the direction of engine rotation. As a result, the ability of the stator to redirect the fluid flow is reduced. Under cruising conditions, the stator is eventually forced to rotate on its one-way clutch in the direction of engine rotation. Under these conditions, the torque converter begins to behave almost like a solid shaft, with the torus and turbine speeds being almost equal.

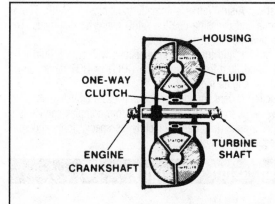

The torque converter housing is rotated by the engine's crankshaft, and turns the impeller—The impeller then spins the turbine, which gives motion to the turbine shaft, driving the gears

PLANETARY GEARBOX

The ability of the torque converter to multiply engine torque is limited. Also, the unit tends to be more efficient when the turbine is rotating at relatively high speeds. Therefore, a planetary gearbox is used to carry the power output of the turbine to the driveshaft.

Planetary gears function very similarly to conventional transmission gears. However, their construction is different in that three elements make up one gear system, and, in that all three elements are different from one another. The three elements are: an outer gear that is shaped like a hoop, with teeth cut into the inner surface; a sun gear, mounted on a shaft and located at the very center of the outer gear; and a set of three planet gears, held by pins in a ring-like planet carrier, meshing with both the sun gear and

the outer gear. Either the outer gear or the sun gear may be held stationary, providing more than one possible torque multiplication factor for each set of gears. Also, if all three gears are forced to rotate at the same speed, the gearset forms, in effect, a solid shaft.

Most automatics use the planetary gears to provide various reductions ratios. Bands and clutches are used to hold various portions of the gearsets to the transmission case or to the shaft on which they are mounted. Shifting is accomplished, then, by changing the portion of each planetary gearset which is held to the transmission case or to the shaft.

SERVOS & ACCUMULATORS

The servos are hydraulic pistons and cylinders. They resemble the hydraulic actuators used on many other machines, such as bulldozers. Hydraulic fluid enters the cylinder, under pressure, and forces the piston to move to engage the band or clutches.

The accumulators are used to cushion the engagement of the

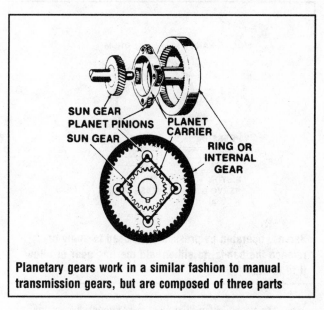

Planetary gears work in a similar fashion to manual transmission gears, but are composed of three parts

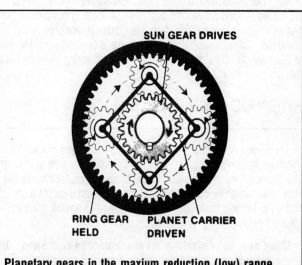

Planetary gears in the maximum reduction (low) range. The ring gear is held and a lower gear ratio is obtained

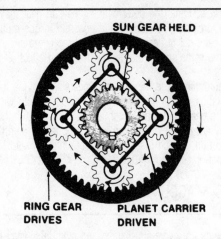

Planetary gears in the minimum reduction (drive) range. The ring gear is allowed to revolve, providing a higher gear ratio

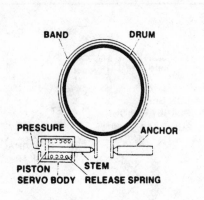

Servos, operated by pressure, are used to apply or release the bands, to either hold the ring gear or allow it to rotate

servos. The transmission fluid must pass through the accumulator on the way to the servo. The accumulator housing contains a thin piston which is sprung away from the discharge passage of the accumulator. When fluid passes through the accumulator on the way to the servo, it must move the piston against spring pressure, and this action smooths out the action of the servo.

HYDRAULIC CONTROL SYSTEM

The hydraulic pressure used to operate the servos comes from the main transmission oil pump. This fluid is channeled to the various servos through the shift valves. There is generally a manual shift valve which is operated by the transmission selector lever and an automatic shift valve for each automatic upshift the transmission provides.

➡ **Many new transmissions are electronically controlled. On these models, electrical solenoids are used to better control the hydraulic fluid. Usually, the solenoids are regulated by an electronic control module.**

There are two pressures which affect the operation of these valves. One is the governor pressure which is effected by vehicle speed. The other is the modulator pressure which is effected by intake manifold vacuum or throttle position. Governor pressure rises with an increase in vehicle speed, and modulator pressure rises as the throttle is opened wider. By responding to these two pressures, the shift valves cause the upshift points to be delayed with increased throttle opening to make the best use of the engine's power output.

Most transmissions also make use of an auxiliary circuit for downshifting. This circuit may be actuated by the throttle linkage the vacuum line which actuates the modulator, by a cable or by a solenoid. It applies pressure to a special downshift surface on the shift valve or valves.

The transmission modulator also governs the line pressure, used to actuate the servos. In this way, the clutches and bands will be actuated with a force matching the torque output of the engine.

Identification

All Mark II, all Crown and 1970–73 (early Corona, use the 3-speed Toyoglide transmissions (A30).

Starting in the spring of 1973, Corona models came equipped with a 3-speed Aisin-Warner automatic transmission (A40). The 1981 Corona and Cressida use the A40D overdrive automatic. The 1982 Cressida models use the A43DE.

Replenish the fluid through the filler tube with type F fluid for all models. Add fluid to the top of the COLD or HOT range, depending upon engine temperature.

This section covers routine service and basic adjustments, which may be performed by the owner. More complex service is best left to an authorized service facility, as special tools and service procedures are required.

Transmission Assembly

REMOVAL & INSTALLATION

3-Speed Toyoglide (A-30)
◆ **See Figure 7a**

1. Disconnect the battery.
2. Remove the air cleaner and disconnect the accelerator torque link or the cable.
3. Disconnect the throttle link rod at the carburetor side, then disconnect the backup light wiring at the firewall (on early models).
4. Jack up the car and support it on stands, then drain the transmission (use a clean receptacle so that the fluid can be checked for color, smell and foreign matter).
5. Disconnect all shift linkage.
6. On early models, remove the cross shaft from the frame.
7. Disconnect the throttle link rod at the transmission side and remove the speedometer cable, cooler lines and parking brake equalizer brake.
8. Loosen the exhaust flange nuts and remove the exhaust pipe clamp and bracket.
9. Remove the driveshaft and the rear mounting bracket, then lower the rear end of the transmission carefully.

3-Speed Automatic Transmission (A30)

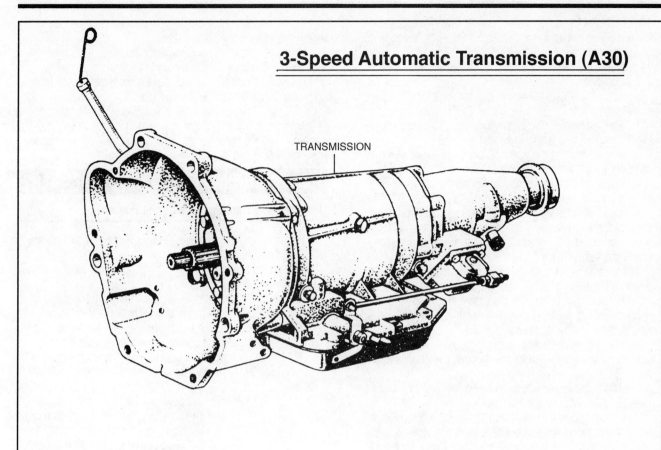

TRANSMISSION

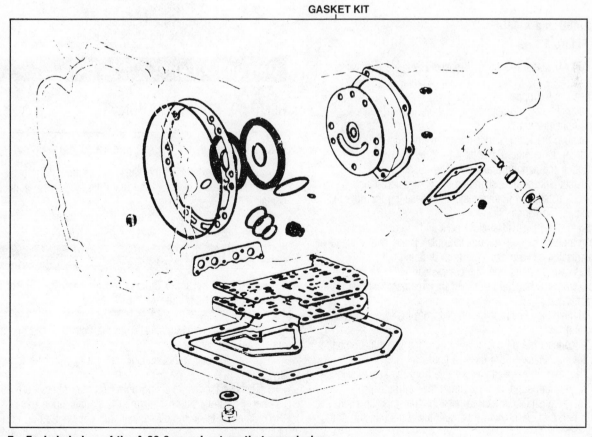

GASKET KIT

Fig. 7a Exploded view of the A-30 3-speed automatic transmission

10. Unbolt the torque converter from the drive plate. Support the engine with a suitable jack stand and remove the seven bolts that hold the transmission to the engine.

11. Reverse the order of the removal procedures with the following precautions:

a. Install the drive plate and ring gear, tighten the attaching bolts to 37–43 ft. lb.

b. After assembling the torque converter to the transmission, check the clearance, it should be about 15mm.

c. Before installing the transmission, place the oil pump locator pin on the torque converter to facilitate installation.

d. While rotating the crankshaft, tighten the converter attaching bolts, a little at a time.

e. After installing the throttle connecting second rod, make sure the throttle valve lever indicator aligns with the mark on the transmission with the carburetor throttle valve fully opened. If required, adjust the rod.

f. To install the transmission control rod correctly, move the transmission lever to N (Neutral), and the selector lever to Neutral. Fill the transmission. Run the engine at idle speed and apply the brakes while moving the selector lever through all positions, then return it to Neutral.

g. After warming the engine, move the selector lever through all positions, then back to Neutral, and check the fluid level. Fill as necessary.

h. Adjust the engine idle to 550–650 rpm with the selector lever at Drive. Road test the vehicle.

i. With the selector lever at 2 or Drive, check the point at which the transmission shifts. Check for shock, noise and slipping with the selector lever in all positions. Check for leaks from the transmission.

A-40, A-40D and A-43DE

▶ See Figure 8

1. Perform Steps 1–3 of the 3-speed Toyoglide removal procedure.

2. Remove the upper starter mounting nuts.

3. Raise the car and support it securely with jackstands. Drain the transmission.

4. Remove the lower starter mounting bolt and lay the starter along side of the engine. Don't let it hang by the wires.

5. Unbolt the parking brake equalizer support.

6. Matchmark the driveshaft and the companion flange, to ensure correct installation. Remove the bolts securing the driveshaft to the companion flange.

7. Slide the driveshaft straight back and out of the transmission. Use a spare U-joint yoke or tie a plastic bag over the end of the transmission to keep any fluid from dripping out.

8. Remove the bolts from the cross-shaft body bracket, the cotter pin from the manual lever, and the cross-shaft socket from the transmission.

9. Remove the exhaust pipe bracket from the torque converter bell housing.

10. Disconnect the oil cooler lines from the transmission and remove the line bracket from the bell housing.

11. Disconnect the speedometer cable from the transmission.

12. Unbolt both support braces from the bell housing.

13. Use a transmission jack to raise the transmission slightly.

14. Unbolt the rear crossmember and lower the transmission about 76mm.

15. Pry the two rubber torque converter access plugs out of their holes at the back of the engine.

16. Remove the six torque converter mounting bolts through the access hole. Rotate the engine with the crankshaft pulley.

17. Cut the head off a bolt to make a guide pin for the torque converter. Install the pin on the converter.

18. Remove the converter bell housing-to-engine bolts.

19. Push on the end of the guide pin in order to remove the converter with the transmission. Remove the transmission rearward and then bring it out from under the car.

✳✳ WARNING

Don't catch the throttle cable during removal.

20. Installation is the reverse of removal. Be sure to note the following, however:

a. Install the two long bolts on the upper converter housing and tighten them to 36–58 ft. lbs.

b. Install the converter-to-flex plate bolts finger-tight, and then tighten them with a torque wrench to 11–16 ft. lbs.

c. When installing the speedometer cable, make sure that the felt dust protector and washer are on the cable end.

d. Tighten the cooling line and exhaust pipe bracket mounting bolts to 37–58 ft. lbs. Tighten the cooling lines to 14–22 ft. lbs.

e. Align the matchmarks made on the driveshaft and the companion flange during removal. Tighten the driveshaft mounting bolts to 11–16 ft. lbs.

f. Be sure to install the oil pan drain plug. Tighten it to 11–14 ft. lbs.

g. Adjust the throttle cable.

h. Fill the transmission to the proper capacity.

i. Road test the car and check for leaks.

Pan and Filter

REMOVAL & INSTALLATION

▶ See Figures 9, 10, 11, 12 and 13 (p. 20–21)

1. Clean the exterior of the transmission around the pan.

2. Remove the drain plug and drain the fluid into a suitable container.

3. Unscrew all the pan retaining bolts and carefully remove the pan assembly. Discard the gasket.

✳✳ WARNING

There will still be some fluid in the oil pan. Be careful not to damage the filler tube or the O-ring.

4. Remove the small magnet from the bottom of the oil pan and clean it thoroughly.

5. Clean the pan with a suitable solvent and allow it to air dry.

6. Remove the five retaining bolts and then remove the oil strainer. Be careful not to puncture the strainer upon removal.

7. Carefully clean the oil strainer with compressed air or a suitable solvent.

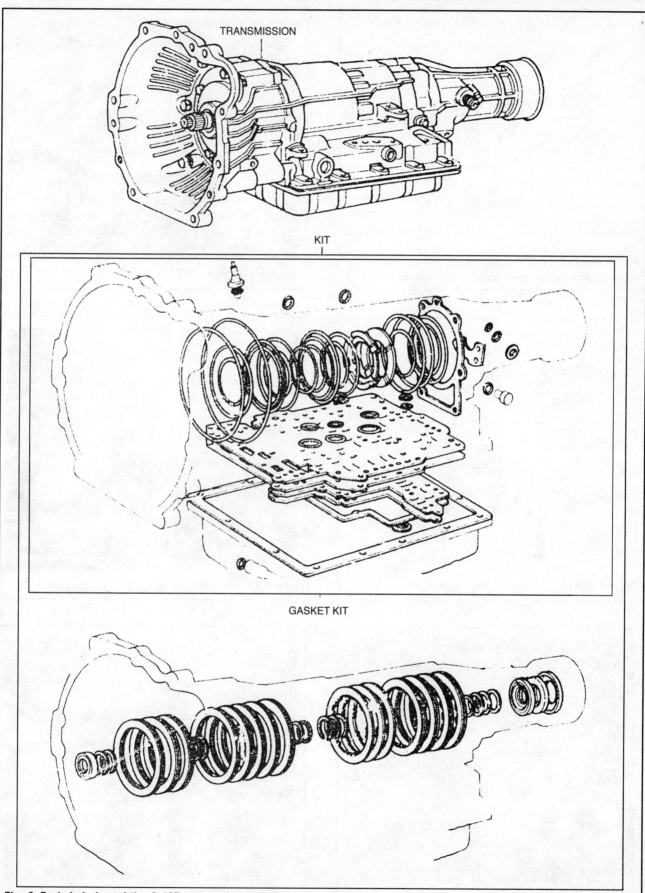

TRANSMISSION

KIT

GASKET KIT

Fig. 8 Exploded view of the A-40D automatic transmission and gaskets

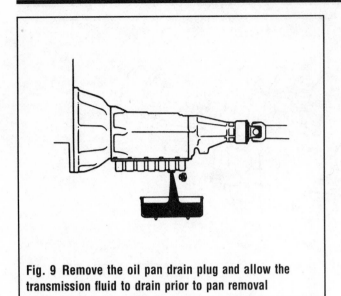

Fig. 9 Remove the oil pan drain plug and allow the transmission fluid to drain prior to pan removal

Remove and discard the old pan gasket

Fig. 10 Remove the transmission pan retaining bolts

Unbolt the filter from the automatic transmission, . . .

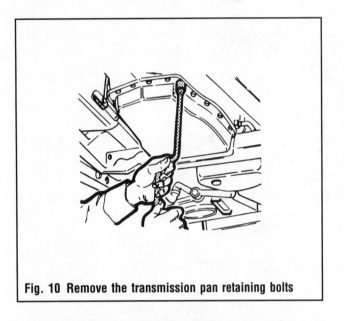

Lower the pan from the transmission

. . . then inspect and clean or replace it as needed

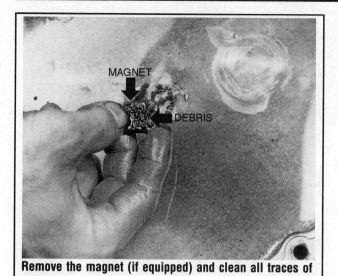

Remove the magnet (if equipped) and clean all traces of debris

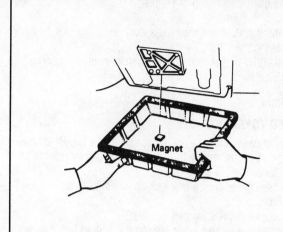

Fig. 13 Position the magnet so that it is directly beneath the oil strainer

8. Installation is in the reverse order of removal. Please note the following:
• Always use a new pan gasket, but never use gasket sealer.
• Before installing the pan, place a clean magnet on the bottom so that it will be positioned directly beneath the oil strainer.
• Tighten the oil strainer retaining bolts to 44–52 inch lbs. (4–5 ft. lbs.)

Adjustments

FRONT BAND

3-Speed Toyoglide
▶ See Figure 14

1. Remove the oil pan as previously outlined.
2. Pry the band engagement lever toward band with a screwdriver.

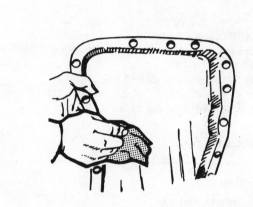

Fig. 11 Clean the pan thoroughly, then allow it to air dry

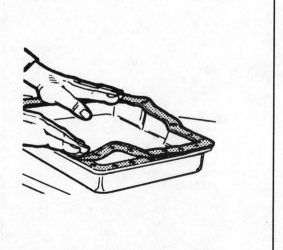

Fig. 12 Install a new pan gasket without sealer

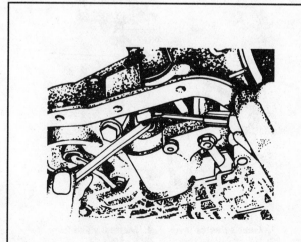

Fig. 14 Toyoglide three-speed front band adjustment

3. The gap between end of the piston rod and the engagement bolt should be 3.5mm.

4. If the gap does not meet the specification, adjust it by turning the engagement bolt.

5. Install the oil pan and refill the transmission as previously outlined.

Rear Band

3-SPEED TOYOGLIDE

The read band adjusting bolt is located on the outside of the case, so it is not necessary to remove the oil pan in order to adjust the band.

1. Loosen the adjusting bolt locknut and fully screw in the adjusting bolt.

2. Loosen the adjusting bolt one turn.

3. Tighten the locknut while holding the bolt so that it cannot turn.

➡ **The 3-speed A-40 transmission has no bands and, therefore, no band adjustments are possible. The only external adjustments are throttle and shift linkages.**

SHIFT LINKAGE

3-Speed Toyoglide
♦ **See Figure 15**

The transmission should be engaged, in the gear selected as indicated on the shift quadrant. If it is not, then adjust the linkage as follows:

1. Check all of the shift linkage bushings for wear. Replace any worn bushings.

2. Loosen the connecting rod swivel locknut.

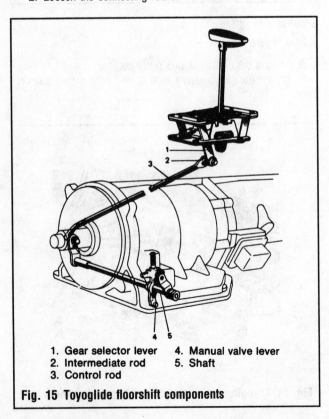

1. Gear selector lever   4. Manual valve lever
2. Intermediate rod   5. Shaft
3. Control rod

Fig. 15 Toyoglide floorshift components

3. Move the selector lever and check movement of the pointer in the shift quadrant.

4. When the control shaft is set in the neutral position the quadrant pointer should indicate N as well.

➡ **Steps 5–7 apply only to cars equipped with column mounted gear selectors.**

5. If the pointer does not indicate Neutral (N), then check the drive cord adjustment.

6. Remove the steering column shroud.

7. Turn the drive cord adjuster with a phillips screwdriver until the pointer indicates Neutral (N).

Steps 8–10 apply to both column mounted and floor mounted selectors:

8. Position the manual valve lever on the transmission so that it is in the Neutral position.

9. Lock the connecting rod swivel with the locknut so that the pointer, selector, and manual valve lever are all positioned in Neutral.

10. Check the operation of the gear selector by moving it through all ranges.

3-Speed A-40

1. Loosen the adjusting nut on the linkage and check the linkage for freedom of movement.

2. Push the manual valve lever toward the front of the car, as far as it will go.

3. Bring the lever back to its third notch (Neutral).

4. Have an assistant hold the shift lever in Neutral, while you tighten the linkage adjusting nut so that it can't slip.

THROTTLE LINKAGE

3-Speed Toyoglide
♦ **See Figures 16 and 17**

1. Loosen the locknut at each end of the linkage adjusting turnbuckle.

2. Detach the throttle linkage connecting rod from the carburetor.

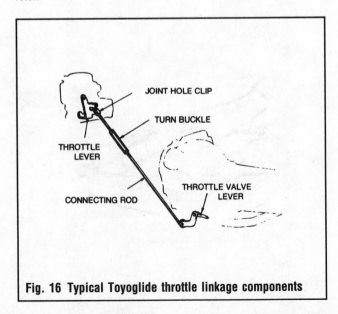

JOINT HOLE CLIP
TURN BUCKLE
THROTTLE LEVER
CONNECTING ROD
THROTTLE VALVE LEVER

Fig. 16 Typical Toyoglide throttle linkage components

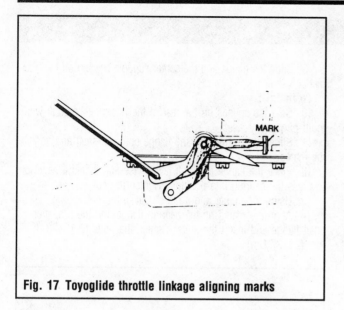

Fig. 17 Toyoglide throttle linkage aligning marks

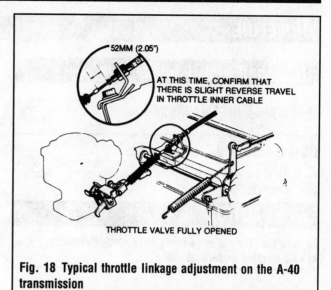

Fig. 18 Typical throttle linkage adjustment on the A-40 transmission

3. Align the pointer on the throttle valve lever with the mark stamped on the transmission case.

4. Rotate the turnbuckle so that the end of the throttle linkage rod and the carburetor throttle lever are aligned.

➡**The carburetor throttle valve must be fully opened during this adjustment.**

5. Tighten the turnbuckle locknuts and reconnect the throttle rod to the carburetor.

6. Open the throttle valve and check the pointer alignment with the mark on the transmission case.

7. Road test the car. If the transmission hunts, i.e., keeps shifting rapidly back and forth between gears at certain speeds or if it fails to downshift properly when going up hills, repeat the throttle linkage adjustment.

3-Speed A-40 and A-40D

♦ **See Figure 18**

1. Remove the air cleaner.

2. Confirm that the accelerator linkage opens the throttle fully. Adjust the link as necessary.

3. Peel the rubber dust boot back from the throttle cable.

4. Loosen the adjustment nuts on the throttle cable bracket (rocker cover) just enough to allow cable housing movement.

5. Have an assistant depress the accelerator pedal fully.

6. Adjust the cable housing so that the distance between its end and the cable stop collar is 52mm.

7. Tighten the adjustment nuts. Make sure that the adjustment hasn't changed. Install the dust boot and the air cleaner.

Neutral Safety Switch

REMOVAL & INSTALLATION

1. Raise and support the front of the vehicle.

2. Disconnect the electrical harness or harnesses leading to the switch.

3. Remove the bolts retaining the switch to the transmission. Remove the switch.

To install:

4. Place the switch into position on the transmission.

5. Tighten the mounting bolts.

6. Attach the harness the switch.

7. Make adjustments as necessary.

ADJUSTMENT

3-Speed Column Selector

The neutral safety switch/reverse lamp switch on the Toyoglide transmission with a column mounted selector is located under the hood on the shift linkage. If the switch is not functioning properly, adjust as follows:

1. Loosen the switch securing bolt.

2. Move the switch so that its arm just contacts the control shaft lever when the gear selector is in Drive (D) position.

3. Tighten the switch securing bolt.

4. Check the operation of the switch. The car should start only in Park (P) or Neutral (N) and the back-up lamps should come on only when Reverse (R) is selected.

5. If the switch cannot be adjusted so that it functions properly, replace it with a new one. Perform the adjustment as previously outlined.

3-Speed Console Shift

Models with a console mounted selector have the neutral safety switch on the linkage located beneath the console.

To adjust it, proceed in the following manner:

1. Remove the screws securing the center console.

2. Unfasten the console multiconnector, if so equipped, and completely remove the console.

3. Adjust the switch in the manner outlined in the preceding column selector section.

4. Install the console in the reverse order of removal after completion of the switch adjustment.

DRIVELINE

Driveshaft and U-Joints

REMOVAL & INSTALLATION

◆ **See Figures 19 thru 26 (p. 24–26)**

1. Raise the rear of the car and support the rear axle housing with jackstands.

✳✳ CAUTION

Be sure that the car is securely supported. Remember, you will be working underneath it!

2. Scribe alignment marks on the two rear flanges (one comes out of the differential and one is attached to the propeller shaft; they are both attached to each other).
3. Loosen the four attaching bolts and remove the U-joint flange from the differential flange.
4. Remove the two bolts which hold the center support bearing to the body.
5. Pull on the driveshaft assembly so as to remove the yoke from the transmission.

➡**Quickly insert a transmission plug or an old rag into the transmission to prevent fluid leakage.**

6. Scribe alignment marks across the two forward flanges of the propeller (rear) shaft.
7. Unscrew the four bolts and remove the propeller shaft from the intermediate (front) shaft.
8. Put alignment marks on the flange (attached to the center support bearing) and the intermediate shaft and then unscrew the retaining nut.

9. Slide the flange and the center support bearing off the intermediate shaft.

To install:

10. Coat the splines on the rear of the intermediate shaft with multi-purpose grease.
11. Slide the bearing and the flange onto the shaft and align the marks.
12. Place the flange in a soft jawed vise and install a new nut to press the bearing into position. Tighten the nut.
13. Using a hammer and a punch, stake the nut.
14. Align the marks on the bearing flange and the propeller shaft flange and insert the bolts. Tighten the bolts to 15–28 ft. lbs. (20–37 Nm).

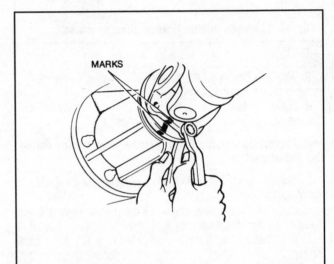

Fig. 19 Scribe alignment marks on the two rear flanges before removal

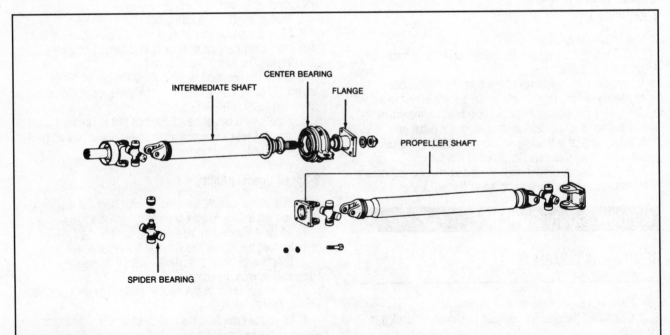

Fig. 20 Exploded view of the driveshaft assembly

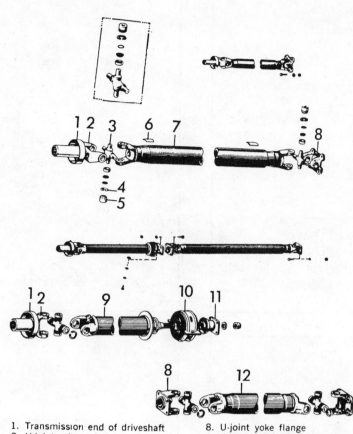

1. Transmission end of driveshaft
2. U-joint yoke and sleeve
3. U-joint spider
4. Snap ring
5. U-joint spider bearing
6. Balancing weight
7. Driveshaft
8. U-joint yoke flange
9. Intermediate driveshaft assembly
10. Center bearing support
11. U-joint flange assembly
12. Driveshaft

Two-piece driveshaft only

Fig. 20a Exploded view of the single-piece and two-piece driveshaft components

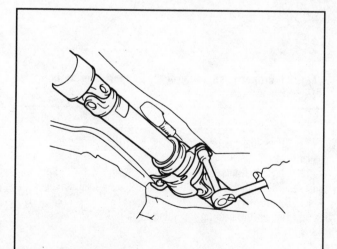

Fig. 21 Remove the center support bearing mounting bolts on the two-piece driveshaft

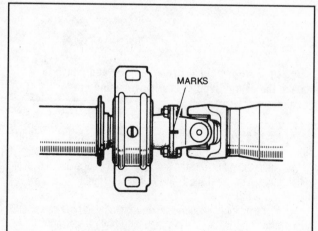

MARKS

Fig. 22 Remove the propeller shaft from the intermediate shaft; the line indicates the matchmarks

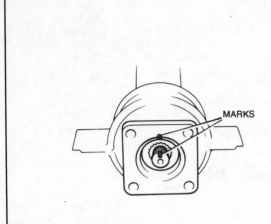

Fig. 23 After removing the retaining nut, slide the center support bearing and flange off the intermediate shaft. Note the matchmarks

Fig. 25 Tighten the support bearing to the body of the car

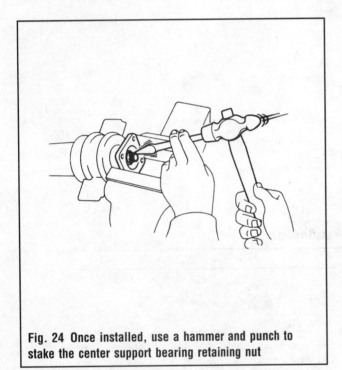

Fig. 24 Once installed, use a hammer and punch to stake the center support bearing retaining nut

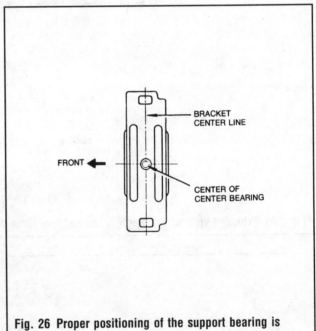

Fig. 26 Proper positioning of the support bearing is crucial

15. Insert the yoke on the intermediate shaft into the transmission.

16. Align the marks on the propeller shaft flange and the differential flange and insert the bolts. Tighten the bolts to 15–28 ft. lbs. (20–37 Nm).

17. Place a height spacer between the body and the center support bearing and install the two mounting bolts finger-tight.

18. Check that the bearing bracket is at right angles to the propeller shaft. Adjust if necessary.

19. Check that the center line of the bearing is set to the center line of the bracket when the car is in the no-load condition. Adjust if necessary.

20. Tighten the bearing mounting bolts to 22–32 ft. lbs. (29–43 Nm).

1. Driveshaft   2. Support bearing

Typical driveline components

U-JOINT OVERHAUL

▶ **See Figure 27**

1. Matchmark the yoke and the driveshaft.
2. Remove the snaprings from the bearings.
3. Position the yoke on vise jaws. Using a bearing remover and a hammer, gently tape the remover until the bearing is driven out of the yoke about ½ inch (12mm).
4. Place the tool in the vise and drive the yoke away from the tool until the bearing is removed.
5. Repeat Steps 3 and 4 for the other bearings.
6. Check for worn or damaged parts. Inspect the bearing journal surfaces for wear.

To install:

7. Install the bearing cups, seals, and O-rings in the spider.
8. Grease the spider and the bearings.
9. Position the spider in the yoke.
10. Start the bearing in the yoke and then press it into place, using a vise.
11. Repeat Step 10 for the other bearings.
12. If the axial play of the spider is greater than 0.002 inches (0.05mm), select snaprings which will provide the correct play. Be sure that the snaprings are the same size on both sides or driveshaft noise and vibration will result.
13. Check the U-joint assembly for smooth operation.

Thickness of snap ring		mm (in.)
Part No.	Thickness	Color code
90521–29070	2.375–2.425 (0.0935–0.0955)	None
90521–29071	2.425–2.475 (0.0955–0.0974)	Brown
90521–29072	2.475–2.525 (0.0974–0.0994)	Blue
90521–29073	2.525–2.575 (0.0994–0.1014)	None

Fig. 27 Snapring assortment chart

REAR AXLE

Determining Axle Ratio

The drive axle of a car is said to have a certain axle ratio. This number (usually a whole number and a decimal fraction) is actually a comparison of the number of gear teeth on the ring gear and the pinion gear. For example, a 4.11 rear means that theoretically, there are 4.11 teeth on the ring gear and one tooth on the pinion gear or, put another way, the driveshaft must turn 4.11 times to turn the wheels once. Actually, on a 4.11 rear, there might be 37 teeth on the ring gear and 9 teeth on the pinion gear. By dividing the number of teeth on the ring gear, the numerical axle ratio (4.11) is obtained. This also provides a good method of ascertaining exactly which axle ratio one is dealing with.

Another method of determining gear ratio is to jack up and support the car so that both rear wheels are off the ground. Make a chalk mark on the rear wheel and the driveshaft. Put the transmission in neutral. Turn the rear wheel one complete turn and count the number of turns that the driveshaft makes. The number of turns that the driveshaft makes in one complete revolution of the rear wheel is an approximation of the rear axle ratio.

Axle Shaft

REMOVAL & INSTALLATION

♦ **See Figures 28, 29 and 30**

1. Raise the rear of the car and support it securely by using jackstands.

✳✳ CAUTION

Be sure that the vehicle is securely supported. Remember, you will be working underneath it.

2. Drain the oil from the axle housing.
3. Remove the wheel cover (if equipped), unfasten the lug nuts, and remove the wheel.
4. Punch matchmarks on the brake drum and the axle shaft to maintain rotational balance.
5. Remove the brake drum and related components, as detailed in Section 9.
6. Remove the backing plate attachment nuts through the access holes in the rear axle shaft flange.
7. Use a slide hammer with a suitable adapter to withdraw the axle shaft from its housing.

✳✳ WARNING

Use care not to damage the oil seal when removing the axle shaft.

8. Repeat the procedure for the axle shaft on the opposite side. Be careful not to mix the components of the two sides.
9. Installation is performed in the reverse order of removal. Coat the lips of the rear housing oil seal with multi-purpose grease prior to installation of the rear axle shaft.

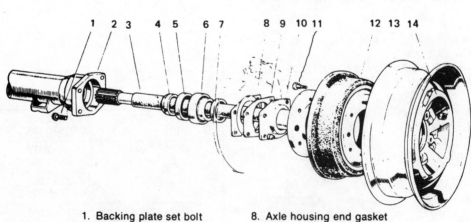

1. Backing plate set bolt
2. Rear axle housing
3. Rear axle shaft
4. Axle bearing inner retainer
5. Oil seal
6. Bearing
7. Spacer
8. Axle housing end gasket
9. Bearing retainer gasket
10. Axle bearing inner retainer
11. Hub bolt
12. Brake drum assembly
13. Wheel
14. Hub nut

Fig. 28 Rear axle shaft component identification

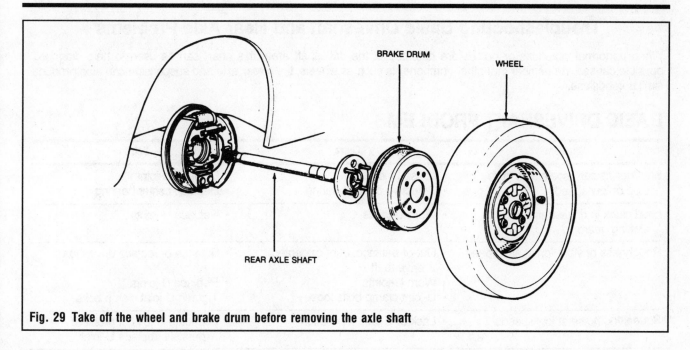

Fig. 29 Take off the wheel and brake drum before removing the axle shaft

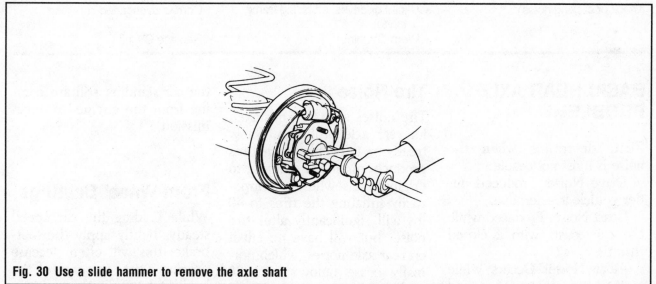

Fig. 30 Use a slide hammer to remove the axle shaft

Troubleshooting Basic Driveshaft and Rear Axle Problems

When abnormal vibrations or noises are detected in the driveshaft area, this chart can be used to help diagnose possible causes. Remember that other components such as wheels, tires, rear axle and suspension can also produce similar conditions.

BASIC DRIVESHAFT PROBLEMS

Problem	Cause	Solution
Shudder as car accelerates from stop or low speed	• Loose U-joint • Defective center bearing	• Replace U-joint • Replace center bearing
Loud clunk in driveshaft when shifting gears	• Worn U-joints	• Replace U-joints
Roughness or vibration at any speed	• Out-of-balance, bent or dented driveshaft • Worn U-joints • U-joint clamp bolts loose	• Balance or replace driveshaft • Replace U-joints • Tighten U-joint clamp bolts
Squeaking noise at low speeds	• Lack of U-joint lubrication	• Lubricate U-joint; if problem persists, replace U-joint
Knock or clicking noise	• U-joint or driveshaft hitting frame tunnel • Worn CV joint	• Correct overloaded condition • Replace CV joint

BASIC REAR AXLE PROBLEMS

First, determine when the noise is most noticeable.

Drive Noise: Produced under vehicle acceleration.

Coast Noise: Produced while the car coasts with a closed throttle.

Float Noise: Occurs while maintaining constant car speed (just enough to keep speed constant) on a level road.

Road Noise

Brick or rough surfaced concrete roads produce noises that seem to come from the rear axle. Road noise is usually identical in Drive or Coast and driving on a different type of road will tell whether the road is the problem.

Tire Noise

Tire noises are often mistaken for rear axle problems. Snow treads or unevenly worn tires produce vibrations seeming to originate elsewhere. **Temporarily** inflating the tires to 40 lbs will significantly alter tire noise, but will have no effect on rear axle noises (which normally cease below about 30 mph).

Engine/Transmission Noise

Determine at what speed the noise is most pronounced, then stop the car in a quiet place. With the transmission in Neutral, run the engine through speeds corresponding to road speeds where the noise was noticed. Noises produced with the car standing still are coming from the engine or transmission.

Front Wheel Bearings

While holding the car speed steady, lightly apply the footbrake; this will often decease bearing noise, as some of the load is taken from the bearing.

Rear Axle Noises

Eliminating other possible sources can narrow the cause to the rear axle, which normally produces noise from worn gears or bearings. Gear noises tend to peak in a narrow speed range, while bearing noises will usually vary in pitch with engine speeds.

WHEELS 8-2
WHEEL ASSEMBLY 8-2
   REMOVAL & INSTALLATION 8-2
   INSPECTION 8-2
FRONT SUSPENSION 8-3
COIL SPRINGS 8-4
   REMOVAL & INSTALLATION 8-4
SHOCK ABSORBERS 8-7
   REMOVAL & INSTALLATION 8-7
   INSPECTION 8-7
MACPHERSON STRUTS 8-7
   REMOVAL & INSTALLATION 8-7
LOWER BALL JOINT 8-9
   INSPECTION 8-9
   REMOVAL & INSTALLATION 8-9
UPPER BALL JOINT 8-11
   INSPECTION 8-11
   REMOVAL & INSTALLATION 8-11
LOWER CONTROL ARM 8-12
   REMOVAL & INSTALLATION 8-12
UPPER CONTROL ARM 8-12
   REMOVAL & INSTALLATION 8-12
FRONT AXLE HUB AND BEARING 8-12
   REMOVAL & INSTALLATION 8-12
FRONT END ALIGNMENT 8-14
   CASTER 8-14
   CAMBER 8-14
   TOE-IN 8-14
REAR SUSPENSION 8-16
LEAF SPRINGS 8-17
   REMOVAL & INSTALLATION 8-17
COIL SPRINGS 8-18
   REMOVAL & INSTALLATION 8-18
SHOCK ABSORBERS 8-20
   REMOVAL & INSTALLATION 8-20
STEERING 8-24
STEERING WHEEL 8-24
   REMOVAL & INSTALLATION 8-24
TURN SIGNAL (COMBINATION)
 SWITCH 8-26
   REMOVAL & INSTALLATION 8-26
IGNITION LOCK/SWITCH 8-29
   REMOVAL & INSTALLATION 8-29
MANUAL STEERING GEAR 8-30
   REMOVAL & INSTALLATION 8-30
POWER STEERING PUMP 8-30
   REMOVAL & INSTALLATION 8-30
   BLEEDING 8-30
STEERING LINKAGE 8-32
   REMOVAL & INSTALLATION 8-32
TIE ROD END 8-35
   REMOVAL & INSTALLATION 8-35
COMPONENT LOCATIONS
 FRONT STEERING AND SUSPENSION
   COMPONENTS 8-3
 REAR SUSPENSION
   COMPONENTS 8-16
SPECIFICATION CHARTS
 FRONT SPRING INSTALLATION
   SPECIFICATIONS 8-4
 TORQUE SPECIFICATIONS 8-10

TORQUE SPECIFICATIONS (FT.
 LBS.) 8-12
PRELOAD SPECIFICATIONS 8-14
WHEEL ALIGNMENT
 SPECIFICATIONS 8-15
SHOCK ABSORBER TIGHTENING
 TORQUE (FT. LBS.) CHART 8-23
STEERING LINKAGE TORQUE
 SPECIFICATIONS (FT. LBS.) 8-34
TROUBLESHOOTING CHARTS
BASIC STEERING AND SUSPENSION
 PROBLEMS 8-37
TROUBLESHOOTING THE STEERING
 COLUMN 8-38
TROUBLESHOOTING THE IGNITION
 SWITCH 8-39
TROUBLESHOOTING THE TURN
 SIGNAL SWITCH 8-40
TROUBLESHOOTING THE MANUAL
 STEERING GEAR 8-41
TROUBLESHOOTING THE POWER
 STEERING GEAR 8-42
TROUBLESHOOTING THE POWER
 STEERING PUMP 8-44

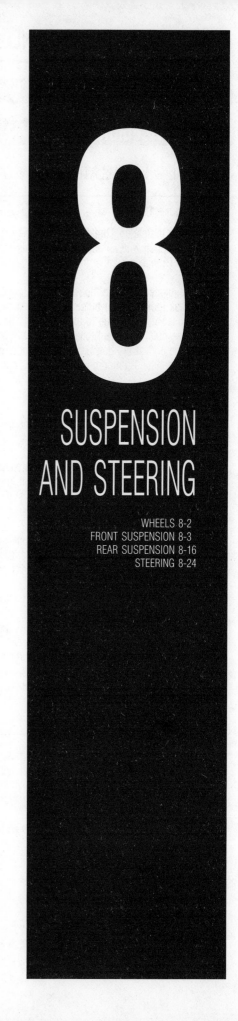

8

SUSPENSION AND STEERING

WHEELS 8-2
FRONT SUSPENSION 8-3
REAR SUSPENSION 8-16
STEERING 8-24

WHEELS

Wheel Assembly

REMOVAL & INSTALLATION

◆ See Figure 1

1. Apply the parking brake and block the opposite wheel.
2. If equipped with an automatic transmission, place the selector lever in **P**; with a manual transmission, place the shifter in Reverse.
3. If equipped, remove the wheel cover or hub cap.
4. Break loose the lug nuts. If a nut is stuck, never use heat to loosen it or damage to the wheel and bearings may occur. If the nuts are seized, one or two heavy hammer blows directly on the end of the bolt head usually loosens the rust. Be careful as continued pounding will likely damage the brake drum or rotor.
5. Raise the vehicle until the tire is clear of the ground. Support the vehicle safely using jackstands.
6. Remove the lug nuts, then remove the tire and wheel assembly.

To install:

7. Make sure the wheel and hub mating surfaces, as well as the wheel lug studs, are clean and free of all foreign material. Always remove rust from the wheel mounting surfaces and the brake rotors/drums. Failure to do so may cause the lug nuts to loosen in service.
8. Position the wheel on the hub or drum and hand-tighten the lug nuts. Make sure that the coned ends face inward.
9. Tighten all the lug nuts, in a crisscross pattern, until they are snug.
10. Remove the supports, if any, and lower the vehicle. Tighten the lug nuts, in a crisscross pattern. Always use a torque wrench to achieve the proper lug nut torque and to prevent stretching the wheel studs.
11. Repeat the torque pattern to assure proper wheel tightening.
12. If equipped, install the hub cap or wheel cover.

INSPECTION

Check the wheels for any damage. They must be replaced if they are bent, dented, heavily rusted, have elongated bolt holes, or have excessive lateral or radial run-out. Wheels with excessive run-out may cause a high-speed vehicle vibration.

Replacement wheels must be of the same load capacity, diameter, width, offset and mounting configuration as the original wheels. Using the wrong wheels may affect wheel bearing life, ground and tire clearance, or speedometer and odometer calibrations.

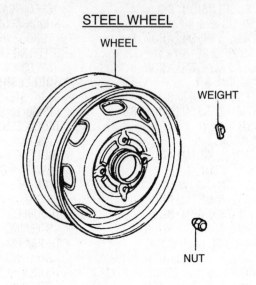

STEEL WHEEL

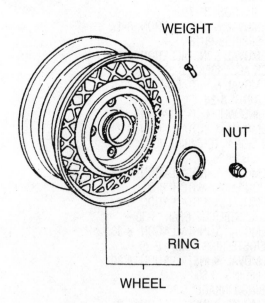

ALUMINUM WHEEL

Fig. 1 Your Toyota may be equipped with either steel or aluminum wheels

FRONT SUSPENSION

FRONT STEERING AND SUSPENSION COMPONENTS

1. Tie rod
2. Lower control arm
3. MacPherson strut
4. Stabilizer bar
5. Strut bar
6. Relay rod
7. Tie rod end
8. Ball joint

Coil Springs

REMOVAL & INSTALLATION

Corona

➥This procedure applies to models without MacPherson struts.

1. Remove the hubcap and loosen the nuts.
2. Raise the front of the car and support it by using jackstands.

✳✳ CAUTION

Be sure that the car is securely supported. Remember, you will be working underneath it.

3. Remove the lug nuts and the wheel.
4. Remove the shock absorber as detailed in the appropriate following section. Unfasten the stabilizer bar from the lower control arm (if equipped).
5. Remove the dust cover.
6. Install a coil spring compressor and compress the spring until there is no load on it. Place a jack under the spring seat for safety.
7. Unfasten the lower ball joint retaining bolts and withdraw the ball joint, complete with the steering knuckle, from the lower control arm.
8. Slowly and carefully loosen the spring compressor and remove the spring. (Lower the jack under the spring seat first).
9. Inspect the spring, ball joint, and related components for wear or damage. Replace any parts necessary.
10. Installation is performed in the reverse order of removal. If the spring is being replaced with a new one, be sure to purchase one of the correct load tolerance for your Corona. The ball joint/steering knuckle assembly securing bolts should be tightened to the following specifications:

1970–73 Models
- 12mm bolts: 58–83 ft. lb.
- 8mm bolts: 11–16 ft. lb.

1974–82 Models
- Steering knuckle bolts: 51–65 ft. lb.

After completing installation of the coil spring, check to ensure that it is properly seated in the lower suspension arm. Check front end alignment.

➥The coil springs are not interchangeable from the right side to the left side.

Mark II and Crown

◆ See Figures 2 and 3

1. Perform Steps 1–3 of the Corona Coil Spring Removal and Installation procedure. Be sure to observe the Caution.
2. Unfasten the stabilizer bar.
3. Measure the distance between the serrated bolt holes on the front side of the torque strut and the attachment nut on the rear side to aid in installation. Remove the strut.
4. On Crown models, disconnect the brake line.
5. Remove the shock absorber, as detailed in the appropriate following section.
6. Install the coil spring compressor on the third coil from the bottom. Tighten the compressor until the load is removed from the spring.
7. Remove the lower ball joint with a ball joint puller.
8. Unbolt and remove the lower control arm.
9. Carefully and slowly remove the spring compressor and withdraw the spring.
10. Inspect the components of the suspension which were removed for signs of wear or damage. Replace parts as required.

To install:

11. Install the lower control arm but do not fully tighten the mounting bolts.
12. Compress the spring with the spring compressor and install the spring.

➥Keep the spring compressed after installation.

13. Install the lower ball joint on the steering knuckle and tighten it to the specifications given in the Front Spring Installation Specifications chart.
14. Install the strut on the lower control arm and temporarily install the other end on the frame.

Front Spring Installation Specifications

Model	Replacment Strut Length (in.)	Ball Joint-to-Steering Knuckle (ft. lbs.)	Torque Specifications (ft. lbs.)		
			Strut-to-Control Arm	Lower Control Arm-to-Member	Strut-to-Frame
Mark II/4	18.70	51–65	50–65	32–43	54–80
Mark II/6	14.16	51–65	51–65	65–87	43–54
Crown 2300	16.00	66–96	50–65	75–110	70–110
Crown 2600	16.14	65–94	50–65	72–108	69–108

a. The distance between the serrations and the nut should be the same as that measured during removal.

b. It a new strut is used, check the chart specifications for the proper installation distance.

c. Carefully install the rear side of the strut to the control arm and tighten the mounting nut to the specifications in the chart.

15. Slowly remove the spring compressor from the coil spring.

16. Install the shock absorber.

17. Install the stabilizer bar bracket and the bar.

➡ **Be sure to assemble the parts of the bracket in the order in which they were removed.**

18. Install the wheel, remove the jackstands, and lower the car.

19. Tighten the lower control arm and strut front mount to the specifications given in the chart.

➡ **These parts should be tightened with the equivalent of passenger weight in the car.**

20. Check the wheel alignment, after completing installation.

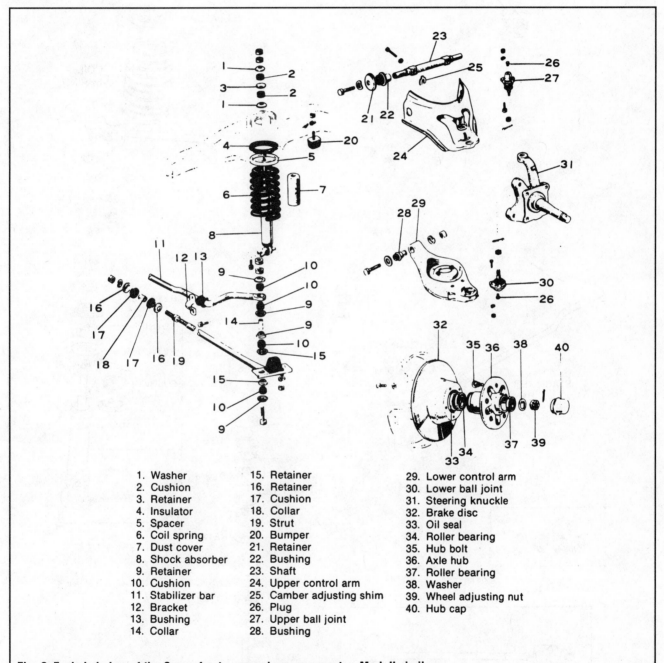

1. Washer	15. Retainer
2. Cushion	16. Retainer
3. Retainer	17. Cushion
4. Insulator	18. Collar
5. Spacer	19. Strut
6. Coil spring	20. Bumper
7. Dust cover	21. Retainer
8. Shock absorber	22. Bushing
9. Retainer	23. Shaft
10. Cushion	24. Upper control arm
11. Stabilizer bar	25. Camber adjusting shim
12. Bracket	26. Plug
13. Bushing	27. Upper ball joint
14. Collar	28. Bushing

29. Lower control arm
30. Lower ball joint
31. Steering knuckle
32. Brake disc
33. Oil seal
34. Roller bearing
35. Hub bolt
36. Axle hub
37. Roller bearing
38. Washer
39. Wheel adjusting nut
40. Hub cap

Fig. 2 Exploded view of the Crown front suspension components—Mark II similar

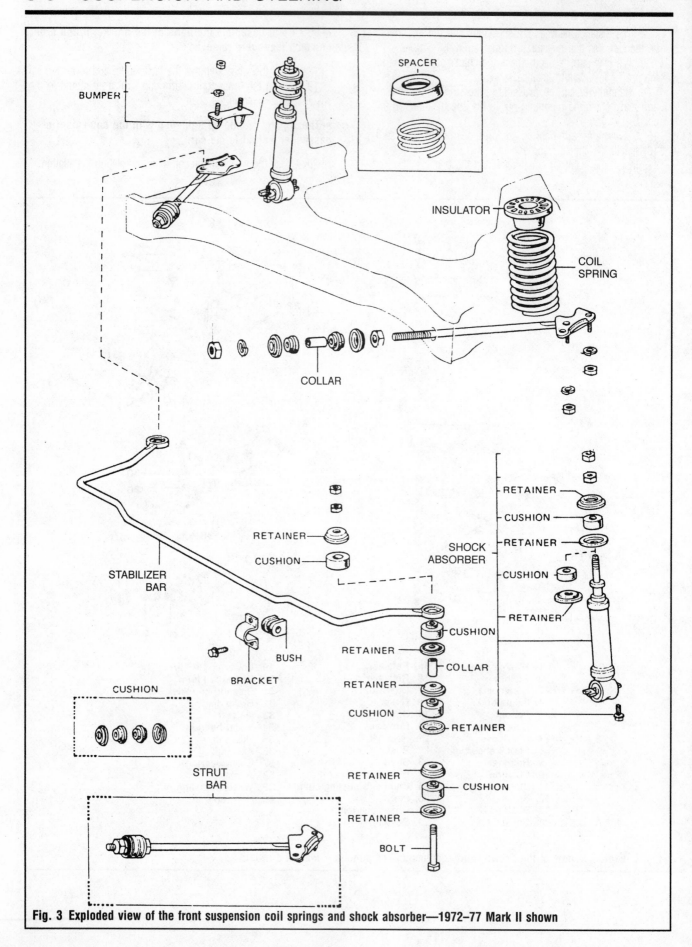

Fig. 3 Exploded view of the front suspension coil springs and shock absorber—1972–77 Mark II shown

Shock Absorbers

REMOVAL & INSTALLATION

1. Remove the hub cap and loosen the lug nuts.
2. Raise the front of the car and support it with jackstands.

✳✳ CAUTION

Be sure that the vehicle is supported securely. Remember, you will be working underneath it.

3. Remove the lug nuts and the wheel.
4. Unfasten the double nuts at the top end of the shock absorber. Remove the cushions and cushion retainers.
5. Remove the two bolts which secure the lower end of the shock absorber to the lower control arm.
6. Remove the shock absorber.
7. Inspect and test the shock as detailed below.
8. Installation of the shock is performed in the reverse order of removal. Tighten the securing nuts and bolts to the following specifications:
   - Upper securing nuts: 14–22 ft. lb.
   - Lower mounting bolts: 11–16 ft. lb.

INSPECTION

With the shock absorber removed from the vehicle, examine it for the following:
- Fluid leaks.
- Damaged housing.
- Weakness.
- Wear.
- Bent or cracked studs.

Test shock absorber operation by placing it in an upright position. Push and pull on the shock. If the shock presents little resistance or binds, replace it with a new one.

MacPherson Struts

REMOVAL & INSTALLATION

▶ **See Figure 4**

1. Disconnect the brake tube and flexible hose.
2. Remove the three nuts and lockwashers from the top of the strut inside the engine compartment.
3. Remove the two bolts and lockwashers attaching the Mac-

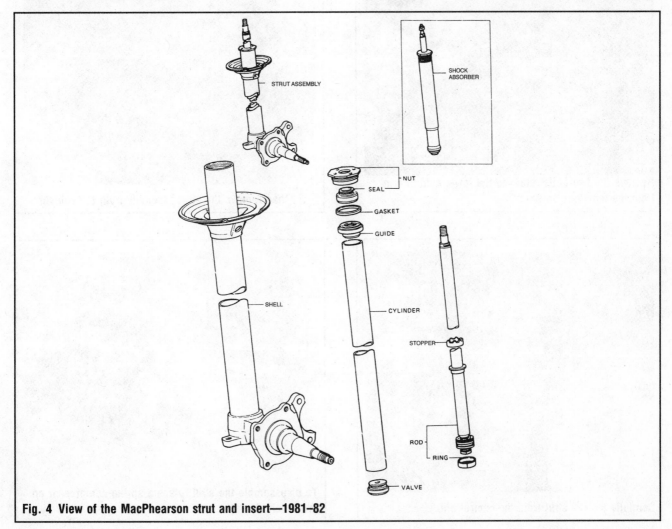

Fig. 4 View of the MacPhearson strut and insert—1981–82

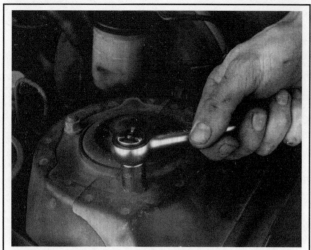

To remove the strut, begin by loosening the three nuts and lockwashers—1979 Corona shown

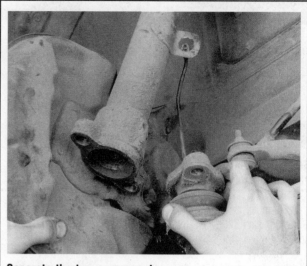

Separate the two components . . .

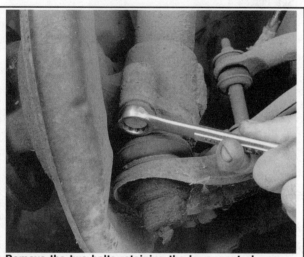

Remove the two bolts retaining the lower control arm from the MacPherson strut

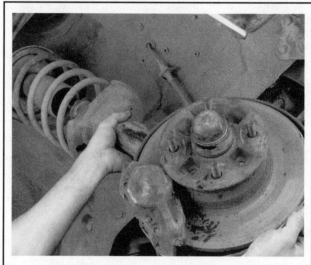

. . . then remove the strut assembly from the vehicle

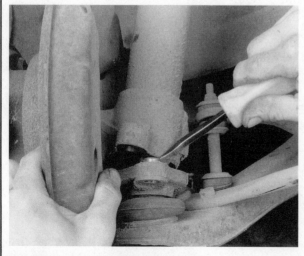

Carefully pry the strut from the control arm

To disassemble the strut, place a spring compressor on the assembly

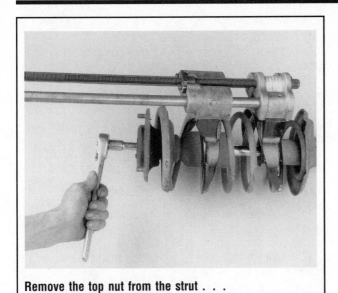

Remove the top nut from the strut . . .

. . . and remove the bearing assembly . . .

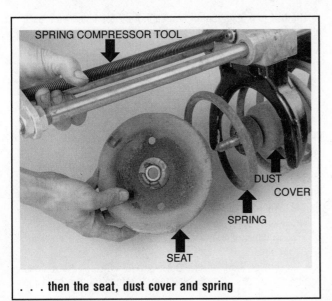

. . . then the seat, dust cover and spring

Pherson strut to the lower control arm. Push the arm downward slightly, and then remove the strut assembly.

4. The strut must be mounted in a vise for further disassembly. It must not be mounted by the shock absorber shell as this part is machined perfectly round and can easily be distorted. A special tool is available from Toyota for this purpose, or you can make some sort of flange that will bolt to the bottom (where the control arm attaches).

5. Using a special tool designed for this purpose, the spring must be compressed so there is no tension on the upper seat.

✷✷ WARNING

Failure to fully compress the spring and hold it securely before performing the next step is extremely hazardous.

6. Hold the shock absorber seat (at top) with a large spanner wrench, and remove the nut from the top of the shock absorber.

7. Remove upper support, upper seat, dust cover, and spring.

8. Install in reverse order. Inspect all parts carefully for wear or distortion, and replace as necessary. Tighten the top shock absorber nut to 32.6–39.8 ft. lb. on Cressida. Pack multipurpose grease into the bearing on the suspension support. Tighten upper support nuts to 21.7–38.6 ft. lb. Lower control arm nuts are tightened to 57.9–86.8 ft. lb.

Lower Ball Joint

INSPECTION

Jack up the lower control arm. Check the front wheel play. Replace the lower ball joint if the play at the wheel rim exceeds 1mm vertical motion or 2mm horizontal motion. Be sure that the dust covers are not torn and they are securely glued to the ball joints.

REMOVAL & INSTALLATION

➡On models equipped with upper and lower ball joints-if both ball joints are to be removed, always remove the lower and then the upper ball joint.

Corona

EXCEPT MACPHERSON STRUT

1. Remove the hubcap and loosen the lug nuts.
2. Raise the front of the car and support it with jackstands.

✷✷ CAUTION

Be sure that the car is securely supported. Remember, you will be working underneath it.

3. Remove the lug nuts and the wheel. Place a jack under the spring seat on 1974–76 models, and compress the spring by raising the jack.

➡On models with Electro Sensor Panel (ESP), unfasten the wiring from the brake sensor, and remove the clamp from the lever control arm.

Torque Specifications

Part(s)	Torque (ft. lbs.)
Ball joint-to-control arm 12 mm bolt	58–83
8 mm bolt	11–16
Ball joint-to-steering knuckle	51–65

4. Remove the cotter pin and the castellated nut from the ball joint.

5. Use a ball joint puller to detach the lower ball joint from the steering knuckle.

6. Remove the securing bolt and withdraw the ball joint as detailed in Chapter 1 and check alignment.

MACPHERSON STRUT

1. Support the vehicle securely by the front suspension cross member.

2. Remove the engine lower cover. Disconnect the stabilizer bar at the lower arm and strut bar at the lower arm. Note the order of disassembly of all rubber bushings and collars.

3. Remove bolts attaching the lower arm to the bottom of the strut.

4. Using a tool designed for the purpose, press the tie rod end out of the steering knuckle arm.

5. Remove the bolt running through the crossmember and remove the control arm from the crossmember.

6. Remove the cotter pin and castle nut, and then press the steering knuckle arm off the lower control arm with an appropriate tool. The lower arm and ball joint must be replaced as an assembly if either is defective.

7. In installation, tighten the parts as follows:
• Control arm-to-crossmember bolt (do not tighten until after the suspension is assembled and weight is put on it so normal ride height is achieved) 65.1–94 ft. lb.
• Steering knuckle castle nut: 50.6–65.1 ft. lb.
• Strut-to-knuckle arm: 57.9–86.8 ft. lb.
• Strut bar-to-lower arm: 43.4–53.2 ft. lb.
• Stabilizer bar-to-lower arm: 10.1–15.9 ft. lb.

Mark II and Crown

1. Remove the hubcap and loosen the lugnuts.
2. Raise and support the front of the vehicle.
3. Remove the lugnuts and wheel.

✳✳ CAUTION

Be sure the car is securely supported.

4. Unfasten the stabilizer bar.

5. Measure the distance between the serrated bolt holes on the front side of the torque strut and the attachment nut on the rear side to aid in installation. Remove the strut.

6. On Crown models, disconnect the brake line.

7. Remove the shock absorber, as detailed in the appropriate following section.

8. Install the coil spring compressor on the third coil from the bottom. Tighten the compressor until the load is removed from the spring.

9. Remove the lower ball joint with a ball joint puller.

10. Unbolt and remove the lower control arm.

11. Carefully and slowly remove the spring compressor and withdraw the spring.

12. Inspect the components of the suspension which were removed for signs of wear or damage. Replace parts as required.

To install:

13. Install the lower control arm but do not fully tighten the mounting bolts.

14. Compress the spring with the spring compressor and install the spring.

➡**Keep the spring compressed after installation.**

15. Install the lower ball joint on the steering knuckle and tighten it to the specifications given in the Front Spring Installation specifications chart.

16. Install the strut on the lower control arm and temporarily install the other end on the frame.

a. The distance between the serrations and the nut should be the same as that measured during removal.

b. If a ne4w strut is used, check, the chart specifications for the proper installation distance.

c. Carefully install the rear side of the strut to the control arm and tighten the mounting nut to the specifications in the chart.

17. Slowly remove the spring compressor from the coil spring.

18. Install the shock absorber.

19. Install the stabilizer bar bracket and the bar.

➡**Be sure to assemble the parts of the bracket in the order in which they were removed.**

20. Install the wheel, remove the jackstands, and lower the car.

21. Tighten the lower control arm and strut front mont to the specifications given in the chart.

➡**These parts should be tightened with the equivalent of passenger weight in the car.**

22. Check the wheel alignment, after completing installation.

Cressida

◆ **See Figure 5**

The ball joint and control arm cannot be separated from each other. If one fails, then both must be replaced as an assembly, in the following manner:

1. Perform Steps 1–7 of the first Front Spring Removal and Installation procedure. Skip Step 6.

2. Remove the stabilizer bar securing bolts.

3. Unfasten the torque strut mounting bolts.

4. Remove the control arm mounting bolt and detach the arm from the front suspension member.

5. Remove the steering knuckle arm from the control arm with a ball joint puller.

6. Installation is the reverse of removal. Note the following, however:

a. When installing the control arm on the suspension member, tighten the bolts partially at first.

b. Complete the assembly procedure and lower the car to the ground.

c. Bounce the front of the car several times. Allow the suspension to settle, then tighten the lower control arm bolts to 51–65 ft. lb.

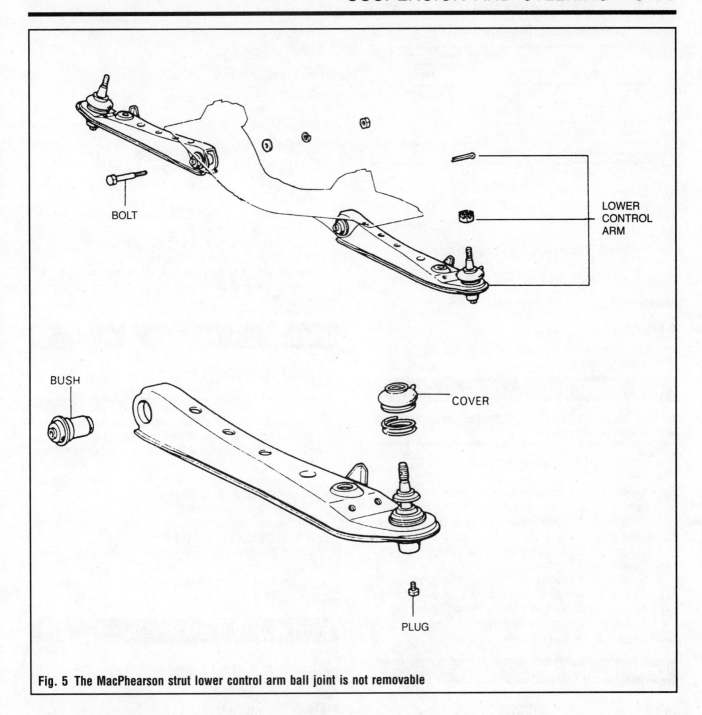

Fig. 5 The MacPhearson strut lower control arm ball joint is not removable

➡️**Use only the bolt which was designed to fit the lower control arm. If a replacement is necessary, see an authorized dealer for the proper part.**

4. Remember to lubricate the ball joint. Check front end alignment.

Upper Ball Joint

INSPECTION

Disconnect the ball joint from the steering knuckle and check free-play by hand. Replace the ball joint, if it is noticeably loose.

REMOVAL & INSTALLATION

➡️**On models equipped with both upper and lower ball joints, if both are to be removed, always remove the lower one first.**

Corona

1. Perform Steps 1–5 of the Corona Lower Ball Joint Removal procedure.
2. Suspend the steering knuckle with a wire.
3. Use an open-end wrench to remove the upper ball joint.
4. Installation is performed in the reverse order of removal. Note the following:

Torque Specifications (ft. lbs.)

Model	Upper Ball Joint-to-	
	Knuckle	Arm
Mark II/4	40–50	15–22
Mark II/6	40–51	15–22
Crown 2300	66–96	11–16
Crown 2600	65–94	11–16

a. Install the upper ball joint dust cover with the escape valve toward the rear.

b. Use sealer on the dust cover before installing it.

c. Tighten the upper ball joint-to-steering knuckle bolt to 29–40 ft. lb. (1970–73) or to 40–51 ft. lb. (1974 and Later).

Mark II and Crown

♦ See Figure 6

1. Remove the wheel cover and loosen the lug nuts.
2. Raise the front of the car and support it with jackstands.

✳✳ CAUTION

Be sure that the car is securely supported. Remember, you will be working underneath it.

3. Remove the lug nuts and the wheel.
4. Place a jack beneath the lower control arm spring seat. Raise the jack until the spring bumper separates from the frame.
5. Detach the flexible hose from the dust cover.
6. Using a ball joint puller, remove the upper ball joint from the steering knuckle.
7. Use an open end wrench to remove the ball joint from the upper control arm.
8. Installation is performed in the reverse order of removal. Tighten the components to the specifications given in the following Torque Specifications chart. Lubricate the ball joint as outlined in Chapter 1. Check front wheel alignment. Remember to bleed the air from the flexible hose.

Lower Control Arm

REMOVAL & INSTALLATION

Cressida

1. Raise and support the front end.
2. Remove the wheel.
3. Disconnect the steering knuckle from the control arm.
4. Disconnect the tie rod stabilizer bar and strut bar from the control arm.
5. Remove the control arm mounting bolts, and remove the arm.
6. Install in reverse of above. Tighten, but do not torque fasteners until car is on ground.
7. Lower car to ground, rock it from side-to-side several times and tighten the control arm mounting bolts to 51–65 ft. lbs., stabi-

lizer bar to 16 ft. lbs., strut bar to 40 ft. lb., and shock absorber to 65 ft. lbs.

Except Cressida

1. Raise and support the vehicle.
2. Remove the front wheel.
3. Remove the shock absorber and disconnect the stabilizer from the lower arm.
4. Install a spring compressor and fully tighten it.
5. Place a jack under the lower arm seat.
6. Disconnect the lower ball joint from the knuckle and lower the jack.
7. Remove the ball joint from the arm, remove the cam plates and bolts and take off the arm.
8. Install in reverse of above. Tighten all fasteners, but do not torque them to specification until vehicle is on ground.
9. Lower vehicle and rock it from side-to-side several times.
10. With no load in vehicle, tighten the lower arm mounting bolts to 94–130 ft. lb.

Upper Control Arm

REMOVAL & INSTALLATION

1. Remove the upper arm mounting nuts from inside the engine compartment, but do not remove the bolts.
2. Raise the vehicle, support the lower arm and remove the wheel.
3. On vehicles equipped with a ball joint wear sensor, remove the wiring from the clamp on the arm.
4. Remove the upper ball joint.
5. Remove the control arm mounting bolts.
6. Pry out the arm with a prybar.
7. Install in reverse of removal. Do not tighten the fasteners until the vehicle is on the ground.
8. Lower the vehicle and tighten the control arm mounting bolts to 95–130 ft. lb.

Front Axle Hub and Bearing

REMOVAL & INSTALLATION

♦ See Figure 7 (p. 14)

1. Raise the front of the vehicle and support it with jackstands. Remove the wheel.
2. Remove the front disc brake caliper mounting bolts and position it safely out of the way.
3. Pry off the bearing cap and then remove the cotter pin, lock cap and the adjusting nut.
4. Remove the axle hub and disc together with the outer bearing and thrust washer.

➡**Be careful not to drop the outer bearing during removal.**

5. Using a small prybar, pry out the oil seal from the back of the hub and then remove the inner bearing.
6. Installation is in the reverse order of removal. Please note the following:

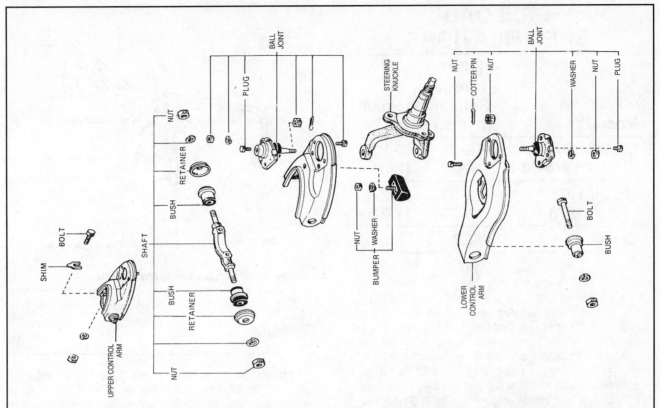

Fig. 6 On models with upper and lower control arms, the ball joints can be replaced—1972–77 Mark II shown, others similar

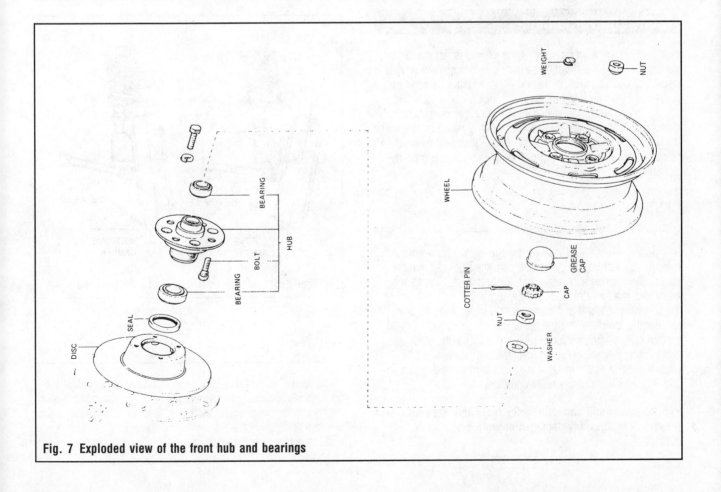

Fig. 7 Exploded view of the front hub and bearings

PRELOAD SPECIFICATIONS

Model/Year	Initial Torque Setting (ft. lbs.)	Preload (oz.)
Corona 1975-77	19-26	10-22
1978-80	19-26	12-31
Mark II 1975	19-23	10-22
1976	19-23	11-24
Cressida	22	37-56

a. Place some axle grease into the palm of your hand and then take the bearing and work the grease into it until it begins to ooze out the other side. Coat the inside of the axle hub and bearing cap with the same grease.

b. Install the bearing adjusting nut and tighten it to 22 ft. lbs. (29 Nm). Snug down the bearing by turning the hub several times. Loosen the nut until it can be turned by hand and then, using a spring scale, retighten it until the preload measures 0.8–1.9 lbs. (2.3 lbs. on 1984–85 models).

c. Use a new cotter pin when installing the lock cap.

Front End Alignment

If the tires are worn unevenly, if the vehicle is not stable on the highway or if the handling seems uneven in spirited driving, wheel alignment should be checked. If an alignment problem is suspected, first check tire inflation and look for other possible causes such a worn suspension and steering components, accident damage or unmatched tires. Repairs may be necessary before the wheels can be properly aligned. Wheel alignment requires sophisticated equipment and can only be performed at a properly equipped shop.

CASTER

Wheel alignment is defined by three different adjustments in three planes. Looking at the vehicle from the side, caster angle describes the steering axis rather than a wheel angle. The steering knuckle is attached to the strut at the top and the control arm at the bottom. The wheel pivots around the line between these points to steer the vehicle. When the upper point is tilted back, this is described as positive caster. Having a positive caster tends to make the wheels self-centering, increasing directional stability. Excessive positive caster makes the wheels hard to steer, while an uneven caster will cause a pull to one side.

➡️**If the caster still cannot be adjusted within the limits, inspect or replace any damaged or worn suspension parts.**

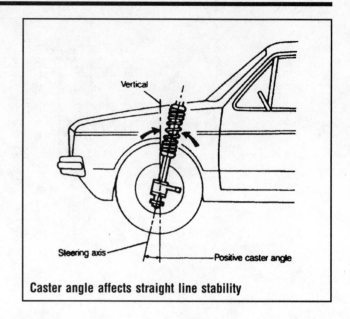

Caster angle affects straight line stability

CAMBER

Looking at the wheels from the front of the vehicle, camber adjustment is the tilt of the wheel. When the wheel is tilted in at the top, this is negative camber. In a turn, a slight amount of negative camber helps maximize contact of the outside tire with the road. Too much negative camber makes the vehicle unstable in a straight line.

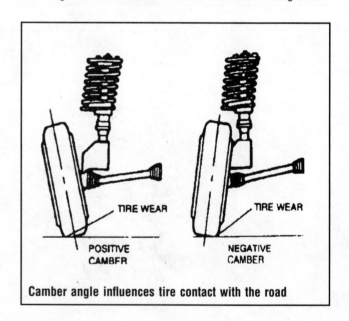

Camber angle influences tire contact with the road

TOE-IN

Toe is the amount measured in a fraction of an inch, that the front wheels are closer together at one end than the other. Toe-in means that the front wheels are closer together at the front of the tire than at the rear; toe-out means that the rear of the tires are closer together than the front.

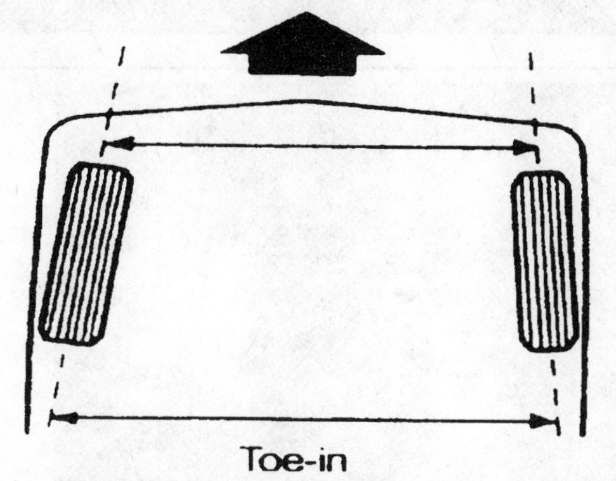

Toe-in means the distance between the wheels is closer at the front than at the rear of the wheels

Although it is recommended that this adjustment be made by your dealer or a qualified shop, you can make it yourself if you make very careful measurement. The wheels must be dead straight ahead. The car must have a full tank of gas, all fluids must be at their proper levels, all other suspension and steering adjustments must be correct and the tires must be properly inflated to their cold specification.

1. Toe can be determined by measuring the distance between the centers of the tire treads, at the front of the tire and the rear. If the tread pattern of your car's tires makes this impossible, you can measure between the edges of the wheel rims, but be sure to move the car and measure in a few places to avoid errors caused by bent rims or wheel run-out.
2. If the measurement is not within specifications, loosen the four retaining clamp lock nuts on the adjustable tie rods.
3. Turn the left and right tie rods EQUAL amounts until the measurements are within specifications.
4. Tighten the lockbolts and then recheck the measurements. Check to see that the steering wheel is still in the proper position. If not, remove it and reposition it as detailed later in this section.

Wheel Alignment Specifications

Model/Year	Caster		Camber		Toe-in (in.)	Steering Axis Inclination	Wheel Pivot Ratio (deg)	
	Range (deg)	Pref Setting (deg)	Range (deg)	Pref Setting (deg)			Inner Wheel	Outer Wheel
Corona 1970–73	0–1P	½P	1P–2P	1½P	0.16–0.24	7P	38½	31
Corona 1974–75	½P–1½P	1P	0–1P	½P	0.06–0.12	7P	—	—
Corona 1976	½P–1½P	1P	0–1P	½P	0.04–0.12	7P	36½–38½	31
Corona 1977	⅓–1⅓	1P	0–1P	½P	0.04–0.12	7P	36½–38½	31
Corona 1978–79	⅓P–1⅓P	⅘P	1/12P–1⅙P	⅗P	0.04–0.12	7P	37½	31
Corona 1980–82	1¼P–2¼P	1¾P	½P–1½P	1P	0–.08	7⅔P	36–38	28–32
Cressida 1978–80	½P–1½P	1P	⅓P–1⅓P	⅚P	0.08–0.16 out	7½P	36–39	30–34
Cressida 1981–82	1P–2P	1½P	⅓P–1⅓P	⅚P	0.08–0.16 out	9P	35–39	30–32
Mark II/4 All	1P–2P	1½P	1P–2P	1P	0.16–0.24	7P	40	32½
Mark II/6 1972–75	0–1P	½P	½P–1½P	1P	0.16–0.24	7P	36½	32½
Mark II/6 1976	1½P–2½P	2P	½P–1½P	1P	0.16–0.24	7P	36½–38½	31–32
Crown 2300	1N–0	½N	0–1P	½P	0.12–0.20	7½P	38	29½
Crown 2600	1N–½P	½N	0–1P	½P	0.12–0.20	7½P	38	29

P Positive
N Negative

REAR SUSPENSION

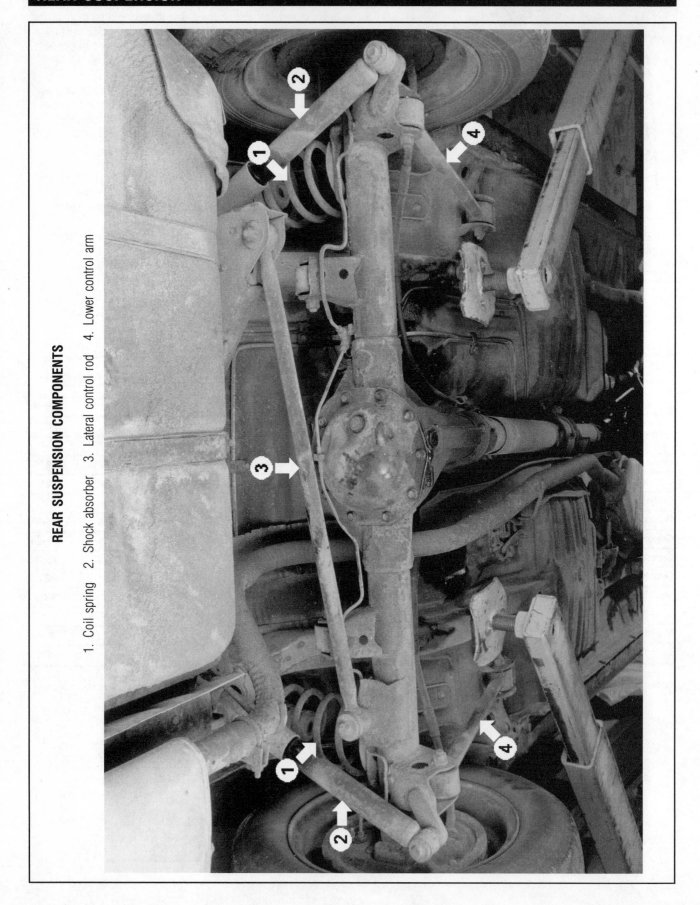

REAR SUSPENSION COMPONENTS

1. Coil spring   2. Shock absorber   3. Lateral control rod   4. Lower control arm

Leaf Springs

REMOVAL & INSTALLATION

◆ **See Figures 8 and 9**

1. Loosen the rear wheel lug nuts.
2. Raise the rear of the vehicle. Support the frame and rear axle housing with stands.

❋❋ CAUTION

Be sure that the vehicle is securely supported.

3. Remove the lug nuts and the wheel.
4. Remove the cotter pin, nut, and washer from the lower end of the shock absorber.
5. Detach the shock absorber from the spring seat pivot pin.
6. Remove the parking brake cable clamp.

➡**Remove the parking brake equalizer, if necessary.**

7. Unfasten the U-bolt nuts and remove the spring seat assemblies.
8. Adjust the height of the rear axle housing so that the weight of the rear axle is removed from the rear springs.
9. Unfasten the spring shackle retaining nuts. Withdraw the spring shackle inner plate. Carefully pry out the spring shackle with a bar.
10. Remove the spring bracket pin from the front end of the spring hanger and remove the rubber bushings.

❋❋ WARNING

Use care not to damage the hydraulic brake line or the parking brake line.

To install:
11. Install the rubber bushings in the eye of the spring.
12. Align the eye of the spring with the spring hanger bracket and drive the pin through the bracket holes and rubber bushings.

➡**Use soapy water as lubricant, if necessary, to aid in pin installation. Never use oil or grease.**

13. Finger-tighten the spring hanger nuts and/or bolts.
14. Install the rubber bushings in the spring eye at the opposite end of the spring.
15. Raise the free end of the spring. Install the spring shackle through the bushings and the bracket.
16. Fit the shackle inner plate and finger-tighten the retaining nuts.
17. Center the bolt head in the hole which is provided in the spring seat on the axle housing.

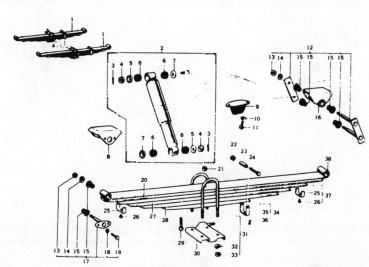

1. Rear spring	14. Spring washer	27. Rear spring leaf
2. Rear shock absorber	15. Bushing	28. Rear spring leaf
3. Cotter pin	16. Spring bracket	29. Rear spring center bolt
4. Castle nut	17. Rear spring hanger pin	30. U-bolt seat
5. Shock absorber cushion washer	18. Spring washer	31. U-bolt
6. Bushing	19. Bolt	32. Spring washer
7. Shock absorber cushion washer	20. Rear spring leaf	33. Nut
8. Spring bracket	21. Nut	34. Rear spring leaf
9. Rear spring bumper	22. Nut	35. Rear spring clip
10. Spring washer	23. Rear spring clip bolt	36. Round rivet
11. Bolt	24. Clip bolt	37. Rear spring leaf
12. Rear spring shackle	25. Rear spring clip	38. Rear spring leaf
13. Nut	26. Round rivet	

Fig. 8 Typical rear leaf spring components

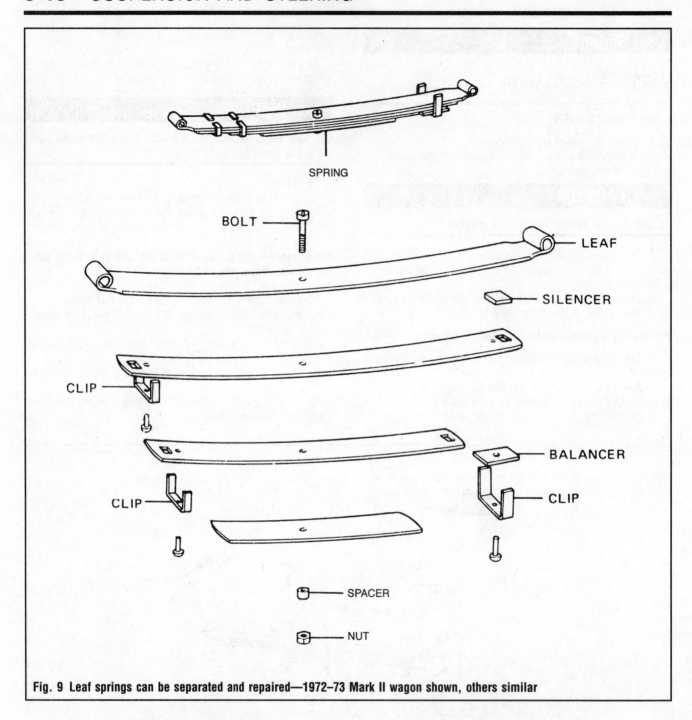

Fig. 9 Leaf springs can be separated and repaired—1972–73 Mark II wagon shown, others similar

18. Fit the U-bolts over the axle housing. Install the lower spring seat.

19. Tighten the U-bolt nuts to the specifications listed in the following Rear Suspension Torque Specifications Chart.

➡**Some models have two sets of nuts, while others have a nut and lockwasher.**

20. Install the parking brake cable clamp. Install the equalizer, if it was removed.

21. Install the shock absorber end at the spring seat. Tighten the nuts to the specified torque.

22. Install the wheel and lug nuts. Lower the car to the ground.

23. Bounce the car several times.

24. Tighten the spring bracket pins and shackles.

25. Repeat Step 13 and check all of the torque specifications again.

Coil Springs

REMOVAL & INSTALLATION

▶ **See Figures 10, 11 and 12 (p. 19–21)**

1. Remove the hubcap and loosen the lug nuts.

2. Jack up the rear axle housing and support the frame with jackstands. Leave the jack in place under the rear axle housing.

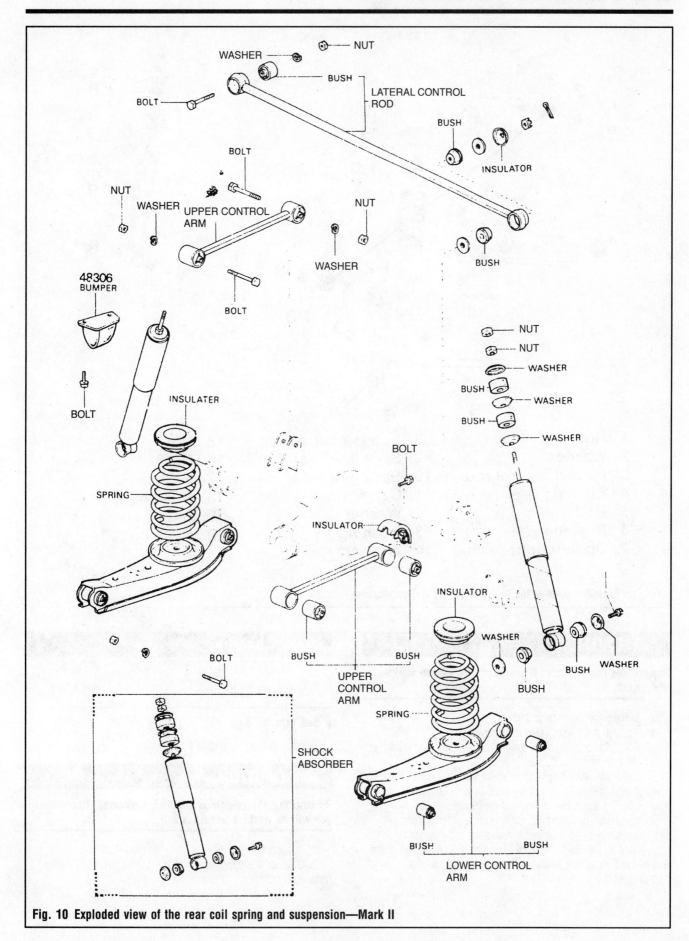

Fig. 10 Exploded view of the rear coil spring and suspension—Mark II

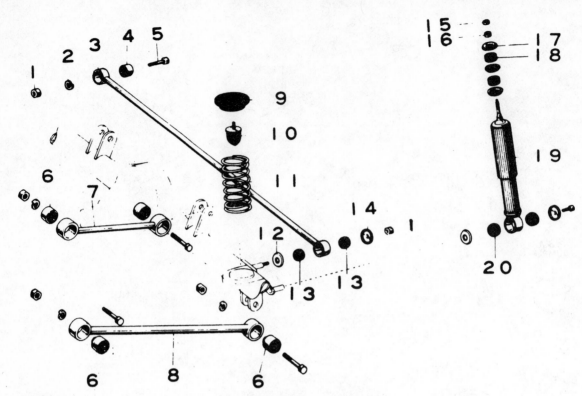

1. Nut
2. Washer
3. Lateral control rod
4. Bushing
5. Bolt
6. Bushing
7. Upper control arm
8. Lower control arm
9. Spring insulator
10. Spring bumper
11. Coil spring
12. Washer
13. Bushing
14. Washer
15. Nut
16. Nut
17. Washer
18. Bushing
19. Shock absorber
20. Bushing

Fig. 11 Exploded view of the rear coil spring and suspension—Crown

❉❉ CAUTION

Support the car securely. Remember, you will be working underneath it.

3. Remove the lug nuts and wheel.
4. Unfasten the lower shock absorber end.
5. Slowly lower the jack under the rear axle housing until the axle is at the bottom of its travel.
6. Withdraw the coil spring, complete with its insulator.
7. Inspect the coil spring and insulator for wear, cracks, or weakness. Replace either or both, as necessary.
8. Installation is performed in the reverse order of removal. Tighten the lower shock absorber mounting to the specifications listed in the Shock Absorber Tightening Torque chart at the end of the Rear Shock Absorber Removal and Installation section.

Shock Absorbers

REMOVAL & INSTALLATION

▶ **See Figure 13 (p. 23)**

1. Jack up the rear end of the vehicle.

❉❉ CAUTION

Be sure that the vehicle is securely supported. Remember, you will be working underneath it.

2. Support the rear axle housing with jackstands.
3. Unfasten the upper shock absorber retaining nuts and/or bolts from the upper frame member.

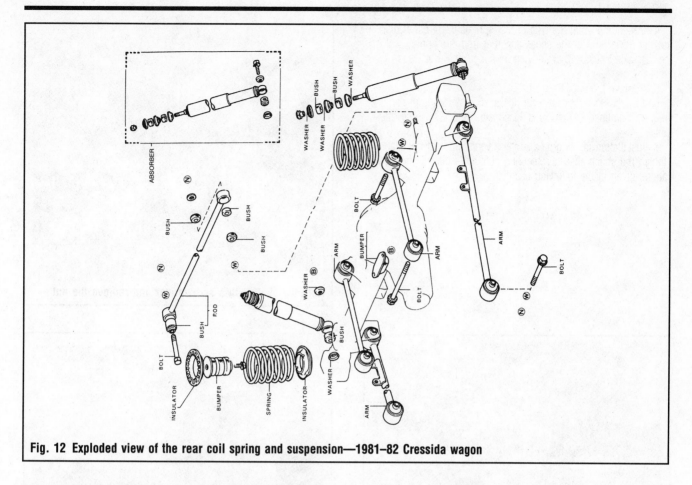

Fig. 12 Exploded view of the rear coil spring and suspension—1981–82 Cressida wagon

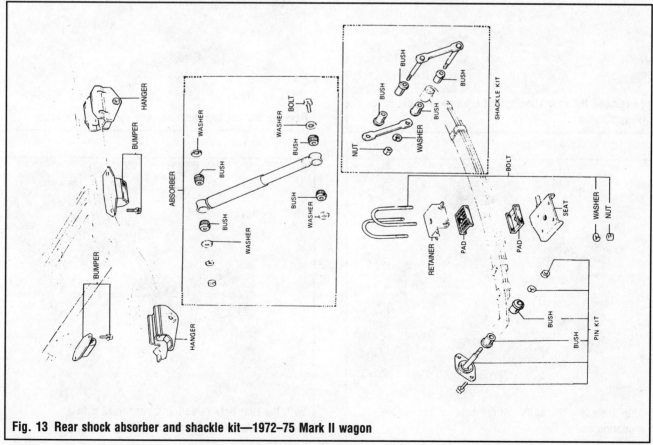

Fig. 13 Rear shock absorber and shackle kit—1972–75 Mark II wagon

4. Depending upon the type of rear springs used, either disconnect the lower end of the shock absorber from the spring seat or the rear axle housing by removing its cotter pins, nuts, and/or bolts.

5. Remove the shock absorber.

6. Inspect the shock for wear, leaks, or other signs of damage. Test it as outlined in the Front Suspension Shock Absorber section.

7. Installation is performed in the reverse order of removal. Tighten the shock absorber securing nuts and bolts to the specifications given in the following chart.

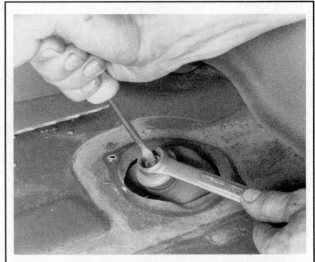

Hold the shaft with a screwdriver and remove the nut

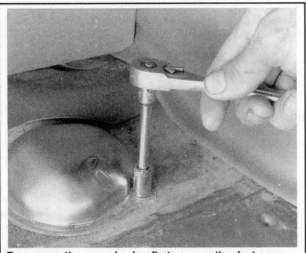

To remove the rear shocks, first remove the dust cover (if applicable)

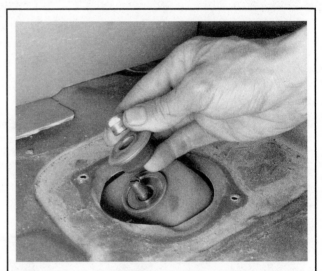

Remove the nut and bushing from the shock absorber

After removing the bolts, lift the cover to expose the mounting nut

With the rear axle raised and supported with a jackstand, loosen the lower mounting bolt

Remove the bolt and washer then place them aside

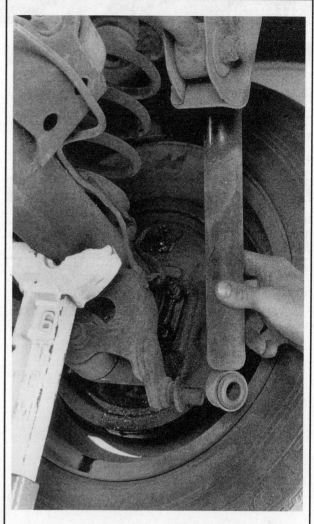

Slide the shock off the lower mounting bracket

Shock Absorber Tightening Torque (ft. lbs.)

Model	Upper Mounting	Lower Mounting
Corona	—	25–40
Mark II/4	—	25–40
Mark II/6 Sedan and Coupe	14–22	26–33
Station Wagon	36–58	14–22
Crown 2300	11–16	22–23
Crown 2600 Sedan and Coupe	11–16	22–33

STEERING

Steering Wheel

REMOVAL & INSTALLATION

Three-Spoke

♦ **See Figures 14 and 15**

✳✳ CAUTION

Do not attempt to remove or install the steering wheel by hammering on it. Damage to the energy absorbing steering column could result.

1. Unfasten the horn and turn signal multiconnector(s) at the base of the steering column shroud.

2. Loosen the trim pad retaining screws from the back side of the steering wheel.

3. Lift the trim pad and horn button assembly(ies) from the wheel.

4. Remove the steering wheel hub retaining nut.

5. Scratch matchmarks on the hub and shaft to aid in correct installation.

6. Use a steering wheel puller to remove the steering wheel.

7. Installation is performed in the reverse order of removal. Tighten the wheel retaining nut to 15–22 ft. lb., except for the Mark II 6 cylinder and 1974–77 Corona, which should be tightened to 22–29 ft. lb.

Two-Spoke

♦ **See Figure 16 (p. 28)**

The two-spoke steering wheel is removed in the same manner as the three-spoke, except that the trim pad should be pried off

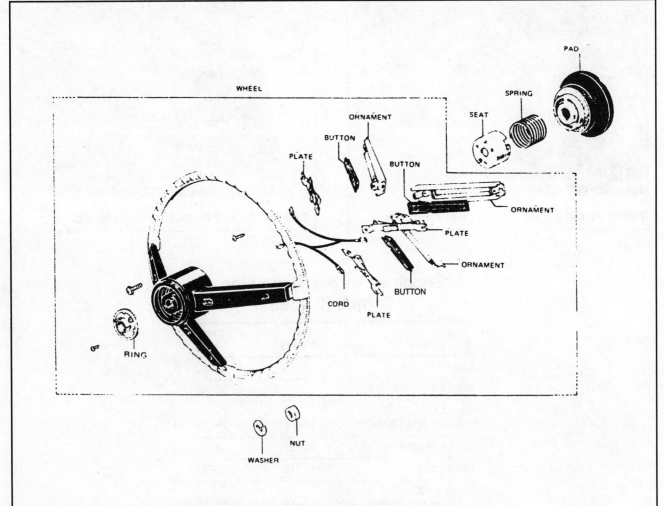

Fig. 14 Exploded view of the three-spoke steering wheel—1971–72 Crown

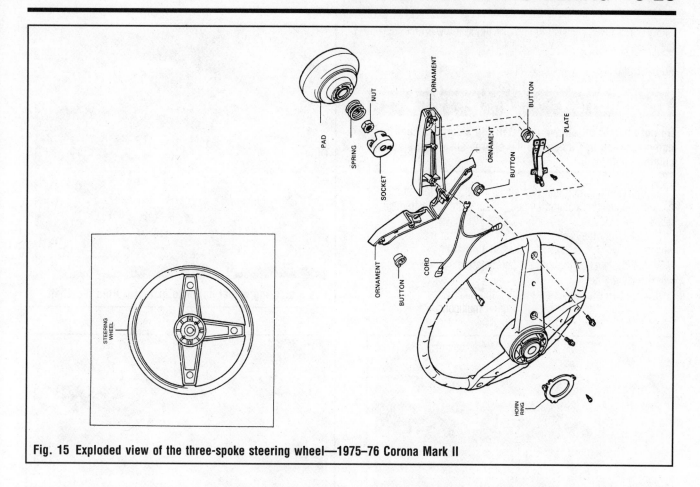

Fig. 15 Exploded view of the three-spoke steering wheel—1975–76 Corona Mark II

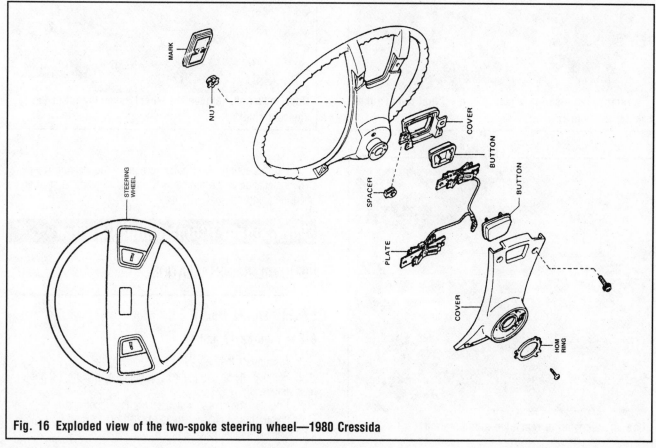

Fig. 16 Exploded view of the two-spoke steering wheel—1980 Cressida

with a screwdriver. Remove the pad by lifting it toward the top of the wheel.

Four-Spoke

✳✳ CAUTION

Do not attempt to remove or install the steering wheel by hammering on it. Damage to the energy absorbing steering column could result.

1. Unfasten the horn and turn signal multiconnectors at the base of the steering column shroud (underneath the instrument panel) if possible.
2. Gently pry the center emblem off the front of the steering wheel.
3. Insert a wrench through the hole and remove the steering wheel retaining nut.
4. Scratch matchmarks on the hub and shaft to aid installation.

Use a steering wheel puller to extract it from the shaft

To remove the steering wheel, you must first remove the center emblem

Once loosened, remove the wheel assembly off of the steering shaft

5. Use a steering wheel puller to remove the steering wheel.
6. Installation is the reverse of removal. Tighten the steering wheel retaining nut to 15–22 lbs.

Turn Signal (Combination) Switch

REMOVAL & INSTALLATION

Except 1970–72 Mark II 4 Cylinder

▶ **See Figures 17 and 18**

1. Disconnect the negative (−) battery cable.
2. Remove the steering wheel, as outlined in the appropriate preceding section.
3. Unfasten the screws which secure the upper and lower steering column shroud halves. On 1974–76 Corona models, remove the lower instrument panel garnish first.

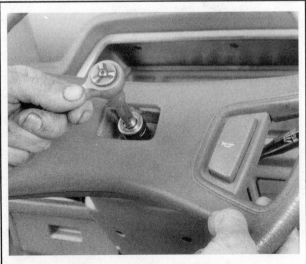

Use an extension to reach the mounting nut

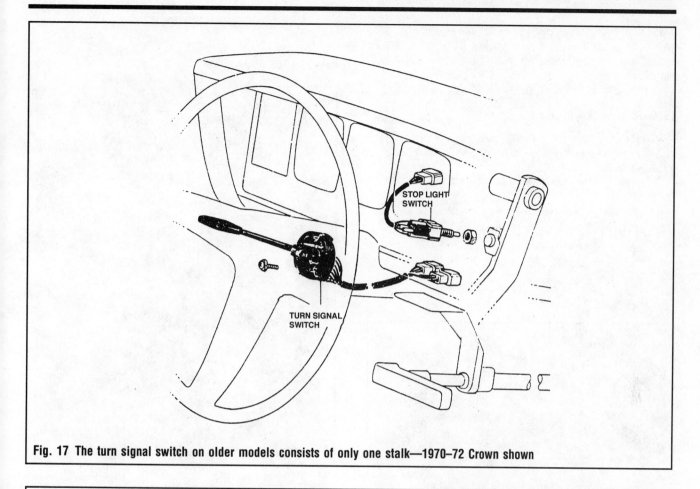

Fig. 17 The turn signal switch on older models consists of only one stalk—1970–72 Crown shown

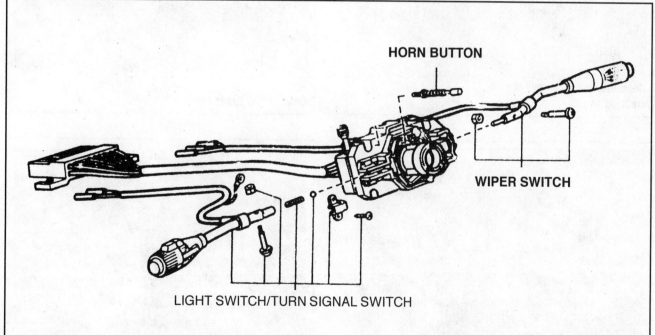

Fig. 18 On later models, a combination switch incorporates the turn signal switch as well as the wiper switch—1980–82 Cressida shown

4. Unfasten the screws which retain the turn signal switch and remove the switch from the column. On later Coronas the hazard warning and windshield wiper switches are part of the assembly, and will be removed as well.

5. Installation is performed in the reverse order of removal.

1970–72 Mark II 4 Cylinder

1. Disconnect the negative battery cable.

2. Remove the steering wheel as outlined in the appropriate preceding section.

3. Remove the turn signal switch housing and the turn signal switch.

4. Installation is performed in the reverse order of removal.

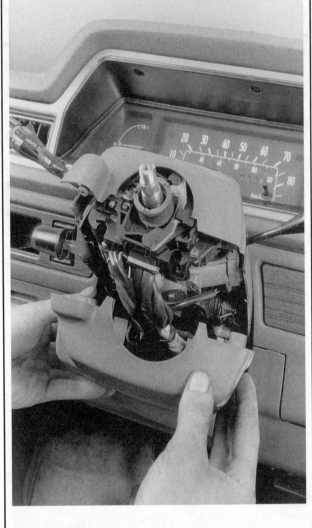

Remove the lower cover

Once loosened, remove the wheel assembly off of the steering shaft

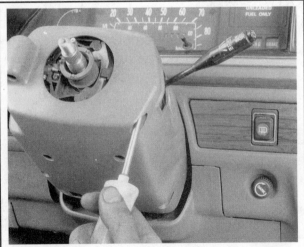

To access the combination switch, remove the steering wheel then the cover screws

Next, pull off the upper cover

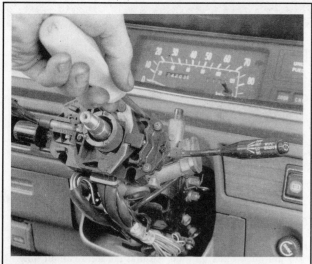

Remove the combination switch mounting screws

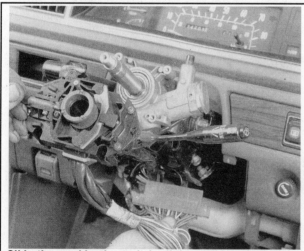

Slide the combination switch off the steering shaft as an assembly—1979 Corona shown, others similar

Ignition Lock/Switch

REMOVAL & INSTALLATION

Except 1970–72 Mark II 4 Cylinder

♦ See Figures 19 and 20

1. Disconnect the negative battery cable.
2. Unfasten the ignition switch multiconnector underneath the instrument panel.
3. Remove the screws which secure the upper and lower halves of the steering column cover. Remove the lower instrument panel garnish on 1974–77 Corona models first.
4. Turn the lock cylinder to the ACC position with the ignition key.
5. Push the lock cylinder stop in with a small, round object (cotter pin, punch, etc).

➡On some models it may be necessary to remove the steering wheel and turn signal switch first.

6. Withdraw the lock cylinder from the lock housing while depressing the stop tab.
7. To remove the ignition switch, unfasten its securing screws and withdraw the switch from the lock housing.

To install:

8. Align the locking cam with the hole in the ignition switch and insert the switch in the lock housing.
9. Secure the switch with its screw(s).
10. Make sure that both the lock cylinder and the column lock are in the ACC position. Slide the cylinder into the lock housing until the stop tab engages the hole in the lock.
11. The rest of installation is performed in the reverse order of removal.

1970–72 Mark II 4 Cylinder

1. Disconnect the negative battery cable.
2. Remove the steering wheel, turn signal switch housing, and turn signal switch as previously outlined.

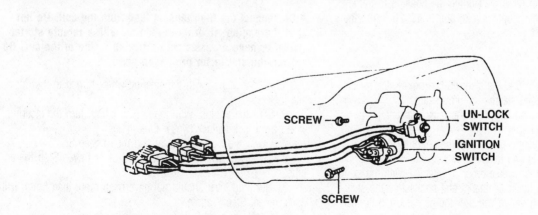

Fig. 19 The ignition switch is the electrical portion attached to the lock cylinder

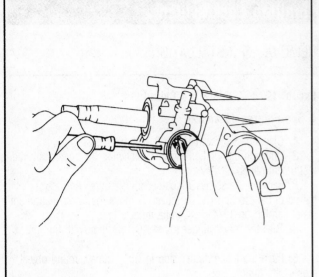

Fig. 20 Push down the stop key with a thin rod and pull out the lock cylinder

3. Remove the lock assembly retaining screw.
4. Withdraw the switch assembly from the column by pulling it out with the ignition key.
5. Installation is performed in the reverse order of removal.

Manual Steering Gear

REMOVAL & INSTALLATION

Corona

1. Remove the bolt attaching the coupling yoke to the steering worm.
2. Disconnect the relay rod from the pitman arm.
3. Remove the steering gear housing down and to the left.
4. Install in reverse of removal. Tighten the housing-to-frame bolts to 25–36 ft. lb.; the coupling yoke bolt to 15–20 ft. lb.; the relay rod to 36–50 ft. lb.

Cressida

1. Open the hood, and find the steering gearbox. Place matchmarks on the coupling and steering column shaft.
2. Disconnect the pitman arm from the relay rod using a tie rod puller on the pitman arm set nut.
3. Disconnect the steering gearbox at the coupling. Unbolt the gearbox from the chassis and remove.
4. Installation is in the reverse order of removal, with the exception of first aligning the matchmarks and connecting the steering shaft to the coupling before you bolt the gearbox into the car permanently.

Power Steering Pump

REMOVAL & INSTALLATION

▶ **See Figure 21**

1. Remove the fan shroud.
2. Unfasten the nut from the center of the pump pulley.

➡ **Use the drive belt as a brake to keep the pulley from rotating.**

3. Withdraw the drive belt.
4. Remove the pulley and the woodruff key from the pump shaft.
5. Detach the intake and outlet hoses from the pump reservoir.

➡ **Tie the hose ends up high, so that the fluid cannot flow out of them. Drain or plug the pump to prevent fluid leakage.**

6. Remove the bolt from the rear mounting brace.
7. Remove the front bracket bolts and withdraw the pump.
8. Installation is performed in the reverse order of removal. Note the following, however:
   a. Tighten the pump pulley mounting bolt to 25–39 ft. lb.
   b. Adjust the pump drive belt tension. The belt should deflect 8–10mm when 22 lbs. pressure is applied midway between the air pump and the power steering pump.
   c. Fill the reservoir with Dexron® automatic transmission fluid. Bleed the air from the system, as detailed following.

BLEEDING

1. Raise the front of the car and support it securely with jackstands.
2. Fill the pump reservoir with DEXRON® automatic transmission fluid.
3. Rotate the steering wheel from lock-to-lock several times. Add fluid as necessary.
4. With the steering wheel turned fully to one lock, crank the starter while watching the fluid level in the reservoir.

➡ **Disconnect the high tension lead from the coil. Do not start the engine. Operate the starter with a remote starter switch or have an assistant do it from inside of the car. Do not run the starter for prolonged periods.**

5. Repeat Step 4 with the steering wheel turned to the opposite lock.
6. Start the engine. With the engine idling, turn the steering wheel from lock-to-lock two or three times.
7. Lower the front of the car and repeat Step 6.
8. Center the wheel at the midpoint of its travel. Stop the engine.
9. The fluid level should not have risen more than 5mm. If it does, repeat Step 7 again.
10. Check for fluid leakage.

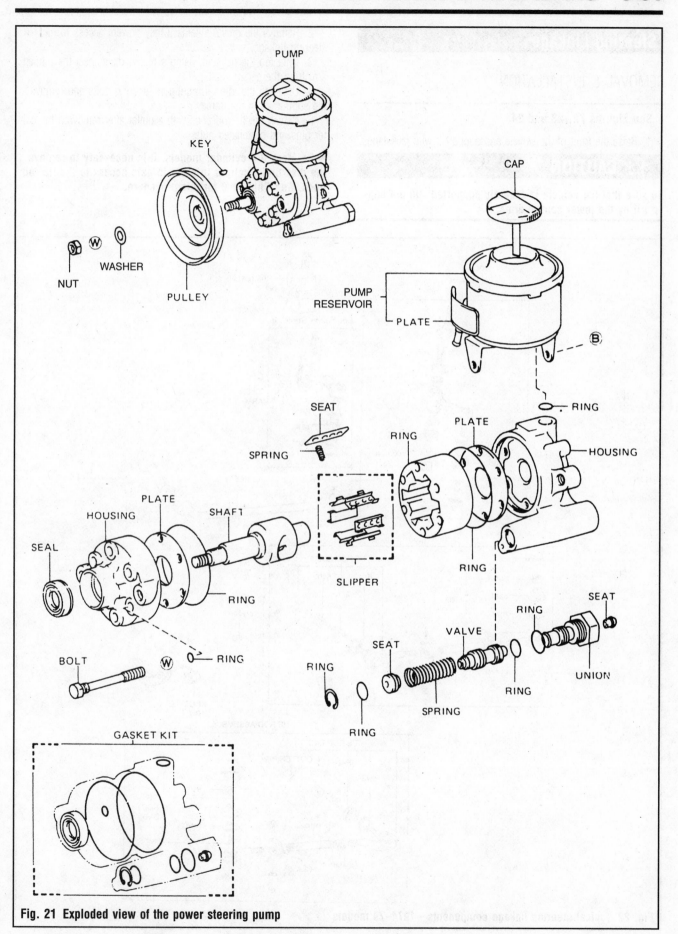

Fig. 21 Exploded view of the power steering pump

Steering Linkage

REMOVAL & INSTALLATION

◆ **See Figures 22, 23 and 24**

1. Raise the front of the vehicle and support it with jackstands.

⁂ **CAUTION**

Be sure that the vehicle is securely supported. Do not support it by the lower control arms.

2. Remove the gravel shields if they prevent access to the steering linkage.

3. Unfasten the nut and, using a puller, disconnect the pitman arm from the sector shaft.

4. Unfasten the idler arm support securing bolts and remove the support from the frame.

5. Detach the tie rod ends with a puller after removing the cotter pins and castellated nuts.

➡ **On Mark II 6 cylinder models, it is necessary to remove the disc brake caliper in order to gain access to the tie rod ends. See Chapter 9 for this procedure.**

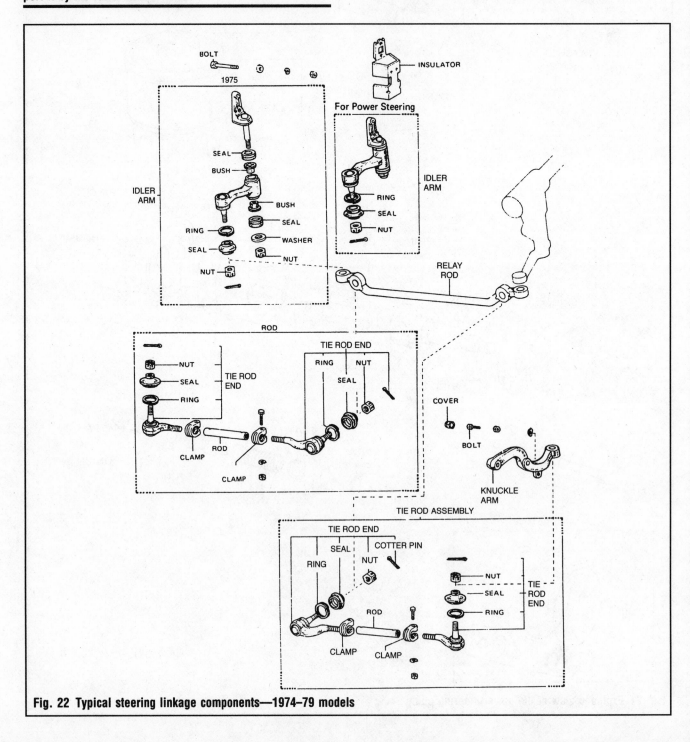

Fig. 22 Typical steering linkage components—1974–79 models

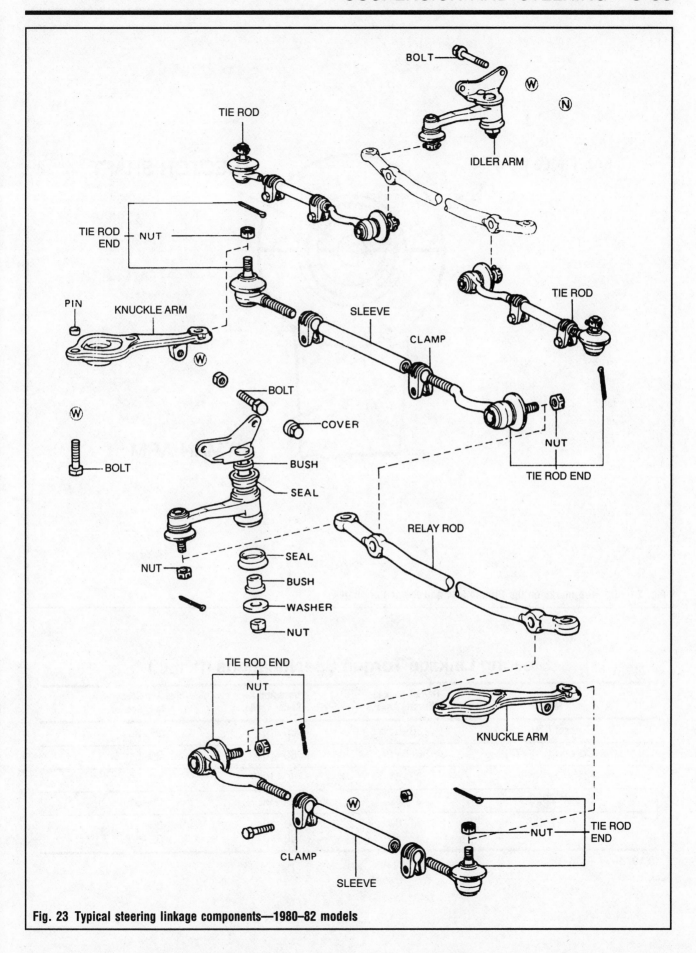

Fig. 23 Typical steering linkage components—1980–82 models

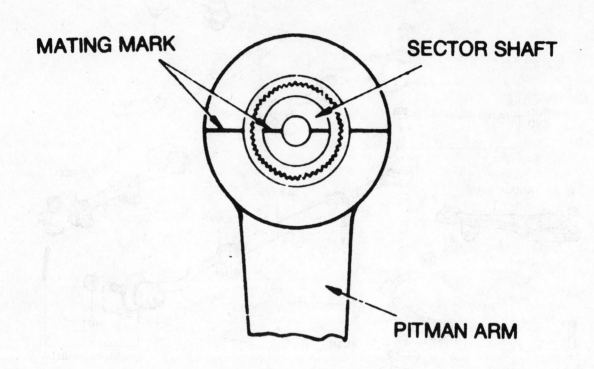

MATING MARK   SECTOR SHAFT

PITMAN ARM

Fig. 24 Align the marks on the Pitman arm and the sector shaft

Steering Linkage Torque Specifications (ft. lbs.)

Model	Tie-Rod Ends-to-Knuckle Arms	Pitman Arm-to-Sector Shaft	Idler Arm-Support-to-Frame
Corona ('70–'73)	36–51	80–101	25–36
Corona ('74–'77)	36–51 ①	80–101	36–51
Mark II	36–51	80–101	29–40
Crown 2300	37–52	80–90	36–51
Crown 2600	54–80 32–50	80–101 80–101	36–51 32–50

① 1976–77—36–65

6. Remove the steering linkage as an assembly.

7. Installation is performed in the reverse order of removal. Note the following however:

  a. Tighten the linkage parts to the torque figures given in the Steering Linkage Torque Specifications chart.

  b. Align the marks on pitman arm and sector shaft before installing the pitman arm.

  c. The self locking nut used on some models, on the idler arm, may be reused if it cannot be turned by hand when fitted to the bolt.

  d. Adjust the toe-in specifications after completing the steering linkage installation procedure.

Tie Rod End

REMOVAL & INSTALLATION

1. Scribe alignment marks on the tie rod and rack end (rack and pinion cars only).

2. Working at the steering knuckle arm, pull out the cotter pin and then remove the castellated nut.

3. Using a tie rod end puller, disconnect the tie rod from the steering knuckle arm.

4. Repeat the first two steps on the other end of the tie rod (where it attaches to the relay rod).

To install:

5. On the non-rack and pinion cars, turn the tie rods in their adjusting tubes until they are of equal lengths. They should be approximately 12.60 inch long.

  a. Turn the tie rod ends so that they cross at 90°. Tighten the adjusting tube clamps so that they lock the ends in position.

  b. Connect the tie rods and tighten the nuts to 37–50 ft. lbs. (50–67 Nm).

  c. Check the toe. Adjust if necessary.

6. On the rack and pinion cars align the alignment marks on the tie rod and rack end.

  a. Install the tie rod end.

  b. Tighten the nuts to 11–14 ft. lbs. (14–18 Nm).

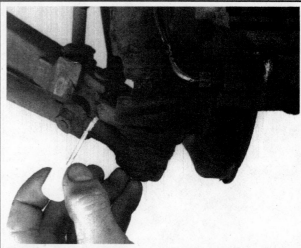

Before separating the tie rod end, scribe threads where it meets the sleeve

Remove the cotter pin . . .

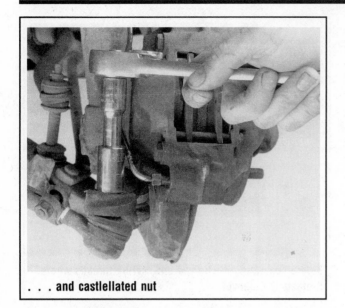

. . . and castlellated nut

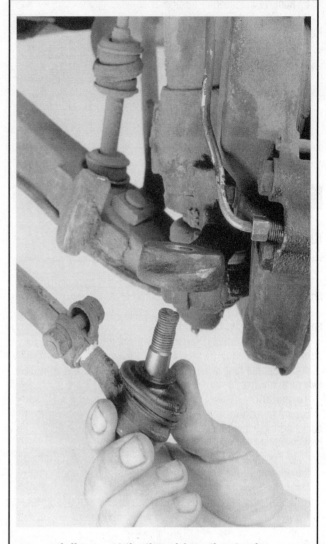

. . . and disconnect the tie rod from the steering knuckle arm

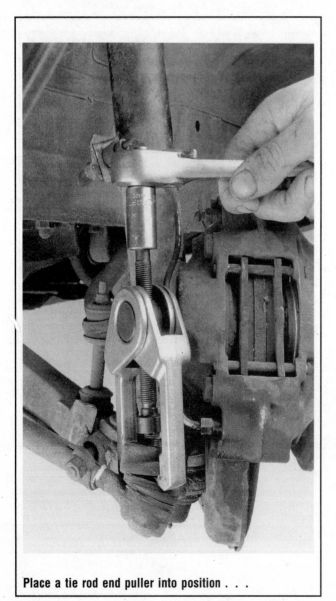

Place a tie rod end puller into position . . .

Unscrew the tie rod end from the sleeve

Troubleshooting Basic Steering and Suspension Problems

Problem	Cause	Solution
Hard steering (steering wheel is hard to turn)	• Low or uneven tire pressure • Loose power steering pump drive belt • Low or incorrect power steering fluid • Incorrect front end alignment • Defective power steering pump • Bent or poorly lubricated front end parts	• Inflate tires to correct pressure • Adjust belt • Add fluid as necessary • Have front end alignment checked/adjusted • Check pump • Lubricate and/or replace defective parts
Loose steering (too much play in the steering wheel)	• Loose wheel bearings • Loose or worn steering linkage • Faulty shocks • Worn ball joints	• Adjust wheel bearings • Replace worn parts • Replace shocks • Replace ball joints
Car veers or wanders (car pulls to one side with hands off the steering wheel)	• Incorrect tire pressure • Improper front end alignment • Loose wheel bearings • Loose or bent front end components • Faulty shocks	• Inflate tires to correct pressure • Have front end alignment checked/adjusted • Adjust wheel bearings • Replace worn components • Replace shocks
Wheel oscillation or vibration transmitted through steering wheel	• Improper tire pressures • Tires out of balance • Loose wheel bearings • Improper front end alignment • Worn or bent front end components	• Inflate tires to correct pressure • Have tires balanced • Adjust wheel bearings • Have front end alignment checked/adjusted • Replace worn parts
Uneven tire wear	• Incorrect tire pressure • Front end out of alignment • Tires out of balance	• Inflate tires to correct pressure • Have front end alignment checked/adjusted • Have tires balanced

Troubleshooting the Steering Column

Problem	Cause	Solution
Will not lock	• Lockbolt spring broken or defective	• Replace lock bolt spring
High effort (required to turn ignition key and lock cylinder)	• Lock cylinder defective	• Replace lock cylinder
	• Ignition switch defective	• Replace ignition switch
	• Rack preload spring broken or deformed	• Replace preload spring
	• Burr on lock sector, lock rack, housing, support or remote rod coupling	• Remove burr
	• Bent sector shaft	• Replace shaft
	• Defective lock rack	• Replace lock rack
	• Remote rod bent, deformed	• Replace rod
	• Ignition switch mounting bracket bent	• Straighten or replace
	• Distorted coupling slot in lock rack (tilt column)	• Replace lock rack
Will stick in "start"	• Remote rod deformed	• Straighten or replace
	• Ignition switch mounting bracket bent	• Straighten or replace
Key cannot be removed in "off-lock"	• Ignition switch is not adjusted correctly	• Adjust switch
	• Defective lock cylinder	• Replace lock cylinder
Lock cylinder can be removed without depressing retainer	• Lock cylinder with defective retainer	• Replace lock cylinder
	• Burr over retainer slot in housing cover or on cylinder retainer	• Remove burr
High effort on lock cylinder between "off" and "off-lock"	• Distorted lock rack	• Replace lock rack
	• Burr on tang of shift gate (automatic column)	• Remove burr
	• Gearshift linkage not adjusted	• Adjust linkage
Noise in column	• One click when in "off-lock" position and the steering wheel is moved (all except automatic column)	• Normal—lock bolt is seating
	• Coupling bolts not tightened	• Tighten pinch bolts
	• Lack of grease on bearings or bearing surfaces	• Lubricate with chassis grease
	• Upper shaft bearing worn or broken	• Replace bearing assembly
	• Lower shaft bearing worn or broken	• Replace bearing. Check shaft and replace if scored.
	• Column not correctly aligned	• Align column
	• Coupling pulled apart	• Replace coupling
	• Broken coupling lower joint	• Repair or replace joint and align column
	• Steering shaft snap ring not seated	• Replace ring. Check for proper seating in groove.
	• Shroud loose on shift bowl. Housing loose on jacket—will be noticed with ignition in "off-lock" and when torque is applied to steering wheel.	• Position shroud over lugs on shift bowl. Tighten mounting screws.
High steering shaft effort	• Column misaligned	• Align column
	• Defective upper or lower bearing	• Replace as required
	• Tight steering shaft universal joint	• Repair or replace
	• Flash on I.D. of shift tube at plastic joint (tilt column only)	• Replace shift tube
	• Upper or lower bearing seized	• Replace bearings
Lash in mounted column assembly	• Column mounting bracket bolts loose	• Tighten bolts
	• Broken weld nuts on column jacket	• Replace column jacket
	• Column capsule bracket sheared	• Replace bracket assembly

Troubleshooting the Steering Column (cont.)

Problem	Cause	Solution
Lash in mounted column assembly (cont.)	• Column bracket to column jacket mounting bolts loose	• Tighten to specified torque
	• Loose lock shoes in housing (tilt column only)	• Replace shoes
	• Loose pivot pins (tilt column only)	• Replace pivot pins and support
	• Loose lock shoe pin (tilt column only)	• Replace pin and housing
	• Loose support screws (tilt column only)	• Tighten screws
Housing loose (tilt column only)	• Excessive clearance between holes in support or housing and pivot pin diameters	• Replace pivot pins and support
	• Housing support-screws loose	• Tighten screws
Steering wheel loose—every other tilt position (tilt column only)	• Loose fit between lock shoe and lock shoe pivot pin	• Replace lock shoes and pivot pin
Steering column not locking in any tilt position (tilt column only)	• Lock shoe seized on pivot pin	• Replace lock shoes and pin
	• Lock shoe grooves have burrs or are filled with foreign material	• Clean or replace lock shoes
	• Lock shoe springs weak or broken	• Replace springs
Noise when tilting column (tilt column only)	• Upper tilt bumpers worn	• Replace tilt bumper
	• Tilt spring rubbing in housing	• Lubricate with chassis grease
One click when in "off-lock" position and the steering wheel is moved	• Seating of lock bolt	• None. Click is normal characteristic sound produced by lock bolt as it seats.
High shift effort (automatic and tilt column only)	• Column not correctly aligned	• Align column
	• Lower bearing not aligned correctly	• Assemble correctly
	• Lack of grease on seal or lower bearing areas	• Lubricate with chassis grease
Improper transmission shifting— automatic and tilt column only	• Sheared shift tube joint	• Replace shift tube
	• Improper transmission gearshift linkage adjustment	• Adjust linkage
	• Loose lower shift lever	• Replace shift tube

Troubleshooting the Ignition Switch

Problem	Cause	Solution
Ignition switch electrically inoperative	• Loose or defective switch connector	• Tighten or replace connector
	• Feed wire open (fusible link)	• Repair or replace
	• Defective ignition switch	• Replace ignition switch
Engine will not crank	• Ignition switch not adjusted properly	• Adjust switch
Ignition switch wil not actuate mechanically	• Defective ignition switch	• Replace switch
	• Defective lock sector	• Replace lock sector
	• Defective remote rod	• Replace remote rod
Ignition switch cannot be adjusted correctly	• Remote rod deformed	• Repair, straighten or replace

Troubleshooting the Turn Signal Switch

Problem	Cause	Solution
Turn signal will not cancel	• Loose switch mounting screws • Switch or anchor bosses broken • Broken, missing or out of position detent, or cancelling spring	• Tighten screws • Replace switch • Reposition springs or replace switch as required
Turn signal difficult to operate	• Turn signal lever loose • Switch yoke broken or distorted • Loose or misplaced springs • Foreign parts and/or materials in switch • Switch mounted loosely	• Tighten mounting screws • Replace switch • Reposition springs or replace switch • Remove foreign parts and/or material • Tighten mounting screws
Turn signal will not indicate lane change	• Broken lane change pressure pad or spring hanger • Broken, missing or misplaced lane change spring • Jammed wires	• Replace switch • Replace or reposition as required • Loosen mounting screws, reposition wires and retighten screws
Turn signal will not stay in turn position	• Foreign material or loose parts impeding movement of switch yoke • Defective switch	• Remove material and/or parts • Replace switch
Hazard switch cannot be pulled out	• Foreign material between hazard support cancelling leg and yoke	• Remove foreign material. No foreign material impeding function of hazard switch—replace turn signal switch.
No turn signal lights	• Inoperative turn signal flasher • Defective or blown fuse • Loose chassis to column harness connector • Disconnect column to chassis connector. Connect new switch to chassis and operate switch by hand. If vehicle lights now operate normally, signal switch is inoperative • If vehicle lights do not operate, check chassis wiring for opens, grounds, etc.	• Replace turn signal flasher • Replace fuse • Connect securely • Replace signal switch • Repair chassis wiring as required
Instrument panel turn indicator lights on but not flashing	• Burned out or damaged front or rear turn signal bulb • If vehicle lights do not operate, check light sockets for high resistance connections, the chassis wiring for opens, grounds, etc. • Inoperative flasher • Loose chassis to column harness connection • Inoperative turn signal switch • To determine if turn signal switch is defective, substitute new switch into circuit and operate switch by hand. If the vehicle's lights operate normally, signal switch is inoperative.	• Replace bulb • Repair chassis wiring as required • Replace flasher • Connect securely • Replace turn signal switch • Replace turn signal switch
Stop light not on when turn indicated	• Loose column to chassis connection • Disconnect column to chassis connector. Connect new switch into system without removing old.	• Connect securely • Replace signal switch

Troubleshooting the Turn Signal Switch (cont.)

Problem	Cause	Solution
Stop light not on when turn indicated (cont.)	Operate switch by hand. If brake lights work with switch in the turn position, signal switch is defective.	
	• If brake lights do not work, check connector to stop light sockets for grounds, opens, etc.	• Repair connector to stop light circuits using service manual as guide
Turn indicator panel lights not flashing	• Burned out bulbs	• Replace bulbs
	• High resistance to ground at bulb socket	• Replace socket
	• Opens, ground in wiring harness from front turn signal bulb socket to indicator lights	• Locate and repair as required
Turn signal lights flash very slowly	• High resistance ground at light sockets	• Repair high resistance grounds at light sockets
	• Incorrect capacity turn signal flasher or bulb	• Replace turn signal flasher or bulb
	• If flashing rate is still extremely slow, check chassis wiring harness from the connector to light sockets for high resistance	• Locate and repair as required
	• Loose chassis to column harness connection	• Connect securely
	• Disconnect column to chassis connector. Connect new switch into system without removing old. Operate switch by hand. If flashing occurs at normal rate, the signal switch is defective.	• Replace turn signal switch
Hazard signal lights will not flash— turn signal functions normally	• Blow fuse	• Replace fuse
	• Inoperative hazard warning flasher	• Replace hazard warning flasher in fuse panel
	• Loose chassis-to-column harness connection	• Conect securely
	• Disconnect column to chassis connector. Connect new switch into system without removing old. Depress the hazard warning lights. If they now work normally, turn signal switch is defective.	• Replace turn signal switch
	• If lights do not flash, check wiring harness "K" lead for open between hazard flasher and connector. If open, fuse block is defective	• Repair or replace brown wire or connector as required

Troubleshooting the Manual Steering Gear

Problem	Cause	Solution
Hard or erratic steering	• Incorrect tire pressure	• Inflate tires to recommended pressures
	• Insufficient or incorrect lubrication	• Lubricate as required (refer to Maintenance Section)
	• Suspension, or steering linkage parts damaged or misaligned	• Repair or replace parts as necessary
	• Improper front wheel alignment	• Adjust incorrect wheel alignment angles
	• Incorrect steering gear adjustment	• Adjust steering gear
	• Sagging springs	• Replace springs

Troubleshooting the Manual Steering Gear (cont.)

Problem	Cause	Solution
Play or looseness in steering	· Steering wheel loose	· Inspect shaft spines and repair as necessary. Tighten attaching nut and stake in place.
	· Steering linkage or attaching parts loose or worn	· Tighten, adjust, or replace faulty components
	· Pitman arm loose	· Inspect shaft splines and repair as necessary. Tighten attaching nut and stake in place
	· Steering gear attaching bolts loose	· Tighten bolts
	· Loose or worn wheel bearings	· Adjust or replace bearings
	· Steering gear adjustment incorrect or parts badly worn	· Adjust gear or replace defective parts
Wheel shimmy or tramp	· Improper tire pressure	· Inflate tires to recommended pressures
	· Wheels, tires, or brake rotors out-of-balance or out-of-round	· Inspect and replace or balance parts
	· Inoperative, worn, or loose shock absorbers or mounting parts	· Repair or replace shocks or mountings
	· Loose or worn steering or suspension parts	· Tighten or replace as necessary
	· Loose or worn wheel bearings	· Adjust or replace bearings
	· Incorrect steering gear adjustments	· Adjust steering gear
	· Incorrect front wheel alignment	· Correct front wheel alignment
Tire wear	· Improper tire pressure	· Inflate tires to recommended pressures
	· Failure to rotate tires	· Rotate tires
	· Brakes grabbing	· Adjust or repair brakes
	· Incorrect front wheel alignment	· Align incorrect angles
	· Broken or damaged steering and suspension parts	· Repair or replace defective parts
	· Wheel runout	· Replace faulty wheel
	· Excessive speed on turns	· Make driver aware of conditions
Vehicle leads to one side	· Improper tire pressures	· Inflate tires to recommended pressures
	· Front tires with uneven tread depth, wear pattern, or different cord design (i.e., one bias ply and one belted or radial tire on front wheels)	· Install tires of same cord construction and reasonably even tread depth, design, and wear pattern
	· Incorrect front wheel alignment	· Align incorrect angles
	· Brakes dragging	· Adjust or repair brakes
	· Pulling due to uneven tire construction	· Replace faulty tire

Troubleshooting the Power Steering Gear

Problem	Cause	Solution
Hissing noise in steering gear	· There is some noise in all power steering systems. One of the most common is a hissing sound most evident at standstill parking. There is no relationship between this noise and performance of the steering. Hiss may be expected when steering wheel is at end of travel or when slowly turning at standstill.	· Slight hiss is normal and in no way affects steering. Do not replace valve unless hiss is extremely objectionable. A replacement valve will also exhibit slight noise and is not always a cure. Investigate clearance around flexible coupling rivets. Be sure steering shaft and gear are aligned so flexible coupling rotates in a flat plane and is not distorted as shaft rotates. Any metal-to-metal contacts through flexible cou-

Troubleshooting the Power Steering Gear (cont.)

Problem	Cause	Solution
Hissing noise in steering gear (cont.)		pling will transmit valve hiss into passenger compartment through the steering column.
Rattle or chuckle noise in steering gear	· Gear loose on frame	· Check gear-to-frame mounting screws. Tighten screws to 88 N·m (65 foot pounds) torque.
	· Steering linkage looseness	· Check linkage pivot points for wear. Replace if necessary.
	· Pressure hose touching other parts of car	· Adjust hose position. Do not bend tubing by hand.
	· Loose pitman shaft over center adjustment	· Adjust to specifications
	NOTE: A slight rattle may occur on turns because of increased clearance off the "high point." This is normal and clearance must not be reduced below specified limits to eliminate this slight rattle.	
	· Loose pitman arm	· Tighten pitman arm nut to specifications
Squawk noise in steering gear when turning or recovering from a turn	· Damper O-ring on valve spool cut	· Replace damper O-ring
Poor return of steering wheel to center	· Tires not properly inflated	· Inflate to specified pressure
	· Lack of lubrication in linkage and ball joints	· Lube linkage and ball joints
	· Lower coupling flange rubbing against steering gear adjuster plug	· Loosen pinch bolt and assemble properly
	· Steering gear to column misalignment	· Align steering column
	· Improper front wheel alignment	· Check and adjust as necessary
	· Steering linkage binding	· Replace pivots
	· Ball joints binding	· Replace ball joints
	· Steering wheel rubbing against housing	· Align housing
	· Tight or frozen steering shaft bearings	· Replace bearings
	· Sticking or plugged valve spool	· Remove and clean or replace valve
	· Steering gear adjustments over specifications	· Check adjustment with gear out of car. Adjust as required.
	· Kink in return hose	· Replace hose
Car leads to one side or the other (keep in mind road condition and wind. Test car in both directions on flat road)	· Front end misaligned	· Adjust to specifications
	· Unbalanced steering gear valve	· Replace valve
	NOTE: If this is cause, steering effort will be very light in direction of lead and normal or heavier in opposite direction	
Momentary increase in effort when turning wheel fast to right or left	· Low oil level	· Add power steering fluid as required
	· Pump belt slipping	· Tighten or replace belt
	· High internal leakage	· Check pump pressure. (See pressure test)
Steering wheel surges or jerks when turning with engine running especially during parking	· Low oil level	· Fill as required
	· Loose pump belt	· Adjust tension to specification
	· Steering linkage hitting engine oil pan at full turn	· Correct clearance
	· Insufficient pump pressure	· Check pump pressure. (See pressure test). Replace relief valve if defective.
	· Pump flow control valve sticking	· Inspect for varnish or damage, replace if necessary

Troubleshooting the Power Steering Gear (cont.)

Problem	Cause	Solution
Excessive wheel kickback or loose steering	• Air in system	• Add oil to pump reservoir and bleed by operating steering. Check hose connectors for proper torque and adjust as required.
	• Steering gear loose on frame	• Tighten attaching screws to specified torque
	• Steering linkage joints worn enough to be loose	• Replace loose pivots
	• Worn poppet valve	• Replace poppet valve
	• Loose thrust bearing preload adjustment	• Adjust to specification with gear out of vehicle
	• Excessive overcenter lash	• Adjust to specification with gear out of car
Hard steering or lack of assist	• Loose pump belt	• Adjust belt tension to specification
	• Low oil level **NOTE:** Low oil level will also result in excessive pump noise	• Fill to proper level. If excessively low, check all lines and joints for evidence of external leakage. Tighten loose connectors.
	• Steering gear to column misalignment	• Align steering column
	• Lower coupling flange rubbing against steering gear adjuster plug	• Loosen pinch bolt and assemble properly
	• Tires not properly inflated	• Inflate to recommended pressure
Foamy milky power steering fluid, low fluid level and possible low pressure	• Air in the fluid, and loss of fluid due to internal pump leakage causing overflow	• Check for leak and correct. Bleed system. Extremely cold temperatures will cause system aeriation should the oil level be low. If oil level is correct and pump still foams, remove pump from vehicle and separate reservoir from housing. Check welsh plug and housing for cracks. If plug is loose or housing is cracked, replace housing.
Low pressure due to steering pump	• Flow control valve stuck or inoperative	• Remove burrs or dirt or replace. Flush system.
	• Pressure plate not flat against cam ring	• Correct
Low pressure due to steering gear	• Pressure loss in cylinder due to worn piston ring or badly worn housing bore	• Remove gear from car for disassembly and inspection of ring and housing bore
	• Leakage at valve rings, valve body-to-worm seal	• Remove gear from car for disassembly and replace seals

Troubleshooting the Power Steering Pump

Problem	Cause	Solution
Chirp noise in steering pump	• Loose belt	• Adjust belt tension to specification
Belt squeal (particularly noticeable at full wheel travel and stand still parking)	• Loose belt	• Adjust belt tension to specification
Growl noise in steering pump	• Excessive back pressure in hoses or steering gear caused by restriction	• Locate restriction and correct. Replace part if necessary.

BRAKE OPERATION SYSTEM 9-2
BASIC OPERATING PRINCIPLES 9-2
    DISC BRAKES 9-2
    DRUM BRAKES 9-3
    POWER BOOSTERS 9-3
ADJUSTMENTS 9-3
    DRUM BRAKES 9-3
    DISC BRAKES 9-3
MASTER CYLINDER 9-4
    REMOVAL & INSTALLATION 9-4
    OVERHAUL 9-5
PROPORTIONING VALVE 9-7
    REMOVAL & INSTALLATION 9-8
BRAKE HOSES AND LINES 9-8
    REMOVAL & INSTALLATION 9-8
    BRAKE LINE FLARING 9-11
BLEEDING THE BRAKE SYSTEM 9-12
    MASTER CYLINDER 9-12
    LINES AND WHEEL CIRCUITS 9-12
FRONT DISC BRAKES 9-13
BRAKE PADS 9-13
    REMOVAL & INSTALLATION 9-13
BRAKE CALIPER 9-14
    REMOVAL & INSTALLATION 9-14
    OVERHAUL 9-15
BRAKE DISC (ROTOR) 9-17
    REMOVAL & INSTALLATION 9-17
    INSPECTION 9-19
REAR DRUM BRAKES 9-20
BRAKE DRUMS 9-20
    REMOVAL & INSTALLATION 9-20
    INSPECTION 9-21
BRAKE SHOES 9-22
    REMOVAL & INSTALLATION 9-22
WHEEL CYLINDERS 9-27
    REMOVAL & INSTALLATION 9-27
    OVERHAUL 9-28
PARKING BRAKE 9-29
CABLES 9-29
    ADJUSTMENT 9-29
    REMOVAL & INSTALLATION 9-29
COMPONENT LOCATIONS
  REAR DRUM BRAKE
  COMPONENTS 9-24
SPECIFICATION CHARTS
  DISC AND PAD SPECIFICATIONS
  (IN.) 9-19
  BRAKE DRUM DIAMETER
  CHART 9-22
  PARKING BRAKE ADJUSTMENT
  CHART 9-29
TROUBLESHOOTING CHARTS
  TROUBLESHOOTING THE BRAKE
  SYSTEM 9-33

9

BRAKES

BRAKE OPERATION SYSTEM 9-2
FRONT DISC BRAKES 9-13
REAR DRUM BRAKES 9-20
PARKING BRAKE 9-29

BRAKE OPERATING SYSTEM

Basic Operating Principles

Hydraulic systems are used to actuate the brakes of all modern automobiles. The system transports the power required to force the frictional surfaces of the braking system together from the pedal to the individual brake units at each wheel. A hydraulic system is used for two reasons.

First, fluid under pressure can be carried to all parts of an automobile by small pipes and flexible hoses without taking up a significant amount of room or posing routing problems.

Second, a great mechanical advantage can be given to the brake pedal end of the system, and the foot pressure required to actuate the brakes can be reduced by making the surface area of the master cylinder pistons smaller than that of any of the pistons in the wheel cylinders or calipers.

The master cylinder consists of a fluid reservoir along with a double cylinder and piston assembly. Double type master cylinders are designed to separate the front and rear braking systems hydraulically in case of a leak. The master cylinder coverts mechanical motion from the pedal into hydraulic pressure within the lines. This pressure is translated back into mechanical motion at the wheels by either the wheel cylinder (drum brakes) or the caliper (disc brakes).

Steel lines carry the brake fluid to a point on the vehicle's frame near each of the vehicle's wheels. The fluid is then carried to the calipers and wheel cylinders by flexible tubes in order to allow for suspension and steering movements.

In drum brake systems, each wheel cylinder contains two pistons, one at either end, which push outward in opposite directions and force the brake shoe into contact with the drum.

In disc brake systems, the cylinders are part of the calipers. At least one cylinder in each caliper is used to force the brake pads against the disc.

All pistons employ some type of seal, usually made of rubber, to minimize fluid leakage. A rubber dust boot seals the outer end of the cylinder against dust and dirt. The boot fits around the outer end of the piston on disc brake calipers, and around the brake actuating rod on wheel cylinders.

The hydraulic system operates as follows: When at rest, the entire system, from the piston(s) in the master cylinder to those in the wheel cylinders or calipers, is full of brake fluid. Upon application of the brake pedal, fluid trapped in front of the master cylinder piston(s) is forced through the lines to the wheel cylinders. Here, it forces the pistons outward, in the case of drum brakes, and inward toward the disc, in the case of disc brakes. The motion of the pistons is opposed by return springs mounted outside the cylinders in drum brakes, and by spring seals, in disc brakes.

Upon release of the brake pedal, a spring located inside the master cylinder immediately returns the master cylinder pistons to the normal position. The pistons contain check valves and the master cylinder has compensating ports drilled in it. These are uncovered as the pistons reach their normal position. The piston check valves allow fluid to flow toward the wheel cylinders or calipers as the pistons withdraw. Then, as the return springs force the brake pads or shoes into the released position, the excess fluid reservoir through the compensating ports. It is during the time the pedal is in the released position that any fluid that has leaked out of the system will be replaced through the compensating ports.

Dual circuit master cylinders employ two pistons, located one behind the other, in the same cylinder. The primary piston is actuated directly by mechanical linkage from the brake pedal through the power booster. The secondary piston is actuated by fluid trapped between the two pistons. If a leak develops in front of the secondary piston, it moves forward until it bottoms against the front of the master cylinder, and the fluid trapped between the pistons will operate the rear brakes. If the rear brakes develop a leak, the primary piston will move forward until direct contact with the secondary piston takes place, and it will force the secondary piston to actuate the front brakes. In either case, the brake pedal moves farther when the brakes are applied, and less braking power is available.

All dual circuit systems use a switch to warn the driver when only half of the brake system is operational. This switch is usually located in a valve body which is mounted on the firewall or the frame below the master cylinder. A hydraulic piston receives pressure from both circuits, each circuit's pressure being applied to one end of the piston. When the pressures are in balance, the piston remains stationary. When one circuit has a leak, however, the greater pressure in that circuit during application of the brakes will push the piston to one side, closing the switch and activating the brake warning light.

In disc brake systems, this valve body also contains a metering valve and, in some cases, a proportioning valve. The metering valve keeps pressure from traveling to the disc brakes on the front wheels until the brake shoes on the rear wheels have contacted the drums, ensuring that the front brakes will never be used alone. The proportioning valve controls the pressure to the rear brakes to lessen the chance of rear wheel lock-up during very hard braking.

Warning lights may be tested by depressing the brake pedal and holding it while opening one of the wheel cylinder bleeder screws. If this does not cause the light to go on, substitute a new lamp, make continuity checks, and, finally, replace the switch as necessary.

The hydraulic system may be checked for leaks by applying pressure to the pedal gradually and steadily. If the pedal sinks very slowly to the floor, the system has a leak. This is not to be confused with a springy or spongy feel due to the compression of air within the lines. If the system leaks, there will be a gradual change in the position of the pedal with a constant pressure.

Check for leaks along all lines and at wheel cylinders. If no external leaks are apparent, the problem is inside the master cylinder.

DISC BRAKES

Instead of the traditional expanding brakes that press outward against a circular drum, disc brake systems utilize a disc (rotor) with brake pads positioned on either side of it. An easily-seen analogy is the hand brake arrangement on a bicycle. The pads squeeze onto the rim of the bike wheel, slowing its motion. Automobile disc brakes use the identical principle but apply the braking effort to a separate disc instead of the wheel.

The disc (rotor) is a casting, usually equipped with cooling fins between the two braking surfaces. This enables air to circulate between the braking surfaces making them less sensitive to heat buildup and more resistant to fade. Dirt and water do not drastically affect braking action since contaminants are thrown off by the centrifugal action of the rotor or scraped off the by the pads. Also, the equal clamping action of the two brake pads tends to ensure uniform, straight line stops. Disc brakes are inherently self-adjusting. There are three general types of disc brake:

1. A fixed caliper.
2. A floating caliper.
3. A sliding caliper.

The fixed caliper design uses two pistons mounted on either side of the rotor (in each side of the caliper). The caliper is mounted rigidly and does not move.

The sliding and floating designs are quite similar. In fact, these two types are often lumped together. In both designs, the pad on the inside of the rotor is moved into contact with the rotor by hydraulic force. The caliper, which is not held in a fixed position, moves slightly, bringing the outside pad into contact with the rotor. There are various methods of attaching floating calipers. Some pivot at the bottom or top, and some slide on mounting bolts. In any event, the end result is the same.

DRUM BRAKES

Drum brakes employ two brake shoes mounted on a stationary backing plate. These shoes are positioned inside a circular drum which rotates with the wheel assembly. The shoes are held in place by springs. This allows them to slide toward the drums (when they are applied) while keeping the linings and drums in alignment. The shoes are actuated by a wheel cylinder which is mounted at the top of the backing plate. When the brakes are applied, hydraulic pressure forces the wheel cylinder's actuating links outward. Since these links bear directly against the top of the brake shoes, the tops of the shoes are then forced against the inner side of the drum. This action forces the bottoms of the two shoes to contact the brake drum by rotating the entire assembly slightly (known as servo action). When pressure within the wheel cylinder is relaxed, return springs pull the shoes back away from the drum.

Most modern drum brakes are designed to self-adjust themselves during application when the vehicle is moving in reverse. This motion causes both shoes to rotate very slightly with the drum, rocking an adjusting lever, thereby causing rotation of the adjusting screw. Some drum brake systems are designed to self-adjust during application whenever the brakes are applied. This on-board adjustment system reduces the need for maintenance adjustments and keeps both the brake function and pedal feel satisfactory.

POWER BOOSTERS

Virtually all modern vehicles use a vacuum assisted power brake system to multiply the braking force and reduce pedal effort. Since vacuum is always available when the engine is operating,

the system is simple and efficient. A vacuum diaphragm is located on the front of the master cylinder and assists the driver in applying the brakes, reducing both the effort and travel he must put into moving the brake pedal.

The vacuum diaphragm housing is normally connected to the intake manifold by a vacuum hose. A check valve is placed at the point where the hose enters the diaphragm housing, so that during periods of low manifold vacuum brakes assist will not be lost.

Depressing the brake pedal closes off the vacuum source and allows atmospheric pressure to enter on one side of the diaphragm. This causes the master cylinder pistons to move and apply the brakes. When the brake pedal is released, vacuum is applied to both sides of the diaphragm and springs return the diaphragm and master cylinder pistons to the released position.

If the vacuum supply fails, the brake pedal rod will contact the end of the master cylinder actuator rod and the system will apply the brakes without any power assistance. The driver will notice that much higher pedal effort is needed to stop the car and that the pedal feels harder than usual.

Vacuum Leak Test

1. Operate the engine at idle without touching the brake pedal for at least one minute.
2. Turn off the engine and wait one minute.
3. Test for the presence of assist vacuum by depressing the brake pedal and releasing it several times. If vacuum is present in the system, light application will produce less and less pedal travel. If there is no vacuum, air is leaking into the system.

System Operation Test

1. With the engine **OFF**, pump the brake pedal until the supply vacuum is entirely gone.
2. Put light, steady pressure on the brake pedal.
3. Start the engine and let it idle. If the system is operating correctly, the brake pedal should fall toward the floor if the constant pressure is maintained.

Power brake systems may be tested for hydraulic leaks just as ordinary systems are tested.

Adjustments

DRUM BRAKES

These models are equipped with self-adjusting rear drum brakes. No adjustment is possible or necessary.

DISC BRAKES

Front disc brakes require no adjustment, as hydraulic pressure maintains the proper brake pad-to-disc contact at all times.

➡**The brake fluid level should be checked regularly. (Refer to Section 1).**

Master Cylinder

REMOVAL & INSTALLATION

▶ See Figures 1 and 2

✳✳ WARNING:

Be careful not to spill brake fluid on the painted surfaces of the vehicle. It will damage the paint.

1. Using a siphon, remove as much fluid from the master cylinder as possible, then reinstall the cap.
2. Unfasten the hydraulic lines from the master cylinder.
3. Detach the hydraulic fluid pressure differential switch wiring connectors. On models with ESP (brake fluid level warning device), disconnect the fluid level sensor wiring connectors, as well.
4. On models with manual brakes and on the Crown 2300, re-

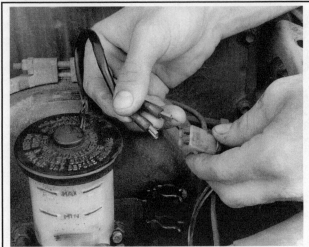

Disconnect the ESP sensor (brake fluid warning level sensor) if equipped

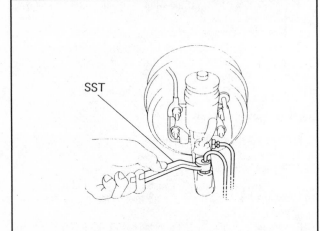

Fig. 1 Using a brake line wrench, disconnect the hydraulic lines from the master cylinder

Siphon as much fluid out of the master cylinder as possible

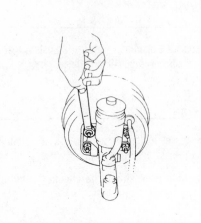

Fig. 2 Remove the mounting nuts to separate the cylinder from the booster

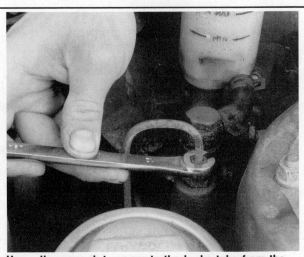

Use a line wrench to separate the brake tube from the master cylinder

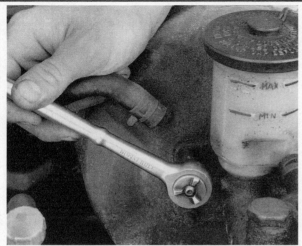

Remove the mounting nuts retaining the master cylinder to the brake booster

If so equipped, attach the ESP wiring and install the cap

Hold the cylinder upright so as not to spill any fluid

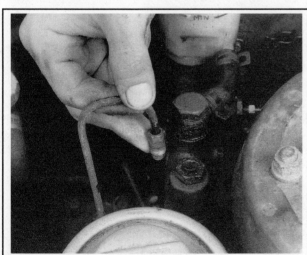

Once the master cylinder is installed, be sure to thread in and tighten the line fittings

move the master cylinder securing bolts and the clevis pin from the brake pedal. Remove the master cylinder.

5. On the other models with power brakes, unfasten the nuts and remove the master cylinder assembly from the power brake unit.

6. Installation is performed in the reverse order of removal. Note the following, however:

    a. Before tightening the master cylinder mounting nuts or bolts, screw the hydraulic line into the cylinder body, a few turns.

    b. After installation is completed, bleed the master cylinder and the brake system.

OVERHAUL

▶ **See Figures 3 thru 10 (p. 6–7)**

1. Remove the reservoir caps and floats. Unscrew the bolts and secure the reservoirs to the main body.

2. Remove the pressure differential warning switch assembly (if equipped). Then, working from the rear of the cylinder, remove the boot, snapping, stop washer, piston No. 1, spacer, cylinder cup, spring retainer, and spring, in that order.

➡**Depending on the model, it may be necessary to remove the side mounted stop bolt before the pistons can be removed.**

3. Remove the endplug and gasket from the front of the cylinder, then remove the front piston stop-bolt from underneath. Pull out the spring, retainer, piston No. 2, spacer, and the cylinder cup.

4. Remove the two outlet fittings, washers, check valves and springs.

5. Remove the piston cups from their seats only if they are to be replaced.

6. After washing all parts in clean brake fluid, dry them with compressed air (if available). Inspect the cylinder bore for wear, scuff marks, or nicks. Cylinders may be honed slightly, but the limit is 0.15mm. In view of the importance of the master cylinder,

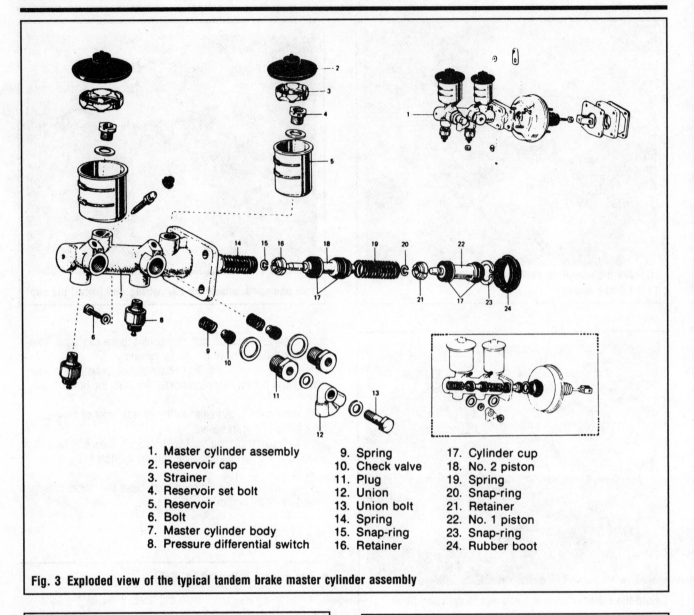

1. Master cylinder assembly
2. Reservoir cap
3. Strainer
4. Reservoir set bolt
5. Reservoir
6. Bolt
7. Master cylinder body
8. Pressure differential switch
9. Spring
10. Check valve
11. Plug
12. Union
13. Union bolt
14. Spring
15. Snap-ring
16. Retainer
17. Cylinder cup
18. No. 2 piston
19. Spring
20. Snap-ring
21. Retainer
22. No. 1 piston
23. Snap-ring
24. Rubber boot

Fig. 3 Exploded view of the typical tandem brake master cylinder assembly

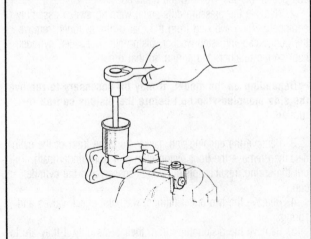

Fig. 4 With the cylinder in a vise, separate the reservoir from the unit

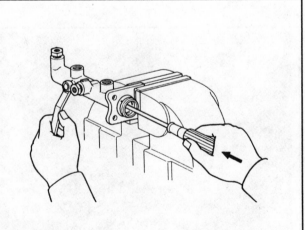

Fig. 5 Push the pistons in all the way and remove the stopper bolt

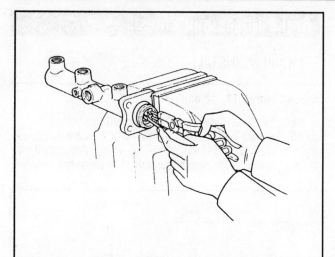

Fig. 6 Use a pair of snapring pliers to remove the snapring

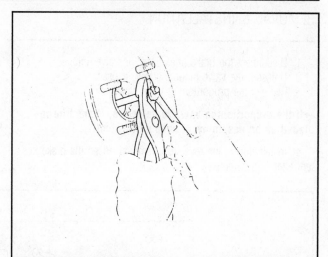

Fig. 9 Adjust the length of the booster pushrod before installing the master cylinder

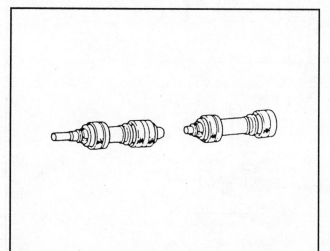

Fig. 7 Apply lithium grease to the rubber parts of the piston

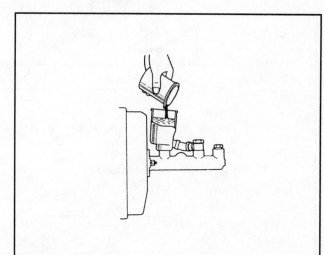

Fig. 10 Fill the reservoir and bleed the system of air BEFORE driving

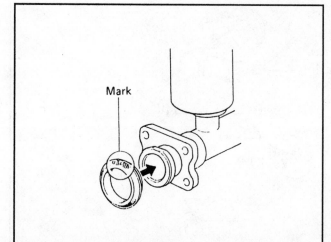

Mark

Fig. 8 When installing, confirm that the UP mark of the boot is in the correct position

it is recommended that it is replaced rather than overhauled if worn or damaged.

7. Assembly is performed in the reverse order of disassembly. Absolute cleanliness is important. Coat all parts with clean brake fluid prior to assembly.

Bleed the hydraulic system after the master cylinder is installed, as detailed following.

Proportioning Valve

A proportioning valve is used to reduce the hydraulic pressure to the rear brakes because of weight transfer during high speed stops. This helps to keep the rear brakes from locking up by improving front-to-rear brake balance.

On 1970–71 Crown models, the proportioning valve is attached to the side frame side rail, about halfway between the front and rear wheels. On all other models, it is located in the engine compartment, near the master cylinder.

REMOVAL & INSTALLATION

1. Disconnect the brake lines from the valve unions.
2. Unfasten the valve mounting bolt, if used.
3. Remove the proportioning valve assembly.

➡**If the proportioning valve is defective, it must be replaced as an assembly. It cannot be rebuilt.**

4. Installation is the reverse of removal. Bleed the brake system after it is completed.

Brake Hoses and Lines

REMOVAL & INSTALLATION

♦ **See Figures 11, 12 and 13**

Metal lines and rubber brake hoses should be checked frequently for leaks and external damage. Metal lines are particularly prone to crushing and kinking under the vehicle. Any such deformation can restrict the proper flow of fluid and therefore impair

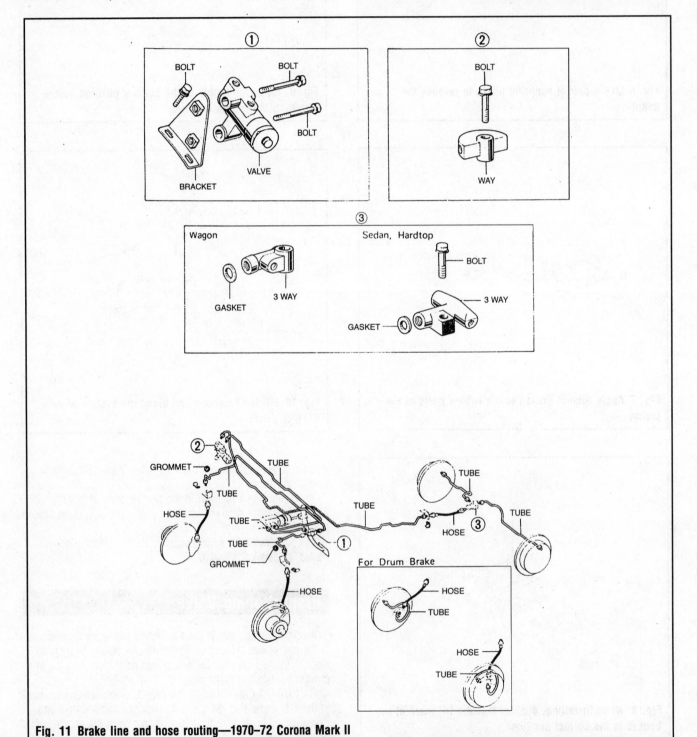

Fig. 11 Brake line and hose routing—1970–72 Corona Mark II

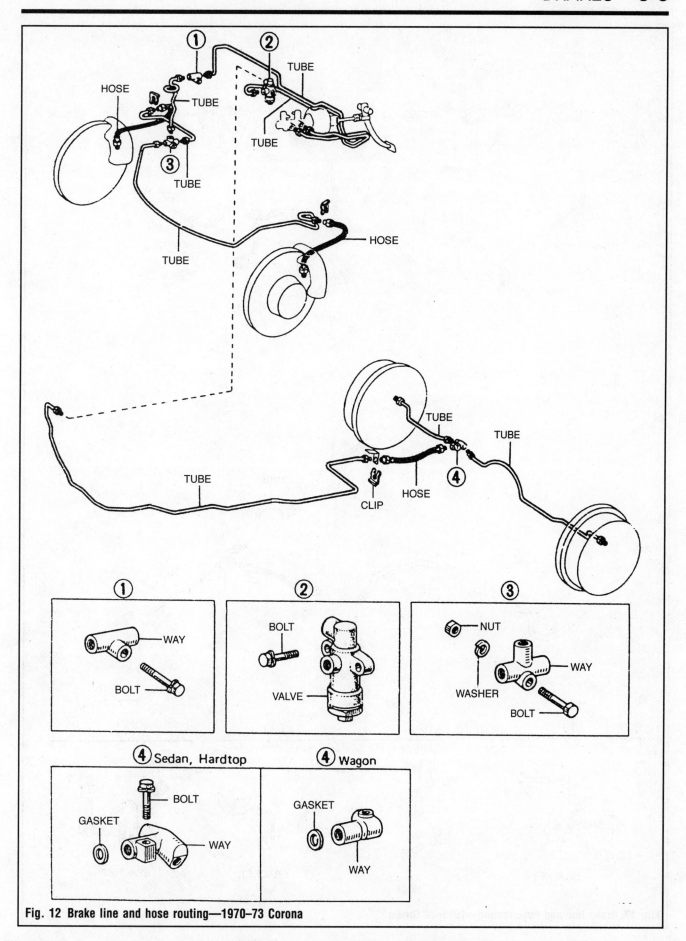

Fig. 12 Brake line and hose routing—1970–73 Corona

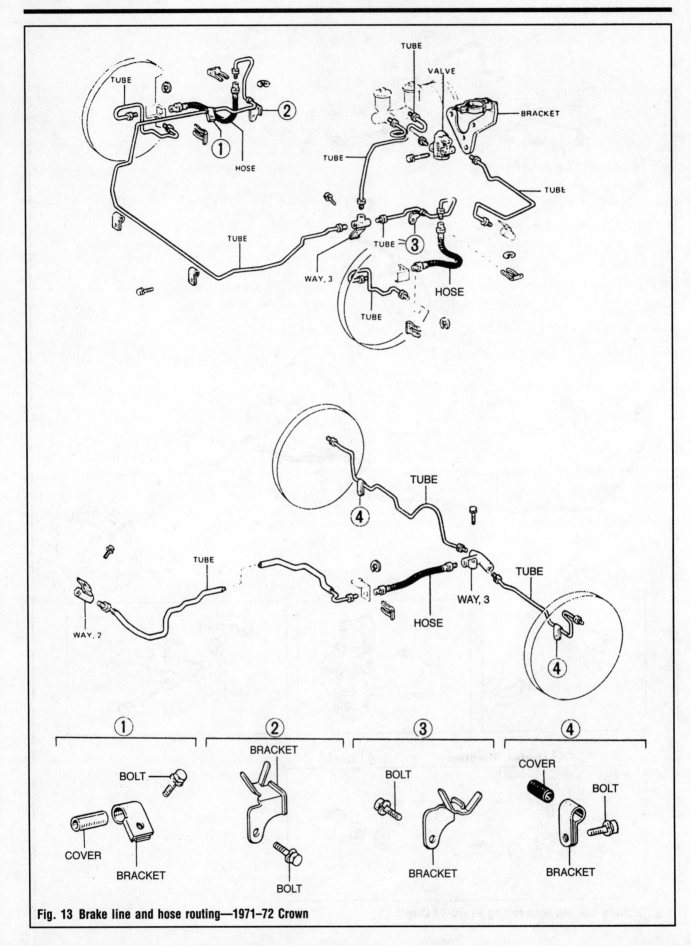

Fig. 13 Brake line and hose routing—1971–72 Crown

braking at the wheels. Rubber hoes should be checked for cracking or scraping; such damage can create a weak spot in the hose and it could fail under pressure.

Any time the lines are removed or disconnected, extreme cleanliness must be observed. The slightest bit of dirt in the system can plug a fluid port and render the brakes defective. Clean all joints and connections before disassembly (use a stiff brush and clean brake fluid) and plug the lines and ports as soon as they are opened. New lines and hoses should be blown or flushed clean before installation to remove any contamination. To replace a line or hose:

Brake Hose

1. Raise the end of the vehicle which contains the hose to be repaired, then support the vehicle safely using jackstands.
2. If necessary, remove the wheel for easier access to the hose.
3. Disconnect the hose from the wheel cylinder or caliper and plug the opening to avoid excessive fluid loss or contamination.
4. Disconnect the hose from the brake line and plug the openings to avoid excessive fluid loss or contamination.

To install:

5. Install the brake hose to the brake line and tighten to 14 ft. lbs. (19 Nm) for rear brakes or 18 ft. lbs (24 Nm) for front brakes.
6. If installing a front brake hose, make sure the hose is routed properly.
7. Install the hose to the wheel cylinder or caliper using NEW washers, then tighten the retainer to 36 ft. lbs. (49 Nm).
8. Properly bleed the brake system, then check the connections for leaks.
9. Remove the supports and carefully lower the vehicle.

Brake Line

There are 2 options available when replacing a brake line. The first, and probably most preferable, is to replace the entire line using a line of similar length which is already equipped with machined flared ends. Such lines are usually available from auto parts stores and usually require only a minimum of bending in order to properly fit them to the vehicle. The second option is to bend and flare the entire replacement line (or a repair section of line) using the appropriate tools.

Buying a line with machined flares is usually preferable because of the time and effort saved, not to mention the cost of special tools if they are not readily available. Also, machined flares are usually of a much higher quality than those produced by hand flaring tools or kits.

1. Raise the end of the vehicle which contains the hose to be repaired, then support the vehicle safely using jackstands.
2. Remove the components necessary for access to the brake line which is being replaced.
3. Disconnect the fittings at each end of the line, then plug the openings to prevent excessive fluid loss or contamination.
4. Trace the line from one end to the other and disconnect the line from any retaining clips, then remove the line from the vehicle.

To install:

5. Try to obtain a replacement line that is the same length as the line that was removed. If the line is longer, you will have to cut it and flare the end. If you have decided to repair a portion of the line, see the procedure on brake line flaring.

6. Use a suitable tubing bender to make the necessary bends in the line. Work slowly and carefully; try to make the bends look as close as possible to those on the line being replaced.

➡**When bending the brake line, be careful not to kink or crack the line. If the brake line becomes kinked or cracked, it must be replaced.**

7. Before installing the brake line, flush it with brake cleaner to remove any dirt or foreign material.
8. Install the line into the vehicle. Be sure to attach the line to the retaining clips, as necessary. Make sure the replacement brake line does not contact any components that could rub the line and cause a leak.
9. Connect the brake line fittings and tighten to 18 ft. lbs. (24 Nm), except for the rear line-to-hose fitting which should be tightened to 14 ft. lbs. (19 Nm).
10. Properly bleed the brake system and check for leaks.
11. Install any removed components, then remove the supports and carefully lower the vehicle.

BRAKE LINE FLARING

Use only brake line tubing approved for automotive use; never use copper tubing. Whenever possible, try to work with brake lines that are already cut to the length needed. These lines are available at most auto parts stores and have machine made flares, the quality of which is hard to duplicate with most of the available inexpensive flaring kits.

When the brakes are applied, there is a great amount of pressure developed in the hydraulic system. An improperly formed flare can leak with resultant loss of stopping power. If you have never formed a double-flare, take time to familiarize yourself with the flaring kit; practice forming double-flares on scrap tubing until you are satisfied with the results.

The following procedure applies to the SA9193BR flaring kit, but should be similar to commercially available brake-line flaring kits. If these instructions differ in any way from those in your kit, follow the instructions in the kit.

1. Determine the length necessary for the replacement or repair and allow an additional ⅛ in. (3.2mm) for each flare. Select a length of tubing according to the repair/replacement charts in the figure, then cut the brake line to the necessary length using an appropriate saw. Do not use a tubing cutter.
2. Square the end of the tube with a file and chamfer the edges. Remove burrs from the inside and outside diameters of the cut line using a deburring tool.
3. Install the required fittings onto the line.
4. Install SA9193BR, or an equivalent flaring tool, into a vice and install the handle into the opening cam.
5. Loosen the die clamp screw and rotate the locking plate to expose the die carrier opening.
6. Select the required die set (4.75mm DIN) and install in the carrier with the full side of either half facing clamp screw and counter bore of both halves facing punch turret.
7. Insert the prepared line through the rear of the die and push forward until the line end is flush with the die face.
8. Make sure the rear of both halves of the die rest against the hexagon die stops, then rotate the locking plate to the fully closed position and clamp the die firmly by tightening the clamp screw.

9. Rotate the punch turret until the appropriate size (4.75mm DIN) points towards the open end of the line to be flared.

10. Pull the operating handle against the line resistance in order to create the flare, then return the handle to the original position.

11. Release the clamp screw and rotate the locking plate to the open position.

12. Remove the die set and line, then separate by gently tapping both halves on the bench. Inspect the flare for proper size and shape. Measurement should be 0.272–0.286 in. (6.92–7.28mm).

13. If necessary, repeat the steps for the other end of the line or for the end of the line which is being repaired.

14. Bend the replacement line or section using SA91108NE, or an equivalent line bending tool.

15. If repairing the original line, join the old and new sections using a female union and tighten.

Bleeding the Brake System

♦ **See Figure 14**

✳✳ WARNING

Clean, high quality brake fluid is essential to the safe and proper operation of the brake system. You should always buy the highest quality brake fluid that is available. If the brake fluid becomes contaminated, drain and flush the system, then refill the master cylinder with new fluid. Never reuse any brake fluid. Any brake fluid that is removed from the system should be discarded.

It is necessary to bleed the hydraulic system any time the system has been opened or has trapped air within the fluid lines. It may be necessary to bleed the system at all four brakes if air has been introduced through a low fluid level or by disconnecting brake pipes at the master cylinder.

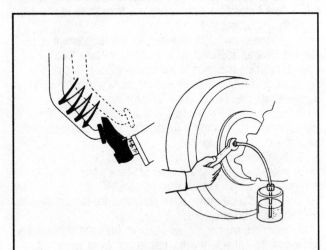

Fig. 14 Bleed the brakes into a half-filled jar of brake fluid

If a line is disconnected at one wheel only, generally only that brake needs bleeding. If lines are disconnected at an fitting between the master cylinder and the brake, the system served by the disconnected pipe must be bled.

✳✳ WARNING

Do not allow brake fluid to splash or spill onto painted surfaces; the paint will be damaged. If spillage occurs, flush the area immediately with clean water.

MASTER CYLINDER

If the master cylinder has been removed, the lines disconnected or the reservoir allowed to run dry, the cylinder must be bled before the lines are bled. To bleed the master cylinder:

1. Check the level of the fluid in the reservoir. If necessary, fill with fluid.

2. Disconnect the brake lines from the master cylinder. Plug the lines to keep dirt from entering.

3. Place a pan or rags under the cylinder.

4. Have an assistant slowly depress the brake pedal and hold it down.

5. Block off the outlet ports with your fingers. Be sure to wear gloves. Have the assistant release the pedal. Make a tight seal with your fingers; do not allow the cylinder to ingest air when the pedal is released.

6. Repeat three or four times.

7. Connect the brake lines to the master cylinder and top up the fluid reservoir.

LINES AND WHEEL CIRCUITS

1. Insert a clear vinyl tube onto the bleed plug at the wheel. If all four wheels are to be bled, begin with the right rear.

2. Insert the other end of the tube into a jar which is half filled with brake fluid. Make sure the end is submerged in the fluid.

3. Have an assistant slowly pump the brake pedal several times. On the last pump, have the assistant hold the pedal fully depressed. While the pedal is depressed, open the bleeder plug until fluid starts to run out, then close the plug.

➥**If the brake pedal is pumped too fast, small air bubbles will form in the brake fluid which will be very difficult to remove.**

4. Repeat this procedure until no air bubbles are visible in the hose. Close the bleeder port.

➥**Constantly replenish the brake fluid in the master cylinder reservoir, so that it does not run out during bleeding.**

5. If bleeding the entire system, repeat the procedure at the left rear wheel, the right front wheel and the left front wheel in that order.

6. Bleed the load sending proportioning and bypass valve.

FRONT DISC BRAKES

An inspection slot is provided, in most cases, in the top of the caliper for checking the brake pad thickness. However, if the thickness seems marginal, the pads should be removed from the caliper and checked.

➡**Always replace the pads on both front wheels. When inspecting or replacing the brake pads, check the surface of the disc rotors for scoring, wear and run-out. The rotors should be resurfaced if badly scored or replaced if badly worn.**

Fixed Caliper

The fixed caliper design uses two pistons mounted on either side of the rotor. The caliper is rigidly mounted and does not move.

Sliding Caliper

The sliding caliper design uses one piston mounted on the inboard side of the disc rotor. The caliper, which is not held in a fixed position, moves slightly when the brake is applied. The movement of the caliper brings the outside brake pad into contact with the rotor.

Brake Pads

REMOVAL & INSTALLATION

Fixed Caliper

1. Loosen the front wheel lugs slightly, then raise and safely support the front of the car. Remove the front wheel(s).
2. Remove the center spring, the retaining clips and the mounting pins from the caliper.
3. Remove the brake pads and antisqueal shims. A pair of locking pliers will help when you are pulling the pads from the caliper.

To install:

4. Remove the master cylinder cap and take a small amount of brake fluid from the reservoir. Force the pistons back into their bores to accommodate the greater thickness of the new brake pads.
5. Clean all caliper and pad locating parts.
6. Check the disc rotor for excessive runout. (See following section on disc rotors).
7. Apply a light coating of grease on the shims and on the metal backing of the pad.
8. Install the brake pads with the antisqueal shims (be sure the arrows are pointed in the right direction), the retaining pins and clips and the center spring in the reverse order of removal.
9. Pump the brake pedal several times to adjust the caliper pistons. Road test the car. If the brake pedal feels soft, it may be necessary to bleed the system.

Sliding Caliper

1. Loosen the front wheel lugs slightly, then raise and safely support the front of the car. Remove the front wheel(s).
2. Remove the guide key retainers. Apply light pressure to the

The brake pads are located inside the caliper mounted on the brake rotor

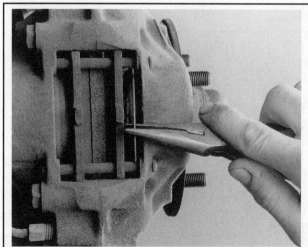

On a fixed caliper, remove the center spring and retaining clips, then . . .

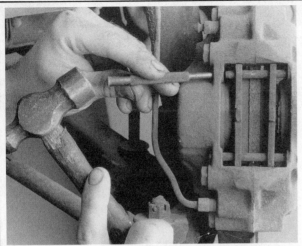

. . . punch out the pins retaining the brake pads in the caliper

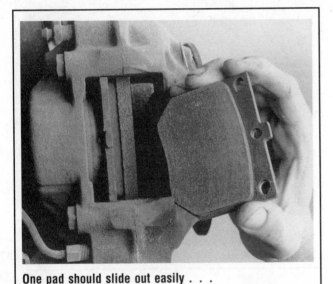

One pad should slide out easily . . .

. . . but the other may need help

caliper housing and slide the guide keys from (between) the caliper housing and the pad support.

3. Remove the caliper housing. Suspend the housing (with wire) so there is no strain on the brake hose.

4. Remove the brake pads and the support springs. Note the various positions of the parts removed.

To install:

5. Clean all of the parts that will be used over again. Remove the master cylinder cap and take a small amount of brake fluid from the reservoir. Force the piston back into the caliper bore to accommodate the greater thickness of the new brake pads.

6. Install the support springs, the brake pads, and the antirattle clips into the pad support.

7. Position the caliper housing on the support and install the guide keys and retainers.

8. Pump the brake pedal several times to adjust the caliper piston. Road test the car. If the brake pedal feels soft, it may be necessary to bleed the system.

Brake Caliper

REMOVAL & INSTALLATION

1. Remove the disc brake pads as previously described.
2. Disconnect the brake hose from the caliper. The fixed cali-

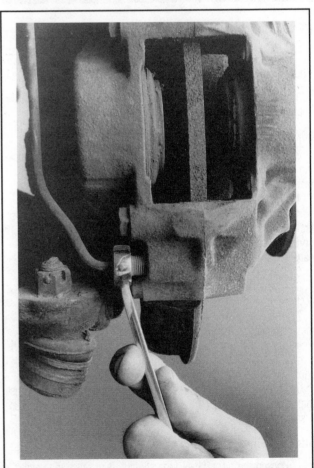

Prior to removing the caliper, disconnect the attached brake line

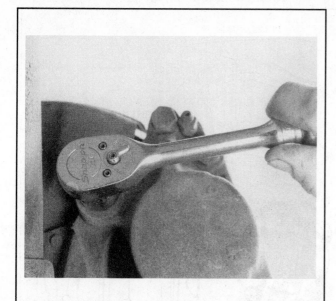

Remove the caliper mounting bolts, then . . .

. . . slide the caliper off the rotor

per is mounted by two bolts, cut the safety wire and remove the bolts. Remove the caliper. The sliding caliper support is held on by two mounting bolts, cut the safety wire and remove the bolts. Remove the caliper support.

3. Installation is the reverse of removal. Be sure to safety wire the mounting bolts.

OVERHAUL

Fixed Caliper
▶ See Figure 15

1. Remove the caliper as previously described.

The caliper halves must not be separated. If brake fluid leaks from the bridge seal, replace the caliper assembly.

2. Clean the caliper assembly of all accumulated mud and dust.

3. Remove the retaining rings. Remove the dust covers.

4. Hold one piston with a finger so that it will not come out and gradually apply air pressure to the brake line fitting. This should cause the other piston to come out, but if the piston you are holding begins moving before the other, switch your finger over and remove the more movable one first.

5. Carefully remove the other piston.

6. With a finger, carefully remove both piston seals.

7. Thoroughly clean all parts in brake fluid.

8. Inspect, as follows:

   a. Check cylinder walls for damage or excessive wear. Light rust, etc. should be removed with fine emery paper. If the wall is heavily rusted, replace the caliper assembly.

   b. Inspect the pad, as previously described.

   c. Inspect the piston for uneven wear, damage or any rust. Replace the piston if there is any rust, as it is chrome plated and cannot be cleaned.

   d. Replace piston seals and dust covers.

9. Coat the piston seal with brake fluid and carefully install the piston seal.

10. Install the dust seal onto the piston. Coat the piston with brake fluid. Install the piston and seal assembly and install the retaining ring.

11. Repeat Steps 9 and 10 for the other piston.

12. Install the caliper assembly. Fill the master cylinder and bleed the system.

Sliding Caliper
▶ See Figure 16

1. Remove the caliper cylinder from the car. (See the appropriate preceding Brake Pad Removal procedure).

2. Carefully remove the dust boot from around the cylinder bore.

3. Place a folded towel between the piston and housing. Apply compressed air to the brake line union to force the piston out of its bore. Be careful, the piston may come out forcefully.

4. Remove the seal from the piston. Check the piston and cylinder bore for wear and/or corrosion. Replace components as necessary.

To assemble:

5. Coat all components with clean brake fluid.

6. Install the seal and piston in the cylinder bore, after coating them with the rubber lubricant supplied in the rebuilding kit. Seat the piston in the bore.

7. Fit the boot into the groove in the cylinder bore.

8. Install the caliper cylinder assembly on to the support.

9. Fill the master cylinder and bleed the system.

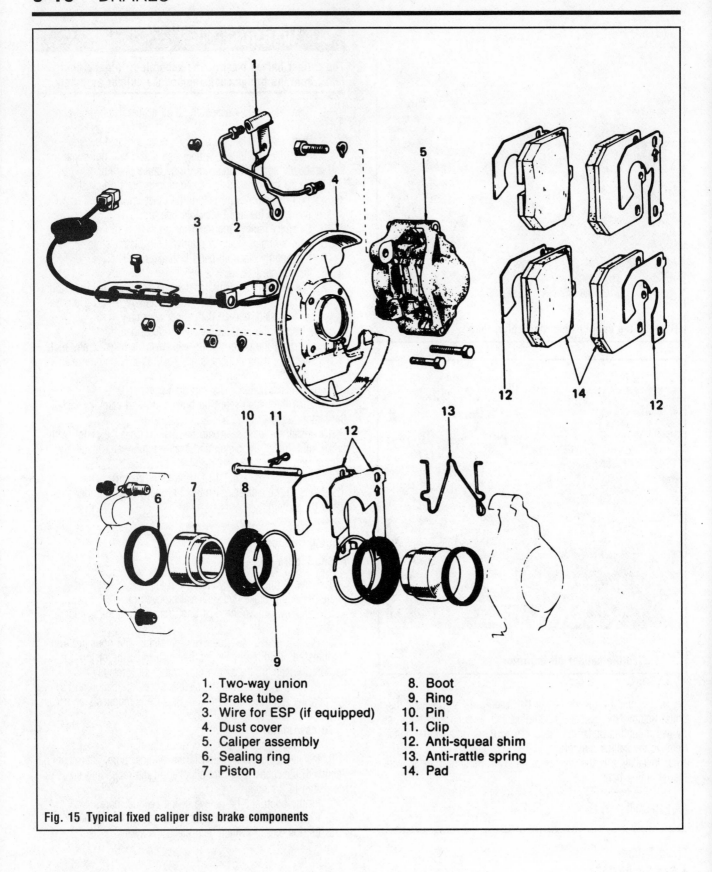

1. Two-way union
2. Brake tube
3. Wire for ESP (if equipped)
4. Dust cover
5. Caliper assembly
6. Sealing ring
7. Piston
8. Boot
9. Ring
10. Pin
11. Clip
12. Anti-squeal shim
13. Anti-rattle spring
14. Pad

Fig. 15 Typical fixed caliper disc brake components

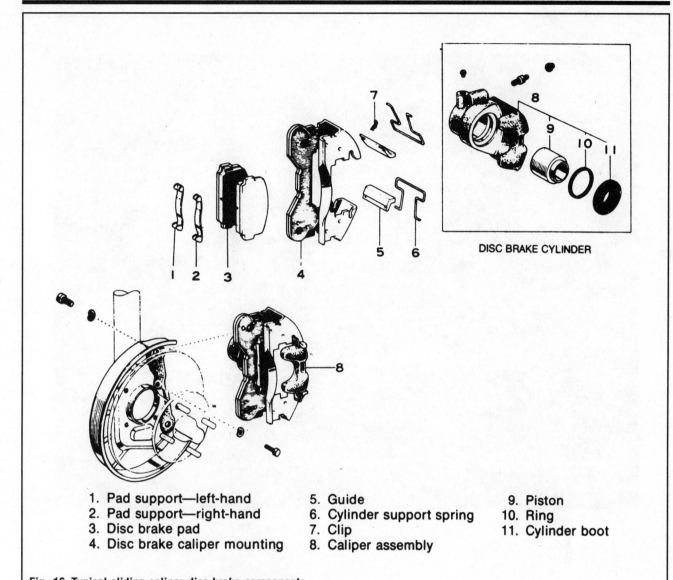

1. Pad support—left-hand
2. Pad support—right-hand
3. Disc brake pad
4. Disc brake caliper mounting
5. Guide
6. Cylinder support spring
7. Clip
8. Caliper assembly
9. Piston
10. Ring
11. Cylinder boot

Fig. 16 Typical sliding caliper disc brake components

Brake Disc (Rotor)

REMOVAL & INSTALLATION

1. Remove the brake pads and caliper, or caliper and support as previously described.
2. Check the disc run-out with a dial indicator, if available. See the rotor inspection section for details.
3. Remove the grease cap from the center of the hub. Remove the cotter pin, castellated nut and bearing.
4. Remove the wheel hub with the disc rotor attached.
5. Inspect the rotor. See the rotor inspection section for details.
6. Check the wheel bearings, repack them with grease if necessary.
7. Installation is the reverse of removal. Before installation, coat the hub oil seal with multi-purpose grease. Install the hub

To remove the rotor, first pry off the grease cap

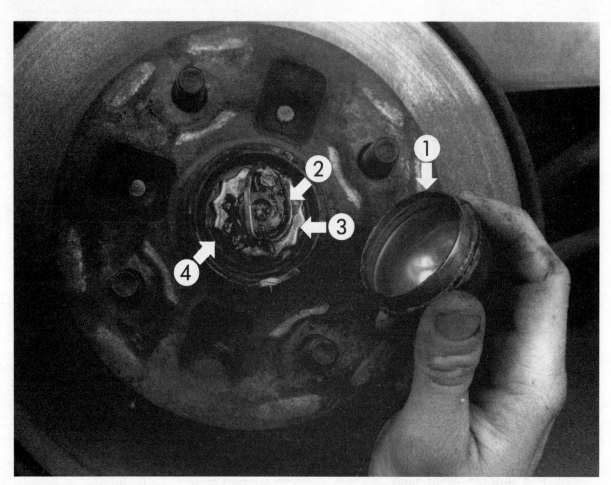

1. Grease cap
2. Cotter pin
3. Castellated nut
4. Wheel bearing

Under the grease cap are several components to be removed

Straighten the cotter pin and remove it from the axle stub

Slide off the castellated nut

Remove the axle nut . . .

With two hands, remove the brake rotor from the axle stub

. . . to access the washer and bearing

and disc rotor. Adjust the wheel bearing preload. See the wheel bearing section.

INSPECTION

Examine the disc. If it is worn, warped or scored, it must be replaced. Check the thickness of the disc against the specifications given in the Disc and Pad Specifications chart. If it is below specifications, replace it. Use a micrometer to measure the thickness.

The disc run-out should be measured before the disc is removed and again, after the disc is installed. Use a dial indicator mounted on a stand to determine run-out. If run-out exceeds 0.15mm (all models), replace the disc.

➡ **Be sure that the wheel bearing nut is properly tightened. If it is not, an inaccurate run-out reading may be obtained. If different run-out readings are obtained with the same disc, between removal and installation, this is probably the cause.**

Disc and Pad Specifications (in.)

Model	New Disc Thickness	Disc Service Limit Thickness	Run-Out Limit	Pad Thickness Limit
Corona ('70–'73)	0.39	0.35	0.006	0.35
Corona ('74–'84)	0.49	0.45	0.006	0.04 ①
Mark II/4	0.39	0.37	0.006	0.08
Mark II/6	0.49	0.45	0.006	0.28 ②
Crown 2300	0.46	0.40	0.006	0.40
Crown 2600	0.50	0.45	0.006	0.27
Cressida	③	④	0.006	0.040

① 1976—0.08 in.   ③ 1978–80: 0.50   ④ 1978–80: 0.45
② 1976—0.45 in.   1981–82: 0.70   1981–82: 0.67

REAR DRUM BRAKES

Brake Drums

REMOVAL & INSTALLATION

▶ **See Figure 17**

1. Remove the hub cap (if used) and loosen the lug nuts. Release the parking brake.

2. Block the front wheels, raise the rear of the car, and support it with jackstands.

✳✳ CAUTION

Support the car securely with jackstands and block the front wheels.

3. Remove the lug nuts and the wheel.

4. Unfasten the brake drum retaining screws.

5. Tap the drum lightly with a mallet in order to free it. If the drum is difficult to remove use a puller. But first be sure that the parking brake is released.

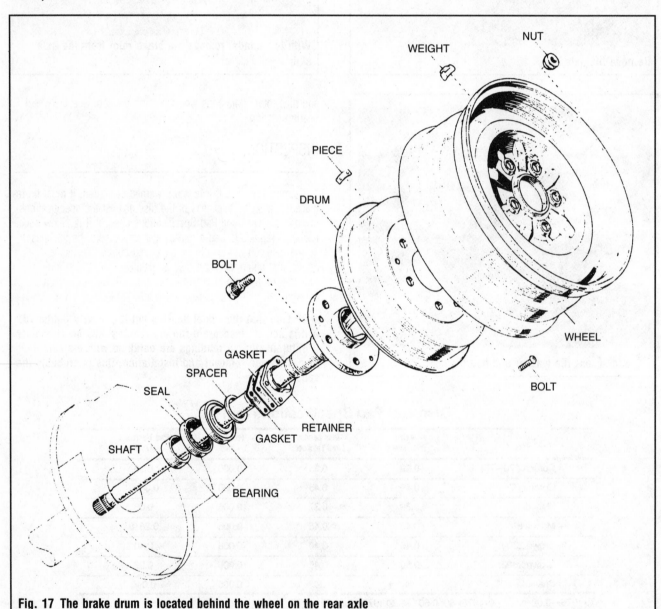

Fig. 17 The brake drum is located behind the wheel on the rear axle

On some models, you can screw bolts into the drums threaded holes to ease removal

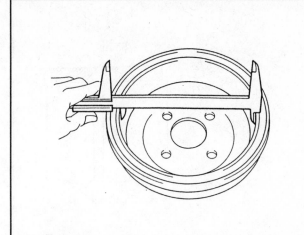

Fig. 18 Measure the inside diameter of the brake drum with an H-gauge (caliper)

Pull off the brake drum

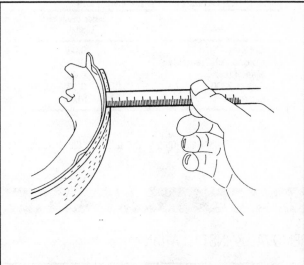

Fig. 19 Measure the shoe lining thickness with a ruler

✳✳ WARNING

Don't depress the brake pedal once the drum has been removed.

6. Inspect the brake drum as detailed following.
7. Brake drum installation is performed in the reverse order of removal.

INSPECTION

▶ See Figures 18, 19, 20 and 21

1. Clean the drum.
2. Inspect the drum for scoring, cracks, grooves and out-of-roundness. Replace or turn the drum, as required.
3. Light scoring may be removed by dressing the drum with fine emery cloth.
4. Heavy scoring will require the use of a brake drum lathe to

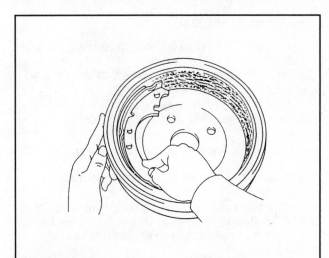

Fig. 20 Inspect the brake lining and drum for proper contact

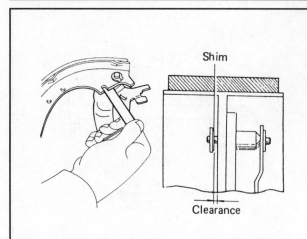

Fig. 21 Measure the clearance between the brake shoe and the parking brake lever

BRAKE DRUM DIAMETER

Model	Inside Diameter Limit (in.)
Corona	9.08
Corona (1977 and later)	9.0
Mark II (all)	9.08
Crown 2300	9.13
Crown 2600	10.08

turn the drum. The service limits of the drum inside diameter are as follows:

Brake Shoes

REMOVAL & INSTALLATION

Corona (1974–82), Crown, Cressida

♦ **See Figures 22 and 23**

1. Perform the Brake Drum Removal procedure as previously detailed.
2. Unhook the shoe tension springs from the shoes with the aid of a brake spring removing tool.
3. Remove the brake shoe securing springs.
4. Disconnect the parking brake cable at the parking brake shoe lever.
5. Withdraw the shoes, complete with the parking brake shoe lever.
6. Unfasten the C-clip and remove the adjuster assembly from the shoes.
7. Inspect the shoes for wear and scoring. Have the linings replaced if their thickness is less than 1mm (1.5mm on the Crown).
8. Check the tension springs to see if they are weak, distorted or rusted.
9. Inspect the teeth on the automatic adjuster wheel for chipping or other damage.

→**Grease the point of the shoe which slides against the backing plate. Do not get grease on the linings.**

To install:

10. Attach the parking brake shoe lever and the automatic adjuster lever to the rear side of the shoe.
11. Fasten the parking brake cable to the lever on the brake shoe.
12. Install the automatic adjuster and fit the tension spring on the adjuster lever.
13. Install the securing spring on the rear shoe, then install the securing spring on the front shoe.

→**The tension spring should be installed on the anchor, before performing Step 13.**

14. Hook one end of the tension spring over the rear shoe with the tool used during removal. Hook the other end over the front shoe.

Spray an aerosol brake cleaner on the brake components before disassembly

Unhook the brake shoe return springs . . .

. . . and anchor spring with appropriate tools

Pull the shoes apart . . .

With an appropriate brake tool, depress, turn and carefully release the hold-down spring retainers . . .

. . . and remove the adjuster

. . . then remove the springs, retainers and pins

Unhook the parking brake cable from the shoe

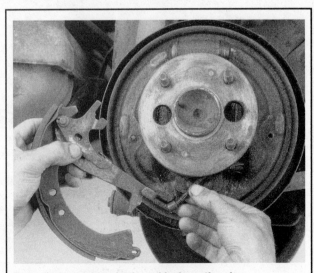

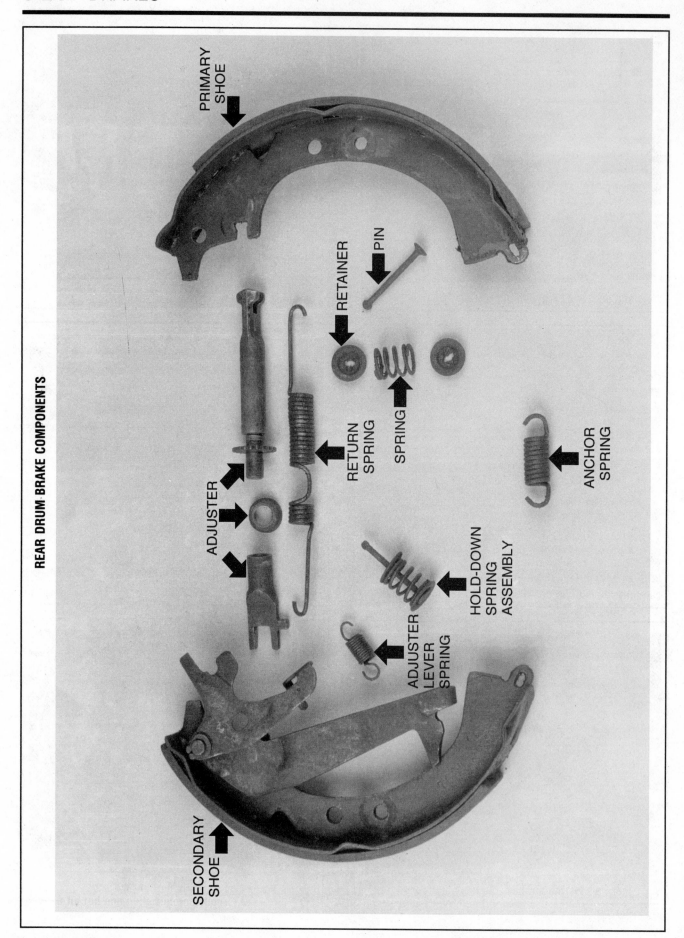

REAR DRUM BRAKE COMPONENTS

PRIMARY SHOE

RETAINER

PIN

RETURN SPRING

SPRING

ANCHOR SPRING

ADJUSTER

HOLD-DOWN SPRING ASSEMBLY

ADJUSTER LEVER SPRING

SECONDARY SHOE

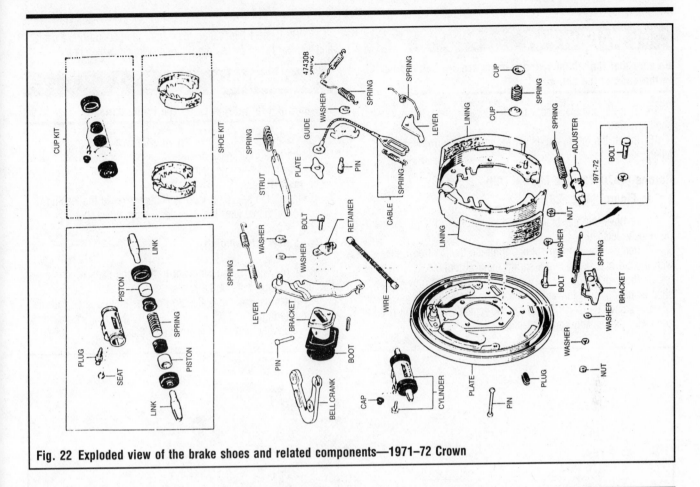

Fig. 22 Exploded view of the brake shoes and related components—1971–72 Crown

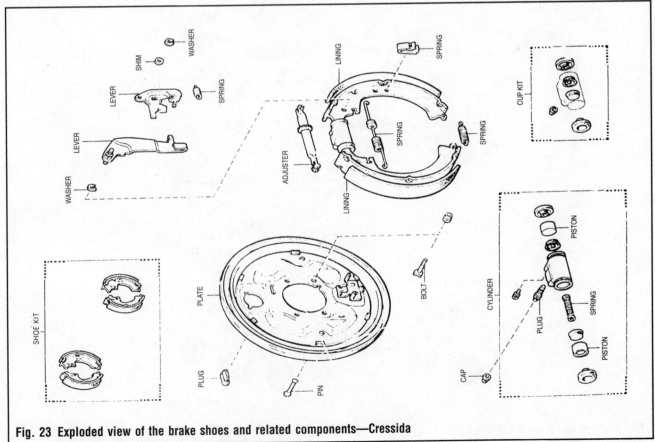

Fig. 23 Exploded view of the brake shoes and related components—Cressida

Be sure that the wheel cylinder boots are not being pinched in the ends of the shoes.

15. Test the automatic adjuster by operating the parking brake shoe lever.

16. Install the drum and adjust the brakes as previously detailed.

Corona (1970–73) and Mark II (All)

♦ **See Figure 24 (p. 28)**

1. Remove the rear brake drum by performing the procedure previously detailed.

2. Remove the tension springs from the trailing (rear) shoe with the aid of a brake return spring removal tool.

3. Press down on the brake adjuster ratchet and move the shoe adjusting lever forward, to the center of the drum.

4. Remove the securing spring and remove the leading (front) shoe with the tension spring attached.

5. Disconnect the trailing shoe from the parking brake cable and remove the shoe retaining spring. Withdraw the shoe.

Use care not to get grease on the lining surface.

6. Inspect all of the parts removed for wear or damage. Check the lining thickness. It should be no less than 1.5mm. If it is less than this have the brakes relined.

To install:

7. Install the adjusting lever and ratchet on to the leading shoe. Attach the parking brake cable to the trailing shoe.

➡**Use a new retaining clip.**

8. Apply non-melting lubricant to the shoe parts which contact other components of the brake.

9. Install the parking brake strut on the trailing shoe with its retaining spring.

10. Attach the parking brake cable to the lever.

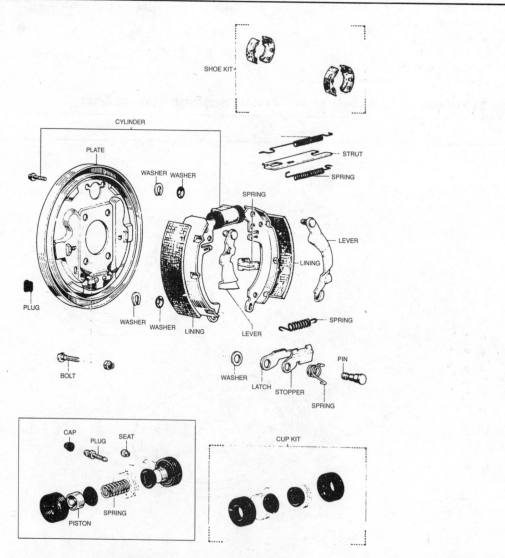

Fig. 24 Exploded view of the brake shoes and related components—1970–73 Corona

11. Fasten the trailing shoe with its security spring.

12. Push the adjusting lever toward the center of the brake and install it with the tension spring. Fasten the shoe retaining spring.

➡**The longer hook of the tension spring attaches to the leading shoe.**

13. Push the adjusting ratchet downward, while returning the lever, so that it contacts the rim of the shoe.

14. Install the retaining spring.

15. Attach the tension spring to the shoes with the tool used during removal. Install the brake drum.

Wheel Cylinders

REMOVAL & INSTALLATION

◆ **See Figure 25**

1. Plug the master cylinder inlet to prevent hydraulic fluid from leaking.

2. Remove the brake drums and shoes as detailed in the appropriate preceding section.

3. Working from behind the backing plate, disconnect the hydraulic line from the wheel cylinder.

4. Unfasten the screws retaining the wheel cylinder and withdraw the cylinder.

5. Installation is performed in the reverse order of removal. However, once the hydraulic line has been disconnected from the wheel cylinder, the union seat must be replaced.

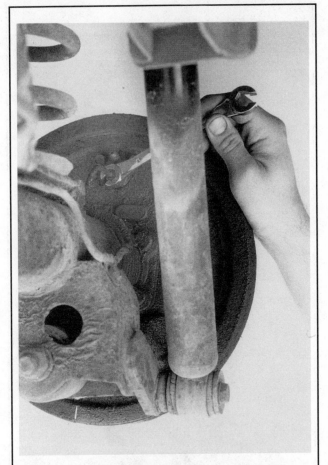

Working from behind the brake backing plate, disconnect the brake line attached to the wheel cylinder

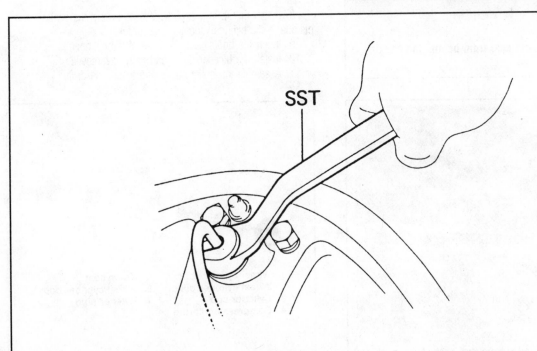

SST

Fig. 25 Using a brake line tool, disconnect the brake line from the back of the wheel cylinder

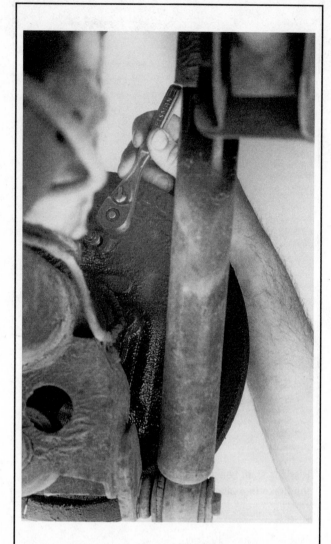

Also unbolt the wheel cylinder from behind the backing plate

Remove the wheel cylinder from the front of the backing plate

Seat Replacement

➡**This procedure is not required on Crown models.**

1. Use a screw extractor with a diameter of 2.5mm and having reverse threads, to remove the union seat from the wheel cylinder.
2. Drive in the new union seat with an 8mm bar, used as a drift.
3. Bleed the brake system after completing wheel cylinder, brake shoe and drum installation.

OVERHAUL

◆ **See Figure 26**

It is not necessary to remove the wheel cylinder from the backing plate if it is only to be inspected or rebuilt.

1. Remove the brake drum and shoes. Remove the wheel cylinder only if it is going to be replaced.
2. Remove the rubber boots from either end of the wheel cylinder.
3. Withdraw the piston and cup assemblies.
4. Take the compression spring out of the wheel cylinder body, except on Crown models.
5. Remove the bleeder plug (and ball), if necessary.
6. Check all components for wear or damage. Inspect the bore for signs of wear, scoring, and/or scuffing. If in doubt, replace or hone the wheel cylinder (with a special hone). The limit for honing a cylinder is 0.127mm oversize. Wash all the residue from the cylinder bore with clean brake fluid and blow dry.

To assemble:

7. Soak all components in clean brake fluid, or coat them with the rubber grease supplied in the wheel cylinder rebuilding kit.
8. Install the spring, cups, (recesses toward the center), and pistons in the cylinder body, in that order.
9. Insert the boots over the ends of the cylinder.
10. Install the bleeder plug (and ball), if removed.
11. Assemble the brake shoes and install the drum.

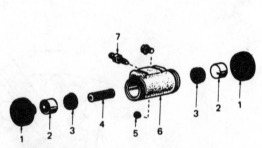

1. Wheel cylinder boot
2. Wheel cylinder piston
3. Cylinder cup
4. Compression spring
5. Union seat
6. Wheel cylinder body
7. Bleeder plug

Fig. 26 Exploded view of a disassembled wheel cylinder

PARKING BRAKE

Cables

ADJUSTMENT

Floor Mounted Lever

1. Ensure that the rear brake shoes are correctly adjusted.
2. Without depressing the button, pull the parking brake handle up slowly, and count the number of notches before the brake is applied. It should take 3–6 notches. If not, proceed with Step 3.
3. Working from underneath of the car, loosen the locknut on the parking brake equalizer.
4. Screw the adjusting nut in, just enough so that the parking brake cables have no slack.
5. Hold the adjusting nut in this position while tightening the locknut.
6. Check the rotation of the rear wheels, with the parking brake off, to be sure that the brake shoes aren't dragging.

Parking Brake Adjustment

Model	Adjusting Range (Notches)
Corona	7–12 ①
Mark II 4-Cylinder ('70–'72)	5–9
Mark II 6-Cylinder ('72–'76)	8–10 ②
Crown 2300 ('70–'71)	5–9
Crown 2600 ('72)	8–11
Cressida	5–8

① 1976 and later—3–6   ② 1976—8–12

Dash Mounted Lever

1. Loosen the parking brake warning light switch bracket.
2. Push the parking brake lever in until it is stopped by the pawl.
3. Move the switch so that it will be off at this position, but on when the handle is pulled out.
4. Tighten the switch bracket and push the brake lever in again.
5. Working from underneath the vehicle, loosen the locknut on the parking brake cable equalizer.
6. Screw the adjusting nut in, just enough so that the brake cables have no slack.
7. Hold the adjusting nut in this position while tightening the locknut.
8. Check the rotation of the rear wheels to make sure that the brakes are not dragging.
9. Pull out on the parking brake lever, and count the number of notches needed to apply the parking brake. Adjust cable if necessary.

REMOVAL & INSTALLATION

▶ **See Figures 27, 28 and 29**

1. Remove the rear console box.
2. Remove the cable adjusting nut.
3. Unscrew the four mounting bolts and remove the parking brake lever.
4. Working under the car, disconnect the parking brake cable equalizer.
5. Remove the two cable clamps from each side of the driveshaft tunnel.
6. Remove the rear brakes and then disconnect the parking brake cable from the lever.
7. Remove the cable from the brake backing plate.
8. Installation is in the reverse order of removal.

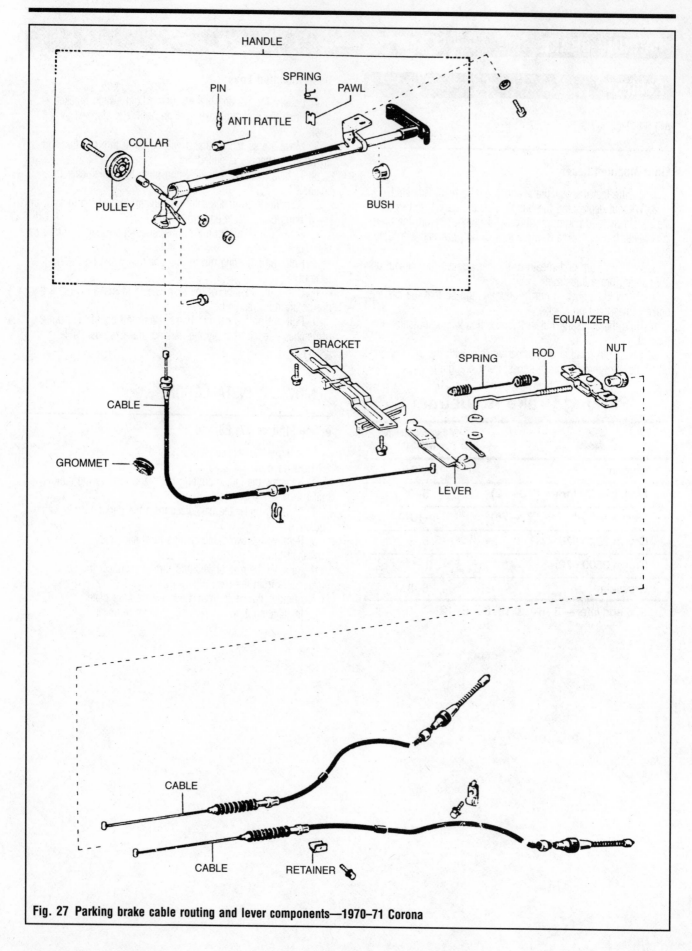

Fig. 27 Parking brake cable routing and lever components—1970–71 Corona

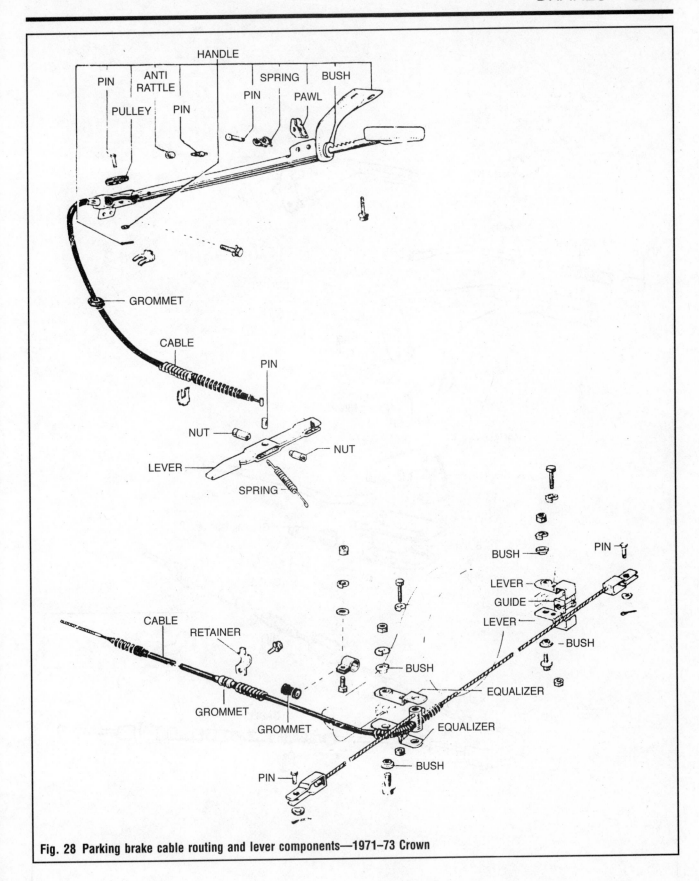

Fig. 28 Parking brake cable routing and lever components—1971–73 Crown

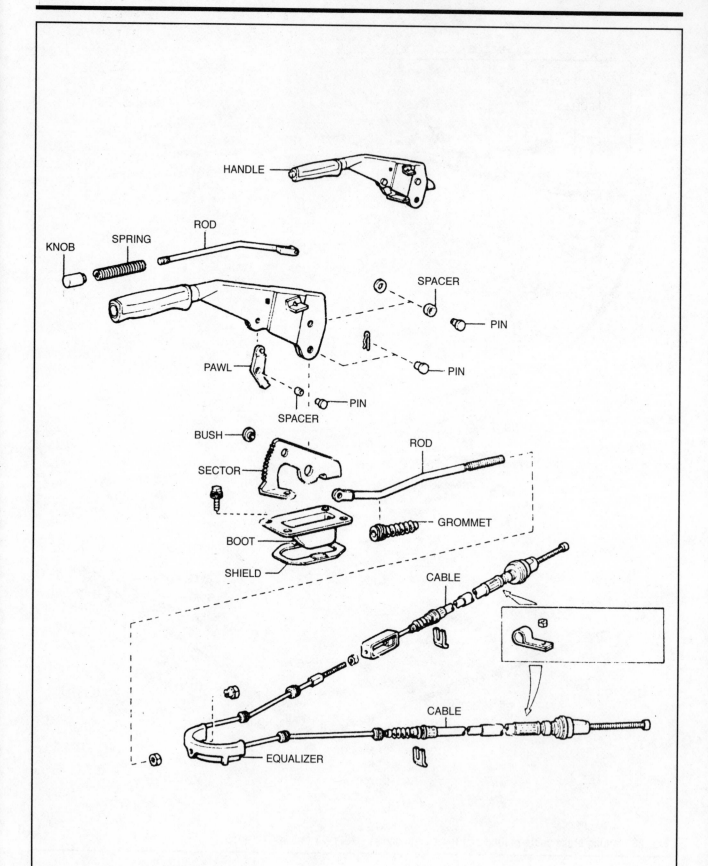

Fig. 29 Parking brake cable routing and lever components—1978–80 Cressida

Troubleshooting the Brake System

Problem	Cause	Solution
Low brake pedal (excessive pedal travel required for braking action.)	• Excessive clearance between rear linings and drums caused by inoperative automatic adjusters	• Make 10 to 15 alternate forward and reverse brake stops to adjust brakes. If brake pedal does not come up, repair or replace adjuster parts as necessary.
	• Worn rear brakelining	• Inspect and replace lining if worn beyond minimum thickness specification
	• Bent, distorted brakeshoes, front or rear	• Replace brakeshoes in axle sets
	• Air in hydraulic system	• Remove air from system. Refer to Brake Bleeding.
Low brake pedal (pedal may go to floor with steady pressure applied.)	• Fluid leak in hydraulic system	• Fill master cylinder to fill line; have helper apply brakes and check calipers, wheel cylinders, differential valve tubes, hoses and fittings for leaks. Repair or replace as necessary.
	• Air in hydraulic system	• Remove air from system. Refer to Brake Bleeding.
	• Incorrect or non-recommended brake fluid (fluid evaporates at below normal temp).	• Flush hydraulic system with clean brake fluid. Refill with correct-type fluid.
	• Master cylinder piston seals worn, or master cylinder bore is scored, worn or corroded	• Repair or replace master cylinder
Low brake pedal (pedal goes to floor on first application—o.k. on subsequent applications.)	• Disc brake pads sticking on abutment surfaces of anchor plate. Caused by a build-up of dirt, rust, or corrosion on abutment surfaces	• Clean abutment surfaces

Troubleshooting the Brake System (cont.)

Problem	Cause	Solution
Fading brake pedal (pedal height decreases with steady pressure applied.)	• Fluid leak in hydraulic system	• Fill master cylinder reservoirs to fill mark, have helper apply brakes, check calipers, wheel cylinders, differential valve, tubes, hoses, and fittings for fluid leaks. Repair or replace parts as necessary.
	• Master cylinder piston seals worn, or master cylinder bore is scored, worn or corroded	• Repair or replace master cylinder
Decreasing brake pedal travel (pedal travel required for braking action decreases and may be accompanied by a hard pedal.)	• Caliper or wheel cylinder pistons sticking or seized	• Repair or replace the calipers, or wheel cylinders
	• Master cylinder compensator ports blocked (preventing fluid return to reservoirs) or pistons sticking or seized in master cylinder bore	• Repair or replace the master cylinder
	• Power brake unit binding internally	• Test unit according to the following procedure: (a) Shift transmission into neutral and start engine (b) Increase engine speed to 1500 rpm, close throttle and fully depress brake pedal (c) Slow release brake pedal and stop engine (d) Have helper remove vacuum check valve and hose from power unit. Observe for backward movement of brake pedal. (e) If the pedal moves backward, the power unit has an internal bind—replace power unit
Spongy brake pedal (pedal has abnormally soft, springy, spongy feel when depressed.)	• Air in hydraulic system	• Remove air from system. Refer to Brake Bleeding.
	• Brakeshoes bent or distorted	• Replace brakeshoes
	• Brakelining not yet seated with drums and rotors	• Burnish brakes
	• Rear drum brakes not properly adjusted	• Adjust brakes
Hard brake pedal (excessive pedal pressure required to stop vehicle. May be accompanied by brake fade.)	• Loose or leaking power brake unit vacuum hose	• Tighten connections or replace leaking hose
	• Incorrect or poor quality brakelining	• Replace with lining in axle sets
	• Bent, broken, distorted brakeshoes	• Replace brakeshoes
	• Calipers binding or dragging on mounting pins. Rear brakeshoes dragging on support plate.	• Replace mounting pins and bushings. Clean rust or burrs from rear brake support plate ledges and lubricate ledges with molydisulfide grease. **NOTE:** If ledges are deeply grooved or scored, do not attempt to sand or grind them smooth—replace support plate.
	• Caliper, wheel cylinder, or master cylinder pistons sticking or seized	• Repair or replace parts as necessary
	• Power brake unit vacuum check valve malfunction	• Test valve according to the following procedure: (a) Start engine, increase engine speed to 1500 rpm, close throttle and immediately stop engine (b) Wait at least 90 seconds then depress brake pedal

Troubleshooting the Brake System (cont.)

Problem	Cause	Solution
Hard brake pedal (excessive pedal pressure required to stop vehicle. May be accompanied by brake fade.) (*continued*)	• Power brake unit has internal bind	(c) If brakes are not vacuum assisted for 2 or more applications, check valve is faulty • Test unit according to the following procedure: (a) With engine stopped, apply brakes several times to exhaust all vacuum in system (b) Shift transmission into neutral, depress brake pedal and start engine (c) If pedal height decreases with foot pressure and less pressure is required to hold pedal in applied position, power unit vacuum system is operating normally. Test power unit. If power unit exhibits a bind condition, replace the power unit.
	• Master cylinder compensator ports (at bottom of reservoirs) blocked by dirt, scale, rust, or have small burrs (blocked ports prevent fluid return to reservoirs). • Brake hoses, tubes, fittings clogged or restricted	• Repair or replace master cylinder **CAUTION:** Do not attempt to clean blocked ports with wire, pencils, or similar implements. Use compressed air only. • Use compressed air to check or unclog parts. Replace any damaged parts.
	• Brake fluid contaminated with improper fluids (motor oil, transmission fluid, causing rubber components to swell and stick in bores • Low engine vacuum	• Replace all rubber components, combination valve and hoses. Flush entire brake system with DOT 3 brake fluid or equivalent. • Adjust or repair engine
Grabbing brakes (severe reaction to brake pedal pressure.)	• Brakelining(s) contaminated by grease or brake fluid • Parking brake cables incorrectly adjusted or seized • Incorrect brakelining or lining loose on brakeshoes • Caliper anchor plate bolts loose • Rear brakeshoes binding on support plate ledges • Incorrect or missing power brake reaction disc • Rear brake support plates loose	• Determine and correct cause of contamination and replace brakeshoes in axle sets • Adjust cables. Replace seized cables. • Replace brakeshoes in axle sets • Tighten bolts • Clean and lubricate ledges. Replace support plate(s) if ledges are deeply grooved. Do not attempt to smooth ledges by grinding. • Install correct disc • Tighten mounting bolts
Dragging brakes (slow or incomplete release of brakes)	• Brake pedal binding at pivot • Power brake unit has internal bind • Parking brake cables incorrrectly adjusted or seized • Rear brakeshoe return springs weak or broken • Automatic adjusters malfunctioning • Caliper, wheel cylinder or master cylinder pistons sticking or seized • Master cylinder compensating ports blocked (fluid does not return to reservoirs).	• Loosen and lubricate • Inspect for internal bind. Replace unit if internal bind exists. • Adjust cables. Replace seized cables. • Replace return springs. Replace brakeshoe if necessary in axle sets. • Repair or replace adjuster parts as required • Repair or replace parts as necessary • Use compressed air to clear ports. Do not use wire, pencils, or similar objects to open blocked ports.

Troubleshooting the Brake System (cont.)

Problem	Cause	Solution
Vehicle moves to one side when brakes are applied	• Incorrect front tire pressure	• Inflate to recommended cold (reduced load) inflation pressure
	• Worn or damaged wheel bearings	• Replace worn or damaged bearings
	• Brakelining on one side contaminated	• Determine and correct cause of contamination and replace brakelining in axle sets
	• Brakeshoes on one side bent, distorted, or lining loose on shoe	• Replace brakeshoes in axle sets
	• Support plate bent or loose on one side	• Tighten or replace support plate
	• Brakelining not yet seated with drums or rotors	• Burnish brakelining
	• Caliper anchor plate loose on one side	• Tighten anchor plate bolts
	• Caliper piston sticking or seized	• Repair or replace caliper
	• Brakelinings water soaked	• Drive vehicle with brakes lightly applied to dry linings
	• Loose suspension component attaching or mounting bolts	• Tighten suspension bolts. Replace worn suspension components.
	• Brake combination valve failure	• Replace combination valve
Chatter or shudder when brakes are applied (pedal pulsation and roughness may also occur.)	• Brakeshoes distorted, bent, contaminated, or worn	• Replace brakeshoes in axle sets
	• Caliper anchor plate or support plate loose	• Tighten mounting bolts
	• Excessive thickness variation of rotor(s)	• Refinish or replace rotors in axle sets
Noisy brakes (squealing, clicking, scraping sound when brakes are applied.)	• Bent, broken, distorted brakeshoes	• Replace brakeshoes in axle sets
	• Excessive rust on outer edge of rotor braking surface	• Remove rust
Noisy brakes (squealing, clicking, scraping sound when brakes are applied.) (cont.)	• Brakelining worn out—shoes contacting drum of rotor	• Replace brakeshoes and lining in axle sets. Refinish or replace drums or rotors.
	• Broken or loose holdown or return springs	• Replace parts as necessary
	• Rough or dry drum brake support plate ledges	• Lubricate support plate ledges
	• Cracked, grooved, or scored rotor(s) or drum(s)	• Replace rotor(s) or drum(s). Replace brakeshoes and lining in axle sets if necessary.
	• Incorrect brakelining and/or shoes (front or rear).	• Install specified shoe and lining assemblies
Pulsating brake pedal	• Out of round drums or excessive lateral runout in disc brake rotor(s)	• Refinish or replace drums, re-index rotors or replace

EXTERIOR 10-2
DOORS 10-2
    REMOVAL & INSTALLATION 10-2
    ADJUSTMENT 10-3
DOOR LOCKS 10-3
    REMOVAL & INSTALLATION 10-3
HOOD 10-5
    REMOVAL & INSTALLATION 10-5
    ALIGNMENT 10-7
LUGGAGE COMPARTMENT LID 10-7
    REMOVAL & INSTALLATION 10-7
    ADJUSTMENT 10-7
FENDERS 10-7
    REMOVAL & INSTALLATION 10-7
GRILLE 10-12
    REMOVAL & INSTALLATION 10-12
OUTSIDE MIRRORS 10-12
    REMOVAL & INSTALLATION 10-12
INTERIOR 10-13
DOOR PANEL 10-16
    REMOVAL & INSTALLATION 10-16
DOOR GLASS 10-17
    REMOVAL & INSTALLATION 10-17
REGULATOR 10-18
    REMOVAL & INSTALLATION 10-18
ELECTRIC WINDOW MOTOR 10-18
    REMOVAL & INSTALLATION 10-18
QUARTER GLASS 10-19
    REMOVAL & INSTALLATION 10-19
LIFTGATE GLASS 10-19
    REMOVAL & INSTALLATION 10-19
SEATS 10-22
    REMOVAL & INSTALLATION 10-22
SEAT BELTS 10-31
    REMOVAL & INSTALLATION 10-31

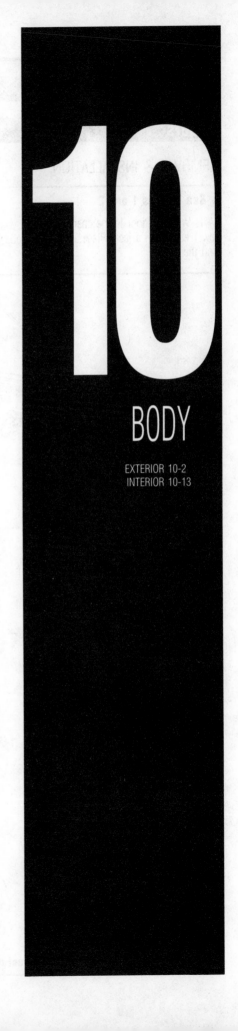

10

BODY

EXTERIOR 10-2
INTERIOR 10-13

EXTERIOR

Doys

REMOVAL & INSTALLATION

▶ **See Figures 1 and 2**

1. With the door in the opened position, support the outer lower edge with a jack. Place a block of wood between the jack and the door.

2. Raise the jack until the wood is against the door, then put a slight upward pressure on the lower door edge. This will help support the door when the hinge mounting bolts are loosened.

3. On models so equipped, remove the door open check pin. Lower the hinge and remove the body side mounting bolts.

4. Remove the door.

5. Install the door in the reverse order of removal. Adjust the door as required.

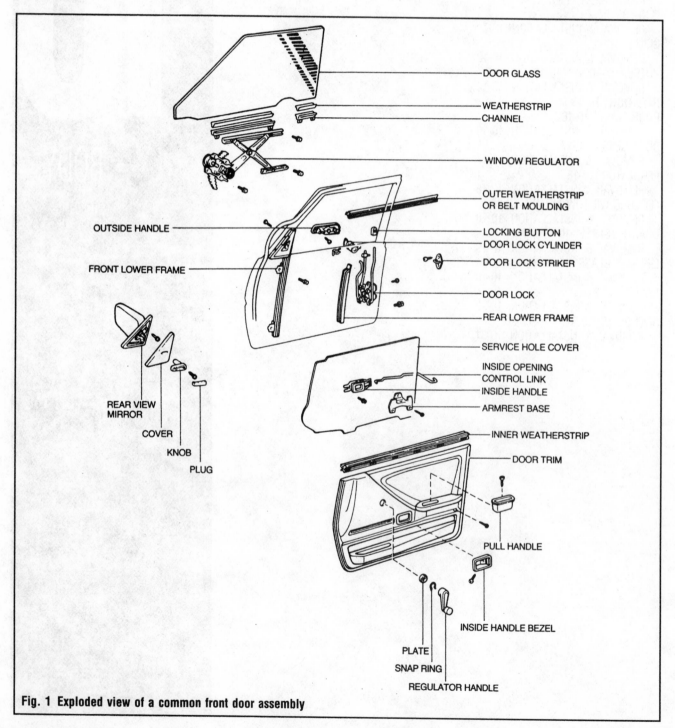

Fig. 1 Exploded view of a common front door assembly

Labels in figure:
- DOOR GLASS
- WEATHERSTRIP
- CHANNEL
- WINDOW REGULATOR
- OUTER WEATHERSTRIP OR BELT MOULDING
- OUTSIDE HANDLE
- LOCKING BUTTON
- DOOR LOCK CYLINDER
- DOOR LOCK STRIKER
- FRONT LOWER FRAME
- DOOR LOCK
- REAR LOWER FRAME
- SERVICE HOLE COVER
- INSIDE OPENING CONTROL LINK
- INSIDE HANDLE
- ARMREST BASE
- REAR VIEW MIRROR
- COVER
- KNOB
- PLUG
- INNER WEATHERSTRIP
- DOOR TRIM
- PULL HANDLE
- INSIDE HANDLE BEZEL
- PLATE
- SNAP RING
- REGULATOR HANDLE

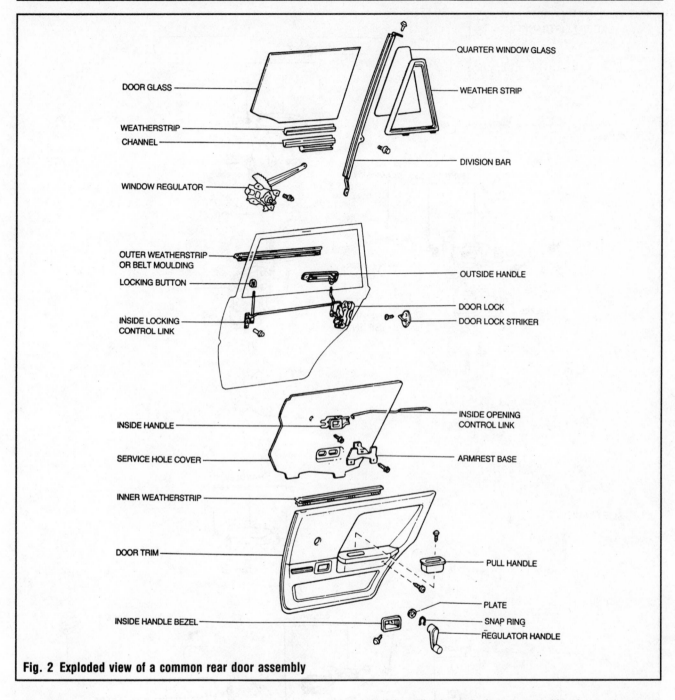

Fig. 2 Exploded view of a common rear door assembly

ADJUSTMENT

➡️**A special tool is required to adjust the door. Tool 09812–22010 or equivalent.**

1. To adjust the door in the forward-backward or up-down position, loosen the body hinge bolts slightly and use the tool to aid in proper door alignment.

2. To adjust the door in the left-right or up-down position, loosen the door side hinge bolts and use the tool to aid proper door alignment.

3. Tighten the door/body side hinge bolts and check the alignment. Readjust if necessary. Check the position of the door lock striker.

4. If the striker is not in the correct position, loosen the mounting bolts slightly, and tap the striker (with a plastic hammer) into the correct position. Tighten the mounting bolts.

Door Locks

REMOVAL & INSTALLATION

◆ **See Figures 3, 4, and 5 (p. 4–6)**

1. Remove the inside door trim panel and access cover.

2. Disconnect the links from the outside handle and door lock cylinder.

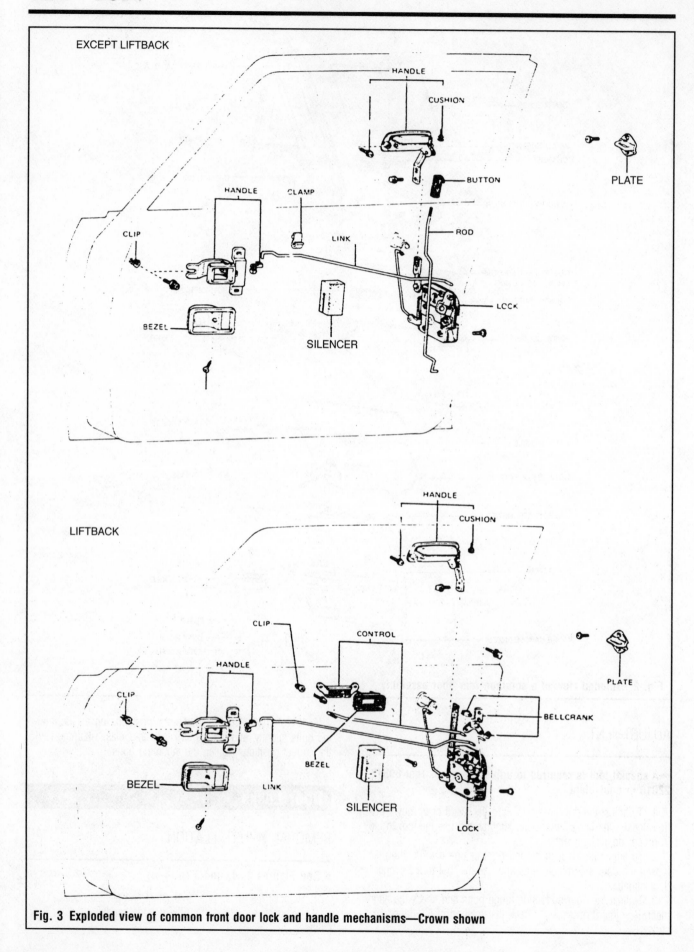

Fig. 3 Exploded view of common front door lock and handle mechanisms—Crown shown

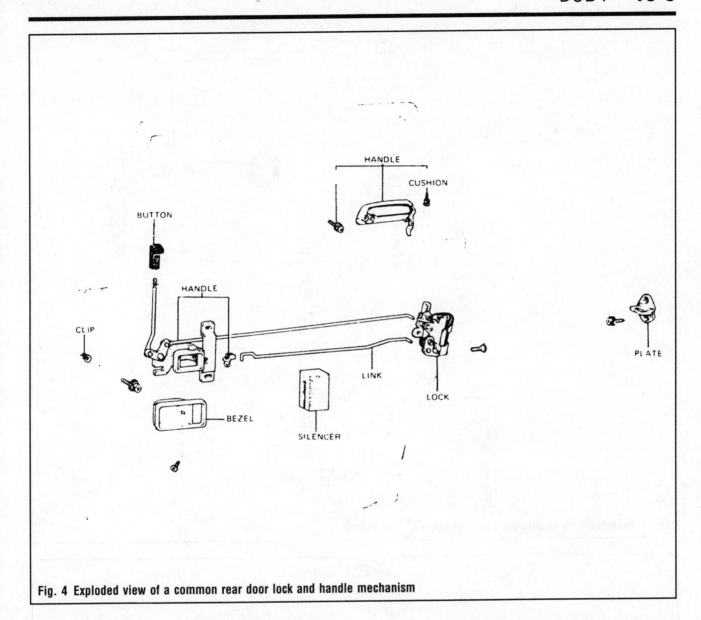

Fig. 4 Exploded view of a common rear door lock and handle mechanism

3. On models with power locks, it will be necessary to unplug the connectors from the door lock solenoid and key unlock switch.

4. Remove the door lock retaining bolts or screws and remove the door lock.

5. Installation is the reverse of removal.

Hood

REMOVAL & INSTALLATION

♦ **See Figure 6**

1. Protect the painted areas such as the fenders with a protective cover.

2. Loosen the hood retaining bolts.

3. With the aid of an assistant remove the retaining bolts and lift the hood away from the car.

4. Installation is the reverse of removal. Align the hood to the proper position.

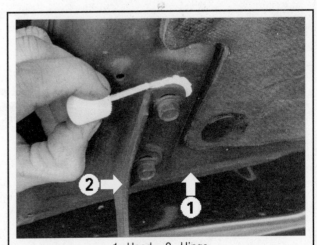

1. Hood 2. Hinge

When removing the hood, scribe or paint markings where the hinge mates to the hood

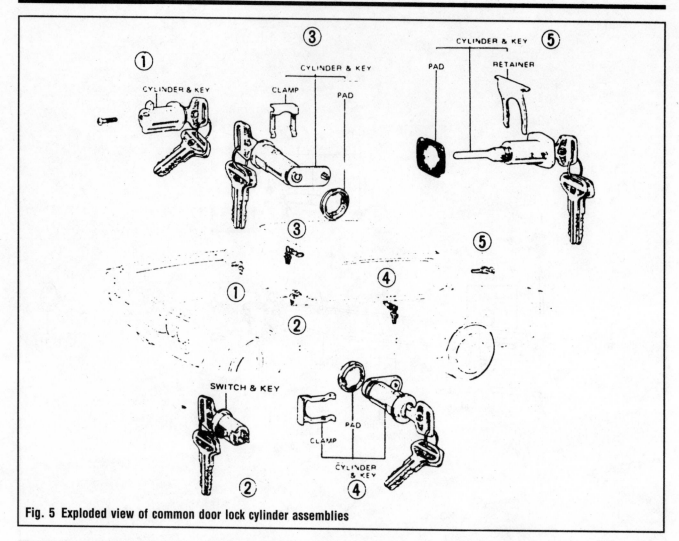

Fig. 5 Exploded view of common door lock cylinder assemblies

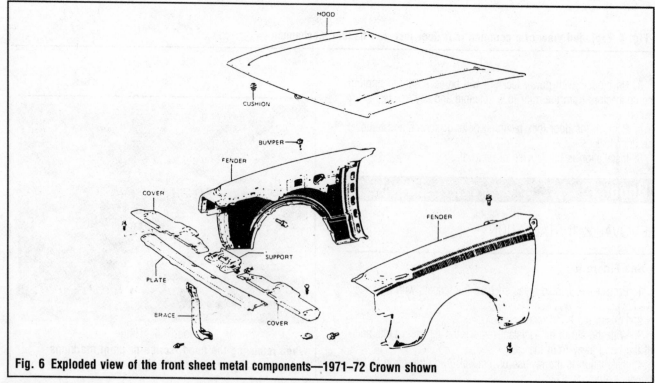

Fig. 6 Exploded view of the front sheet metal components—1971–72 Crown shown

Loosen the hinge retaining bolts . . .

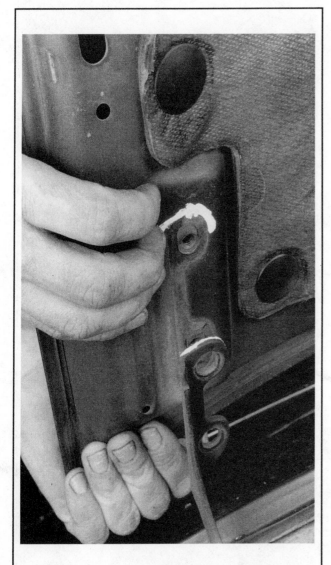

. . . then, with an assistant, lift the hood off the hinges

ALIGNMENT

▶ See Figure 7 (p. 8)

1. For forward/rearward and left/right adjustments, loosen the bolts and move the hood the desired position.
2. For vertical adjustment of the hoods front edge, turn the cushion.
3. For vertical adjustment of the hoods rear end, increase or decrease the number of shims.
4. Adjust the hood lock if necessary by loosening the bolts.

Luggage Compartment Lid

REMOVAL & INSTALLATION

Sedan and Coupe

▶ See Figure 8 (p. 9)

1. Matchmark the position of the hinges on the lid.
2. Remove the hinge mounting bolts.
3. Carefully lift the lid from the vehicle.
4. Installation is the reverse of installation

Liftback
▶ See Figure 9 (p. 10)

1. Disconnect the damper stay from the body.
2. Matchmark the position of the hinges to the lid.
3. Have an assistant secure the lid.
4. Remove the hinge bolts and remove the lid.
5. Installation is the reverse of removal. Adjust as necessary.

ADJUSTMENT

1. For forward/rearward and left/right adjustments, loosen the bolts and move the luggage compartment lid the desired position.
2. For vertical adjustment of the front edge of the lid, increase or decrease the number of shims between the hinge and the compartment lid.
3. Adjust the lock striker, loosen the mounting bolts and move the lock striker assembly in the correct position.

Fenders

REMOVAL & INSTALLATION

▶ See Figure 10 (p. 11)

1. Protect the painted areas with a protective cover.
2. Remove the retainers securing the inner fender liner to the fender.
3. Raise the hood.
4. Remove the front turnsignal/parking light housing assembly if necessary.

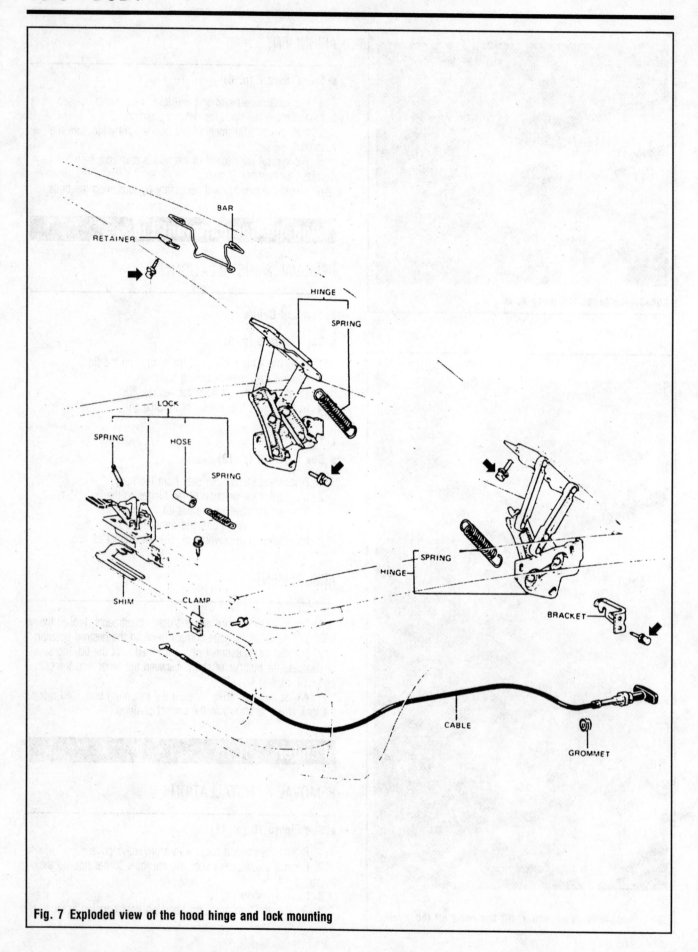

Fig. 7 Exploded view of the hood hinge and lock mounting

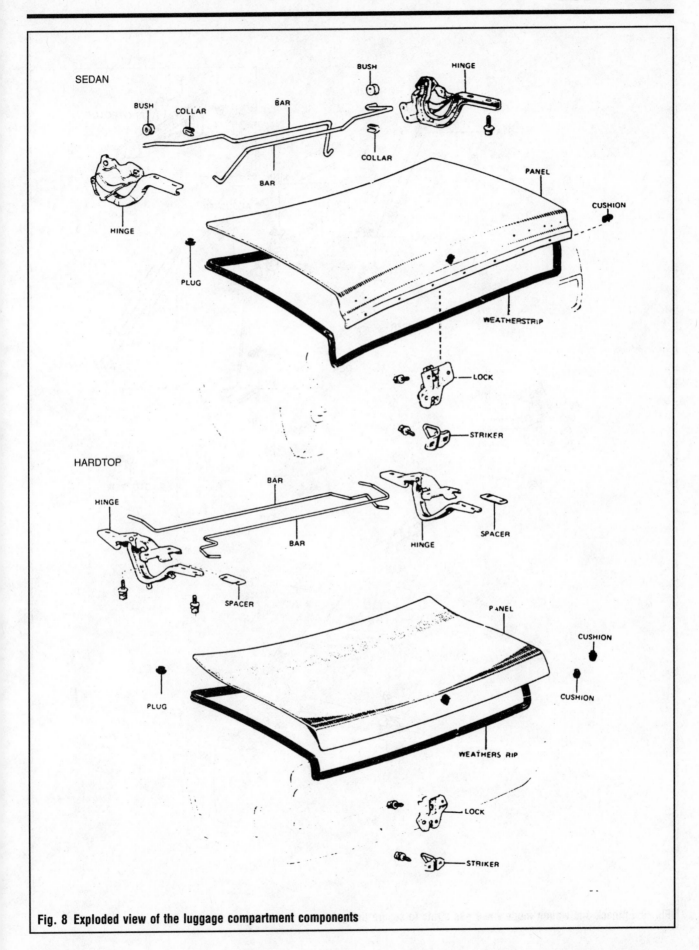

Fig. 8 Exploded view of the luggage compartment components

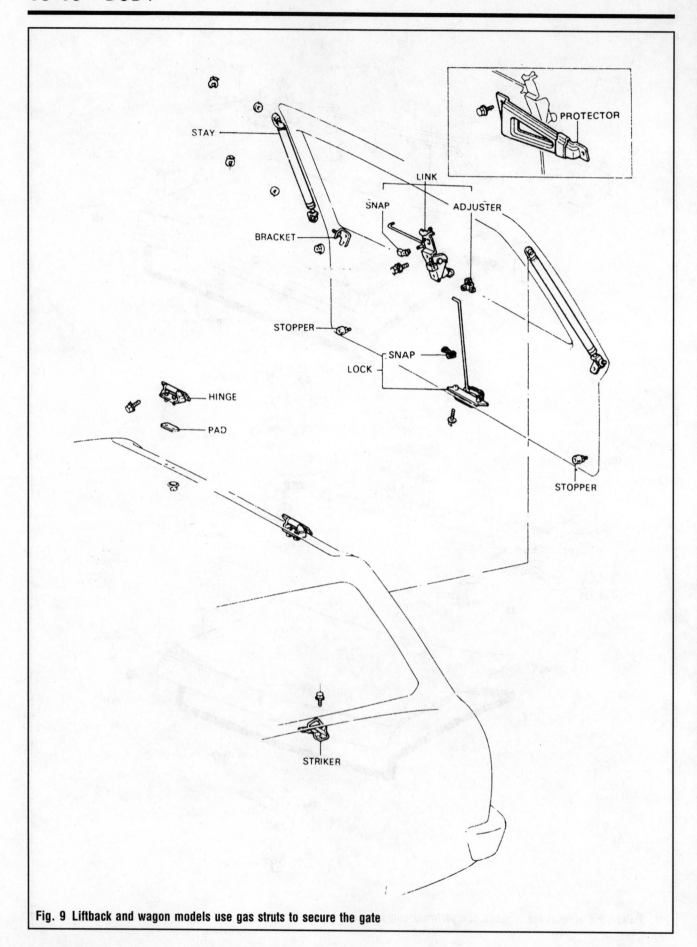

STAY

PROTECTOR

LINK

SNAP   ADJUSTER

BRACKET

STOPPER

SNAP

LOCK

HINGE

PAD

STOPPER

STRIKER

Fig. 9 Liftback bond wagon models use gas struts to secure the gate

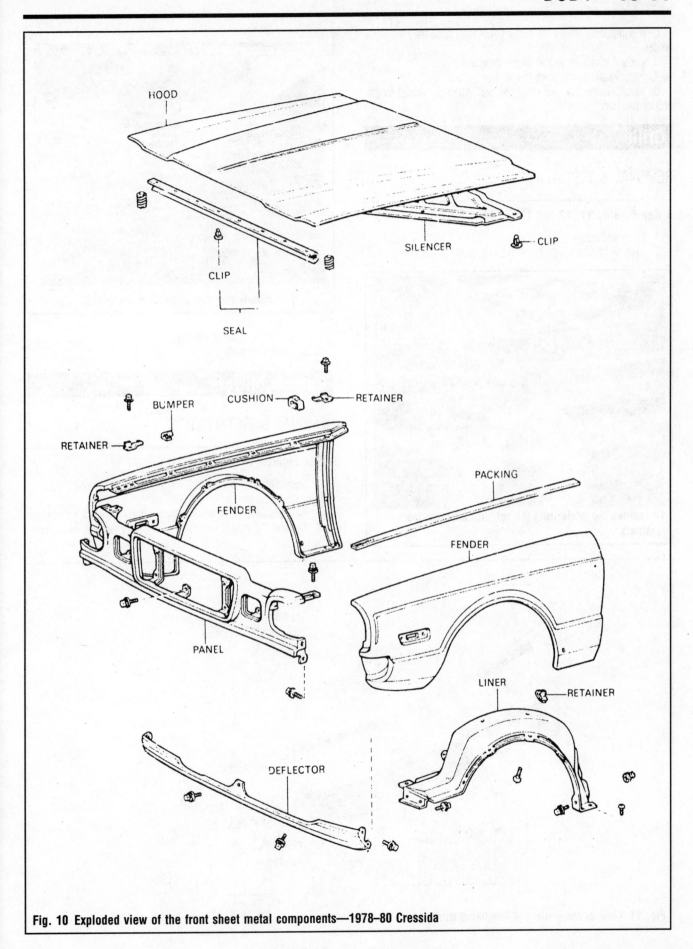

Fig. 10 Exploded view of the front sheet metal components—1978–80 Cressida

5. If equipped, remove the side marker light assembly from the fender.

6. Loosen and remove the fender retaining bolts.

7. Remove the fender from the vehicle.

8. Installation is the reverse of removal. Align the fender to the proper position.

Grille

REMOVAL & INSTALLATION

▶ **See Figures 11, 12 and 13 (p. 14)**

1. Open and support the hood.
2. Remove the turn signal and parking lamps if necessary.

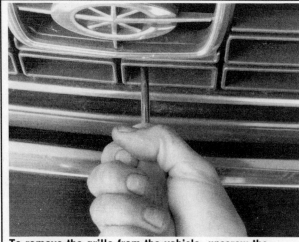

To remove the grille from the vehicle, unscrew the retainers . . .

. . . then simply pull the grille from the vehicle

3. Unscrew the grille assembly.
4. Reverse to install.

Outside Mirrors

REMOVAL & INSTALLATION

▶ **See Figures 14 and 15 (p. 15)**

1. Open the door and pry off the mirror garnish which covers the retaining screws.
2. Role the window down and hold onto the mirror assembly.
3. Remove the mirror retaining screws and remove the mirror

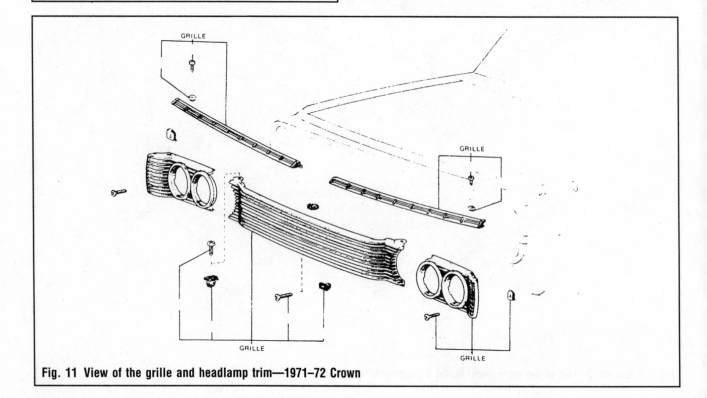

Fig. 11 View of the grille and headlamp trim—1971–72 Crown

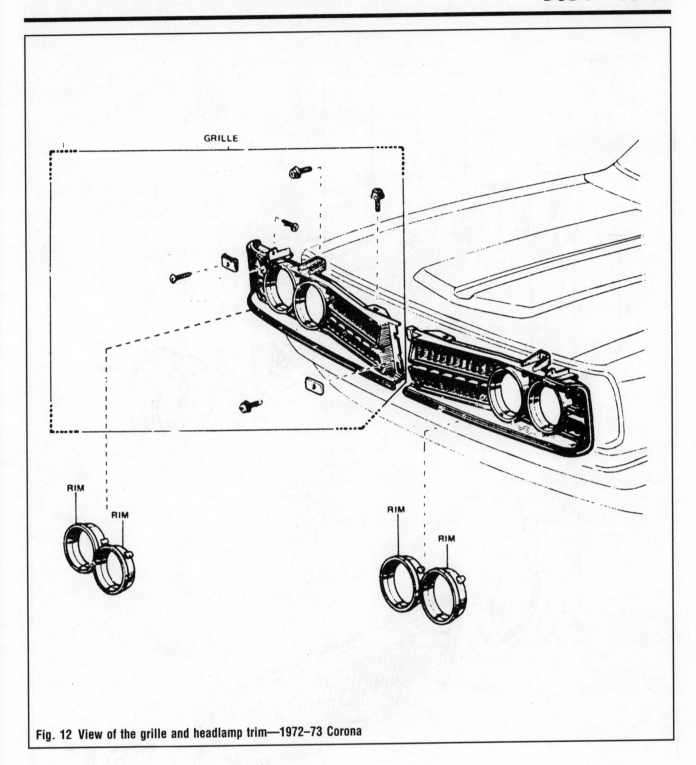

GRILLE

RIM

RIM

RIM

RIM

Fig. 12 View of the grille and headlamp trim—1972–73 Corona

from the door. If equipped with a power mirror, disconnect the electrical wiring.

➡**On some models equipped with power mirrors, it may be necessary to remove the door panel in order to gain access to the electrical harness to the power mirror.**

4. Installation is the reverse order of removal.

INTERIOR

➡**These procedures apply to most models, some variations may be needed depending on the year.**

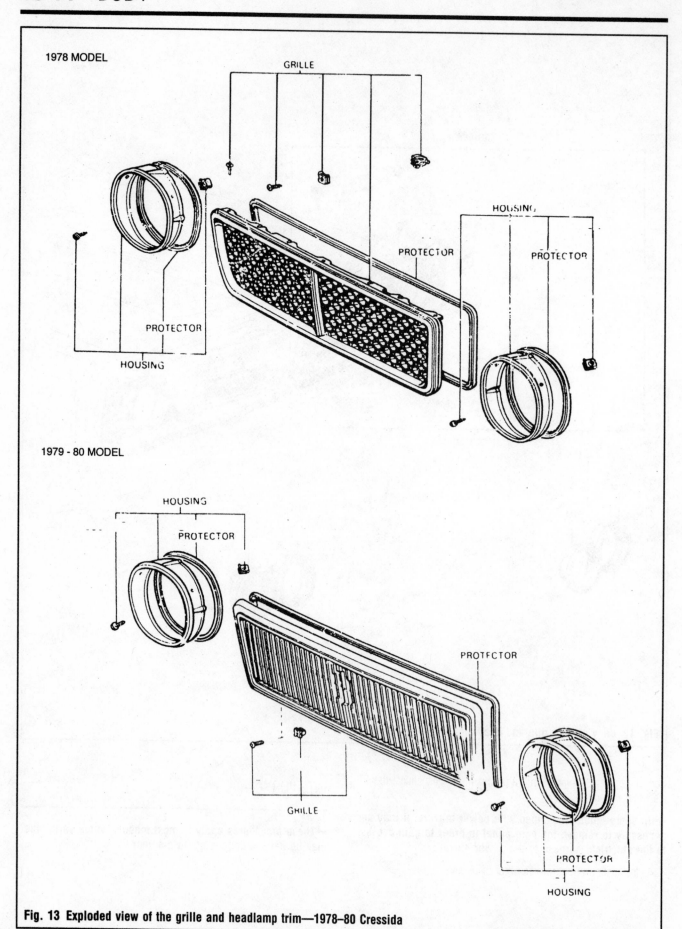

Fig. 13 Exploded view of the grille and headlamp trim—1978–80 Cressida

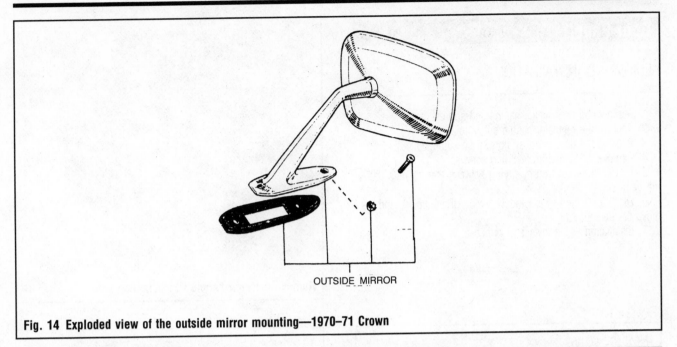

Fig. 14 Exploded view of the outside mirror mounting—1970–71 Crown

OUTSIDE MIRROR

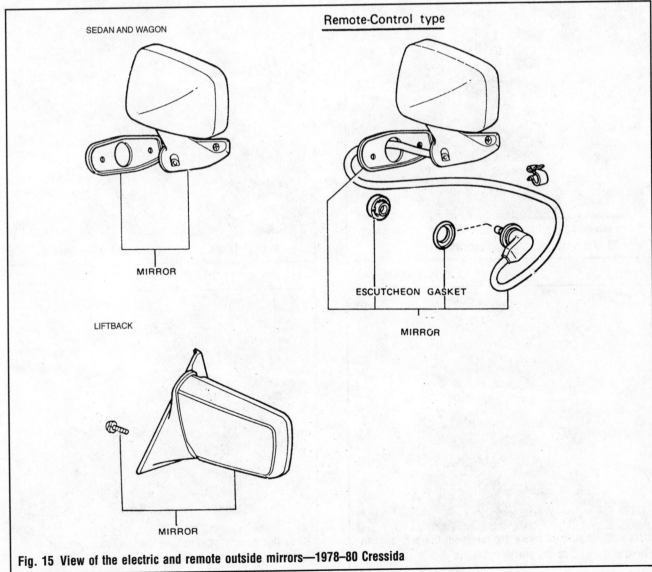

SEDAN AND WAGON

Remote-Control type

MIRROR

ESCUTCHEON GASKET

MIRROR

LIFTBACK

MIRROR

Fig. 15 View of the electric and remote outside mirrors—1978–80 Cressida

Door Panel

REMOVAL & INSTALLATION

1. Remove the door inside handle and armrest.
2. Remove the regulator handle snapring.
3. Remove the door courtesy light, if so equipped.
4. Remove the door trim retaining screws.
5. Loosen the door trim by prying between the retainers and the door trim.
6. Disconnect the power window switch (if equipped), and remove the door panel.
7. Installation is the reverse of removal.

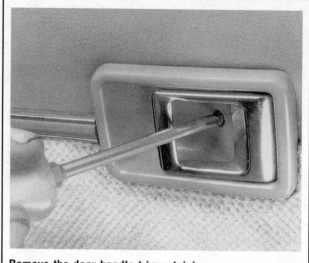

Remove the door handle trim retaining screw . . .

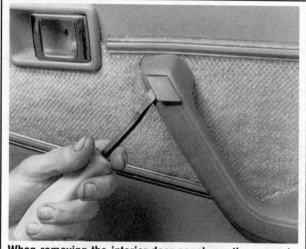

When removing the interior door panel, pry the armrest trim off to access the retaining screws

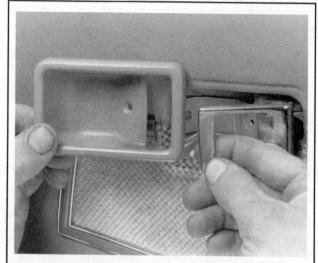

. . . then slide the trim out from behind the handle

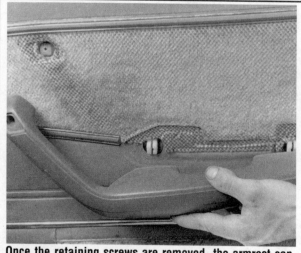

Once the retaining screws are removed, the armrest can be snapped off of the plastic retainers

Slide this special tool behind the window regulator handle . .

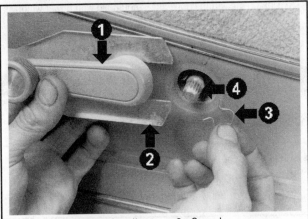

1. Regulator handle   3. Snapring
2. Clip remover tool   4. Regulator shaft

. . . to remove the snapring retaining the handle to the regulator shaft

With the trim separated, lift the panel over the door lock button

Carefully pry the outer edges around the trim panel to separate it from the door shell

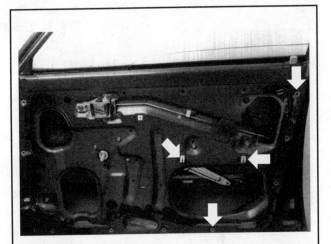

Check for any damaged retaining clips and replace as needed

Door Glass

REMOVAL & INSTALLATION

1. Lower the window fully.
2. Remove the door inner trim panel.
3. Remove the service hole cover.
4. Remove the side view mirror.
5. Remove the top of the weatherstrip on both sides of the door, remove the screws and the belt molding if necessary.
6. Raise the window about an inch and remove the bolt holding the window guide in place. Pull the window guide upward out of the door.
7. Move the window downward and remove the forward stabilizer hook.
8. Move the window forward and down and remove the rear stabilizer hook.

9. Separate the regulator roller by sliding it from the door glass bracket.
10. Remove the door glass by pulling it upward.
11. Installation is the reverse of removal.

Regulator

REMOVAL & INSTALLATION

▶ **See Figure 16**

1. Remove the door trim panel and service hole cover.
2. Raise the window and secure the glass.

3. Unplug the wiring connector, if equipped with power windows.
4. Remove the regulator mounting bolts.
5. Remove the regulator through the service hole.
6. Installation is the reverse of removal.

Electric Window Motor

REMOVAL & INSTALLATION

▶ **See Figure 17**

1. Remove the door trim panel and service hole cover.
2. Raise the window and secure the glass.

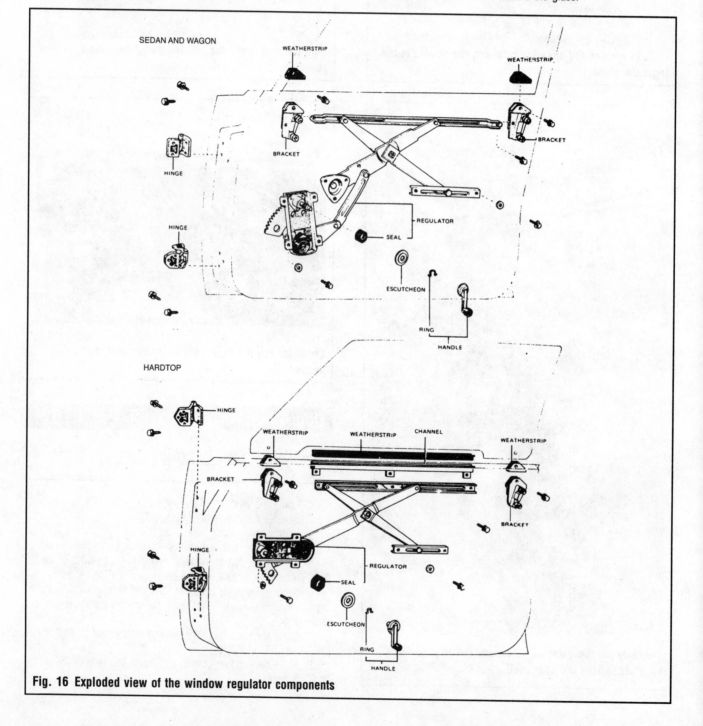

Fig. 16 Exploded view of the window regulator components

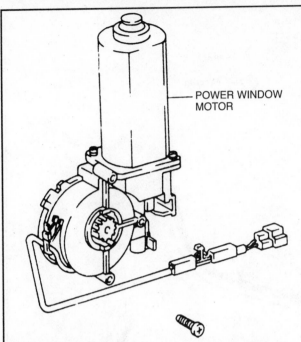

POWER WINDOW MOTOR

Fig. 17 Power windows are raised and lowered by an electric motor

3. Unplug the wiring connector.
4. Remove the regulator mounting bolts.
5. Remove the regulator and motor through the service hole.
6. Installation is the reverse of removal.

Quarter Glass

REMOVAL & INSTALLATION

These procedures apply to most models, some variations may be needed depending on the year.

Sedan
▶ **See Figure 18 (p. 20)**

1. Remove the rear seat cushion and rear seat backrest.
2. Using a flatbladed tool, pry out the garnish on the rear side window.
3. Pry the garnish off the roof side trim.
4. Using a knife, cut loose the adhesive on the glass. Remove the glass and the molding.
Install:
5. Purchase a sealant kit from your local dealer.
6. Wipe off any adhesive left on the body or glass with alcohol.
7. Using a sponge, oat the glass adhering surface with primer. Allow the primer coating to dry for 10 minutes.
8. Before installing the glass, apply butyl tape. Tape over 0.79 in. (20mm) of the upper area.
9. Place the molding on. Install the glass as a guide for the molding stud.

10. Install the roof trim garnish, rear window side garnish and rear seat backrest and cushion.

Wagon
▶ **See Figure 19 (p. 21)**

1. Separate the trim from the vehicle using a clip remover.
2. Working from the outside, loosen the weatherstrip lip from the body with a flatbladed tool.
3. Force the weatherstrip lip from the interior to the body flange outside. Pull the glass outwards and remove it with the weathertstrip.
To install:
4. Clean off any adhesive left on the body and glass with alcohol.
5. Attach the weatherstrip to the glass. If the weatherstrip is hardened, it may develop leaks. Replace it with a new one if necessary.
6. Apply a working cord along the weathetrstrip groove.
7. Apply soapy water to the contact face of the weatherstrip lip and to the body flange.

➡**Begin installation in the middle of the lower portion of the glass.**

8. Hold the glass into position on the body. Install the glass by pulling the string from the interior, while pushing on the outside of the weathertstrip with your open and.
9. To snug the glass into place, tap from the outside with your open hand.
10. Place masking tape around the weather strip to protect the paint surface.
11. Apply adhesive between the weatherstrip and the glass; and between the weatherstrip and body.
12. When the adhesive is dry, remove the masking tape.
13. Install any remaining components.

Liftgate Glass

REMOVAL & INSTALLATION

▶ **See Figure 20 (p. 22)**

1. Separate the trim from the vehicle using a clip remover.
2. Remove the rear wiper arm.
3. Remove the rear defogger wire harness from the glass.
4. Working from the outside, loosen the weatherstrip lip from the body with a flatbladed tool.
5. Force the weatherstrip lip from the interior to the body flange outside. Pull the glass outwards and remove it with the weathertstrip.
To install:
6. Clean off any adhesive left on the body and glass with alcohol.
7. Attach the weatherstrip to the glass. If the weatherstrip is hardened, it may develop leaks. Replace it with a new one if necessary.
8. Apply a working cord along the weathetrstrip groove.
9. Apply soapy water to the contact face of the weatherstrip lip and to the body flange.

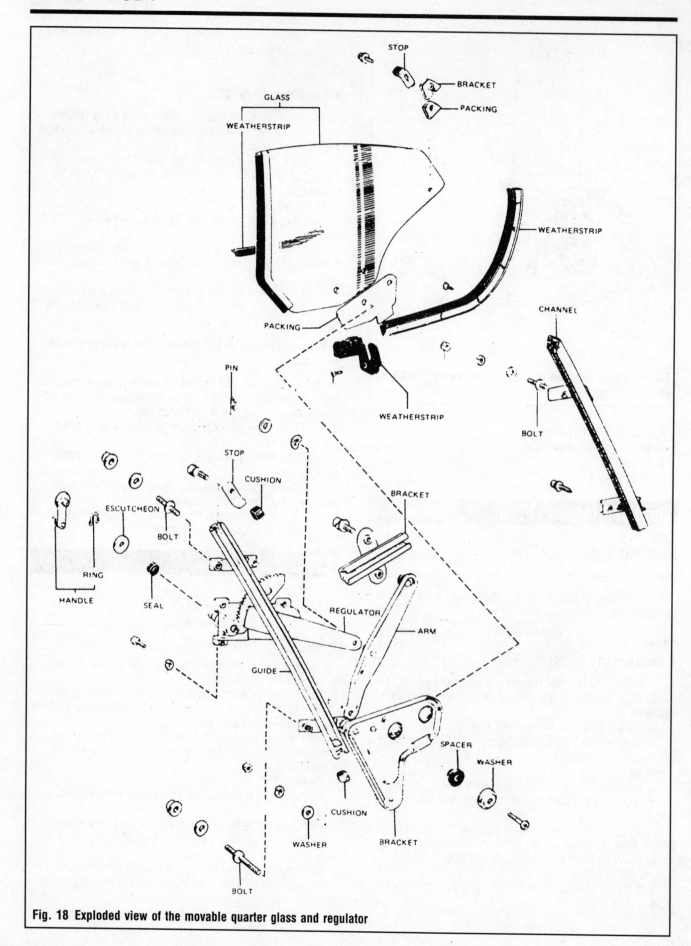

Fig. 18 Exploded view of the movable quarter glass and regulator

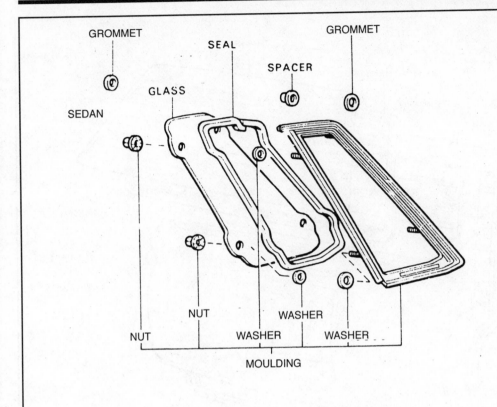

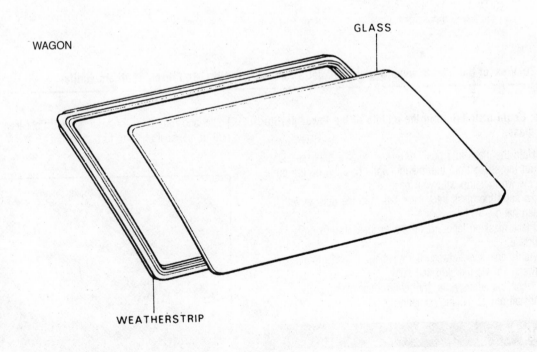

Fig. 19 View of the stationary quarter glass—Cressida sedan and wagon

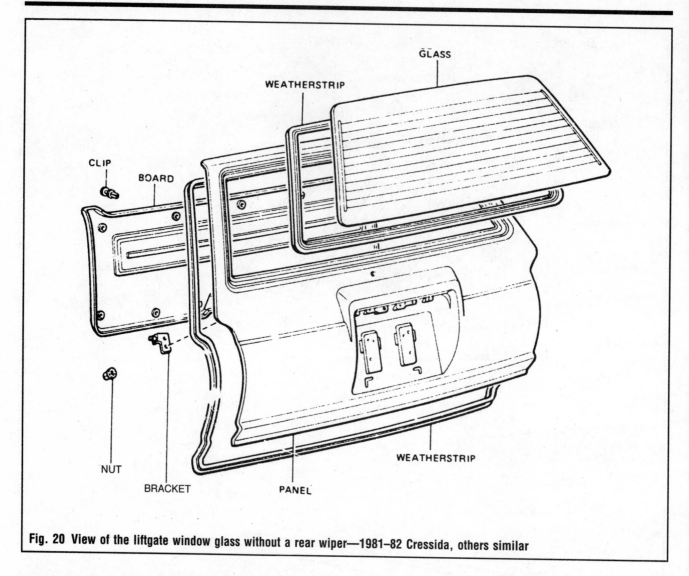

Fig. 20 View of the liftgate window glass without a rear wiper—1981–82 Cressida, others similar

➡Note: Begin installation in the middle of the lower portion of the glass.

10. Hold the glass into position on the body. Install the glass by pulling the string from the interior, while pushing on the outside of the weatherstrip with your open and.

11. To snug the glass into place, tap from the outside with your open hand.

12. Place masking tape around the weather strip to protect the paint surface.

13. Apply adhesive between the weatherstrip and the glass; and between the weatherstrip and body.

14. When the adhesive is dry, remove the masking tape.

15. Install any remaining components.

Seats

REMOVAL & INSTALLATION

◆ **See Figures 21 thru 28 (p. 23–30)**

Most of these models front seats are held on the floor with four bolts each. Some of the models rear seats are mounted in by

hooks and rods. Pull the front left and right levers forward and pull up the seat cushion to remove.

Remove the bolts securing the seat to the floor

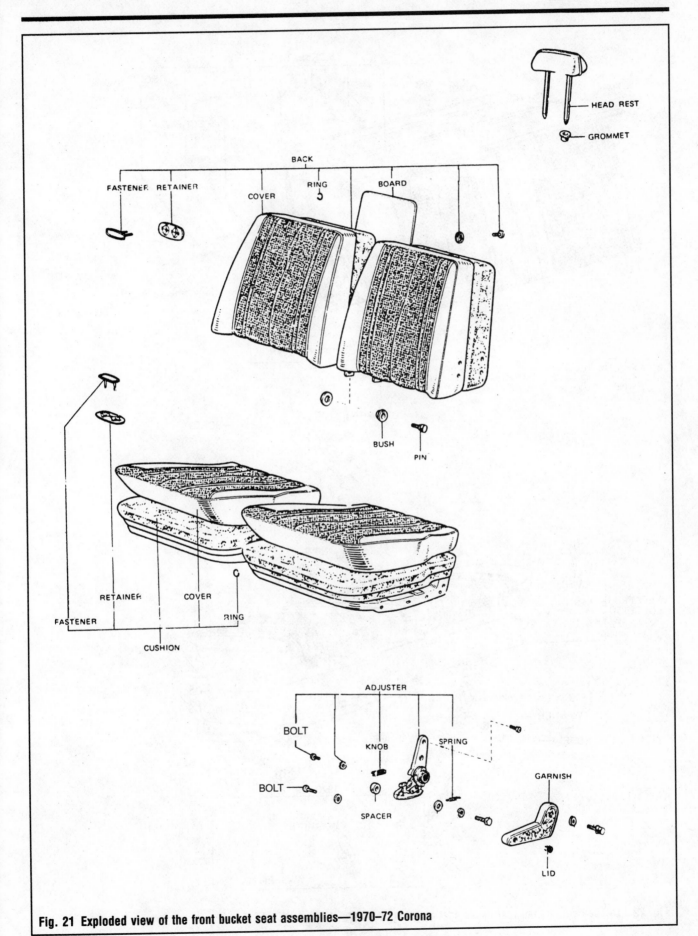

Fig. 21 Exploded view of the front bucket seat assemblies—1970–72 Corona

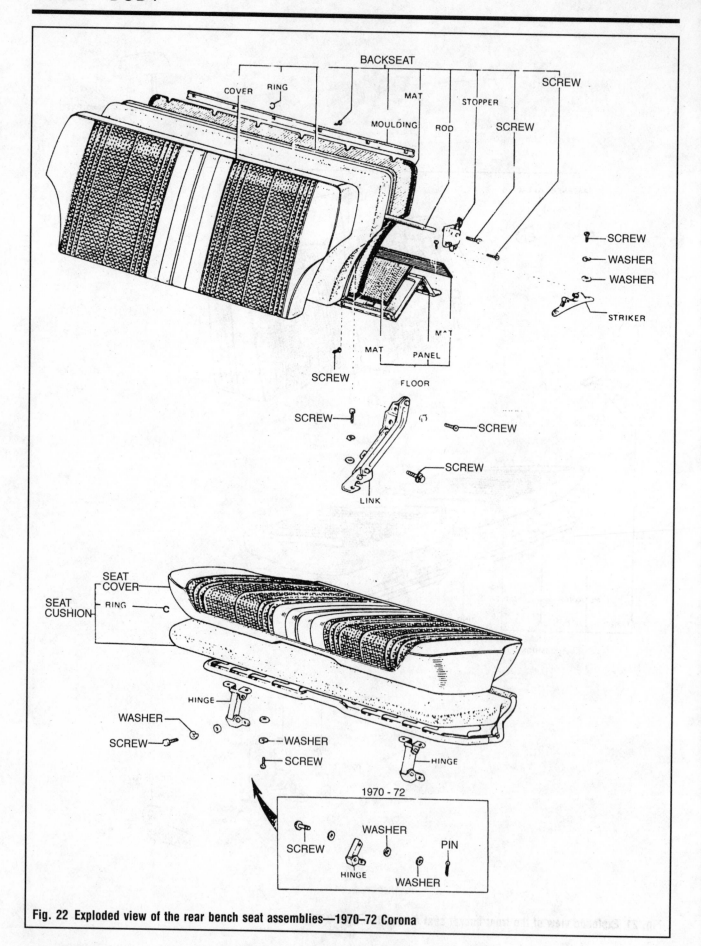

Fig. 22 Exploded view of the rear bench seat assemblies—1970–72 Corona

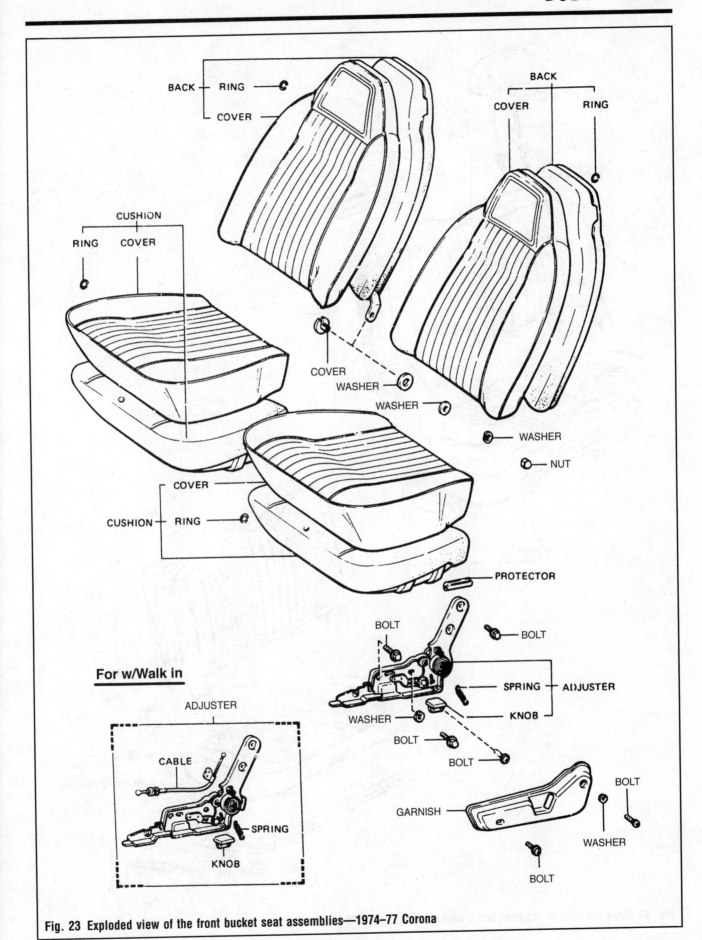

Fig. 23 Exploded view of the front bucket seat assemblies—1974–77 Corona

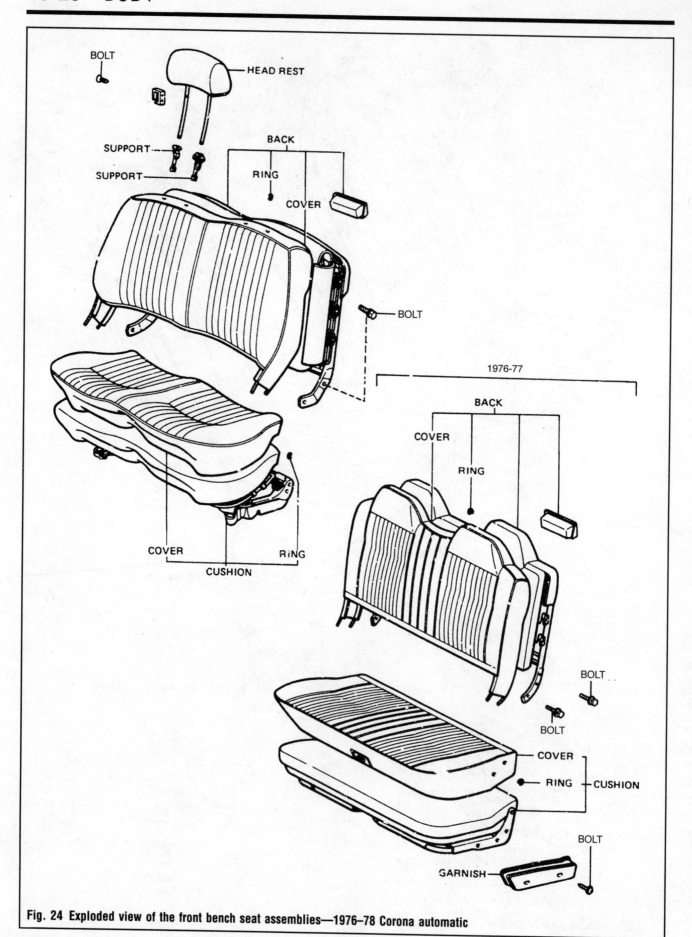

Fig. 24 Exploded view of the front bench seat assemblies—1976–78 Corona automatic

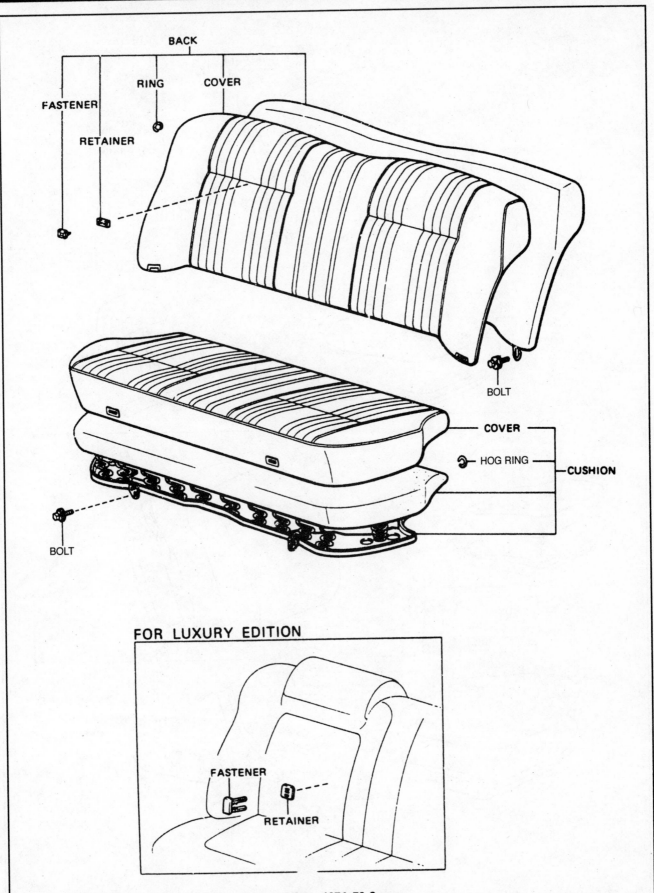

Fig. 25 Exploded view of the rear bench seat assemblies—1974–78 Corona

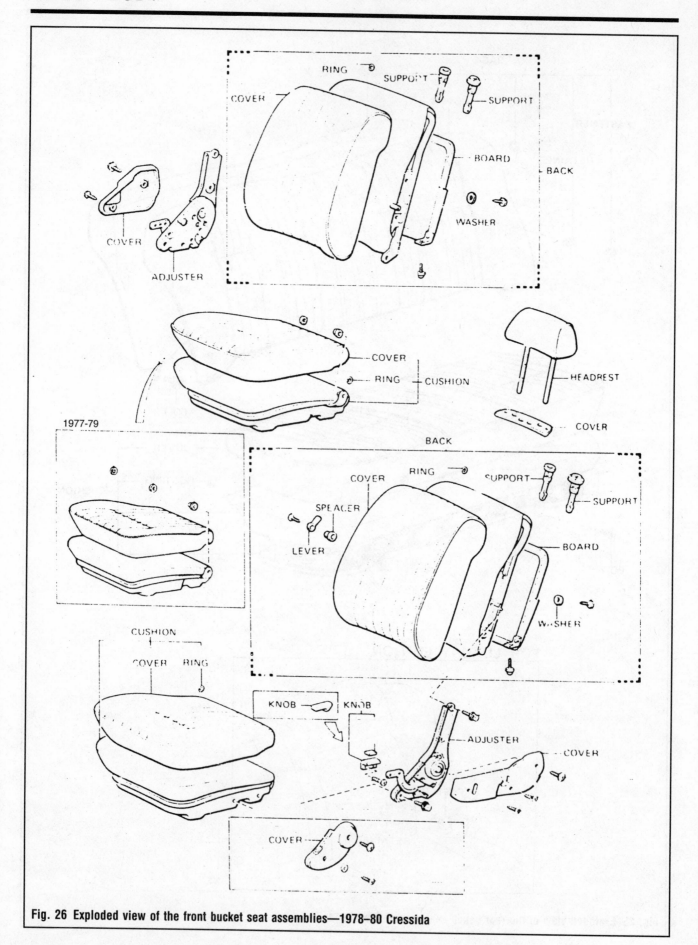

Fig. 26 Exploded view of the front bucket seat assemblies—1978–80 Cressida

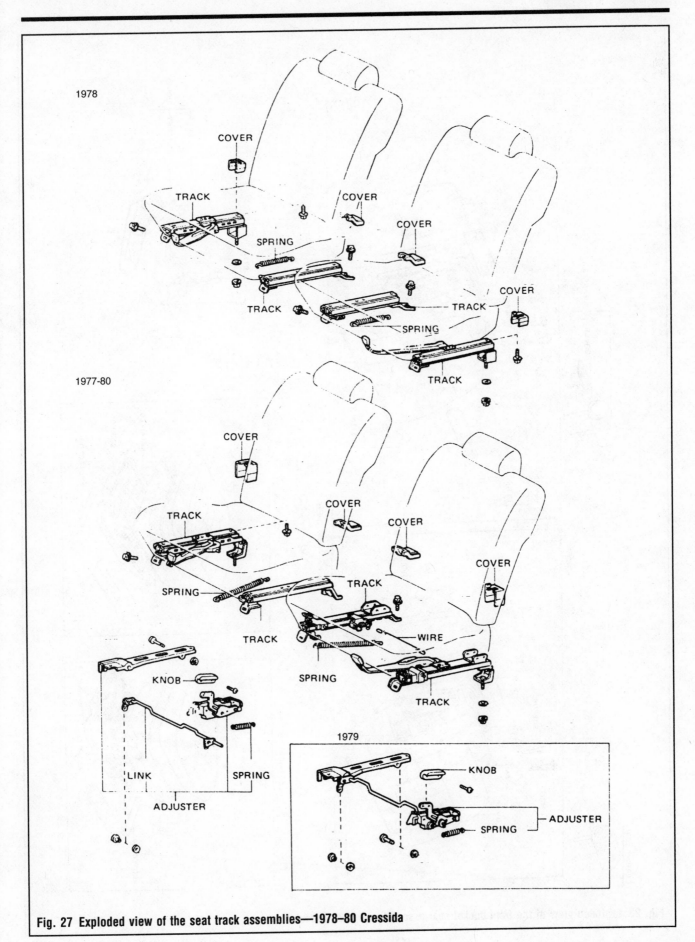

Fig. 27 Exploded view of the seat track assemblies—1978–80 Cressida

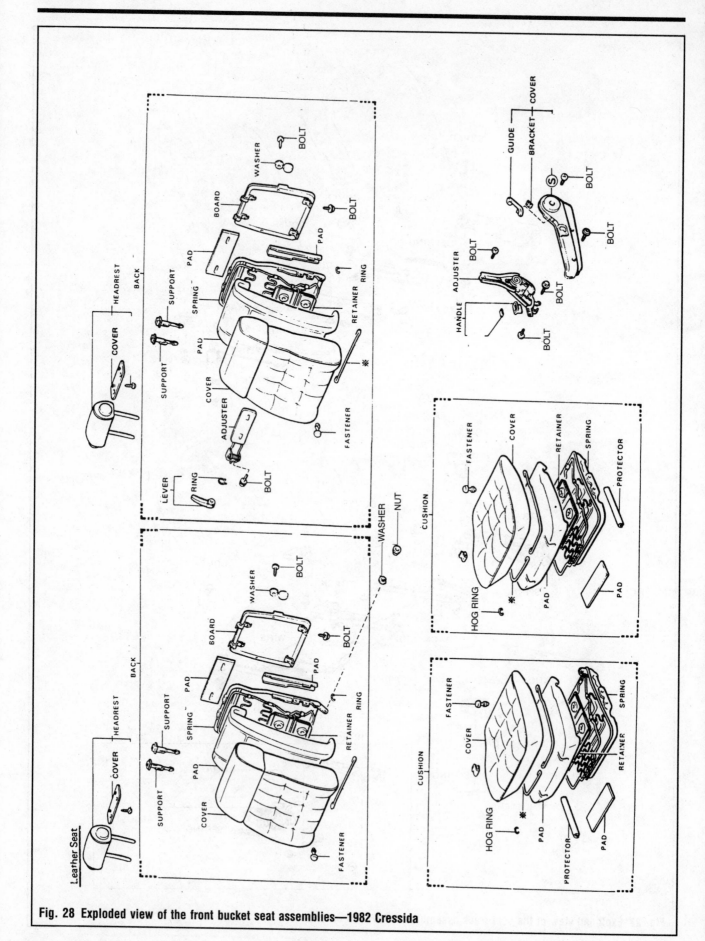

Fig. 28 Exploded view of the front bucket seat assemblies—1982 Cressida

Seat Belts

REMOVAL & INSTALLATION

▶ **See Figures 29, 30, 31 and 32 (p. 31–34)**

The following procedures are to be used as reference. All of these models slightly differ, and the instructions may need altering.

Front

1. Remove the trim cover at the upper shoulder anchor bolt.
2. Remove the anchor bolt.
3. Remove the lower cover on the outer retractor from the inner floor panel.
4. Remove the retractor portion of the seat belt.

5. To remove the buckle end of the seat belt, remove the cover on the base of the belt and the mounting bolt.
6. Installation of the belt is reverse removal. Tighten the mounting bolts.

Rear

1. Remove the trim cover at the upper shoulder anchor bolt.
2. Remove the upper anchor bolt.
3. Unbolt the outer belt anchor from the body panel. Removal of the rear seat belt is required. Unbolt the lower end of the belt under the retractor from the side panel.
4. Remove the retractor portion of the seat belt.
5. To remove the center belt buckle off the seat belt, remove the seat cushion and the belt mounting bolt.
6. Installation of the belt is reverse of removal. Tighten the mounting bolts.

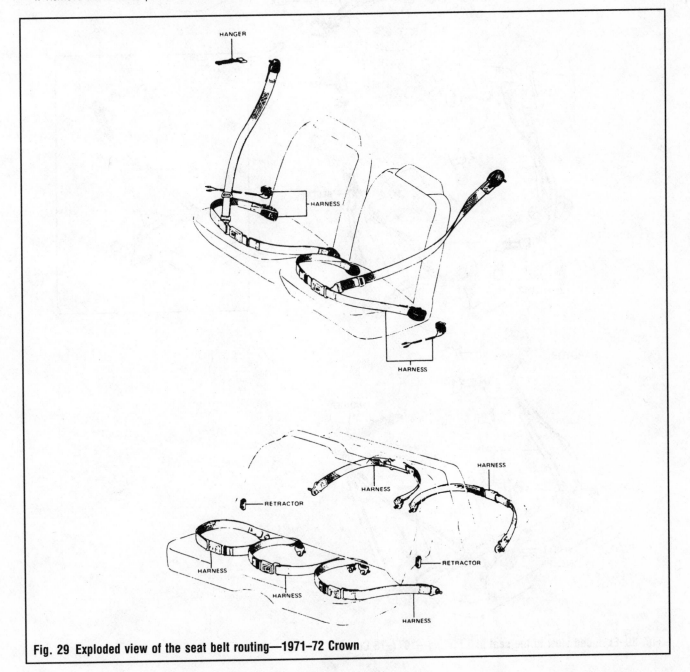

Fig. 29 Exploded view of the seat belt routing—1971–72 Crown

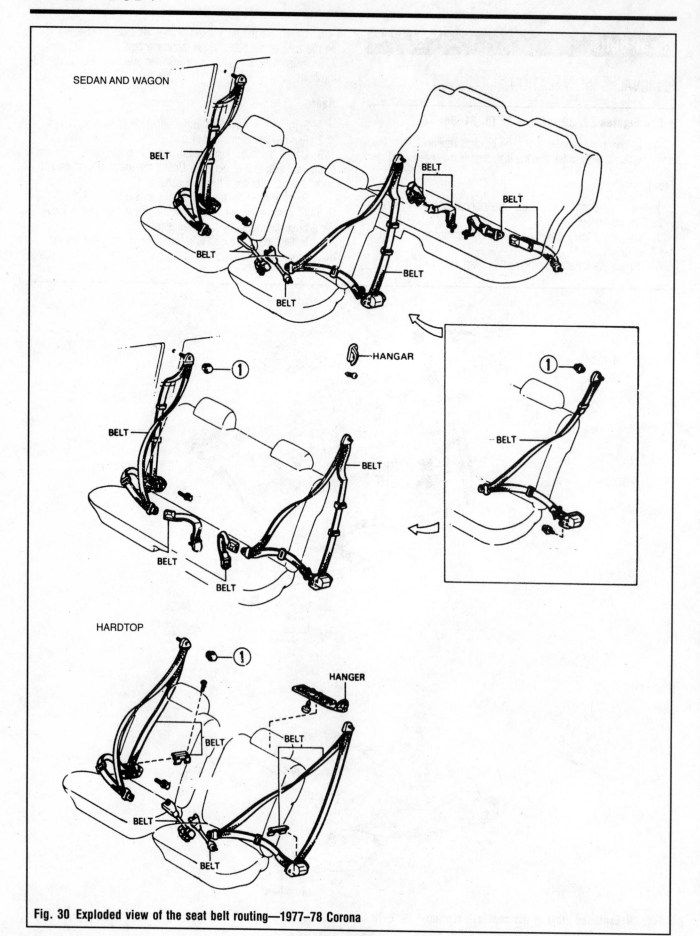

Fig. 30 Exploded view of the seat belt routing—1977–78 Corona

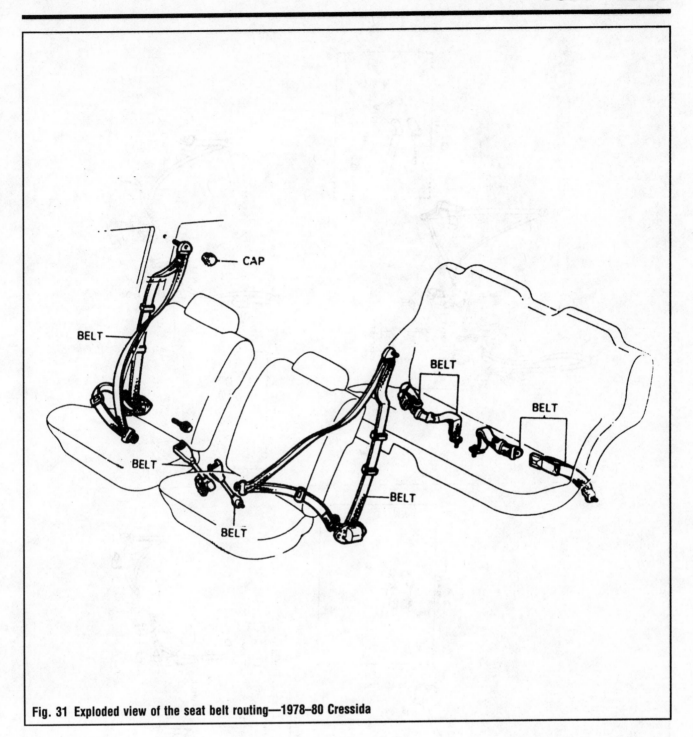

Fig. 31 Exploded view of the seat belt routing—1978–80 Cressida

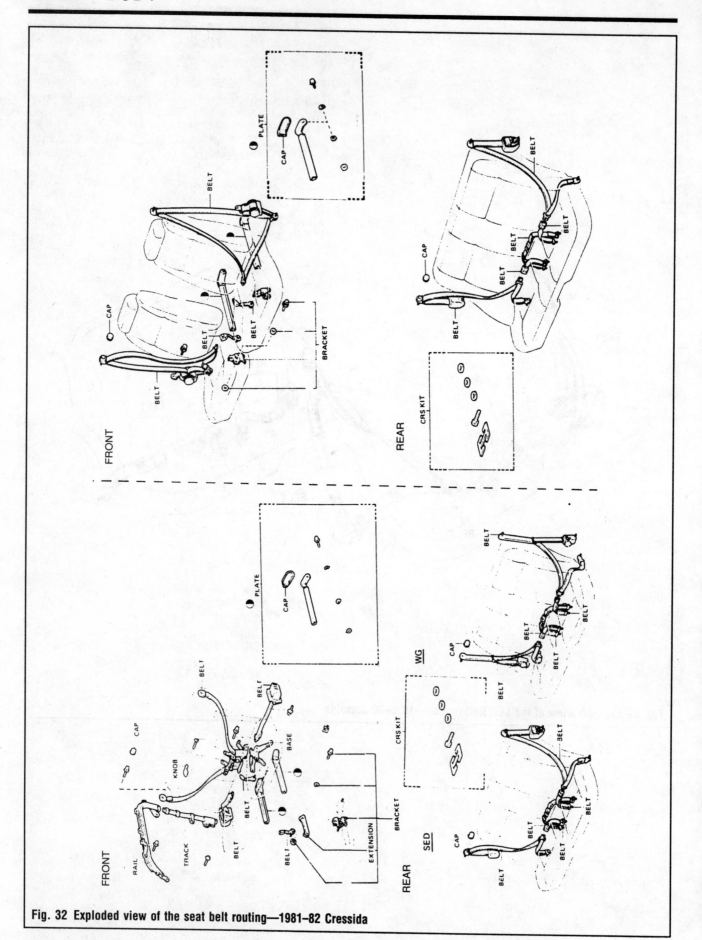

Fig. 32 Exploded view of the seat belt routing—1981–82 Cressida

GLOSSARY

AIR/FUEL RATIO: The ratio of air-to-gasoline by weight in the fuel mixture drawn into the engine.

AIR INJECTION: One method of reducing harmful exhaust emissions by injecting air into each of the exhaust ports of an engine. The fresh air entering the hot exhaust manifold causes any remaining fuel to be burned before it can exit the tailpipe.

ALTERNATOR: A device used for converting mechanical energy into electrical energy.

AMMETER: An instrument, calibrated in amperes, used to measure the flow of an electrical current in a circuit. Ammeters are always connected in series with the circuit being tested.

AMPERE: The rate of flow of electrical current present when one volt of electrical pressure is applied against one ohm of electrical resistance.

ANALOG COMPUTER: Any microprocessor that uses similar (analogous) electrical signals to make its calculations.

ARMATURE: A laminated, soft iron core wrapped by a wire that converts electrical energy to mechanical energy as in a motor or relay. When rotated in a magnetic field, it changes mechanical energy into electrical energy as in a generator.

ATMOSPHERIC PRESSURE: The pressure on the Earth's surface caused by the weight of the air in the atmosphere. At sea level, this pressure is 14.7 psi at 32°F (101 kPa at 0°C).

ATOMIZATION: The breaking down of a liquid into a fine mist that can be suspended in air.

AXIAL PLAY: Movement parallel to a shaft or bearing bore.

BACKFIRE: The sudden combustion of gases in the intake or exhaust system that results in a loud explosion.

BACKLASH: The clearance or play between two parts, such as meshed gears.

BACKPRESSURE: Restrictions in the exhaust system that slow the exit of exhaust gases from the combustion chamber.

BAKELITE: A heat resistant, plastic insulator material commonly used in printed circuit boards and transistorized components.

BALL BEARING: A bearing made up of hardened inner and outer races between which hardened steel balls roll.

BALLAST RESISTOR: A resistor in the primary ignition circuit that lowers voltage after the engine is started to reduce wear on ignition components.

BEARING: A friction reducing, supportive device usually located between a stationary part and a moving part.

BIMETAL TEMPERATURE SENSOR: Any sensor or switch made of two dissimilar types of metal that bend when heated or cooled due to the different expansion rates of the alloys. These types of sensors usually function as an on/off switch.

BLOWBY: Combustion gases, composed of water vapor and unburned fuel, that leak past the piston rings into the crankcase during normal engine operation. These gases are removed by the PCV system to prevent the buildup of harmful acids in the crankcase.

BRAKE PAD: A brake shoe and lining assembly used with disc brakes.

BRAKE SHOE: The backing for the brake lining. The term is, however, usually applied to the assembly of the brake backing and lining.

BUSHING: A liner, usually removable, for a bearing; an anti-friction liner used in place of a bearing.

CALIPER: A hydraulically activated device in a disc brake system, which is mounted straddling the brake rotor (disc). The caliper contains at least one piston and two brake pads. Hydraulic pressure on the piston(s) forces the pads against the rotor.

CAMSHAFT: A shaft in the engine on which are the lobes (cams) which operate the valves. The camshaft is driven by the crankshaft, via a belt, chain or gears, at one half the crankshaft speed.

CAPACITOR: A device which stores an electrical charge.

CARBON MONOXIDE (CO): A colorless, odorless gas given off as a normal byproduct of combustion. It is poisonous and extremely dangerous in confined areas, building up slowly to toxic levels without warning if adequate ventilation is not available.

CARBURETOR: A device, usually mounted on the intake manifold of an engine, which mixes the air and fuel in the proper proportion to allow even combustion.

CATALYTIC CONVERTER: A device installed in the exhaust system, like a muffler, that converts harmful byproducts of combustion into carbon dioxide and water vapor by means of a heat-producing chemical reaction.

CENTRIFUGAL ADVANCE: A mechanical method of advancing the spark timing by using flyweights in the distributor that react to centrifugal force generated by the distributor shaft rotation.

CHECK VALVE: Any one-way valve installed to permit the flow of air, fuel or vacuum in one direction only.

CHOKE: A device, usually a moveable valve, placed in the intake path of a carburetor to restrict the flow of air.

CIRCUIT: Any unbroken path through which an electrical current can flow. Also used to describe fuel flow in some instances.

CIRCUIT BREAKER: A switch which protects an electrical circuit from overload by opening the circuit when the current flow exceeds a predetermined level. Some circuit breakers must be reset manually, while most reset automatically.

COIL (IGNITION): A transformer in the ignition circuit which steps up the voltage provided to the spark plugs.

COMBINATION MANIFOLD: An assembly which includes both the intake and exhaust manifolds in one casting.

COMBINATION VALVE: A device used in some fuel systems that routes fuel vapors to a charcoal storage canister instead of venting them into the atmosphere. The valve relieves fuel tank pressure and allows fresh air into the tank as the fuel level drops to prevent a vapor lock situation.

COMPRESSION RATIO: The comparison of the total volume of the cylinder and combustion chamber with the piston at BDC and the piston at TDC.

CONDENSER: 1. An electrical device which acts to store an electrical charge, preventing voltage surges. 2. A radiator-like device in the air conditioning system in which refrigerant gas condenses into a liquid, giving off heat.

CONDUCTOR: Any material through which an electrical current can be transmitted easily.

CONTINUITY: Continuous or complete circuit. Can be checked with an ohmmeter.

COUNTERSHAFT: An intermediate shaft which is rotated by a mainshaft and transmits, in turn, that rotation to a working part.

CRANKCASE: The lower part of an engine in which the crankshaft and related parts operate.

CRANKSHAFT: The main driving shaft of an engine which receives reciprocating motion from the pistons and converts it to rotary motion.

CYLINDER: In an engine, the round hole in the engine block in which the piston(s) ride.

CYLINDER BLOCK: The main structural member of an engine in which is found the cylinders, crankshaft and other principal parts.

CYLINDER HEAD: The detachable portion of the engine, usually fastened to the top of the cylinder block and containing all or most of the combustion chambers. On overhead valve engines, it contains the valves and their operating parts. On overhead cam engines, it contains the camshaft as well.

DEAD CENTER: The extreme top or bottom of the piston stroke.

DETONATION: An unwanted explosion of the air/fuel mixture in the combustion chamber caused by excess heat and compression, advanced timing, or an overly lean mixture. Also referred to as "ping".

DIAPHRAGM: A thin, flexible wall separating two cavities, such as in a vacuum advance unit.

DIESELING: A condition in which hot spots in the combustion chamber cause the engine to run on after the key is turned off.

DIFFERENTIAL: A geared assembly which allows the transmission of motion between drive axles, giving one axle the ability to turn faster than the other.

DIODE: An electrical device that will allow current to flow in one direction only.

DISC BRAKE: A hydraulic braking assembly consisting of a brake disc, or rotor, mounted on an axle, and a caliper assembly containing, usually two brake pads which are activated by hydraulic pressure. The pads are forced against the sides of the disc, creating friction which slows the vehicle.

DISTRIBUTOR: A mechanically driven device on an engine which is responsible for electrically firing the spark plug at a predetermined point of the piston stroke.

DOWEL PIN: A pin, inserted in mating holes in two different parts allowing those parts to maintain a fixed relationship.

DRUM BRAKE: A braking system which consists of two brake shoes and one or two wheel cylinders, mounted on a fixed backing plate, and a brake drum, mounted on an axle, which revolves around the assembly.

DWELL: The rate, measured in degrees of shaft rotation, at which an electrical circuit cycles on and off.

ELECTRONIC CONTROL UNIT (ECU): Ignition module, module, amplifier or igniter. See Module for definition.

ELECTRONIC IGNITION: A system in which the timing and firing of the spark plugs is controlled by an electronic control unit, usually called a module. These systems have no points or condenser.

END-PLAY: The measured amount of axial movement in a shaft.

ENGINE: A device that converts heat into mechanical energy.

EXHAUST MANIFOLD: A set of cast passages or pipes which conduct exhaust gases from the engine.

FEELER GAUGE: A blade, usually metal, of precisely predetermined thickness, used to measure the clearance between two parts.

FIRING ORDER: The order in which combustion occurs in the cylinders of an engine. Also the order in which spark is distributed to the plugs by the distributor.

FLOODING: The presence of too much fuel in the intake manifold and combustion chamber which prevents the air/fuel mixture from firing, thereby causing a no-start situation.

FLYWHEEL: A disc shaped part bolted to the rear end of the crankshaft. Around the outer perimeter is affixed the ring gear. The starter drive engages the ring gear, turning the flywheel, which rotates the crankshaft, imparting the initial starting motion to the engine.

FOOT POUND (ft. lbs. or sometimes, ft.lb.): The amount of energy or work needed to raise an item weighing one pound, a distance of one foot.

FUSE: A protective device in a circuit which prevents circuit overload by breaking the circuit when a specific amperage is present. The device is constructed around a strip or wire of a lower amperage rating than the circuit it is designed to protect. When an amperage higher than that stamped on the fuse is present in the circuit, the strip or wire melts, opening the circuit.

GEAR RATIO: The ratio between the number of teeth on meshing gears.

GENERATOR: A device which converts mechanical energy into electrical energy.

HEAT RANGE: The measure of a spark plug's ability to dissipate heat from its firing end. The higher the heat range, the hotter the plug fires.

HUB: The center part of a wheel or gear.

HYDROCARBON (HC): Any chemical compound made up of hydrogen and carbon. A major pollutant formed by the engine as a byproduct of combustion.

HYDROMETER: An instrument used to measure the specific gravity of a solution.

INCH POUND (inch lbs.; sometimes in.lb. or in. lbs.): One twelfth of a foot pound.

INDUCTION: A means of transferring electrical energy in the form of a magnetic field. Principle used in the ignition coil to increase voltage.

INJECTOR: A device which receives metered fuel under relatively low pressure and is activated to inject the fuel into the engine under relatively high pressure at a predetermined time.

INPUT SHAFT: The shaft to which torque is applied, usually carrying the driving gear or gears.

INTAKE MANIFOLD: A casting of passages or pipes used to conduct air or a fuel/air mixture to the cylinders.

JOURNAL: The bearing surface within which a shaft operates.

KEY: A small block usually fitted in a notch between a shaft and a hub to prevent slippage of the two parts.

MANIFOLD: A casting of passages or set of pipes which connect the cylinders to an inlet or outlet source.

MANIFOLD VACUUM: Low pressure in an engine intake manifold formed just below the throttle plates. Manifold vacuum is highest at idle and drops under acceleration.

MASTER CYLINDER: The primary fluid pressurizing device in a hydraulic system. In automotive use, it is found in brake and hydraulic clutch systems and is pedal activated, either directly or, in a power brake system, through the power booster.

MODULE: Electronic control unit, amplifier or igniter of solid state or integrated design which controls the current flow in the ignition primary circuit based on input from the pick-up coil. When the module opens the primary circuit, high secondary voltage is induced in the coil.

NEEDLE BEARING: A bearing which consists of a number (usually a large number) of long, thin rollers.

OHM: (Ω) The unit used to measure the resistance of conductor-to-electrical flow. One ohm is the amount of resistance that limits current flow to one ampere in a circuit with one volt of pressure.

OHMMETER: An instrument used for measuring the resistance, in ohms, in an electrical circuit.

OUTPUT SHAFT: The shaft which transmits torque from a device, such as a transmission.

OVERDRIVE: A gear assembly which produces more shaft revolutions than that transmitted to it.

OVERHEAD CAMSHAFT (OHC): An engine configuration in which the camshaft is mounted on top of the cylinder head and operates the valve either directly or by means of rocker arms.

OVERHEAD VALVE (OHV): An engine configuration in which all of the valves are located in the cylinder head and the camshaft is located in the cylinder block. The camshaft operates the valves via lifters and pushrods.

OXIDES OF NITROGEN (NOx): Chemical compounds of nitrogen produced as a byproduct of combustion. They combine with hydrocarbons to produce smog.

OXYGEN SENSOR: Used with the feedback system to sense the presence of oxygen in the exhaust gas and signal the computer which can reference the voltage signal to an air/fuel ratio.

PINION: The smaller of two meshing gears.

PISTON RING: An open-ended ring which fits into a groove on the outer diameter of the piston. Its chief function is to form a seal between the piston and cylinder wall. Most automotive pistons have three rings: two for compression sealing; one for oil sealing.

PRELOAD: A predetermined load placed on a bearing during assembly or by adjustment.

PRIMARY CIRCUIT: The low voltage side of the ignition system which consists of the ignition switch, ballast resistor or resistance wire, bypass, coil, electronic control unit and pick-up coil as well as the connecting wires and harnesses.

PRESS FIT: The mating of two parts under pressure, due to the inner diameter of one being smaller than the outer diameter of the other, or vice versa; an interference fit.

RACE: The surface on the inner or outer ring of a bearing on which the balls, needles or rollers move.

REGULATOR: A device which maintains the amperage and/or voltage levels of a circuit at predetermined values.

RELAY: A switch which automatically opens and/or closes a circuit.

RESISTANCE: The opposition to the flow of current through a circuit or electrical device, and is measured in ohms. Resistance is equal to the voltage divided by the amperage.

RESISTOR: A device, usually made of wire, which offers a preset amount of resistance in an electrical circuit.

RING GEAR: The name given to a ring-shaped gear attached to a differential case, or affixed to a flywheel or as part of a planetary gear set.

ROLLER BEARING: A bearing made up of hardened inner and outer races between which hardened steel rollers move.

ROTOR: 1. The disc-shaped part of a disc brake assembly, upon which the brake pads bear; also called, brake disc. 2. The device mounted atop the distributor shaft, which passes current to the distributor cap tower contacts.

SECONDARY CIRCUIT: The high voltage side of the ignition system, usually above 20,000 volts. The secondary includes the ignition coil, coil wire, distributor cap and rotor, spark plug wires and spark plugs.

SENDING UNIT: A mechanical, electrical, hydraulic or electromagnetic device which transmits information to a gauge.

SENSOR: Any device designed to measure engine operating conditions or ambient pressures and temperatures. Usually electronic in nature and designed to send a voltage signal to an on-board computer, some sensors may operate as a simple on/off switch or they may provide a variable voltage signal (like a potentiometer) as conditions or measured parameters change.

SHIM: Spacers of precise, predetermined thickness used between parts to establish a proper working relationship.

SLAVE CYLINDER: In automotive use, a device in the hydraulic clutch system which is activated by hydraulic force, disengaging the clutch.

SOLENOID: A coil used to produce a magnetic field, the effect of which is to produce work.

SPARK PLUG: A device screwed into the combustion chamber of a spark ignition engine. The basic construction is a conductive core inside of a ceramic insulator, mounted in an outer conductive base. An electrical charge from the spark plug wire travels along the conductive core and jumps a preset air gap to a grounding point or points at the end of the conductive base. The resultant spark ignites the fuel/air mixture in the combustion chamber.

SPLINES: Ridges machined or cast onto the outer diameter of a shaft or inner diameter of a bore to enable parts to mate without rotation.

TACHOMETER: A device used to measure the rotary speed of an engine, shaft, gear, etc., usually in rotations per minute.

THERMOSTAT: A valve, located in the cooling system of an engine, which is closed when cold and opens gradually in response to engine heating, controlling the temperature of the coolant and rate of coolant flow.

TOP DEAD CENTER (TDC): The point at which the piston reaches the top of its travel on the compression stroke.

TORQUE: The twisting force applied to an object.

TORQUE CONVERTER: A turbine used to transmit power from a driving member to a driven member via hydraulic action, providing changes in drive ratio and torque. In automotive use, it links the driveplate at the rear of the engine to the automatic transmission.

TRANSDUCER: A device used to change a force into an electrical signal.

TRANSISTOR: A semi-conductor component which can be actuated by a small voltage to perform an electrical switching function.

TUNE-UP: A regular maintenance function, usually associated with the replacement and adjustment of parts and components in the electrical and fuel systems of a vehicle for the purpose of attaining optimum performance.

TURBOCHARGER: An exhaust driven pump which compresses intake air and forces it into the combustion chambers at higher than atmospheric pressures. The increased air pressure allows more fuel to be burned and results in increased horsepower being produced.

VACUUM ADVANCE: A device which advances the ignition timing in response to increased engine vacuum.

VACUUM GAUGE: An instrument used to measure the presence of vacuum in a chamber.

VALVE: A device which control the pressure, direction of flow or rate of flow of a liquid or gas.

VALVE CLEARANCE: The measured gap between the end of the valve stem and the rocker arm, cam lobe or follower that activates the valve.

VISCOSITY: The rating of a liquid's internal resistance to flow.

VOLTMETER: An instrument used for measuring electrical force in units called volts. Voltmeters are always connected parallel with the circuit being tested.

WHEEL CYLINDER: Found in the automotive drum brake assembly, it is a device, actuated by hydraulic pressure, which, through internal pistons, pushes the brake shoes outward against the drums.

ADD-ON ELECTRICAL EQUIPMENT 6-10
ADJUSTMENT (MANUAL TRANSMISSION) 7-2
   LINKAGE 7-2
ADJUSTMENTS (AUTOMATIC TRANSMISSION) 7-21
   FRONT BAND 7-21
   SHIFT LINKAGE 7-22
   THROTTLE LINKAGE 7-22
ADJUSTMENTS (BRAKE OPERATION SYSTEM) 9-3
   DISC BRAKES 9-3
   DRUM BRAKES 9-3
ADJUSTMENTS (CLUTCH) 7-5
   FREE-PLAY 7-6
   PEDAL HEIGHT 7-5
ADJUSTMENTS (TRANSISTORIZED IGNITION) 2-12
   DWELL 2-12
   PICKUP AIR GAP 2-12
   POINT GAP 2-12
AIR CLEANER 1-22
   REMOVAL & INSTALLATION 1-22
AIR CONDITIONING 1-40
   DISCHARGING, EVACUATING & CHARGING 1-42
   GENERAL SERVICING PROCEDURES 1-41
   SAFETY PRECAUTIONS 1-40
   SYSTEM INSPECTION 1-42
AIR INJECTION SYSTEM 4-8
   OPERATION 4-8
   REMOVAL & INSTALLATION 4-14
   TESTING 4-15
AIR INJECTION SYSTEM DIAGNOSIS CHART 4-16
AIR POLLUTION 4-2
AIR VALVE 5-14
   REMOVAL & INSTALLATION 5-14
   TESTING 5-14
ALTERNATOR 3-12
   PRECAUTIONS 3-12
   REMOVAL & INSTALLATION 3-15
ALTERNATOR AND REGULATOR SPECIFICATIONS 3-16
AUTOMATIC TRANSMISSION 7-14
AUTOMATIC TRANSMISSION (FLUIDS & LUBRICANTS) 1-55
   DRAIN & REFILL 1-55
   LEVEL CHECK 1-55
AUTOMOTIVE EMISSIONS 4-3
AUTOMOTIVE POLLUTANTS 4-2
   HEAT TRANSFER 4-3
   TEMPERATURE INVERSION 4-2
AUXILIARY ACCELERATION PUMP SYSTEM 4-27
   OPERATION 4-27
   TESTING 4-28
AUXILIARY ENRICHMENT SYSTEM 4-29
   TESTING 4-30
AVOIDING THE MOST COMMON MISTAKES 1-2
AVOIDING TROUBLE 1-2
AXLE SHAFT 7-28
   REMOVAL & INSTALLATION 7-28
BASIC DRIVESHAFT AND REAR AXLE PROBLEMS 7-30
BASIC FUEL SYSTEM DIAGNOSIS 5-2
BASIC OPERATING PRINCIPLES 9-2
   DISC BRAKES 9-2
   DRUM BRAKES 9-3
   POWER BOOSTERS 9-3
BASIC STEERING AND SUSPENSION PROBLEMS 8-37
BATTERY (ENGINE ELECTRICAL SYSTEM) 3-18
   REMOVAL & INSTALLATION 3-19
BATTERY (ROUTINE MAINTENANCE) 1-31
   BATTERY FLUID 1-32
   CABLES 1-33
   CHARGING 1-34
   GENERAL MAINTENANCE 1-31
   REPLACEMENT 1-34
BATTERY DIMENSIONS (INCHES) 1-35

MASTER
INDEX

BATTERY, STARTING AND CHARGING SYSTEMS 3-4
   BASIC OPERATING PRINCIPLES 3-4
BELTS 1-35
   INSPECTION 1-35
BI-METAL VACUUM SWITCHING VALVE 4-35
   TESTING 4-35
BLEEDING THE BRAKE SYSTEM 9-12
   LINES AND WHEEL CIRCUITS 9-12
   MASTER CYLINDER 9-12
BLOCK HEATERS 3-76
   REMOVAL & INSTALLATION 3-76
BLOWER MOTOR 6-12
   REMOVAL & INSTALLATION 6-12
BODY LUBRICATION 1-59
BOLTS, NUTS AND OTHER THREADED RETAINERS 1-8
BRAKE AND CLUTCH MASTER CYLINDERS 1-56
   LEVEL CHECK 1-56
BRAKE CALIPER 9-14
   OVERHAUL 9-15
   REMOVAL & INSTALLATION 9-14
BRAKE DISC (ROTOR) 9-17
   INSPECTION 9-19
   REMOVAL & INSTALLATION 9-17
BRAKE DRUM DIAMETER CHART 9-22
BRAKE DRUMS 9-20
   INSPECTION 9-21
   REMOVAL & INSTALLATION 9-20
BRAKE HOSES AND LINES 9-8
   BRAKE LINE FLARING 9-11
   REMOVAL & INSTALLATION 9-8
BRAKE OPERATION SYSTEM 9-2
BRAKE PADS 9-13
   REMOVAL & INSTALLATION 9-13
BRAKE SHOES 9-22
   REMOVAL & INSTALLATION 9-22
BREAKER POINTS AND CONDENSER 2-10
   ADJUSTMENT 2-11
   INSPECTION AND CLEANING 2-10
   OPERATION 2-10
   REMOVAL & INSTALLATION 2-11
CABLES 9-29
   ADJUSTMENT 9-29
   REMOVAL & INSTALLATION 9-29
CAMSHAFT AND BEARINGS 3-64
   CAMSHAFT INSPECTION 3-66
   REMOVAL & INSTALLATION 3-64
CAPACITIES CHART 1-72
CARBURETED FUEL SYSTEM 5-2
CARBURETED VEHICLES 2-19
   IDLE SPEED & MIXTURE 2-19
CARBURETOR 5-5
   ADJUSTMENTS 5-7
   OVERHAUL NOTES 5-7
   REMOVAL & INSTALLATION 5-5
CARBURETOR AUXILIARY SLOW SYSTEM 4-23
   OPERATION 4-23
   REMOVAL & INSTALLATION 4-23
   TESTING 4-23
CATALYTIC CONVERTER (EXHAUST SYSTEM) 3-78
   REMOVAL & INSTALLATION 3-78
CATALYTIC CONVERTERS (EMISSION CONTROLS) 4-40
   PRECAUTIONS 4-40
   REMOVAL & INSTALLATION 4-42
   WARNING LIGHT CHECKS 4-42
CHASSIS GREASING 1-59
   CROWN 4M ENGINE 1-59
   EXCEPT CROWN 4M ENGINE 1-59
CHOKE BREAKER SYSTEM 4-34

   ADJUSTMENT 4-34
CHOKE OPENER SYSTEM 4-32
   OPERATION 4-32
CHOKE UNLOADER ADJUSTMENT CHART 5-10
CIRCUIT BREAKERS 6-48
CIRCUIT OPENING RELAY 5-15
   TESTING 5-15
CIRCUIT PROTECTION 6-47
CLUTCH 7-4
CLUTCH PEDAL FREE-PLAY ADJUSTMENTS CHART 7-6
CLUTCH TORQUE SPECIFICATIONS (FT. LBS.) 7-11
COIL SPRINGS (FRONT SUSPENSION) 8-4
   REMOVAL & INSTALLATION 8-4
COIL SPRINGS (REAR SUSPENSION) 8-18
   REMOVAL & INSTALLATION 8-18
COMBINATION MANIFOLD 3-54
   REMOVAL & INSTALLATION 3-54
COMPLETE SYSTEM EXHAUST 3-79
   REMOVAL & INSTALLATION 3-79
COMPONENT LOCATIONS
   DRIVELINE COMPONENTS 7-27
   ENGINE COMPONENT LOCATIONS—20R ENGINE 3-20
   FRONT STEERING AND SUSPENSION COMPONENTS 8-3
   MAINTENANCE COMPONENT LOCATIONS—20R ENGINE 1-21
   REAR DRUM BRAKE COMPONENTS 9-24
   REAR SUSPENSION COMPONENTS 8-16
   TYPICAL EMISSION COMPONENT LOCATIONS—20R ENGINE 4-13
   WINDSHIELD WIPER COMPONENTS 6-21
COMPRESSION TESTING 3-23
CONTROL ASSEMBLY 6-15
   REMOVAL & INSTALLATION 6-15
CONTROL CABLES 6-15
   REMOVAL & INSTALLATION 6-15
COOLING 1-63
   ENGINE 1-63
   TRANSMISSION 1-63
COOLING SYSTEM 3-85
COOLING SYSTEM (ROUTINE MAINTENANCE) 1-38
   DRAIN & REFILL 1-39
   INSPECTION 1-38
   LEVEL CHECK 1-38
CRANKCASE EMISSIONS 4-5
CRANKCASE VENTILATION SYSTEM 4-5
   OPERATION 4-5
   REMOVAL & INSTALLATION 4-7
   TESTING 4-7
CRANKSHAFT AND CONNECTING ROD SPECIFICATIONS 3-25
CRANKSHAFT AND MAIN BEARINGS 3-73
   BEARING CLEARANCE CHECK 3-75
   BEARING REPLACEMENT 3-75
   INSPECTION 3-74
   REMOVAL & INSTALLATION 3-73
CYLINDER HEAD 3-28
   CLEANING & INSPECTION 3-39
   REMOVAL & INSTALLATION 3-28
   RESURFACING 3-40
DECELERATION FUEL CUT SYSTEM 4-35
   TESTING 4-35
DESCRIPTION 3-21
   8R-C AND 18R-C ENGINES 3-21
   20R AND 22R ENGINES 3-21
   2M, 4M, 4M-E AND 5M-E ENGINES 3-21
DESCRIPTION AND OPERATION 2-11
   SERVICE PRECAUTIONS 2-12
DESCRIPTION OF SYSTEM 5-13
DETERMINING AXLE RATIO 7-28
DISC AND PAD SPECIFICATIONS (IN.) 9-19
DISTRIBUTOR 3-7

INSTALLATION 3-11
REMOVAL 3-7
DISTRIBUTOR CAP AND ROTOR 2-9
INSPECTION 2-9
REMOVAL & INSTALLATION 2-9
DOME LAMPS 6-44
REMOVAL & INSTALLATION 6-44
DON'TS 1-8
DOOR GLASS 10-17
REMOVAL & INSTALLATION 10-17
DOOR LOCKS 10-3
REMOVAL & INSTALLATION 10-3
DOOR PANEL 10-16
REMOVAL & INSTALLATION 10-16
DOORS 10-2
ADJUSTMENT 10-3
REMOVAL & INSTALLATION 10-2
DO'S 1-7
DRIVE AXLE 1-57
DRAIN & REFILL 1-57
LEVEL CHECK 1-57
DRIVELINE 7-24
DRIVELINE COMPONENTS 7-27
DRIVEN DISC AND PRESSURE PLATE 7-6
REMOVAL & INSTALLATION 7-6
DRIVESHAFT AND U-JOINTS 7-24
REMOVAL & INSTALLATION 7-24
U-JOINT OVERHAUL 7-27
DUAL DIAPHRAGM DISTRIBUTOR 4-30
TESTING 4-30
ELECTRIC FUEL PUMP (CARBURETED FUEL SYSTEM) 5-4
REMOVAL & INSTALLATION 5-4
TESTING 5-5
ELECTRIC FUEL PUMP (GASOLINE FUEL INJECTION SYSTEM) 5-13
REMOVAL & INSTALLATION 5-13
TESTING 5-13
ELECTRIC WINDOW MOTOR 10-18
REMOVAL & INSTALLATION 10-18
EMISSION CONTROLS 4-5
ENGINE (ENGINE MECHANICAL) 3-26
REMOVAL & INSTALLATION 3-26
ENGINE (FLUIDS AND LUBRICANTS) 1-52
OIL LEVEL CHECK 1-52
ENGINE (SERIAL NUMBER IDENTIFICATION) 1-14
ENGINE COMPONENT LOCATIONS—20R ENGINE 3-20
ENGINE ELECTRICAL SYSTEM 3-2
ENGINE IDENTIFICATION CHART 1-20
ENGINE MECHANICAL 3-20
ENGINE MECHANICAL PROBLEMS 3-90
ENGINE MODIFICATIONS SYSTEM 4-31
INSPECTION 4-32
OPERATION 4-31
ENGINE OVERHAUL TIPS 3-21
INSPECTION TECHNIQUES 3-21
OVERHAUL TIPS 3-21
REPAIRING DAMAGED THREADS 3-22
TOOLS 3-21
ENGINE PERFORMANCE 3-93
ENGLISH TO METRIC CONVERSION CHARTS 1-73
ENTERTAINMENT SYSTEM 6-17
EVAPORATIVE CANISTER 1-29
SERVICING 1-29
EVAPORATIVE EMISSION CONTROL SYSTEM 4-17
OPERATION 4-17
REMOVAL & INSTALLATION 4-21
TESTING 4-21
EVAPORATIVE EMISSIONS 4-5
EXHAUST GAS RECIRCULATION (EGR) SYSTEM 4-36

OPERATION 4-36
SYSTEM CHECKS 4-40
TESTING 4-38
EXHAUST GASES 4-3
CARBON MONOXIDE 4-4
HYDROCARBONS 4-3
NITROGEN 4-4
OXIDES OF SULFUR 4-4
PARTICULATE MATTER 4-4
EXHAUST MANIFOLD 3-52
REMOVAL & INSTALLATION 3-52
EXHAUST SYSTEM 3-77
EXTERIOR 10-2
FAST IDLE ADJUSTMENT CHART 5-9
FAST IDLE SPEED CHART 5-10
FAST IDLE CAM BREAKER 4-33
TESTING 4-33
FASTENERS, MEASUREMENTS AND CONVERSIONS 1-8
FENDERS 10-7
REMOVAL & INSTALLATION 10-7
FIRING ORDERS 2-9
FLOAT LEVEL ADJUSTMENTS CHART 5-8
FLUID DISPOSAL 1-51
FLUIDS & LUBRICANTS 1-51
FLYWHEEL AND RING GEAR 3-77
REMOVAL & INSTALLATION 3-77
FREEZE PLUGS 3-76
REMOVAL & INSTALLATION 3-76
FRONT AXLE HUB AND BEARING 8-12
REMOVAL & INSTALLATION 8-12
FRONT DISC BRAKES 9-13
FRONT END ALIGNMENT 8-14
CAMBER 8-14
CASTER 8-14
TOE-IN 8-14
FRONT SPRING INSTALLATION SPECIFICATIONS 8-4
FRONT STEERING AND SUSPENSION COMPONENTS 8-3
FRONT SUSPENSION 8-3
FUEL CAP GASKET 1-29
REMOVAL & INSTALLATION 1-29
FUEL FILTER 1-26
REMOVAL & INSTALLATION 1-26
FUEL INJECTED VEHICLES 2-23
IDLE ADJUSTMENT 2-23
FUEL RECOMMENDATIONS 1-52
FUEL TANK 5-15
FUSES AND FUSIBLE LINK 6-48
REPLACEMENT 6-48
GASOLINE FUEL INJECTION SYSTEM 5-13
GENERAL ENGINE SPECIFICATIONS 3-24
GENERAL INFORMATION 3-77
GENERAL RECOMMENDATIONS 1-63
GRILLE 10-12
REMOVAL & INSTALLATION 10-12
HANDLING A TRAILER 1-64
HEADLIGHTS 6-34
REMOVAL & INSTALLATION 6-34
HEATER 6-12
HEATER CONTROL VALVE 6-15
REMOVAL & INSTALLATION 6-15
HEATER CORE 6-14
REMOVAL & INSTALLATION 6-14
HIGH ALTITUDE COMPENSATION SYSTEM 4-35
HISTORY 1-14
HITCH (TONGUE) WEIGHT 1-63
HOOD 10-5
ALIGNMENT 10-7
REMOVAL & INSTALLATION 10-5

HOSES 1-36
    INSPECTION 1-36
    REMOVAL & INSTALLATION 1-37
HOT AIR INTAKE SYSTEM 4-36
HOT IDLE COMPENSATION VALVE 4-35
    TESTING 4-35
HOW TO BUY A USED VEHICLE 1-68
HOW TO USE THIS BOOK 1-2
IC REGULATOR 3-16
    REMOVAL & INSTALLATION 3-16
    TESTING 3-16
IDENTIFICATION 7-16
IDLE SPEED AND MIXTURE ADJUSTMENT 2-19
IGNITION LOCK/SWITCH 8-29
    REMOVAL & INSTALLATION 8-29
IGNITION SWITCH 6-32
IGNITION TIMING 2-13
INDUSTRIAL POLLUTANTS 4-2
INSTRUMENT CLUSTER 6-27
    REMOVAL & INSTALLATION 6-27
INSTRUMENTS AND SWITCHES 6-27
INTAKE MANIFOLD 3-50
    REMOVAL & INSTALLATION 3-50
INTERIOR 10-13
JACKING 1-65
JACKING PRECAUTIONS 1-66
JUMP STARTING A DEAD BATTERY 1-67
JUMP STARTING PRECAUTIONS 1-67
JUMP STARTING PROCEDURE 1-67
KICK-UP ADJUSTMENT CHART 5-12
LEAF SPRINGS 8-17
    REMOVAL & INSTALLATION 8-17
LIFTGATE GLASS 10-19
    REMOVAL & INSTALLATION 10-19
LIGHTING 6-34
LOWER BALL JOINT 8-9
    INSPECTION 8-9
    REMOVAL & INSTALLATION 8-9
LOWER CONTROL ARM 8-12
    REMOVAL & INSTALLATION 8-12
LUGGAGE COMPARTMENT LID 10-7
    ADJUSTMENT 10-7
    REMOVAL & INSTALLATION 10-7
MACPHERSON STRUTS 8-7
    REMOVAL & INSTALLATION 8-7
MAINTENANCE COMPONENT LOCATIONS—20R ENGINE 1-21
MAINTENANCE OR REPAIR? 1-2
MAINTENANCE SCHEDULE CHART 1-70
MANUAL STEERING GEAR 8-30
    REMOVAL & INSTALLATION 8-30
MANUAL TRANSMISSION 7-2
MANUAL TRANSMISSION (FLUIDS & LUBRICANTS) 1-54
    DRAIN & REFILL 1-54
    LEVEL CHECK 1-54
MASTER CYLINDER (BRAKE OPERATION SYSTEM) 9-4
    OVERHAUL 9-5
    REMOVAL & INSTALLATION 9-4
MASTER CYLINDER (CLUTCH) 7-12
    OVERHAUL 7-12
    REMOVAL & INSTALLATION 7-12
MECHANICAL FUEL PUMP 5-2
    REMOVAL & INSTALLATION 5-2
MIXTURE CONTROL VALVE 4-25
    REMOVAL & INSTALLATION 4-27
    TESTING 4-27
MODEL IDENTIFICATION 1-14
MUFFLER AND/OR TAILPIPE 3-78
    REMOVAL & INSTALLATION 3-78

NATURAL POLLUTANTS 4-2
NEUTRAL SAFETY SWITCH 7-23
    ADJUSTMENT 7-23
    REMOVAL & INSTALLATION 7-23
NON-TRANSISTORIZED REGULATOR 3-15
    ADJUSTMENTS 3-15
    REMOVAL & INSTALLATION 3-15
OCTANE SELECTOR 2-14
    ADJUSTMENT 2-14
OCTANE SELECTOR TEST SPEEDS 2-15
OIL CHANGES 1-52
    OIL & FILTER CHANGE 1-52
OIL PAN 3-59
    REMOVAL & INSTALLATION 3-59
OIL PUMP 3-60
    OVERHAUL 3-61
    REMOVAL & INSTALLATION 3-60
OIL RECOMMENDATION 1-51
OUTSIDE MIRRORS 10-12
    INTERIOR 10-13
    REMOVAL & INSTALLATION 10-12
PAN AND FILTER 7-18
    REMOVAL & INSTALLATION 7-18
PARKING BRAKE 9-29
PARKING BRAKE ADJUSTMENT CHART 9-29
PARTS REPLACEMENT 2-13
    BREAKER POINTS 2-13
PCV VALVE 1-29
    REMOVAL & INSTALLATION 1-29
PEDAL HEIGHT SPECIFICATIONS 7-5
PISTON AND RING SPECIFICATIONS 3-25
PISTONS AND CONNECTING RODS 3-67
    CLEANING & INSPECTION 3-69
    CONNECTING ROD INSPECTION & BEARING REPLACEMENT 3-72
    CYLINDER BORE INSPECTION 3-72
    HONING 3-69
    PISTON & CONNECTING ROD IDENTIFICATION 3-68
    PISTON RING REPLACEMENT 3-70
    REMOVAL & INSTALLATION 3-67
    WRIST PIN REMOVAL & INSTALLATION 3-71
POINT TYPE IGNITION 2-10
POWER STEERING PUMP 8-30
    BLEEDING 8-30
    REMOVAL & INSTALLATION 8-30
POWER STEERING RESERVOIR 1-59
    LEVEL CHECK 1-59
PRELOAD SPECIFICATIONS 8-14
PRESSURE REGULATOR 5-14
    REMOVAL & INSTALLATION 5-14
PRINTED CIRCUIT BOARD 6-32
    REMOVAL & INSTALLATION 6-32
PROPORTIONING VALVE 9-7
    REMOVAL & INSTALLATION 9-8
QUARTER GLASS 10-19
    REMOVAL & INSTALLATION 10-19
RADIATOR 3-85
    REMOVAL & INSTALLATION 3-85
RADIO 6-17
    REMOVAL & INSTALLATION 6-17
REAR AXLE 7-28
REAR DRUM BRAKE COMPONENTS 9-24
REAR DRUM BRAKES 9-20
REAR MAIN OIL SEAL 3-59
    REMOVAL & INSTALLATION 3-59
REAR SUSPENSION 8-16
REAR SUSPENSION COMPONENTS 8-16
REGULATOR 10-18
    REMOVAL & INSTALLATION 10-18

ROCKER ARM (VALVE) COVER 3-46
  REMOVAL AND INSTALLATION 3-46
ROCKER ARMS 3-48
  INSPECTION 3-49
  REMOVAL AND INSTALLATION 3-48
ROCKER SHAFTS 3-45
  REMOVAL & INSTALLATION 3-45
ROUTINE MAINTENANCE 1-21
SAFETY PRECAUTIONS (EXHAUST SYSTEM) 3-77
SAFETY PRECAUTIONS (UNDERSTANDING AND TROUBLESHOOTING
  ELECTRICAL SYSTEMS) 6-2
SEAT BELTS 10-31
  REMOVAL & INSTALLATION 10-31
SEATS 10-22
  REMOVAL & INSTALLATION 10-22
SECONDARY SLOW CIRCUIT FUEL CUT SYSTEM 4-35
  TESTING 4-35
SERIAL NUMBER IDENTIFICATION 1-14
SERVICING YOUR VEHICLE SAFELY 1-7
SHOCK ABSORBER TIGHTENING TORQUE (FT. LBS.) CHART 8-23
SHOCK ABSORBERS (FRONT SUSPENSION) 8-7
  INSPECTION 8-7
  REMOVAL & INSTALLATION 8-7
SHOCK ABSORBERS (REAR SUSPENSION) 8-20
  REMOVAL & INSTALLATION 8-20
SIGNAL AND MARKER LIGHTS 6-37
  REMOVAL & INSTALLATION 6-37
SLAVE CYLINDER 7-12
  HYDRAULIC SYSTEM BLEEDING 7-12
  OVERHAUL 7-12
  REMOVAL & INSTALLATION 7-12
SPARK DELAY VALVE 4-30
  TESTING 4-30
SPARK PLUG WIRES 2-8
  REMOVAL & INSTALLATION 2-8
  TESTING 2-8
SPARK PLUGS 2-3
  INSPECTION & GAPPING 2-7
  REMOVAL & INSTALLATION 2-6
  SPARK PLUG HEAT RANGE 2-6
SPARK PLUGS AND WIRES 2-2
SPEAKERS 6-19
  REMOVAL & INSTALLATION 6-19
SPECIAL TOOLS 1-6
SPECIFICATION CHARTS
  ALTERNATOR AND REGULATOR SPECIFICATIONS 3-16
  BATTERY DIMENSIONS (INCHES) 1-35
  BRAKE DRUM DIAMETER CHART 9-22
  CAPACITIES CHART 1-72
  CHOKE UNLOADER ADJUSTMENT CHART 5-10
  CLUTCH PEDAL FREE-PLAY ADJUSTMENTS CHART 7-6
  CLUTCH TORQUE SPECIFICATIONS (FT. LBS.) 7-11
  CRANKSHAFT AND CONNECTING ROD SPECIFICATIONS 3-25
  DISC AND PAD SPECIFICATIONS (IN.) 9-19
  ENGINE IDENTIFICATION CHART 1-20
  ENGLISH TO METRIC CONVERSION CHARTS 1-73
  FAST IDLE ADJUSTMENT CHART 5-9
  FAST IDLE SPEED CHART 5-10
  FLOAT LEVEL ADJUSTMENTS CHART 5-8
  FRONT SPRING INSTALLATION SPECIFICATIONS 8-4
  GENERAL ENGINE SPECIFICATIONS 3-24
  KICK-UP ADJUSTMENT CHART 5-12
  MAINTENANCE SCHEDULE CHART 1-70
  OCTANE SELECTOR TEST SPEEDS 2-15
  PARKING BRAKE ADJUSTMENT CHART 9-29
  PEDAL HEIGHT SPECIFICATIONS 7-5
  PISTON AND RING SPECIFICATIONS 3-25
  PRELOAD SPECIFICATIONS 8-14

SHOCK ABSORBER TIGHTENING TORQUE (FT. LBS.) CHART 8-23
STANDARD TORQUE SPECIFICATIONS AND FASTENER
  MARKINGS 1-10
STEERING LINKAGE TORQUE SPECIFICATIONS (FT. LBS.) 8-34
TORQUE SPECIFICATIONS 3-25
TORQUE SPECIFICATIONS 8-10
TORQUE SPECIFICATIONS (FT. LBS.) 8-12
TOWING POINTS—1970–77 CHART 1-64
TUNE-UP SPECIFICATIONS 2-2
VACUUM AT IDLE (IN. HG) CHART 2-20
VALVE SPECIFICATIONS 3-24
WHEEL ALIGNMENT SPECIFICATIONS 8-15
SPEEDOMETER CABLE 6-32
  REMOVAL & INSTALLATION 6-32
SPEEDOMETER, TACHOMETER, AND GAUGES 6-32
  REMOVAL & INSTALLATION 6-32
STANDARD AND METRIC MEASUREMENTS 1-12
STANDARD TORQUE SPECIFICATIONS AND FASTENER
  MARKINGS 1-10
STARTER 3-17
  REMOVAL & INSTALLATION 3-17
  STARTER OVERHAUL 3-17
STEERING 8-24
STEERING GEAR 1-58
  LEVEL CHECK 1-58
STEERING LINKAGE 8-32
  REMOVAL & INSTALLATION 8-32
STEERING LINKAGE TORQUE SPECIFICATIONS (FT. LBS.) 8-34
STEERING WHEEL 8-24
  REMOVAL & INSTALLATION 8-24
TANK ASSEMBLY 5-15
  REMOVAL & INSTALLATION 5-15
THERMOSTAT 3-88
  REMOVAL & INSTALLATION 3-88
THROTTLE BODY 5-14
  REMOVAL & INSTALLATION 5-14
THROTTLE POSITIONER 4-23
  ADJUSTMENT 4-25
  OPERATION 4-23
THROTTLE POSITIONER SETTINGS (RPM) 4-25
TIE ROD END 8-35
  REMOVAL & INSTALLATION 8-35
TIMING 2-13
  INSPECTION & ADJUSTMENT 2-14
TIMING CHAIN AND TENSIONER 3-56
  REMOVAL & INSTALLATION 3-56
TIMING CHAIN COVER OIL SEAL 3-56
  REPLACEMENT 3-56
TIMING GEAR COVER 3-55
  REMOVAL & INSTALLATION 3-55
TIPS 1-68
  ROAD TEST CHECKLIST 1-69
  USED VEHICLE CHECKLIST 1-68
TIRES AND WHEELS 1-47
  CARE OF SPECIAL WHEELS 1-50
  INFLATION & INSPECTION 1-48
  TIRE DESIGN 1-48
  TIRE ROTATION 1-47
  TIRE STORAGE 1-48
TOOLS AND EQUIPMENT 1-3
TORQUE 1-9
  TORQUE ANGLE METERS 1-12
  TORQUE WRENCHES 1-11
TORQUE SPECIFICATIONS (FT. LBS.) 8-12
TORQUE SPECIFICATIONS (SPECIFICATION CHARTS) 8-10
TORQUE SPECIFICATIONS (SPECIFICATION CHARTS) 3-25
TOWING POINTS—1970–77 CHART 1-64
TOWING THE VEHICLE 1-64

TRAILER TOWING   1-63
TRAILER WEIGHT   1-63
TRAILER WIRING   6-46
TRANSISTORIZED IGNITION   2-11
TRANSISTORIZED IGNITION SYSTEM   3-5
   PRECAUTIONS   3-6
   REMOVAL & INSTALLATION   3-7
   TESTING   3-6
TRANSMISSION ASSEMBLY (AUTOMATIC TRANSMISSION)   7-16
   REMOVAL & INSTALLATION   7-16
TRANSMISSION ASSEMBLY (MANUAL TRANSMISSION)   7-2
   REMOVAL & INSTALLATION   7-2
TROUBLESHOOTING   6-3
   BASIC TROUBLESHOOTING THEORY   6-4
   TEST EQUIPMENT   6-4
   TESTING   6-6
TROUBLESHOOTING CHARTS
   AIR INJECTION SYSTEM DIAGNOSIS CHART   4-16
   BASIC DRIVESHAFT AND REAR AXLE PROBLEMS   7-30
   BASIC STEERING AND SUSPENSION PROBLEMS   8-37
   ENGINE MECHANICAL PROBLEMS   3-90
   ENGINE PERFORMANCE   3-93
   THROTTLE POSITIONER SETTINGS (RPM)   4-25
   TROUBLESHOOTING THE BRAKE SYSTEM   9-33
   TROUBLESHOOTING THE IGNITION SWITCH   8-39
   TROUBLESHOOTING THE MANUAL STEERING GEAR   8-41
   TROUBLESHOOTING THE POWER STEERING GEAR   8-42
   TROUBLESHOOTING THE POWER STEERING PUMP   8-44
   TROUBLESHOOTING THE STEERING COLUMN   8-38
   TROUBLESHOOTING THE TURN SIGNAL SWITCH   8-40
TUNE-UP SPECIFICATIONS   2-2
TURN SIGNAL (COMBINATION) SWITCH   8-26
   REMOVAL & INSTALLATION   8-26
TURN SIGNALS AND FLASHERS   6-47
   REMOVAL & INSTALLATION   6-47
TYPICAL EMISSION COMPONENT LOCATIONS—20R ENGINE   4-13
**UNDERSTANDING AND TROUBLESHOOTING ELECTRICAL
  SYSTEMS   6-2**
UNDERSTANDING AUTOMATIC TRANSMISSIONS   7-14
   HYDRAULIC CONTROL SYSTEM   7-16
   PLANETARY GEARBOX   7-15
   SERVOS AND ACCUMULATORS   7-15
   TORQUE CONVERTER   7-14
UNDERSTANDING BASIC ELECTRICITY   6-2
   AUTOMOTIVE CIRCUITS   6-3
   CIRCUITS   6-2
   SHORT CIRCUITS   6-3
   THE WATER ANALOGY   6-2
UNDERSTANDING ELECTRICITY   3-2
   BASIC CIRCUITS   3-2
   TROUBLESHOOTING   3-3
UNDERSTANDING THE CLUTCH   7-4
UNDERSTANDING THE MANUAL TRANSMISSION   7-2
UPPER BALL JOINT   8-11
   INSPECTION   8-11

REMOVAL & INSTALLATION   8-11
UPPER CONTROL ARM   8-12
   REMOVAL & INSTALLATION   8-12
VACUUM AT IDLE (IN. HG) CHART   2-20
VACUUM DIAGRAMS   4-43
VACUUM LIMITER SYSTEM   5-13
   REMOVAL & INSTALLATION   5-13
   TESTING   5-13
VALVE GUIDES   3-45
   INSPECTION   3-45
   REPLACEMENT   3-45
VALVE LASH   2-15
   ADJUSTMENT   2-15
VALVE SEATS   3-45
VALVE SPECIFICATIONS   3-24
VALVES AND SPRINGS   3-40
   ADJUSTMENT (AFTER ENGINE SERVICE)   3-40
   INSPECTION   3-42
   REFACING   3-44
   REMOVAL & INSTALLATION   3-41
   VALVE LAPPING   3-44
VEHICLE   1-14
WASHER FLUID RESERVOIR   6-24
   REMOVAL & INSTALLATION   6-24
WASHER PUMP   6-27
   REMOVAL & INSTALLATION   6-27
WATER PUMP   3-86
   REMOVAL & INSTALLATION   3-86
WATER THERMO SENSOR   5-15
   TESTING   5-15
WHEEL ALIGNMENT SPECIFICATIONS   8-15
WHEEL ASSEMBLY   8-2
   INSPECTION   8-2
   REMOVAL & INSTALLATION   8-2
WHEEL BEARINGS   1-60
   PRELOAD ADJUSTMENT   1-62
   REMOVAL & INSTALLATION   1-60
WHEEL CYLINDERS   9-27
   OVERHAUL   9-28
   REMOVAL & INSTALLATION   9-27
WHEELS   8-2
WHERE TO BEGIN   1-2
WINDSHIELD WIPER BLADE AND ARM   6-21
   REMOVAL & INSTALLATION   6-21
WINDSHIELD WIPER COMPONENTS   6-21
WINDSHIELD WIPER MOTOR   6-22
   REMOVAL & INSTALLATION   6-22
WINDSHIELD WIPERS   1-42
   ELEMENT (REFILL) CARE & REPLACEMENT   1-42
WINDSHIELD WIPERS AND WASHERS   6-21
WIPER LINKAGE   6-22
   REMOVAL & INSTALLATION   6-22
WIRING DIAGRAMS   6-51
WIRING HARNESSES   6-8
   WIRING REPAIR   6-8